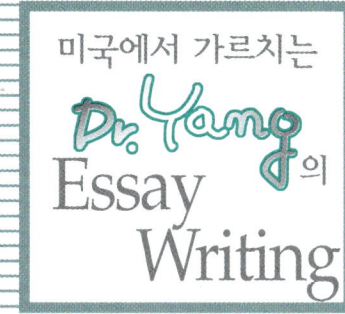

미국에서 가르치는

Dr. Yang의

Essay
Writing

미국에서 가르치는
Dr. Yang Essay Writing

초판 1쇄 발행 2002년 1월 1일
초판 6쇄 발행 2009년 10월 15일

지은이 양규철
발행인 김태진
펴낸 곳 에디터
주소 서울특별시 마포구 공덕동 105-219 정화빌딩 3층
문의 02-753-2700, 2778 **FAX** 02-753-2779
등록 1991년 6월 18일 제1-1220호

ⓒ 에디터, 2002
값 25,000원

ISBN 89-85145-61-4   03740

미국에서 가르치는
Dr. Yang 의
Essay
Writing

양규철 박사 지음

필라델피아 템플대 교수

에디터

Preface

영어다운 영어 에세이를 쓰려면

문맹자가 아니라면 사람은 누구나 글을 써서 어느정도 의사소통을 할 수 있다. 그러나 글을 효과적으로 잘 쓴다는 것은 결코 쉬운 일이 아니다. 이는 한국어, 영어, 또는 어떠한 언어를 사용하여 글을 써도 마찬가지일 것이다. 글을 쓴다는 게 왜 그렇게 쉽지 않을까? 이에 대한 주요한 이유는 글을 쓴다는 것은 , 첫째, 정리된 생각(Organized Thinking)을 바탕으로한 창의적 아이디어(Creative Process)가 필요한데 이에대한 훈련이 부족하고, 둘째, "나는 잘 쓰지 못한다." 라는 마음가짐(Attitude)때문이다.

"정리된 생각"이라함은, 글 쓰기 전에 글 쓰는 목적및 과정(예: 구상, 토픽선정, 대상, 어조, 글의형태 등)등을 계획, 분류및 조직함을 말한다. 글 쓰기전에 토픽선정이 필요한데 토픽은 범위가 넓을수록 글 쓰기가 막연하고 다루기가 힘들기 때문에, 최대한으로 정확하고 객관성 있는 토픽으로 좁혀야한다. 예를 들어 어떤 음식에 대한 글을 쓴다고 하자. 먼저 음식을 주제로 정했으나 음식 가운데도 채소음식, 채소음식에서 다시 범위를 좁혀서 한국채소음식, 또 그중에 이름난 전주김치, 더 주제를 좁혀서 '전주배추 김치' 로 정한다. 그러면, 글을 쓰는 목적과 형태는 어떻게 해야하나? '전주배추김치' 의 맛, 모양, 색깔, 냄새등에 마음이 끌려 그것을 표현함을 목적으로 한다면, 형태는 묘사 (Descriptive)로 분류하고 이에대한 지침을 활용하여, 쓰는이의 "창의적 아이디어"로 글을 쓰는 게 효과적이다. 김치담는 방법을 알리고 싶으면 유익한 정보를 주는(Informative)형태로, 김치와 깍두기의 공통점과 차이점을 들어 서술할려면 자세히 설명하는(Expository) 김치를 상품화하여 판매목적에 중점을 둘때는 설득력(Persuasive) 있게, 그리고 김치에 대한 어떤 특성연구(예, 발달과정, 영양분석, 건강에 미치는 이해관계)는 조사보고서(Research Paper)지침하에 글을 창의적으로 쓰는 게 효과적이다. 이와같이 "정리된 생각"을 바탕으로 "창의적"으로 글을 써야되기 때문에, 글을 쓴다는 것이 결코 쉬운 일이 아니다.

이에 본서는 정리된 생각에 근거한 창의적 아이디어를 주로 돕기위한 목적으로 편찬되었다. 즉, 제1장에서 글을 쓰는 다양한 준비과정을 많은 예를 들어 그림과 같이 보여주고 있으며; 제 3장에서는 에세이의 중요한 뼈대가 되는 문단구조(Paragraph Structure)((1)요지및주제, (2)뒷바침자료, (3)통일성, (4)일관성)에 대하여 상세한 실예를 들어 선명히 보여주고 있고; 제4장에서는 에세이구조 (서론, 본론, 결론)와 특히 유형(Type)을 철저히 다루었다. 유형을 분석, 평가하기 위하여 각 유형마다 모범작품을 예를 들고, 설정된 평가기준에 의하여 에세이의 질을 독자로 하여금 평가토록 하였다. 이렇게 세밀하고 철저한 에세이 평가방법은 이곳 어느출판사에서도 아직 시도치 못 하였다. 끝으로 제5장에서는 글을 더욱 효과적으로 쓰는 다양한 Techniques을 상세한 예를 들고 다루었으며, 특히 글 쓰는데 쉽게 범할 수 있는 논리적 오류(Logical Fallacies)를 고국의 독자에게 소개하여 언론의 횡포를 알게하는 데 기여하였다. 그리고, 각 장 끝에 요약과 연습문제를 출제하여 읽은 내용을 독자가 철저히 응용하고 복습이 되도록 시도하였다. 이렇게 본서의 제 1,3,4,5장은 "정리된 생각"을 바탕으로한 "창의적인 글"을 쓸 수 있도록 집필하였다.

둘째, "나도 할수 있다"라는 긍정적 마음가짐(Attitude)대신에, "나는 할 수 없다"라는 부정적 태도 때문에, 그동안 우리는 할 수 있는 것을 매우 적게 표현했다고 할 수 있다. 이는 자신을 포함하여 가족, 사회에게 매우 불행한 일이다. 우리 능력과 사고방식은 영어를 모국어로 쓰는 사람과 비교해 볼때 절대로 떨어지지 않으며, 이는 비단 영어구사 능력, 특히 작문에서는 큰 차이가 없다. 고국의 독자와 이곳 미국 독자와의 영어구사능력을 비교하여 볼때, 가장 크게 차이가 나는 점은 청취력이고, 다음은 말하기, 그 다음은 독해력, 그리고 글쓰기에서 가장 차이가 적다. 또는 기초 한국어를 공부한 미국사람과 고국 독자와의 한국어 구사능력을 비교하면 같은 결과가 나온다. 이유는 앞에서 말하였듯이, 글 쓴다는 것은 "정리된 생각"에 기준한 "창의적 아이디어"가 필요하기 때문에, 이곳 미국학생도 글을 쓰는데 많은 어려움이 있음은 한국학생과 비교하여 별 차이가 없다. 이는 한국학생이 한국어로 기사, 논술, 상업용광고, 정치연설, 논문 등을 쓸때 겪는 어려움과 마찬가지이다.

1960년대초부터 이곳에 불어닥친 자유주의는 학교에도 Liberal Education의 영향을 받아 수학, 과학은 물론 모국어인 영어, 특히 작문에 심각한 문제를 야기시켰고, 1970년대 후반부터는 "Johnny&Sue can't read and write"라는 말로, 읽고 쓰지도 못하는 학교영어교육을 신랄히 비판하였다. 이에 90년대 초부터는 SAT에 작문시험이 첨가되었고, 요사이는 각종시험에 Essay Writing이 요구되고 있어서 싫으나 좋으나 작문은 공부하여야 된다. 특히 이곳 학생도 "명확하고 생생한 언어(Specific Use of Language)"사용이 매우 서툴러서, 대부분 영어교재출판사는 "명확하고 생생한 언어"를 많이 다루고, 이의 사용을 무척 강조하고 있다.

언어는 문화와 뗄 수 없는 관계를 맺고, 문화를 반영하고 있는 것이 사실이다. 미국과 한국문화는 차이점도 있으나, 공통된 점이 훨씬 더 많다. 공통된 점은 못 보고, 차이점만 크게 보는 견해는 매우 위험하고 좁은 생각이다. 이에 영어를 가르치는 분중에서, 회화체에 사용되는 속어를, 예를들어 "미국식 표현은 어떻고, 한국식 표현은 저렇다"라고 독자들에게 과장하는 글을 접하게 되면 무척 기분이 서글퍼진다. 이유는 능력있는 독자들에게 자신감을 빼앗아 가기 때문이다. 본서의 제 2장에서는 문화의 차이에서 발생되는 글씀의 독특성을 소개하고 있지만, 본질적으로는 "명확하고 생생한 언어" 사용의 어려움은 한국과 미국학생을 비교할때 큰차이가 나지 않으니 걱정하지 않기를 바란다. 요점을 말하면, 글 쓴다는 것이 쉽지 않음은 동서양 거의 비슷하니, "나도 잘 쓸 수 있다"라는 긍정적 마음가짐을 갖는 것이 더욱 중요하다.

끝으로, 항상 양서를 출판하여 독자들의 알찬 실력 향상만을 위하여 노력하는 에디터 출판사의 김석성 사장님에게, 그리고 어려운 영문원고를 훌륭히 다듬어준 편집부에게 깊은 감사를 드린다.

스프링필드, 펜실베니아에서 양 규 철

CONTENTS

CHAPTER 1 · 작문이란 (AN OVERVIEW OF WRITING)

□ 작문의 목적 (Aims of Writing) ··· 12

□ 작문과정 (Writing Process) ··· 13

  1. 구상(Prewriting)

    1-1. 주제 선정과 범위 축약 (Choosing a Topic & Narrowing the Scope of the Topic)········ 14
    1-2. 작문의 목적, 대상, 어조 결정 (Considering Purpose, Audience and Tone) ·········· 16
    1-3. 자료수집 및 아이디어 찾기 (Gathering Information & Ideas) ························ 20
    1-4. 주제문과 문단 구성 (Structuring a Topic Sentence & a Paragraph) ··············· 22
    1-5. 문단조직 (Organizing a Paragraph) ·· 26

  2. 초고 (Drafting) ·· 28

  3. 수정 (Revising)

    3-1. 문장구조 점검 (Checking Sentence Structure) ··· 31
    3-2. 기교, 용법, 문체 점검 (Checking Mechanics, Usage and Style) ················· 35
    3-3. 문단구조 점검 (Checking Paragraph Structure) ·· 36
    3-4. 글 전체의 구성 점검 (Checking Organization) ·· 38
    3-5. 내용 점검 (Checking Content) ··· 44

  4. 교정 (Proofreading) ·· 47

□ 요약과 연습(Chapter Summary and Exercises) ··· 49

CHAPTER 2   명확하고 생생한 언어 사용 (SPECIFIC USE OF LANGUAGE)

□ 언어와 문화(Language and Culture) ·· 54

□ 형용사와 명사의 구체적인 사용(Specific Use of Adjective and Noun) ················· 57

□ 감각단어(Sensory Words) ··· 66

   1. 시각적 단어 (SIGHT WORDS)

      1-1 색상 (Colors) ··· 69
      1-2 외양 (Appearance) ··· 76
      1-3 형태 (Shapes) ··· 78
      1-4 시력 (Light/Vision) ··· 78

   2. 미각 단어 (TASTE WORDS) ·· 82
   3. 후각 단어 (SMELL WORDS) ··· 83
   4. 촉각 단어 (TOUCH WORDS) ·· 86

□ 동사와 부사의 명확한 사용(SPECIFIC USE OF VERB & ADVERB)

   1. 구체적인 '행위동사' 사용에 따른 역동적인 구조 (Dynamic Structure with the Specific 'Action Verb') ····· 90
   2. 구체적인 '행동' 단어에 따른 역동적인 구조(Dynamic Structure with the Specific 'Movement' Word) ····· 102

      2-1. 행동단어(Movement words) ·· 102

   3. 명확한 소리단어로 된 인상적인 구조 (Effective Structure with the specific 'Hearing' Words) ·················· 105

      3-1. 큰 소리(Loud Sounds) ·· 106
      3-2. 부드러운 소리(Soft Sounds) ··· 107
      3-3. 대화/연설의 소리(Speech Sounds) ·· 107
      3-4. 자연스런 소리(General Sounds) ·· 107

□ 요약과 연습 (Chapter Summary and Exercises) ·· 112

□ 해답 ··· 127

CHAPTER 3 　문단(PARAGRAPH)

3.1. 문단구조(Paragraph Structure) ·· 146

    3.1.1. 요지 및 주제문 전개(Developing a main idea & a topic sentence) ················· 148

    3.1.2. 뒷받침 세부자료 전개(Developing Supporting Details) ······························· 178

        3.1.2.1. 효과적인 뒷받침 세부자료로서의 감각적 세부사항, 사실과 통계, 사례, 일화(Sensory Details, Facts &

        Statistics, Examples, Anecdotes as Effective Supporting Details) ················ 190

        3.1.2.1.1. 감각적 세부사항(Sensory Details) ··· 190

        3.1.2.1.2. 사실과 통계(Facts and Statistics) ··· 192

        3.1.2.1.3. 사례(Examples) ··· 196

        3.1.2.1.4. 일화(Anecdotes) ··· 198

    3.1.3. 통일성(Unity) ·· 202

    3.1.4. 일관성(Coherence) ·· 206

        3.1.4.1 연대순(Chronological Order) ··· 206

        3.1.4.2. 공간순(Spatial Order) ··· 208

        3.1.4.3. 중요도순(Order of Importance) ··· 212

        3.1.4.4. 논리순(Logical Order) ··· 212

        3.1.4.5. 아이디어 사이의 연관(Connections Between Ideas) ····························· 214

            3.1.4.5.1. 직접적인 언급(Direct References) ··· 214

            3.1.4.5.2. 이행장치들(Transitional Devices) ··· 216

3.2. 요약과 연습(Chapter Summary and Exercise) ····································· 218

CHAPTER 4 　에세이 쓰기(WRITING AN ESSAY)

4.1. 구조(Structure) ·· 238

    4.1.1. 서론(Introduction – The First Paragraph) ································· 242

    4.1.2. 본론(Body Paragraphs –The second, third, and fourth) ··············· 248

    4.1.3. 결론(Conclusion) ··· 260

4.2. 에세이의 유형(Types) ··· 266

    4.2.1. 묘사(Descriptive) ··· 276

    4.2.2. 설명(Expository) ··· 286

    4.2.3. 정보제공(Informative) ··· 298

    4.2.4. 나레이션(Narrative) ··· 312

    4.2.5. 사적인 이야기(Personal) ··· 324

    4.2.6 설득(Persuasive) ··· 338

    4.2.7. 연구논문(Research Paper) ··· 354

4.3. 요약과 연습(Chapter Summary and Exercises) ····················· 376

5.1. 단어선택(Choosing Word) ·· 408

    5.1.1. 정확한 단어(Accurate Words) ··· 408

    5.1.2. 효과적인 단어(Effective Words) ··· 414

5.2. 장황함 피하기(Reducing Wordiness) ·· 424

    5.2.1. 반복되는 단어나 불필요한 동의어 없애기(Eliminating Repeated or Unnecessary Synonyms) ········· 424

    5.2.2. 긴 어구를 한 단어로 바꾸기(Replacing a Long Phrase with One Word) ················· 436

5.3. 간결한 글쓰기(Concise Writing) ··· 440

5.4. 압축하기(Condensing) ··· 446

5.5. 문장의 완결성(Sentence Completeness) ·· 460

    5.5.1. 문장의 파편(Sentence Fragments) ·· 460

    5.5.2. 다음 행으로 이어지는 문장(Run-on Sentences) ······························ 462

    5.5.3. 병렬구조(Parallel Structure) ·· 468

        5.5.3.1. 대등한 아이디어(Coordinated Ideas) ·· 468

        5.5.3.2. 상관구성(Correlative Constructions) ·· 472

5.6. 잘못된 접속사 바꾸기(Replacing Faulty Conjunctions) ····················· 476

5.7. 오류피하기(Avoiding Fallacies) ··· 482

    5.7.1. 무지에의 호소(Appeal to Ignorance) ··· 482

    5.7.2. 인신공격(Attacking the Person) ·· 484

    5.7.3. 시류에 편승하기(Bandwagon) ·· 484

    5.7.4. 순환논법(Circular Reasoning) ·· 484

    5.7.5. 그릇된 유추(False Analogy) ··· 486

    5.7.6. 잘못된 이분법(False Dichotomy) ·· 486

    5.7.7. 지나친 일반화(Overgeneralization) ·· 486

    5.7.8. 포스트 학 팰러시(Post hoc Fallacy) ··· 488

    5.7.9. 세력암시(Prestige Suggestion) ··· 488

    5.7.10. 정형화(Stereotyping) ··· 488

5.8. 요약과 연습(Chapter Summary and Exercises) ······························· 496

CHAPTER

1

작문이란?

An Overview of Writing

□ AIMS OF WRITING (작문의 목적)

우리는 좋든 싫든 매일 글을 보고 산다. 글은 우리 주위 곳곳에 널려 있다. 아침마다 등교 · 출근 길에 만나는 길거리 간판의 글만 해도 엄청나다. 거기다 책, 신문, 광고, 편지, 공문서, 일기, 영화자막, 취직 시험 문제, 논문, 컴퓨터와 이메일 등에 나오는 글까지…, 석기 시대에 살지 않는 한 글과 떨어져 산다는 것은 불가능하다.

글은 많은 뜻을 가지고 있으나, 나름의 특정한 목적을 직 · 간접적으로 내포하고 있다. 상업 광고를 목적으로 신문이나 잡지에 쓰여진 글과 화산 폭발 과정이 설명된 지질학 교재에 나오는 글은 각각 그 목적이 다르다. 전자가 '설득'을 주목적으로 하고 있다면, 후자는 '설명 및 개발'을 주목적으로 한다. 그렇다면, 글을 쓰는 주목적은 어디에 있는가? 그 목적은 대체로 4가지로 분류할 수 있다.

작문의 목적
1. **의사표현** : 글쓴이가 자기 자신을 더 많이 알리며 인생의 뜻이 어디에 있고, 또 무엇인지 알리려고 할 때
2. **설명 및 개발** : 원하는 사람들에게 여러 가지 자연 및 사회적 현상을 설명하고, 어떤 사상 및 문제를 더 개발시키고자 할 때
3. **설득** : 상대방의 가치(value), 믿음(belief), 태도(attitude) 기준 등을 부정적인 쪽에서 긍정적인 쪽으로 바꾸려 할 때
4. **문예창작** : 어떤 사상이나 문학 작품을 독자적으로 창작하려고 할 때

교사가 교실에서의 강의를 목적으로 글을 쓴다면 '설명 및 개발' 목적이 큰 비중을 차지하며, 상업 광고용으로 쓰이는 글은 '설득'을 주목적으로 한다. 안네 프랑크 (1929~1945)가 2차대전 때 쓴 일기는 '의사표현', 김소월의 시 '진달래꽃'은 '문예창작'을 주목적으로 보는 것이 타당하다.

(※참고 : 글은 여러 가지 내용과 목적을 복합적으로 내포하고 있으며, 100% '설득' 또는 '설명' 등을 목적으로 쓰여진 글은 찾아보기 힘들다. 따라서 글의 주된 목적을 찾아야 한다.)

□ WRITING PROCESS (작문과정)

일기류를 제외하면 글은 주로 남을 의식하고 쓰여진다. 과연 남이 나의 글을 재미있게 읽어줄까? 싫증은 느끼지 않을까? 글을 잘 쓴다는 것은 우리말로 쓰든 영어로 쓰든 결코 쉬운 일이 아니지만, 그렇다고 그렇게 어려운 일도 아니다.

모든 일에 다 연습이 필요하듯이, 글쓰기에도 연습이 필요하다. 작문은 누구나 연습으로 습득할 수 있는 기술이다 (Writing is a skill that anyone can learn with practice!).

그렇다면 '연습' 을 하고자 할 때, 도대체 어떤 방법으로 어떤 과정을 거쳐야 할까? 글 쓰는 목적이 다양하듯이, 글의 주제와 소재를 찾는 방법도 다양하다.

글의 소재와 주제를 찾는 방법

1. **Remembrance**(기억) : 잊혀지지 않는 장소, 사람, 사건 등을 떠올려 글을 생생하고 자세히 쓰는 것.

2. **Observation**(관찰) : 직접 목격한 사건(예를 들면 일식, 허리케인 등)을 사건이 일어난 순서(chronological order)에 따라 흥미롭게 쓰는 것.

3. **Description of a place**(장소묘사) : 어떤 장소의 이미지를 형상화하고 어떤 점이 독특한 지를 충분히 해설함으로써 독자들에게 실제로 가본 듯한 느낌을 안겨주는 것.

4. **Character profile**(인물묘사) : 실제 또는 가공 인물의 모습, 성격 등을 독자가 고스란히 볼 수 있도록 쓰는 것.

5. **Travel Brochure**(여행 안내) : 휴가 기간을 활용하여 독자들이 가 볼만한 장소를 소개하는 것으로, 어떤 곳에서는 무엇을 보고 즐길 수 있는지, 또 무엇을 얻을 수 있는지 권유하는 것.

그렇다면 이 다양하고 아름다운 소재들을 어떻게 이용하여 글을 써야 하는가? 이제 다음과 같은 작문 과정을 살펴보기로 하자.

1 작문이란?

> **작문과정**
>
> 1. Prewriting(구상);
>   Choosing a Topic & Narrowing the Scope of the Topic (주제 선정 및 주제의 범위 축약)
>   Considering Purpose, Audience and Tone (작문의 목적, 대상, 어조 결정)
>   Gathering Information & Ideas (자료수집 및 아이디어 찾기)
>   Structuring a Topic Sentence & a Paragraph (주제문과 문단 구성)
>   Organizing a Paragraph (문단 조직)
> 2. Drafting (초고)
> 3. Revising (수정); and
>   Checking Sentence Structure (문장구조 점검)
>   Checking Mechanics, Usage and Style (기교, 용법, 문체 점검)
>   Checking Paragraph Structure (문단구조 점검)
>   Checking Organization (글 전체의 구성 점검)
>   Checking Content (내용 점검)
> 4. Proofreading (교정)

1. Prewriting (구상)

1-1. Choosing a Topic & Narrowing the Scope of the Topic (주제 선정과 범위 축약)

　주제는 (1) **자신이 잘 아는 분야**, (2) **독자의 흥미를 유발시킬 수 있는 것**, (3) **자기 생각과 의견 중에서 중요하다고 판단되는 것**으로 선정해야 한다. 주제의 범위 축약은 주제가 너무나 광범위하면 제한된 시간에 효과적으로 연구하여 글을 쓰기 힘들기 때문에, 보다 구체적인 영역으로 좁혀야 한다는 것을 의미한다.

Q1 다음 주제 중에서 가장 구체적인 것은 무엇인가 살펴보자.

A. ⓐ Plants ⓑ Flowers ⓒ Tropical flowers ⓓ Tree ⓔ Lily

B. ⓐ Vulture ⓑ Migrating birds ⓒ Birds in Korea ⓓ Magpie ⓔ Birds

C. ⓐ Mammal ⓑ Fish ⓒ Cicada ⓓ Insect ⓔ Animal

D. ⓐ 99Ford LX ⓑ Vehicle ⓒ Automobile ⓓ Car ⓔ Passenger car

E. ⓐ People ⓑ Relatives ⓒ Parents ⓓ nephews ⓔ uncles

A1

A항의 경우, ⓐ식물은 동물과 비교되는 개념으로 범위가 너무 광범위하고; ⓑ는 식물보다는 범위가 적지만 '꽃' 의 종류 역시 어마어마하다. ⓒ는 ⓑ보다 범위가 적지만 열대지방 꽃(Tropical flowers)의 종류 또한 셀 수 없이 많고; ⓓ나무는 식물에 속하긴 하지만 그 종류가 무수하다. 마지막으로 ⓔ백합이 ⓐⓑⓒⓓ에 비해 가장 범위가 작다. 이렇게 볼 때, B항에서는 ⓓ; C항은 ⓒ; D항은 ⓐ, 그리고 E항은 ⓒ가 가장 범위가 좁혀진 주제이다.

주제 선정은 매우 중요하다. 특히 논문/보고서를 써 본 경험이 적은 사람은 주제를 너무 광범위(too broad)하거나 너무 주관적(too subjective)인 것으로 선정하는 경우가 많다. 다음은 연구 논문을 쓰기에 좋은 주제와 나쁜 주제의 특성이다.

연구 논문 쓰기의 좋은 주제

1. Interesting(흥미롭다) : 자신이 흥미가 있어서 더 많이 연구하고 싶은 분야

2. Manageable(다루기 쉽다) : 주어진 과제 분량에 맞추어 적절한 양의 연구로
   다룰 수 있는 주제

3. Available(자료 수집이 가능하다) : 자료를 구할 수 있는 주제

4. Worthwhile(가치 있다) : 연구 가치가 있는 주제란, 가치 기준(value judgement)
   에 따라 달라질 수 있지만, 무엇보다 실용 가치 (something of substance)가

있어야 한다.

5. Original(독창적이다) : 민족주의자 김 구의 자서전을 다시 쓰는 것은 창의적 (Original/Creative)이지 못하지만, 그가 어렸을 때 읽은 책들이 후에 그의 사상에 어떠한 영향을 끼쳤는지 연구하는 것은 매우 독창적이다.

연구 논문 쓰기의 나쁜 주제

1. Too broad(너무 광범위하다) : 학생들이 가장 범하기 쉬운 실수(예 : The Ice Age, The Great Wall of China 등은 약 1,500~2,000자로 다루기에는 너무나 광범위한 주제이다).

2. Too narrow(너무 제한적이다) : 몇 줄의 글 또는 차트를 이용하여 보고될 수 있는 주제(예 : 한국 내 외제 자동차 판매량, 2000년도, 1999년도 외국관광객 수).

3. Too trivial(너무 사소하다) : 연구 가치가 적은 것(예 : 교통 신호 준수, 밥짓는 법).

4. Too subjective (너무 주관적이다) : 개인의 의견, 편견, 주장이 객관적 증거 없이 많이 도출되는 주제(예 : 특정언어의 우수성, 특정종교의 우월성).

5. Too Controversial(너무 논쟁적이다) : 너무나 상반된 의견으로 인해 충돌을 야기시킬 수 있는 주제는 객관성을 잃기 쉽다(예 : 낙태문제, 창조론 대 진화론).

6. Too Technical(너무 전문적이다) : 너무 전문적인 술어를 많이 쓰면 독자와 거리가 생기며, 독자가 싫증을 느끼고 이해하는 데도 힘들어 한다.

7. Too New(너무 새롭다) : 너무 새로운 주제는 아무리 흥미롭다 할지라도, 연구 자료를 충분히 찾을 수 없다.

1-2. Considering Purpose, Audience and Tone
(작문의 목적, 대상, 어조 결정)

글을 쓰는 데는 여러 가지 목적이 있다. 누군가에게 무엇을 설명하거나 설득하기 위해 글을 쓰기도 하고, 즐거움 때문에, 혹은 자신의 감정이나 생각을 표현하고 싶어서 글을 쓰기도 한다. 글의 목적이 단 하나가 아니라 설명, 설득, 즐거움 등이 함께 섞여 다목적으로 되는 경우도 있다. 이처럼 글의 목적이 다양하듯이, 글을 쓰는 형태도 다양하다.

Q2 다음의 글 형태는 대체로 어떤 목적을 갖고 있는지 생각해 보고 해당란에 표시하여 보자.

ⓐ 자기표현 　　　ⓑ 문학작품 　　　ⓒ 설명 　　　ⓓ 설득

1. Journal, Personal essay, Letter : ⓐ (　) ⓑ (　) ⓒ (　) ⓓ (　)

2. Short story, Poem, Play : ⓐ (　) ⓑ (　) ⓒ (　) ⓓ (　)

3. Scientific report, Newspaper or Magazine articles, Biography, Autobiography, Travel essay, Brochure : ⓐ (　) ⓑ (　) ⓒ (　) ⓓ (　)

4. Letter to the editor, Pamphlet, Advertisement, Political speech, Religious speech, Poster : ⓐ (　) ⓑ (　) ⓒ (　) ⓓ (　)

A2

각각의 답은 1항 ⓐ, 2항 ⓑ, 3항 ⓒ, 4항 ⓓ이며, 형태에 따라 각각 그런 목적을 가진다.

독자층(Audience)을 고려하는 것 또한 매우 중요하다. 말을 할 때에도 연령, 성, 신분, 나와의 관계 등을 고려하여 예의에 맞게 적절한 말을 골라 쓰듯이, 글을 쓸 때도 독자층에 맞게 글을 써야 한다.

글을 쓰기 전에 다음 사항을 고려하여 보자.

글 쓰기 전 고려사항

1. 독자층은 주로 누가 될까? (독자의 연령, 성별, 교육수준, 흥미, 필요, 관심 등) 그

작문이란?

렇다면 글은 쉽게 쓸까 아니면 어렵게 쓸까? 친숙하게? 엄하게?

2. 독자는 나의 주제에 대하여 얼마나 알고 있을까? 배경설명(Background Information) 또는 전문용어(Technical Terms)설명이 필요할까?

3. 주제에 대하여 어떤 강한 거부감을 갖게 되지는 않을까?

4. 어떻게 해야 나의 글이 내가 겨냥한 독자층을 흥미롭고 가치있게 만들 수 있을까?

어조(Tone)도 글 쓰는 데 매우 중요하다. 어조란 글쓴이의 태도 또는 감정을 글로 나타내는 것으로, 어떤 '부당한 사건을 반박' 할 때의 어조는 보통 노한 상태가 되며, '연구 보고서' 는 중립적이고 객관적(Neutral and Objective)이어야 한다. '창문에 가볍게 떨어지는 비' 는 로맨틱(Romantic), '낙엽 떨어질 때' 의 어조는 슬프게 전개된다.

어조는 글 쓰는 이가 취하는 단어, 숙어, 묘사 및 문장구조(Sentence structure)에 따라 여러 가지로 달라진다. 다음 예를 보자.

> ① A half-starved wolf was jealous of a sheep who appeared to be well fed, fat and strong. "Come to our house." the sheep said to him. "You'll find everything to eat there." The wolf was very happy and started to go home with the sheep. On the way, however, he noticed something on the sheep's neck. ②"What's that?" ③"Not much."answered the sheep. ④"It's only the mark of my chain." ⑤"Your chain? ⑥ Does that mean you're tied?" And with these words, the wolf ran away. He thought he'd rather be hungry than be without leisure.

(배고픈 늑대 한 마리가 잘 먹어서 살찌고 튼튼해 보이는 양을 부러워했다. 그러자 양이 늑대에게 말했다. "우리 집으로 가자. 거긴 먹을 게 아주 많으니까." 늑대는 아주 뿌듯한 마음으로 양과 함께 양의 집으로 가기 시작했다. 그런데 가는 도중에 양의 목에 뭔가 걸려 있는 모습이 눈에 띄었다. "그건 뭐니?" "별 거 아냐"라고 양이 대답했다.

"그냥 내 목줄일 뿐이니까." "네 목줄? 그럼 너 묶여있단 말이야?" 그 말과 함께 늑대는 도망쳤다. 자유도 없이 사느니 차라리 배고픈 것이 낫다고 생각했기 때문이다.)

①번 "A half-starved wolf...strong."은 문장 구조상 우화를 소개하는 부분이므로 어조가 "중립적이고 객관적(Neutral and Objective)"이며,

② "What's that?"은 '호기심이 강한(Curious)' 어조,

③ "Not much(별 거 아냐)"는 ②항에 대한 '방어적(Defensive)' 느낌,

④ "It's … chain"은 "Not much"에 대한 '확인(Confirming)',

⑤ "Your chain?"은 ④항의 "my chain"에 대한 '의구심을 띤 질문(Inquiring)',

⑥ "Does...tied?"는 "your chain"에 대한 '확인(Confirming)'의 어조를 띠고 있다.

Q3 다음과 같은 상황(situation)에서는 어조가 대체로 어떻게 될 지 생각해 보자.

1. 성난 사람을 진정시킬 때 : ⓐ Cynical ⓑ Perfunctory ⓒ Quiet ⓓ Enthusiastic

2. 판매원이 상품을 선전할 때 : ⓐ Obsequious ⓑ Warm ⓒ Serious ⓓ Enthusiastic

3. 두 사람이 심하게 언쟁할 때 : ⓐ Solemn ⓑ Sarcastic ⓒ Furious ⓓ Sincere

4. 유치원 교실에서 선생님이 보통 사용하는 어조 : ⓐ Sincere ⓑ Warm
　　ⓒ Humorous ⓓ Quiet

5. 뉴스를 방송할 때 : ⓐ Neutral ⓑ humorous ⓒ Pedantic ⓓ Serious

A3

정답은 1번 ⓒ, 2번 ⓓ, 3번 ⓒ, 4번 ⓑ, 5번 ⓐ 이다. 이처럼 글에 사용되는 어조는 상황에 따라 많이 달라진다.

1-3. Gathering Information & Ideas
(자료수집 및 아이디어 찾기)

주제와 관련된 아이디어 및 자료 수집은 어떻게 해야 할까? 글을 쓰려면 일단 아이디어를 찾고 그와 관련된 정보를 수집해야 된다. 아이디어는 다음에서 찾아볼 수 있다.

1. Journal Writing : 매일 주변에서 일어나는 일, 경험, 관찰, 느낌, 의견 등을 적은 기록에서 아이디어를 찾는다.

2. Freewriting : 떠오르는 생각을 잠시 써 본다.

3. Brainstorming : 주제와 관련된 아이디어를 혼자 또는 타인과 같이 적어 본다.

4. Clustering : 주제와 관련된 사항들을 생각나는 대로 열거해 놓고, 관련된 사항을 서로 연결시켜 본다.

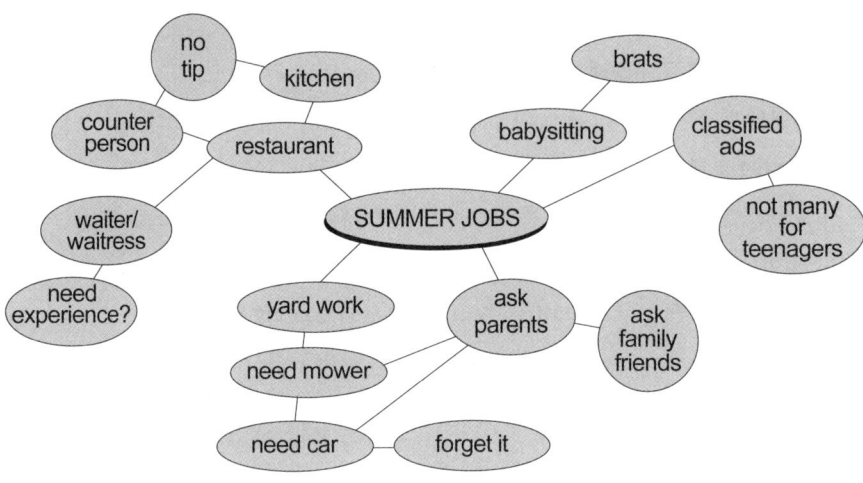

5. Imaging : 창의력 있는 작가는 기발한 상상력(active imaginations)도 많이 활용한다 What if I had $10,000,000? What if I had lived during the Silla Dynasty? 등 이러한 상상력을 통해 아이디어를 찾을 수도 있다.

6. Asking Questions : 신문, 방송 기자들이 사건을 기사화 할 때 5W-How (Who? What? Where? When? Why? and How?)라는 공식을 쓰듯이, 5W–How 사용은 정확하고 논리적인 아이디어를 줄 수 있다. 예를 들면,

> Topic : Today□s Most Popular Recording Artist
>
> **Who?** Who is number one on the pop charts?
>
> **What?** What record or album won this year's Grammy Award?
>
> **Where?** Where do most people see or hear this artist's
>
> music performed?
>
> **When?** When did the artist first achieve stardom?
>
> **Why?** Why do so many people like this star?
>
> **How?** How did the star get his or her start in popular music?

> **주제 : 오늘날 가장 인기 있는 대중 가요 아티스트**
>
> **누구?** 팝 차트 1위는 누구인가?
>
> **무엇?** 무슨 레코드와 앨범이 금년 그래미 상을 받았나?
>
> **어디?** 대부분의 사람들은 이 예술가의 음악 공연을 어디에서 보거나 듣나?
>
> **언제?** 이 가수는 언제 처음으로 스타덤에 올랐나?
>
> **왜?** 왜 그렇게 많은 사람들이 이 스타를 좋아하나?
>
> **어떻게?** 이 스타는 어떻게 대중 음악을 시작하게 되었나?

7. Reading with a Focus : 주제와 관련된 자료를 찾아 효율적으로 읽어 본다.

8. Observing : 감각기관을 통하여 사물을 세밀히 관찰하고 서술한다. 예를 들어, 캠핑에 가서 관찰하고 서술한 내용은 다음과 같다.

SIGHT : trout leaping high out of the water ; campers struggling to win a tug of war ; moonlit nights around the campfire

SOUND : roar of the river water ; chatter of crickets ; crackling fire
     ; campers shouting and laughter

SMELL : tangy odor of wet leaves and grass ; musty smell of wet
     swimsuits drying ; savory odor of fish frying

TASTE : toasted marshmallows ; tart lemonade from a bottle in
     an ice-filled tub

TOUCH : rough, splintery firewood ; shoulders aching from
     carrying backpacks ; dry, crackling leaves underfoot

시각 : 물 밖으로 높이 솟구치는 송어; 줄다리기에 이기려는 야영자들 ;
   캠프파이어 주위로 달빛이 쏟아지는 밤

청각 : 포효하듯 흐르는 강물; 귀뚜라미의 재잘거림 ; 딱딱 소리내며 타는 장작
   ; 웃고 떠드는 야영자들

후각 : 풀과 나뭇잎에서 나는 톡 쏘는 향 ; 젖은 수영복이 마르면서 나는
   곰팡내 ; 물고기가 구워지면서 나는 향긋한 냄새

미각 : 구운 마시맬로 과자 ; 얼음통에 병째 넣어두었던 톡 쏘는 레몬네이드

촉각 : 거칠고 깔쭉깔쭉한 장작 ; 배낭을 짊어져서 아픈 어깨 ; 발 밑으로
   사각사각 밟히는 나뭇잎

1-4. Structuring a Topic Sentence & a Paragraph
(주제문과 문단 구성)

주제문 구성

 주제문은 정보를 제공하고(informative), 흥미로우며(interesting), 직설적(direct)
으로 구성되어야 한다. Informative and direct란 주제에서 벗어나지 않고 한 가지
아이디어(single idea)에 초점을 맞추며 불필요한 정보는 피해야 한다는 뜻이다.

다음 문장을 보자.

Soonsin Lee was a naval captain and patriot who was born at Ahsan, and he prepared for the Japanese invasion by building iron-clad turtle boats, and he was also a devoted humanitarian.

Soonsin Lee

불필요한 정보(naval captain, patriot, was born at Ahson, the Japanese invasion, iron-clad turtle boats 등)가 소개되었고, 또 주어진 정보가 하나의 아이디어에 초점을 맞추지 못하고 산만하여, 주제문으로서는 좋지 못하다.

□Soonsin Lee, one of the Imjin War heroes, was a devoted humanitarian□로 고쳐 쓰는 게 하나의 아이디어에 초점을 맞춤으로써 정보가 산만하지 않아 좋다.

좋은 주제문은,

1. 문단의 요지(main idea)를 분명히 나타냄으로써 독자들이 다음에 올 내용을 알 수 있도록 정보를 제공해야 하고,
2. 독자들의 관심을 끌 수 있도록 재미있어야 하며,
3. 저자를 소개하지 말고, 주제를 소개하는 직설적인 정보를 제시해야 한다.

구체적으로 말하면 "I think, I feel, or I believe"라는 말은 쓰지 말고, 또 장황한 문장(wordy sentence)은 피하여야 한다. 다음은 직설적이지 않고 장황한 문장이다.

I want to write about the fact that Admiral Soonsin Lee actually made three famous victories, not two.

직설적으로 고쳐 쓰면 :

Admiral Soonsin Lee actually made three famous victories, not two.

1 작문이란?

문단구성

일단 주제문를 구성한 뒤에는 주제문의 요지를 설명, 보충할 수 있는 뒷받침 세부 자료(supporting details)를 찾아 요지를 전개시킴으로써 문단을 구성해야 한다. 주제문 구성 여하에 따라서 문단 구성도 많이 달라진다. 다음 주제문을 예로 들어보자.

"Seventeen is not too young to drive."

이 주제문은 명백히 '의견'을 말하고 있다. 의견을 말할 때는 그 의견을 정당화할 수 있는 구체적인 세부사항, 또는 이유를 먼저 제시해야 한다. (※ 참고 : 문단 수는 많을수록 좋은 게 아니며, 독자가 읽어서 기억하기 좋은 분량이 좋다. 대체로 3~5개의 문단이 바람직하다).

그렇다면 "열 일곱은 운전하기에 너무 어린 나이가 아니다"라는 주제문를 정당화시키기 위해 어떠한 '뒷받침 세부자료'가 좋을까?

첫째, 17세라는 '정신적 나이(Mental age)'를 설명하고 그 나이가 운전에 어리지 않음을 실례와 통계 자료를 들어 주장하고, 둘째, '신체적 나이(Physical age)'를 들어서 사실 및 의학적 통계 자료를 들어 주장하며, 셋째, 세계 각국에서 17세 이상에게 운전 면허증을 주는 나라 또는 주(state)를 들어 비교, 주장할 수 있다.

Topic sentence : 17 is not too young to drive.
  1st paragraph : Mental age (··· with supporting details & statistical data)
  2st paragraph : Physical age (··· with supporting details & data)
  Final paragraph : Examples (··· with specific data for comparison)

위와 같이 주제문이 어떠한 의견을 말할 때는, 사실 및 통계자료를 이용한다.

그렇다면 주제문이 묘사문일 때는 문단 구성을 어떻게 하는 것이 좋을까? 어떤 암시·시사를 줄 때는? 또 어떤 사물을 설명 및 정의할 때는?

Q4 다음 주제문을 살펴보고, 문단을 어떻게 구성할지 생각해 보자.

① Lion tamers go through intense training. (사자 조련사는 강도 높은 훈련을 거쳐야 한다.)

② The sun is an important source of energy. (태양은 중요한 에너지원이다.)

③ The earth is the mother of all people, and all people should have equal rights upon it. (땅은 모든 사람의 어머니이고, 땅 위의 모든 사람은 동등한 권리를 가져야 한다.)

④ I feel sad whenever I remember the Memorial Day. (나는 전몰 장병 기념일을 떠올릴 때마다 슬프다)

A4

주제문 ①은 어떠한 '사실을 주지(prove a point)' 시키는 말이며, ②는 일반 사실을 '설명·정의' 하고 있다. ③은 '의견(All people should… it)' 을 주장하고 있고, 끝으로 ④는 남에게 무언가를 주지시키거나 주장하는 것이 아니라 묘사문(Descriptive sentence)으로 자기 감정을 표현하고 있다.

'사실을 주지시키는' 주제문 ①의 경우, 문장을 어떻게 구성하는 것이 가장 효과적일까? 다음 중에서 해당되는 사항 하나를 골라보자:

( ) ⓐ 구체적인 사례(specific examples)를 들어 사실을 설명 및 정의한다.

( ) ⓑ 사실 및 통계 자료를 이용하여 의견을 강화시킨다.

( ) ⓒ 감각적 세부사항(sensory details)을 많이 사용하여 어떤 개체, 사물의 모양, 냄새, 맛, 소리, 감정·느낌 등을 서술한다.

( ) ⓓ 사건과 일화를 들어 어떤 사실을 설명한다.

주제문 ①에서는 '사자 조련사' 가 받는 '강도 높은 훈련' 을 알려야 한다. ⓐ는 일반 사실·생각을 설명할 때는 적합하지만, 합리적으로 알리는 데에는 적합치 않으며, ⓑ는 의견을 말할 때, ⓒ는 묘사문을 써서 어떠한 사물, 개체, 그리고 감정을 표현할 때, ⓓ는 일화(anecdotes)를 들어 어떤 사실을 알리는 데 가장 적합하다. 따라서 ①은 ⓓ로 문장을 구성함이 타당하다. 주제문 ②는 ⓐ; ③은 ⓑ; ④는 ⓒ로 문장을 구성하는 게 적합하다.

1-5. Organizing a Paragraph (문단조직)

저자가 자신의 생각 및 설명을 논리적으로 배열 또는 조직하지 못하면, 독자는 그 글이 도대체 무슨 뜻인지 이해하기 힘들다. 따라서 저자는 문단을 유기적으로 조직할 필요가 있는데, 이것이 바로 문단조직이다.

1. **Chronological order**(연대기적 순서) : 이야기를 하거나 또는 나름의 노하우를 설명할 때 사건을 순서적으로 기술하는 것.

2. **Spatial order**(공간적 순서) : 어떤 사물을 감각적으로 묘사할 때 공간/장소와 관련지어 사물을 기술하는 것.

3. **Order of Importance**(중요도 순서) : 어떤 의견을 보충하기 위하여 이유, 사실, 또는 예를 들 때 사용되는 것으로, 제시될 세부 사항들을 가장 덜 중요한 개념에서 가장 중요한 개념의 순서로 기술하는 것.

4. **General to Specific**(일반적인 것에서 구체적인 것으로) : 어떤 사물 또는 개념을 정의할 때, 일반적 서술(general statement)로 시작하여 차츰 구체적인 세부 사항(Specific details)으로 기술하는 것.

5. **Most Familiar to least Familiar**(가장 친숙한 것에서 덜 친숙한 것으로) : 어떤 사물이나 개념을 정의 또는 기술할 때, 독자가 잘 아는 세부사항을 먼저 기술하고, 독자가 잘 모르는 세부사항 또는 개념은 나중에 소개하는 것.

6. **Comparison and Contrast**(비교와 대조) : 두 사물의 비슷한 점과 다른 점을 보여줄 때 사용하는 것으로, 두 사물의 비슷한 점을 먼저 기술하고, 다른 점을 나중에 기술한다. 또는 반대로 순서를 바꿀 수도 있다.

Q5 다음 주제문은 어떤 방법으로 문단을 조직하는 것이 좋을까?

(1) The emu and the penguin are both flightless birds, yet they lead very different lives.

(2) Toxic waste is a problem that deserves our attention.

(3) Changing a tire is a simple process.

(4) Perseverance is a special quality that is defined in the motto, "If you don't succeed, don't be discouraged. Try, try, again."

(5) Uncle John's home is a gorgeous, colonial house, filled with treasured antiques and furniture.

A5

(1) 번의 경우, 에뮤와 펭귄은 둘 다 날지 못하는 새이지만 매우 다른 삶을 산다는 뜻. 따라서 '비교와 대조'를 이용하여 두 동물의 공통점과 차이점을 비교한다.

(2) 번은 유독성 폐기물은 충분히 주의를 기울여야 할 문제라는 뜻이므로, '가장 친숙한 것에서 덜 친숙한 것으로' 기법을 이용하여 가장 중요하고 독자가 잘 아는 사실을 먼저 기술하고 차츰 독자가 잘 모르는 사실을 서술하는 것이 적합하다.

(3) 번은 타이어 교체는 간단한 과정이라는 뜻이므로, 과정을 순서에 따라 설명하는 연대기적 순서를 이용하도록.

(4) 번은 중요도 순서에 따라 가장 덜 중요한 개념에서 가장 중요한 개념 순으로 기술하는 것이 좋다. 인내란 "실패하더라도, 낙담하지 말라. 다시 시도하고, 또 다시 시도하라."라는 금언으로 정의되는 특별한 자질이라는 의미.

(5) 번은 존 아저씨의 집은 귀중한 골동품과 가구로 가득한 호화로운 식민지풍 건물이라는 뜻. 따라서 공간적 순서를 따르는 것이 좋다.

2. Drafting(초고)

Prewriting(구상) 단계에서 ① 주제를 선정하고, ② 자료수집 및 아이디어를 찾는 것도 매우 중요하지만, 구상이 아무리 훌륭하더라도, 종이에 직접 써보지 않고는 (drafting) 아무 소용이 없다. 초고를 작성하는 데 어떤 특정한 방법이 있는 것은 아니다. 그저 글쓰는 이의 마음대로 천천히 또는 빨리 쓸 수 있으나, 다음 사항을 고려하기 바란다.

초고 작성시 고려사항

1. Prewriting(구상)에 사용했던 메모 및 전체적인 윤곽을 지침으로 사용한다. 그러나 모든 메모를 다 사용할 필요는 없고, 중복되거나 불필요한 메모와 개념은 생략한다.
2. 초고를 작성할 때에는 '자기 생각을 표현하는(Expressing your ideas)'데에만 집중하여 아무 걱정없이 자유롭게 쓴다.
3. 초고를 작성할 때 새로운 아이디어가 떠오르면 그 생각을 포함시킨다.
4. 문법, 철자, 관용어와 관련된 실수는 걱정 말고, '자기 생각을 표현하는'데에만 전념한다. 실수는 나중에 고친다. 오로지 염두에 둘 것은 나의 글을 읽을 독자와 내가 글을 쓰는 목적이다.

그럼 이제 다음에 제시된 메모와 세부 사항을 참고하여, 그것을 문단에 따라 분류하고, 초고를 작성해 보자.

당신이 마이클 잭슨(Michael Jackson)과 같은 유명 연예인이 되었다고 가정해 보라. 그럼 다음과 같은 구상 단계의 메모와 세부사항을 열거할 수 있으며, 상상력이 풍부한 사람이라면 더 많은 것들을 생각할 수 있을 것이다.

구상 단계의 메모와 세부사항 (Prewriting notes/details)

① 큰 저택 소유
② 개인 생활을 갖기 힘들다.

③ 여행을 자주 한다.

④ 비싼 옷을 입는다.

⑤ 내가 모르는 사람이 나를 사랑/좋아한다.

⑥ 수많은 호텔에서 유숙한다.

⑦ 신변보호를 위해 보디가드가 필요하다.

⑧ 어디를 가나 사람들이 떼를 지어 따라다닌다.

⑨ 1년에 몇 백만 불 이상의 수입을 올린다.

⑩ 군중 앞에서 연기하는 것에 만족한다.

위의 사항들을 문단으로 나눈 뒤 초고를 작성해야지, 그냥 ①~⑩까지 순서대로 쓴다면 너무나 산만하고 초점 없는 글이 된다.

문단에 따라 분류해 보면,

문단 A. 수입과 관련된 notes/details : ①, ④, ⑨

문단 B. 직업 만족과 관련된 notes/details : ⑤, ⑩

문단 C. 직업 불만과 관련된 notes/details : ②, ⑦, ⑧

문단 D. 여행과 관련된 notes/details : ③, ⑥

(비고 : 문단 D는 '여행을 좋아할 경우'에는 문단 B에 속할 수 있으며, 싫어할 경우에는 문단 C에 속할 수 있다.)

그렇다면, 초고를 작성할 때 구상 단계의 메모와 세부사항(Prewriting notes/detail)을 지침으로 해서, 문단 A(수입과 관련된 세부사항으로 이용), 문단 B(직업 만족과 관련된 세부사항으로 이용), 문단 C(직업 불만족과 관련된 세부사항으로 이용), 문단 D (여행과 관련된 세부사항으로 이용)로 분류하여 초고를 작성하는 것이 좋다.

분류된 그룹 및 이와 연관된 메모와 세부사항을 이용하여 우리말로 초고를 작성해 보면, 다음과 같은 모델이 나올 수 있다.

초고

문단 1) 나는 마이클 잭슨 같은 유명 연예인이 되고 싶다. 그 이유는 다음과 같다.

문단 2) 첫째, 경제적으로 궁핍한 생활에서 벗어나고 싶다. 궁핍에서 벗어나려면 상당한 수입이 필요하다(전면 ①, ④, ⑨항을 참조, 세부사항과 메모를 들어 열거하고 확대한다).

문단 3) 둘째, 연예인으로서 직업적 만족을 찾고 싶다(⑤, ⑩을 차례로 열거하고 세부 사항을 확장한다). 게다가 나는 여행을 좋아하는데, 유명 연예인이 되면 여행을 많이 할 수 있어서 직업적 만족이 극대화될 것이다(③, ⑥을 열거하고 확장한다).

문단 4) 마지막으로, 유명 연예인이 누리는 이점도 많지만, 그와 반대로 불편한 점(②, ⑦, ⑧을 참조하여 구체적인 예를 든다)이 있다는 것도 잘 알고 있다. 그러나 이런 것들은 장점에 비하면 너무나 사소한 일이다. 따라서 나는 유명 연예인이 되기 위해 최대한 노력하겠다.

이렇게 구상 단계의 메모와 세부사항을 분류, 이용하여 적절한 문단을 구성하고, 초고를 작성해 보았다. 이런 연습을 충분히 하면, "Writing is a fun"이 된다.

3. Revising(수정)

수정이란 완성된 초고를 평가하여 부족한 점을 첨가, 삭제, 수정함으로써 독자로 하여금 글을 더 흥미 있게, 쉽게, 정확히 읽게 하는 것을 목적으로 한다. 수정할 때에는 다음 다섯 가지 사항을 점검해야 한다(연구 논문에서는 이 과정이 특히 중요하다) : (A) 내용; (B)구성(Organization), (C) 문단 구조(Paragraph Structure), (D) 문장 구조(Sentence Structure), (E) 기교, 용법, 문체(Mechanics, Usage and style).

3-1. Checking Sentence Structure (문장구조 점검)

먼저 우리가 학교에서 오랫동안 배운 문장구조부터 살펴보기로 하자. 문장구조가 어색, 모호, 중복되거나 불필요한 단어, 구 등은 좀더 간결하고, 구체적이며, 명확하게 고친다.

① See your dentist at 3:45 <u>pm</u> <u>in the afternoon</u>
　　　　　　　　　　　　ⓐ　　　　ⓑ

　　(Note : ⓐ와 ⓑ가 같은 의미로 중복됐으므로, 하나를 지운다)

② Dr. Jeong explained everything <u>in a clear way</u>.
　　　　　　　　　　　　　　　　부사구

　　(Note : 부사구를 부사로 대체한다. 이를 테면, clearly)

③ Every building <u>in the city</u> should not be taller than that of the City Hall <u>in height</u>.
　　　　　　　　　ⓐ　　　　　　　　　　　　　　　　　　　　　　　　　　ⓑ

　　(Note : ⓐ와 ⓑ 불필요한 구를 대체, 또는 삭제할 것. 이를 테면, Every city building should
　　　　　 not be taller than that of the City Hall.)

④ Mr. Kim was fired <u>because of fact that</u> he accepted bribe.

　　(Note : 간결하지 못하다. Mr. Kim was fired because he accepted bribe.)

⑤ John blinked <u>his eyes</u> just before kissing Susan.

　　(Note : his eyes는 불필요한 단어. blink는 '눈을 깜박이다' 라는 뜻으로 단어 자체에 이미
　　eyes가 포함되어 있다. 따라서 his eyes를 삭제시켜야 한다.)

⑥ Please see the bank teller <u>who is</u> in charge of all the transactional activities.

　　(Note : 절 who is … 를 지우고 구 in charge of로 간결하게 표현해야.)

⑦ The <u>sparkling</u> <u>glitter</u> of the diamonds and rubies almost blinded my eyes.
　　　　　　ⓐ　　　　ⓑ

(Note : ⓐ와 ⓑ는 동의어이므로, 하나를 삭제해야.)

⑧ All the players <u>who are in the basketball</u> warmed up for the game.

(Note : All the basketball players warmed up for the game.)

⑨ The convicted criminal was <u>shot dead</u> and <u>killed.</u>
　　　　　　　　　　　　　　　　　　　ⓐ　　　　　ⓑ

(Note : ⓐ와 ⓑ가 중복되었으므로, ⓑ를 삭제해야 한다. was shot and killed로 고칠 수도 있으나, shot dead가 더 간결한 표현이다.)

⑩ <u>What I want to say is that</u> I love heart.

(Note : ⑨번과 마찬가지로, "What I want …"는 삭제해야 문장이 더 간결해진다. 물론 삭제했다고 해서 뜻이 바뀌는 것은 아니다.)

좋은 문장 (Good sentence structure)이란

1. 모호한 단어를 피하고 구체적인 단어를 사용한다.
2. 글의 전체적인 흐름을 중시하여 아이디어 및 문장을 이어주는 접속사를
   사용한다.
3. 아이디어를 중시하여 단문, 중문, 복문 등을 섞어 사용한다.
4. 병렬 구조(대구법)를 사용한다.
5. 반복을 피한다.

그럼 이제 구체적인 문장을 통해 좋은 문장을 실습해 보자.

1. 모호한 단어를 피하고 구체적인 단어를 사용한다.

① It was a <u>nice</u> day.

　어떤 점에서 nice한지 정확히 말해야 한다.

→ It was a mild spring day for walking. 또는 It was a perfect day
　for skating.

② Susan's birthday will be <u>soon</u>.

　soon은 특정한 날짜를 지칭하는 것이 아니므로, on next Friday 등으로
　고치면 보다 구체적인 표현이 된다.

③ Susan went to get her <u>thing</u>.

thing도 모호한 단어. 특정한 물건 이름을 사용할 것.

④ Let's have a good dinner <u>sometimes</u>.

가끔 근사한 저녁 식사나 하자. 가끔? 도대체 언제? 근사한? 도대체 어떻게 근사한? 구체적인 시간, 날짜, 장소 표시가 없는 말은, 그냥 인사치레에 불과한 것으로 간주해도 무방하다.

⑤ The movie was <u>interesting</u>.

구체적인 배역, 줄거리, 테마 등을 들어 무엇이 어떻게 흥미로웠는지를 말해야 구체적인 표현이 된다.

2. 아이디어 및 문장을 잇는 적절한 접속사를 사용한다.

<u>초고</u> : I did not notice anything. It began to occur to me that something went wrong. I was not sure what had happened. I did not know what to do with it.

이 글을 적절한 접속사를 사용하여 고치면:

I did not notice anything <u>at first</u>. Then it began to occur to me that something went wrong. <u>Since</u> I was not sure what had happened. I did not know what to do with it (처음에는 아무 것도 눈치채지 못했다. 그 뒤, 뭔가 잘못됐다는 생각이 떠오르기 시작했다. 도대체 무슨 일이 생긴 건지 확신할 수 없었으므로, 나는 어떻게 해야 할지 알 수 없었다.)

3. 아이디어를 중시하고 여러 형태의 문장을 섞어 사용한다.

<u>초고</u> : Helen walked down the Fifth Avenue. She saw several people. They were homeless. She ignored them.

→ Walking down the Fifth Avenue, Helen ignored several homeless people she saw. (헬렌은 5번 가를 걸어 내려가는 동안, 자신이 본 몇몇 홈리스들을 그냥 무시했다.)

초고 : The small lake in my mountain village was always too cold to swim in June, and even though I knew what to expect the icy water always numbed me and I would come out as fast as I went in I would run back to the shack where I could drink hot tea.

→ The small lake in my mountain village was always too cold to swim in June. Even though I knew what to expect, the icy water always numbed me. I would come out as fast as I went in and run back to the shack where I could drink hot tea. (내 고향 산골 마을의 작은 호수는 6월에 수영하기는 항상 너무 차가웠다. 어떤 일이 벌어질지 잘 알고 있긴 했지만, 그 차가운 물은 항상 나를 마비시켰다. 나는 들어갈 때만큼이나 재빨리 물에서 나와 뜨거운 차를 마실 수 있는 오두막집으로 뛰어 돌아왔다.)

4. 병렬 구조를 사용하여 독자의 기억에 남도록 한다.

초고 : Mr. Kim worked as director. He worked as actor. Also he worked as producer.

→ Mr. Kim worked as <u>director</u>, <u>actor</u> and <u>producer</u>.(미스터 김은 감독 겸 배우 겸 제작자로 일했다.)

초고 : Helen got a job. She saved her money. She paid for her college tuition.

→ By <u>getting a job</u> and <u>saving her money</u>, Helen paid for her college tuition. (헬렌은 일자리를 얻고 돈을 저축함으로써, 대학 등록금을 냈다.)

초고 : Let every nation know, whether it wishes us well or ill, that we shall pay any price, we shall bear any burden, we shall meet any hardship, we shall support any friend, or we shall oppose any foe to assure the survival and success of liberty.

→ Let every nation know, whether it wishes us well or ill, that we shall <u>pay any price</u>, <u>bear any burden</u>, <u>meet any hardship</u>, <u>support any friend</u>,

or oppose any foe to assure the survival and the success of liberty.(John
F. Kennedy)

(우리가 잘 되기를 바라는 국가는 그렇지 않은 국가든, 그 모든 나라에게 알려줍시다.
우리는 자유 수호와 성공을 보증하기 위해서 어떤 대가든 치를 것이며, 어떤 부담도
견딜 것이고, 어떠한 고난과도 맞닥뜨릴 것이며, 친구는 누구든 지지하고 또 적은
누구든 반대할 것입니다.)

5. 중복을 피한다

초고 : Many American people began <u>moving west</u> in <u>1848</u>.

<u>1848</u> was the beginning of a great <u>westward movement</u>.

➡ 1848 was the beginning of an American great westward movement.

(1848년은 미국인들이 대거 서부로 이동하기 시작한 해였다.)

초고 : <u>The Korean War</u> was a <u>difficult time to live in</u>.

<u>Life was very hard</u> during the <u>Korean War</u>.

➡ The Korean War created a difficult time to live in.(한국 전쟁은 살기
힘든 시기를 창조했다.)

3-2. Checking Mechanics, Usage and Style
(기교, 용법, 문체 점검)

이제 기교와 용법, 그리고 문체를 수정해 보자.

(1) 주어진 동사를 일치시킨다.

<u>A cup</u> of coffee <u>sit</u> on the table.(Incorrect)

<u>A cup</u>   <u>sits</u>   (Revised/improved)

(2) 대명사들을 일치시킨다.

<u>Everyone</u> should buy <u>their</u> textbooks.(Incorrect)

<u>Everyone</u>　　　　　<u>his/her</u>　　　　(Improved)

(3) 3인칭을 사용하여 자기 의견을 시종일관한다.

· <u>Most female high school students</u> love classical music, but if <u>you</u> prefer

nonclassical music, let me recommend a good one.(Incorrect)

· <u>Most female high school students</u> love classical music, but for <u>those</u>

<u>who prefer</u> nonclassical music, this is a good one.(Improved)

(4) 줄임말은 가능한 한 피한다.

· The new economic policy <u>won't</u> solve the existing social

problems.(Informal)

· The new economic policy <u>will not</u> solve the existing social

problems.(Improved)

(5) 가능한 한 수동형보다는 능동형(active voice)을 쓴다.

· Computer games are enjoyed by many teenagers(수동)(Draft)

· Many teenagers enjoy computer games.(능동)(Revised)

3-3. Checking Paragraph Structure (문단구조 점검)

좋은 문단은 다음과 같은 점을 포함한다.

1. 주제문이 있어야 한다.

2. 앞 문단과의 연관성을 보여주는 접속어나 구, 문장 등이 있어야 한다.

3. 주제문 또는 요지를 뒷받침할 수 있는 뒷받침 세부자료로서, 사례,

감각적 세부사항 사실/통계, 일화 등이 있어야 한다.

다음 두 개의 문단을 보자.

1) <u>Two kinds of goats are famous for their wool.</u> <u>One</u> is the Cashmere goat

which is raised in Asia and India. It's wool is called cashmere. <u>The other</u> is

the Angora goat which is raised in Texas. It's wool is called mohair. <u>Many</u>

farmers would like to raise them for their handsome income.

(털로 유명한 염소는 두 종류다. 그 중 하나는 아시아와 인도에서 사육되는 캐시미어다. 그 털은 캐시미어라 불린다. 나머지 하나는 텍사스에서 사육되는 앙고라 염소다. 그 털은 모헤어라 불린다. 많은 농부들은 충분한 수입을 위해 그것들을 기르고 싶어한다.)

The topic sentence is "Two kinds of goats are famous for their wool."

The supporting details are given here as specific examples.

(1) One is the Cashmere goat which is raised in Asia and India.

(2) It's wool is called cashmere.

(3) The other(Transitional phrase) is the Angora goat which is raised in Texas.

(4) It's wool is called mohair.

(5) Many farmers would like to raise them for their handsome income.

(종결을 짓는 아이디어)

주제문이 있고, One과 The other가 접속어 기능을 함으로써 앞 문장(Previous sentence)과 적절한 연관성을 갖게 하였다. 끝으로 "Many farmers…"문장이 종결을 맺는 아이디어를 포함하고 있다.

2) ① Every country has a variety of national symbols, which is usually represented on its flag. ② For example, the national symbol of Laos displayed on its flag shows a three-headed elephant with a white parasol over it and a five-step platform under it. ③ The three-headed elephant signifies the three sixteenth century kingdoms of Laos; the

parasol as a symbol of royalty; and the five-step of the platform as the five commandment of the Laotian official religion that proscribe killing, stealing, lying, adultery, and abuse of alcohol.

(나라마다 다양한 국가의 상징물이 있다. 그리고 그것들은 대개 국기에 포함된다. 예를 들면 국기에 나타난 라오스의 국가상징은 흰 파라솔 아래 머리가 셋 달린 코끼리와 그 아래에 있는 5개의 계단으로 된 연단이다. 3두 코끼리는 라오스의 16세기 3개 왕국을 의미하며 파라솔은 왕권의 상징이고 5계단으로 된 연단은 살생, 도둑질, 거짓말, 간음 그리고 술의 남용을 금지하는 라오스 공식 종교의 5계명을 의미한다.)

①은 주제문이며, ②와 ③은 예문을 통해 주제문을 뒷받침하는 구체적인 세부사항이다. 그러나 "This type of national symbol signifies its unique meanings not only through flag but also national flower of bird."라는 식으로 종결을 짓는 문장이 있으면 더 좋은 문단이 될 수 있다.

3-4. Checking Organization (글 전체의 구성 점검)

글 전체의 구성을 점검하고 필요하면 고친다.

다음에 나열한 단어들을 논리적으로 분류하여 조직해 보자.
① cheese ② cherry ③ cucumber ④ fruit ⑤ food ⑥ mango ⑦ ham
⑧ cabbage ⑨ butter ⑩ cauliflower ⑪ pear ⑫ milk ⑬ persimmon
⑭ apricot ⑮ egg ⑯ vegetable ⑰ scallion ⑱ lettuce ⑲ dairy product

제일 중요하고 범위가 큰 화제를 (Theme)라 하고, 그 다음을 주제(main topic), 그리고 주제에 속하는 나머지를 부주제(sub topic)라 하자.

테마 하나, 주제 셋, 부주제 열 다섯 가지를 골라보면, 다음과 같이 분류할 수 있다:

Theme : Food

Main topic 1:**Fruit** → mango, pear, persimmon, apricot, cherry(Sub topics)

Main topic 2:**Vegetable** → cucumber, cabbage, cauliflower, scallion, lettuce(〃)

Main topic 3:**Dairy product**(유제품) → cheese, ham, milk, butter, egg(〃)

이런 방식으로 다음 테마 또는 논제 "Korean gold mining during the colonial period"(식민지 시대 한국의 금광업)를 주제와 부주제로 분류하면 다음과 같다.

Theme : Korean gold mining during the colonial period.

Main topic 1:**Korean miners** → ① Seasonal activities ② Limited resources
③ Prized results(Sub topics)

Main topic 2:**Japanese settlers** → ① Permanent settlement
② Socioeconomic control
③ War effort(Sub topics)

'초고 작성' 편에서 살펴보았듯이, 특히 연구 논문에서는 주제를 선정하고, 테마에서 논제를 이끌어내며, 이와 관련하여 구상 단계의 메모와 세부 사항을 포함한 최종 개요가 필요하다. 그러면 연구 논문에서 핵심인 논제(central idea)란 무엇인가?

'논제 진술(Thesis statement)'이란 자신이 쓸 연구 논문의 내용을 간단히 요약한 것으로, 다음과 같은 특성을 가지고 있다.

논제 진술의 특징

1. 연구 논문에서 논할 명확한 논점을 보여준다.
2. 논문 쓰는 사람의 의견, 사상, 답을 보여주거나, 논제의 내용 전개를 보여준다.
   결론(Conclusion)이 어떻게 나올지 암시한다.
3. 부정 또는 의문형 문장이 아닌, 하나의 평서문(single declarative sentence)을
   사용해야 한다.

예를 들면 :

Question : What should we do to solve the pollution problem?

　　　　　(공해 문제를 해결하기 위해서는 어떻게 해야 하나?)

Thesis : Government, business organizations, and individuals should work

　　　　　together to solve the pollution.

　　　　　(정부와 기업체, 개인들이 공해 문제를 해결하기 위해 힘을 합쳐 일해야 한다.)

Main topic 1 **Government** → ① Local government ② Internal government

　　　　　　　　　　　　　③ World government(Sub topic)

Main topic 2 **Business Organizations** → ① Local business Organizations

　　　　　　　　② Domestic business Organizations

　　　　　　　　③ Foreign business Organizations(Sub topic)

Main topic 3 **Individuals** → Unit as ① Self ② Family(Sub topic)

그렇다면 이제 감기(The common cold)라는 주제로 논문을 쓸 때, 일반적인 글의 구성은 어떻게 짜여질까?

Topic : The common cold

Question : What exactly is the common cold, and what is the best thing to

　　　　　do when you got one?

(※ 글쓰는 이가 논제를 끌어내기 위해 스스로에게 던지는 질문. 이 질문은 논문에는 쓰지 않는다.)

★★★Thesis : The common cold is a contagious virus that can be treated by

　　　　　the traditional remedy of rest, aspirin, and plenty of fluids.

Main topic 1 : The common cold is a viral infection of the upper respiratory

　　　　　system.(※What exactly is the common cold?에 대한 대답)

Sub topics : (1) An infection caused by over 120 different viruses.

　　　　　(2) Symptoms are dry, scratchy sensation in nose or throat.

　　　　　(3) Body temperature drops.

　　　　　(4) Nasal discharge becomes thick.

Main topic 2 : For a long time people have tried many traditional remedies to
combat the common cold. (※What is the treatment?에 대한 대답)

Sub topics : (1) Rest helps your body fight the virus.

(2) Aspirin reduces fever, and helps you combat the minor
pains of cold.

(3) Liquid helps loosen thickness in the chest.

(4) Moderate amount of alcohol helps you get comfort and
sleep.

Conclusion : Simply put, there is no magic care for the common cold
caused by variety of viruses. The best we can do is resting, and
taking aspirin and plenty of fluids.

테마 : 감기

질문 : 감기란 정확히 무엇이며, 또 감기에 걸렸을 때 가장 좋은 치료책은 무엇인가?

논제 : 감기란 휴식, 아스피린, 그리고 다량의 액체라는 전통적인 치료법으로
대처할 수 있는 전염성 바이러스이다.

주제 1 : 감기란 호흡기 계통의 바이러스 감염이다.(감기란 정확히 무엇인가에 대한
대답)

부주제 : (1) 감염은 120종 이상의 다양한 바이러스에 의해 야기된다.

(2) 증상은 코나 목이 건조하거나 따끔거린다.

(3) 체온이 떨어진다.

(4) 콧물이 탁해진다.

주제 2 : 감기를 퇴치하기 위해 사람들은 오랫동안 전통적인 치료책을 상당수
시도해왔다. (치료책은 무엇인가에 대한 대답)

부주제 : (1) 휴식은 몸이 바이러스와 싸우는데 도움이 된다.

(2) 아스피린은 열을 내려주고, 감기의 여타 사소한 통증과 싸우는데 도움을
준다.

(3) 액체는 가슴의 답답함을 완화시키는 데 도움이 된다.

(4) 적당한 양의 술은 몸을 진정시켜 숙면을 취할 수 있도록 도와준다.

결론 : 간단히 말해서, 다양한 바이러스에 의해 야기된 감기의 기적적 치료책은 없다. 최선의 방법은 휴식을 취하고, 아스피린을 복용하며, 다량의 액체를 마시는 것이다.

그럼 이제 ★★★표를 한 논제("The common cold is a contagious virus that can be treated by the traditional remedy of rest, aspirin, and plenty of fluids.") 를 다시 한번 살펴보자. 이 논제는,

① 한 문장의 평서문인가? Yes(X) No(   )

② 논문이 논할 논점을 보여주었는가? (※ 논점은 둘 : ①감기는 무엇인가? ②치료는 무엇인가?) Yes(X) No(   )

③ 쓰는 사람이 답 또는 주제에 대한 내용 전개를 보여주는가? (※답은 논점이며, 내용전개는 논점을 중심으로 Main topic 및 sub topic에 보여준다) Yes(X) No(   )

④ 결론이 어떻게 나올지 보여주고 있는가? (※ '전염성 바이러스' 를 설명하고, '치료책' 을 설명할 결론을 예측할 수 있다) Yes(X) No(   )

'논제' 는 이처럼 학술 논문에서 논할 구체적인 논점을 보여줄 뿐 아니라 내용을 전개하고 결론을 이끌어내게 하는 매우 중요한 열쇠이다.

연구 논문의 구성은 1-5(문단 조직)에서 살펴보았듯이 ① **연대기적 순서**, ② **공간적 순서**, ③ **중요도 순서**, ④ **일반적인 것에서 구체적인 것으로**; ⑤ **가장 친숙한 것에서 가장 덜 친숙한 것으로**, ⑥ **비교와 대조** 등으로 분류된다.

Q6 다음 '독서와 인생(이희승,1998)' 이란 글을 보고, 구성(Organization)에 대해 살펴보자.

독서와 인생   이 희 승

사람은 무엇을 위해 사는가? 이상(理想)을 위하여 산다. 이상을 위하여 산다는 것은 오직 인간만이 누릴 수 있는 특권(特權)이다. 여타의 동물은 이상이라는 것이 없다. 다만, 현실(現實)만을 위하여 산다. 즉, 먹기 위하여 살고, 살기 위하여 먹는다. 그러나 인생(人生)은 그렇지가 않다. 먹기도 해야겠지만, 먹는 것만으로는 만족하지를 않는다. 그리하여 사람은 빵만으로 사는 동물이 아니라고 하였다.

이상을 위하여 산다는 것은 어떠한 꿈을 그리며 산다는 말이 된다. 이 꿈이란 것은 현실이 아니란 말이다. 현실 이상의 것, 초현실적(超現實的)인 것을 의미한다.

그런데 꿈과 이상은 꼭 같지가 않다. 꿈은 허탄(虛誕)한 가공(架空)의 환상(幻想)을 가리키는 일이 많다. 그러나 이상은 결코 허황한 망상(妄想)이 아니다. 초현실적이고, 따라서 비현실적(非現實的)인 점에서는 이상과 꿈이 상통하는 면이 있다고 하겠지만, 그러나 이상은 실현의 가능성(可能性)이란 것을 수반하는 사고작용(思考作用)이다. 이상은 비현실적인 것, 초현실적인 것이란 점에서 우리 현실의 권외(圈外)에 있으면서도, 이것을 추구(追求)하기 위하여 연구하고 노력하면 도달할 수도 있다는 점에서 꿈과 다르고, 따라서 공상(空想)이 아니다. 꿈과 이상은 이와 같이 정신세계(精神世界)의 차원이 다르다.

어떠한 이상을 추구하여 그것을 실현하면, 그것은 벌써 현실이 되어 버리고, 이상은 아닌 것이다. 그렇게 되면, 이번에는 그 이상(以上)의 것을 추구하게 되며, 그 이상의 것이 다시 이상이 되고 마는 것이다. 현실과 이상의 차이는, 그것이 실현되었느냐 않았느냐에 달려 있는 것이라 하겠다. 가령, 사람이 월세계(月世界)에서 가서 살려고 그 방법을 연구하고 있다고 하자. 이것은 어디까지나 이상이요, 아직 현실은 아니다. 우리의 월세계에서의 생활은 오늘날까지도 이상에 지나지 않는 것이요, 현실로는 이루어지지 못하였다. 그러나 그 가능성(可能性)만은 충분히 보이고 있다. 그리하여 만일, 우리가 월세계에서 몇몇 사람의 이상과 마찬가지로 별장(別莊)도 짓고, 농장도 건설하게 되면, 그 때에는 이것이 현실이 되고 말 것이다.

문제 1) 이 글의 Topic은?

문제 2) 이 글의 Organization 형태는?

ⓐ Chronological( ) ⓑ Spatial( ) ⓒ Order of importance( )

ⓓ General to specific( ) ⓔ Comparison & Contrast

문제 3) 이 글의 Thesis는?

ⓐ 사람은 무엇을 위하여 사는가( ) ⓑ 사람은 이상을 위하여 산다( )

ⓒ 사람은 어떠한 꿈을 그리며 산다( )

ⓓ 사람은 특권을 누리기 위하여 산다( )

ⓔ 사람은 먹기 위하여 살고, 살기 위하여 먹는다( )

문제 4) 이 글의 Main Topic은?

ⓐ 현실과 이상의 차이( ) ⓑ 현실추구( ) ⓒ 꿈의 추구( )

ⓓ 이상추구( ) ⓔ 현실과 꿈의 차이

문제 5) 이 글의 Sub Topic은?

ⓐ 현실과 실현가능성( ) ⓑ 환상과 초현실( ) ⓒ 꿈과 현실( )

ⓓ 현실과 이상( ) ⓔ 꿈과 실현가능성( )

A6

발췌한 '독서와 인생' 이라는 글에서 Topic은 독서와 인생, Organization의 형태는 ⓓ가 가장 타당성이 많으며('이상' 이라는 General Concept을 Specific하게 전개 및 설명하고 있음), Thesis는 ⓑ(Paper가 논할 Specific issue를 보여주고 저자의 의견, 사상을 전개시켜 나타냄), Main Topic은 ⓓ(나온 Thesis를 꿈과 현실을 들어 설명하고 있음), 그리고 Sub Topic은 ⓔ가 가장 적합하다(Thesis는 '이상', Main topic은 '이상추구' 인데 Main topic에 대한 보완설명으로 즉, '꿈과 실현 가능성이 이상추구' 이다).

3-5. Checking Content (내용점검)

끝으로 내용을 점검하고 수정을 끝낸다. 내용을 점검할 때에는 다음 사항을 유의해야 한다.

내용점검시 유의사항

1. 연구 논문을 쓰고 난 뒤에는, 충분한 시간(24시간 이상)을 가진 후에 내용을 검토한다.

2. 문법, 철자 등의 오류는 우선 무시하고, 글이 일관성을 갖고 있는지 살핀다. 다시 말해, 각 문단이 논제를 뒷받침하고 있는지 점검한다.

3. 글의 어조는 적절한가?

4. 문단과 개요를 비교해 보고, 중요한 세부 사항이 빠지지 않았는지 살펴본다.

5. 배정된 분량과 비교할 때, 쓴 글의 분량이 적으면 부가적인 뒷받침 세부자료 (additional supporting details)를 첨가하고, 이와 반대로 쓴 분량이 너무 많으면 개요를 점검하면서 그다지 중요치 않은 문단 등은 생략한다. (참고 : 중요한 문단이란 논제를 충분히, 효과적으로 설명한 문단을 말한다.)

　　지금까지 우리는 ① 내용(Content), ② 문장 구조(Sentence structure), ③ 문단 구조(Paragraph structure), ④ 글 전체의 조직(Organization) ⑤ 기교, 용법, 문체 (Mechanics, Usage and style) 등을 점검해 보았다. 참고로, 정말 잘 쓴 A급 연구 논문은 다음과 같은 특징을 가지고 있다.

STANDARDS FOR ENGLISH PAPER

－Characteristics of an A paper

(1) The subject is focused, significant, interesting, and manageable, mechanical.

(2) The paper's purpose is identified clearly by the thesis statement.

(3) The paper is correctly organized and supplies transitions which keep the organization from seeming

(4) Each topical paragraph has a controlling idea, solid detail, and smooth transitions.

(5) The sentences are varied in length and structure according to the author's

purpose and emphasis.

(6) The word choice is almost uniformly good. Words are chosen for precise denotation, connotation, and tone

(7) The author clearly designed his essay for a definite an appropriate level of complexity and has maintained that level consistently.

(8) If sources were used, documentation is consistently and accurately employed.

(9) Mechanically the paper is correct except for excusable errors of inadvertence and violation of extremely technical rules.

영어 논문의 표준

논문의 성격

(1) 주제가 명확하고, 의미 있으며, 재미있고, 다루기 쉽다.

(2) 논문의 목적이 논제 진술에 명확히 제시되어 있다.

(3) 논문이 잘 조직되어 있으며, 기교상으로 볼 때 그 구성을 유지시키는 이행 장치를 제공한다.

(4) 각각의 주제 문단에는 지배적인 아이디어와 탄탄한 세부 사항, 부드러운 이행 장치 등이 들어 있다.

(5) 문장은 작가의 목적 및 강조점에 다라 길이상으로나 구조적으로나 다양화되어 있다.

(6) 단어 선택이 거의 한결같이 뛰어나다. 단어는 명시적 의미와 언외의 의미는 물론 어조 면에서도 정확하게 선택되어 있다.

(7) 작가는 특정 독자를 대상으로 하여 자신의 글을 기획하였다. 그는 적절한 수준의 언어와 문장 구조를 선택했으며, 그 수준을 일관되게 유지하였다.

(8) 인용문을 사용할 경우, 증거 자료를 정확하고 일관되게 제시한다.

(9) 기교상으로 볼 때, 논문이 부주의로 인한 사소한 실수나 극단적으로 전문적인 규칙 위반 등을 제외하고는 사실과 일치한다.

4. Proofreading (교정)

수정된 초고를 주로 문법, 용법, 기교 면에서 교정하는 작문 과정의 마지막 단계. 이 단계에서는 특히 다음 사항을 주의해야 한다.

1. 모든 문장은 완벽한 문장인가? 또한 문장 첫 글자 및 고유 명사는 대문자로 쓰여져 있는가?

2. 오자는 없는가?

3. 구두점 점검 – 특히 중문 또는 복합문에서 구두표가 제대로 사용되었는지 검토한다.

4. 문법상의 실수는 없는가?

   예 : ⓐ Subject - verb agreement(주어 – 동사 일치)

   A bowl of oranges (sit, sits) on the table.

   ⓑ Pronoun-Antecedent agreement(대명사 – 전위(前位)와 일치)

   Everyone should spend (his/her, their) time wisely.

5. 동사의 시제를 시종일관 일치시킨다.

   예 : John Steinbeck's the grapes of wrath (is, was) set during the great depression and (describes, described) a family's struggle with socioeconomic crisis. (존 스타인벡의 「분노의 포도」는 대공황기를 배경으로, 사회경제적 위기에 대항하는 한 가족의 투쟁을 다루고 있다.)

6. 일관된 관점을 견지하고 있는가?

   예 : ⓐ The issue seems to be paradoxical to me.(1인칭)

   ⓑ You may be confused with the paradoxical issue.(2인칭)

   ⓒ The issue presents a paradoxical question.(3인칭)

   (※ 연구 논문에서는 3인칭 관점을 견지한다.)

7. 연구 논문에서는 준말(Contractions), 속어(slang) 및 구어체(colloquialism) 등은 피한다. 끝으로 연구 논문을 수정하고 교정할 때 미국 교사들이 흔히 사용하는 부호를 소개한다.

CHAPTER

1 작문이란?

※ 미국의 영문 교정부호

SYMBOLS FOR REVISING AND PROOFREADING

SYMBOL	EXAMPLE	MEANING OF SYMBOL
cap ≡	Spence college	Capitalize a lowercase letter.
lc /	our Best quarterback	Lowercase a capital letter.
∧	the on the fourth of july	Insert a missing word, letter, or punctuation mark.
/	a endurence	Change a letter.
∧	Ohio the capital of Iowa	Change a word.
⌐	hoped for to go	Leave out a word, letter, or punctuation mark.
⌐	on that occassion	Leave out and close up.
⌒	today's home work	Close up space.
∐	nieghbor	Change the order of the letters.
tr ∐	the councell general of the corporation	Transpose words. (Write tr in nearby margin.)
¶	¶ "Wait!" I shouted.	Begin a new paragraph.
⊙	She was right⊙	Add a period.
∧	Yes∧that's true.	Add a comma.
#	# centerfield	Add a space.
⊙	the following items⊙	Add a colon.
∧	Evansville, Indiana∧ Columbus, Ohio	Add a semicolon.
=	Self=control	Add a hyphen.
∨	Mrs. Ruiz's office	Add an apostrophe.
stet	a very tall building	Keep the crossed-out material. (Write stet in nearby margin.)

◻ CHAPTER SUMMARY & EXERICISES

Choose the best answer provided

1. A religious sermon can be largely considered as a/an (ⓐ entertaining
   ⓑ Informative ⓒ Persuasive ⓓ Expressive ⓔ Creative) speech.

2. One of the best topic to research for a paper of about 1,000 words is:
   ⓐ Ancient cosmetics ⓑ World language ⓒ Pythagoras
   ⓓ How to audition   ⓔ Potential health problems for joggers

3. One of the best and the most specific topic for an academic paper is:
   ⓐ Civil rights movements in the United States
   ⓑ Civil rights movements in the 1960s
   ⓒ Martin Luther King's activities
   ⓓ Martin Luther King's civil rights movement
   ⓔ Leadership role of Martin L. King during the early civil rights protests.

4. Choose the best topic progression that is generated from the general to the
   specific.
   ⓐ History → Korean history → Korean war history → The Korean Conflict
      → Inchon Landing → MacArther's strategy of employing naval forces
      for the Inchon Landing.
   ⓑ History → Korean war history → Korean history → Inchon Landing →
      The Korean Conflict → MacArther's strategy of employing naval forces
      for the Inchon Landing.
   ⓒ Korean war history → Korean history → History → Inchon Landing →
      The Korean Conflict → MacArther's strategy of employing naval forces
      for the Inchon Landing.

ⓓ History → Korean history → Korean war history → Inchon Landing → The Korean Conflict → MacArther's strategy of employing naval forces for the Inchon Landing.

ⓔ Korean history → Korean war history → The Korean Conflict → Inchon Landing → History → MacArther's strategy of employing naval forces for the Inchon Landing.

5. One of the best topic sentences is:

ⓐ Bears are fascinating animals.

ⓑ Bears are fascinating, aggressive, and hostile animals.

ⓒ Bears are clumsy and ugly animals.

ⓓ The reason I am writing is to tell you bears are incredible animals.

ⓔ To me, bears are fascinating animals.

연습문제 해답

1. 종교적 설교는 주로 설득형 연설로 간주될 수 있다.

　정답 : ⓒ persuasive

2. 1000단어 분량의 연구 논문을 작성하는데 가장 적합한 주제는?

　정답 : ⓔ 조깅하는 사람들의 잠재적인 건강 문제 – ⓐ 고대의 화장품, ⓑ 세계의 언어, ⓒ 피타고라스, ⓓ 오디션 하는 방법 등은 주제가 너무 광범위하다.

3. 연구 논문에 가장 적합하고 또 가장 구체적인 주제는?

　정답 : ⓔ 초기 민권 운동 기간의 마틴 루터 킹의 리더쉽 – 미국의 민권 운동, 1960년대의 민권 운동, 마틴 루터 킹의 활동, 마틴 루터 킹의 민권 운동 등 기타 주제들은 ⓔ에 비해 너무 광범위하고, 학술적으로 초점을 맞추기에도 너무 넓고 모호하다.

4. 다음은 주제를 '일반적인 것에서 구체적인 것으로' 좁히는 과정이다. 가장 잘 된 것은?

　정답 : ⓐ가 단계적으로 가장 논리적으로 전개되었다. 즉 '역사' → 어떤 역사? '한국역사' → 어떤 한국역사? '한국전쟁역사' → 어떤 전쟁역사? '6·25전쟁 → 6·25전쟁 중에서 어떤 것? '인천 상륙 작전' → 상륙 작전의 어떤 면? → '인천 상륙 작전을 위한 맥아더의 해군력 동원작전'

5. 가장 좋은 주제문은?

　정답 : ⓐ 곰은 매혹적인 동물이다. single idea(즉 fascinating)로 직설적으로 소개시켰기 때문에 독자에게 흥미를 준다. – ⓑ는 'aggressive'와 'hostile'이 redundancy (중복)을 가져와 좋지 않을 뿐 아니라 세 가지 ideas를 가져와 독자에게 혼란을 주며; ⓒ도 'clumsy'와 'ugly'가 redundant; ⓓ Too personal(사적 교신에는 쓰여도 무방하다), 그리고 ⓔ도 Too personal.

CHAPTER

2

명확하고 생생한 언어사용

Specific Use of Language

명확하고 생생한 언어 사용

이 장에서는 언어와 문화의 상호 관계를 이해하고, 문화의 영향을 받는 언어가 특정 사회에서 어떻게 표현되고 있는지 살펴보기로 하겠다. 또한 애매모호하고 생생치 않은 영문을 구체적이고 생생하게 쓸 수 있는 능력을 기르는 데 초점을 맞췄다. 한국적 문화 및 사고방식에 따라 한국어로 소통하면서 살아온 우리로서는 한국어와 영어를 혼용하듯이 영작을 하게 되어 '영어다운 영어'를 쓰기가 결코 쉽지 않다. 특히 영어를 구체적이고 생생하게 쓴다는 것은 영어를 외국어로(English as a foreign language)로 쓰는 한국 학생한테나 영어를 모국어로 쓰는 미국 학생한테나 모두 어려운 일이며, 미국 사회에 살지 않는 한국 학생에게는 더욱 힘들다.

그러나 두려워할 필요는 없다. 한국과 미국의 문화 차이에서 기인하는 언어 표현은 서로 다른 것보다 비슷한 것이 더 많으며, 조금만 더 노력해서 미국의 문화 및 사고방식에서 기인한 표현들을 이해하고 습득하면 되기 때문이다.

그럼 지금부터 '영어다운 영어'를 쓰기 위해 몇 가지 공부해 보기로 하자.

□ LANGUAGE AND CULTURE
(언어와 문화)

언어는 사회문화와 뗄 수 없는 관계를 맺고 있으며, 문화가 변함에 따라 언어도 그 영향을 받아 변한다. 언어란 문화의 일부로서, 특정 문화와 긴밀한 관계 속에서 발달한다.

문화(Culture)란 무엇인가? 문화란 "인간이 주변 자연 환경과 공존하면서 형성, 발전시킨 적절한 사회규범 및 습관"을 말하며, 그에 반해 문명(Civilization)은 "주변 자연과 자원을 개척, 이용하여 사회의 실리를 축적하는 것"이다. 일본과 뉴기니는 '실리적인 자원이용(Civilization)' 면에서는 우열을 말할 수 있지만, '자연과 공존하면서 형성, 발전시킨 사회습관(Culture)' 면에서는 우열을 가릴 수 없다.

나라마다 주변 환경이 서로 다르다. 사람들은 다른 이 주변 환경에 적응하면서 독특한 문화를 형성, 발전시킨다. 동양 문화를 오랫동안 연구한 Keyserling, Herman(1963)은 동서양의 문화적 차이를 다음과 같이 일반화하였다:

EAST(동양)	←→	West(서양)
contemplative	←→	active (동양인은 사색적, 서양인은 활동적)
placid	←→	restless (차분 ↔ 불안)
gentle	←→	rough (온화 ↔ 난폭)
courteous	←→	sincere (정중 ↔ 성실)
patient	←→	impatient (끈기 ↔ 조급)
quietude	←→	bustling (조용 ↔ 떠들썩)
thinkers	←→	doers (사색가 ↔ 행동가)
introspective	←→	objective (내성적 ↔ 객관적)
conservative	←→	progressive (보수적 ↔ 진보적)
communalistic	←→	individualistic (공동체적 ↔ 개인적)
imitative	←→	initiative (모방적 ↔ 독창적)
religious	←→	ethical (종교적 ↔ 윤리적)
heteronomous	←→	autonomous (타율적 ↔ 자율적)
weak	←→	strong (허약 ↔ 튼튼)
passive	←→	aggressive (수동적 ↔ 공격적)
negative	←→	positive (부정적 ↔ 긍정적)
feminine	←→	masculine (여성적 ↔ 남성적)
submissive	←→	masterful (순종적 ↔ 지배적)
onlookers	←→	participators (방관적 ↔ 참여적)
mystical	←→	realistic (초자연적 ↔ 현실적)
traditional	←→	liberal (전통적 ↔ 자유주의적)
drifty	←→	purposeful (표류성 ↔ 목적의식성)
profound	←→	superficial (심오 ↔ 피상적)
mythological	←→	scientific (신화적 ↔ 과학적)
pessimistic	←→	optimistic (비관적 ↔ 낙천적)
authoritarian	←→	self-determinative (권위주의적 ↔ 자기 결정적)

이와 별도로, Kaplan(1972)은 미국으로 유학 온 동양계 학생과 미국 학생의 작문 구성을 비교·연구했다. 그 결과 미국 학생은 '평행선 구성(parallel construction)' 을 취하여 주제 또는 먼저 나온 아이디어를 이어지는 문장에서 설명하여 끝을 맺은 뒤 계속해서 같은 순서로 다음 아이디어로 나아가는데 반해, 동양계 유학생은 '원형 (Circularity)' 작문 구성 방식을 취하여 주제나 먼저 나온 소주제를 곧바로 설명하지 않고 여러 각도로 빙빙 돌리고 난 뒤, 주제 또는 소주제를 다루는 경향이 있다고 지적했다.

1. Parallel construction, with the first idea completed in the second part:

    (첫 번째 아이디어가 두 번째 부분에서 완결되는 평행선 구성 방식)

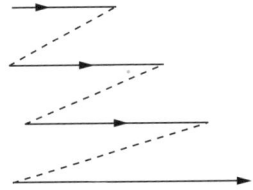

2. Circularity, with the topic looked at different tangents.

    (주제를 다른 각도에서 비춰보는 원형 구성 방식)

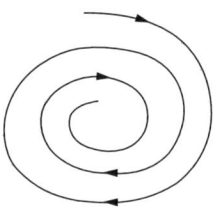

이와 같이 언어와 문화는 서로 긴밀한 상호관계를 맺고 있다. 다만 여기 실린 두 가지 가설 및 일반론은 직접적인 실험 및 증명을 거친 진리가 아니라 가설 또는 일반론에 불과하다는 점은 분명히 알아두기 바란다.

□ # SPECIFIC USE OF ADJECTIVE AND NOUN
(형용사와 명사의 구체적인 사용)

알다시피, 형용사와 명사의 관계는 무척 긴밀하다. 형용사는 명사를 수식함으로써, 오감(Five senses : ① Sight, ② Smell, ③ Sound, ④ Taste, ⑤ Touch)을 자극할 뿐 아니라 애매하고 추상적인 명사의 개념을 명확히 해 준다. "Good Writing should be specific, vivid, clear, and detailed."(좋은 글은 구체적이고, 생생하고, 명확하고, 상세해야 한다.) 이 파트에서는 명사와 형용사를 "일반적인 것에서 구체적인 것으로" 바꿔 쓰는 연습을 해보기로 하자.

> **Q1** 다음 예를 든 문장들을 보면, 밑줄 친 명사와 형용사가 구체적이며 상세하지 못하고 일반적이다. 주어진 보기들 가운데 밑줄 친 명사나 형용사를 대신할 '구체적이고, 생생하고, 명확하고, 상세한(specific, vivid, clear, and detailed)' 단어를 골라라. 〈해답은 2장 끝에 있음, 이하 모두〉

1. My grandfather packed a few <u>things.</u>

   (a) items   (b) stuff   (c) personal possessions

   (d) objects   (e) boxes of Godiva chocolates

2. Helen's garden is very <u>beautiful.</u>

   (a) filled with flowering shrubs and trees   (b) colorful

   (c) cute   (d) pretty   (e) gorgeous

3. The movie, Titanic, was very <u>interesting.</u>

   (a) fascinating   (b) well acted and written

   (c) appealing   (d) amusing   (d) delightful

4. Mr. David Greenberg is very <u>tall.</u>

   (a) high   (b) giant   (c) towering at 7 feet 4 inches

(d) great   (e) lofty

5. Flying an airplanes is great.

   (a) important   (b) excellent   (c) unbelievably thrilling

   (d) pleasant   (e) amazing

6. Mr. Kim ate a lot of beef.

   (a) a big portion of   (b) a large amount of   (c) a large piece of

   (d) 3 pounds of   (e) a large quantity of

7. It was a nice day.

   (a) charming   (b) beautiful   (c) perfect day for hiking

   (d) lovely   (e) charming

8. The two English professors had their big fight last week.

   (a) bitter, last Monday (b) large, a few days ago (c) great, several days ago

   (d) enormous, last Tuesday   (e) massive, last Monday

9. Mr. Goldman is heavy.

   (a) overweight   (b) plump   (c) obese

   (d) chubby   (e) tipping the scale at 350 pounds

10. That house is made of wood.

    (a) lumber   (b) oak 2' x 4'   (c) timber

    (d) logs   (e) boards

Q2 다음 10개의 문장을 읽고 각 문장에 포함된 명사와 형용사를 분류하라.

(1) The animal ran away.

(2) The boy walked along the street.

(3) My uncle bought a car.

(4) The dog did not seem to like the cat.

(5) The girl was shy.

(6) The woman was very emotional.

(7) Her teacher was very strict.

(8) The fish smells bad.

(9) The people liked the food.

(10) My friend loves flowers.

이 10개의 문장을 분류했다면 이렇게 분류된 형용사와 명사는 각각 specific, vivid, clear, and detailed한가? 형용사와 명사가 'specific and clear' 하지 못하고 'general' 하기 때문에 (1)~(10)번 문장을 몇 번이고 다시 읽어도 사진을 보는 듯한 선명한 뜻을 알아내기 어렵다. 문법적으로는 문제가 없지만, 여기서 학습하고 있는 'Specific, vivid, clear, and detailed' 면에서는 적절하지 못한 것이다. 명확하고 상세한 문장은 독자가 읽었을 때 뜻을 명확히 파악할 수 있는 '문장다운 문장' 이라 볼 수 있다. 그렇다면, 예를 든 문장 하나 하나를 자세히 살펴보자.

(1)번 문장의 경우(The animal ran away.)의 경우, '동물(Animal)' 이라는 개념이 너무 광범위하여, 독자들은 도대체 그 동물이 어떤 동물인지 종잡을 수 없다. 만일 가족 간의 대화에서 'The animal ran away.' 라고 한다면, 그 집에서 기르는 동물이 하나일 경우 서로 의사 소통될 수 있지만, 글은 대화와는 명확히 다르다. 글 쓴 사람이 글로써 어떤 상황을 명확하고 상세하게 말해주지 않으면, 독자는 그 상황을 이해하는데 어려움을 느끼고, 혼동을 일으키게 된다. 그래서 막연한 명사 animal을 특정한 종류 (horse, dog, calf 등)로 먼저 분류하고, 나이(Age), 성(sex(male, female)), 색상(color(brown, gray, milky등)), 형태(shape(chubby, skinny, flat 등)) 등을 넣어야 일반적인 'animal'이 '명확하고 생생한' 의미를 지니게 된다.

이처럼 모호한 문장을 명확하고 생생하게 구성하고자 할 경우, 각자의 취향에 따라 답은 수십, 수백 가지가 나올 수 있으며, 단 하나의 정답이란 있을 수 없다. 예문마다 두 가지 문장((a)와 (b))로 영작해 보았으니, 참조하기 바란다.

(1) The animal ran away.

→(a) The <u>five-year-old</u>, <u>female</u>, <u>brown</u> and <u>chubby</u> <u>German shepherd</u> ran away.

→(b) The <u>six-month-</u> <u>old</u>, <u>male</u>, <u>white</u>, <u>tiger cub</u> <u>with black stripes</u> ran away.

　작문은 '창조적인 예술(Writing is a creative art)' 이라고 한다. animal이라는 막연한 명사에 'Age, sex, color, shape, specific kind/type' 등을 창의적으로 첨가하여 (1)번 문장을 좀 더 'specific, clear, vivid, and detailed' 하게 만들어 보았다. 즉 (a)에서는 five-year-old가 age, female은 sex, brown은 color, chubby는 shape, German shepherd는 '특정종류(specific Kind)', 그리고 (b)에서는 six-month-old가 age, male은 sex, white는 color, tiger cub은 specific Kind, 그리고 with black stripes은 shape/color인 셈이다. 앞에서 말했듯이, 독자의 취향에 따라 답은 수십, 수백 가지가 나올 수 있으므로, 이에 대해 많은 연습이 있기를 바란다.

(2) The boy walked along the street.

→(a) The <u>fifteen-year-old</u>(age), <u>blonde</u>(color) and <u>skinny</u>(shape) <u>guy</u>(type/kind, sex) walked along <u>Chestnut Street between 42nd and 43rd</u>(specific street).

→(b) The <u>seventeen-year-old</u>(age), <u>dark skinned</u>(color) and <u>tall</u>(shape) <u>boy</u>(type/kind, sex) <u>with curly hair</u>(shape) walked along <u>Broad Street by City Hall</u>(specific street).

　(이 두 문장은 두 명사 boy와 street를 구체적이고 명확하게 만든 예문이다.)

(3) My <u>uncle</u> bought a <u>car</u>.

→(a) My uncle Larry, bought a brand new 2000 green Lexus XKE.

→(b) One of my uncles, Joe, bought a secondhand 1995 metallic blue Ford Mustang LX.

(4) The <u>dog</u> did not seem to like the <u>cat</u>.

→(a) The five-year-old, brown bulldog with strong square jaws growled and snarled at the fat black Siamese cat.

→(b) The four-year-old, yellow Labrador snarled at the stocky Persian cat with long silky fur, and was about to attack it.

(5) The girl was <u>shy</u>.

→(a) The seventeen-year-old girl with a white blouse and black skirt had her head down like her spirits.

→(b) Susan, the first ranking student among the 560 seniors, was afraid of meeting and talking with others present at John's wedding party.

(6) The <u>woman</u> was very <u>emotional</u>.

→ (a) The lady who lost her beloved husband a few days ago sobbed in distress.

→(b) Mrs. Elizabeth Lincoln burst out in tears at her only son's wedding ceremony.

(7) Her <u>teacher</u> was very <u>strict</u>.

→(a) Jane's high school English teacher neither allowed lateness nor accepted late papers.

→(b) Susan's homeroom teacher never allowed any student to chew gum, drink soda, or even talk during the advisory period.

(8) The <u>fish</u> smells <u>bad</u>.

→ (a) The 3-day-old whiting with red eyes stinks awful.

→(b) The huge shark, dead for several days, hanging in the fish market choked me with a decaying and foul stench.

(9) The <u>people</u> liked the <u>food</u>.

➜(a) The 7 delegates from Delaware for the Republican Convention devoured all the 200 pounds of succulent and spicy Thai dishes.

➜(b) My five tourist group members in Munich, Germany ate more than 73 delicious white sausages in a minute.

(10) My <u>friend</u> loves <u>flowers</u>.

➜(a) My girlfriend, Ok hee, loves all types of roses for their aroma and vibrant color.

➜(b) One of my best friends, Julie, is beside herself with joy whenever I send her a bouquet of tulips, carnations, tropical orchids, and hyacinths.

앞에서 살펴보았듯이, 'Specific, clear, vivid, and detailed' 라는 것은 다음과 같은 특성을 가지고 있다.

  1. 특정 개체를 분명히 지정한다.

  2. 그 특정 개체에 대한 중요 설명을 빠뜨리지 않는다.

  3. Five senses(오감 : ⓐ sight, ⓑ smell, ⓒ sound, ⓓ taste, ⓔ touch)에 해당하는 단어 또는 숙어가 하나 이상 포함되어 있어서 독자에게 생생하고 구체적 (vivid & concrete)인 개념 및 느낌을 전달한다.

Q3 다음에 열거한 15개의 추상적인 명사를, 위에서 본 3가지의 특성을 고려하여 'specific & vivid' 하게 고쳐 창작해 보자. 예문의 (a)항을 참조하여 빈 칸의 (b)항을 채워넣어라.

GENERAL   SPECIFIC & VIVID

	(a)	(b)
1. aircraft	non-stop, Boeing 747	I get on a non-stop, Boeing 747 jumbo jet.

	(a)	(b)
	jumbo jet	
2. athlete	6-foot-tall, female volleyball player	
3. building	flat red brick warehouse	
4. fruit	Washington red delicious (apple)	
5. game	Sony Playstation Final Fantasy VII	
6. hat	wide brimmed straw sombrero	
7. house	split-level, 5-bedroom ranch	
8. liquor	100-year-old, Napoleon Cognac	
9. meat	5-pound juicy pork tenderloin	
10. medicine	over-the-counter, medicated cough syrup	
11. toy	3.5□ GI Joe action figure	
12. shoes	old, dirty leather boots	
13. snake	6-foot, poisonous King Cobra	
14. vehicle	4-wheel drive, Toyota pick-up truck	

	(a)	(b)
15. weapon	short range, Patriot missile	

> **Q4** 다음 글을 읽고 저자가 어떻게 명사와 형용사를 'specific & vivid' 하게 사용하여 우리의 감각적 경험(sensory experience)을 강화시켰는지 알아보자. 이 글은 Cynthia Kadohata가 1991년에 쓴 소설, <The Floating World>에서 발췌한 글이다.

We hurried along. The ①<u>white daytime moon</u> showed on ②<u>a patch of turquoise sky between clouds</u>. ③<u>The rain was fine, like sifted flour.</u> My mother was in a mood but seemed aware this could easily pass. She looked at the rain and the sky as if they were possessions someone might take from her at any moment. The clouds suddenly seemed to be turning over themselves, and in a second they broke. ④ <u>We got drenched.</u>

● 다음 물음에 답해 보자.

1. 밑줄 친 구(phrase) ①에서 명사 moon을 수식하는 형용사는 무엇인가? 그리고 moon은 무엇을 말하는가?

2. 밑줄 친 구 ②에서 명사 patch를 꾸미는 형용사구는?

3. 밑줄 친 절(clause) ③에서 명사 The rain을 수식하는 형용사는 무엇인가? 그리고 절 ③에서 형용사 fine을 꾸며주는 구는 무엇이며, ③을 우리말로 번역하면 어떻게 되겠는가?

4. 밑줄친 문장 ④에서 대명사 We를 꾸며주는 형용사를 찾아보고, 문장 ④를 번역해 보아라.

5. 윗글의 무대 배경(setting)을 생각해 보자. 장소는 어떤 곳이며, 계절 및 시간은 몇 시경으로 느껴지는지 ⓐ~ⓒ중에서 골라보자.

   ⓐ 넓고 한산한 들, 여름, 3~6시경.

   ⓑ 소음 많고 번잡한 도시거리, 가을, 2:00~4:00 a.m.

   ⓒ 시끄러운 어린이 놀이터, 겨울, 3:00~6:00 p.m.

6. "The rain was fine, ⋯ She looked at the rain ⋯ at any moment."에서 My mother의 mood는?

   ⓐ 상쾌하다

   ⓑ 큰비가 곧 닥칠까 불안, 초조하다.

   ⓒ 무서운 비극이 닥칠까 두렵다.

7. 이 글은 주로 어떤 면을 구체적으로 서술하여, 독자로 하여금 생생한 이미지를 갖게 하는가?

   ⓐ Revealing characters

   ⓑ Making the setting beautiful and concrete

   ⓒ Creating mood and making setting concrete by using vivid and specific Verbs, adjectives, and nouns.

8. 형용사와 명사의 명확한 사용이라는 이 장의 주내용을 고려해 볼 때, 훌륭한 작가는 작품을 쓸 때, 특히 묘사적인 작품(Descriptive composition)에서 어떤 결론을 내릴 수 있겠는가?

   ⓐ General and Specific & vivid words를 같이 병행하여 쓰지만, 구체적인 단어(특히 오감에 호소하는)를 많이 사용하여, 읽는 사람에게 생생한 이미지를 전달한다.

ⓑ General words는 피하고, Specific words를 사용하여 독자들에게 생생한 이미지를 갖게 한다.

ⓒ Specific words, 특히 우리 오감에 호소하는 단어/숙어만 사용하여, 독자들에게 생생한 이미지를 갖게 한다.

□ SENSORY WORDS (감각단어)

글을 잘 쓰는 작가는 특정한 사물 또는 행위를 묘사하는데 5감(시각, 후각, 청각, 미각, 촉각 및 느낌)과 관련된 단어, 숙어를 잘 쓴다. 그 결과, 글을 읽는 독자가 현장에서 직접 보고, 냄새를 맡고, 듣고, 맛볼 수 있고, 느낄 수 있게 하는 것이다. 5감과 관련된 단어를 '감각 단어(Sensory words)' 라 하는데, 형용사가 제일 많긴 하지만, 문장에 어떻게 쓰였는가에 따라서 명사, 동사, 부사 및 다른 품사들도 감각 단어/구로 쓰인다.

> **Q5** 다음 문장을 읽고, 밑줄 친 단어 또는 구가 오감 중 어디에 주로 해당되는지 ( )안에 번호로 표시하라. 편의상 시각(Sight)은 ①번, 후각(Smell)은 ②번, 청각(Sound)은 ③번, 미각(Taste)은 ④번, 촉각/느낌(Touch)은 ⑤번으로 하자.

1. I found myself in the center of a <u>noisy</u>( ) crowd.

2. When the first snow falls, one awakens in the morning to find the <u>world white and clean</u>.( )

3. A cloud in the sky suddenly <u>lighted</u>( ) as if turned on by a switch.

4. I love the <u>feeling</u>( ) of <u>smooth, rich</u>( ) ice cream <u>coating</u>( ) my lips and <u>sliding down</u>( ) my throat.

5. I like the <u>quiet crackling</u>( ) of root beer foaming, but not the <u>violent slamming</u> ( ) of a steel door.

6. He was <u>tall</u>(   ), and his shoulder were so <u>wide</u>(   ) and <u>powerful</u>(   ) that they seemed to be armored in steel instead of muscle.

7. It was <u>cool and sweet</u>(   )to be on the grass and there was the <u>scent of freshly cut lemons or melons</u>(   ) in the air.

8. In the center of the bedroom was <u>maple</u>(   ) bed. On the table was a <u>marble</u>(   ) clock with <u>red and blue</u>(   ) birds. On the wall was an <u>oval</u>(   ) mirror. On the opposite wall were two <u>scratched and worn</u>(   )chests.

9. There are all the human <u>odors</u>(   ) of the hundreds of people who filled the Boardwalk in Atlantic City : ladies in <u>print</u>(   ) dress <u>smelling like passing gardens</u>(   ), and beach guys with <u>their scent of sun-tan and body lotions</u>(   ).

10. It was then that the <u>crashing</u>(   ) began. First a <u>sharp</u>(   ) <u>crackling</u>(   ) like a <u>monstrous</u>(   ) <u>snapping</u>(   ) of twigs; then a <u>roar</u>(   ) like the <u>fall</u>(   ) of whole forest trees.

11. I used to treasure the <u>flavored</u>(   ) ice-crystals of snow cones as they <u>melted into</u>(   ) <u>sweet</u>(   ) streams of <u>cherry-flavored</u>(   ) syrup.

12. He was <u>freezing</u>(   ); he couldn't lie there all night. <u>Inch by inch</u>(   ) he crawled away. <u>Silent as a shadow</u>(   ) he went back across the lake.

13. Volcanoes have always <u>fascinated</u>(   ) me. I have seen <u>color</u>(   ) photographs of one of Hawaii's active volcanoes, <u>shooting</u>(   ) flames and molten, and <u>glowing</u>(   ) lava.

14. Between them was a <u>transparent</u>( ) pool in the mountain pass. Every rock <u>on the bottom</u>( ) <u>shimmered</u>( ) in <u>green-gold helicoid light.</u>( )

15. As he tired to make his inept way, <u>the pain</u>( ) was with him. Every time he tired to inhale, <u>the night air</u>( ) hit the holes in his teeth and <u>attacked the open nerves</u>( ).

16. A tornado is <u>violent</u>( ) windstorm. It can be recognized by its <u>dark, funnel-shaped</u>( ) cloud.

17. Above me the clouds roll in, <u>unfurling and smoking</u>( ) billows of <u>malignant</u>( ) violet, <u>dense as wool</u>( ). Most of the sky is lidded over but the sun remains <u>clear</u>( ), <u>halfway down the west</u>( ), <u>shining</u>( ) beneath the storm.

18. Bonsai, the Japanese art of growing miniature tree is my <u>new</u>( ) hobby. My bonsai tree is a <u>prickly</u>( ) juniper, only 19 inches <u>high</u>( ). I have carefully shaped my <u>dwarf</u>( ) tree so that it resembles an umbrella.

19. <u>The odors of onions, garlics, oranges, and kerosene</u>( ) in the grocery store had been mixing all night and wouldn't <u>be disturbed</u>( ) until the doors were wide open and <u>early morning air</u>( ) forced its way in.

20. I remember the <u>small</u>( ) village near Chingmai, Thailand, was a place of entrancing odors. The earth smell was <u>pungent</u>( ), spiced <u>with the odor of cattle manure</u>( ), <u>the deep pots of greens and beans cooking for hours with smoked or cured pork</u>( ).

　지금까지 살펴보았듯이, 감각 단어(Sensory words)는 사물 및 인물을 사진과 같이 명확하고 생생하게 기술한다.

　그럼 이제 감각단어, 즉 ① Sight, ② Taste ③ Smell ④ Touch ⑤ Hearing과 관련된 단어들을 살펴보기로 하자. 단어 공부한다는 생각으로, 모르는 단어는 꼭 사전을 찾아 정확한 뜻을 익혀서, 앞으로 영작하는데 활용하기 바란다. 각각의 감각 단어를 큰 틀로 분류하면 다음과 같다.

1. Sight Words:

　(1) Colors　　　　(2) Appearance　　　(3) Shapes　　　(4) Light/Vision

2. Taste Words

3. Smell Words

4. Touch Words

5. Hearing Words:

　(1) Loud sounds　(2) Soft sounds　　(3) Speech sounds　(4) General sounds

1. Sight Words (시각적 단어)

　시각적 단어란 시각과 관련된 단어, 구절, 문장을 말하며, 이것은 다시 Colors, Appearance, Shapes, Light/Vision 등으로 구분된다.

1-1. Colors (색상)

색상의 종류는 무수하나, 우리가 일상 생활에 보통 쓰는 색상의 종류는 다음과 같다.

Black				
Charred	Coal	Ebony	Jet	Licorice

Blue

Aqua	Aquamarine	Azure	Baby Blue	Cobalt	Delft
Inky	Navy	Peacock	Porcelain	Powder	Royal
Sapphire	Sky	Teal	Turquoise	Violet	Wedgwood

Brown

Almond	Amber	Bronze	Cinnamon	Coffee	Copper
Chocolate	Foxy	Ginger	Hazel	Mahogany	Nutmeg
Rust	Sandy	Tawny	Walnut		

Gray

Ashen	Dove	Steel

Green

Apple	Chartreuse	Celery	Emerald	Kelly	Lime
Mint	Moss	Olive	Pea	Pistachio	

Purple

Amethyst	Fuchsia	Lavender	Lilac	Magenta	Mauve
Mulberry	Orchid	Pansy	Plum		

Red

Blood	Burgundy	Cardinal	Carmine	Cherry	Coral
Crimson	Currant	Flame	Garnet	Maroon	Pink
Raspberry	Rose	Ruby	Salmon	Strawberry	Tomato
Vermilion	Wine				

White					
Bleached	Bone	Chalky	Creamy	Ivory	Marble
Milky	Oyster	Pale	Pearl	Platinum	Silver
Snow					

Yellow					
Apricot	Beige	Buff	Butter	Buttercup	Butterscotch
Canary	Chartreuse	Chrome	Citron	Gold	Lemon
Mustard	Ochre	Orange	Peach	Persimmon	Saffron
Straw	Sulfur	Tangerine	topaz		

General					
Bland	Colorless	Drab	Rainbow	Stark	Vibrant
Vivid					

Q6 다음은 색상 용어(color term)와 관련된 형용사로서 직유법(simile)으로 쓰여졌다. 주어진 보기 중에서 답을 <u>고르고</u>, 1번을 참조하여 2~10번까지 영어로 직접 써 보아라.

1. As((a)black, (b)purple, (c)gray, (d)brown) as coal.

   As black as coal.

   →_____

2. As((a)yellow, (b)gray, (c)black, (d)green) as the night.

   →_____

3. As((a)blue, (b)brown, (c)sandy, (d)foxy) as the sea.

   →_____

4. As((a)brown, (b)blue, (c)foxy, (d)red) as the sky.

→ _____

5. As((a)brown, (b)crimson, (c)ashen, (d)orange) as blood

→ _____

6. As((a)blue, (b)green, (c)pale, (d)red) as emerald.

→ _____

7. As((a)green, (b)pale, (c)red, (d)bleached) as a rose.

→ _____

8. As((a)pale, (b)green, (c)purple, (d)white) as grass.

→ _____

9. As((a)blue, (b)pale, (c)violet, (d)white) as snow.

→ _____

10. As((a)blue, (b)pale, (c)yellow, (d)crimson) as the sun.

→ _____

Q7 다음은 유명한 작가들이 남긴 주옥같은 글에서 발췌한 것이다. 색상용어 (Color term)와 관련된 가장 옳은 답을 고르되, '시의 제목과 문맥에 상응하는 뜻'을 고려하라. 그리고 1번을 참조하여 완성된 문장을 한번씩 써 보아라.

1. O, my love is like a ((a)blue, (b)green, (c)red, (d)purple), ((a)white, (b)red, (c)yellow, (d)black) rose.

("A red, red rose," Robert Burns)

→ O, my love is like a red, red rose.

2. When all at once I saw a crowd,

   A host of ((a)silver, (b)royal, (c)almond, (d)golden) daffodils.

   ("Daffodils," William Wordsworth)

   →

3. And the wheel's kick and the wind's song

   And the ((a)black, (b)olive, (c)white, (d)foxy) sail's shaking.

   ("Sea fever," John Masefield)

   →

4. When I was down beside the sea,

   A wooden spade they gave to me

   To dig the ((a)black, (b)sandy, (c)violet, (d)rainbow) shore.

   ("At the seaside," Robert Louis Stevensen)

   →

5. A lemon looks like a little ((a)yellow, (b)purple, (c)green, (d)hazel) orange.

   But look out! It is very sour. You bite it and it bites you!

   →

6. How do squirrels remember

   When woods are ((a)inky, (b)white, (c)azure, (d)tawny) with snow

   Where they hid the pine cones they buried months ago?

   ("Buried treasure." Aileen Fisher)

   →

7. Then the ((a)blue, (b)white, (c)green, (d)purple) grass sprouted

   And the little ((a)black, (b)purple, (c)green, (d)red) flowers blossomed.

   ("Creation," James Weldon Johnson)

   → _____

8. The ((a)gray, (b)green, (c)brown, (d)yellow) sea

   And the long ((a)red, (b)yellow, (c)green, (d)black) land;

   And the ((a)yellow, (b)red, (c)green, (d)blue) half-moon large and low,...

   ("Meeting at night," Robert Browning)

   → _____

9. The sun is an eagle old;

   There in the windless west,

   Atop of the spirit-cliffs

   He builds him a ((a)aqua, (b)green, (c)crimson, (d)purple) nest.

   ("An Indian summer day on the prairie," Vachel Lindsy)

   → _____

10. Let the rain beat upon your head

    With ((a)silver, (b)gold, (c)bronze, (d)green) liquid drops.

    → _____

11. Listen a while, the moon is a lovely woman,

    A lovely woman lost in a ((a)gold, (b)silver, (c)porcelain, (d)brown) dress.

    ("The moon," Carl Sandburg)

    → _____

12. Between the under and upper ((a)blue, (b)white, (c)green, (d)yellow)

All day the seagulls climb and swerve and soar,

Arc intersecting arc, curve over curve.

("Seagulls," Robert Francis)

→ _____

13. The lake roared in. A vast stream leaped up, ((a)green, (b)blue, (c)yellow,

(d)white) in the sudden dark under the moon.

There was a hiss, a gushing whirl, and silence.

("The Hobbit," J. R. R. Tolkien)

→ _____

14. ((a)Brown, (b)White, (c)Dark, (d)Yellow) hair, ((a)brown, (b)white,

(c)dark, (d)yellow) skin.

These are the dominant measure of

My sense of beauty

Which explains possibly why being a ((a)black, (b)white, (c)yellow,(d)pink) girl

In a country of ((a)black, (b)white, (c)yellow, (d)pink) strangers.

I am so pleased with myself.

("The way it is," Gloria Oden)

→ _____

15. Della finished crying... She stood by the window and looked out with little

interest at a ((a)black, (b)gray, (c)white, (d)blue) cat walking along a

((a)black, (b)gray, (c)white, (d)blue) fence in a ((a)black, (b)gray,

(c)crimson, (d)hazel) backyard. Tomorrow would be Christmas day, and

she had only one dollar and eight-seven cents with which to buy Jim, her husband, a present.

("The Christmas Present," O' Henry)

$\longrightarrow$ _____

1-2. Appearance(외양)

　외양(Appearance)이란 특정한 장소, 시간, 환경 등에 비춰진 어떤 사물 또는 사람의 일반적 생김새나 상태를 말한다. 즉, 어떤 사람이 특정한 장소와 시간에 '화' 를 냈다거나 기분이 '상쾌' 했다거나 '눈물을 글썽거렸다' 는 등의 상태 및 생김새(예 : tall, heavy, skinny, beautiful)등을 나타내는 것이다. 다음에 열거한 단어를 잘 익히고, 특히 뜻이 모호한 단어는 사전을 찾아보아라.

APPEARANCE

Animated	Apprehensive	Arid	Arrogant	Ashen	Attractive
Awkward	Beautiful	Blazing	Blotched	Boiling	Bold
Bright	Brilliant	Bruised	Bubbling	Bulky	Bumpy
Burning	Bushy	Calm	Cheap	Chintzy	Chubby
Clean	Clear	Cluttered	Coarse	Colorless	Congested
Crisp	Crooked	Curved	Dark	Dazzling	Decorative
Dim	Dingy	Dismal	Distinctive	Dotted	Drab
Dramatic	Drenched	Dripping	Dull	Dusty	Elegant
Energetic	Erect	Exhausted	Exotic	Expansive	Exuberant
Fearful	Feathery	Fiery	Fine	Flamboyant	Flashy
Flat	Flowery	Fluffy	Fluid	Flushed	Foamy
Foggy	Formal	Fragile	Frail	Freckled	Fresh
Frightened	Furry	Fuzzy	Gigantic	Glassy	Glazed

Glimmering	Glossy	Glowing	Gorgeous	Graceful	Grainy
Greasy	Grimy	Hairy	Handsome	Hard	Hazy
Healthy	Heavy	Hideous	Huge	Hysterical	Immense
Imposing	Iridescent	Irresistible	Jammed	Jeweled	Jutting
Keen	Knobbed	Lacy	Large	Lavish	Lean
Leathery	Light	Lit	Lithe	Lively	Long
Loose	Lopsided	Lovely	Lumpy	Massive	Matted
Messy	Metallic	Miniature	Mottled	Muddy	Muscular
Mushy	Narrow	Neat	Nerveless	Nervous	Nondescript
Oily	Old	Opaque	Opulent	Orderly	Overloaded
Packed	Pale	Pasty	Patterned	Perky	Pleasant
Pocked	Pointed	Powdered	Pretty	Prickly	Pulpy
Radiant	Ramshackle	Regal	Rigid	Robust	Rocky
Rotted	Rough	Round	Ruffled	Sandy	Scrubbed
Scummy	Serene	Shabby	Shadowy	Shaggy	Sharp
Sheer	Shimmering	Shiny	Short	Showy	Shy
Sickly	Silky	Skinny	Slender	Slick	Slimy
Small	Smooth	Sooty	Sparkling	Spiky	Splintered
Spongy	Spotless	Spotted	Square	Squeezed	Stately
Statuesque	Steamy	Stolid	Stout	Straight	Stretched
Striped	Strong	Stubbly	Stunning	Sturdy	Sunny
Supple	Swollen	Tall	Tangled	Tantalizing	Tearful
Terrified	Thick	Thin	Tidy	Tide	Timid
Tiny	Tired	Translucent	Transparent	Twinkling	Ugly
Unruffled	Untidy	Used	Verdant	Vivid	Wavy
Waxy	Wet	Wide	Wild	Wiry	Woolly
Worn	Wrinkled	Young			

1-3. Shapes (형태)

형태는 특정한 장소 및 시간에 비춰진, 외양(Appearance)보다 좀더 구체적인 생김 새나 꼴을 말한다.

SHAPES

Angular	Branching	Broken	Clustered	Conical	Crimped
Crinkled	Crooked	Curved	Cylindrical	Domed	Flared
Flat	Frilled	Globular	Hexagonal	Hollow	Irregular
Jutting	Long	Lumpy	Narrow	Octagonal	Oval
Padded	Patterned	Pendulous	Portly	Proportioned	Pyramidal
Rectangular	Rolled	Rotund	Round	Ruffled	Scalloped
Scrolled	Shapeless	Shapely	Short	Skinny	Spindly
Split	Square	Straight	Stretched	Swollen	Tapering
Thin	Top Heavy	Triangular	Tubular	Tufted	Twiggy
Wavy	Wide	Winged	Wiry		

1-4. Light/Vision (시력)

Light/Vision은 주로 시력과 관련된 단어를 말한다.

Blind	Blinding	Blurred	Cloudy	Dim	Dusky
Dusty	Faint	Foggy	Gaudy	Gazing	Glancing
Glaring	Gleaming	Glimpsing	Glittering	Hazy	Inspecting
Invisible	Leering	Microscopic	Misty	Myopic	Ogling
Peeking	Peeping	Peering	Perceiving	Recognizing	Scanning

Scrutinizing   Shadowy   Shiny   Squinting   Staring   Steamy

Transparent   20/20   Twilit   Twinkling

Q8 다음 글에 나오는 밑줄친 형용사가 Appearance로 쓰여졌다고 생각되면 ( )에 ［A］, Shapes는 ［S］ 그리고 Light/Vision은 ［LV］로 표기한 뒤, 1번의 예를 참조하여 문장을 한번씩 써 보아라.

1. The <u>little</u>(   ) boat at anchor

   In the black water sat murmuring

   To the <u>tall</u>(   ) black sky. ("Fourth of July," Carl Sandburg)

   → The little boat at anchor in the black water sat murmuring to the tall black sky.

2. Wintermelon has light green or orange flesh with <u>smooth</u>(   ) or <u>ridged</u>(   ) skin.

   →

3. There were fogs so <u>thick</u>(   ) that you could cut houses out of them, The way they did with snow and ice in the far north.("Paul Bunyan's been there," Maurice Dobier)

   →

4. It is a cold and snowy night. The main street is <u>deserted</u>(   ). The only things moving are swirls of snow. ("Driving to town late to mail a letter," Robert Bly)

   →

5. When we arrived on the scene, fire-fighters were aiming gigantic(   ) water hoses at the upper floors.

→ _____

6. During the 1970's, there was a gasoline shortage. Drivers waited in long(   ) lines at filling stations and the gas price skyrocketed.

→ _____

7. We drove past a barbed-wire(   ) fence, through a gate, and into an open(   ) space.

→ _____

8. He was tall(   ), and his shoulders were so wide(   ) and powerful that they seemed to be armored in steel instead of muscle.

→ _____

9. The set is magnificent(   ). the left half of the stage depicts a hillside in cherry blossom, and the other half does a thatched(   ) entrance gateway.

→ _____

10. When John first arrived at our school, he was carrying a natty(   ) little briefcase and wore a pink spotted(   ) tie and short trousers.

→ _____

11. Following the unsuccessful operation, the vision in his right eye fell to 20/20(   ).

→ _____

12. My bonsai tree is <u>prickly</u>(   ) juniper, only 12 inches <u>high</u>(   ). Below this cluster of needles, the tiny trunk is <u>twisted</u>(   ) and <u>wrinkled</u>(   ).

→ _____

13. When I reached the top of the mountain, I scanned the horizon. It was a <u>bright</u>(   ), <u>beautiful</u>(   ) noon.

→ _____

14. The well-known professor's room was a <u>peculiar</u>(   ), <u>triangular</u>(   ) one. It had an old, musk oder to it.

→ _____

15. Spring skips lightly on a <u>thin</u>(   ) crust of snow,

Pokes her fragrant fingers in the ground far below,

Searches for the sleeping seeds hiding in <u>cracked</u>(   ) earth,

Sticks a straw of sunshine down and whispers words to grow. ("A circle of season," Myra Cohn Livingston)

→ _____

16. The brittle air stung Sonja's cheeks as her sleigh along the <u>snow-packed</u>(   ) road. As the horse clip-clopped homeward, his <u>brass</u>(   ) harness bells jingled.

→ _____

17. The old store, <u>lighted</u>(   ) only by three 50-watt bulbs smelled of coal oil and baking bread. In the middle of the <u>rectangular</u>(   ) room stood an iron stove.

→ _____

18. A woman with <u>shorn</u>(   ) white hair is standing at the kitchen window. She is wearing tennis shoes and a <u>shapeless</u>(   ) gray sweater over a summery calico dress. she is small and <u>sprightly</u>(   ), like a bantam hen; but, due to a long youthful illness, her shoulders are pitifully <u>hunched</u>(   ).

→ _____

19. In a hole in the ground, there lived a hobbit. Not a nasty, <u>dirty</u>(   ), wet hole, filled with the ends of worms and an oozy smell, nor yet a dry, <u>bare</u>(   ) sandy hole with nothing in it to sit down on or to eat; it was a hobbit-hole, and that means comfort. ("The Hobbit," J.R.R. Tolkien)

→ _____

20. She was a big, <u>awkward</u>(   ) woman, with big bones and hard, <u>rubbery</u> flesh. Her short arms ended in ham hands, and her neck was a <u>squat</u>(   ) roll of fat that protruded behind her head as a big bump. Her skin was <u>rough</u>(   ) and <u>puffy</u>(   ), with <u>plump</u>(   ), <u>mole</u>(   ) like freckles down her cheeks. (Alice Walker)

→ _____

2. Taste Words(미각 단어)

다음은 미각과 관련된 단어들(주로 형용사)이다. 맛에 대한 표현은 문화와 개개인의 습성에 따라 조금씩 다르기 때문에 사실 이런 저런 맛을 정확히 표현하기는 어렵다. 이와 관련된 세부 사항은 후각 단어(Smell Words)까지 알아본 후에 설명하기로 하겠다. 앞에서와 마찬가지로, 모르는 단어는 사전을 찾으면서 뜻을 읽히기 바란다.

Acid	Alkaline	Appetizing	Bitter	Bittersweet	Bland
Burnt	Buttery	Cajun Hot	Catsup	Crisp	Delicious
Dull	Edible	Fishy	Foul-tasting	Fruity	Garlicky
Gingery	Grueling	Hearty	Honeyed	Hot	Lemony
Liquorice	Medicinal	Mellow	Mild	Minty	Mustard
Oily	Overripe	Peppery	Pickled	Plain	Pulpy
Raw	Rich	Ripe	Rotten	Salty	Savory
Slopping	Smoked	Sour	Spicy	Spoiled	Stale
Succulent	Sugary	Sweet	Tangy	Tarted	Tasteless
Unripe	Vanilla	Vinegary	Watered-down		

3. Smell Words(후각 단어)

Acidic	Acrid	Aroma	Aromatic	Balmy	Boutique
Briny	Burnt	Damp	Dank	Decaying	Deodorizing
Disinfected	Dry	Earthy	Faint Smell	Fishy	Flowery
Foul-smelling	Fragrant	Fresh	Freshness	Gamy	Garlicky
Gaseous	Heady	Herb	Lemony	Mildewed	Minty
Moldy	Musky	Musty	Odorous	Offensive	Overpowering
Perfumed	Piney	Plastic	Pungent	Putrid	Rancid
Rank	Reeking	Rotten	Rubbery	Savory	Scented
Sea Air	Sewer	Sharp	Sickly	Smelly	Sour
Spicy	Spoiled	Stagnant	Stale	Stench	Stinking
Sweaty	Sweet	Tempting	Unwashed	Vile	Whiff

　　맛(Taste)과 냄새(Smell)는, 시각(Sight)과 청각(Sound)에 비해 주관적인 표현이기 때문에 객관적으로 정확히 기술하기가 힘들다. 맛에 대한 표현은 음식의 생김새와

냄새, 또는 혀와 입에 느껴지는 감촉에 따라 개개인마다 달라질 수 있다. 우리 입맛에는 된장찌개가 '구수하다, 맛있다' 등으로 표현될 수 있지만, 외국 사람들에게는 '별의별 불유쾌한' 맛으로 표현될 수 있다. 게다가 우리 인간은 다른 동물에 비해 후각 기능이 매우 떨어지기 때문에, 가까운 곳에서 강한 냄새를 풍기지 않는 한 냄새를 잘 맡지 못하며, 강한 냄새조차도 오래 맡으면 그 냄새에 면역이 되어 후각이 둔화된다.

그러나 맛과 냄새는 우리의 유쾌한 또는 불유쾌한 기억, 감정, 분위기(memories, emotion, and moods)를 불러일으키는 중요한 감각 단어이다. 이렇게 표현하기 힘든 맛과 냄새는 특정된 형용사로 기술하기가 힘들어, 보통 맛과 냄새에 관련된 다른 관련 단어(references words)를 많이 사용한다. 예를 들어 '푹 익은 김치 맛/냄새, 삶은 계란 맛/냄새, 끓는 된장찌개 맛/냄새' 등에서 '김치, 계란, 찌개'는 감각 단어는 아니지만 맛/냄새와 관련된 관련 단어로서, 어떤 맛/냄새와 관련된 형용사(짜다, 시다, 맵다, 구수하다)보다 더욱 정확하고 객관적인 기술을 할 수 있다.

> **Q9** 다음 문장에서 밑줄 친 부분이 맛을 기술하고 있으면 (　　)안에 'T'를, 냄새를 기술하고 있다면 'S'를 써놓고, 보기 문장과 같이 각 문장을 한번 써 보아라.

Example : I crunched happily on bags of popcorn that were usually too salty(T) and always slightly stale(T).

(1) I love the smooth, sweet and rich ice cream(　) coating my lips and sliding down my throat.

(2) Mingled breath and smell(　)

So close mingled

Black and white

So near no room for fear.

("Subway rush hour," Langston Hughes)

(3) I drew in a deep breath and held it, savoring the smell of <u>rich earth, sweet, and damp hay</u>( ).

(4) To the left of them are strings of <u>fragrant sausage</u>( ) and speckled salamis. Beside these meats are blocks of cheese from <u>mild-flavored Gouda</u>( )to pungent Limburger.

(5) In the memory, my wife used to open the window of the white house by the seashore, and <u>the breeze smells of salt and the sea</u>( ).

(6) Water voices drift up from the river, while from the forest emanates an <u>odor made up of all the winter decomposition and the summer blooming</u>( ); <u>exotic, pungent, heady</u>( ).

(7) There were all the smells of <u>salt and seaweed, of fish, water and wind</u>( ). There were all the human smells too <u>of the hundreds of people who filled the boardwalk</u>( ). (Jessamyn West)

(8) In my memory, the village was a place of entrancing odors. The earth smell was pungent, spiced with the odor of cattle manure, the yellowish acid of the ponds and river, <u>the deep pots of greens and cooking for hours with smoked or cured pork</u>( ). <u>Flowers added their heavy aroma</u>( ). (Maya Angelou)

(9) What happens to a dream deferred?
Does it dry up like a raisin in the sun?
Or fester like a sore-And then run?

<u>Does it stink like rotten meat</u>(　)?

Or crust and sugar over-<u>Like a syrup sweet</u>(　)?

Maybe it just sags like a heavy load

Or does it explode? ("Harlem," Langston Hughes)

(10) The wolf wrinkled its nose in disgust, its wary expression contorting with a grimace of distaste. The <u>scent of the man was strong here</u>(　), much more so than at any time in the past several hours. <u>The acrid odor of the clothing alerted the wolf</u>(　) first-the musty smell of an ancient wool coat saturated with a <u>disagreeable, sickly-sweet stench of sweat and fear</u>(　). And then there was the oppressive odor of the man himself, the heavy musky smell of warm skin and racing blood.

4. Touch Words(촉각 단어)

촉각이란 오감, 특히 피부를 통해 느끼는 물체적(예 : cold, soft, oily), 정서적(예 : suffering, dull, stimulating) 느낌 및 감촉을 말한다.

Q10 일단 다음 문장을 읽고 영문으로 답하라.

① 만질 수 있는 물체를 20개 이상 열거하라(예 : water)
② 현재 느낌은? 더운가, 추운가, 편안한가? 어떻게, 왜 그렇게 느끼는가?
③ 거친 것과 부드러운 물체를 10개씩 열거하라.(예 : ⓐ Rough : rock ⓑ Soft : velvet 등)
④ 손으로 만지지 말고 Five senses와 cognition을 통해 느낄 수 있는 것들을 10개 이상 열거하라(예 : wind).
⑤ 다른 교통 수단(비행기, 버스, 기차 등)을 이용하여 여행할 때 느끼는 기분은?

TOUCH WORDS

Aching	Abrasive	Arthritic	Balmy	Battering	Biting
Bleeding	Blistering	Blushed	Boiling	Bruised	Brushed
Bubbly	Bulky	Bumpy	Burning	Bushy	Caressing
Chilly	Clammy	Clutching	Coarse	Cold	Cool
Cottony	Cramping	Crisp	Cuddling	Cushioned	Cut
Damp	Downy	Drenched	Dripping	Dry	Dull
Dusty	Elastic	Feathery	Feverish	Fine	Fleshy
Fluffy	Flushed	Foamy	Fondling	Fragile	Freezing
Frosty	Furry	Gashing	Glassy	Gluey	Gnawing
Grabbing	Grainy	Grasping	Grazing	Greasy	Gripping
Gritty	Groping	Gushy	Hairy	Hard	Headache
Heavy	Hot	Hugging	Humid	Hurt	Icy
Itching	Keen	Kissing	Knobbed	Lacy	Leathery
Light	Lukewarm	Mangling	Massaging	Matted	Mauling
Metallic	Moist	Mushy	Nippy	Numbing	Oily
Pampering	Pang	Perspiring	Petting	Piercing	Pinching
Plastic	Pocked	Poking	Pointed	Pounding	Prickling
Pulpy	Punching	Puncturing	Raw	Rocky	Rough
Rubbery	Rubbing	Sandy	Satiny	Scalded	Scorching
Scratching	Scummy	Shaggy	Sharp	Shivering	Silky
Skimming	Slashing	Slick	Slimy	Slippery	Sloppy
Smashed	Smooth	Smothering	Soapy	Soft	Sore
Sopping	Soupy	Spasm	Splitting	Spoiled	Spongy
Sprained	Steamy	Steely	Sticky	Stifled	Stimulating
Stinging	Stony	Stroking	Stubby	Suffering	Sun-baked
Sweated	Sweltering	Tangled	Tearful	Tender	Tepid
Thick	Thin	Throbbing	Tickling	Tingling	Tough

Tugged	Twinge	Ulcer	Velvety	Warm	Waxy
Wet	Wiry	Woolly	Wounded	Wring	Yank

Q11 다음 문장에서 피부를 통해 직접 느껴지거나 정서적(emotional feeling)으로 느껴지는 촉각 단어/구/절(Touch words/phrase/clauses)에 밑줄을 쳐라.

Example : I wouldn't let him <u>touch</u> me unless I am <u>in mood.</u>

(1) The metal was so hot that I couldn't touch it.

(2) It was cool and sweet to be on the grass during that summer day.

(3) Into each life some rain must fall; Some days must be dark and dreary.

(4) He was freezing; he could not lie there all night. Inch by inch he crawled away.

(5) All those who are contended with this life pass like a shadow or a dream, or wither like the flower of the field.

(6) She stands in the quiet darkness,

This troubled woman bowed by weariness and pain

Like an autumn flower in the frozen rain,

Like a wind-blown autumn flower

That never lifts its head again.

("Troubled woman," Langston Hughes)

(7) It is a cold and snowy night. The main street is deserted.

   The only things moving are swirls of snow

   As I left the mailbox door, I feel its cold iron.

   There is a privacy I love in this snowy night.

   Driving around, I will waste more time.

   ("Driving to town late to mail a letter," Robert Bly)

(8) Are you Chinese? Yes

   American? Yes

   Really Chinese? No... not quite.

   Really American? Well, actually, you see...

   But I would rather say, Yes

   Not neither nor, not maybe, but both, only not only.

   The homes I've had, the ways I am.

   I'd rather say it twice, Yes.

   ("Saying Yes," Diana Chang)

(9) As he tried to make his inept way, the pain was with him. Every time he

   tried to inhale, the night air hit the holes in his teeth and attacked the open

   nerve. (William Goldman)

(10) The rain hit his face. He covered his face with his hands. The rain hit his

   back. He turned over on his stomach in the mud on the rubbery plants,

   and the rain hit his back and hit his legs. (Ray Bradbury)

명확하고 생생한 언어 사용

□ SPECIFIC USE OF VERB & ADVERB
(동사와 부사의 구체적인 사용)

앞에서 우리는 일반적/모호한 명사와 형용사를 구체적/상세한 것으로 바꿔보았다. "The animal ran away"라는 문장은 구문상으로는 잘못이 없다. 단지 The animal... 이 너무 일반적/모호하기 때문에 The five-year-old, brown German Shepherd.... 로 명확하게 고쳐 줄 경우, 독자들에게 생생하고 분명하며 상세한 묘사를 전하게 된다. 감각 단어 또한 마찬가지다.

1. Dynamic Structure with the Specific 'Action Verb'
(구체적인 '행위 동사' 사용에 따른 역동적인 구조)

지금부터 살펴보게 될 동사와 부사 역시 구문상(Syntatic or grammatical rules)의 하자를 따지기보다는 '일반적인 것에서 구체적인 것으로' 라는 측면에 역점을 두고 있다. 또한 영작을 할 때 문장을 좀더 역동적이고 효과적으로 만드는 방법을 익히는 데 중점을 두기로 하겠다.

알다시피, 형용사의 주요 기능은 명사 수식이며, 부사는 동사를 수식한다. 명사와 동사는 언어사용에 있어서 가장 중요한 기능을 하며, 문장 구성에 필수불가결한 요소이다. 다시 말해, 명사, 동사 없이는 문장을 구성(Syntax)하지 못한다. 이런 측면에서 볼 때, 명사와 동사가 지나치게 '일반적/모호' 하지 않고 보다 '구체적/분명' 해야 문장 및 문단이 역동적이고 효과적으로 구성될 수 있다. 우선 다음 사항을 유의하자.

1. 문장을 수동태(Passive Voice)보다는 능동태(Active Voice)로 쓰는 게 보다 역동적이고 효과적이다. 단, 다음과 같은 경우는 제외된다

(a) 행위자를 모를 때, 또는 밝히고 싶지 않을 때

The pianist(행위자) played the waltz.

The waltz was played beautifully.

(b) 행위자보다 행위 자체를 강조할 때

The Waltz was applauded wildly(행위자체)by the audience.

(c) 행위자를 문장 끝에 놓고 강조할 때

The waltz was played by the well-known pianist, Ray Charles himself

(행위자 강조).

그럼 다음 능동태와 수동태를 보면서, 어떤 문장이 더 역동적이고 효과적인지 비교하라. 알다시피, 능동태가 항상 구체적이고, 역동적이며, 효과적이다.

(1) Music videos are enjoyed by many teenagers. (Passive)

Many teenagers enjoy music videos. (Active)

(2) Many trees in the park were damaged by the gale last night. (Passive)

The gale damaged many trees in the park last night. (Active)

(3) A great deal of time is spent by teachers marking papers. (Passive)

Teachers spend a great deal of time marking papers. (Active)

2. 연결 동사(Linking verbs : be, become, feel, sound 등)는 가능한 한 피하고, 행위 동사(Action verbs : 특정한 행위를 묘사하거나 보여주는 동사. kick, send, kiss, speak, swim 등)로 대체한다. 또한 행위 동사라도 뜻이 너무 일반적일 때는 구체적인 행위를 보여주는 동사로 대체한다.

예 : (1) (a) She is a beautiful dancer. (연결동사 'is')

(b) She dances beautifully. (연결 동사를 대치)

(2) (a) She went down the stairs. (구체적이지 못한 행위동사)

(b) She <u>charged</u> down the stairs. (구체적인 행위 동사)

3. 행위를 설명하는 동사보다는 행위를 보여주는 동사가 보다 역동적이고 효과적이다.

   (1) (a) She <u>entered</u> the room happily. (행위 설명)

      (b) She <u>bounced</u> into the room. (행위 보여줌)

   (2) (a) The 60ton German Panzer tank <u>ruined</u> the small jeep. (행위 설명)

      (b) The 60ton German Panzer tank <u>flattened</u> the small jeep. (행위 보여줌)

4. 동사 혼자서도 부사의 도움 없이 문맥의 뜻을 분명히 나타내는 동사가 좋다.

   (1) (a) Larry <u>sat quickly</u> on the sofa. (부사 도움 필요)

      (b) Larry <u>plopped</u> on the sofa. (부사 도움 필요 없음)

   (2) (a) Larry <u>looked intently into</u> her eyes. (부사 도움 필요)

      (b) Larry <u>stared into</u> her eyes. (부사 도움 필요 없음)

> **Q12** 다음 문장에서 밑줄 친 동사 및 부사를 좀더 역동적이고 효과적으로 만들
> 어줄 동사를 고르고, 문장을 다시 한 번 써 보아라.

Example : Mary <u>walked fast</u> ((a)went, (b)scampered, (c)sprinted, (d)hurried, (e)chased) to the school cafeteria.

  →Mary hurried to the school cafeteria.

(1) The horse <u>ran fast</u> ((a)chased, (b)flew, (c)galloped, (d)scampered, (e)hurled) down the hill with his ears flat to his head.

  →

(2) Four female hyenas <u>ran after</u> ((a)chased, (b)raced, (c)rushed, (d)streaked,

(e)bolted) a large, striped zebra persistently.

→ _____

(3) Several colorful hummingbirds <u>flew fast</u> ((a)dashed, (b)darted, (c)rushed, (d)shoved, (e)loitered) from one flower to another.

→ _____

(4) All afternoon the tired, old man <u>walked up and down</u> ((a)stride, (b)drifted, (c)strayed, (d)fluctuated, (e)waddled) the street, looking at the shops displaying a variety of items and the people shopping here and there.

→ _____

(5) That night I <u>walked out of</u> ((a)loitered, (b)lumbered, (c)stalked, (d)staggered, (e)sneaked) my dormitory without being noticed to meet John, my sweetheart.

→ _____

(6) I felt the horrified little creatures <u>climbing up</u> ((a)dragging, (b)cantering, (c)ambling, (d)crawling, (e)swatting) my neck.

→ _____

(7) The price of stocks <u>fell hard and fast</u> ((a)sank, (b)crashed, (c)plummeted, (d)soared, (e)immersed) these days.

→ _____

(8) Portrait studios <u>gradually appeared</u> ((a)emerged, (b)erupted, (c)existed, (d)arrived, (e)prolonged) in every Korean city and large town during the 1920s.

$\longrightarrow$ _____

(9) The small boy <u>called loudly</u> ((a)shrilled, (b)roared, (c)complained, (d)sobbed, (e)shouted) from the top of the tree.

$\longrightarrow$ _____

(10) The fighter interceptor took off and <u>flew through</u> the blue sky. ((a)soared into, (b)disappeared from, (c)travelled to, (d)fluttered in, (e)passed by)

$\longrightarrow$ _____

(11) Susan <u>entered</u> the family room happily. ((a)went into, (b)bumped into, (c)bounced into, (d)arrived in, (e)slipped into

$\longrightarrow$ _____

(12) He who rides the tiger can never <u>get off</u> (Chinese proverb) ((a)dismiss, (b)dismantle, (c)dismount, (d)dismay, (e)alright)

$\longrightarrow$ _____

(13) A man does not have to <u>go to</u> ((a)check in, (b)attend, (c)visit, (d)drop in, (e)care for) church to be a Christian.

$\longrightarrow$ _____

(14) Trees often transplanted seldom <u>grow well</u> ((a)prosper, (b)produce, (c)succeed, (d)generate, (e)advance). (Dutch proverb)

$\longrightarrow$ _____

(15) A young man is likely to love the first woman who <u>speaks too well of</u>

((a)flatters, (b)compliments, (c)enhances, (d)flirts, (e)blesses) him.

→ _____

(16) Confucius did not <u>make up</u> ((a)discover, (b)envision, (c)initiate, (d)coin,
(e)invent) a system of morale; he found it in the hearts of mankind.
(Voltaire)

→ _____

(17) Susan <u>took</u> his hand <u>fearfully.</u> ((a)gripped, (b)caught, (c)grabbed,
(d)captured, (e)jerked)

→ _____

(18) The new techniques <u>affected</u> ((a)directed, (b)thrilled, (c)changed,
(d)disturbed, (e)modified) photographers and customers since it yielded
lifelike tone.

→ _____

(19) The hungry man <u>ate</u> the food <u>heartily</u>, and <u>liked it very much.</u>
((a)consumed the food and liked it, (b)nibbled the food and liked it,
(c)disposed of the food and enjoyed it, (d)devoured the food and enjoyed
each mouthful, (e)picked at the food and enjoyed each mouthful)

→ _____

(20) The tired old lady <u>walked</u> home <u>heavily.</u> ((a)shoved, (b)trudged,
(c)strode, (d)strayed, (e)loitered)

→ _____

(21) The mother <u>rubbed</u> her baby's face <u>softly</u>. ((a)caressed, (b)embraced, (c)squeezed, (d)snuggled, (e)cuddled)

$\longrightarrow$ _____

(22) The rotten fish <u>smells awful</u>. ((a)stinks, (b)has foul-smelling, (c)smells offensive, (d)smells rotten, (e)smells stagnant)

$\longrightarrow$ _____

(23) This black shirt <u>got smaller</u> ((a)decreased, (b)shrank, (c)minimized, (d)retreated, (e)reduced) in the hot water.

$\longrightarrow$ _____

(24) The frustrated teenager <u>broke</u> the huge beautiful vase <u>into tiny pieces</u>. ((a)destroyed, (b)damaged, (c)violated, (d)tore, (e)shattered)

$\longrightarrow$ _____

(25) John's grandfather <u>speaks haltingly</u> ((a)murmurs, (b)mumbles, (c)grumbles, (d)stammers, (e)repeats) when he is very nervous.

$\longrightarrow$ _____

위의 연습문제를 통해, 우리는 쓰임이 단조롭고 모호한 행위 동사 또는 동사와 부사를 좀더 정밀한 행위동사로 바꿈으로써 문장을 좀더 역동적이고 효과적으로 만들어보았다. 즉, 문장(1)의 ran fast를 '말(馬)이 뛰는 동사' galloped로, (2)의 ran after를 chased로, ... (25) speaks haltingly를 stammers등으로 고쳐본 것이다. 또한 앞에서 살펴보았듯이, 연결 동사(be, become, sound, feel 등)가 들어 있는 문장은 가능한 행위 동사로 고쳐 쓸 경우, 문장이 좀더 역동적이고 효과적으로 변화한다.

예 : (1) (a) Once upon a time there <u>was</u> a little girl named Milgrig.(Linking verb)

(b) Once upon a time there <u>lived</u> a little girl named Milgrig.(Action verb)

(2) (a) A flower <u>can be</u> a nice gift.(Linking verb)

(b) A flower <u>serves</u> a nice gift.(Action verb)

(3) (a) She <u>became terribly frightened</u>.(Linking verb)

(b) She <u>fainted from fear</u>.(Action verb)

Q13 대체로 글을 쓰는 영미 작가는 명사와 동사를 풍부하게 활용하며, 형용사와 부사는 가능한 적게 씀으로써 문장을 더욱 역동적이고 인상적이게 한다. 다음에 열거한 문장에서 (a)와 (b)를 비교해 보고, 왜 문장 (b)가 문장 (a)보다 생생하고 인상적인지를, 우선 우리가 공부한 '네 가지 지침'(1.수동형보다는 능동형을, 2. 연결 동사는 행위 동사로 대치, 3. 행위를 설명하는 동사보다는 행위를 보여주는 동사를 사용할 것, 4. 부사의 도움 없이 동사 혼자서도 뜻을 분명히 나타내는 동사를 사용할 것)을 근거로 판단해 보아라(문장 끝부분의 Clue(s)란에 표시된 부호는 네 가지 지침을 가리키고 있다. 이 네가지 이외의 이유에 대해서는 번호 외에 따로 간단히 기재하였으니, 독자의 의견과 비교해 보기 바란다).

(1) 수동형보다는 능동형   (2) 연결동사를 행위동사로

(3) 행위설명보다 행위를 보여줌   (4) 부사의 도움없이 의미전달

---

(1) (a) John <u>looked intently into</u> Helen's beautiful eyes.

(b) John <u>stared into</u> Helen's beautiful eyes.

*Clue(s) : (4)

(2) (a) This beautiful plant easily <u>shrinks, dries up, and dies</u> under the sun.

(b) This beautiful plant easily <u>withers</u> under the sun.

*Clue(s) : (3)&(4) – 문장 (a)는 동사가 셋이나 사용되어 장황하고 비경제적이다.

(3) (a) The wind <u>blew very hard</u> last night.

    (b) The wind <u>lashed</u> the trees <u>furiously</u> last night.

    *Clue(s) : (3)문장 – (b)가 (a)보다 역동적이고 정확하다.

(4) (a) The smoke trail <u>blew lightly</u> toward the north.

    (b) The smoke trail <u>floated</u> toward the north.

    *Clue(s) : (3)&(4)

(5) (a) The child <u>took</u> his hand <u>away</u> from the hot stove.

    (b) The child <u>pulled</u> his hand from the hot stove.

    *Clue(s) : (3)&(4)

(6) (a) The long river <u>travels slowly and indirectly</u> to the sea.

    (b) The long river <u>wanders</u> to the sea.

    *Clue(s) : (3)&(4)

(7) (a) The old lady <u>spoke softly and indistinctly</u> into her husband' s ear.

    (b) The old lady <u>murmured</u> into her husband' s ear.

    *Clue(s) : (3)&(4)

(8) (a) The policeman <u>pushed</u> the suspect <u>sharply</u>.

    (b) The policeman <u>shoved</u> the suspect.

    *Clue(s) : (3)&(4)

(9) (a) That guy <u>showed considerable anger</u> as he <u>went out of</u> the room.

    (b) That guy <u>cursed and slammed the door</u> as he <u>left</u> the room.

    *Clue(s) : (3) – 문장 (3)과 마찬가지로 문장 (b)는 정확히 행동을 보여주는 동사

를 썼기 때문에 독자가 보다 생생하게 느낄 수 있다.

(10)(a) The standard of living <u>has risen significantly</u> over the last few decades.

(b) The average worker <u>makes twice as much today</u> as in the 1980s.

*Clue(s) : (3)&(4)

(11)(a) My teacher <u>looked briefly</u> at Madame X.

(b) My teacher <u>glanced</u> at Madame X.

*Clue(s) : (3)&(4)

(12)(a) Don <u>gently threw</u> the ball to Mary.

(b) Don <u>lobbed</u> the ball to Mary.

*Clue(s) : (3)&(4)

(13)(a) A distinction <u>is made</u> by sociologists between achieved and ascribed status.

(b) Sociologists <u>make</u> a distinction between achieved and ascribed status.

*Clue(s) : (1)

(14)(a) A deer <u>ran very fast</u> across the highway.

(b) A deer <u>sprinted</u> across the highway.

*Clue(s) : (3)&(4)

(15) (a) Jimmy <u>smiled happily</u> at the stewardess.

(b) Jimmy <u>beamed</u> on the stewardess.

*Clue(s) : (3)&(4)

(16) (a) The little girl <u>looked curiously</u> at the stranger.

(b) The little girl <u>observed</u> the stranger.

*Clue(s) : (3)&(4)

(17) (a) Prof. Ecroyd <u>carefully read</u> the instructions.

(b) Prof. Ecroyd <u>deciphered</u> the instructions.

*Clue(s) : (3)&(4)

(18) (a) These planes <u>were flown</u> by the experienced pilots.

(b) The experienced pilots <u>flew</u> these planes.

*Clue(s) : (1)

(19) (a) The student <u>asked repeatedly</u> to postpone the examination.

(b) The student <u>restated</u> to postpone the examination.

*Clue(s) : (4)

(20) (a) The doctor <u>hastily wrote</u> the prescription.

(b) The doctor <u>scribbled</u> the prescription.

*Clue(s) : (3)&(4)

(21) (a) The hungry soldier <u>was terribly cold.</u>

(b) The hungry soldier's teeth <u>chattered</u>.

*Clue(s) : (3)&(4)

(22) (a) Susan <u>seemed to be nervous</u> at the party last night.

(b) Susan <u>avoided looking at them in the eye and whispered</u> at the party

lastnight.

*Clue(s) : (2)&(3) – 구체적 행동을 보여주는 동사

(23) (a) The stout woman <u>was terribly hot and sweaty</u>.

(b) <u>Sweat ran down from</u> the shout woman's <u>face and neck</u>.

*Clue(s) : (2)&(3) − 구체적 행동을 보여주는 동사

(24) (a) Mr. Shaw <u>was</u> a terribly ugly man.

(b) Babies <u>cried</u> when they saw Mr. Shaw.

*Clue(s) : (2)&(3)

(25) (a) Snow <u>fell very heavily</u> last night.

(b) Snow <u>blanketed the city</u> last night.

*Clue(s) : (3)&(4) − 구체적 행동을 보여주는 동사

2. Dynamic Structure with the Specific 'Movement' Word
(구체적인 '행동' 단어에 따른 역동적인 구조)

앞에서 지적했듯이, 행위 동사는 행동(movement)을 나타내는데, 그 행동이 'fast' 인지 아니면 'slow'인지를 구별하여 알아두면, 영작을 할 때 문장을 좀더 생생하고 역동적으로 쓰는 데 도움이 된다. 다음에 열거한 동사는 행동의 'fast'와 'slow'에 따른 것이다. 모르는 단어는 사전을 찾아보고 정확한 뜻을 익히기 바란다.

2-1. Movement Words(행동 단어)

FAST

Bolt	Bounce	Careen	Chase	Dart	Dash
Drive	Drop	Flick	Fly	Gallop	Hurl
Hurry	Plummet	Plunge	Propel	Race	Ram
Rip	Run	Rush	Sail	Scramble	Scamper
Shove	Skip	Smash	Speed	Spin	Spring
Sprint	Streak	Stride	Swat	Swerve	Swing
Swoop	Trot	Whisk	Zip	Zoom	

SLOW

Amble	Bend	Canter	Crawl	Creep	Drag
Drift	Droop	Edge	Heave	Lift	Loiter
Lope	Lumber	Plod	Saunter	Slink	Slouch
Sneak	Soar	Stagger	Stalk	Stray	Sway
Tiptoe	Waddle				

Q14 각 항의 두 문장, (a)와 (b)를 행동(movement) 면에서 비교해 보고, 어떤 문장이 더 역동적이며 독자에게 실감을 주는지 살펴보자. 그리고 '보기'와 같이 실감을 더 주는 문장을 써 보자. (해답생략)

보기 : (a) The boy _walked_ to school in the morning.

(b) The boy _hurried_ to school in the morning.

The boy hurried to school in the morning.

(1)　(a) People _went out_ into the street to see what was happening.

(b) People _dashed out_ to the street to see what was happening.

(2)　(a) He _lifted_ his wrist and _looked at_ his watch.

(b) He _flicked out_ his wrist and _glanced at_ his watch.

(3)　(a) He _took_ all his books, and _disposed of_ them out of the window.

(b) He _grabbed_ all his books, and _hurled_ them out of the window.

(4)　(a) The hare and the tortoise _took part in a race_ against other to the tall tree.

(b) The hare and the tortoise _raced_ each other to the tall tree.

(5)　(a) She _opened_ the envelope containing the money.

(b) She _ripped open_ the envelope containing the money.

(6)　(a) Military cadets _walked fast_ to the platform to shake hands with the President.

(b) Military cadets _rushed_ to the platform to shake hands with the President.

(7)　(a) Carl Lewis _ran fast_ for the finishing line.

(b) Carl Lewis _sprinted_ for the finishing line.

(8)　(a) John lay awake all night _repelling_ mosquitoes.

(b) John lay awake all night _swatting_ mosquitoes.

(9)　(a) I just _ambled_ home through the peaceful village.

(b) I just _hurried_ home through the peaceful village.

(10)   (a) A family of ducks <u>waddled</u> past pond.

      (b) A family of ducks <u>streaked</u> past pond.

Q15 다음 문단의 문장에 들어있는 5개의 동사 중에서, 문맥에 가장 적합한 동사 하나를 골라 ○표 하여라.

(1) Puppies here, puppies there! Fat, furry puppies are everywhere. Their fat bodies ((a)tremble, (b)wiggle, (c)shake, (d)jerk, (e)jingle). Friendly tails ((a)rattle, (b)wave, (c)wag, (d)move, (e)rock).

(2) A long time ago in Italy, There ((a)was, (b)lived, (c)resided, (d)dwelt, (e)existed) a wood-carver named Geppetto. Geppetto ((a)carved, (b)dissected, (c)sliced, (d)indented, (e)trimmed) a puppet and named him Pinochio. The puppet came to life, but ((a)managed, (b)controlled, (c)observed, (d)played, (e)behaved) badly. He spent money carelessly, and played hooky. Worst of all, Pinochio lied. when he told a lie, his nose would grow. Each time he lied, it ((a)emerged, (b)grew, (c)prospered, (d)developed, (e)flourished).

(3) The chipmunk sat up on its hind legs, chewing an acorn. Looking around, the chipmunk ((a)froze, (b)frosted, (c)solidified, (d)refrigerated, (e)glaciated) when it spied the farmer's dog. The dog ((a)smelled, (b)sniffed, (c)inhaled, (d)inspired, (e)exhaled) the air, ((a)saw, (b)caught, (c)distinguished, (d)spotted, (e)encountered) the chipmunk, and

((a)accused, (b)bolted out, (c)supervised, (d)invaded, (e)charged) toward it.

(4) We ((a)hurried, (b)walked, (c)sauntered, (d)tiptoed, (e)waddled) along. The white daytime moon showed on a patch of turquoise sky between clouds. The rain was fine, like sifted flour. My mother was in a good mood but seemed aware this could easily pass. She looked at the rain and the sky as if they were possessions someone might take from her at any moment. The clouds suddenly seemed to be turning over themselves, and in a second they ((a)fell, (b)broke, (c)came, (d)dropped, (e)descended). We ((a)were wet, (b)got chilled, (c)got dampened, (d)got drenched, (e)got drowned).("The floating world," Cynthia Kadohata)

(5) It stopped raining at noon, but dark clouds continued to ((a)bend, (b)fall, (c)crawl, (d)come, (e)drop) down the craggy mountain into the valley below. Despite the weather, we were determined to hike up at least one mountain in Switzerland. We ((a)trotted, (b)went, (c)trudged, (d)scampered, (e)tiptoed) up the steep slope behind the hotel. After an hour of slab to revive ourselves with fresh water.

3. Effective Structure with the specific "Hearing" Words (명확한 소리 단어로 된 인상적인 구조)

소리 단어(Hearing words)란 우리가 들을 수 있는 소리에 대한 단어이다. 눈을 감고 주위에서 들리는 소리를 들어 보자. 어디에 있느냐에 따라 달라지긴 하겠지만, 보통 여러 가지 소리를 들을 수 있을 것이다. 시각 장애인을 포함한 청각 전문가들은 일반인들보다 월등히 많은 소리를 듣고 감별할 수 있다고 한다. 젖 먹는 아기의 울음소리도 '배가 고플 때', '몸이 아플 때', '대소변을 보고 싶을 때', '무서울 때', '놀랐을 때', '불만을 표할 때' 등 상황에 따라 다르다고 한다.

소리 단어는 4종류로 구분할 수 있다 : (1) Loud Sounds (예 : 천둥소리, 총소리), (2) Soft Sounds(예 : Whisper, murmur), (3) Speech Sounds (예 : Talk, speak), (4) General sounds(예 : Sob, cough) 등이 그것이다. 누군가 '사자가 짖는다(The lion barks)' 라고 글을 쓰면, 미국인이든 한국인이든 글이 잘못됐다고 말한다(한국인은 '사자가 포효 또는 으르렁거린다, 개가 짖는다.' 라고 말하고, 미국인은 'The lion roars, The dog barks.' 라 표현한다). 문맥에 맞는 적절한 소리 단어를 쓰면 인상적이고 역동적인 글을 쓸 수 있다. 다음 단어들을 잘 익히고, 모르는 단어는 꼭 사전을 찾아보아라.

3-1. Loud Sounds(큰 소리)

Bang	Bark	Bawl	Bedlam	Blare	Blast
Blatant	Bluster	Boom	Brawl	Bray	Bump
Caterwaul	Clamor	Clang	Clap	Clash	Crash
Deafening	Discord	Drum	Earsplitting	Explode	Grate
Gunfire	Honk	Howl	Hubbub	Jangle	Noise
Outburst	Pandemonium	Peal	Piercing	Pop	Racket
Rage	Rasp	Raucous	Riot	Roar	Rowdy
Rumble	Scream	Screech	Shatter	Shout	Shriek
Siren	Slam	Smash	Squeal	Squawk	Stamp
Stomp	Thud	Thump	Thunder	Tumult	Uproar
Wail	Whack	Whine	Whistle	Yell	Yowl

3-2. Soft Sounds(부드러운 소리)

Bleat	Buzz	Chime	Chuckle	Click	Clink
Chuck	Crackle	Drip	Drone	Faint	Fizz
Gasp	Groan	Gurgle	Harmony	Heartbeat	Hiss
Hum	Hush	Inaudible	Lisp	Melody	Moan
Muffle	Murmur	Musical	Mute	Mutter	Patter
Peep	Purr	Resonance	Rush	Rustle	Rumble
Shush	Sigh	Snap	Speechless	Still	Swish
Tap	Tinkle	Twitter	Weep	Whir	Whisper
Woofing	Zing				

3-3. Speech Sounds(대화/연설의 소리)

Babble	Bellow	Chatter	Drawl	Eavesdrop	Gag
Giggle	Growl	Guffaw	Hiss	Jeer	Laugh
Mumble	Murmur	Mutter	Pitch	Scream	Screech
Sing	Snarl	Snort	Speak	Stammer	Stutter
Talk	Whimper	Whisper	Yell		

3-4. General Sounds(자연스런 소리)

Alarm	Audible	Belch	Boo	Burp	Cheer
Chirp	Clank	Coke	Cough	Croak	Crunch
Cry	Earshot	Echo	Fart	Grunt	Gurgle
Jangle	Jingle	Hiccup	Hoot	Knock	Muzzle
Ouch	Quiet	Racket	Rattle	Ring	Rip

Scratch	Scrunch	Silent	Sizzle	Smack	Sneeze
Snore	Snort	Sob	Splash	Squeak	Squish
Tear	Tick	Tweet	Wheeze	Whiz	Whoop
Yelp	Yippee	Yodel	Zap		

Q16 다음 ( )속에 주어진 'hearing' words 중에서, 문맥에 가장 맞은 단어를 골라 ○표 하여라.

(1) Lions ((a) roar, (b) hoot, (c) creak, (d) squeal), while horses ((a) croak, (b) quack, (c) neigh, (d) squeak).

(2) Owls ((a) cluck, (b) hoot, (c) bark, (d) roar), while coyotes ((a) croak, (b) creak, (c) chatter (d) howl).

(3) Doves ((a) snore, (b) coo, (c) squeal, (d) howl), while frogs ((a) growl, (b) croak, (c) buzz, (d) moo).

(4) Church bells ((a) rang, (b) yelled, (c) jangled, (d) rumbled) across the nation when the first transcontinental railroad was completed.

(5) There is a time of ((a) chattering, (b) laughing, (c) speaking, (d) babbling) and a time of being silent.

(6) The wheel that ((a) cries, (b) clangs, (c) sizzles, (d) squeaks) the loudest is the one that gets the grease.

(7) ((a) Gag, (b) Silence, (c) Eavesdropping, (d) Drawling) is the language of

all strong passions : love, anger, surprise, fear.

(8) The unpleasant man is the one who will come in and wake a person who has just gone asleep in order to ((a) bellow, (b) mumble, (c) chat, (d) jeer) with him.

(9) If you wish to share this room with me, dog, stop that ((a) growling and bellowing, (b) bumping and screaming, (c) drawling and shouting, (d) stammering and whimpering). I can't have such a noisy comrade near me. ('Faust,' Goethe)

(10) "Villains!" I ((a) exploded, (b) clanged, (c) howled, (d) shrieked), "I admit the deed! Tear up the planks! Here, here! It is the beating of his hideous heart!" ("The Tell-tale Heart," Edgar Allan Poe)

Q17 다음 글을 읽고 물음에 답하라.

It was as if, in the midst of a film concerning an avalanche, a tornado, a hurricane, a volcanic eruption, something had, first, gone wrong with the sound apparatus, thus muffling and finally cutting off all noise, all the blasts and repercussions and thunders, and then second, ripped the tremor. The world ground to a standstill. The silence was so immense and unbelievable that you felt your ears had been stuffed or you had lost your hearing altogether. (Ray Bradbury)

(1) Strong actions(요란한 행위)와 관련된 Loud sounds를 열거하면?
(2) Silent images(조용한 이미지)와 관련된 Soft sounds를 열거하면?

Q18 다음 시에서 밑줄 친 hearing word가 Loud sound에 속하면 괄호 안에 (L), Soft sound는 (S), 그 이외의 소리는 General sound (G)라고 써보아라.

Weather is full

of the nicest sounds:

it <u>sings</u> (   )

and <u>rustles</u> (   )

and <u>pings</u> (   )

and <u>pounds</u> (   )

and <u>hums</u> (   )

and <u>tinkles</u> (   )

and <u>strums</u> (   )

and <u>twangs</u> (   )

and <u>whishes</u> (   )

and <u>sprinkles</u> (   )

and <u>splashes</u> (   )

and <u>bangs</u> (   )

and <u>mumbles</u> (   )

and <u>grumbles</u> (   )

and <u>rumbles</u> (   )

and <u>flashes</u> (   )

and <u>crashes</u> (   )

I wonder

if thunder

frightens a bee,

a mouse in her house,

a bird in a tree,

a bear

or a hare

or a fish in the sea?

Not me!

("Weather is full of the nicest sounds," Aileen Fisher -Children's Author)

Q19 다음 두 시의 문맥에 가장 알맞은 감각단어(sensory word)를 아래 보기에서 골라 ( )안에 써 넣어라.

보기 hear, see, smell, taste, feel, hearing, sight, feeling

A. Autumn is (   );

I (   ) the colors of the leaves that fall from the trees

Autumn is (   );

I (   ) apple pie a-cooking in the oven

Autumn is (   );

I (   ) the sweet apple cider

Autumn is (   );

I (   ) the leaves crunch when I walk on them

Autumn is (   );

I (   ) the cool breeze that blows by.(Snoopy' s Special, Peggy Hoffman)

보기 hear, smell, taste, feel, see

B. I (   ) the scratchy, cracking dry leaves on my leg.

I (   ) the crunchy, cracking leaves when I walk.

I (   ) the crispy crust of the pumpkin pie.

명확하고 생생한 언어 사용

I (　　　) the crispy burning leaves in the flaming red fire.

I (　　　) the red, bright yellow and lightish tan leaves on the trees.

(Snoopy's Special, Richard Drinkwater)

◘ CHAPTER SUMMARY AND EXERCISES

이 장에서 우리는 영작을 하거나 영문을 읽을 때 꼭 유념해야 할 사항들을 다음과 같이 살펴보았다:

1. 언어와 문화는 서로 뗄래야 뗄 수 없는 관계(inseparable relations)를 맺고 있으며, 특정한 언어는 특정한 사회 문화 속에서 형성, 사용, 발전 또는 퇴화한다. 그러므로 특정한 문화적 맥락을 고려치 않고, 영작을 하거나 또는 영문을 독해한다는 것은 위험한 일이다.

2. 효과적으로 글을 잘 쓰는 작가는 독자에게 어떤 행위 및 사건을 설명한다기 보다 그것을 선명하게 보여주는 글을 많이 쓴다.

3. 상황을 선명하게 보여주기 위해서는 구체적이고, 역동적이며, 효과적인 '형용사/명사', '동사/부사' (Specific, dynamic, and effective 'Adjective/Noun' and 'Verb/Adverb') 단어를 골라 써야 한다.

그러면, 지금까지 다루지 못한 ① 접속사, ② 전치사, ③ 대명사, ④ 감탄사 등이 명확하고 역동적으로 쓰여지는 경우는 어떠한가? 이들 4품사는 'Adjective/Noun', 'Verb/Adverb'에 비해 구체적인 용법을 논하는 데 있어서 쓰임새의 폭이 적으므로, 따로 절을 만들어 다루지는 않겠다.

그럼 이제부터 실질적인 연습 문제를 풀면서 (1)언어와 문화의 관계, (2)설명하는 글보다는 보여주는 글, (3)Specific, dynamic and effective use of 'Adjective/Noun' and 'Verb/Adverb'를 익히기로 하자.

연습 1) 다음은 우리말을 영어로 옮겨보았다. 영작을 할 때 겪는 어려움은 언어 혼용 (Interlanguage)의 영향 때문이다. 다시 말해 우리는 영어를 우리식대로 옮기는 잘못을 쉽게 범한다. 뜻이 비슷한 말도 영어식 표현과 우리식 표현은 종종 다른 경우가 많다. 다음 문장을 읽어보고 문맥에 가장 적합한 동사를 골라라. 그리고 영어와 우리말의 차이점도 비교해 보자.

(1) 안아주세요.

Please ((a)embrace, (b)enclose, (c)hold, (d)hug) me.

(2) 꽃은 좋은 선물이 됩니다.

A flower ((a)becomes, (b)creates, (c)serves, (d)works) as a nice gift.

(3) 비행기를 타본 적이 있습니까?

Have you ever ((a)driven, (b)flown, (c)mounted, (d)ridden) in an airplane?

(4) 조용히 하세요. 귀가 아프네요.

Please be quiet. My ears ((a)bother, (b)grieve, (c)hurt, (d)pain).

(5) 쉿! 숨소리 내지 말아요.

Shh! ((a)Curtail, (b)Hold, (c)Kill, (d)Silence) your breath.

(6) 까불면 목을 비틀어버릴 거야.

If you make trouble, I' ll ((a)spin, (b)twist, (c)wind, (d)wring) your neck.

(7) 팽이 쳐본 적 있니?

Have you ever ((a)beaten, (b)spun, (c)struck, (d)whipped) a top?

(8) 헌혈할께요.

Please ((a)draw, (b)pick, (c)pluck, (d)remove) my blood for the blood drive.

(9) 전화 좀 받아주세요.

Please ((a)accept, (b)accomodate, (c)answer, (d)receive) the phone.

(10) 연필 좀 깍아주세요.

Please ((a)curtail, (b)cut, (c)reduce, (d)sharpen) my pencil.

(11) 이름을 말해주세요.

Please ((a)explain, (b)instruct, (c)teach, (d)tell) me your name.

(12) 돈 좀 빌려주실래요?

Can you ((a)acquire, (b)borrow, (c)lend, (d)rent) me some money?

(13) 비행기를 조정할 수 있습니까?

Can you ((a)actuate, (b)drive, (c)fly, (d)run) an airplane?

(14) 기차를 운전할 수 있습니까?

Will you ((a)drive, (b)fly, (c)move, (d)operate) this train?

(15) 색소폰 불 수 있니?

Can you ((a)blow, (b)execute, (c)inflate, (d)play) the saxophone?

(16) 원서를 쓰세요.

((a)Fill out, (b)Scribe, (c)Transcribe, (d)Write) the application form.

(17) 수표를 현찰로 바꾸세요.

((a)Change, (b)Cash, (c)Exchange, (d)Trade) the check.

(18) 저녁을 진수성찬으로 차리세요.

((a)Make, (b)Prepare, (c)Set, (d)Settle) the table for the sumptuous dinner.

(19) 많이 아파요. 이를 악물고 참으세요.

It hurts a lot. ((a)Bite, (b)Chew, (c)Eat, (d)Grip) the bullet.

(20) 전구가 나갔다.

The bulb is ((a)burnt, (b)combustion, (c)flashed, (d)gone) out.

(21) 이번 호남지역 홍수로 50여 명 이상의 사상자가 났다.

The recent severe flood in Honam area ((a)alleged, (b)declared, (c)claimed, (d)killed) more than fifty lives.

(22) 그러한 경찰 조사는 수박 겉 핥기 식으로 끝났다.

Such a police investigation concluded in ((a)licking, (b)rubbing, (c)touching, (d) scratching) the surface.

(23) 나 지금 소귀에 경을 읽는 게 아니야.

I'm not ((a)communicating, (b)conveying, (c)saying, (d)talking) to the wall.

(24) 휴지통을 비우세요.

Please ((a)decant, (b)depilate, (c)empty, (d)remove) the trashcan.

(25) 옥희의 생일날, 성대한 파티를 열자.

Let's ((a)cast, (b)deliver, (c)open, (d)throw) a big party for Okhee on her birthday.

(26) 이 상황에서 입 조심하지 않으면 넌 죽을 수도 있어.

If you don't ((a)guard, (b)protect, (c)scrutinize, (d)watch) your tongue in this situation, you may lose even your life.

(27) 햇빛이 없으면, 세상 사람들은 곧 죽고 말거야.

Without the sunlight, the people of the world would soon ((a)be perished, (b)decay, (c)expire, (d)perish).

(28) 맛있는 음식 많이 드세요.

Please ((a)devour,(b)eat,(c)gobble,(d)help) yourself to these delicious dishes.

(29) 심하게 다친 개가 절름거리며 집에 왔다.

The seriously injured dog ((a)chased, (b)dashed, (c)limped, (d)sprinted) home.

(30) 이제 출항하겠습니다. 배에 오르십시오.

Ladies and gentlemen. We are ready to sail now. Please ((a)enter, (b)board, (c)mount, (d)progress) the ship.

(31) 톰, 네가 나한테 좋은 일 해줬으니, 내가 콘에 아이스크림을 떠줄께.

Tom, you did a good job for me. I will ((a)cup, (b)make, (c)scoop, (d)spoon) the ice cream into the cone for you.

(32) 켄사스 농부들이여, 좋은 수확을 거둘 수 있도록 밭을 일구십시오.

You Kansas farmers. ((a)Arrange, (b)Cut, (c)Plow, (d)Prepare) the field, so we may have a good harvest.

(33) 북군 윌리엄 셔만 장군의 군대는 1864년 11월 15일, 조지아주 애틀란타시를
점령한 후 당당하게 행진했다.
General William T. Sherman's army victoriously ((a)marched, (b)rambled,
(c)strolled, (d)waltzed) through Atlanta, Georgia on November 15, 1864.

(34) 의사는 이 약을 복용하라고 말했다.
The doctor told me to ((a)consume, (b)eat, (c)feed, (d)take) this medicine.

(35) 정원의 잡초를 뽑아주시겠습니까?
Would you please ((a)draw, (b)extract, (c)pluck, (d)pull) the weed in the
garden?

(36) 새치기하지 마세요. 제가 더 오래 기다렸어요.
Don't ((a)break, (b)cut, (c)join, (d)mix) in line. I've been waiting here
much longer than you.

(37) 너무 허풍떨지 마세요. 진실을 알고 있으니까요.
Please don't ((a)brag, (b)exclaim, (c)exert, (d)glorify) too much. I know
the truth.

(38) 너무 비행기 태우지 마세요. 전 그런 거 별로 좋아하지 않아요.
Don't ((a)acclaim, (b)flatter, (c)fly an airplane, (d)suit) me too much. I
don't like that.

(39) 인류학 교수인 루스 F. 베네딕트는 1943년, "동일한 경제적 및 교육 조건하에서는
흑백인종이 차이가 없다"고 주장했다. 그 주장은 여전히 유효한가?
Ruth Fulton Benedict, professor of anthropology, claimed in 1943 that
the Negro and white races are equal, if given equal economic and
educational conditions. Does her claim still ((a)contain, (b)detain,
(c)hold, (d)secure) water?

(40) 생존경쟁이 매우 심한 한국 사회에서 영어도 잘 못하면서 보수가 좋은 직장을
구한다는 것은 "하늘의 별따기"다.
Obtaining well paid employment in a highly competitive Korean society

without an advanced level of English proficiency is like ((a)asking, (b)discovering, (c)finding, (d)inventing) a needle in a haystack. (or chasing a rainbow.)

연습 2) 동사 공부용으로 여기 세계 민족 문화를 엿볼 수 있는 유익하고 흥미로운 100개 의 격언을 간추려 보았다. 보기 중에서 문맥에 가장 적합한 동사를 하나 고르고, 더불어 세계 각국의 전통적인 지혜가 담긴 격언을 통해 각자의 지식을 넓혀 보자.

Ashanti (an ethnic group in central & southern part of Ghana)

(1) Only when you have ((a)crossed, (b)cruised, (c)drifted, (d)driven) the river, you can say the crocodile has a lump on his snout.

(2) Rain ((a)beats, (b)crushes, (c)defeats, (d)punches) a leopard's skin, but it does not wash off the spots.

American (The United States):

(3) Great trees ((a)grip, (b)hold, (c)keep, (d)maintain) little ones down.

(4) The bad gardener ((a)attacks, (b)breaks, (c)disagrees, (d)quarrels) with his rake.

(5) Laws too gentle are seldom ((a)accepted, (b)conducted, (c)honored, (d)obeyed), too severe, seldom executed.

(6) If you cut down the trees, you will ((a)conceives, (b)detect, (c)find, (d)seek) the wolf.

(7) ((a)Conduct, (b)Hold, (c)Keep, (d)Make) your eyes wide open before marriage, half afterwards.

(8) Calm weather in June ((a)allocates, (b)arranges, (c)declares, (d)sets) the corn in tune.

(9) It does not always rain when the pig ((a)complains, (b)protects, (c)shouts, (d)squeals).

Arabic (Saudi Arabia & other countries where Arabic is spoken):

(10) ((a)Chase, (b)Explore, (c)Invite, (d)Seek) counsel of him who makes you weep, and not of him who makes you laugh.

(11) A thousand curses never ((a)broke, (b)cracked, (c)cut, (d)tore) a shirt.

(12) If you buy cheap meat, when it boils you smell what you have ((a)deposited, (b)loaned, (c)saved, (d)spent).

(13) Live together like brothers, and ((a)do, (b)draw, (c)make, (d)shoot) business like strangers.

Bulgarian (Bulgaria):

(14) A tree falls the way it ((a)leans, (b)prefers, (c)sinks, (d)twists).

Burmese (Burma/Myanmar):

(15) Sparrows who emulate peacocks are likely to ((a)break, (b)burst, (c)demolish, (d)destroy) their thighs.

Canadian (Canada):

(16) The devil places a pillow for a drunken man to ((a)descend, (b)fall, (c)jump, (d)sink) upon.

Chinese (China):

(17) Give a man a fish, and you ((a)fatten, (b)feed, (c)foster, (d)nurse) him for a day. Teach him to fish, and you feed him a lifetime.

(18) He who rides the tiger can never ((a)decline, (b)descend, (c)dismount, (d)spring).

(19) A man without a smiling face must not ((a)develop, (b)inaugurate, (c)launch, (d)open) shop.

(20) The wise adapt themselves to circumstances as water ((a)forms, (b)molds, (c)shrinks, (d)splashes) to the pitcher.

(21) He who would rise in the world should ((a)change, (b)protect, (c)shield, (d)veil) his ambition with the forms of humanity.

(22) Life is partly what makes it, and partly it is made by the friends whom we ((a)appoint, (b)choose, (c)elect, (d)nominate).

▶ Czech (Czechoslovakia):

(23) Many doctors, death ((a)accepted, (b)accomplished, (c)authorized, (d)tolerated).

(24) Many a friend was lost through a joke, but none was ever ((a)accomplished, (b)advanced, (c)gained, (d)purchased).

⊞ English (United Kingdom):

(25) Lend your money, and ((a)displace, (b)escape, (c)lose, (d)waste) your friend.

(26) Experience is good, if not ((a)associated, (b)blended, (c)bought, (d)correlated) too dear.

(27) An empty purse ((a)agitates, (b)frightens, (c)horrifies, (d)terrifies) away friends.

(28) A wicked book gets a wicked man because it cannot ((a)read, (b)repeal, (c)repel, (d)repent).

(29) ((a)Build, (b)Create, (c)Form, (d)Set) a thief to catch a thief.

(30) Autumn ((a)loots, (b)robs, (c)steals, (d)takes possession of) the summer like a thief.

(31) Only the wearer knows where the shoe ((a)costs, (b)discomforts, (c)pinches, (d)shrivels).

(32) An ill workman always ((a)blames, (b)charges, (c)indict, (d)sues) his tools.

▬ Ethiopian (Ethiopia):

(33) Evil enters like a needle and ((a)advertises, (b)declares, (c)publicizes, (d)spreads) like an oak tree.

(34) When spider webs ((a)coincide, (b)equal, (c)identify, (d)unite), they can tie up a lion.

▮▮ French (France):

(35) God ((a)conciliates, (b)heals, (c)medicates, (d)recovers) and the physician takes the fee.

(36) Marriage often ((a)associates, (b)incorporates, (c)synthesizes, (d)unites) for life two people who scarcely know each other.

(37) The laws of love unite man and woman so strongly that no human laws can ((a)dichotomize, (b)divorce, (c)remove, (d)separate) them.

(38) Don't ((a)follow, (b)imitate, (c)immigrate, (d)resemble) the fly before you have wings.

(39) The doctor's office is often more to be ((a)agitated, (b)disturbed, (c)feared, (d)intimidated) than the disease.

▬ German (Germany):

(40) He who has once burnt his month always ((a)blows, (b)enlarges, (c)inflates, (d)swells) his soup.

(41) There are many preachers who don't ((a)accept, (b)agree, (c)follow,

(d)watch) their own instruction.

(42) The cats that ((a)attack, (b)bark, (c)catch, (d)drive) mice away are as good as the cats that catch them.

(43) The silent dog is always the first to ((a)bite, (b)grab, (c)grip, (d)tear).

(44) He who begins too much ((a)accomplishes, (b)arrives, (c)manages, (d)wins) too little.

▤ **Greek** (Greece):

(45) Act quickly, ((a)speculate, (b)study, (c)think, (d)understand) slowly.

(46) In hospitality it is the spirit that ((a)awaits, (b)counts, (c)experts, (d)thinks).

(47) The shepherd, even when he becomes a gentleman, ((a)mind, (b)perceives, (c)smells, (d)smiles) of lamb.

▤ **Hindu** (India):

(48) The great tree ((a)casts, (b)displays, (c)exhibits, (d)shows,) its shade, upon all, even the woodcutter.

▤ **Hungarian** (Hungary):

(49) An ox remains an ox, even if ((a)driven, (b)gone, (c)induced, (d)operated) to Vienna.

▥ **Irish** (Ireland):

(50) The law of lending is to ((a)breach, (b)break, (c)cut, (d)violate) the dish.

(51) Where everyone goes, the grass never ((a)advances, (b)amplifies, (c)develops, (d)grows).

(52) A new broom ((a)clears, (b)drives, (c)removes, (d)sweeps) clean, but the

old brush knows all the corners.

🟥 **Italian** (Italy):

(53) Give neither counsel nor salt till you are ((a)asked, (b)charged, (c)interrogated, (d)questioned) for it.

(54) When ill luck falls asleep, let one ((a)dispute, (b)excite, (c)stimulate, (d)wake) her.

(55) When the sun is the highest, it ((a)casts, (b)distributes, (c)drops, (d)shines) the least shadow.

⬜ **Japanese** (Japan):

(56) The tongue is more to be ((a)agitated, (b)alarmed, (c)disturbed, (d)feared) than the sword.

(57) A single arrow is easily ((a)broken, (b)detached, (c)eradicated, (d)torn), but not ten in a bundle.

(58) To ((a)endure, (b)exist, (c)permit, (d)support) what is unendurable is true endurance.

(59) When folly passes by, reason ((a)attracts, (b)conveys, (c)draws, (d)rakes) back.

🔵 **Korean** (Korea):

(60) If a man fails, he ((a)blames, (b)condemns, (c)denounces, (d)indict) his ancestors.

(61) In a fight between whales, the back of a shrimp ((a)bursts, (b)cracks, (c)explodes, (d)splits).

(62) A sparrow does not ((a)aviate, (b)skim, (c)soar, (d)travel) over a rice mill.

☐ **Latin** (The Roman Empire):

(63) Nothing ((a)bakes, (b)dries, (c)fades, (d)scorches) sooner than tears.

(64) Let a fool ((a)endure, (b)entertain, (c)hold, (d)support) his tongue and he will pass for a sage.

(65) A physician is an angel when ((a)applied, (b)employed, (c)operated, (d)selected), but a devil when one must pay for him.

(66) The fool ((a)remains, (b)departs, (c)hikes, (d)wanders), the wise travels.

(67) When the old dog barks, it is time to ((a)regards, (b)gaze, (c)watch, (d)focus) it.

■■ **Malay** (Malaysia):

(68) When a dead tree falls, the woodpecker ((a)distributes, (b)divides, (c)shares, (d)splits) in its death.

(69) Although it may rain, do not ((a)cast, (b)drop, (c)scatter, (d)sprinkle) the watering pot away.

(70) Though a tree grows ever so high, the falling leaves ((a)rebate, (b)refund), (c)reimburse, (d)return) to the root.

■ **Nigerian** (Nigeria):

(71) When the mouse ((a)animates, (b)disbelieves, (c)fears, (d)laughs at) the cat, there is a hole nearby.

■ **Persian** (Iran):

(72) He who has been bitten by a snake ((a)alarms, (b)concerns, (c)fears, (d)worries) a piece of string.

(73) He who wants a rose must ((a)appreciate, (b)obey, (c)respect, (d)value)

the thorn.

(74) A broken hand ((a)drives, (b)employs, (c)holds, (d)works), but not a broken heart.

(75) The larger a man's roof, the more snow it ((a)arrays, (b)collects, (c)converts, (d)digs).

Polish (Poland):

(76) Love ((a)arrives in, (b)enters, (c)inserts, (d)makes an entrance into) a man through his eyes, women through her ears.

Portuguese (Portugal):

(77) He who ((a)acquires, (b)delivers, (c)nurses, (d)serves) two master has to lie to one.

(78) Where the iron goes, there ((a)goes, (b)moves, (c)travels, (d)withdraws) also rust.

Russian (Russian Federation):

(79) With seven nurses the child ((a)capitulates, (b)consumes, (c)loses, (d)reduces) its eyes.

(80) The horses of hope ((a)chase, (b)gallop, (c)hunt, (d)run after), but the asses of experience go slowly.

(81) The wife is twice precious only; when ((a)compelled, (b)conducted, (c)driven, (d)led) into the house, and when taken out.

(82) If you put your nose into water, you will also ((a)spray, (b)sprinkle, (c)sprint, (d)wet) your cheek.

(83) They bow to you when borrowing, you bow to them when ((a)assembling, (b)flocking, (c)collapsing, (d)collecting).

Senegalese (Senegal):

(84) A healthy ear can ((a)locate, (b)place, (c)stand, (d)twist) hearing sick words.

Spanish (Spain & other countries where Spanish is spoken):

(85) He who knows most ((a)converses, (b)speaks, (c)utters, (d)verbalizes) least.

(86) Do not ((a)celebrate, (b)glorify, (c)rejoice, (d)triumph) at my grief, for when mine is old, yours will be new.

(87) To whom you tell your secrets, to him you ((a)adjust, (b)notice, (c)resign, (d)vacate) your liberty.

(88) If you want good service, ((a)nurse, (b)observe, (c)satisfy, (d)serve) yourself.

(89) It is better to conceal one's knowledge than to ((a)admit, (b)affirm, (c)broadcast, (d)reveal) one's ignorance.

(90) We make more enemies by what we((a) announce, (b) communicate, (c) declare, (d) say)than friends by what we do.

(91) When fortune ((a)abuses, (b)batters, (c)hurts, (d)knocks) upon the door, open it widely.

Swiss (Switzerland):

(92) The night rinses what day has ((a)disgraced, (b)soaped, (c)stained, (d) tainted).

Turkish (Turkey):

(93) A man does not ((a)explore, (b)probe, (c)seek, (d)struggle) his luck, luck

seeks its man.

(94) The devil ((a)courts, (b)fascinates, (c)motivates, (d)tempts) all other men, but idle men tempt the devil.

(95) Smoke does not make a pot ((a)agitate, (b)boil, (c)bubble, (d)simmer).

(96) He who ((a)conceals, (b)obscures, (c)preserves, (d)shelters) his grief finds no remedy for it.

Yiddish (Israel & other areas where Yiddish is spoken as a Jewish ethnic language):

(97) To be rich is not everything, but it certainly ((a)helps, (b)performs, (c)runs, (d)works).

(98) All things ((a)flourish, (b)generate, (c)grow, (d)multiply) with time except grief.

(99) The world would ((a)conclude, (b)destroy, (c)expire, (d)perish) if all men were learned.

(100) If you lose an hour in the morning, you have to ((a)chant, (b)charge, (c)chase,(d)chasten) it all day.

ANSWER

A1

(1) 할아버지께서 몇 가지 휴대품들을 꾸리셨다. ('things'는 너무나 general하며, (a)(b)(c)(d)도 마찬가지. specific & clear한 것은 (e). 따라서 답은 (e)).

(2) 헬렌의 정원은 무척 아름답다. (beautiful은 general한 형용사. (b)(c)(d)(e)도 마찬가지다. Specific한 것은 (a))

(3) 영화 <타이타닉>은 무척 흥미로웠다. 답은 (b)

(4) 데이비드 그린버그 씨는 키가 무척 크다. 답은 (c)

(5) 비행기 조종은 신나는 일이었다. 답은 (c)

(6) 김 씨는 많은 고기를 먹었다. 답은 (d)

(7) 화창한 날이었다. 답은 (c)

(8) 영문과 교수 두 분이 지난주에 크게 다퉜다. 답은 (a)

(9) 골드만 씨는 육중하다. 답은 (e)

(10) 그 집은 목조 건물이다. 답은 (b)

A2

Noun	Adjective
(1) animal	none
(2) boy, street	none
(3) uncle, car	none
(4) dog, cat	none
(5) girl	shy
(6) woman	emotional
(7) teacher	strict
(8) fish	bad
(9) people, food	none
(10) friend, flowers	none

A4

우리는 서둘러 나아갔다. 흰 구름 사이에 언뜻 파란 헝겊처럼 비친 하늘 위로 하얀 대낮의 달이 나타났다. 빗줄기는 체로 친 고운 밀가루처럼 가늘었다. 어머니는 기분이 좋았지만, 이 기분이 금방 변할 수 있다는 걸 알고 계신 것 같았다. 그녀는 비와 하늘을 쳐다보았다. 그것들이 누군가가 순식 간에 가져갈 수 있는 소유물이라도 된 것처럼. 갑자기 구름이 몸을 뒤척이는가 싶더니, 금세 부서 졌다. 우리는 비에 흠뻑 젖었다.

1. White daytime. 따라서 white daytime moon은 sun을 말한다.

2. of turquoise sky between clouds

3. fine, like sifted flour. 이 문장의 뜻은, "빗줄기는 체로 친 고운 밀가루처럼 가늘었다."

4. drenched. 이 문장의 뜻은, "우리는 소낙비에 흠뻑 젖었다."

5. 저자는 대자연 속에서 일어나는 자연 현상(비내리는 과정)에 무력하게 휩쓸려 들어가는 인간상 에 초점을 맞춰, 비오는 과정과 비맞는 과정이라는 두 가지 현상을 비교·서술함으로써, 두 현상 에 대한 생생한 이미지를 창조했다. 따라서 번잡한 도시거리와 어린이 놀이터는 두 현상을 극대 화시키기에 적합치 않다. 따라서 답은 ⓐ.

6. ⓑ

7. ⓒ

8. ⓐ

A5 (※ ①/③은 ①도 ③도 다 맞다는 뜻)

1. ③ (나는 떠들썩한 군중 한 가운데 서 있는 나를 발견했다.)

2. ① (첫 눈이 내릴 때, 사람들은 아침에 잠에서 깨어 온 세상이 하얗고 투명하게 변했다는 사실을 발견하게 된다.)

3. ① (마치 스위치라도 켠 듯 하늘에서 갑자기 구름 한 점이 빛났다.)

4. ⑤④⑤⑤ (나는 내 입술을 뒤덮으며 목구멍으로 미끄러져 내려가는 부드럽고 맛있는 아이스크 림의 느낌을 사랑한다.)

5. ③③ (나는 파삭파삭한 루트 비어 거품소리를 좋아하지만, 철문이 쾅 닫히는 소리는 좋아하지 않는다.)

6. ①①⑤ (그는 키가 컸고, 어깨는 또 어찌나 넓고 탄탄했던지 근육이 아니라 강철 갑옷을 입은 듯 했다.)

7. ⑤② (풀밭을 거닐기에 선선하고 쾌적한 날씨였고, 공기중에는 보통 갓 자른 레몬이나 멜론 향내가 있었다.)

8. ①①①① (침실 중앙에는 단풍나무 침대가 있었다. 탁자 위에는 빨간색과 파란색 새들이 있는 대리석 시계가 있었다. 벽에는 타원형 거울이 있었다. 반대편 벽에는 여기 저기 긁힌 낡은 장롱 두 개가 있었다.)

9. ②①②② (애틀랜틱 시의 보드워크(바닷가 등의 판자 산책로)를 가득 채운 수백명의 사람들은 모두 냄새를 풍긴다. 사라사 옷을 입은 숙녀들은 정원을 지나칠 때 나는 향내를 풍기고, 해변의 청년들은 선탠 크림과 바디로션 향기를 풍긴다.)

10. ③⑤③⑤③③③ (붕괴가 시작된 것은 바로 그 때였다. 먼저 소름끼치는, 가지를 툭툭 꺾는 듯 예리한 소리가 났고, 뒤이어 숲의 나무가 모두 쓰러지는 듯한 포효가 있었다.)

11. ④⑤④④ (나는 체리향 시럽이 달콤하게 녹는 것처럼 향기로운 하얀 아이스크림 콘의 얼음 결정체를 소중히 여기곤 했다.)

12. ⑤⑤ ③/⑤ (그는 얼어붙고 있었다. 그는 밤새도록 거기 누워있을 수 없었다. 차츰, 그는 크롤로 헤엄쳤다. 그림자처럼 소리없이 그는 호수를 가로질러 돌아갔다.)

13. ⑤①①/③① (화산은 언제나 나를 매혹시켰다. 불꽃과 녹아서 타오르는 용암을 내뿜는 하와이의 한 활화산의 컬러 사진을 보았다.)

14. ①①①① (그것들 사이로 산길에 투명한 연못이 있었다. 연못 바닥에 있는 자갈들은 녹색이 감도는 나선형 금빛을 받아 희미하게 반짝였다.)

15. ⑤⑤⑤ (그릇된 길로 나아가려 하자, 고통이 그와 함께 했다. 그가 숨을 들이마시려 할 때마다, 밤공기가 이 사이의 구멍들을 때렸고, 열려 있는 신경을 공격했다.)

16. ⑤① (토네이도는 격렬한 폭풍이다. 그것은 깔때기 모양의 어두운 구름에 의해 식별될 수 있다.)

17. ①⑤⑤①①① (내 위로 양털처럼 빽빽한 구름이 불길한 자주빛 소용돌이 형태로 뭉게뭉게 피어오른다. 하늘 대부분이 구름에 뒤덮이지만, 태양은 서쪽으로 반쯤 기운 채 폭풍 아래서 여전히 또렷하게 빛나고 있다.)

18. ⑤①①① (작은 나무를 기르는 일본 예술 분재가 나의 새 취미이다. 나의 분재 나무는 가시 투

성이 곱향나무로, 높이가 19인치에 불과하다. 나는 내 난쟁이 나무가 우산처럼 보이도록 주의깊게 더듬었다.)

19. ②③② (야채 가게의 양파, 마늘, 등유 냄새가 밤새도록 뒤섞인 나머지, 문을 활짝 열어 이른 아침 공기로 환기를 시키기 전까지 결코 사라지지 않곤 했다.)

20. ①②②② (나는 태국 칭마이 근처의 작은 마을이 매혹적인 향기의 마을이었다는 것을 기억하고 있다. 흙냄새가 코를 찔렀고, 가축 퇴비 냄새, 그리고 속 깊은 냄비에 큰 야채와 콩, 훈제 또는 말린 돼지고기를 넣어 몇 시간 동안 요리하는 냄새가 흥취를 더했다.)

A6

1.(a) 2.(c) 3.(a) 4.(b) 5.(b) 6.(b) 7.(c) 8.(b) 9.(d) 10.(c)

A7

1. 오, 내 사랑은 빨간, 빨간 장미 같아라.

   답은 (b), (b) -- 사랑의 정열을 표현하는 색상이므로.

2. 갑자기 나는 군중을 보았나니 / 황금빛 수선화 무리를 /

   답은 (d) -- 수선화는 노랑색

3. 바퀴의 발길질 / 바람의 노래 / 흰 돛의 떨림

   답은 (c) -- 돛의 색은 대부분 흰색.

4. 내가 바다 곁에 누웠을 때 / 나무 가래를 그들이 내게 주었나니, / 해안의 모래를 파라고

   답은 (b) -- 해안가는 모래투성이.

5. 레몬은 자그만 노란색 오렌지처럼 보이지 / 그러나 명심하게! 아주 시큼하니까. 당신이 레몬을 깨물면, 레몬이 당신을 깨문다! 답은 (a) -- 레몬은 노란색.

6. 나무가 온통 하얀 눈에 뒤덮일 때 / 다람쥐들은 / 몇 달 전에 솔방울을 숨겨뒀던 장소를 / 어떻게 기억할까? 답은 (b) -- 눈덮힌 숲은 하얀색.

7. 그러자 초록 풀이 돋아났고 / 어린 자줏빛 꽃들이 피어났다.

   답은 (c), (d) -- 봄에 눈에 잘 띄는 풀과 꽃의 색.

8. 잿빛 바다와 / 길다랗게 뻗어있는 검은 땅 / 그리고 나지막히 떠 있는 노란 반달...

답은 (a), (d), (a) -- 밤에 본 바다, 육지, 달의 색.

9. 태양은 늙은 독수리;/ 저기, 바람 없는 서쪽, / 영혼의 낭떠러지 꼭대기에 / 그는 스스로에게 진홍 색 둥지를 지어주네. 답은 (c) -- 해가 질 때의 색.

10. 비가 그대 머리 위에서 / 은빛의 물방울인 채 퍼붓게 하라.

답은 (a) -- 비의 색.

11. 귀 기울여 보니, 달은 사랑스런 여자./ 은빛 옷에 싸인 사랑스런 여자.

답은 (b) -- 밤에 비치는 달의 색.

12. 파란 하늘을 위아래로 누비며/ 갈매기들은 하루종일 올라가고 빗나가고 솟구치나니,/ 호와 호가 교차하고, 곡선과 곡선이 겹쳐지네.

답은 (a) -- 청명한 대낮, 바닷가에서 본 하늘의 색.

13. 호수가 으르렁거렸다. 달빛 아래 갑작스런 어둠 속에서 거대한 파도가 하얗게 솟아올랐다. 쏴 하는 소리, 분출하는 소용돌이, 그리고 침묵.

답은 (d) -- 어두운 달빛 아래서 바라본 파도의 색.

14. 갈색 머리카락, 갈색 피부./ 그것이 바로 내가 아름다움을 바라보는 / 지배적인 척도/ 그것이야 말로 낯선 백인들의 나라에서 / 내가 왜 흑인 소녀여야 하는지 설명해주네./ 나는 나 자신이 너무 나 만족스러운 것을.

답은 (a), (a), (a), (b) -- 백인 사회에서 차별받는 흑인 여성의 감정을 묘사한 글. 머리카락과 피부 는 갈색, 인종은 흑인.

15. 델라는 울음을 멈췄다...그녀는 창가에 서서 별 관심도 없이 잿빛 고양이가 잿빛 뒤뜰의 잿빛 담 장을 따라 걸어가는 모습을 쳐다보았다. 내일이면 크리스마스이건만, 그녀는 남편 짐에서 선물 을 사줄 돈이 기껏 1달러 87센트밖에 없었다.

답은 (b), (b), (b) --- 돈이 없어 선물을 살 수 없는 심정을 잿빛으로 표현하였다.

A8

1. (A), (A) -- 검은 바다에 정박하고 있는 작은 배는 높고 검은 하늘에다 대고 속삭이고 있었다.

2. (A), (A) -- 겨울 멜론은 밝은 초록 또는 오렌지빛 과육에 부드럽거나 융기한 껍질을 가지고 있다.

3. (A) -- 안개가 너무 짙게 끼어 있어서 안개로 집을 지을 수도 있으리니, 멀리 북쪽지방에서 눈과

얼음으로 집을 짓듯이.

4. (A) -- 춥고 눈내리는 밤이다. 중심가에는 인적이 끊겼다. 움직이는 것이라곤 소용돌이치는 눈 뿐이다.

5. (A) -- 우리가 현장에 도착했을 때, 소방수들은 거대한 호스로 위층을 조준하고 있었다.

6. (A) -- 1970년대에는 가솔린 부족 사태가 있었다. 운전자들은 주유소에서 길다랗게 줄을 서서 기다렸고, 가스 가격이 급등했다.

7. (A),(A) -- 우리는 철조망을 지나 문을 통과하여 탁 트인 공간으로 차를 몰았다.

8. (A),(A) -- 그는 키가 컸고, 어깨가 어찌나 넓고 탄탄했는지, 근육이 아니라 강철 갑옷을 입은 듯했다.

9. (A),(A) -- 무대는 화려했다. 무대의 왼쪽 절반은 벚꽃 만발한 산허리를 묘사하고 있고, 나머지 반쪽은 짚으로 엮은 출입구를 묘사하고 있다.

10. (A),(A) -- 처음 우리 학교에 도착했을 때, 존은 산뜻한 작은 서류 가방을 들고 있었고, 분홍색 물방울 무늬 타이와 짧은 바지를 입고 있었다.

11. (L/V) -- 수술 실패 후, 그의 오른쪽 눈 시력은 떨어졌다.

12. (A),(A),(A),(A) -- 나의 분재 나무는 가시 투성이 곱향나무로, 키가 기껏 12인치에 불과하다. 이 바늘 더미 아래의 작은 가지는 서로 얽히고 구부러져 있다.

13. (A),(A) -- 산 꼭대기에 이르자, 나는 수평선을 뚫어져라 쳐다보았다. 화창하고 아름다운 한낮이었다.

14. (A),(S) -- 그 저명한 교수의 방은 색다른 삼각형이었다. 그 방은 오래된 사향 냄새를 풍겼다.

15. (A),(A) -- 봄은 얇은 눈 껍질 위에서 가볍게 뛰어다니고,/ 향긋한 손가락을 땅 깊숙이 찌르네/ 갈라진 땅에 숨어 자고 있던 씨앗들을 찾아내고, / 한줄기 햇빛을 비춰주며 어서 자라라고 속삭이네.

16. (A),(A) -- 썰매가 눈쌓인 길을 따라 미끄러지듯 움직이는 사이, 매서운 공기가 손자의 뺨을 얼얼하게 만들었다. 말이 집을 향해 따가닥 따가닥 달릴 때, 그의 목에 걸린 황동 벨이 짤랑짤랑 울렸다.

17. (A),(S) -- 50와트 전구 세 개에 의지해 불을 밝힌 그 낡은 가게는 등유 냄새와 빵굽는 냄새를 풍겼다. 직사각형 모양의 방 한가운데에는 철제 난로가 있었다.

18. (A),(A),(A),(A) -- 백발 머리 여성이 부엌 창문에 서 있다. 그녀는 여름용 사라사 원피스 위에 엉성한 회색 스웨터를 걸치고, 테니스화를 신고 있다. 그녀는 작고 쾌활하다, 마치 밴텀닭처럼. 그

러나 젊은 시절의 오랜 병 때문에, 그녀의 어깨는 안스러울 정도로 구부러져 있다.

19. (A),(A) -- 땅 속 한 구멍 안에 호빗이 살았다. 그것은 벌레와 보드라운 흙냄새로 가득찬 추잡하고, 더럽고, 축축한 구멍도 아니었고, 반면 앉을 자리나 먹을거리가 전혀 없는 건조하고, 텅 빈 모래투성이 구멍도 아니었다. 그것은 호빗의 구멍이었고, 그것은 곧 안락함을 의미한다.

20. (A),(A),(A),(A),(A),(A),(A) -- 그녀는 덩치가 크고 꼴사나운 여자였고, 커다란 골격에 튼튼하고 탄력있는 살갗을 갖고 있었다. 짧은 팔 끝에 굉장히 큰 손이 달려 있었고, 목은 커다란 혹처럼 머리 뒤에 튀어나온 쪼그라진 지방 덩어리였다. 그녀의 피부는 거칠고 부풀어 있었고, 빰 아래로 오동통하고, 사마귀같은 주근깨가 있었다.

A9

(1) T -- 나는 내 입술을 감싸며 내 목구멍으로 미끄러져 내려가는 부드럽고, 달콤하고, 풍부한 아이스크림을 사랑한다.

(2) S -- 숨결과 냄새가 뒤섞여 있네/ 너무 가까이 뒤섞여 있네/ 흑인과 백인도/ 너무 가까이 있어서 두려움을 가질 여지가 없네.

(3) S -- 나는 숨을 깊이 들이마시고 내쉬지 않은 채 풍성하고 달콤한 땅과 축축한 풀 냄새를 즐겼다.

(4) S, T -- 왼쪽으로는 향기로운 소세지가 늘어서 있다. 이 고기 옆에는 부드러운 맛의 네덜란드산 구다 체즈에서부터 자극적인 림버거에 이르기까지 치즈 더미가 있다.

(5) S -- 기억컨대, 내 아내는 해변가 하얀 집 창문을 열곤 했는데, 불어오는 바람을 타고 소금과 바다 냄새가 풍기곤 했다.

(6) S, S -- 강에서는 물소리가 떠다니는 반면, 숲에서는 겨울의 온갖 시듦과 여름의 온갖 만발함이 어우러진, 이국적이고, 얼얼하고, 자극적인 향내가 퍼져나온다.

(7) S, S -- 소금과 해초, 물고기와 바다와 바람 냄새가 가득했다. 산책로를 채운 수백 명의 사람들의 냄새 또한 거기 함께 있었다.

(8) S, S -- 기억컨대, 그 마을은 매혹적인 향기가 있는 곳이었다. 흙냄새가 코를 찔렀고, 가축 퇴비 냄새, 연못과 강의 누르스름한 물, 그리고 속 깊은 냄비에 큰 야채와 콩, 훈제 또는 말린 돼지고기를 넣어 몇 시간 동안 요리하는 냄새가 흥취를 더했다. 꽃들도 진한 향기를 내뿜었다.

(9) S, T -- 무슨 일로 꿈이 연기되는가?/ 태양을 받은 건포도처럼 바싹 말라버렸나?/ 아니면 상처처

럼 곪았나? - 그리고 나서 사라져버렸나?/ 썩은 고기처럼 악취를 풍기는가?/ 아니면 딱딱해져서 설탕을 넣었나?-- 달콤한 시럽처럼?/혹시 무거운 짐처럼 그냥 축 처진 건가?/ 아니면 폭발했나?

(10) S, S, S -- 늑대는 넌더리가 나서 코에 주름을 잡았다. 싫증이 났다는 걸 나타내는 신중한 표현이었다. 여기서는 사람 냄새가 아주 강했다. 지난 몇 시간 전보다 훨씬 더. 처음 늑대에게 경고를 발한 자극적인 옷냄새 -- 오래된 털코트에서 나는 곰팡내는 땀과 두려움으로 얼룩진 불쾌하고 메스꺼운 냄새에 흠뻑 젖어 있었다. 그리고 나서 인간 자체의 음침한 냄새, 따뜻한 피부와 힘차게 뛰는 피의 진한 사향 냄새가 이어졌다.

A11

(1) hot -- 금속이 너무 뜨거워서 나는 그것을 만져볼 수 없었다.

(2) cool and sweet -- 그 여름 하루 동안은 풀밭을 거닐기에 선선하고 쾌적했다.

(3) some rain must fall, dark and dreary-- 모든 생명체 속으로 약간의 비는 내려야 하거늘 ; 음울하고 쓸쓸한 날도 있으리.

(4) freezing; lie there all night, Inch by inch he crawled away -- 그는 얼어붙고 있었다. 그는 밤새도록 거기 누워있을 수 없었다. 조금씩 그는 크롤로 헤엄쳤다.

(5) are contended with this life, like a shadow or a dream, like the flower of the field -- 인생과 겨루는 사람들은 모두 그림자나 꿈처럼 사라지거나 들판의 꽃처럼 시든다.

(6) in the quiet darkness, bowed by weariness and pain, Like an autumn flower in the frozen rain, Like a wind-blown autumn flower, That never lifts its head again. -- 그녀는 고요한 어둠 속에 서 있네, / 근심에 시달리는 이 여자는 피로와 고통에 굴종하였으니, / 다시는 결코 고개를 들지 못하는 / 얼어붙은 비 속의 가을 꽃처럼, / 바람에 날리는 가을 꽃처럼/

(7) cold and snowy night, deserted, swirls of snow, its cold iron, a privacy I love in this snowy night -- 춥고 눈내리는 밤. 중심가는 인적이 끊겼다./ 움직이는 것이라곤 오직 소용돌이 치는 눈 뿐/ 우체통 문을 떠나면서, 나는 쇠의 차가움을 느낀다/ 이렇게 눈내리는 밤엔 내가 사랑하는 나만의 사생활이 있나니/ 차로 근처를 돌아다니며, 좀더 시간을 낭비하리라.

(8) "Yes", "Yes", "No... not quite", "Well, actually", "Yes", "Yes" -- "중국인이세요?" "네."/ "미국인?" "네."/ "정말 중국인이에요?" "아니오... 딱히 그런 건 아니에요."/ "정말 미국인이에

요?" "저, 사실은, 알다시피..."/ 그러나 난 차라리 "네,"라고 말하고 싶다./ 둘다 아닌 것도 아니요, 어쩌면 아닐 지도 모르지만, 둘다 맞고, 단지 어느 하나가 아닐 뿐/ 내가 가져온 가정, 있는 그대로의 내 방식들./ 난 차라리 "네"라고 두 번 말하고 싶다.

(9) the pain was with him, the night air hit the holes in his teeth, attacked the open nerve -- 그릇된 길로 나아가려 하자, 고통이 그와 함께 했다. 그가 숨을 들이마시려 할 때마다, 밤공기가 이 사이의 구멍들을 때렸고, 열려 있는 신경을 공격했다

(10) 문장 전체에 밑줄 -- 비가 그의 얼굴을 때렸다. 그는 손으로 얼굴을 감쌌다. 비가 그의 등을 때렸다. 그는 진흙의 질긴 풀 위에 배를 깔고 누웠고, 비는 그의 등을 때렸고, 다리를 때렸다.

A12

(1) (c) 말은 귀를 머리에 꼭 붙인 채 재빨리 언덕을 뛰어내려왔다.

(2) (a) 암컷 하이에나 네 마리가 커다란 줄무늬 얼룩말을 집요하게 추적했다.

(3) (b) 화려한 벌새 몇 마리가 한 꽃에서 다른 꽃으로 재빨리 날아갔다.

(4) (b) 늙고 지친 한 남자가 다양한 품목들을 진열하고 있는 가게들과 여기 저기서 쇼핑하는 사람들을 쳐다보면서 오후 내내 거리를 오락가락했다.

(5) (c) 그날 밤, 나는 아무도 모르게 기숙사에서 빠져나와 애인 존을 만났다.

(6) (d) 나는 겁에 질린 작은 생물들이 내 목을 기어오르는 것을 느꼈다.

(7) (c) 이즈음 주가가 명백히 떨어졌다.

(8) (a) 1920년대에 한국의 모든 도시와 큰 읍에는 초상화 스튜디오가 차츰 생겨났다.

(9) (e) 작은 소년이 나무 꼭대기에서 큰 소리로 외쳤다.

(10) (a) 전투 요격기가 이륙하여 파란 하늘로 날아올랐다.

(11) (c) 수잔은 행복하게 거실로 들어갔다.

(12) (c) 호랑이를 타고 있는 남자는 결코 내릴 수 없다.

(13) (b) 기독교도가 되기 위해 교회에 갈 필요는 없다.

(14) (a) 종종 이식된 나무는 대부분 잘 자라지 않는다.

(15) (a) 젊은 남성은 자기에 대해 아주 좋게 말해주는 첫 번째 여성을 사랑하게 되는 것 같다.

(16) (e) 공자는 도덕 체계를 창안한 것이 아니라 인류의 마음 속에서 그것을 발견했다.

(17) (a) 수잔은 두려워하며 그의 손을 잡았다.

(18) (b) 새로운 기술들은 실물 그대로의 분위기를 산출함으로써 사진사들과 고객들을 감동시켰다.

(19) (d) 그 배고픈 남자는 음식을 실컷 먹었고, 그것을 무척 즐겼다.

(20) (b) 지친 노부인이 힘겹게 집으로 걸어갔다.

(21) (a) 어머니가 아기의 얼굴을 부드럽게 문질렀다.

(22) (a) 썩은 물고기는 지독한 냄새를 풍긴다.

(23) (b) 이 검정 셔츠는 뜨거운 물에 담그자 줄어들었다.

(24) (e) 좌절감에 빠진 틴에이저가 아름다운 꽃병을 산산조각 냈다.

(25) (d) 존의 할아버지는 신경이 무척 예민해질 때면 더듬거리며 말한다.

A15

(1) (b), (c) -- 여기에도 강아지, 저기에도 강아지! 부드러운 털을 가진 살찐 강아지들은 어디에나 있다. 그들의 살찐 몸이 흔들린다. 정답게 꼬리를 친다.

(2) (b), (a), (e), (b) -- 먼 옛날, 이탈리아에 제페토라는 목각사가 살았다. 제페토는 목각 인형을 만들어 피노키오라 이름지었다. 인형은 소생했지만, 행동이 서툴렀다. 그는 돈을 부주의하게 썼고, 학교를 빼먹었다. 그중에서도 가장 나쁜 점은 거짓말을 한다는 것이었다. 그가 거짓말을 하면, 코가 길어지곤 했다. 그가 거짓말을 할 때마다, 코가 자랐던 것이다.

(3) (a), (b), (d), (e) -- 북미산 다람쥐가 뒷다리로 일어나 앉아 도토리를 씹고 있었다. 주위를 둘러보다가, 다람쥐는 농부의 개를 발견하고 그만 자리에 얼어붙고 말았다. 개는 코를 킁킁거리더니, 다람쥐를 발견하고는 그를 향해 돌격했다.

(4) (a), (b), (d) -- 우리는 서둘러 나아갔다. 흰 구름 사이로 언뜻 파란 헝겊처럼 하늘 위로 하얀 대낮의 달이 나타났다. 빗줄기는 체로 친 고운 밀가루처럼 가늘었다. 어머니는 기분이 좋았지만, 이 기분이 금방 변할 수 있다는 걸 알고 계신 것 같았다. 그녀는 비와 하늘을 쳐다보았다. 그것들이 누군가가 순식간에 가져갈 수 있는 소유물이라도 된 것처럼. 갑자기 구름이 몸을 뒤척이는가 싶더니, 금세 부서졌다. 우리는 비에 흠뻑 젖었다.

(5) (c), (c), (d) -- 정오가 되자 비는 그쳤지만, 검은 구름은 계속해서 바위가 울퉁불퉁한 산을 따라 저 아래 계곡으로 내려가고 있었다. 이런 날씨에도 불구하고, 우리는 최소한 스위스의 산 하나

만은 오르기로 결정했다. 우리는 호텔 뒤쪽의 가파른 비탈을 힘겹게 올랐다. 한 시간 가량의 힘든 산행 뒤, 우리는 냉랭한 널빤지 위에 앉아 신선한 물로 기운을 돋궜다.

A16

(1) (a), (c) -- 사자는 으르렁거리고, 말은 히힝거린다.

(2) (b), (d) -- 올빼미는 부엉부엉 울고 코요테는 청승맞게 운다.

(3) (b), (b) -- 비둘기는 구구거리고, 개구리는 개굴거린다.

(4) (a) -- 최초의 대륙횡단 철도가 완공되었을 때, 전국에 교회 종이 울렸다.

(5) (c) -- 말할 때가 있고, 침묵할 때가 있다.

(6) (d) -- 가장 크게 끽끽거리는 바퀴는 기름친 바퀴다.

(7) (b) -- 침묵은 사랑, 분노, 놀람, 두려움 등 강한 열정의 언어다.

(8) (c) -- 싫은 사람은 잡담을 하기 위해 막 잠든 사람을 깨우는 사람이다.

(9) (a) -- 나랑 이 방을 함께 쓰고 싶으면, 투덜거리거나 고함치지 마. 그렇게 시끄러운 친구는 곁에 둘 수 없으니까.

(10) (d) -- "이런 악한들!" 내가 날카롭게 소리쳤다. "인정하네! 증서를 다 찢어버리게! 여기 있네, 여기! 그건 그의 그 흉칙한 마음을 때리는 거니까!"

A17

그건 마치 산사태, 토네이도, 허리케인, 화산 폭발 등과 관련된 영화 중간에, 처음에는 사운드 장치에 뭔가 이상이 생겨서 소리가 지워지고 결국 모든 소음, 폭풍과 반향과 천둥소리가 모두 끊어졌다가 뒤이어 영사기에서 필름을 빼고 그 자리에 움직임이나 떨림이 없는 평화로운 열대지방의 슬라이드를 삽입한 것 같았다. 그 침묵이 어찌나 엄청나고 믿을 수 없는 것이었던지 사람들은 귀가 솜으로 막혔거나 청각을 잃어버린 듯한 기분을 느꼈다.

(1) Loud sounds : avalanche, tornado, hurricane, volcanic eruption, ripped, blasts, repercussions, thunders

(2) Soft sounds : a peaceful tropical slide... tremor, muffling, cutting off, The world... standstill, The silence was... had been stuffed or... your hearing altogether.

CHAPTER 2

명확하고 생생한 언어 사용

A18

날씨는 지극히/ 미묘한 소리들로 가득하다./ 노래하고, / 살랑거리고/ 핑 소리도 내고/ 쿵쾅거리고, / 윙윙거리고, / 딸랑거리고, / 가볍게 줄을 튕기고, / 윙하고 울기도 하고, / 쉿 소리도 내고, / 물을 뿌리고, / 철벅거리고, / 쾅 부딪치고, / 웅얼거리고, / 으르렁거리고, / 우르르 울리고, / 번쩍거리고, / 와르르 부서진다./ 궁금하다./ 천둥은 벌을 놀라게 할까,/ 쥐구멍의 쥐나 / 나무 위의 새, / 곰이나 / 토끼나 / 바다 속 물고기를 놀라게 할까? / 난 놀라지 않는다!

답 : G, S, G, L, S, S, G, G, G, G, G, L, S, S, S, G, L

A19

A. 가을은 풍경; / 나는 나무에서 떨어지는/ 색색의 나뭇잎을/ 보네. /

가을은 향기; / 나는 오븐에서 요리되고 있는/ 사과 파이의 냄새를 맡네./

가을은 맛; / 나는 감미로운 / 사과주를 마시네.

가을은 소리; / 나뭇잎을 밟을 때/ 나는 나뭇잎이/ 바삭거리는 소리를 듣네.

가을은 느낌; / 나는 내게 불어오는/ 시원한 바람을 느끼네.

답 : sight, see, smell, smell, taste, taste, hearing, hear, feeling, feel

B. 나는 내 다리에 아무렇게나 떨어지는/ 파삭파삭한 마른 나뭇잎을 느끼네.

나는 저벅저벅 내 발에 밟히는/ 파삭파삭한 나뭇잎 소리를 듣네.

나는 아삭아삭 씹히는 / 호박 파이의 조각을 맛보네.

나는 빨간 불꽃 속에서/ 바삭바삭 타오르는 나뭇잎 냄새를 맡네.

나는 나무에 매달린/ 빨강, 노랑, 황갈색 나뭇잎을 보네.

답 : feel., hear, taste, smell, see

연습문제 1

(1)(d)	(2)(c)	(3)(b)	(4)(c)	(5)(b)	(6)(d)	(7)(b)	(8)(a)	(9)(c)
(10)(d)	(11)(d)	(12)(c)	(13)(c)	(14)(d)	(15)(d)	(16)(a)	(17)(b)	(18)(c)
(19)(a)	(20)(a)	(21)(c)	(22)(d)	(23)(d)	(24)(c)	(25)(d)	(26)(d)	(27)(d)
(28)(d)	(29)(c)	(30)(c)	(31)(c)	(32)(c)	(33)(a)	(34)(d)	(35)(d)	(36)(b)
(37)(a)	(38)(b)	(39)(c)	(40)(c)					

연습문제 2

(1) (a) -- 강을 건너본 사람만이 악어 주둥이에 혹이 있다고 말할 수 있다.

(2) (b) -- 비는 표범 가죽을 구기지만, 얼룩을 씻어내지는 못한다.

(3) (c) -- 큰 나무는 작은 나무들을 보호한다.

(4) (d) -- 서투른 정원사가 연장만 나무란다.

(5) (d) -- 너무 너그러운 법은 거의 지켜지지 않으며, 너무 가혹한 법은 거의 집행되지 않는다.

(6) (c) -- 나무를 자르면, 늑대와 만나게 된다.

(7) (c) -- 결혼 전에는 눈을 크게 뜨고, 결혼 후에는 반만 떠라.

(8) (d) -- 6월의 평온한 날씨는 옥수수를 잘 자라게 한다.

(9) (d) -- 돼지가 꿀꿀거린다고 항상 비가 오는 것은 아니다.

(10)(d) -- 자기를 웃게 만드는 사람이 아니라 자기를 울게 만드는 사람에게 상담을 구하라.

(11)(d) -- 아무리 저주를 퍼부어도 셔츠를 찢을 순 없다.

(12)(c) -- 값싼 고기를 사면, 고기가 익어갈 때, 당신이 소중히 하여 아낀 것이 무엇인지 냄새로 알게
되다.

(13)(a) -- 함께 살 때는 형제처럼, 사업할 때는 타인처럼.

(14)(a) -- 나무는 기댄 방향으로 쓰러진다.

(15)(a) -- 참새가 공작을 흉내내다가는 다리가 부러진다.

(16)(b) -- 악마는 술 취한 사람이 쓰러져 누울 베개를 놓아둔다.

(17)(b) -- 물고기를 주는 것은 하루의 양식을 주는 것이오, 물고기 잡는 법을 가르쳐주면, 평생 먹여
살리는 것이다.

(18)(c) -- 호랑이를 탄 사람은 결코 내릴 수 없다.

(19)(d) -- 미소가 없는 사람은 가게를 열어선 안 된다.

(20)(b) -- 현명한 사람은 주전자에 물 맞추듯이 환경에 적응한다.

(21)(d) -- 출세하려는 사람은 인간성으로 자신의 야망을 감춰야 한다.

(22)(b) -- 인생이란 어느 정도는 이미 주어진 것이지만, 어느 정도는 우리가 선택한 친구들에 의해
만들어진다.

(23)(a) -- 많은 의사들은 죽음을 받아 들인다.

(24)(c) -- 많은 친구를 농담으로 잃으며, 어느 누구도 농담으로 친구를 얻지 못한다.

(25)(c) -- 돈을 빌려주면, 친구를 잃게 된다.

(26)(c) -- 경험은 유익하다. 단, 너무 비싼 대가를 치르지만 않는다면.

(27)(b) -- 텅 빈 지갑은 친구들을 쫓아버린다.

(28)(d) -- 나쁜 책은 회개할 수 없기 때문에 더 나빠진다.

(29)(d) -- 도둑을 잡으려면 도둑을 배치하라.

(30)(c) -- 가을은 도둑처럼 여름을 훔친다.

(31)(c) -- 구두 어디가 죄는지는 신어 본 사람만 안다.

(32)(a) -- 일 못하는 사람이 늘 연장 탓을 한다.

(33)(d) -- 불행은 바늘처럼 들어와서 떡갈나무처럼 퍼진다.

(34)(d) -- 거미줄이 합쳐지면, 사자도 묶을 수 있다.

(35)(b) -- 치료는 신이 하고, 돈은 의사가 받는다.

(36)(d) -- 결혼은 종종 서로를 거의 알지 못하는 두 사람을 평생 동안 결합시킨다.

(37)(d) -- 사랑의 법칙이 남녀를 어찌나 강하게 묶어놓는지 인간의 어떤 법도 그 둘을 갈라놓을 수
없다.

(38)(b) -- 날개를 갖기 전에는 파리를 흉내내지 말라.

(39)(c) -- 병원이 종종 병 그 자체보다 더 무섭다.

(40)(a) -- 한번 입을 데인 사람은 항상 수프를 불어 먹는다.

(41)(c) -- 자신의 가르침대로 행하지 않는 설교자가 많다.

(42)(d) -- 쥐를 쫓아버리는 고양이는 쥐를 잡는 고양이만큼이나 훌륭하다.

(43)(b) -- 짖지 않는 개가 항상 제일 먼저 잡아챈다.

(44)(a) -- 너무 많이 시작하는 사람은 성취하는 것이 거의 없다.

(45)(c) -- 행동은 빠르게, 생각은 천천히.

(46)(b) -- 환대할 때, 중요한 것은 마음이다.

(47)(c) -- 양치기는 신사가 되고 나서도 양 냄새를 맡는다.

(48)(a) -- 큰 나무는 모든 것들에 그늘을 드리워준다. 심지어 나무꾼에게도.

(49)(a) -- 황소는 비엔나로 데려가도 황소로 남는다.

(50)(b) -- 빌려줄 때의 법칙은 접시를 깨는 것이다.

(51)(d) -- 누구나 가는 곳에는 풀이 결코 자라지 않는다.

(52)(d) -- 새 빗자루는 청소에 열심이지만, 오래된 솔은 구석 구석 모르는 곳이 없다.

(53)(a) -- 요청받기 전에는 조언도 주지 말고 소금도 주지 말라.

(54)(d) -- 불운이 잠잘 때, 어느 누가 그것을 깨우게 한다.

(55)(a) -- 태양이 가장 높이 떴을 때, 그늘은 가장 적게 드리운다.

(56)(d) -- 칼보다 더 무서운 것이 혀.

(57)(a) -- 화살 하나는 쉽게 부러지지만, 화살 한 묶음은 그렇지 않다.

(58)(a) -- 참을 수 없는 것을 참는 것이 진정한 인내다.

(59)(c) -- 어리석은 행동을 그냥 두면, 이성이 물러난다.

(60)(a) -- 안되면 조상 탓.

(61)(a) -- 고래 싸움에 새우등 터진다.

(62)(b) -- 참새가 방앗간을 그냥 지나가랴.

(63)(b) -- 눈물보다 더 빨리 마르는 것은 없다.

(64)(c) -- 바보가 잠자코 있으면 현자로 통한다.

(65)(b) -- 의사는 일할 땐 천사지만, 돈 받을 땐 악마다.

(66)(d) -- 바보는 떠돌아다니고, 현자는 여행한다.

(67)(c) -- 늙은 개가 짖으면, 조심해야 한다.

(68)(c) -- 죽은 나무가 쓰러지면, 딱따구리는 그 죽음을 함께 한다.

(69)(a) -- 비가 오더라도, 물뿌리개를 버리지 말라.

(70)(d) -- 나무가 아무리 높이 자라도, 낙엽은 뿌리로 돌아온다.

(71)(d) -- 쥐가 고양이를 보고 웃을 땐, 근처에 함정이 있다.

(72)(c) -- 뱀에 물린 적이 있는 사람은 실 한 오라기만 봐도 무서워한다.

(73)(c) -- 장미를 원하는 사람은 가시를 주의해야 한다.

(74)(d) -- 다친 손은 움직이지만, 상처받은 마음은 그렇지 않다.

(75)(b) -- 사람의 지붕이 크면 클수록, 눈이 더 많이 모인다.

(76)(b) -- 남자는 눈으로 사랑을 받아들이고, 여자는 귀로 받아들인다.

(77)(d) -- 주인을 둘 섬기는 사람은 둘 중 한 명에게는 거짓말을 해야 한다.

(78)(a) -- 철이 있는 곳에 녹도 있다.

(79)(c) -- 유모가 일곱이면, 아이가 시력을 잃는다.

(80)(b) -- 희망이라는 말은 전속력으로 질주하지만, 경험이라는 나귀는 천천히 간다.

(81)(d) -- 아내는 오직 집으로 이끌 때, 집밖으로 내보낼 때, 두 번만 귀중하다.

(82)(d) -- 코를 물 속에 넣으면, 뺨도 적시게 된다.

(83)(d) -- 꿔 줄 때는 절을 받지만, 받을 때는 도리어 절을 한다.

(84)(c) -- 건강한 귀는 병든 이야기 듣기를 거부한다.

(85)(b) -- 많이 아는 사람이 말은 가장 적게 한다.

(86)(c) -- 나의 슬픔을 알고 즐거워하지 말라. 내 슬픔이 해묵은 것일 때, 네 슬픔은 새로운 슬픔일
것이므로.

(87)(c) -- 누군가에게 비밀을 털어놓으면, 그 사람한테 자신의 자유까지 양도하는 것이다.

(88)(d) -- 훌륭한 서비스를 원한다면, 당신 자신을 섬겨라.

(89)(d) -- 무지를 드러내기보다는 지식을 숨기는 것이 더 낫다.

(90)(d) -- 행동으로 얻는 친구보다 말로 얻는 적이 더 많다.

(91)(d) -- 행운이 문을 두드리면, 문을 활짝 열어라.

(92)(b) -- 낮이 비누칠한 것을 밤이 헹군다.

(93)(c) -- 사람이 행운을 찾는 것이 아니라 행운이 사람을 찾아간다.

(94)(d) -- 악마는 사람을 유혹하지만, 오직 게으른 사람만이 악마를 유혹한다.

(95)(b) -- 연기가 항아리를 끓게 만들지는 못한다.

(96)(a) -- 자신의 슬픔을 숨기는 사람은 어떤 해결책도 찾지 못한다.

(97)(a) -- 부자가 되는 것이 전부는 아니지만, 확실히 도움은 된다.

(98)(c) -- 시간과 더불어 모든 것이 자라지만, 슬픔은 그렇지 않다.

(99)(d) -- 사람들이 모두 학식이 있다면, 세상은 멸망할 것이다.

(100)(c) -- 아침에 한 시간을 낭비하면, 하루종일 그것을 쫓아다녀야 한다.

CHAPTER 3

문단

Paragraph

This section, PART 3 is designed to intensively prepare for a variety of essays along with their styles and types

that will be studied in PART 4. As you know, a paragraph as a core unit of an essay serves as a key role for developing well-organized writings. Without fundamental skills for paragraph development, writing a good essay is as difficult as "finding a needle in a haystack." The following sections in PART 3 are devoted to distinctive skills for developing an organized paragraph.

3.1. Paragraph Structure

A paragraph is a series of written expressions usually constructed with more than two sentences that explicitly or implicitly support one specific topic of a passage presented. Some of the sentences in a paragraph express major points that directly support the topic, whereas others express minor supporting details.

The first sentence of a paragraph usually begins on a new line with the first word indented as a way of showing distinct units on the page. This helps the writer organize his/her ideas clearly and coherently, and the reader can easily group and follow related thoughts in a paper.

A paragraph includes: (l) the main idea; (2) the topic sentence; and, (3) the supporting details. The main idea refers to the key point or topic presented in a paragraph. The main idea of a paragraph is often stated as a single sentence called the topic sentence. This sentence often appears at the beginning, but it can occur anywhere in a paragraph. Some paragraphs have no topic sentence at all if the sentences presented relate a sequence of events as in a narrative description. In this case, be sure to ask these questions to yourself: (a) What is each sentence about? (b) How do all the sentences relate to each other?, and, (c) Think about the details of (a) and (b), and generate the topic sentence of the paragraph. The supporting details in a paragraph help explain or support the topic sentence clearly and interestingly to the reader by using a variety of communicative skills such as (A) sensory details, (B) facts and statistics, (C) examples, and (D) anecdotes, which will be extensively exemplified with comprehensive practices for a sound grip in the following sections.

이장은 4장에서 공부하게 될 문체 및 유형에 따른 다양한 에세이를 집중적으로 준비해 보는 장이다. 알다시피, 에세이의 핵심 단위인 문단은 잘 짜인 글을 전개시키는 데 핵심적인 역할을 담당한다. 문단 전개의 기본 기술도 없이 좋은 에세이를 쓴다는 것은 "건초더미에서 바늘을 찾는 것"만큼이나 어렵다. 이 장을 통해 잘 짜인 문단을 전개시키는 데 필요한 독특한 기술을 익혀보기로 하자.

3.1. 문단 구조

문단이란 제시된 절의 특정한 주제를 명시적 또는 암시적으로 뒷받침하는 두 문장 이상으로 구성된 문자화된 표현이다. 한 절의 일부 문장은 주제를 직접적으로 뒷받침하는 중요한 요점들을 표현하지만, 다른 문장들은 기타 뒷받침 세부자료들을 표현한다.

한 문단의 첫 문장은 그 페이지상의 차별적인 단위임을 보여주는 한 방식으로서 보통 줄을 바꾸고 첫 단어를 몇 칸 들여 쓴다. 이렇게 하면, 작가 입장에서는 자신의 아이디어를 분명하고 조리 있게 구성할 수 있고, 독자들은 글 전체에 서술된 사고를 쉽게 분류하여 이해할 수 있다.

한 문단에는 (1) 요지, (2) 주제문, (3) 뒷받침 세부자료(보충설명) 등이 포함되어 있다. 요지는 한 절에 제시된 요점 또는 주제를 가리킨다. 한 문단의 요지는 종종 주제문이라 불리는 단문으로 시작된다. 이 문장은 종종 처음에 나오지만, 문단 어디에나 쓸 수 있다. 제시된 문장들은 일련의 사건들을 이야기식으로 서술할 뿐 주제문이 전혀 없는 문단들도 있다. 이런 경우, 스스로에게 이런 질문들을 던져야 한다. (a) 각각의 문장은 무엇에 대해 말하고 있는가? (b) 모든 문장들은 서로 어떤 연관을 가지고 있는가? (c) (a)와 (b)의 세부사항들에 대해 생각해보고, 문단의 주제문을 결정한다. 한 문단의 뒷받침 세부자료는 (A) 감각적 세부사항, (B) 사실과 통계, (C) 사례, (D) 일화 등과 같은 다양한 전달 기법을 사용하여 독자들에게 주제문을 분명하고 재미있게 설명할 수 있게 한다. 이러한 표현 기법은 이어지는 장에 나오는 포괄적인 실전 연습을 통해 광범위하게 살펴보게 될 것이다.

Note

devote	*v.*	To give time or attention entirely to a particular person, purpose or activity
		-- I devoted my life to music
indent	*v.*	To begin the first line of a paragraph farther in from the margine then the other line
exemplify	*v.*	Clarify by giving an example of
narrative	*n.*	An account describing incidents or events
	a.	Consisting of or characterized by the telling of a story

3.1.1. Developing a main idea & a topic sentence

To develop a main idea, first, decide on the main topic of your paragraph. The main idea of a paragraph or a passage can be drawn or defined in a single word, phrase, or sentence. Based on this single thought, you should generate a complete sentence focused on the main idea. This is the topic sentence, which should be broad enough to be supported or developed by supporting details through the remainder of the paragraph or passage. Therefore, the topic sentence summarizes the whole paragraph/passage, and makes a general statement. It is wider in scope than the rest of the sentences in the paragraph.

The topic sentence can include several sub-topics from which the supporting details are developed and illustrated so as to support the sub-topic or the topic sentence. These linguistic terms such as "the topic sentence and the main idea" can be compared to our body structure as illustrated below:

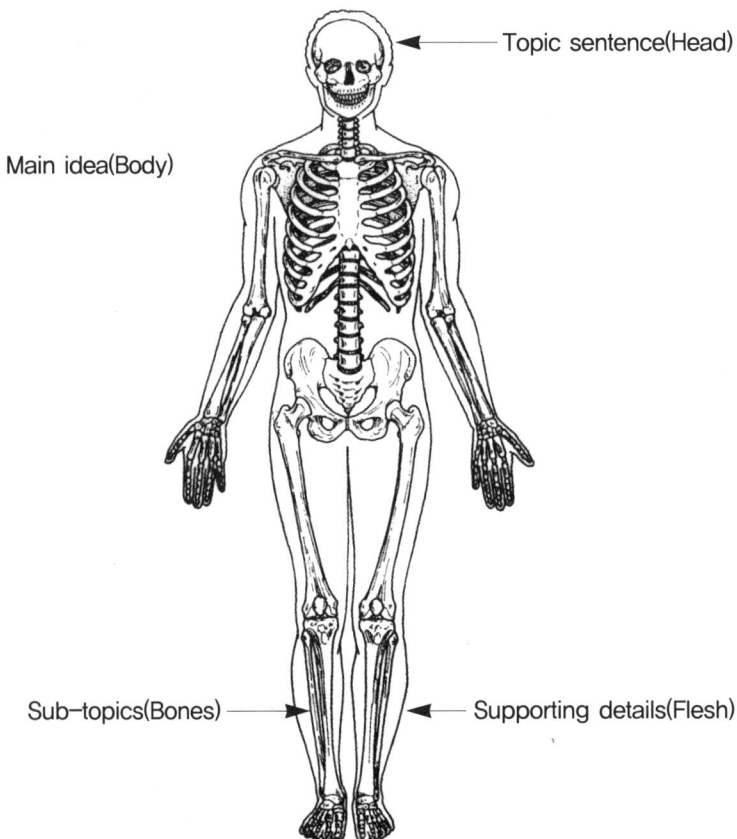

Topic sentence(Head)

Main idea(Body)

Sub-topics(Bones)   Supporting details(Flesh)

Basic Structure of a Paragraph

3.1.1. 요지 및 주제문 전개

요지를 전개시키려면, 일단 문단의 주제문을 결정해야 한다. 한 문단이나 절의 요지는 한 단어나 구, 또는 한 문장에서 도출되거나 명확히 규정될 수 있다. 따라서 이러한 한 가지 생각에 근거해서 요지에 초점을 맞춘 완전한 문장을 만들어야 한다. 이것이 바로 주제문이며, 주제문은 그 문단이나 절의 여타 뒷받침 세부자료들에 의해 뒷받침되거나 전개될 수 있을 만큼 충분히 폭넓어야 한다. 따라서 주제문은 문단이나 절 전체를 요약하고 포괄적인 설명을 제시한다. 그것은 문단 속의 다른 문장들보다 범위가 더 넓다.

주제문에는 몇 가지 부주제가 포함될 수 있으며, 부주제나 주제문을 뒷받침하기 위해 뒷받침 세부자료들이 전개되고 설명된다. '주제문과 요지' 등과 같은 언어학적 용어들은 아래에 예시된 우리의 신체 구조에 비유될 수 있다.

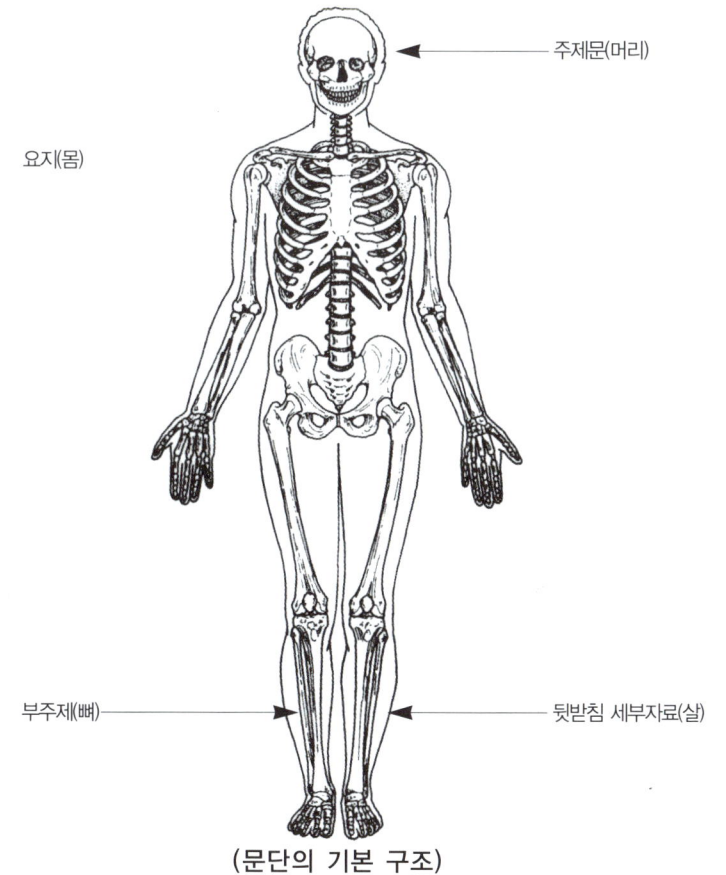

(문단의 기본 구조)

Below in the left are several words listed. One choice, for example, serves as a main idea from which a topic sentence can be generated as follows:

Elementary school
Kindergarten
Middle school
High school
School division
College/University

* <u>Main idea</u>: School division

*<u>Topic sentence</u>: School has several divisions such as kindergarten, elementary school, middle school, high school, and college. *(Note: This topic sentence is just a model. There are quite a few ways to generate a topic sentence. For example, "School division is classified into kindergarten, elementary school, middle school, high school, and college.")*

*<u>Sub-topics</u>: kindergarten, elementary school, middle school, high school, and college.

*<u>Supporting details</u>: <u>Kindergarten</u> is a nursery school for children under the age of 6. In many countries, the kindergarten is organized on informal instruction with the emphasis on social development and basic academic preparation for elementary schooling. Children attend it for a year. *(Note: These supporting details are provided only for the sub-topic, kindergarten)*

*<u>Basic structure of a paragraph</u>: School has several divisions such as kindergarten, elementary school, middle school, high school, and college. Kindergarten is a nursery school...Children attend it for a year.

Elementary school: Supporting details are omitted.
Middle school: Omitted.
High school: Omitted.
College/University: Omitted.

C H A P T E R 3

왼쪽에 몇 가지 단어들이 나열되어 있다. 예를 들어, 요지로 기능하는 단어를 선택하면, 그에 따라 주제문을 도출할 수 있다.

초등학교
유치원
중학교
고등학교
학교 분과
대학교

●**요지** : 학교 분과

●**주제문** : 학교는 유치원, 초등학교, 중학교, 고등학교, 대학 등과 같은 몇 가지 분과를 가지고 있다. (Note : 이 주제문은 단지 하나의 모델에 불과하다. 주제문을 도출하는 데는 몇 가지 방법이 있다. 예를 들어, 학교 분과는 유치원, 초등학교, 중학교, 고등학교, 대학교 등으로 분류된다.)

●**부주제** : 유치원, 초등학교, 중학교, 고등학교, 대학교

●**뒷받침 세부자료** : 유치원은 6세 이하의 어린이들을 위한 보육 학교이다. 상당수의 나라에서 유치원은 사회성 함양 및 초등학교 교육을 받기 위한 기초 과정 준비에 역점을 두는 비공식적 지침에 따라 설립된다. 아이들은 1년 동안 유치원에 다닌다. (Note : 여기 실린 뒷받침 세부자료는 단지 유치원이라는 부주제를 설명하기 위한 것이다.)

●**문단의 기본 구조** : 학교는 유치원, 초등학교, 중학교, 고등학교, 대학교 등과 같은 몇 가지 분과를 가지고 있다. 유치원은 보육학교이며... 아이들은 1년 동안 유치원에 다닌다.

초등학교 : 뒷받침 세부자료 생략

중학교 : 생략

고등학교 : 생략

대학교 : 생략

Note

generate *v.* Bring about or produce
--Water and steam generate electricity
nursery *n.* 1. A room or place set apart for babies or young children.
2. A place where plants and young trees are raised, often to be sold

Below in the left are five lists. In each list, one choice serves as a main idea from which you should generate a topic sentence. The other words or phrases can work as supporting details. Write the choice as a main idea, and generate a topic sentence focused on the main idea. The following 1 and 2 are exemplified for you.

l. Arabic
   Hindi
   Language
   Swahili
   Swedish

Main idea: Language

Topic sentence: People speak a variety of languages such as Arabic, Hindi, Swahili, and Swedish.

2. Caucasian
   Malayan
   Mongoloid
   Negroid
   Race

Main idea: Race

Topic sentence: In general, race can be classified into four: Caucasian, Malayan, Mongoloid, and Negroid.

3. Good morning.
   Greeting
   Hello, there.
   Good night.
   How do you do?

Main idea: _____

Topic sentence: _____
_____

4. Conclusion
   Main idea
   Research paper
   Supporting details
   Topic sentence

Main idea: _____

Topic sentence: _____
_____

5. Appetizer
   Entree
   Dessert
   Dinner
   Soup

Main idea: _____

Topic sentence: _____
_____

6. Causes of poor health
   Lack of exercise
   Lack of medical care
   Unbalanced diet
   Unsanitary conditions

Main idea: _____

Topic sentence: _____
_____

왼쪽에 다섯 가지 단어 또는 구가 나열되어 있다. 요지로 기능하는 단어를 선택하고, 주제문을 작성하라. 그밖의 단어 또는 구는 뒷받침 세부자료로 기능하게 된다. 요지를 써 넣고, 그 요지에 초점을 맞춘 주제문을 만들어라. 1,2의 두 가지 예를 참조하라.

1. 아라비아어 | 힌디어 | 언어 | 스와힐리어 | 스웨덴어

Main idea : Language

Topic sentence : People speak a variety of languages such as Arabic, Hindi, Swahili, and Swedish.

● **요지** : 언어

● **주제문** : 사람들은 아라비아어, 힌디어, 스와힐리어, 스웨덴어 등과 같은 다양한 언어로 말한다.

2. 코카서스인(백인) | 말레이인 | 몽고인 | 흑인 | 인종

Main idea : Race

Topic sentence : In general, race can be classified into four: Caucasian, Malayan, Mongoloid, and Negroid.

● **요지** : 인종

● **주제문** : 인종은 대개 코카서스인, 말레이인, 몽고인, 흑인 등 네 가지로 분류될 수 있다.

3. 좋은 아침입니다 | 인사 | 안녕 | 잘자 | 처음 뵙겠습니다

Main idea : Greeting

Topic sentence : Based on situations and time, we use various expressions for greetings: Good morning, Hello, there, Good night, and How do you do?.

4. 결론 | 요지 | 연구 논문 | 뒷받침 세부자료 | 주제문

Main idea : Research paper

Topic sentence : Research paper should include several important features such as a main idea, a topic sentence, supporting details, and a conclusion.

5. 애피타이저 | 앙트레 | 디저트 | 만찬 | 수프

Main idea : Dinner

Topic sentence : A good dinner often includes appetizer, soup, entree, and dessert.

6. 건강 악화의 원인들 | 운동 부족 | 의학적 관심 부족 | 불균형적 식단 | 비위생적 환경

Main idea : Causes of poor health

Topic sentence : Poor health is often caused by a lack of exercise and medical attention/care, unbalanced diet, and unsanitary conditions.

7. Brushing habits
   Dental care
   Eating too many sweets
   Regular checkups
   Smoking habits

Main idea: _____

Topic sentence: _____

_____

8. Getting a job
   Having an interview
   Preparing a resume
   Sending a letter of-
   -application
   Studying the want ads

Main idea: _____

Topic sentence: _____

_____

9. Advantages of city life
   Places of entertainment
   Places of cultural
   activities
   Convenient transportation
   Wide choices of career

Main idea: _____

Topic sentence: _____

_____

10. Flies
    Insect pests
    Fleas
    Mosquitoes
    Ticks

Main idea: _____

Topic sentence: _____

_____

11. Jean-Francois Millet's
    "The Gleaners."
    Leonard da Vinci's
    "Mona Lisa."
    Masaccio's
    "The Expulsion of Adam &
    Eve from Paradise."
    Sandra Botticelli's
    "The Birth of Venus."
    Publicized Western
    paintings

Jean-Francois Millet's "The Gleaners."

7. 칫솔질 습관 | 치아 관리 | 단 음식 과다 섭취 | 정기 진단 | 흡연 습관

   Main idea : Dental care

   Topic sentence : Dental care is maintained through regular checkups and proper
   brushing habits, while refraining from eating too many sweets and
   smoking habits.

8. 일자리 얻기 | 면접보기 | 이력서 준비 | 입사 지원서 보내기 | 구인 광고 보기

   Main idea : Getting a job

   Topic sentence : Getting a job often requires studying the want ads, preparing a resume,
   sending a letter of application, and having an interview.

9. 도시 생활의 이점 | 오락 시설 | 문화 시설 | 교통 편의 | 직업 선택의 다양성

   Main idea : Advantages of city life

   Topic sentence : City life provides us with a lot of advantages such as places of
   entertainment and cultural activities, wider choices of career,
   and transportation convenience.

10. 파리 | 해충 | 벼룩 | 모기 | 진드기

    Main idea : Insect pests

    Topic sentence : Flies, fleas, mosquitoes, and ticks constitute major insect pests.

11. 쟝 프랑소와 밀레의 '이삭줍는 사람들' | 레오나르드 다빈치의 '모나리자' | 마사치오의
    '아담과 이브의 낙원 추방' | 산드라 보티첼리의 '비너스의 탄생' | 유명한 서양화

    Main idea : Publicized Western paintings

    Topic sentence : Several well publicized classical Western paintings are Millets
    "The Gleaners", Leonard da Vinci's "Mona Lisa", Masaccio's
    "The Expulsion of Adam & Eve from Paradise", and Botticelli's
    "The Birth of Venus".

Botticelli's
"The Birth of Venus".

Choose the best main idea, and generate a defensive topic sentence as shown in 12, 13, and 14.

<u>12.</u>   Honeybees work together in several ways to build a bee colony. The drones mate with the queen. The queen lays all the eggs to provide new workers and drones for the colony. The worker bees build the honeycomb, gather the nectar from flowers, make honey, and care for the young bees.

(1) **The main idea**:

    (a) Making a bee colony   (d) Caring for the young bees

    (b) Building the honeycomb   (e) *<u>How honeybees build a colony</u>

    (c) Making honey.

(2) **The topic sentence**:

    <u>*Honeybees work together in several ways to build a colony.</u>

<u>13.</u>   Now, there are two different attitudes towards learning from others. One is the dogmatic attitude of transplanting everything, whether or not it is suited to our conditions. This is no good. The other attitude is to use our heads and learn those things which suit our conditions, that is, to absorb whatever experience is useful to us. That is the attitude we should adopt. *(Source: On the Correct Handling of Contradictions among the People. (Feb.27,1957). <u>Quotations from Chairman Mao Tse-Tung, 1967)</u>*

(1) **The main idea**:

    (a) Dogmatic attitude

    (b) Different attitudes

    (c) <u>*Different attitudes in learning</u>

    (d) The attitude we should adopt

    (e) Absorbing useful experience & attitude

Mao Tse-Tung

(2) **The topic sentence**:

    <u>*There are two different attitudes towards learning from others.</u>

가장 적절한 요지를 선택하고, 12,13,14에서 보이는 것처럼, 그 요지에 맞는 주제문을 만들어라.

12. 꿀벌들은 벌 군거지를 만들기 위해 몇 가지 방식으로 함께 일한다. 수벌들은 여왕벌과 교미한다. 여왕벌은 알을 낳아 군거지에 새로운 일벌과 수벌을 제공한다. 일벌은 벌집을 짓고, 꽃에서 화밀(花蜜)을 따오며, 꿀을 만들고, 어린 벌들을 보살핀다.

Main idea : (e)

Topic sentence : Honeybees work together in several ways to build their colony.
　　　　　　　　　(꿀벌들은 군거지를 만들기 위해 몇 가지 방식으로 함께 일한다.)

Note

drone	*n.* A male bee, especially a honeybee
	v. To make or talk with a low, dull humming sound
	--An airplane droned far overhead
nectar	*n.* A sweet liquid found in many flowers

13. 다른 사람으로부터 무언가를 배우는 데는 서로 다른 두 가지 자세가 있다. 그 하나는 우리 조건과 상관없이 모든 것을 이식하는 교조적인 자세이다. 이것은 결코 좋은 자세가 아니다. 나머지 자세는 머리를 써서 우리의 조건에 맞는 것들을 배우는 것, 다시 말해 우리에게 유용한 경험은 모두 흡수하는 것이다. 그것이 바로 우리가 채택해야 할 자세이다. (마오쩌뚱)

Main idea : (c)

Topic sentence : There are two different attitudes towards learning from others
　　　　　　　　　(다른 사람으로부터 무언가를 배우는 데는 서로 다른 두 가지 자세가 있다.)

Note

dogmatic	*a.* 1. Of, pertaining to, or characteristic of dogma
	2. Asserting beliefs and opinions as though they were proven facts.
absorb	*v.* 1. Take in, soak up --A sponge absorbs water.
	2. Take in and make part of something -- The United States has absorbed people from all over the world.
	3. Take in and keep from going back or through --Thick rugs absorb sound.
	4. Hold the attention, engross --The movie absorbed the audience from start to finish.
adopt	*v.* 1. Take another person's child and raise it as one's own.
	2. Take and make one's own --Samuael Clemens adopted the name Jone.
	3. Accept and use or follow --Our school has adopted a new method of teaching geography.

14. The first type of volcano, the active one, always shows signs of volcanic action. The second type, the dormant volcano, is one that has not erupted yet, but it might someday. The third type, the extinct, is one that has not erupted in hundreds of years; it is dead.

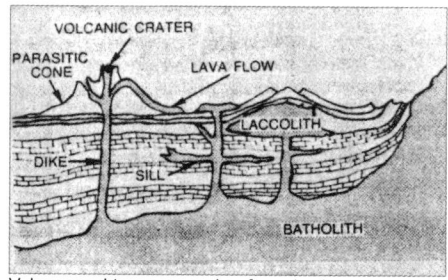

Volcano ; subterranean and surface structure

(1) The main idea:

    (a) Active volcano   (b) Dormant volcano   (c) Volcanic eruption

    (d) *Types of volcano   (e) Extinct volcano

(2) The topic sentence:

    *There are three types of volcano: active, dormant, and extinct.

    (Note: There is no topic sentence in the above paragraph. In this case, ask yourself;

    (a) What is each sentence about? (b) How do all sentences relate to each other?, and

    (c) Think about the details of (a) and (b), and generate the topic sentence of the

    paragraph. The above paragraph clearly defines three types of volcano as you see.)

15. The role of an American President's wife is a difficult and demanding one. She as the First Lady must provide support and encouragement for her husband. Since her husband's job is one of the most burdensome in all the world, her help is crucially important. She must be a hostess at many official dinners and receptions. She must participate in many social activities outside the White House. When her husband is criticized, she must encourage him.

(1) The main idea:

    (a) Duty of the First Lady of U.S.   (b) Job of an American President's wife

    (c) Rights of an American First Lady (d) Partnership of the First Lady of the U.S.

    (e) Role of the First Lady of the U. S.

(2) The topic sentence:_____

14. 화산의 첫 번째 유형인 활화산은 항상 화산 활동의 징조를 보여준다. 두 번째 유형인 휴화산은 아직까지 폭발하진 않았지만, 언젠가는 폭발할 화산이다. 세 번째 유형인 사화산은 수백년간 폭발하지 않았던 화산으로서, 죽은 화산이다.

Main idea : (d)

Topic sentence: There are 3 types of volcano: active, dormant, and extinct.

(Note : 위의 문단에는 주제문이 없다. 이런 경우, 스스로에게 이런 질문을 던져라. (a) 각각의 문장은 무엇에 대해 이야기하고 있는가? (b) 모든 문장들은 서로 어떤 연관을 가지고 있는가? (c) (a)와 (b)의 세부사항들에 대해 생각해보고, 문단의 주제문을 만들어라. 위의 문단은 알다시피 화산의 세 가지 유형을 명확히 정의하고 있다.)

Note

dormant	*a.* Not active for a time
erupt	*v.* Burst out violently --Lava and ash erupted from the volcano.
extinct	*a.* 1. No longer existing in living form --The dodo bird been extinct for 300 years
	2. No longer active, extinguished --A lake can form in the crater of an extinct volcano.

15. 미국 대통령 부인의 역할은 어렵고 힘들다. 그녀는 영부인으로서 남편을 지원하고 남편에게 용기를 주어야 한다. 남편의 업무가 세계에서 가장 부담스러운 것이기에, 그녀의 도움은 결정적으로 중요하다. 그녀는 수많은 공식 만찬 및 리셉션의 안주인이 되어야 한다. 그녀는 백악관 밖의 수많은 사회 활동에 참여해야 한다. 남편이 비난받을 때면, 그에게 용기를 북돋워야 한다.

Main idea : (e)

Topic sentence: The role of an American Presidents wife is a difficult and demanding one.

(미국 대통령 부인의 역할은 어렵고 힘들다.)

Note

demand	*v.* 1. Ask as one's right --I demanded the money that was owed me.
	2. Ask urgently and with authority --The investigators demanded the suspect's name.
	3. Call for as necessary, require --The work of a lawyer demands skill and concentration.
participate	*v.* Join with others -- We participated in the athletic program.

16. Both President Lincoln and President Kennedy were attacked by an assassin on Friday, and each in the presence of his wife. Each man was shot in the head; in each instance, crowds of people watched the shooting. Lincoln's secretary, named Kennedy, had advised him not to go to the theater where the attack occurred. Kennedy's secretary, named Lincoln, had advised him not to go to Dallas where the attack occurred.

(1) The main idea:

(a) Similar fate of President Lincoln & President Kennedy

(b) Some common factors related to the assassin of President Lincoln & President Kennedy

(c) The same fate of President Lincoln & President Kennedy

(d) An unavoidable fate for President Lincoln & President Kennedy

(e) A mystery of assassinating President Lincoln & President Kennedy

(2) The topic sentence: _____

_____

17. Fidel Castro overthrew the Bastista regime in 1958, and initiated ambitious social reforms, diversifying Cuba's economy and redistributing the land based on socialist economic ideology. Since then, almost a million Cubans have left Cuba, and came to the United States. At least half of them went to Miami, Florida, to start a new life there. Miami is not far from Cuba, and the climate there is not much different from that of Cuba. Thus, they began to settle in Miami, developing a part of the city they called "Little Havana." Now, it is not difficult to see why the Cubans want to live in Little Havana. It reminds them of home. They want to live in an environment which can provide them with as much closeness of home as possible.

(1) The main idea:

(a) When Castro seized power

(b) How Castro initiated reforms

(c) Why Cubans left Cuba

(d) Why Cubans live in Little Havana

(e) Living in Little Havana

Fidel Castro

(2) The topic sentence: _____

16. 링컨 대통령과 케네디 대통령은 둘 다 금요일, 아내의 면전에서 암살당했다. 둘 다 머리에 총상을 입었고, 두 경우 모두, 수많은 군중이 저격 장면을 지켜보았다. 링컨의 비서 케네디는 링컨에게 사건이 일어난 극장에 가지 말라고 충고했었다. 케네디의 비서 링컨은 케네디에게 사건이 일어난 달라스에 가지 말라고 충고했었다.

Lincoln

Kennedy

Main idea : (b)

Topic sentence : Both President Lincoln and President Kennedy were attacked by an assassin on Friday, and each in the presence of his wife.

Note

assassin *n.* Murderer, especially one who kills an important person.

advise *v.* 1. Give advice to or offer advice
        2. Give information to; notify

17. 피델 카스트로는 1958년, 바스티스타 정권을 전복하고 야심찬 사회 개혁에 착수했다. 쿠바 경제를 다각화하고, 사회주의 경제 이념에 입각하여 토지를 재분배하였다. 그 이후로, 거의 백만 명에 달하는 쿠바인들이 쿠바를 떠나 미국으로 왔다. 그들 가운데 최소한 절반은 플로리다주 마이애미로 가서 새로운 인생을 시작했다. 마이애미는 쿠바에서 그리 멀지 않고, 기후 또한 쿠바와 그다지 다르지 않다. 따라서 그들은 마이애미에 정착하여 도시 한 곳에 '리틀 하바나' 라는 구역을 발전시키기 시작했다. 그렇다면, 쿠바인들이 왜 리틀 하바나에 살고 싶어하는지를 이해하기란 어렵지 않다. 그곳은 그들에게 고향을 상기시킨다. 그들은 가능한 한 고향과 비슷한 것을 제공해주는 환경에서 살고 싶어한다.

Main idea : (d)

Topic sentence : Cuban refugees live in Little Havana since it reminds them of their original home environment as much as possible.

Note

overthrow *v.* Cause the fall or destruction of --The rebels overthrew the government.

initiate *v.* 1. Set going, start --Who initiated this rumor ?
        2. Admitted to membership in a club, often with a special ceremony.

diversify 1. Give variety to; vary: diversify a menu.
        2. Distribute (investments) among different companies or securities in order to limit losses in the event of a fall in a particular market or industry.

18. The electric light was invented by Thomas Alva Edison in 1879. Many people knew that a very hot wire gives off light. But what kind of wire is best for a light bulb? It must have a high resistance, give off a lot of light, and last a long time. In his search for the suitable material, Edison tried hundreds of different substances. The first successful electric lamp used a carbon filament. Filaments in light bulbs today are made of tungsten which has a high resistance and gives off a lot of light when it gets hot. But, the tungsten wire would quickly burn out if it were in air. So the air is removed from inside the bulb, and nitrogen or argon is forced in.

Thomas Alva Edison

(1) The main idea:

    (a) How Edison improved the quality of the light bulb

    (b) How the electric light was developed

    (c) What substances constitute the light bulb

    (d) Why tungsten wire easily burns out

    (e) Why nitrogen or argon is forced in

(2) The topic sentence: _____

_____

Taj Mahal

19. Advertisements lure us to travel. They strongly invite us to see the splendors of the Taj Mahal in India, the Great Wall of China, the pyramids and the Sphinx in Egypt, and to fish, relax or swim in the gorgeous waters of Tahiti, South Pacific and in the beautiful beaches of the Hawaiian Islands such as Maui, Molokai, Kuanai, and Oahu, or elsewhere in the Caribbean Islands. However, the ads do not mention the wearing trials of travel. They do not mention the burden of paying later. They do not mention all the hassles of traveling that have to be tackled. These considerations make "home sweet home."

(1) The main idea:

    (a) The travel ads   (b) Landmarks around the world

    (c) Travel costs   (d) Travel hassles

    (e) Home sweet home

(2) The topic sentence: _____

18. 전등은 1879년, 토마스 앨버 에디슨에 의해 발명되었다. 뜨겁게 달구어진 철선이 빛을 낸다는 사실은 많은 사람들이 알고 있었다. 그러나 어떤 종류의 철선이 전구에 가장 적합할까? 그것은 저항력이 높고, 많은 빛을 발산해야 하며, 오랜 시간 지속되어야 한다. 에디슨은 적당한 재료를 찾기 위해 수백 가지의 물질을 시험했다. 최초의 성공적인 전기 램프는 탄소 필라멘트를 사용했다. 오늘날의 전구 필라멘트는 저항력이 높고 뜨거워졌을 때 빛도 많이 발산하는 텅스텐으로 만들어진다. 그러나 텅스텐 철선은 공기 중에 노출되면 재빨리 타버린다. 따라서 전구 속의 공기를 빼 내고, 대신 질소나 아르곤을 주입한다.

Main idea : (b)

Topic sentence : After hundreds of scientific experiments with different substances, the electric light was finally invented by Thomas Edison in 1879.

Note

invent	*v.*	Make or produce something that did not exist before
		---Who invented the elevator?
substance	*n.*	1. Something that has weight and takes up space; matter.
		2. That material that a thing is made of.
		3. The content of what is said or written rather than its form or style, meaning.
		4. Truth or reality
		--Is there any substance to these charges?

19. 광고물들은 우리에게 여행을 부추긴다. 인도의 타지마할, 중국의 만리장성, 이집트의 피라미드와 스핑크스 같은 장관을 구경하고, 남태평양 타히티 섬의 멋진 바닷가와 마우이, 몰로카이, 쿠아나이, 오아후 같은 하와이 섬들의 아름다운 해변가, 또는 카리브해 섬 어딘가에서 낚시나 휴식, 또는 수영을 즐기라며 맹렬히 우리를 초대한다. 그러나 광고물들은 여행이 안겨주는 성가신 일들에 대해서는 언급하지 않는다. 나중에 지불해야 할 돈 이야기도 하지 않는다. 불가피하게 맞부딪쳐야 할 여행의 괴로움에 대해서는 한마디 언급이 없다. 이러한 생각들은 집을 '즐거운 안식처' 로 만든다.

Main idea : (e)

Topic sentence : Although travel ads strongly lure us to visit, home sweet home is often a better place considering all the travel hassles.

Note

gorgeous	*ad.*	Extremely beautiful.
hassle	*n.*	Argue or fight
tackle	*v.*	1. To begin to deal with .
		2. To grab hold of and throw a person to the ground.

20. English is not an easy one to write and its grammar is monstrously difficult...
It's not only the grammar that makes English a difficult language to write. English
has an enormous vocabulary—how large you can see for yourselves by comparing
a French dictionary of synonyms with Roget's Thesaurus. The French dictionary is
a slim volume of 300 loosely printed pages; Roget is a volume of nearly 1000
pages printed in double columns... English, as everybody knows, is an amalgam of
several languages, and it is this amalgam that has made it more difficult for us to
write prose... None of us can expect never to make mistakes. The best we can
hope is that we shall not make many.

   (Source: William Somerset Maugham (1874-1965), English novelist and playwright)

William Somerset Maugham

(1) The main idea:

   (a) Writing English is not easy.

   (b) English grammar is difficult

   (c) None of us can expect never to make mistakes

   (d) English includes monstrously difficult vocabulary

   (e) English has an amalgam of several languages

(2) The topic sentence: _____

21. Study is a good way to transform small-scale individuals into large-scale
individuals. We are now moving from local citizenship to world citizenship. In our
homes, our communities, our everyday person-to-person contacts, we need to know.
He who does not know, and does not know that he does not know, he is a fool—
shun him; he who does not know, and knows that he does not know, he is simple—
teach him; he who knows that he does not know, he is asleep—wake him; he who
knows, and knows that he knows, he is wise—follow him. *(Source: Anonymous)*

(1) The main idea:

   (a) How to be a world citizen   (b) What makes a wise man

   (c) How to be large-scale individuals   (d) What study makes us

   (e) What makes people different

(2) The topic sentence:_____

20. 영어는 쓰기도 쉽지 않고, 문법 또한 무척 어렵다... 영어를 쓰기 어려운 언어로 만드는 것이 비단 문법만은 아니다. 어휘 또한 엄청나게 많다. 어휘가 얼마나 많은지는 프랑스어 동의어 사전과 '로제 시소러스 사전' 만 비교해보면, 금방 알 수 있다. 프랑스어 사전은 느슨하게 인쇄된 300페이지의 얇은 책인데 반해, 로제 시소러스 사전은 2단으로 인쇄된 거의 1000페이지에 달하는 책이다... 모두가 알고 있다시피, 영어는 몇 가지 언어의 혼합물이며, 이러한 혼합이야말로 글 쓰기를 더욱 어렵게 만들었다... 우리 가운데 어느 누구도 실수를 전혀 하지 않는다고 장담할 수 없다. 우리가 바랄 수 있는 최선은 그 실수가 많지 않게 하는 것이다.

Main idea : (a)

Topic sentence : English is not an easy one to write and its grammar is monstrously difficult.

Note

monstrously	*ad.*	Extremely large. ; oversize ; huge
amalgam	*n.*	1. Any of various alloys of mercury with other metals,
		2. A combination of diverse elements; a mixture.

21. 공부란 소인을 대인으로 바꾸는 좋은 방법이다. 우리는 지금 지역 시민에서 세계 시민으로 옮아가고 있다. 가정에서, 공동체 속에서, 일상적인 대인 접촉에서, 우리는 이제 알아야 한다. 무식하면서도 자기가 무식하다는 것을 모르는 사람은 바보다. 그런 사람은 피하라. 무식하긴 하지만 자기가 무식하다는 것을 아는 사람은 순박한 사람이다. 그런 사람은 가르쳐라. 자기가 무식하다는 것을 아는 사람은 자고 있는 사람이니, 그런 사람은 깨워라. 그리고 유식할 뿐 아니라 자기가 유식하다는 것을 알고 있는 사람은 현명하다. 그를 따르라.

Main idea : (d)

Topic sentence : Study is a good way to transform small-scale individuals into large-scale individuals

Note

transform	*v.*	1. To change very much in form or appearance
		--The cold weather transformed the green leaves into gold ones.
		2. To change the nature, function, or condition of; convert
		--A steam engine transforms heat into energy
shun	*v.*	Avoid on purpose.

<u>22.</u>   Psychology is important because it tells us the little that is known about attention, association, memory, and interest. Without a knowledge of these, advertising people would have little idea of the best way to attract the attention of perspective buyers, or of the way to hold interest after it is secured. The aim of advertising people is to present the target commodity in such a way that pleasant association will be aroused. If the prospective buyer is pleased with the advertisement, he will be interested in the commodity; and when the need for it comes, he will remember that particular brand. The function of advertisement is to attract attention, to create desire to build confidence, and finally, to stimulate action for purchase.

(1) The main idea: (a) To attract attention

(b) Psychology is used for advertisement

(c) To stimulate action

(d) To build confidence

(e) To present the commodity with association

(2) The topic sentence: _____

Commerical Advertisement

22. 심리학은 중요하다. 왜냐하면 주의, 연상, 기억, 흥미 등에 대한 것들을 가르쳐 주기 때문이다. 이런 것들을 모르면, 광고업계 종사자들은 잠재적 고객의 주의를 끄는 최선의 방법이나 흥미를 끌어 그것을 지속시키는 방법을 모르게 될 것이다. 광고업계 종사자들의 목표는 유쾌한 연상이 일어날 수 있는 방식으로 목표 상품을 소개하는 것이다. 그 광고가 만족스러우면, 잠재적 고객은 그 상품에 관심을 가지게 될 것이며, 그 상품이 필요할 때면, 그 특정 상표를 기억할 것이다. 광고의 기능은 주의를 끌고, 욕구를 창출하며, 신뢰를 쌓고, 최종적으로 구매활동을 자극하는 것이다.

Main idea : (b)

Topic sentence : Psychology is important because it tells us the little we know about attention, association, memory, and interest.

Note

association *n.* 1 The act of associating or the condition of being associated
2. A group of people organized for a common purpose.
3. A mental connection made between thoughts or feelings and a person, place, or thing
--What association do you have with the word 'teenager'?
secure *a.* 1. Safe against danger or risk of loss.
2. Not frightened or worried.
3. Firm or strong --The door has a secure lock.
4. Assured; certain --The future of our school band is secure
v. 1. To make safe.　　2. To fasten tightly
3. To get; acquire --The workers tried to secure higher wages.
commodity *n.* Something that is bought and sold.
prospective *ad.* 1. Likely to happen --The president spoke of prospective budget cuts
2. Likely to be or become --The prospective bride and groom received many gifts.

<u>23.</u>　Washington, December 7, 1941. —- Japanese airplanes today attacked American defense bases at Hawaii and Manila. President Roosevelt ordered the Army and Navy to carry out undisclosed orders prepared for the defense of the United States. The White House announced that Japanese airplanes had attacked Pearl Harbor, principal American base in the Hawaiian Islands, and Manila, capital city of the Philippines. At 3:20 p.m. (Eastern Standard Time) a supplementary statement said the Japanese attacks were still in progress as far as this Government knew. The White House later said Naval reports from Hawaii indicated heavy loss of life and damage.

(1) The main idea:

(a) Japanese airplanes attacked Pearl Harbor, Hawaii

(b) Japanese airplanes bombed Hawaii and Manila today

(c) President Roosevelt ordered the Army and Navy to defend the U.S.

(d) The Japanese attacks were still in progress in Hawaii and Manila

(e) The Japanese air attacks caused heavy loss of life and damage in Hawaii

(2) The topic sentence: _____

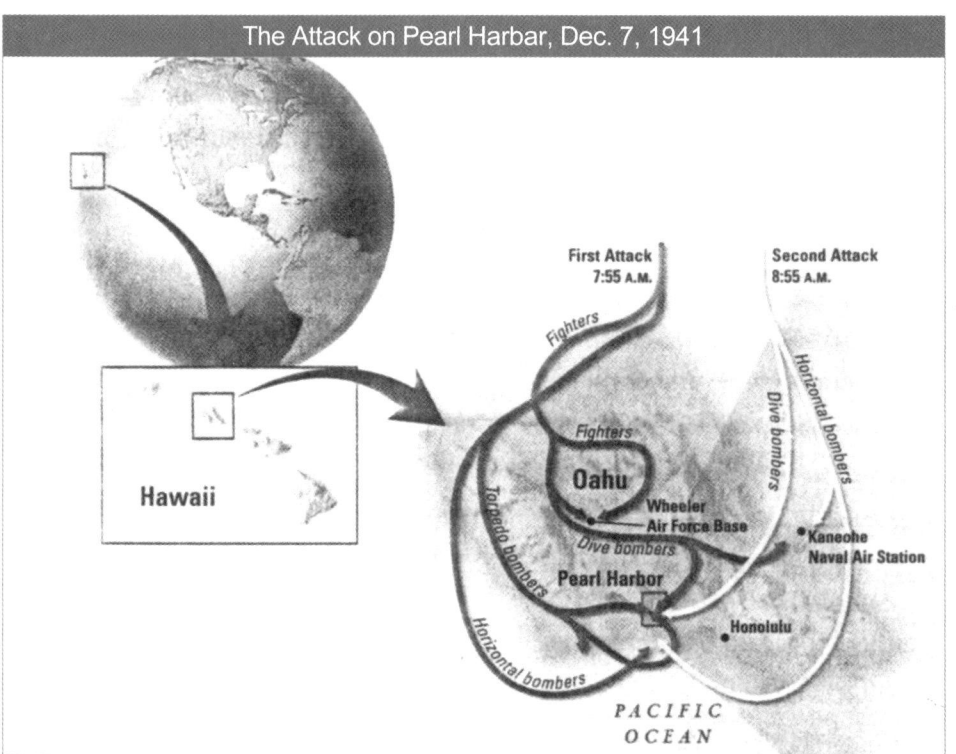

The Attack on Pearl Harbar, Dec. 7, 1941

First Attack
7:55 A.M.

Second Attack
8:55 A.M.

Fighters

Fighters

Horizontal bombers

Dive bombers

Oahu

Wheeler
Air Force Base

Kaneohe
Naval Air Station

Torpedo bombers

Dive bombers

Pearl Harbor

Honolulu

Horizontal bombers

Hawaii

PACIFIC
OCEAN

CHAPTER 3

23. 1941년 12월 7일, 워싱턴 -- 일본군 항공기들이 오늘 하와이와 마닐라에 있는 미군 방위 기지를 공격했다. 루스벨트 대통령은 육군과 해군에 대해 미국을 수호하기 위해 준비해둔 비밀 명령을 수행하라고 지시했다. 백악관은 일본군 항공기가 하와이의 주요 미군 기지인 진주만과 필리핀의 수도 마닐라를 공격했다고 발표했다. 동부 기준시(그리니치 표준시보다 5시간 늦다)로 오후 3시 20분에 발표된 추가 성명에 따르면, 일본군의 공격은 현 정부가 아는 한, 아직도 계속되고 있다고 한다. 나중에 백악관은 하와이에서 온 해군 보고서를 인용, 인명피해가 심각하다고 밝혔다.

Main idea : (b)

Topic sentence : Japanese airplanes today attacked American defense bases at Hawaii and Manila

Pearl Harber

Note

attack	*v.* 1.	To make a sudden violent move against
	2.	To criticize strongly or in an unfriendly way
	3.	To afflict -- Flu attacked many people.
	4.	To start work with purpose and energy
	n. 1.	The act of attacking.
	2.	Sudden illness -- I had an attack of indigestion.
announce	*v.* 1.	To make known to people officially -- The principal announced a holiday.
	2.	To make known the presence, readiness, or arrival of -- Dad announced supper.
	3.	To serve as announcer of --She announced the game on the radio.
indicate	*v.* 1.	To show or point out --A compass indicates direction
	2.	To serve as a sign of --The dark clouds indicated rain.

<u>24.</u>　On June 25, 1950, North Korean forces crossed over the 38th parallel, which divides the two zones established in Korea after World War II.　The Security Council of the United Nations authorized military sanctions against the North. Consequently, 16 nations contributed to the U.N. forces, mostly U.S. troops led by Gen. Douglas MacArthur.

　　In the first months of war, the North Korean forces drove the U.N. forces back to an area near Taegu. But, by counterattacks, especially the amphibious Inchon landing, the U.N. forces pushed them close to the Manchurian border. On November 25, l950, Chinese ground troops crossed the Yalu River, making the U.N. forces lose ground again. Differences arose over American policies, especially regarding the extension of military operations beyond the Yalu. President Truman removed Mac Arthur from command in l951, replacing him with Gen. Matthew Ridgway.

　　Truce negotiations started July 10, l951, and the cease-fire was signed on July 27, l953, setting the existing battle line between the two Koreas as the border still existing today. This has been one of the most destructive and ungraceful seesawing wars in American military history.

(1) The main idea:　(a) Facts about the Korean war

　　　　　　　　　(b) The invasion of the North Korean forces to the South

　　　　　　　　　(c) Development of the Korean war

　　　　　　　　　(d) General Mac Arthur's Inchon landing

　　　　　　　　　(e) A history of the Korean war

(2) The topic sentence: _____

NOT MUCH HELP, BUT IT'S NICE
TO HAVE COMPANY
(JENSEN, CHICACO DAILY NEWS).

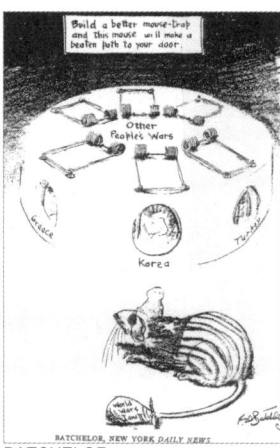

BATCHELOR,
NEW YORK DAILY NEWS.

24. 1950년 6월 25일, 북한군이 2차 세계대전 이후 한반도를 양분하고 있던 38선을 넘어왔다. 유엔 안전 보장 이사회는 무력 제재를 결의했다. 그 결과, 16개국이 유엔군에 참여했고, 그 대부분은 더글 라스 맥아더 장군이 이끄는 미군이었다.

　전쟁 초기 몇 달 간, 북한군은 유엔군을 대구 근처까지 후퇴시켰다. 그러나 인천 상륙 작전 같은 반격에 의해, 유엔군은 그들을 만주 국경 근처까지 밀어 올렸다. 1950년 11월 25일, 중국군이 압록강 을 넘어와 또다시 유엔군을 퇴각시켰다. 미국의 정책, 특히나 압록강 너머로 군사 작전을 확대하는 문제와 관련하여 의견 차가 불거졌다. 트루만 대통령은 1951년, 맥아더의 지휘권을 박탈하고 그 자 리에 매튜 리지웨이 장군을 임명했다.

　1951년 7월 10일, 휴전 협상이 시작되었고, 1953년 7월 27일, 현존하는 두 개의 한국 사이의 전선 을 오늘날에도 존재하는 경계선으로 확정하는 휴전협정이 체결되었다. 이것은 미군 역사상 가장 파 괴적이고 볼품없는 시소 같은 전쟁 가운데 하나였다.

Main Idea : (a)

Topic sentence : The Korean War has been one of the most destructive and ungraceful
seesawing wars in American military history.

Note

establish　*v.* 1. To begin or set up ; found ; create
　　　　　　　-- My grandparents established the lumber company in 1920
　　　　　　2. To show to be true -- I established my identity by showing my passport
sanction　*n.* Permission or approval.
　　　　　v. To give approval to.
contribute　*v.* 1. To give along with others -- Our family contributes time to conservation projects.
　　　　　　2. To aid in bringing about --Exercise contributes to better health
　　　　　　3. To submit for publication especially in a magazine
remove　*n.* 1. To move or take from a position or place -- Remove the fruit from the box.
　　　　　2. To take off or away -- The new cleaner removed stains from my coat.
command　*v.* 1. To begin orders to; direct -- The officer commanded the solders to leave.
　　　　　　2. To have control or authority over; rule -- The admiral commanded 25 ships
　　　　　　3. To deserve and receive -- Honesty commands respect.
　　　　　n. 1. An order or direction
　　　　　　2. The authority to give orders -- The major was in command.
　　　　　　3. Ability to control or use;mastery -- The student has a good command of two
　　　　　　　languages.
　　　　　　4. A signal that tells a computer to start, stop, or continue a specific operation

Elvis Presley

25. Elvis Presley (1935 ~ 1977) was born in Tupelo, Mississippi. His close-knit family attended a Pentecostal church, where he first heard gospel music. Given a guitar at age 11, he picked hillbilly songs and later, the blues. After graduating from high school, he worked as a movie usher and truck driver. One day he went into a Sun Records studio in Memphis, Tennessee to make a recording for his mother's birthday. There he caught the attention of the entrepreneur, Tom Parker, which led to aggressive promotion of his career.

In 1956, "Heartbreak Hotel" sold millions of copies, and his performances featuring much hip-wriggling and sexual innuendo incited hysteria among teenagers. When he sang "Heartbreak Hotel" or "Don't Be Cruel," he swiveled his hips and twitched his legs. When he crooned "Love Me Tender," the girls would swoon.

After acquiring a manager, he toured the South and signed with a major label. By 1958, when he joined the Army, he had 14 consecutive million sellers of his eventual 79, and had begun making Hollywood B movies such as "Jailhouse Rock," "Loving You," and "GI Blues," earning one million dollars for each.

Personal excesses overtook him in 1977 when he died of a drug overdose at Graceland, his Memphis mansion. By then he had become one of the greatest stars of the 20th century.

(1) The main idea: (a) Elvis Presley should be respected as one of the greatest rock singers

(b) E. Presley is remembered as one of the greatest movie stars

(c) E. Presley is remembered as one of the greatest entertainers

(d) E. Presley is remembered as one of the greatest country music singers

(e) E. Presley is remembered as one of the greatest stars of the 20th century

(2) The topic sentence: _____

C H A P T E R 3

25. 엘비스 프레슬리(1935-1977)는 미시시피주 튜펠로에서 태어났다. 결속력이 강한 그의 가족은 펜테코스트파(20세기초 미국에서 시작된 원리주의 교파에 가까운 파) 교회에 다녔고, 그는 거기서 처음 복음 음악을 들었다. 11살 때, 기타를 받자, 그는 힐빌리 음악(미국 남부 산악 지대의 민요조 음악)과 블루스를 연주했다. 고등학교를 졸업한 뒤, 그는 극장 안내인 겸 트럭 운전사로 일했다. 어느 날, 그는 어머니의 생일 선물로 노래를 녹음하기 위해 테네시주 멤피스의 선 레코드 스튜디오에 갔다. 거기서 그는 기획자 탐 파커의 눈에 띄게 되었고, 그 결과 의욕적인 가수활동에 들어가게 되었다. 1956년, "하트브레이크 호텔"이 수백만 장 팔렸고, 엉덩이를 흔들고 성적 풍자를 특징으로 하는 그의 몸짓은 십대들 사이에 병적인 흥분을 불러일으켰다. "하트브레이크 호텔"이나 "돈 비 크루얼"을 부를 때, 그는 엉덩이를 돌리고 다리를 씰룩거렸다. 그가 나지막히 "러브 미 텐더"를 부를 때, 소녀들은 기절하곤 했다.

그는 매니저를 구한 뒤, 남부를 순회 공연했고, 대형 레코드사와 계약했다. 군에 입대한 1958년까지, 그는 총 79개의 밀리언셀러 가운데 14개의 밀리언셀러를 연속 기록했고, "제일하우스 락," "러빙 유," "GI 블루스" 같은 헐리우드 B급 영화를 만들기 시작하여 각각 백만 달러를 벌어들였다.

1977년, 개인적인 무절제가 그를 덮쳤고, 그는 멤피스에 있는 자신의 저택 그레이스랜드에서 약물 과용으로 사망했다. 그 즈음, 그는 이미 20세기 최고의 스타 가운데 한 명이었다.

Main idea : (e)

Topic sentence : At the time of his death, Elvis Presley had become one of the greatest stars of the 20th century.

Note

attend   *v.* 1. To be present at --All our friends attended party.
           2. To act as a servant or companion to --The page attended the king.
           3. To take care of --Parents attend their babies
           4. To apply oneself --Attend to your tasks   5. To pay attention.

incite   *v.* 1. To move to action; urge on --The speaker incited us to acts of patriotism
innuendo *n.* An artful, indirect, often derogatory hint.
swivel   *v.* To move, as a gun, laterally
twitch   1. A sudden motion, such as a pull   2. A nervous shaking of the body
swoon   *v.* To suffer temporary lack of consciousness

Below topic sentence of (a) is not good. Generate a good topic sentence in (b).

(1)   (a) Smoking is harmful.

(b) Smoking is very harmful for four reasons.

(2)   (a) Korea is a beautiful country.

(b) Korea is very beautiful in terms of climate and unspoiled mountain streams.

(3)   (a) There are some new devices to help deaf people.

(b) A new device for hearing-impaired persons converts a telephone touch tones into printed messages.

(4)   (a) Swimming is a good sport.

(b) _____

_____

(5)   (a) Many old people have problems.

(b) _____

_____

(6).   (a) Cheating examination is wrong.

(b) _____

_____

(7)   (a) English is not an easy one to write.

(b) _____

_____

(8)   (a) Prof. Lee's lecture is boring.

(b) _____

_____

(9)   (a) Safety is very important.

(b) _____

_____

(a)항의 주제문은 좋지 못하다. (b)항에 좋은 주제문을 만들어라(정답 생략)

(1) a. 흡연은 해롭다.

   b. 흡연은 네 가지 이유로 매우 해롭다.

(2) a. 한국은 아름다운 나라이다.

   b. 한국은 기후와 훼손되지 않은 계곡 측면에서 볼 때 매우 아름답다.

(3) a. 농아들을 돕는 몇 가지 새로운 기기가 있다.

   b. 듣는 기능이 손상된 사람들을 위한 새로운 기기는 전화기 누름단추(푸시 버튼)를 인쇄된 메시지로 전환시킨다.

(4) a. 수영은 좋은 운동이다.

   b. _____

(5) a. 상당수의 노인들이 문제를 가지고 있다.

   b. _____

(6) a. 커닝은 잘못된 것이다.

   b. _____

(7) a. 영어는 쓰기가 쉽지 않다.

   b. _____

(8) a. 이교수의 강의는 지루하다.

   b. _____

(9) a. 안전은 매우 중요하다.

   b. _____

An advertisement from the American Cancer Society.

(10) (a) The coming of that summer vacation made every student happy.

     (b) _____

          _____

(11) (a) An apple a day keeps the doctor away.

     (b) _____

          _____

(12) (a) Two captains will sink the ship.

     (b) _____

          _____

(12) (a) Some people are really annoying.

     (b) _____

          _____

(13) (a) Love makes the time pass.

     (b) _____

          _____

(14) (a) The world is worried about energy.

     (b) _____

          _____

(15) (a) A penny saved is a penny earned. *(Benjamin Franklin)*

     (b) _____

Benjamin Franklin

(10)a. 여름방학이 다가왔다는 사실은 모든 학생들을 행복하게 했다.

b. _____

(11) a. 하루에 사과 한 알이면 의사가 필요 없다.

b. _____

(12)a. 선장이 두 명이면 배가 가라앉는다.

b. _____

(12)a. 정말 성가신 사람들도 있다.

b. _____

(13)a. 사랑을 하면 시간이 빨리 흐른다.

b. _____

(14)a. 전세계가 에너지 문제를 걱정하고 있다.

b. _____

(15)a. 한 푼 저축하면 한 푼 버는 것과 같다.

b. _____

Benjamin Franklin proved that lighting is actually electricity--a fact unknown at the time--in a dangerous experiment, Lighting struck his kite, traveled down the string, and caused key to glow.

3.1.2. Developing Supporting Details.

As we have seen, the topic sentence is what the paragraph/passage is about; therefore, it should be broad enough to be supported or developed by supporting details through the remainder of the paragraph. The supporting details in the paragraph help explain or support the topic sentence. Imagine what communication would be like if you read such topic sentences as follows:

" *The Hankyoreh Daily Newspaper reports that Korea will be reunified within ten years.*"
" *Some scientists claim that males can be pregnant.*"
" *From the year of 2003, only the American-English will be used as a medium of instruction in all educational institutes in Korea.*"

These are really surprising statements as topic sentences, and readers will not accept these statements without supporting details that give details or feasible reasons to support or prove them. This is why we need the supporting details for a sound paragraph/passage. Several ways that the supporting details explain or support the topic sentence include the use of (1) Sensory Details; (2) Facts & Statistics; (3) Examples; and, (4) Anecdotes.

The following paragraph includes a main topic and support details.

Line 1   Two kinds of goats are famous for their wool.
One is the Cashmere goat which is raised in Asia and India.
Its wool is called cashmere.
The other is the Angora goat which is raised in Texas.
Line 5 Its wool is called mohair.

3.1.2. 뒷받침 세부자료 전개

앞에서 살펴보았듯이, 주제문은 문단/절이 무엇에 대해 이야기하고 있는지 알려준다. 따라서 주제문은 그 문단이나 절의 여타 뒷받침 세부자료들에 의해 뒷받침되거나 전개될 수 있을 만큼 충분히 폭넓어야 한다. 문단 속의 뒷받침 세부자료들은 주제문을 설명하거나 뒷받침한다. 다음과 같은 주제문을 읽을 경우, 어떤 대화가 가능할지 생각해 보라.

"한겨레 신문은 한국이 십 년 이내에 통일될 것이라고 밝히고 있다."
"일부 과학자들은 남성도 임신이 가능하다고 주장한다."
"2003년부터 한국의 모든 교육 기관에서는 미국식 영어만이 교육의 매개체로 사용될 것이다."

이 글들은 주제문만큼이나 놀라운 진술이며, 독자들은 세부사항을 알려주는 보충설명 또는 그 진술을 뒷받침하거나 증명해줄 그럴듯한 이유가 없는 한, 이 주장을 받아들이지 않을 것이다. 탄탄한 문단/절에 뒷받침 세부자료가 필요한 것도 다 그 때문이다. 보조적 세부사항들이 주제문을 설명하거나 뒷받침하는 방식으로는 (1) 감각적 세부사항, (2) 사실과 통계, (3) 사례, (4) 일화 등이 사용된다.

다음 문단에는 주제문과 기타 뒷받침 세부자료가 포함되어 있다.

Line 1. 털로 유명한 염소는 두 종류다. (주제문)
Line 2. 그 중 하나는 아시아와 인도에서 사육되는 캐시미어다.
Line 3. 그 털은 캐시미어라 불린다.
Line 4. 나머지 하나는 텍사스에서 사육되는 앙고라 염소다.
Line 5. 그 털은 모헤어라 불린다.

뒷받침 세부자료

Cashmere goat

Angora goat

The sentence in line 1 is the topic sentence, and the sentences from line 2 to 5 are the supporting details which give explanations to support the topic sentence.

Another example is to be diagrammed to show basic features of the supporting details.

Line 1   Trees are the most useful plants.
        They help the soil in place.
        They add oxygen to the air.
        They provide wood.
Line 5   Trees help keep soil from washing away.
        Farmers often plant trees to stop rain from washing away the soil.
        Trees make oxygen.
        People and other animals need oxygen to survive.
        Trees provide wood for people.
Line 10   Many people heat their houses with wood.

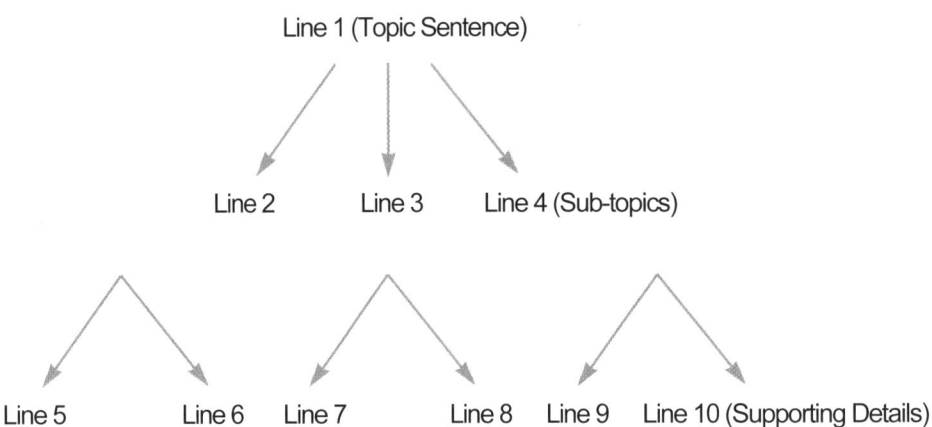

Line 1의 문장이 주제문이며, Line 2-5 까지는 주제문을 뒷받침해주는 보충설명이 담긴 뒷받침 세부자료이다.

또하나의 예는 뒷받침 세부자료의 기본적 특징을 보여주기 도표로 표시해 보았다.

Line 1. 나무는 매우 유용한 식물이다. (주제문)
Line 2. 그들은 흙이 제자리에 있도록 도와준다. ⎫
Line 3. 그들은 공기에 산소를 더해준다. ⎬ 부주제
Line 4. 그들은 목재를 제공한다. ⎭
Line 5. 나무는 토양 유실을 막아준다. ⎫
Line 6. 농부들은 종종 토양 유실을 막기 위해 나무를 심는다. ⎪
Line 7. 나무는 산소를 만든다. ⎪
Line 8. 사람들을 비롯한 여타 동물들은 생존을 위해 산소가 필요하다. ⎬ 뒷받침 세부자료 ; 사례
Line 9. 나무는 인간에게 목재를 제공한다. ⎪
Line10. 많은 사람들이 나무를 때서 집을 따뜻하게 한다. ⎭

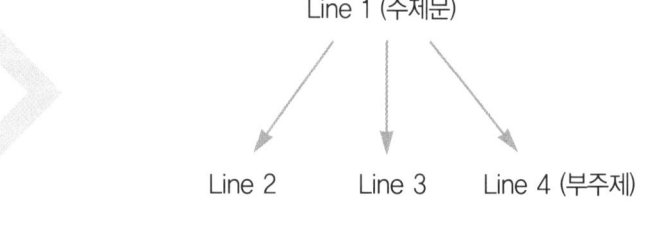

Read the following paragraph, and identify the topic sentence and the
supporting details of each paragraph.

Line 1 <u>1.</u> Dozens of enterprising businessmen made American life richer, safer,
and more comfortable. Gail Borden invented condensed milk, a healthy
and safe product in a time of 1895 when fresh milk was often dangerous.
Willis Carrier named his 1902 invention "air conditioning." Clarence
Line 5 Birdseye discovered frozen foods, and Aaron
Montgomery Ward brought the department store to the most isolated farm
through the innovation of the mail order catalog.

The topic sentence._____.
The supporting details: (1)_____.
       (2)_____.
       (3)_____.
       (4)_____.

Line 1 <u>2.</u> The spread of Islam was rapid for the following reasons. Muslims held
that all believers were equal; therefore, they did not need priests or a
church to practice their religion. They fought for one God, Allah, to
spread Islam. Mohammed died in A.D.632, which was two years after he
Line 5 had taken over Mecca. By that time, his army had taken over most of
Arabia. In the next 100 years, Islam spread from Arabia
to all of the Middle East, Egypt, North Africa, and a part of Spain. It also
spread to Persia, and parts of India.

The topic sentence: ._____.
The supporting details: (1) _____.
       (2) _____.
       (3) _____.
       (4) _____.
       (5) _____.

다음 문단을 읽고, 각 문단의 주제문과 뒷받침 세부자료를 밝혀라.

1. 수십 명의 진취적인 기업가들이 미국인의 삶을 더 풍부하고, 더 안전하며, 더 편안하게 만들었다. 게일 보든은 생우유가 위험했던 1895년, 건강에 좋고 안전한 제품인 농축 우유를 발명했다. 윌리스 캐리어는 1902년에 만든 자신의 발명품을 '공기 조절기(에어컨)'라 이름 붙였다. 클레어런스 버즈아이는 냉동 식품을 발견했고, 아론 몽고메리 워드는 통신 판매 카탈로그를 혁신하여 적지의 외딴 농장에 백화점을 도입했다.

    The topic sentence: Dozens of ...._____.
    The supporting details: (1) Gail..._____.
                          (2) Willis..._____.
                           (3) Clarence..._____.
                           (4) Aaron..._____.

2. 이슬람교는 다음과 같은 이유로 급속히 전파되었다. 이슬람교도들은 모든 신자가 평등하다고 생각했다. 따라서 그들은 종교 의식을 수행할 성직자나 교회가 필요치 않았다. 그들은 유일신 알라를 위해 싸웠고, 이슬람교를 전파했다. 마호메트는 메카를 차지한 지 2년 뒤인 서기 632년에 죽었다. 그 즈음, 그의 군대는 아라비아 대부분을 점령한 상태였다. 이후 100년간, 이슬람교는 아라비아로부터 중동 전역, 이집트, 북아프리카, 스페인 일부 지역까지 전파되었다. 그리고 페르시아와 인도 일부 지역까지 퍼졌다.

    The topic sentence: The spread of Islam..._____.
    The supporting details: (1) Muslims ...._____.
                           (2) They..._____.
                           (3) Mohammed..._____.
                           (4) By..._____.
                           (5) It..._____.

Note

spread *v.* 1. To open out wide or wider --I spread the tablecloth on the ground.
               2. To push or move apart ; stretch--Spread your fingers as much as you can when holding the basketball.
               3. To distribute a layer of over a surface --I spread paint on the wall.
               4. To make or become widely known --The news spread rapidly.
      n. 1. The act or process of spreading.
               2. The extent to which something can be spreading --The wings of the bird have a 12-inch spread.
               3. A cloth cover for bed.
practice *v.* 1. To do or work over and over in order to acquire skill -- I practice the piano everyday.
               2. To make a habit of --Learn to practice self-control.
               3. To work at a profession --I would like to practice medicine.

Line 1   <u>3.</u> For everything there is a season, and a time for everything under heaven:

a time to be born, and a time to die;

a time to plant, and a time to pluck up what is planted;

Line 5   a time to kill, and a time to bear;

a time to break down, and a time to build up;

a time to weep, and a time to laugh;

a time to mourn, and a time to dance;

a time to cast away stones, and a time to gather stones together;

Line 10   a time to embrace, and a time to refrain from embracing;

a time to seek, and a time to lose;

a time to keep, and a time to cast away;

a time to rend, and a time to sew;

a time to keep silence, and a time to speak;

Line 15   a time to love, and a time to hate;

a time for war, and a time for peace.

(Revised Standard Version of the Bible)

The topic sentence: _____

The supporting details : <u>From.</u>   to. _____

3. 만물에는 다 때가 있나니, 하늘 아래 모든 것은 다 때가 있어라. (주제문)

태어날 때와 죽을 때;

심을 때와 뽑을 때;

죽일 때와 참을 때;

파괴할 때와 지을 때;

울 때와 웃을 때;

슬퍼할 때와 춤출 때;

돌을 던질 때와 돌을 모을 때;

포옹할 때와 포옹을 삼갈 때;

찾을 때와 잃을 때;

지킬 때와 버릴 때;

찢을 때와 꿰맬 때;

침묵을 지킬 때와 말할 때;

사랑할 때와 미워할 때;

싸울 때와 화해할 때;

뒷받침 세부자료

The topic sentence : Line 1.
The supporting details : From Line 2 to Line 16.

Note

embrace　*v.*　1. To clasp or hold in the arms, especially as a sign of affection ; hug --They embraced and then said good-bye.

2. To take up willingly or eagerly --We left the city and embraced life in the suburbs.

3. To take in as a part or member ; include --My education embraced all the language arts.

n.　An act of clasping in the arts.

refrain　*v.*　To hold oneself back.

Line 1   <u>4.</u> People have not always written things down. The "prehistorical" refers
to a time before writing was invented, while the "historical" means a time
in which writing was invented and has been used. In the first stage of
developing writing, drawings called "pictograms" were used to describe
Line 5   objects. The Sumerians who lived between the Tigris and Euphrates rivers
were the first to draw pictograms around 3200 B.C. These drawings of
objects were gradually changed into picture scripts and then into symbols.
The Sumerians invented a way of making symbols to represent the early
drawings called "cuneiform" writing, whereas the ancient Egyptians had a
Line 10   form of writing: hieroglyphics. The Phoenicians invented the first
alphabet in which a letter stands for a specific sound. This sound-based
writing was invented in 1000 B.C., and the variations of this writing
system are still used today.

The topic sentence: _____

The supporting details : <u>From.</u>   <u>to.</u> _____

EGYPTIAN HIEROGLYPHICS

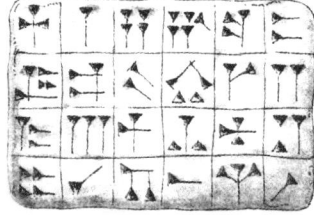

CUNEIFORM WRITING

4. 사람들이 늘상 이런 저런 상황을 문자로 기록한 것은 아니다. '선사시대' 란 문자가 발명되기 이전 시기를 가리키며, '역사시대' 란 문자가 발명되어 사용된 시대를 뜻한다. 문자의 발전 첫 단계에서는 대상을 묘사하는 데 '그림문자' 라는 그림이 사용되었다.

티그리스와 유프라테스강 사이에 살았던 수메르인들은 기원전 3200년 경, 인류 최초로 그림문자를 사용했다. 이러한 그림들은 차츰 그림 글씨에서 다시금 심볼로 변해갔다. 수메르인들은 심볼을 사용하여 '설형문자' 라 불리는 초기 그림 글자를 나타내는 방식을 발명한 반면, 고대 이집트인들은 상형문자라는 글자 형태를 갖게 되었다. 페니키아인들은 한 문자가 특정한 소리를 대표하는 최초의 알파벳을 발명했다. 음성에 근거한 이러한 문자는 기원전 1000년 경에 발명되었고, 오늘날까지도 여전히 이러한 글자 체계의 변형이 사용되고 있다.

The topic sentence: People have not always written things down.
The supporting details: From The prehistorical... to the rest of the paragraph

Phoenician Letter	Greek Letter	Roman Letter	English Letter
⟨	A	A	A
⟨	B	B	B
7	Γ	C	C
◁	△	D	D
∃	E	E	E
目	日	H	H
W	M	M	M
W	Σ	S	S
+	T	T	T

This chart shows how the English alphabet developed from the Phoenician alphabet.
The Greeks borrowed the Phoenician alphabet, making some changes in the letters.
Later, the Romans borrowed the Greek alphabet and made more changes. The English alphabet is very much like the Roman alphabet.

Note

describe *v.* To use words to tell about --We described our trip around the world.
cuneiform *n.* Any of several wedge - shaped bones, such as the tarsus.
  a. In the shape of a wedge

Line 1   <u>5.</u> Over 200 Military Occupational Specialties are listed in the back of this booklet. Select the one you want to learn before you join. If you qualify and there is an opening, it is yours. And the Army guarantees it. Perhaps you have completed post secondary vocational/technical schooling or have

Line 5   on-the-job experience in a certain skill. If so, you could earn a substantial bonus to enlist in that particular specialty. Bonuses are determined by the Army's current manpower needs for certain skill specialties. Prior experience can lead to faster promotions which bring increased responsibility and higher pay. Regardless of your experience level, you

Line 10   will receive comprehensive instruction and training in a valuable skill specialty. You will become proficient in the latest technology using high-tech equipment and procedures. Besides advancing your military career, you will be mastering the skills that employers seek. You should get an edge on the next century with an Army skill.

Line 15   *(Source: Adapted from a booklet, "Army. Be All You Can Be." Sept.1997)*

The topic sentence: _____

The supporting details : <u>From.</u> _____ to. _____

BROADCAST JOURNALIST

5. 이 책자 뒷면에는 200가지가 넘는 군사 주특기(MOS)가 열거되어 있습니다. 입대에 앞서서 당신이 배우고 싶은 것을 선택하십시오. 자격증을 따고 일자리가 생기면, 그건 바로 당신의 이익입니다. 군에서 보장해 드립니다. 중등과정 이후에 직업/기술 교육을 완수했거나 특정 기술 분야의 현장 경험이 있는 분도 있을 겁니다. 그럴 경우, 그 특정 전문 분야에 입대하여 실질적인 보너스를 받을 수 있습니다. 보너스는 일정한 기술 분야에 대한 군대의 현재 인력 수요에 의해 결정됩니다. 이전의 경험은 더 빠른 승진으로 이어져 더 큰 책임과 더 높은 임금을 받게 해 줍니다. 또한 경험 정도와 무관하게, 귀중한 기술 분야에 대한 포괄적인 교육과 훈련도 받게 됩니다. 따라서 하이테크 장비 및 과정을 이용하는 최신 기술에 숙달케 될 것입니다. 게다가 군 생활이 길어질수록, 고용주가 찾는 기술들을 마스터하게 될 것입니다. 군대의 기술과 더불어, 다음 세기를 준비하십시오.

The topic sentence: You should get an edge on the next century with an Army skill.
The supporting details: From Line 1 to Line 11.

PERSONNEL
INFORMATION SYSTEMS
MANAGEMENT
SPECIALIST

Note

qualify	*v.*	1. To make, be, or became fit for a particular position, purpose, or task
		--Your grades qualify you for honor society.
		2. To limit the meaning of ; modify ; -- Adjectives qualify nouns and adverbs qualify verbs
substantial	*a.*	1. Of, relating to, or having substance 2. Not imaginary ; real.
		3. Solidly built ; strong ; The tower was a substantial structure .
		4. Large in amount ; ample.
enlist	*v.*	1. To join or persuade to join the armed forces as a volunteer
		--They enlisted in the navy after they finished high school.
		2. To get the help or support of -- I enlisted my best friend in planning the party.

3.1.2.1. Sensory Details, Facts & Statistics, Examples, Anecdotes as Effective Supporting Details.

Supporting details help explain or support a topic sentence of a paragraph. Most sentences in a paragraph are the supporting details that are supposed to effectively support the topic sentence. The use of (1) Sensory Details; (2) Facts & Statistics; (3) Examples; and, (4) Anecdotes serves as an effective and clear way of supporting the topic sentence. As previously studied in PART 2, the Sensory Details are effective and powerful as supporting details for Descriptive paragraphs; Facts & Statistics for Persuasive as well as Informative; Examples for Explanatory and Expository; and, Anecdotes for Informative and Explanatory paragraphs.

3.1.2.1.1. Sensory Details

"Sensory details" refer to the descriptions/explanations that we observe through our five senses: sight, sound, smell, touch, taste. As we have thoroughly studied in PART 2, the use of the sensory details clearly helps readers create vivid and powerful pictures or images in their mind.

Read the following paragraph, and notice how the writer uses details of sound, sight, smell, touch, and taste, to describe the situation, event, or object concerned. Pay a special attention to the underlined sentences for which a variety of sensory details are effectively used.

1. Della was crying. As she cried, she counted her money. One dollar and eighty-seven cents. That was all... And the next day would be Christmas... She stood by the window and looked out with little interest at a gray cat walking along a gray fence in a gray backyard... She put her old brown coat. She put on her old brown hat.

* The sight word, "gray" is used 3 times as a way of intensifying Della's feeling of sadness.
* Another sight word, "old brown" is used twice as a symbolic implication of poverty.
(Source: O. Henry (1862~1910). "The Christmas Present."
O.Henry (pen name), William Sydney Porter)

O. Henry

3.1.2.1. 효과적인 뒷받침 세부자료로서의 감각적 세부사항, 사실과 통계, 사례, 일화

뒷받침 세부자료는 주제문이나 문단을 설명하거나 뒷받침하는 데 도움을 준다. 한 문단에 있는 대부분의 문장은 주제문을 효과적으로 뒷받침하는 뒷받침 세부자료들이다. (1) 감각적 세부사항, (2) 사실과 통계, (3) 사례, (4) 일화 등을 사용하면, 효과적이고 분명하게 주제문을 뒷받침할 수 있다. 2부에서 공부했듯이, 감각적 세부사항은 묘사적 문단의 뒷받침 세부자료로서 매우 효과적이다. 사실과 통계는 설득이나 정보 전달을 목적으로 하는 문단에 적합하며, 설명이나 해설문에는 사례, 정보 전달이나 설명문에는 일화를 이용하는 것이 좋다.

3.1.2.1.1. 감각적 세부사항

'감각적 세부사항' 이란 시각, 청각, 후각, 촉각, 미각 등 5감을 통해 관찰하는 묘사문/설명문을 가리킨다. 2장에서 철저하게 공부했듯이, 감각적 세부사항을 이용할 경우, 독자들은 마음 속에 생생하고 효과적인 그림이나 이미지를 창출할 수 있게 된다.

다음 문단을 읽고, 작가가 관련된 상황이나 사건, 대상 등을 서술하기 위해 청각, 시각, 후각, 촉각, 미각 등을 어떻게 사용했는지 잘 살펴보아라. 다양한 감각적 세부사항이 효과적으로 사용된 밑줄 친 문장에 특히 주목하라.

1. 델라는 울고 있었다. 그녀는 울면서 돈을 헤아렸다. 1달러 87센트. 그게 전부였다... 그리고 다음날은 크리스마스였다... 그녀는 창가에 서서 밖을 내다보았다. 잿빛 뒤뜰에서 잿빛 담장을 따라 걷고 있는 잿빛 고양이한테는 거의 관심도 두지 않았다... 그녀는 낡은 갈색 코트를 입었다. 그녀는 낡은 갈색 모자를 썼다.

※ 시각적 단어 '잿빛'은 델라의 슬픈 마음을 두드러지게 하기 위한 한 방식으로 3번이나 사용되고 있다.
※ 또 다른 시각적 단어 '낡은 갈색'은 빈곤을 암시하는 상징적 단어로서 두 번 사용되고 있다.

2. My favorite place is my basement. It is the place my friends and I play very often. It has lots of great hiding places for hide-and-seek. In this place, <u>I see a light green floor and brown walls. Silver and copper pipes are above me. I hear the chugging of the washing machine and smell soap.</u>

3. <u>We noticed that storm clouds were rolling in. Soon the wind suddenly changed into the gale. The sky changed into darkness</u> by the time we finally finished pitching our tent. Squashed inside our tiny space, <u>we ate several pieces of cold cheese and drank icy water for dinner. It was too cold for us to fall asleep.</u> Our first camping experience was quite an adventure.

3.1.2.1.2. Facts and Statistics

  Facts and Statistics serve as effective supporting details to support and prove the topic sentence. As such, they are often used for persuasive purposes. A "fact" is something that can be proven true *(e.g. Juneau is the state capital of Alaska)*; whereas a "statistics" is a fact based on numbers *(e.g. According to the report from the U.S. Environmental Protection Agency (EPA) in 1999, an average American family throws out 2,460 pounds of paper per year).*

  Read the following paragraph, and notice how the use of "Facts and Statistics" supports and proves the topic sentence.

1. The damage, however, is more than cosmetic. The same ultraviolet rays that dry and shrivel your skin can also cause cancer. As a result of your quest for the perfect tan, <u>says the American Cancer Society, more than 500,000 Americans will get skin cancer every year.</u>

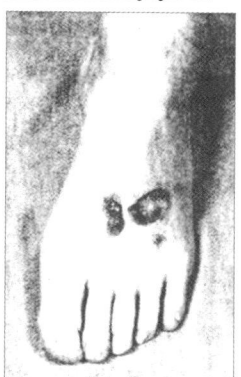  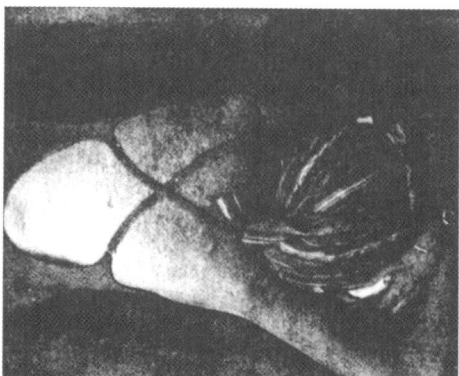

Overexposure to the sun can result in cleft to right'skin cancer, premature aging of the skin, and sunburn.

2. 내가 가장 좋아하는 곳은 나의 지하실이다. 그곳은 나와 내 친구가 자주 놀곤 하는 곳이다. 거기에는 숨바꼭질할 때 숨을 장소가 무척 많다. 이 장소에서 나는 연두색 마룻바닥과 갈색 벽을 본다. 은과 동 파이프들은 내 위에 있다. 나는 세탁기 돌아가는 소리를 듣고, 비누 냄새를 맡는다.

Note

chug   *n.* A sound that is like a muffled explosion made by or as if by an engine running slowly.
       v. To make such sounds.

3. 우리는 폭풍우를 몰고 올 구름이 모여드는 것을 감지했다. 잠시 후 바람이 갑자기 강풍으로 변했다. 우리가 텐트를 다 쳤을 무렵, 하늘은 암흑으로 변했다. 그 작은 공간 안에 쭈그리고 앉아 우리는 차가운 치즈 몇 조각과 싸늘한 물로 저녁을 때웠다. 잠을 자기에는 날씨가 너무 추웠다. 우리의 첫 캠핑 경험은 모험에 가까웠다.

Note

gale   *n.* 1. A very strong wind
              2. A noisy outburst --I heard gales of laughter coming from the kitchen.
squash ¹ *n.* Any of various fleshy fruits that are relate to pumpkins and are eaten as a vegetable.
squash ² *v.* To press or be pressed into a flat mass or pulp ; crush.
          n. A game played in a walled court. The players hit s hard rubber ball with a racket.

3.1.2.1.2. 사실과 통계

사실과 통계는 주제문을 뒷받침하고 증명하는 효과적인 보충 설명으로 기능한다. 그런 까닭에 종종 설득을 목적으로 사용되기도 한다. 하나의 '사실'은 진실로 증명될 수 있는 중요한 것이다(예를 들면, 쥬노는 알래스카의 주도이다). 그에 대해 '통계'란 수치에 근거한 사실이다(예를 들면, 1999년 미국 환경보호국(EPA)의 보고서에 따르면, 평균적인 미국 가정은 일년에 2,460파운드의 종이를 버린다).
다음 문단을 읽고, '사실과 통계'가 주제문을 어떻게 뒷받침하고 증명하는지 살펴보아라.

1. 그러나 그 피해는 미용의 차원을 뛰어넘는다. 피부를 건조하게 하고 주름지게 하는 자외선은 암을 유발할 수도 있다. 미국 암 협회에 따르면, 완벽한 선텐을 추구하다가는, 매년 500,000명 이상의 미국인들이 피부암에 걸리게 될 것이라고 한다.

Note

cosmetic *n.* A preparation, as powder, rouge, or skin cream, used to make the hair, skin, or complexion beautiful.
shrivel *v.* To shrink and wrinkle ; wither.

2. As we gaze out into the sky on a clear moonless night, it seems as if we see millions upon millions of stars. Actually, this is an exaggeration; <u>the naked human eye can see a total of only 6,000 stars across the sky... Of course, there are countless billions of stars in the universe.</u> But aside from the 6,000 stars visible to the naked eye, all the rest are so dim and distant that powerful telescopes must be used to reveal them.

(Source: William Kaufmann, "Stars & Nebules.")

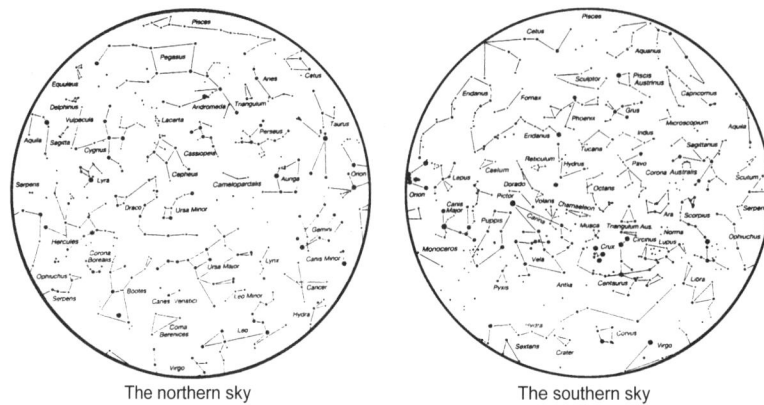

The northern sky   The southern sky

3. In Hong Kong the shark fin is such <u>an important luxury food that an industry worth more than $10 billion a year has grown up around its capture, sale, and preparation.</u> Many Hong Kong fishermen make their living catching sharks in the South China Sea and other waters near Hong Kong. The fins are so highly valued that their importation from such places as India, Singapore, the Philippines, Norway, Mexico, and South America is a big business. <u>Fins are auctioned twice a day in Hong Kong, and more than 3,000 tons a year find their way to the city's restaurants through its 20 auction houses and more than 100 professional buyers.</u>

(Source: Adapted from Eileen Yin-fel Lo's writing)

About 250 species of shark exist today, of which 10 have been known to attack people. They are all carnivorous. The thresher shark(Top)uses the long upper lobe of its tail fin to herd prey into a compact group.
The mako shark(bottom left) is a fast, Stream - lined swimmer that can overtake swordfish. Hammerhead(bottom right)has eyes on either side of the projecting lobes.

CHAPTER 3

2. 달도 없는 선명한 밤하늘을 뚫어져라 응시하다 보면, 우리가 마치 수 조에 달하는 별들을 보는 것만 같다. 사실 이것은 과장이다. 사람의 육안으로 볼 수 있는 별은 총 6,000개뿐이다. 물론 우주에는 셀 수 없이 많은 수 조의 별이 있다. 그러나 육안으로 볼 수 있는 6,000개의 별을 제외하면, 그밖의 별들은 너무나 희미하고 멀리 있기 때문에, 그 별들을 보려면 성능 좋은 망원경이 사용되어야 한다.

Note

gaze *v.* To look steadily and long --They gazed in wonder at the high mountains.
naked *a.* 1. Wearing no clothing.
      2. Lacking the usual covering --In winter many trees naked branches.
      3. Not helped by an optical instrument --Some Planets can be seen with the naked eye.

3. 홍콩에서는 상어 지느러미가 어찌나 고급 요리인지 상어 포획과 판매, 요리 등을 둘러싸고 일년에 100조 달러 이상의 산업이 성장해왔다. 홍콩의 많은 어부들은 남지나해 및 홍콩 연안 바다에서 상어를 잡아 생계를 유지한다. 지느러미는 가격이 무척 높기 때문에, 인도, 싱가포르, 필리핀, 노르웨이, 멕시코, 남아메리카 등에서 지느러미를 수입하는 것도 엄청난 사업이다. 홍콩에서는 지느러미가 하루에 두 번 경매에 부쳐지며, 20개의 경매장과 100명 이상의 전문 바이어를 통해 매년 300톤 이상의 지느러미가 홍콩 각지의 레스토랑으로 팔려간다.

Fin

Note

value *n.* 1. What something is worth in exchange for something else --These shoes will give you good value for your money.
      2. The quality that makes something worth having ; importance --You should recognize the value of a good education
      3. Estimated or determined worth --The jeweler put a value of $ 9,000 on the diamond ring
  v. 1. To believed to be of great worth or importance --I value your opinions
      2. To estimate or determine how much something is worth.

3.1.2.1.3. Examples

Another way to support a main idea/topic sentence of a paragraph is the use of "Examples." Examples are specific instances or illustrations of a general idea. As such, examples are often used for explanatory and expository purposes.

Read the following paragraph, and notice how the writer uses specific examples as a way of supporting the main idea/topic sentence for both explanatory and expository purposes.

<u>1.</u> Today American public schools face serious disciplinary problems. A survey conducted in the 1940s listed the top seven problems: <u>talking in the classroom, chewing gum, making noise, running in the halls, getting out of turn in line, wearing inappropriate clothes, not putting paper in wastebaskets.</u> A 1990s survey lists the top seven: <u>drug abuse, alcohol abuse, pregnancy, suicide, assault with weapons, rape, robbery.</u>

<u>2.</u> Sometimes there seems to be a kind of telepathic communication between identical twins. <u>In Singapore, for example, Yanling and Meiling Lee sat in separate rooms for their college admission tests in 1998. Five topics were given to them to choose one for an essay question. Not only did both choose the same topic, but also they wrote word for word the same answer.</u>

<u>3.</u> In Japan, recycling has been practiced for hundreds of years. <u>In public places such as city parks, you will see separate containers for paper and cans...</u> Retired or disabled people work in these recycling centers, repairing old furniture or household appliances and then selling them again. <u>And in Machida City, they have a program called "Chirigami Kokan (tissue - paper exchange)" in which you receive free recycled paper products such as tissue paper, napkins, and toilet paper in exchange for your old newspapers.</u> *(Source: Evan & Janet Hadingham, "Garbage! Where it comes from, Where it goes.")*

3.1.2.1.3. 사례

한 문단의 주제나 주제문을 뒷받침하는 또다른 방법은 "사례"를 이용하는 것이다. 사례란 포괄적 아이디어에 대한 구체적인 예나 실례이다. 따라서 사례는 종종 설명 및 해설을 목적으로 사용된다.

다음 문단을 읽고, 작가가 주제/주제문을 뒷받침하는 방법으로서 설명 및 해설을 목적으로 구체적인 사례를 어떻게 사용했는지 살펴보아라.

1. 오늘날 미국의 공립 학교들은 심각한 규율상의 문제에 직면하고 있다. 1940년대에 이루어진 한 조사에 따르면, 주요한 일곱 가지 문제는 교실에서의 잡담, 껌 씹기, 떠들기, 복도 뛰어다니기, 차례 지키지 않기, 부적절한 옷 입기, 휴지 아무데나 버리기 등이었다. 1990년대의 조사에서는 주요한 일곱 가지 문제로 마약 남용, 술 남용, 임신, 자살, 무기를 사용한 폭행, 강간, 강도 등이 제시되었다.

2. 때로 일란성 쌍둥이 사이에는 일종의 텔레파시가 있는 것 같다. 예를 들어, 싱가포르에서는 1998년, 얀링 리와 메일링 리가 다른 교실에서 대학 입학 시험을 치렀다. 작문 시험으로 다섯 가지 주제 가운데 하나를 골라 글을 쓰라는 지시가 떨어졌다. 두 사람 다 같은 주제를 선택한 것은 물론, 단어 하나하나까지 똑같은 답안을 썼다.

Note

telepathic *n.* Communication through means other than the senses, as by the exercise of an occult power.
admission *n.* 1. The act of admitting.
2. The right to enter --You should apply early for admission to collage.

3. 일본에서는 재활용이 수백 년 동안 시행되어왔다. 공원 같은 공공 장소에서, 당신은 종이를 담는 쓰레기통과 캔을 담는 쓰레기통이 따로 있는 모습을 보게 될 것이다... 은퇴한 사람이나 장애자들은 이러한 재활용 센터에서 일하면서 낡은 가구나 가재 도구를 수선한 뒤 다시 되판다. 마치다 시에는 '치리가미 코칸(박엽지-- 포장, 트레이싱, 도판 덮개용 종이 -- 교환)' 이라 불리는 프로그램이 있는데, 낡은 신문지를 가져가면 대신 박엽지, 냅킨, 화장지 등의 무료 재활용 종이 제품을 받게 된다.

Note

practice *v.* 1. To do or work over and over in order to acquire skill -- I practice the piano every day.
2. To make a habit of --Learn to practice self-control
3. To work at a profession --I would like to practice medicine.
receive *v.* 1. To take or acquire something given, offered, or sent --I receive an allowance every week.
2. To great or welcome

3.1.2.1.4. Anecdotes.

Anecdotes are "extended examples" in the sense that they are longer and more detailed than brief examples. They are often called "illustrations" or "narratives." Anecdotes are used as an effective way to support a main idea/topic sentence, since they as the writer's first-hand experiences add to personal touch to almost any form of writing. The writer draws these experiences to explain or clarify a general idea. Then, the well chosen anecdotes drive a point home sharply and imprint an idea clearly on the reader's mind.

Read the following paragraph, and make notice how the writer uses specific anecdotes (extended examples) based on numerous real-life or imaginary details that help to support the writer's main idea.

<u>1.</u> Children have taught me much of what I know about love. To them, love is nothing fancy, but very real - a feeling to be taken seriously. "If you love somebody," a six-year-old boy named Charlie once told me, "You help him put his boots on when they got stuck." *(Leslie Kenton)*

<u>2.</u> President Kennedy had the ability to inspire people wherever he went. When he visited West Berlin in 1963, he knew the people were afraid. The government of East Berlin had erected a wall to divide the city. West Berliners feared that the city might be cut off from the free world. Kennedy spoke to a huge crowd of West Berliners at the wall. He ended his speech with the words, "Ich bin ein Berliner," which means, "I am a Berliner." The crowd cheered wildly.

C H A P T E R 3

<u>Kennedy at Berlin Wall</u>
June 1963. President Kennedy on platform by Berlin Wall. East German police stare at him. Kennedy made an 8 - hour visit to west Berlin.

The Berlin Wall separated East Berlin and West Berlin.

3.1.2.1.4. 일화

일화란 간략한 사례보다 더 길고 더 상세하다는 점에서 '확장된 사례' 이다. 일화는 종종 '실례' 또는 '이야기' 라 불린다. 일화는 주제/주제문을 뒷받침하는 효과적인 방법으로 사용된다. 작가의 직접적인 경험으로서의 일화는 거의 모든 형태의 글 쓰기에 개인적인 특색을 가미시키기 때문이다. 작가는 포괄적인 아이디어를 설명하거나 분명히 하기 위해 이러한 경험을 끌어들인다. 잘 선택된 일화는 요점을 예리하게 강타하고, 독자의 마음에 주제를 명확히 각인시킨다.

다음 문단을 읽고, 작가가 주제를 뒷받침하기 위해 다양한 실생활이나 가상의 세부사항에 근거한 구체적 일화(확장된 사례)를 어떻게 사용하는지 살펴보아라.

1. 사랑에 대해 내가 알고 있는 것들 상당 부분은 모두 아이들이 가르쳐준 것이다. 그들에게는 사랑이 공상적인 것이 아니라 매우 실제적이다. 심각하게 받아들여야 할 감정인 것이다. 언젠가 찰리라는 여섯 살 소년이 내게 이렇게 말했다. "누군가를 사랑한다면, 부츠가 꽉 끼일 때 부츠 신는 걸 도와줘야 해요."

Explanation

*An anecdotal example describes real-life experiences

2. 케네디 대통령은 가는 곳마다 사람들을 고무시키는 능력을 가지고 있었다. 1963년, 서베를린을 방문했을 때, 그는 주민들이 두려움에 떨고 있다는 사실을 알고 있었다. 동베를린 정부가 베를린을 분할하기 위해 장벽을 세웠기 때문이다. 서베를린 사람들은 베를린이 자유 세계와 단절되지나 않을까 두려웠다. 케네디는 장벽에서 엄청난 서베를린 군중들에게 연설했다. 그는 "이히 벤 아인 베를리너" 다시 말해 "저는 베를린 사람입니다"라는 말로 연설을 마쳤다. 군중들은 열렬한 갈채를 보냈다.

On June 26, 1963 President John F. Kennedy delivered a speech that electrified an adoring crowd gathered in the shadow of the Berlin Wall.

Explanation

*An anecdote structured based on real - life experiences.

Note

inspire *v.* 1. To fill with great emotion --The songs inspired us.
   2. To move to action --The promise of money inspired me to work hard.
   3. To be the cause or source of -- The book inspired a movie.
erect *a.* Standing upright ; vertical --The dancer had a proud, erect posture.

<u>3.</u>   During the winter of 1909, an elderly woman of Flaxman Island, northern Alaska, went out to gather driftwood half a mile from her house. She was wearing only one coat or shirt, hair side turned in. With a sudden onslaught rare in the Flaxman country, a gale descended. She could not find her way home; she had to wait the storm out.

Most Eskimos would have built themselves some sort of a shelter in such a blizzard, but our aged woman thought it too much bother. In the blinding storm, she felt around with her feet until she discovered a tiny knoll. Taking off her mittens, she placed them on the hillock and sat down, using them as insulation to keep her body heat from melting the snow beneath her. Like all good Eskimo garments, her jacket was so designed that she could slip her bare arms out of the sleeves to cross them within the coat upon her bare breast, thus warming them and using them as added radiators to warm the inside of her shirt. With her back to the wind, she settled herself to wait the gale out, leaning slightly forward with elbows on knees so as not to topple over when she fell asleep. Every now and then, stiffened from sitting, she would pick up her mittens and walk around in a small circle. When tired of this, she would sit down again on them and try to sleep. The gale lasted till late afternoon the next day.

When the weather cleared, the old lady came home. She was not very hungry, because she had slept or rested most of the time. It was during the first day that she had been most hungry. No one thought anything of her experience, except that some argued that she should have taken the trouble to build a shelter.

Had she known she was going to be caught out, she would have worn two coats, the entire costume weighing about ten pounds. What she wore weighed six or seven. A Minneapolis businessman going to his office in January would wear from twenty to thirty pounds, and he wouldn't be planning to sit out a two-day blizzard. The difference in their clothing systems explains largely why the average Minnesotan is more eager to move to California than the average Eskimo. In our time, the Eskimo has been the sole possessor of a clothing system adequate in the sense that it permits in January a degree of mobility, efficiency, and comfort similar to that of July. We have taken a long time to understand how it works, and we are still a long way from making full use of its principles.

(Vilhjalmur Stefansson - "Clothes Make the Eskimo")

The belt of Eskimo

3. 1909년 겨울, 알래스카 북부 플랙스맨 섬의 한 나이든 여자가 부목을 모으기 위해 집에서 반 마일 떨어진 곳으로 나갔다. 그녀는 안에 털이 달린 코트 혹은 셔츠 하나만 입고 있었다. 갑자기 플랙스만에서는 드문 폭설과 더불어 강풍이 몰아닥쳤다. 그녀는 집으로 가는 길을 찾을 수 없었고, 결국 폭풍이 지나갈 때까지 기다려야 했다.

대부분의 에스키모들은 그런 폭풍설에 갇히면 일종의 피난처를 지었을 테지만, 나이든 이 여자는 그게 너무 귀찮다고 생각했다. 앞이 보이지 않는 폭풍설 속에서 그녀는 발을 더듬어 마침내 작은 둔덕을 발견했다. 그녀는 장갑을 벗어 둔덕 위에 놓은 뒤, 그 위에 앉았다. 체온으로 인해 그녀 밑에 깔린 눈이 녹지 않도록 장갑을 일종의 단열재로 사용한 것이다. 그녀의 자켓은 훌륭한 에스키모 옷들과 마찬가지로 디자인되어 있었으므로, 그녀는 코트 속에서 맨팔을 소매 밖으로 꺼낸 뒤 맨 가슴 위에 팔짱을 낄 수 있었다. 그렇게 해서 몸을 따뜻하게 한 것은 물론 셔츠 내부를 따뜻하게 하는 추가 난방기로 몸을 이용한 것이다. 등에 바람을 맞으며, 그녀는 바람이 잦아들 때까지 기다리기로 작정하고, 잠들 경우 넘어지지 않도록 팔꿈치를 무릎에 약간 기댔다. 이따금 그녀는 뻣뻣한 자세로 장갑을 들어 주위를 원형으로 걷곤 했다. 걷다가 지치면, 다시 장갑 위에 앉아 잠을 청했다. 강풍은 다음날 오후 늦게까지 계속되었다.

날씨가 개이자, 노부인은 집으로 돌아왔다. 그녀는 그다지 배가 고프지 않았다. 밖에서 보낸 대부분의 시간 동안 잠을 자거나 휴식을 취했기 때문이다. 가장 배가 고팠던 때가 바로 첫날이었다. 어느 누구도 그녀가 겪은 일을 상상도 하지 못했다. 단지 몇몇 사람들이 그녀가 피난처를 짓느라 고생이 많았을 것이라고 주장했을 뿐이다.

폭풍설을 만날 줄 알았더라면, 그녀는 코트 두 벌, 다시 말해 무게가 10파운드에 달하는 완벽한 의상을 갖춰입었을 것이다. 그녀가 입고 있던 옷은 무게가 6파운드 내지 7파운드 정도였다. 1월에 회사에 출근하는 미니애폴리스의 사업가는 20파운드 내지 30파운드의 옷을 입으며, 폭풍설 속에서 이틀이나 보낸다는 건 엄두도 내지 못한다. 그들의 의복 체계의 차이는 평범한 미네소타 사람이 평범한 에스키모보다 캘리포니아로의 이주를 더 열망하는 이유가 무엇인지 잘 설명해준다. 에스키모의 의복은 1월에도 7월과 마찬가지의 이동성과 효율성, 편안함 등을 허용한다는 면에서 우리 시대 유일의 의복 체계라 할만하다. 그 체계가 어떻게 기능하는지 이해하기까지 오랜 시간이 걸렸고, 그 원칙을 온전히 사용하려면 아직도 갈 길이 멀다.

Explanation *A long 'extended example' structured based on real-life details.*

Note

blizzard	*n.*	1 A heavy and widespread snowstorm of lengthy duration.
		2. A violent, intensely cold windstorm, producing heavy snowfall and ice.
mitten	*n.*	A hand covering, worn for warmth, with one section for the thumb and one for all the other fingers.
hillock	*n.*	A relatively small hill or mound
topple	*v.*	1. To fall because of being too heavy on top.;tumble. 2. To cause to topple.
stiffen	*v.*	To make or become stiff or stiffer.

3.1.3. Unity

As we have seen, every sentence in a paragraph should work together as a unit to develop or support one main idea. A paragraph in which every sentence is directly related to the main idea has "unity." Any sentence that does not support the main idea or destroys the paragraph unity should be removed so that it may not distract the reader.

The following paragraphs show that "all sentences" are related to (1) the main idea stated; (2) the implied main idea; and, (3) a sequence of events.

1. When we had a visitor from Korea, we found ourselves tasting foods we had never tried before. Sookhee showed us how to prepare "boolgogee (marinated barbecue beef)" and "kimchee (seasoned pickled cabbage)" with soy sauce, sesame oil, ground garlic, sugar, black pepper for boolgogee, and salt, cabbage, red pepper powder, fish sauce, scallion, ground garlic, and radish for kimchee. My favorite was boolgogee for its rich and flavorful taste with so many different ingredients.

2. One of the first women to commit the shocking act of cutting her hair was the famous American ball dancer Irene Castle. In 1913 she popularized a very short hairstyle called the Castle Clip, worn with a string of pearls around her forehead. It wasn't until after World War I, though, that most women found the courage to bob their hair and exchange their hairpins for the new spring-clip "bobby pin." The shortest cuts of the 1920s flapper age were the "boyish bob" and the "shingle," for which the hair was actually shaved at the back of the neck. For women who wanted their short hair frizzy-curly rather than sleek, there was a new hair treatment called a permanent wave.

(Source: Lila Perl, From Top Hats to Baseball Caps, From Bustles to Blue Jeans: Why We Dress the Way We Do)

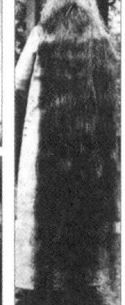

From medieval bun to ballpark Afro, hairstyles have always had a lot in common ; their differences.

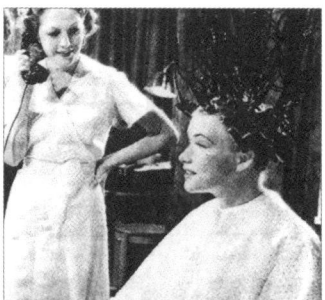

Permanent weave? This 1930's device did a lasting jog of curling hair.

CHAPTER 3

3.1.3. 통일성

지금까지 살펴보았듯이, 한 문단의 모든 문장은 하나의 주제를 전개하거나 뒷받침하기 위한 하나의 단위로 기능해야 한다. 모든 문장이 주제와 직접적으로 연관된 문단은 "통일성"이 있다. 주제를 뒷받침하지 않거나 문단의 통일성을 파괴하는 문장은 그 즉시 제거되어야 독자가 헷갈리지 않는다.

다음 문단은 "모든 문장"이 (1) 명시된 주제, (2) 암시된 주제, (3) 일련의 사건 등과 연관되어 있음을 보여준다.

1. 한국에서 손님이 왔을 때, 우리는 그전까지 엄두도 내지 못했던 음식들을 맛보게 되었다. 숙희는 우리에게 간장, 참기름, 마늘, 설탕, 후춧가루를 이용한 "불고기"(매리네이드에 절인 소고기 바비큐) 요리법과 소금, 고춧가루, 생선 소스, 골파, 마늘, 무를 이용한 "김치"(소금에 절여 양념한 배추) 요리법을 보여주었다. 나는 수많은 재료의 깊고 풍부한 맛이 살아있다는 점에서 불고기를 가장 좋아했다.

Explanation

모든 문장이 "한국에서 손님이 왔을 때, 우리는 그전까지 엄두도 내지 못했던 음식들을 맛보게 되었다"라는 명시된 주제문/주제와 직접적으로 연관되어 있다.

2. 머리를 자른다는 충격적인 행위를 한 최초의 여성들 가운데 한 명이 그 유명한 미국의 댄서 아이린 캐슬이었다. 1913년, 그녀는 이마에 진주를 늘어뜨린 '캐슬 클립'이라 불린 아주 짧은 헤어스타일을 유행시켰다. 그러나 대부분의 여성들은 1차 세계대전이 끝난 뒤에야 머리카락을 짧게 자르고 기존의 머리핀을 스프링 클립의 새로운 "짧은 머리용 핀"으로 바꿀 수 있는 용기를 얻게 되었다. 1920년대 플래퍼(자유를 찾아 복장, 행동 등에서 관습을 깨뜨린 말괄량이) 시대의 가장 짧은 머리는 "소년 같은 단발"과 "싱글 컷"이었는데, 이 헤어스타일은 실제로 목 뒤쪽의 머리카락을 면도했다. 짧은 머리가 매끄럽기보다는 다소 곱슬거리기를 원하는 여성들에게는 퍼머넌트 웨이브라 불리는 새로운 머리 손질법이 있었다.

Explanation

이 문단에는 주제문이 들어있지 않지만, 모든 문장이 "미국 여성들은 1900년대 초반에 짧은 헤어스타일을 실험하기 시작했다"는 암시된 주제문과 연관되어 있다.

Note

bob	*v.*	To move or cause to move with a quick, up-and-down motion
	n.	1. A short haircut. 2. A float or cork for a fishing line.
flap	*n.*	A flat piece attached along one side and hanging loose on the other.
shave	*v.*	1. To remove hair from with a razor 2. To cut or remove thin slices from.
	n.	The act of shaving.
frizzy	*ad.*	Formed into or covered with small tight curls.
sleek	*ad.*	Very smooth and glossy.

<u>3.</u> First came a drizzle. Then groundwater poured from the walls, and I was plunging through a waterfall. The darkest darkroom doesn't begin to compare to the pitch-black inside the mine shaft. I couldn't look upward at the patch of daylight above for fear of drowning. After about three minutes - an eternity - the unseen operator threw on the brake, jerking me to a stop two feet above the mud. To no one in

particular, I sighed, "Welcome to the glamorous world of emeralds."
(Source: Fred Ward, "Emeralds.")

Read the following paragraph, and identify any sentence(s) that destroy(s) the unity of the paragraph.

<u>1.</u> For the Lovedu people of South Africa, rainmaking is an important festival, and their queen is the rainmaker. They call her the Transformer of the Clouds. They believe that she has great powers to influence the weather. When rain is needed, the people bring her gifts. In other places the rainmaker is often a man. The Lovedu queen uses secret medicines and summons the help of ancestors in trying to call forth the rain.

<u>2.</u> The popularity of first names changes with certain names in fashion for a generation or so. For example, in 1928, the ten top names for girls were Mary, Marie, Ann, Margaret, Catherine, Gloria, Helen, Teresa, Jean, and Barbara. None of these names made the top ten list for girls in 1983. That year the ten most popular girls' names were Jennifer, Jessica, Melissa, Nicole, Stephanie, Christina, Tiffany, Michelle, Elizabeth, and Lauren. Unusual-sounding names can cause problems for children. One California lawyer, for example, named his son Shelter because he wanted him to have a unique first name. The most popular boys' names have changed also. John, William, Joseph, James, Richard, Edward, Robert, Thomas, George, and Louis were the most popular boys' names in 1928. In 1983, however, the ten top boys' names were Michael, Christopher, Jason, David, Daniel, Anthony, Joseph, John, Robert, and Jonathan.

3. 처음에는 가랑비가 내렸다. 그리고 나서 벽에서 갱내수가 쏟아져 나왔고, 나는 폭포에 잠기고 있었다. 지극히 어둡다는 암실도 탄광 갱도 안의 칠흑 같은 어둠과는 비교가 되지 않는다. 나는 익사할지도 모른다는 두려움 때문에 고개를 들어 빛을 볼 수조차 없었다. 영원처럼 느껴진 3분 가량의 시간이 흐른 뒤, 보이지 않는 기사가 브레이크를 걸었고, 나는 진흙 2피트 위에 멈춰섰다. 특별히 누구한테라고 할 것도 없이, 나는 한숨을 내쉬며 이렇게 말했다. "매혹적인 에메랄드 세상에 오신 걸 환영합니다."

Explanation

* 위의 문단은 주제문 없이 일련의 사건과 행위를 통해 통일성을 이루고 있다. 모든 문장이 강철 케이블에 부착된 타이어 위의 에메랄드 광산에 들어간 경험과 연관되어 있다.

다음 문단을 읽고, 문단의 통일성을 파괴하는 문장을 모두 골라라.

1. 남아프리카의 로베두족에게는 비를 만드는 일이 중요한 축제이며, 그들의 여왕은 마술로 비가 오게 만드는 사람이다. 그들은 그녀를 '구름을 변화시키는 사람'이라 부른다. 그들은 그녀가 날씨에 영향을 끼칠 수 있는 위대한 권능을 가지고 있다고 믿고 있다. 비가 필요할 때면, 부족민들은 그녀에게 선물을 바친다. 다른 곳에서는 이렇게 비를 만드는 사람이 남자인 경우가 많다. 로베두족의 여왕은 비를 부르기 위해 은밀한 주술을 사용하여 조상들의 도움을 청한다.

Explanation

* "In other places the rainmaker is often a man" 이라는 문장은 "비를 만드는 일은 중요한 축제이며, 그들의 **여왕**은 비가 오게 만드는 사람이다"라는 주제문과 연관이 없다.

2. 인기 세례명은 한두 세대 동안 유행하는 이름과 함께 바뀐다. 예를 들면, 1928년에는 여자아이 이름으로 가장 선호되던 열 개의 이름이 메리, 마리, 앤, 마가렛, 캐더린, 글로리아, 테레사, 진, 바바라 등이었다. 이 열 가지 이름 가운데 1983년의 톱 텐 리스트에 낀 이름은 하나도 없다. 그 해에 가장 인기있는 여자아이 이름 열 개는 제니퍼, 제시카, 멜리사, 니콜, 스테파니, 크리스티나, 티파니, 미셸, 엘리자베스, 그리고 로렌이었다. 특이하게 들리는 이름들은 아이들에게 문제를 야기시킬 수 있다. 예를 들어, 캘리포니아의 한 변호사는 아들에게 셸터라는 이름을 지어주었다. 독특한 세례명을 지어주고 싶었기 때문이다. 인기있는 남자 아이들의 이름 또한 끊임없이 변해왔다. 존, 윌리암, 조지프, 제임스, 리차드, 에드워드, 로버트, 토마스, 조지, 루이스 등이 1928년에 가장 인기있는 남자아이 이름이었다. 그러나 1983년에는 남자아이 이름 톱 텐이 마이클, 크리스톱, 제이슨, 데이빗, 다니엘, 앤소니, 조지프, 존, 로버트, 조나단 등이었다.

Explanation

* "Unusual-sounding names.... because he wanted him to have a unique first name" 라는 문장은 "인기 세례명은..."이라는 주제문과 관련이 없다. 문단의 통일성을 파괴시키기 때문에, 이들 문장은 지워버려야 한다.

<u>3.</u> A whale, one of the largest animals in the world, is killed by Soviet and Japanese whale hunters every 17 minutes. Some day, if this killing continues, whales might be like the dinosaur and disappear forever. One Japanese businessman says, "Many Japanese could not live without whale meat." This makes some people angry, and they are showing their anger in several ways. Some people are writing letters to the Japanese Government officials concerned, and others are asking people not to buy Japanese products. If this hurts Japanese business enough, the Japanese government should stop the whale hunting.

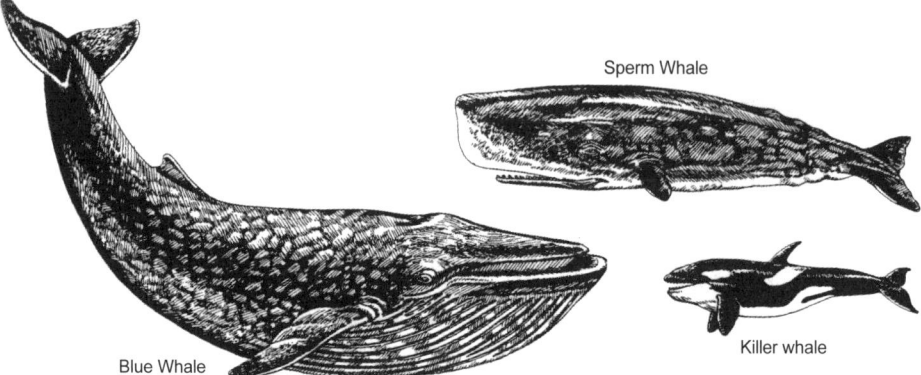

Sperm Whale

Killer whale

Blue Whale

3.1.4 Coherence

A well organized paragraph should include not only "unity," but also "coherence" for a reader so that he/she can easily follow the material and see how it is related to the main idea. If a paragraph loses coherence, the relationship between ideas is not clear; the paragraph does not follow smoothly. You can create coherence in a paragraph by clearly organizing ideas and making connections between them with the following orders and conjunctions.

3.1.4.1 Chronological Order

In a paragraph that describes or narrates an incident or a brief story, the logical way to organize information is to use chronological order: a series of actions or events in the order they happen in time. Chronological order is also used to tell a story, to explain a process, and to explain cause and effect.

3. 세계에서 가장 큰 동물에 속하는 고래가 소련 및 일본의 고래 사냥꾼에 의해 17분마다 한 마리씩 죽어가고 있다. 이런 학살이 계속된다면, 언젠가 고래는 공룡과 마찬가지로 영원히 사라져버릴지도 모른다. 일본의 한 사업가는 "일본인 상당수가 고래 고기 없이는 살 수 없다"고 말한다. 이것은 몇몇 사람들을 분노케 하며, 그들은 몇 가지 방식으로 자신들의 분노를 표현하고 있다. 어떤 사람들은 일본 정부의 관련 각료들에게 편지를 보내고 있고, 또 어떤 사람들은 일본 제품 불매 운동을 펼치고 있다. 이런 운동이 일본의 경기에 충분한 타격을 입힌다면, 일본 정부는 고래잡이를 멈추게 될 것이다.

Explanation

"One Japanese businessman says..." 이라는 문장과 "If this hurts Japanese business..." 라는 문장은 "세계에서 가장 큰 동물에 속하는 고래가..."라는 주제문과 직접적인 연관이 없다. 따라서 문단의 통일성을 기하기 위해 이들 문장은 없어져야 한다.

3.1.4. 일관성

잘 짜여진 문단은 '통일성' 뿐 아니라 '일관성' 을 갖추고 있기 때문에 독자가 자료를 따라가면서 그것이 주제와 어떻게 연관되어 있는지 쉽게 파악할 수 있다. 문단에 일관성이 없으면, 여러 아이디어 사이의 관계가 불분명해지고, 따라서 문단이 부드럽게 이어지지 않는다. 문단에 일관성을 부여하려면, 다음과 같은 순서와 접속사와 더불어 여러 가지 아이디어를 명확히 조직화하고 그것들을 잘 연결시켜야 한다.

3.1.4.1. 연대순

작은 사건이나 짧은 이야기를 묘사하거나 이야기하는 문단에서, 정보를 조직화하는 가장 논리적인 방법은 연대순에 따라 행위나 사건이 일어난 순서대로 써나가는 것이다. 연대순은 이야기를 하거나 어떤 과정을 설명할 때, 그리고 원인과 결과를 설명할 때도 사용된다.

Note

disappear *v.* 1. To pass out of sight; vanish --The ship disappeared over the horizon
　　　　　　2. To cease to exist.
concern *v.* 1. To have to do with; be about --This story concerns our class trip to the local museum.
　　　　　　2. To be of importance or interest to --Their problems don°Øt concern me.
　　　　　　3. To worry or trouble --Your poor grade concerns your parents.
　　　　n. 1. Something of interest or importance 2. Serious care or interest 3. Worry or anxiety
　　　　　　4. A business; firm

<u>1.</u> In 1926 Margaret Mead, American anthropologist, came to Samoa to study the existing cultural behaviors of the island. She feasted on native food and she talked with the daughter of a chief. She led the life of a Samoan for nine months while always keeping careful notes. When she came to the United States, she published her first book, Coming of Age in Samoa (1928), which describes her life among the Samoan natives.

Margaret Mead

<u>2.</u> In the year 1260, two European traders, the Polos, traveled to the distant and unknown land of China. They had many adventures there. Eleven years later in 1271, they made a second trip. But this time, the Polo brothers took along the son of one of them, a boy named Marco. The three Polos stayed in China about seventeen years. After their return to Italy, Marco had the story of his travels written down in book form. From this book, many Europeans became interested in the Far Eastern lands, and traders began to journey there.

Marco Polo in China ; Marco Polo served as an official of kubilai khan, the ruler of China.

3.1.4.2. Spatial Order

"Spatial Order" is used as a logical order to describe an object's location in relation to other objects. This order helps give a reader a visual impression of an object such as a car, chair, building, lake, tree, or mountain. You can describe a target object from left to right, from top to bottom, from far to near, from front to back, and so on.

The following paragraphs include "spatial order," and notice how the writer skillfully arranges this order.

1. 1926년, 미국의 인류학자 마가렛 미드는 사모아의 현행 문화 행동을 연구하기 위해 그곳으로 갔다. 그녀는 원주민의 음식을 먹었고, 족장의 딸과 이야기도 나눴다. 그녀는 아홉 달 동안 사모아인으로 살면서 항상 주의깊게 기록했다. 미국에 돌아오자, 그녀는 자신의 첫 저서 〈Coming of Age in Samoa〉를 출판했는데, 그 책은 사모아 원주민들 속에서 보낸 그녀의 생활을 서술하고 있다.

Explanation   일련의 전기적 사건들이 연대순으로 이야기되었다.

Note

behavior	*n.*	1. The way in which a person behaves
		2. The way in which something acts or reacts under given circumstances
publish	*v.*	To print and offer for public sale or distribution

2. 1260년, 유럽의 두 상인, 폴로 형제는 멀리 중국이라는 미지의 땅까지 갔다. 그들은 거기서 많은 모험을 겪었다. 11년이 지난 1271년, 그들은 두 번째 여행을 했다. 그러나 폴로 형제는 이번 여행에 두 사람 중 한 사람의 아들, 마르코를 데려갔다. 이들 세 명의 폴로는 약 17년 간 중국에 머물렀다. 이탈리아로 돌아온 뒤, 마르코는 자신의 여행기를 책 형태로 적어나갔다. 이 책을 통해, 많은 유럽인들은 극동의 땅에 대해 관심을 가지게 되었고, 상인들은 그곳으로 여행을 가기 시작했다.

Explanation   일련의 역사적 사건들이 연대순으로 서술되었다.

Note

interest	*n.*	1. A feeling of wanting to give special attention to something --The adventure book held my interest from the very first page.
		2. The quality of causing this feeling --A boring movie lacks interest.
	v.	1. To arouse interest in --the story about your trip interested me very much.
		2. To cause to become involved or concerned.

3.1.4.2. 공간순

'공간순'은 다른 대상들과 관련한 한 대상의 위치를 서술하는 논리적 순서로서 사용된다. 이 순서는 자동차, 의자, 건물, 호수, 나무 또는 산과 같은 대상에 대해 독자에게 시각적 효과를 제공한다. 목표로 하는 대상을 왼쪽에서 오른쪽으로, 위에서 아래로, 먼 곳에서 가까운 곳으로, 앞에서 뒤로 등으로 서술할 수 있다.

다음 문단은 '공간순'을 포함하고 있다. 작가가 이러한 순서를 어떻게 기술적으로 배열하는지 살펴보아라.

1. Mary sat on a green, wooden park bench, warming herself in a patch of sun. On her right she had placed the canvas bag that held her crossword puzzle and popcorn for the pigeons. A few pigeons gathered in front of her. On her left sat her husband, John. Behind her, a small group of teenagers practiced playing baseball.

2. ...As we came through the entrance gallery into the walled garden and looked down the long series of oblong pools in which the Taj and the dark cypresses are reflected, I held my breath, unable to speak in the face of so much beauty. The white marble walls, inlaid with semiprecious stones, seemed to take on a mauve tinge with the coming night, and about halfway along I asked to be allowed to sit down on one of the stone benches and just look at it. The others walked on around, but I felt that this first time I wanted to drink in its beauty from a distance. One does not want to talk and one cannot glibly say this is a beautiful thing, but one's silence, I think, says this is a beauty that enters the soul. With its minarets rising at each corner, its dome and tapering spire, it creates a sense of airy, almost floating lightness; looking at it, I decided I had never known what perfect proportions were before...

   As long as I live I shall carry in my mind the beauty of the Taj.

(Source: Eleanor Roosevelt, 1953)

The Taj Mahal - Mumatz was the beloved wife of Shah Jahan. When she died in childbirth in 1631, her heartbroken husband built for her the most glorious tomb in the world - the Taj Mahal.

Mumtaz Mahal

Shah Jahan

* Mumtaz Mahal and the Shah were constant companions, even on his military campaigns. He trusted her opinion in everything from art to politics, and showered her with gifts of roses and diamonds. He was so crushed by her death that his beard turned white overnight.

1. 메리는 공원에 있는 초록색 나무 벤치에 앉아 햇살에 몸을 데우고 있었다. 그녀는 크로스워드 퍼즐과 비둘기에게 줄 팝콘이 들어있는 캔버스 가방을 자기 오른편에 놓아두었다. 비둘기 몇 마리가 그녀 앞에 모여들었다. 그녀의 왼편에는 남편 존이 앉아 있었다. 그녀의 뒤편으로 십대 몇 명이 야구를 하고 있었다.

Explanation "On her right, On the left" 같은 구체적인 위치 용어가 독자에게 강한 시각적 효과를 제공하고 있다.

2. ...현관 안의 회랑을 지나 벽으로 둘러싸인 정원으로 가서 타지와 어두운 사이프러스 나무들을 비추고 있는 길다란 직사각형 연못을 내려다보았을 때, 나는 숨을 죽였고, 그 엄청난 아름다움 앞에서 말조차 할 수 없었다. 준보석으로 세워진 하얀 대리석 벽은 밤이 다가오자 연자줏빛으로 물든 것 같았고, 대략 중간쯤 가서 나는 돌 벤치에 앉아 그 모습을 그저 바라볼 수 없겠느냐고 물었다. 다른 사람들은 주위를 계속 걸었지만, 나는 이번만큼은 멀리서 그 아름다움에 취하고 싶은 기분이었다. 어떤 사람은 말하고 싶어하지 않고, 또 어떤 사람은 아름답다고 그럴듯하게 말할 수 없기도 하겠지만, 누군가의 침묵은 이것이 영혼으로 들어가는 아름다움이라고 말하는 것이라는 생각이 든다. 돔과 첨탑, 그리고 각각의 모서리에 솟아있는 광탑들과 더불어 그것은 공기 같은, 거의 떠다니는 빛 같은 느낌을 창조한다. 그것을 바라보면서, 나는 완벽한 균형이란 것이 어떤 건지 전에는 전혀 몰랐었다고 결론지었다... 살아있는 한, 나는 항상 타지의 미를 마음 속에 담고 다닐 것이다.

Explanation "the entrance gallery... reflected" "The white marble walls... with the coming night" "I wanted to drink in its beauty from a distance" "With its minarets rising at each corner,... almost floating lightness" 등과 같은 구체적인 공간 서술을 이용하여 작가는 타지마할의 숨막히는 정경을 생생하게 묘사하고 있다. 이러한 생생한 묘사는 독자들에게 목표로 하는 대상에 대한 강한 시각적 효과를 제공한다.

Note

oblong	*a.* Greater in length than in width *n.* An oblong object
cypress	*n.* 1. An evergreen tree that grows in warm regions and has small, scale like needles, hard wood, and cones.
	2. A similar, related tree that grows in swamps and sheds its needles each year
inlay	*v.* 1. To set pieces of (wood, metal, ivory, or the like) into a surface to form an ornamental design.
	2. To decorate (something) by setting pieces, usu. in a contrasting material or pattern, into its surface.
semiprecious	*a.* of gems, classed as less valuable than diamonds, rubies, or the like.
glibly	*a.* 1. Speaking or prone to speak easily and fluently, esp. in a careless or thoughtless manner, with little concern for the truth.
	2. Spoken or performed in an offhand manner, with ease or fluency
	3. Careless, thoughtless, or insincere. glib responses.
minaret	*n* A tall, thin tower on a mosque with a balcony from which Muslims are called to prayer.
spire	*n.* A structure, such as a steeple, that becomes narrow at the top.
proportion	*n.* 1. The size, amount, number, or extent of one thing as compared with that of another thing --The proportion of students to teachers in our school is 20 to one.
	2. A pleasing, proper, or balanced relation between parts of a whole --Your face is swollen out of all proportion because of your toothache.

3.1.4.3. Order of Importance

The supporting details in a paragraph can be logically organized in order of importance, from the most to the least important, or vice versa. This type of arrangement is effective for persuasive or informative writing. Also with this arrangement, you can draw your reader's attention to what you think is most important by putting it at the beginning or end of the paragraph.

Read the following paragraph, and notice how the supporting details are arranged to support the topic sentence.

<u>1.</u> I also like to see all the folks write an autobiography. Writing is very therapeutic. In fact, experts say it promotes self-esteem and personal integration. Personally, I think it also clears away the cobwebs and stimulates a fresh way of thinking and looking back at your life. Most important, perhaps, it leaves a private history of yourself and your family. Don't you wish your grandmother and her grandmother before her had done that? *(Source: Helen Hayes, "Hayes: 'There Is So Much to Do.'")*

<u>2.</u> African-Americans in the Army and the Navy during the Civil War played a key role in Union victory. After Richmond fell, black troops were among the first Union presence in the city. Then, the Fifty-fourth Massachusetts Volunteers, the first African-American combat unit, led the charge of Fort Wagner in Charleston Harbor that earned respect for the mettle of black soldiers. Over the course of the war, nearly 35,000 African-American soldiers died for the Union.

3.1.4.4. Logical Order

"Logical order" refers to the grouping of related ideas together. The grouping can be done by the category of classification, division, definition, or comparison/contrast.

Read the following paragraph, and notice how the writer uses his ideas/supporting details for logical order.

<u>1.</u> Trees can be classified in several ways based on their function or use. They are used most commonly for lumber or building products. Pine and oak are among the most popular for this purpose. Besides these uses, trees are considered valuable for landscaping purposes where they provide shade, color, and screening for homes and businesses. Among the most popular are evergreens, maples, and honey-locusts.

3.1.4.3. 중요도순

문단 속의 뒷받침 세부자료들은 중요도 순서, 다시 말해 가장 중요한 것에서 가장 덜 중요한 것 또는 그 역으로 논리적으로 배열할 수 있다. 이런 유형의 배열은 설득이나 정보 전달을 목적으로 하는 글에 매우 효과적이다. 또한 이런 배열을 이용할 경우, 가장 중요한 것을 문단 처음이나 끝에 배치함으로써 당신이 가장 중요하게 생각하는 것에 대해 독자의 주의를 끌 수 있다.

다음 문단을 읽고, 주제문을 뒷받침하기 위해 뒷받침 세부자료들이 어떻게 배열되어 있는지 살펴보아라.

1. 나는 모든 사람이 자서전을 쓰는 모습 또한 보고 싶다. 글 쓰기는 건강 유지에 큰 도움이 된다. 실제로 전문가들은 글 쓰기가 자부심과 인격 통합을 증진시킨다고 말한다. 개인적인 생각이지만, 나는 그것이 또한 혼란을 없애주며, 삶을 신선한 방식으로 생각하고 되돌아볼 수 있게 해준다고 생각한다. 어쩌면 가장 중요한 것은 그것이 당신 자신과 가족의 사적인 역사를 남겨준다는 점일지도 모른다. 당신의 할머니와 할머니의 할머니가 그렇게 했기를 바라지 않는가?

Explanation * 작가는 중요도가 가장 낮은 이유, "the therapeutic value"로 시작해서 가장 중요한 이유, "the preservation of autobiography"로 나아가고 있다.

2. 남북 전쟁 당시 육군과 해군의 아프리카출신 미국인들은 북부의 승리에 핵심적인 역할을 담당했다. 리치몬드가 함락된 뒤, 그 도시 최초의 북부군 속에는 흑인 중대가 있었다. 그 후, 최초의 아프리카출신 미국인 전투 부대인 Fifty-fourth Massachusetts Volunteers가 흑인 병사들의 용기로 명성을 얻은 찰스턴 항 와그너 요새의 책임을 떠맡았다. 전쟁 와중에, 거의 35,000명에 이르는 아프리카출신 미국인 병사가 북부를 위해 싸우다 죽었다.

Explanation * 이 문단에는 "African-Americans in the Army... in Union victory"라는 주제문과 중요성이 가장 낮은 것에서 시작하여 차츰 가장 중요한 것으로 전개되는 뒷받침 세부자료가 들어 있다.

3.1.4.4. 논리순

'논리순'은 관련 아이디어들을 그룹별로 나누는 것을 가리킨다. 이 작업은 분류, 구분, 한정, 또는 비교/대조 등의 범주를 이용하여 행해질 수 있다. 다음 문단을 읽고, 작가가 자신의 아이디어/보충설명 등을 논리순에 따라 어떻게 사용하는지 살펴보아라.

1. 나무는 기능이나 용도에 근거하여 몇 가지 방식으로 분류될 수 있다. 나무는 흔히 재목이나 건축자재로 사용된다. 이런 용도로 쓰이는 가장 인기 있는 나무는 소나무와 오크나무이다. 그밖에도, 나무는 가정과 회사에 그늘과 컬러, 휘장 등을 제공하는 조경이라는 면에서도 귀중한 것으로 간주되고 있다. 이런 용도로 가장 인기 있는 나무는 상록수, 단풍나무, 수엽나무 등이다.

Explanation * 분류를 기초로 논리적 순서가 짜여졌다.

<u>2.</u> In one way, baby-sitting for a two-year-old child is like dog-sitting for a two-month-old puppy. You cannot trust either of them out of your sight. Puppies must be watched constantly because their curiosity is endless and their teeth are sharp. Nothing they can reach is safe. They can happily destroy a shoe or a pillow or a book in a few minutes. If you don't know where a puppy is, you had better worry. Silence does not necessarily mean sleep. Similarly, two-year-olds are never still. They run, climb, fall down, throw things, and disappear suddenly. They try to put everything into their mouths. If you can't see or hear them, you had better investigate. Silence often means mischief.

3.1.4.5. Connections Between Ideas

To give a paragraph "coherence," not only "unity" but also "connections between ideas" is required as a way of connecting ideas smoothly. There are two ways to show connection: (1) Direct References; and, (2) Transitional Devices. The former is used to make references to something or someone else in the paragraph; whereas the latter as a word or phrase is for bridging from one idea to another.

3.1.4.5.1. Direct References

"Direct References" can be made in three ways:

1. Use a noun or pronoun that refers to a noun or pronoun previously used.
2. Repeat a word previously used.
3. Use a word or phrase that refers to the same thing or person as one previously used.

In the following paragraph, the direct references are italicized. The number (1, 2, or 3) beside the reference shows the type of reference illustrated above.

<u>1.</u> Sarah spent Sunday cleaning out the garage. *This (3)* did not seem to *her (1)* to be a proper use of the holiday; but *it (3)* had to be done.

2. 어떤 면에서는 두 살바기 아이를 돌본다는 것이 두 달 짜리 강아지를 돌보는 것과 같다. 아이도 강아지도 눈에 보이지 않으면 안심할 수 없다. 강아지들은 호기심이 무궁무진하고 이빨은 날카롭기 때문에 한시도 눈을 떼선 안 된다. 강아지들 손에 닿을 수 있는 것치고 안전한 것은 아무 것도 없다. 녀석들은 행복한 마음으로 몇 분만에 구두나 베개나 책을 망가뜨릴 수 있다. 강아지가 어디 있는지 모른다면, 걱정을 하는 편이 옳다. 침묵이 반드시 잠을 뜻하는 것은 아니다. 마찬가지로, 두 살바기 아이들은 결코 가만히 있지 못한다. 뛰고, 올라가고, 떨어지고, 뭔가를 던지고, 갑자기 사라진다. 게다가 손에 잡히는 것은 무엇이든 입으로 가져간다. 아이들 모습이 보이지 않거나 소리가 들리지 않는다면, 찾아보는 것이 좋다. 침묵은 종종 못된 장난을 뜻하기 때문이다.

Explanation * 비교/대조를 기초로 논리적 순서가 짜여졌다.

3.1.4.5. 아이디어 사이의 연관

문단에 '일관성'을 부여하려면, 여러 아이디어를 부드럽게 연결하는 한 방식으로서 '통일성' 뿐 아니라 '아이디어 사이의 연관' 또한 필요하다. 연관을 보여주는 방법으로는 (1) 직접적인 언급이나 (2) 이행 장치 등 두 가지가 있다. 전자는 문단의 어떤 것 또는 다른 누군가에 대해 언급하는데 사용되는 반면, 단어 또는 구로서의 후자는 하나의 아이디어를 다른 아이디어와 이어주는데 쓰인다.

3.1.4.5.1. 직접적인 언급

'직접적인 언급'은 세 가지 방식으로 이루어질 수 있다.
1. 이전에 사용된 명사나 대명사를 가리키는 명사 또는 대명사를 사용하라.
2. 이전에 사용된 단어를 반복하라.
3. 이전에 사용된 사물 또는 사람을 가리키는 단어 또는 구를 사용하라.

다음 문단에는 '직접적인 언급' 부분이 이탤릭체로 쓰여져 있다. 그 언급 옆의 숫자(1,2,3)는 위에 예시한 언급의 유형을 보여준다.
(1) 사라는 차고를 치우면서 일요일을 보냈다. 그녀(1) 입장에서 보면, 이것은(3) 휴일을 잘 보내는 방법은 아닌 것 같았다. 그러나 그것(3)을 하지 않을 수 없었다.

Note

curiosity	*n.* 1. A desire to know or learn --We burned with curiosity over what was in the box.
	2. Something unusual, strange, or rare --The old wooden skis are a curiosity.
investigate	*v.* To look into carefully.
mischief	*n.* 1. Naughty or bad behavior.
	2. Harm or damage caused by someone or something.

<u>2.</u> The word Inuit means "people," and *they (1)* prefer this name for themselves. At one time, other American-Indians called *them (1) Eskimos (3)*, which means "eaters of raw meat."

They (1) are thought to have migrated from Asia centuries ago, because *their (1)* appearance is similar to *that (1)* of Central Asian peoples.

Kotzebue Eskimo Woman

3.1.4.5.2. Transitional Devices

   Transitional devices are connecting words or phrases that show the relationship between ideas, details, and examples. Actually, they act as signals for giving directions or telling where the paragraph is going. In this sense, they also act to hold sentences together. Notice the transitional devices as you read the following paragraph.

<u>1.</u> The human body contains three types of muscle cells: smooth muscle, striated muscle, and heart muscle. <u>First</u>, smooth muscle is present in the walls of many internal organs. <u>For</u> <u>example</u>, the walls of the digestive tract and those of the arteries contain smooth muscle. <u>Since</u> smooth muscle is involuntary, you cannot control its movement. <u>Next</u>, striated muscle shows bands (striations) when viewed under the microscope. Striated muscles in your body are under voluntary control, <u>so</u> you can move them at will. <u>For</u> <u>example</u>, when you walk, talk, jump, and run, you use striated muscle. <u>Finally</u>, heart muscle is present in your heart and causes its contraction. Heart muscle is similar to striated muscle <u>since</u> it also contains striations. <u>However</u>, <u>unlike</u> striated muscle, heart muscle is involuntary. The beat of the heart muscle is automatic. The beating is controlled by a small node on the top of the heart.

C H A P T E R 3

   As we have seen, transitional devices are used as a bridge for connecting between words, sentences, paragraphs, and ideas. A good writer uses a lot of appropriate transitional devices which are listed for readers. When you are stuck for a word or phrase, must choose an appropriate transitional device for your essay or thesis. These words or phrases help the flow of the essay and improve the style of writing, especially for those who are writing their essays or dissertations related to Bachelor, Master, or Doctoral degrees.

(2) '이뉴잇' 이라는 단어는 '사람들' 을 뜻하며, 그들은(1) 스스로를 부를 때 이 이름을 선호한다. 한때 다른 미국 인디언들이 그들을 (1) '생고기를 먹는 사람' 이라는 뜻을 가진 에스키모(3)라고 불렀다. 그들은(1) 수세기 전에 아시아에서 이주해온 것으로 여겨진다. 왜냐하면 그들의(1) 생김새가 중앙아시아 민족의 그것(1)과 비슷하기 때문이다.

3.1.4.5.2. 이행 장치들

이행 장치는 아이디어와 아이디어, 세부사항과 세부사항, 사례와 사례 사이의 관계를 보여주는 연결 단어 또는 구를 말한다. 실제로 그것은 방향을 알려주거나 문단이 어디로 가고 있는지 말해주는 신호로 기능한다. 다음 문단을 읽으면서 이행 장치들을 살펴보아라.

1. 인간의 몸에는 평활근, 횡문근, 심근 등 세 가지 유형의 근육세포가 있다. 먼저, 평활근은 많은 내장 벽에 있다. 예를 들어, 소화관과 동맥의 벽은 평활근을 하고 있다. 평활근은 불수의근이기 때문에, 사람의 힘으로 그 운동을 통제할 수 없다. 다음으로, 횡문근은 현미경으로 보면 띠(줄무늬)가 있다. 몸의 횡문근은 수의근이므로, 마음대로 움직일 수 있다. 예를 들어, 걸을 때, 말할 때, 뛰어오를 때, 달릴 때, 우리는 횡문근을 이용한다. 마지막으로, 심근은 심장에 있으며, 심장 수축을 야기시킨다. 심근 또한 줄무늬를 가지고 있다는 점에서 횡문근과 비슷하다. 그러나 횡문근과 달리, 심근은 불수의근이다. 심근 박동은 자동적이다. 맥박은 심장 꼭대기에 있는 작은 결절에 의해 통제된다.

Explanation * 위의 문단에 사용된 이탤릭체로 쓰여진 이행 장치들은 구체적인 연결 목적에 따라 다양한 모습을 보여주고 있다. 구체적으로 보면, 'First, Next, Finally' 는 중요도의 순서를 나타내기 위해 사용된다(이 단어들은 종종 시간이나 결과를 보여주는데 사용된다). 'However, unlike' 는 대조 또는 반대되는 점을 보여주며, 'since' 는 원인, 'For example' 는 설명이나 실례를 들 때, 'so' 는 결과, 'and' 는 비슷한 진술이 이어질 때 사용된다.

지금까지 살펴보았듯이, 이행 장치들은 단어, 문장, 문단, 아이디어 사이를 이어주는 다리로 사용된다. 훌륭한 작가는 독자들을 위해 나열되는 적절한 이행장치를 많이 쓴다. 한 단어나 구가 부족할 때면, 당신이 지금 쓰고 있는 에세이나 논문에 맞는 적당한 이행 장치를 골라라. 이 단어 또는 구는 에세이의 흐름을 도와주고, 글의 문체를 향상시킨다. 학사, 석사, 박사 학위와 관련된 에세이나 논문을 쓰는 사람들에게는 특히 더 그러하다. (이행장치의 분류는 p. 232~235에 있음.)

Note

contain	*v.*	1. To have within itself ; hold --Orange juice contains vitamins.
		2. To consist of or include --A gallon contains four quart.
		3. To hold back ; restrain --I could not contain my laughter.
artery	*n.*	1. A vessel that carries blood away from the heart. (cf. vein.)
		2. A major route or highway.
voluntary	*a.*	1. Made, done, given, or acting of one's own free will --I made a voluntary decision to give up the movies tonight.
		2. Controlled by the will --We move our arms and legs with voluntary muscles. <--->involuntary

3.2.Chapter Summary & Exercises

EXERCISES:

1. Read the following paragraph, and answer the question.

Muslims and Christians have fought "holy war" against one another, which have been anything but holy. And within their own ranks, so-called Christians have persecuted other Christians. Like Saul of Tarsus before he became Christ's apostle to the Gentiles, they think they are doing God a service when actually they are persecuting Jesus. People have treated others with unbelievable cruelty in the name of religion throughout history.
(Source: Adapted from "The Difference Jesus Makes," Our Daily Bread (1997)).

(a) The main idea? : _____

(b) The topic sentence?: _____

(c) The supporting details shown as "examples"? _____
_____

2. Read the following paragraph carefully, and identify the topic sentence supported by specific supporting details such as Sensory Details, Facts & Statistics, Examples, or Anecdotes.

(1) The Beatles came from Liverpool, England. During the 1960s, they often sang in the United States. They were very popular with young Americans. Wherever they sang, crowds cheered and screamed. Young Americans imitated their music, their clothing, and their hairstyles.

The Beatles, shown here on the cover of their album, Sgt. Pepper's Lonely hearts Club Band, influenced fashion with their long hair and psychedelic clothing.

(a) The topic sentence: _____

(b) The topic sentence is supported by Sensory Details (   ); Facts & Statistics (   ); Examples (   ); Anecdotes (   ).

3.2. 요약과 연습

> **연습 문제**

1. 다음 문단을 읽고, 질문에 답하라.

이슬람교도와 기독교도는 상대방에 대항하여 서로 '성전'을 벌였지만, 그것은 결코 성스럽지 않았다. 게다가 소위 기독교도들은 자체 계급 내에서 다른 기독교도들을 박해하였다. 타르수스의 사울(이스라엘 초대 왕. 사도 바울의 원이름. 타르수스는 바울의 탄생지)이 예수의 12사도가 되기 전에 그랬던 것처럼, 그들은 자신들이 사실상 예수를 박해하고 있을 때에도 신께 경배드리고 있다고 생각한다. 인류 역사를 통틀어 사람들은 종교라는 이름아래 다른 사람들을 믿을 수 없을 정도로 잔인하게 대해 왔다.

정답   *(a) Religious persecution*
      (b) People have treated others ... history.
      (c) Muslim and Christians .... holy. And within their own ranks, ... Christians.
         Like Saul of ... Jesus.

> **Note**
>
> persecute   *v.*   To cause constant suffering to, as because of political beliefs ; oppress.
> apostle   *n.*   One of the early missionaries of Jesus, including the twelve disciples and Saint Paul.

2. 다음 문단을 주의 깊게 읽고, 감각적 세부사항, 사실과 통계, 사례 또는 일화 등의 뒷받침 세부자료에 의해 뒷받침되고 있는 주제문을 밝혀라.

(1) 비틀즈는 영국 리버풀 출신이었다. 1960년대에 그들은 종종 미국에서 노래를 불렀다. 그들은 미국 젊은이들에게 매우 인기가 좋았다. 그들이 노래부를 때마다, 군중들은 환호하며 소리를 질렀다. 미국 젊은이들은 그들의 음악, 옷차림, 헤어스타일 등을 흉내냈다.

정답   *(a) The Beatles ... England. (b) Facts & statistics*

> **Note**
>
> cheer   *v.*   1. To shout in happiness, approval, encouragement, or enthusiasm --The audience cheered and clapped.
>   2. To encourage or urge on especially by cheering --The fans cheered the runner on.
>   3. To make or become happier.
> imitate   *v.*   1. To copy the actions, looks, or sounds of --Little children imitate their parents.
>   2. To look like ; resemble --This wallpaper imitates wood paneling.

(2) Lions are among the largest members of the cat family. An adult male usually weighs about 400 pounds. Some males, however, weigh up to 500 pounds. Most male lions are 9 feet long from nose to tail. Females are somewhat smaller and usually weigh about 300 pounds.

(a) The topic sentence: _____

(b) Supported by Sensory Details (SD) (   ); Facts & Statistics (FS) (   ); Examples (EX) (   ); Anecdotes (AD) (   ).

(* Note: Hereafter Sensory Details will be abbreviated as SD, Facts & Statistics FS, Examples EX, and Anecdotes AD for convenience sake).

(3) Most construction workers specialize in certain materials. For example, carpenters use wood in constructing buildings and such building features as floors and frames. Metal workers perform such jobs as pipe fitting and welding. They also install plumbing, heating, and air-conditioning systems.

(a) The topic sentence: _____

(b) Supported by SD (   ); FS (   ); EX (   ); AD (   ).

(4) As Sonya entered the forest, she was surrounded by sound. A stream of water gurgled over the rock. Branches of various trees clacked together in the wind like gossiping neighbors. Nearby, a woodpecker drilled a message into the bark of a tree. The forest was a lively and noisy place.

(a) The topic sentence: _____

(b) Supported by SD (   ); FS (   ); EX (   ); AD (   ).

C H A P T E R 3

(2) 사자는 고양이과 동물들 가운데 가장 큰 축에 속한다. 어른이 된 수컷 사자는 몸무게가 보통 400 파운드이다. 그러나 일부 수컷들은 몸무게가 500파운드에 달하기도 한다. 대부분의 수컷 사자들은 코에서 꼬리까지 길이가 9피트이다. 암컷들은 그보다 좀 작으며, 몸무게도 보통 300파운드이다.

정답   *(a) Lions are among ... family. (b) Facts & Statistics*

(3) 대부분의 건설 공사 인부들은 일정한 재료를 전문으로 한다. 예를 들어, 목수는 건물을 짓는데 목재를 사용하며, 그런 건물은 마룻바닥이나 뼈대를 특징으로 삼는다. 금속공들은 배관공사와 용접 같은 업무를 수행한다. 또한 수도관, 난방 장치, 공기 조절 장치도 설비한다.

정답   *(a) Most construction workers... materials. (b) Examples*

Note

construct   *v.* To make by fitting parts togather; build --We constructed a bookcase.
plumbing   *n.* 1. The equipment, as pipes and fixtures, through which water, sewage, or gas flows in a building.
          2. A plumber's work.

(4) 숲에 들어서자, 소냐는 소리에 둘러싸였다. 바위 위로 개울이 콸콸 흘러내렸다. 수많은 나무 가지들이 마치 서로 수다라도 떠는 이웃들처럼 바람을 맞으며 함께 수근거렸다. 근처에는 딱따구리가 나무껍질 속으로 메시지를 집어놓고 있다. 숲은 활기차고 시끄러운 곳이었다.

정답   *(a) As Sonya entered... by sound. (b) Sensory Details.*

Note

gurgle   *v.* 1. To flow or pour out of the bottle.
          2. To make low, building sounds --The baby gurgled when I came into the room.
        n. A bubbling sound.
clack   *n.* A sudden, sharp sound, as that made by two hard objects that are struck together --We heard the clack of typewriters.
        v. To make this sound.

(5) It is believed that Tahiti was first settled by Polynesians from the Philippines and Micronesia long time ago. Then, in 1767, an English sea captain, Samuel Wallis discovered the island. But in 1768 a French navigator claimed the island for France, and it became a French colony. During the

Paul Gauguin, Self - Portrait with the Yellow christ.

1890s, Paul Gauguin made Tahiti well known by painting its people, flowers, and beaches.

(a) The topic sentence: _____

(b) Supported by SD (   ); FS (   ); EX (   ); AD (   ).

(6) The next morning the three horses arrived, and off we went. We zigzagged along up the precipitous paths, and I enjoyed myself enormously perched on top of what seemed to be an immense horse. A guide led it up, occasionally picking little branches of flowers, handed them to me to stick in my hatband... The guide came running back to us bringing with him a magnificent butterfly he had trapped. "For the little Miss," he said. Taking a pin from his lapel he transfixed the butterfly and stuck it in my hat! Oh, the horror of that moment! The feeling of the poor butterfly fluttering, struggling against the pin, the agony I felt as the butterfly fluttered there... That horrible flapping against my hat! There is only one thing a child can do in these circumstances. I cried. *(Agatha Christie)*

(a) The topic sentence: _____

(b) Supported by SD (   ); FS (   ); EX (   ); AD (   ).

(5) 타히티에 처음 정주한 사람들은 오래 전 필리핀과 미크로네시아에서 온 폴리네시아인으로 보인다. 그 뒤, 1767년, 영국의 선장 사뮤엘 월리스가 그 섬을 발견하였다. 그러나 1768년, 프랑스의 한 탐험가가 그 섬은 프랑스의 것이라고 주장했고, 결국 프랑스의 식민지가 되었다. 1890년대에, 폴 고갱은 타히티 사람, 타히티의 꽃, 타히티 해변 등을 그림으로 그려 타히티를 유명하게 만들었다.

정답 *(a) It is believed ... ago.*　　　*(b) Facts*

Note

settle	*v.* 1. To arrange or decide by agreement --Let's settle the date of the field trip.
	2. To come to rest or cause to come to rest in place --The butterfly settled on a flower.
	3. To make a home or place to live in --Pioneers settled the West.
	4. To go down or to the bottom ; sink --Mud settle fast in calm rivers.
	5. To make or become calm --After the excitement I tried to settle myself so I could study
navigator	*n.* A crew member who plots the course of a ship or aircraft.
claim	*v.* 1. To ask for as something that one owns or has a right to --I claimed my luggage at the airport.
	2. To call for ; deserve --Your homework should claim your full attention.
	3. To state to be the case ; assert --I claim that I can run faster than you.

(6) 다음날 아침, 말 세 마리가 도착했고, 우리는 길을 나섰다. 우리는 가파른 길을 따라 지그재그로 올라갔고, 나는 거대한 말 같은 동물 등에 터무니없이 자리잡고 앉아 있는 나 자신을 즐겼다. 가이드가 앞서가면서, 가끔 꽃나무 가지를 꺾어 모자 띠에 꽂으라며 내게 건네주었다... 그 가이드는 방금 잡은 멋진 나비를 들고 우리한테 되돌아오기도 했다. "어린 숙녀분께 바칩니다."라고 그는 말했다. 그는 옷깃에서 핀을 뽑아들고 나비를 고정시킨 뒤, 그것을 내 모자에 꽂아주었다! 아, 그 순간의 그 공포라니! 불쌍한 나비가 핀에서 빠져나오려고 바둥거리는 느낌, 나비가 거기서 바둥거릴 때 내가 느낀 고통... 내 모자에서 벗어나려는 그 끔찍한 날개 짓! 이런 상황에서 아이가 할 수 있는 일은 오직 하나밖에 없다. 나는 울음을 터트렸다.

정답 *(a) Those circumstances made me cry. (b) Anecdotes*

Note

precipitous	*a.* So sharply inclined as to be almost perpendicular
perch	*v.* To place or be placed on a narrow or insecure surface
lapel	*n.* The part of a garment, such as a coat or jacket, that is an extension of the collar and folds back against the breast.
transfix	*v.* 1. To pierce with or as if with a pointed weapon.　2. To fix fast; impale.
	3. To render motionless, as with terror, amazement, or awe
flutter	*v.* 1. To flap the wings rapidly in flying or trying to fly --A moth fluttered around the porch light.
	2. To wave, flap, or beat rapidly --My heart is fluttering with excitement. The curtains fluttered in the breeze.
	n. A condition of nervous excitement --The cast of the play was in a flutter on opening night.
agony	*n.* Great pain or suffering.

(7) My name I must have written a million times that season on printed programs, in books, on scraps of paper, and even on paper napkins at rural receptions. But, my most personal autograph is, I suppose, obliterated by now. I inscribed it unawares in a small town in Mississippi near the Alabama state line. I was housed with one of the pillars of the church in a tiny house, spotlessly clean and filled, when I arrived, with the fumes of wonderful cooking... At the very last moment, it seemed, in her zeal to have everything spick-and-span, she had even freshly painted the bathtub, outside and in, with white enamel. Unfortunately, the enamel had not dried when I arrived. But, unaware of this fact, I blithely ran the bathtub full of hot water and sat down therein, soaking myself happily as I lathered my hair. But ten minutes late, when I started to get up, I could not tear myself loose. I was stuck to the bottom of the tub! With great deliberateness, slowly and carefully pushing myself upward, I finally managed to rise without leaving my skin behind. But I certainly left imprinted on that bathtub a most personal autograph.

Langston Hughs

(Langston Hughes (1902~1967), "I wonder as I wander.")

(a) The topic sentence: _____

(b) Supported by SD (   ); FS (   ); EX (   ); AD (   ).

(8) The Indian tribes in North America used deer for almost everything. The flesh was used for food, the hide for moccasins and cloth, and the antlers for tool handles. The cords and sinew that connected the muscles of the deer to the bones were used for thread with which to sew clothing. The hooves were made into glue. (Rosebud Yellow Robe)

(a) The topic sentence:

(b) Supported by SD (   ); FS (   ); EX (   ); AD (   ).

(7) 그 시즌에 나는 인쇄물, 책, 종이조각, 심지어 시골 호텔의 냅킨 위에까지 수백만 번이나 내 이름을 써야했다. 그러나 나의 가장 개인적인 육필은 지금쯤은 벌써 지워졌을 거라고 나는 생각한다. 나는 앨라바마주 경계선 근처의 미시시피 주에 있는 작은 마을에서 부지불식 중에 그것을 새겨 넣었다. 나는 어느 작은 집에 교회 기둥 하나와 함께 묵었고, 내가 도착했을 때, 그 집은 티끌 하나 없이 깨끗하고 맛있는 음식 냄새로 가득 차 있었다...바로 그 마지막 순간, 그녀는 모든 것을 깔끔하게 하고 싶은 열망에, 심지어 욕조까지 안팎으로 하얀색 에나멜을 칠한 듯했다. 불행하게도, 내가 도착했을 때, 그 에나멜은 아직 마르지 않은 상태였다. 그러나 이 사실을 모르고 있던 나는 즐거운 마음으로 뜨거운 물이 가득 찬 욕조에 뛰어들어갔고, 거기 앉아 기분 좋게 몸을 푹 담근 채 머리를 감았다. 그러나 10분 뒤, 욕조에서 일어나기 시작했을 때, 나는 도저히 몸을 일으킬 수 없었다. 욕조 바닥에 붙어버린 것이다! 심사숙고하면서 천천히 그리고 조심스럽게 내 몸을 위로 올린 끝에, 나는 마침내 피부를 조금도 다치지 않고 가까스로 몸을 일으킬 수 있었다. 그러나 내가 그 욕조에 나의 가장 개인적인 육필을 찍어놓았다는 점은 분명했다.

정답 *(a) My name … at rural receptions. (b) Anecdotes*

Note

obliterate	*v.*	1. To do away with completely so as to leave no trace.
		2. To wipe out, rub off, or erase (writing or other markings).
		3. Medicine to remove completely (a body organ or part), as by surgery, disease, or radiation.
inscribe	*v.*	To write, print, carve, or engrave something on or in.
pillar	*n.*	1. An upright structure that serves as a support or stands alone as a monument ; column.
		2. Something that is like a pillar --A pillar of flame rose from the volcano.
fume	*n.*	An irritating or strong-smelling smoke, vapor, or gas --The fumes from the cigar were making me sick.
zeal	*n.*	Intense enthusiasm for a person, ideal, cause, or the like.
lather	*n.*	1. A thick, creamy foam made by mixing soap and water.
		2. Foam from heavy sweating, especially on a horse.
imprint	*n.*	1. A maker or pattern made by something pressed on a surface --I saw the imprints of feet in the sand.
		2. A strong influence --Settlers from many countries made a strong imprint in American life.

(8) 북아메리카의 인디안 부족들은 거의 모든 것에 사슴을 이용했다. 고기는 음식으로 사용되었고, 가죽은 신발과 옷으로, 뿔은 연장의 손잡이로 사용되었다. 근육과 뼈를 연결시켰던 사슴의 인대는 옷을 꿰매는 실로 사용되었다. 발굽은 접착제로 만들어졌다.

정답 *(a) The Indian tribes …everything. (b) Examples*

Note

moccasin	*n.*	A soft leather slipper or shoe without a heel.
antler	*n.*	A bony growth on the head of such animals as deer or antelopes. Antlers grow in pairs and are often branched.
sinew	*n.*	A strong cord of tissue in the body that joins a muscle to a bone ; tendon

3. Read the following paragraph, and identify the sentence which destroys the unity of the paragraph.

(1) Spring is my favorite season. Yellow daffodils poke their heads up from the earth. Tulips burst into a rainbow of colors. Crickets creak in the thick bush. Even the rain showers are welcome because they help flowers and plants to grow.

(2) A number of birds cannot fly, but they have other abilities that make up for their ability to fly. The ostrich has powerful legs that allow it to run swiftly. The penguin uses its flippers to swim underwater. Birds such as eagles fly to great heights.

(3) Most persons desire fame; most persons desire wealth; but, for one reason or another, thousands fail to achieve what they desire. They lack either singleness of aim or adequate perseverance, or determined will, or sound judgment, or, instead of mastering circumstances, they permit circumstances to master them. If they are interested in such trivial matters as neighbor's wedding, or other's profits or losses, they can achieve what they desire.

(4) What kind of a liar are you?
People lie because they don't remember clear what they saw.
People lie because they can't help making a story better than it was the way it happened.
People tell "white lies" so as to be decent to others. People lie in a pinch, hating to do it, but lying on because it might be worse.
And people lie just to be liars for a crooked personal gain.
Some people steal, rob, or even kill others to satisfy their desires.
What sort of liar are you?
Which of these liars are you?*(Carl Sandburg, (1878~1967))*

Carl Sandburg

CHAPTER 3

3. 다음 문단을 읽고, 문단의 통일성을 파괴하는 문장을 찾아라.

(1) 봄은 내가 가장 좋아하는 계절이다. 노란 수선화가 땅에서 머리를 내민다. 튤립은 무지개 빛으로 피어난다. 울창한 수풀 속에선 귀뚜라미가 울어 제친다. 비조차도 환영받는다. 꽃과 나무가 자라는 것을 도와주기 때문이다.

정답 *The sentence, Crickets creak in the thick bush, unrelated to the topic sentence, destroys the paragraph unity. Crickets can creak in the thick bush during the late summer or the early fall.*

(2) 날 수 없는 새들도 많다. 그러나 그들은 날 수 있는 능력을 만회할 다른 능력을 가지고 있다. 타조는 신속하게 달릴 수 있는 강한 다리를 가지고 있다. 펭귄은 지느러미 모양의 날개를 이용하여 물 속에서 헤엄칠 수 있다. 독수리와 같은 새들은 아주 높은 곳까지 날아간다.

정답 *Birds such as eagles fly to great heights is not related to the topic sentence*

(3) 대부분의 사람들은 명예를 갈구한다. 또 대부분의 사람들은 부를 소망한다. 그러나 이런 저런 이유로 해서, 상당수의 사람들이 원하는 것을 이루지 못한다. 그들은 목표의 단일성이나 충분한 인내력, 또는 단호한 의지나 건전한 판단력이 부족하다. 다시 말해 그들은 상황을 지배하는 것이 아니라 상황이 자신들을 지배하게 만든다. 만약 그들이 이웃의 결혼이나 여타 손익 등의 사소한 문제에 관심을 가진다면, 원하는 것을 이룰 수 있다.

정답 *If they are interested in trivial matters ..., they can achieve what they desire is not related to the topic sentence at all.*

(4) 당신은 어떤 유형의 거짓말쟁이인가?

사람들은 자신이 본 것을 명확히 기억하지 않기 때문에 거짓말을 한다.

사람들은 실제 상황보다 더 그럴듯하게 이야기를 꾸며내지 않을 수 없기 때문에 거짓말을 한다.

사람들은 다른 사람들한테 예의를 차리느라 '선의의 거짓말' 을 한다.

사람들은 위기에 처하면 거짓말을 한다. 그렇게 하긴 싫지만, 그게 더 나쁠 수도 있기 때문이다.

그리고 사람들은 개인적으로 부정한 이익을 얻기 위해 거짓말쟁이가 된다.

어떤 사람들은 자신의 욕심을 채우기 위해 도둑질하고, 강도질하고, 심지어 다른 사람을 죽이기도 한다.

당신은 어떤 종류의 거짓말쟁이인가?

앞서 말한 거짓말쟁이들 가운데 당신은 어느 유형인가?

정답 *Some people steal, rob, or even kill others ...desires is not related to the topic sentence, What kind of a liar are you?*

(5) The man with money in his pocket not only enjoys a power that men without money do not; he is also in a position to do his work in the world more carefully, more independently, more truthfully, and more successfully. The best artists living today, the men who are doing their finest work, are, without exception, men who have no need longer to worry about financial matters. They have looked out for that first. A destitute and miserable man may write a good book, or paint a good picture, or write a good piece of music, but the records hint that he seldom, in these days, contrives to do another. However, it is true that the man whether with or without money is highly respected in these days. (George Jean Nathan, 1882~1958)

4. For each topic below, identify which "Order of Organization (i.e. Chronological, Spatial, Logical, and Order of Importance)" would make the most sense for your composition.

(1) A discussion of blue whales and sperm whales.

(2) A visit to the Louvre, Paris.

(3) Reasons to celebrate ChooSuk. (a Korean holiday similar to Thanksgiving Day)

(4) A biography of Sir.Koo Kim

(5) How to drive a car.

(6) A discussion of the Korean unification.

(7) Korea should be unified within a year.

(8) Development and spread of Buddhism.

(9) A visit to Mt. Diamond in North Korea.

(10) How to quit smoking.

(5) 주머니에 돈을 가지고 있는 사람은 그렇지 않은 사람들은 감히 즐기지 못하는 파워를 즐긴다. 게다가 그는 보다 신중하게, 보다 독립적으로, 보다 정직하게, 보다 성공적으로 일할 수 있는 지위에 있다. 오늘을 살아가는 최고의 예술가들, 가장 멋진 일을 하는 사람들은 예외 없이 재정적인 문제는 더 이상 걱정할 필요가 없는 사람들이다. 그들은 일단 그 점에 주의했다. 가난하고 불행한 사람이 좋은 책을 쓰거나 멋진 그림을 그리거나 훌륭한 음악을 작곡할 수도 있겠지만, 기록에 따르면, 오늘날 그런 사람은 거의 다른 일을 하려고 하지 않는다. 그러나 돈이 있든 없든 오늘날 그가 매우 존경받는다는 점은 사실이다.

정답 *The last sentence of the paragraph, However, it is true ... in these days does not support the topic sentence at all.*

Note

creak	*v.* To make or move with a squeaking sound --The rusty gate creaked.
persevere	*v.* To continue to try to do something despite obstacles or difficulties.
achieve	*v.* 1. To succeed in doing or accomplishing
	2. To get with great work or effect --They finally achieved success and fame.
pinch	*v.* 1 To squeeze between the thumb and a finger or between edges.
	2. To squeeze or press so hard as to cause pain --The shoes pinched my feet.
	3. To cause to seem shriveled or shrunken --Their faces were pinched with cold.
destitute	*a.* Lacking the resources, as money, needed for life; very poor.
miserable	*a.* 1. Very unhappy --I was miserable on my first night at camp.
	2. Causing real unhappiness or discomfort --We had miserable weather last winter.
	3. Very poor ; inferior --They live in a miserable shack in the woods.
contrive	*v.* To plan in a clever way --They contrived a way to escape. We contrived a little boat out of a large nutshell

4. 아래에 주어진 각각의 주제를 보고, 당신의 작문에 가장 어울릴 "구성 순서(예를 들면, 연대순, 공간순, 논리순, 중요도순)"는 어떤 것인지 밝혀라.

(1) 흰긴수염고래와 향유고래에 대한 논의

정답 *Logical order. Blue whales and sperm whales can be contrasted and compared with.*

(2) 파리 루브르 박물관 견학

정답 *Spatial order.*

(3) '추석' (추수감사절과 유사한 한국의 명절)을 지내야 하는 이유

정답 *Order of importance. It can be based on Logical order, too.*

(4) 김구 선생의 전기

정답 *Chronological order*

(5) 자동차를 운전하는 방법

정답 *Chronological order or Order of importance*

5. Read the following cartoon by Powell, The News and Observer, and answer the questions as directed.

(a) The implied main idea: _____

(b) The topic sentence: _____

(c) The order of organization: _____

(d) The supporting details that support the topic sentence: _____
_____
_____.

(6) 남북 통일에 대한 논의

정답 *Logical order. Advantages or disadvantages related to the Korean unification can be discussed.*

(7) 한국은 1년 안에 통일되어야 한다.

정답 *Order of importance. The topic, Korean should be unified within a year is not only an opinionated but also persuasive one. Therefore, the writer or the speaker needs several points in order of importance to support the topic sentence and to persuade the audience.*

(8) 불교의 발전과 전파

정답 *Chronological order.*

(9) 북한의 금강산 유람기

정답 *Spatial order.*

(10) 금연법

정답 *Chronological order or Order of importance*

5. 〈뉴스 앤 옵저버 (The News and Observer)〉의 파웰이 그린 시사 만화를 보고, 제시된 질문에 답하라.
정답
(a) Education or Academic motivation.

(b) Education makes your life quite different both in economic and social perspectives.

(c) Chronological order.

(d) In terms of economic perspective, Johnny in the cartoon lives in the worlds richest country; whereas Sue Lin lives in a Southeastern Asian country where life is economically challenged. Johnnys community and that of Sue Lins are well contrasted in terms of economic situations; the former, relatively affluent, and, latter, rustically rural.

Both students went to school, but Sue Lin worked hard while Johnny did not think of his educational value too much. As inferred in the international test they took, Sue passed it with high marks while Johnny placed last. Much later, Sue was rewarded for her hard work by becoming a successful doctor with a very comfortable income as evidenced by her ownership of a BMW (BMW is not a typical car for middle class Americans, but for affluent middle-upper people). Johnny, on the other hand, ends up as a manual laborer waxing Sues BMW.

In social perspectives, it is inferred that Johnny, as a student, lived in a community where middle-upper class people owned their residential properties. Chances are that probably, he could easily get whatever he wanted from his parents. He neglected his school work, which could not be obtained without hard work. Consequently, he ended up waxing Sues BMW which is a status symbol of the affluent middle-upper class. To sum up, we have seen the lives of two different students who have lost or gained both economic and social status due to the value of education

1. To Show a Time or Sequence

After	Afterwards	All along	Amid this
As soon as	At a later date	At the onset	At the same time
Beforehand	Beyond that	Before then	Chronologically
Coming after	Continuously	Currently	During
Earlier	Eventually	Finally	First of all
Following	For a time	For the duration	For this occasion
From its inception	Heretofore	Hitherto	Immediately after
In an instant	In the aftermath	In the course of	In a few minutes
Initially	In the first place	In the interim	In the near future
In the end	In the past	In progression	Just before
Later	Let's set in motion	Meanwhile	Next
Next term	Originally	Opening with	Presently
Prior to	Primarily	Previously	Recently
Sequentially	Spontaneously	Subsequently	Suddenly
Then	The secondary	Till now	Ultimately
Without letup			

2. To Show Comparing Points (Similarities)

Agreeable	Akin to	All are	A constant is
And	Another	As it were	As well as
Besides	Closely related to	Coinciding with	Coincidentally
Comparable to	Compared to	Congruent with	Consistent with
Corresponding to	Coupled with	Equally	Equally important
Everything in common	Identical to	Identically	In addition to
In accordance	In comparison	In harmony with	In like manner
In relation to	In similar fashion	In the same vein	In the same way
In unison	In tune with	Just the same	Likewise
On equal terms	Parallel to	Representative of	Similarly
Synonymous with	This reflects	This concurs with	This resembles
The same as	To some extent		

3. To Show a Place

About	Above	Across	After
Against	Along	Among	Around
At	Before	Behind	Below
Beneath	Beside	Between	Beyond
By	Down	From	Here
In	In front of	Inside	Nearby

Next	On	Out of	Outside
Over	There	To	Toward
Under	Underneath	Up	Within

4. To Show Contrasting Points

A different version	A disparate view	A dissenting point	A dissimilar
A divergent idea	After all	Although	Another way
Antagonistically	An incompatible	At odds with this	A variation
But	Conversely	Contrarily	Defiantly
Despite	Even though	However	I disagree
I doubt	In another way	In conflict	In contrast
In contractible	In disharmony	In my view, however	In negation
In opposition	In spite of	Instead	In this way
Inversely	Nevertheless	Nonetheless	Not only
Notwithstanding	Now, let's explain	Of course	On the other hand
Otherwise	Poles apart	Rather than	Regardless
Surely others	This is opposed to	Though	To counterattack
To refute	To the contrary	Unlike	What, though, if
Whether or not	Yet		

5. To Show Cause and Effect

Accordingly	As a result	As might be expected	As long as
Attributing to	Because	Because of	Consequently
Chances are	Considering the	Due to	Ergo
For	For this reason	Hence	It follows that
If...then...	In all likelihood	Inasmuch	In effect
Necessarily	On account of	Owing to	Since
So	Subsequently	Thereby	Thereupon
Therefore	This entails	This gives rise to	This implies
This is caused by	This results	Thus	Whereas

6. To Show an Order of Importance

Finally	First	Last	Mainly
More importantly	Next	Second	Then
To begin with	To start with		

7. To Show a Similar Statement to Follow

Additionally	Again	Also	Another point is
Apart from	Aside from	A supplement to	As well as
Besides	Beyond that	Further	Furthermore
In addition	In conjunction with	In fact	Let alone
Moreover	Next	Not to mention	On top of that
Plus	What's more		

8. To Emphasize a Point for Clarity

As you can see	Beyond question	Certainly	Clearly
Foremost	Honestly	Indeed	Indubitably
In fact	In particular	In reality	In truth
It's essential	It's evident	It's imperative	It's permanent
It's vital	Most important	Obviously	Precisely
Surely	Surprisingly	The critical point	The crucial
The eminent	The exact	The key element	The overriding
The prominent	The urgent	The unique view	To be specific
To be sure	Truly now		

9. To Simplify or State Another Way

Hence	In a nutshell	In all likelihood	In brief
In essence	In other words	In short	Its only
Putting it succinctly	Simply	That is to say	Therefore
Thus	To be concise	To sum up	

10. To Introduce Examples or Explanations

After all	As an illustration	As evident	As proof
As we have seen	Consider	For example	For instance
Inasmuch	In particular	In support of this	Namely
Since	That is		

11. To Open a Statement

From my viewpoint	He alleges	He purports	I assert
I believe that	I maintain	I question whether	I strongly feel
It is my contention	It seems that	It was found that	Many claim

More than ever before	The council proposes	The data indicate	The data suggest
The mayor affirms	The paper state	The study reported	The test concludes
The theory is	To begin with	We affirm	

12. After the Problem Has Been Stated

After all	Afterwards	Despite	Equally important
Granted	In some cases	Interestingly	In view of the foregoing
Its assumed	Keep in mind	Lets propose	Many times
Most importantly	More than ever before	The premise is	The conjecture is
They postulated	We surmised		

13. To End Statements

As you can see	As I have noticed	At last	Eventually
Finally	For the reason above	In any case	In conclusion
In summation	In the long run	Last of all	On the whole
Sooner or later	The result is	To close	To conclude
To summarize	To sum up	Ultimately	

14. To Show Feelings and Emotions

Angrily	Cruelly	Enthusiastically	Happily
Ominously	Regrettably	Sadly	Surprisingly
Tragically	Unfavorably	Unsuccessfully	With disgust
With fervor	With great joy	With hesitation	With satisfaction
Without hesitation			

CHAPTER 4

에세이쓰기

Writing an Essay

As we have studied in PART 3, a paragraph is a series of sentences that focuses on one main idea. It often includes the topic sentence that can be developed by providing sensory details, facts & statistics, examples, and anecdotes. Writing an essay is not much different from writing a paragraph. Structurally, an essay is made up of several extended paragraphs. It just requires the basic elements of a composition: the introduction, the body, and the conclusion. These three elements can serve as a basic structure for a variety of essays: **(1) descriptive; (2) expository; (3) informative; (4) narrative; (5) personal; (6) persuasive; and, (7) research paper which needs the thesis as an additional element.** A basic structure and several essay types are to be introduced and illustrated in the following sections.

4. 1. Structure

As previously mentioned, a basic structure of most essays includes (1) an introduction, (2) a body, and, (3) a conclusion. That is, it contains an opening paragraph as the introduction, several developmental paragraphs as the body, and a closing paragraph as the conclusion, which is framed and exemplified below as **"Five paragraph format."**

Introduction
First Paragraph:

The topic is _____.

The specific issue to discuss is _____.

My view on this issue is _____.

My three main points to discuss are _____.

Style of opening (Choose one from 8 suggestions provided in 4.1.1. Introduction).

Include 1~4 transitional devices (conjunctions) if necessary.

Body
Second Paragraph:

My first main point is _____.

Supporting evidence or example(s) for my first main point are _____.

Related sub-point.

Details, description: Who, What, Where, When?

3장 에서 공부했듯이, 문단이란 하나의 주제에 초점을 맞춘 일련의 문장이다. 문단에는 종종 감각적 세부사항 및 사실과 통계, 사례, 일화 등을 통해 전개될 수 있는 주제문이 포함되어 있다. 에세이를 쓰는 것은 문단을 쓰는 것과 그다지 다르지 않다. 구조적인 측면에서 볼 때, 에세이는 몇 개의 확장된 문단으로 구성된다. 이 경우, '서론, 본론, 결론' 이라는 작문의 기본 요소를 갖추어야 한다. 이 세 가지 요소는 (1)서술, (2)설명, (3)정보제공, (4)이야기체, (5)사적인 이야기, (6)설득, 그리고 (7)부가적인 요소로서 논제를 필요로 하는 연구 논문 등과 같은 다양한 에세이의 기본 구조로 기능할 수 있다. 이제부터 에세이의 기본 구조 및 몇 가지 유형을 살펴보기로 하자.

4.1. 구조

앞에서 언급했듯이, 에세이의 기본 구조는 대부분 (1)서론, (2)본론, (3)결론으로 이루어져 있다. 다시 말해, 대부분의 에세이는 서론 역할을 하는 첫 문단과 본론의 기능을 맡은 몇 개의 문단, 그리고 결론으로 기능하는 마지막 문단으로 나뉘어지는데, 다음에 실린 **다섯 문단 구성**은 그 좋은 예라 할 수 있다.

서론

첫 문단 :

주제는 _____.

여기서 논의하게 될 구체적 문제는 _____.

이 문제에 대한 나의 입장은 _____.

여기서 논의할 세 가지 주요 요지는 _____.

서두의 스타일(4.1.1. 서론 부분에 소개된 8가지 방법 가운데 하나를 선택하라).

필요하다면 1 ~ 4개 정도의 이행 장치(접속사)를 포함시켜라.

본론

두 번째 문단 :

나의 첫 번째 요지는 _____.

이 요지를 뒷받침하는 증거나 사례는 _____.

이와 관련된 부수적인 강조점.

세부 사항, 묘사 : 누가, 무엇을, 어디서, 언제?

Add some information.

Include 1~4 transitional devices (conjunctions) if necessary.

Third Paragraph:

My second main point is _____.

Supporting evidence or example(s) for my second main point

are _____.

Related sub-point.

Details, description: Who, What, Where, When?

Add some information.

Include 1~4 transitional devices (conjunctions) if necessary.

Fourth Paragraph:

My third main point is _____.

Supporting evidence or example(s) for my third main point

are _____.

Related sub-point.

Details, description: Who, What, Where, When?

Add some information.

Include 1~4 transitional devices (conjunctions) if necessary.

Conclusion

Closing Paragraph: Choose a style from 13 suggestions provided in 4.1.3.

Conclusion. Restate the importance, significance, or purpose of the essay.

몇 가지 정보를 첨가하라.
필요하다면 1 ~ 4개 정도의 이행 장치(접속사)를 포함시켜라.

세 번째 문단 :

나의 두 번째 요지는 _____.
이 요지를 뒷받침하는 증거나 사례는 _____,
이와 관련된 부수적인 강조점.
세부사항, 묘사 : 누가, 무엇을, 어디서, 언제?
몇 가지 정보를 첨가하라.
필요하다면 1 ~ 4개 정도의 이행 장치(접속사)를 포함시켜라.

네 번째 문단 :

나의 세 번째 요지는 _____.
이 요지를 뒷받침하는 증거나 사례는 _____,
이와 관련된 부수적인 강조점.
세부사항, 묘사 : 누가, 무엇을, 어디서, 언제?
몇 가지 정보를 첨가하라.
필요하다면 1 ~ 4개 정도의 이행 장치(접속사)를 포함시켜라.

결론
마지막 문단 :

4.1.3. 결론 부분에 소개된 13가지 방법을 참조하여 스타일을 정하라.
이 에세이의 중요성이나 의미, 또는 목적을 다시 한 번 설명하라.

4.1.1. Introduction (The First Paragraph)

The first paragraph as an introduction should accomplish two important functions: (1) it should arouse the reader interest, and, (2) it must state the main idea of the essay. To accomplish these functions, you can consider the following suggestions.

1. Begin with a question as a way of answering the issue/topic raised in the introduction.

   Example: Why do so many high school students pick up the habit of smoking?

2. Begin with a direct statement of the topic so that the first sentence may directly state the essay topic.

   Example: The major problem of smoking is the cost of health care. It affects anyone who smokes and the public pays too.

3. Present a startling or unusual fact or figure.

   Example: According to the 1990 report by the U.S. Surgeon General, 60% of the people who smoke may get lung cancer and other respiratory diseases.

4. Provide an example or anecdote related to the topic.

   Example: One of my neighbors, Mr. Kim, has to spend more than one million dollars for his lung cancer treatment at the Red-Cross Hospital in Seoul.

5. Quote a well-known person or literary work.

   Example: "Many persons have a wrong idea of what constitutes true happiness. It is not attained through self-gratification but through fidelity to a worthy purpose," says Helen Keller. Is smoking a worthy purpose or self-gratification? Indeed, smoking is self-gratification, not a worthy purpose.

4.1.1. 서론 (첫 문단)

서론으로 기능하는 첫 문단은 두 가지 중요한 기능을 달성해야 한다. **(1)독자의 흥미를 유발시켜야 하고, (2)에세이의 주제를 밝혀야 하는 것**이다. 이러한 기능을 달성하기 위해서는 다음과 같은 8가지 방법을 참조할 필요가 있다.

1. 질문으로 시작함으로써 서론에서 제기된 문제/주제에 답하는 방법

   예〕 고등학생 상당수가 흡연 습관에 빠져드는 까닭은 무엇일까?

2. 첫 문장에서 글의 주제를 직접적으로 언급할 수 있도록 주제에 대한 직접적인 언급으로 시작하는 방법

   예〕 흡연의 일차적인 문제는 건강 관리 비용이다. 그것은 담배를 피는 사람 모두에게 작용하며, 일반 대중들 역시 그 비용을 지불한다.

3. 놀랍거나 유별난 사실 또는 그림을 제시하는 방법

   예〕 공중 위생국장이 1990년에 제출한 보고서에 따르면, 흡연 인구의 60%가 폐암을 비롯한 여타 호흡기 질환에 걸릴 가능성이 높다고 한다.

4. 주제와 관련된 사례 또는 일화를 소개하는 방법

   예〕 내 이웃 김씨는 서울 적십자병원에서 폐암을 치료하는데 백만 달러 이상을 들여야 한다.

5. 유명인이나 저명한 문학 작품을 인용하는 방법

   예〕 "진정한 행복의 구성 요소에 대해 많은 사람들이 그릇된 생각을 가지고 있다. 그것은 자기 만족을 통해 얻어지는 것이 아니라 숭고한 목적에의 헌신을 통해 달성된다."고 헬렌 켈러는 말한다. 흡연은 숭고한 목적일까, 아니면 자기 만족일까? 흡연은 진정 숭고한 목적이 아니라 자기 만족이다.

Helen keller, both deaf and blind, was taught to communicate by Anne Sullivan. Here Helen Keller "listens" to what her teacher is saying by feeling her nose, lips, and throat.

6. Use a vivid and concrete description of a person, place, or object related to the topic.

   Example: *One of my friend fathers, Mr. Lee who smoked for more than 40 years, walks in with a sickly look, yellow teeth, and a hacking cough.*

7. Introduce a significant past event.

   Example: *More than half a century ago, smoking was part of popular culture and was considered as "Cool" or fashionable, evidenced by such prominent figures as Winston Churchill, Douglas MacArthur, and Fidel Castro.*

8. Present a current event related to the topic/issue.

   Example: *Today, American Tobacco Companies have to pay millions of dollars to settle the class-action law suit against them.*

Among many, these 8 techniques are effective to draw the reader attention to the main idea of your essay. In addition to the use of these techniques, you should consider the styles of introduction and include one you like in your opening paragraph. Remember what you should include in the introduction. Some of them are provided as follows:

(1) A recognizable style of opening.
(2) The topic and its importance.
(3) The specific issue and how it relates.
(4) The viewpoint or tone.
(5) The three major points.
(6) Two or three transitional devices.

6. 주제와 관련된 인물, 장소, 대상 등에 대해 구체적이고 생생하게 묘사하는 방법

> **예]** 40년 넘게 담배를 피워온 내 친구의 아버지 이씨는 병자 같은 모습, 누런 이, 끊임없이 나오는 기침 소리를 달고 다니신다.

7. 과거의 중요한 사건을 소개하는 방법

> **예]** 윈스턴 처칠, 더글라스 맥아더, 피델 카스트로와 같은 유명인들이 증명하고 있듯이, 반세기 전만 해도, 흡연은 대중 문화의 일부였고, 최신 유행의 '멋진' 모습으로 간주되었다.

8. 주제/문제와 관련된 현재의 사건을 제시하는 방법

> **예]** 오늘날 미국의 담배 회사들은 자신들을 상대로 한 집단 소송 건을 처리하는데 수백만 달러를 지불 해야 한다.

Note

affect *a.* 1. To cause a change in ; have an effect on --Eating junk food can affect your health. 2. To touch the feeling of. 3. To pretend to feel or have ; assume --They affected deep sorrow, but it was all an act.

constitute *v.* To make up ; form -Twelve units constitute a dozen.

attain *v.* 1. To achieve a goal --I hope to attain my ambition of becoming a lawyer. 2. To arrived at ; reach

vivid *a.* 1. Bright and strong ; brilliant --The coat was a vivid blue. 2. Actively ; lively --You have a vivid imagination. 3. Sharp and clear --We still have vivid memories of our trip to New York.

concrete *n.* A building material made of cement, sand, pebbles, and water. Concrete becomes very hard when it dries.

prominent *a.* 1. Sticking out --I have a long, prominent nose.
2. Very easy to see --The meat counter is in a prominent place in the supermarket.
3. Widely known --Our neighbor is a prominent scientist.

수많은 방법 중에서도 여기 소개된 8가지 기법들이야말로 글의 주제에 대한 독자의 관심을 끄는 데 가장 효과적이다. 이 8가지 기법 외에도, 서론의 스타일을 결정하고 그것을 서두 문단에 포함시켜야 한다. 서론에 무엇을 포함시켜야 하는지 항상 기억하라. 그 중 일부는 다음과 같다.

(1) 인식 가능한 서두의 스타일
(2) 주제와 그것의 중요성
(3) 구체적인 문제와 그것을 설명하는 방법
(4) 관점 또는 논조
(5) 세 가지 주요 요지
(6) 두세 가지 이행 장치

Now, based on the suggestions and the first paragraph format (the introduction), let's generate an introduction paragraph.

The format of the first paragraph:

* The topic: Teenagers' smoking.
* The specific issue to discuss: The smoking habit of high school students.
* My view on this issue: High school students should free themselves from the habit of smoking.
* My three main points to discuss: My three main points against the habit of smoking are (1) the health related problems; (2) the image building; and, (3) the cost of purchasing tobacco products.

Based on the above format, the introduction focused on the topic, "Teenagers' smoking" can be generated as below.

Introduction

Why do so many high school students pick up the habit of smoking these days? This is a very negative social phenomenon developing in our school communities, from which our high school students should free themselves. This issue is to be discussed based on three perspectives: (1) the health related problems; (2) the image building; and, (3) the cost of purchasing tobacco products.

● A specific issue to discuss while arousing the reader's interest and stating the main idea of the essay.
→ " Why do so many high school students pick up the habit of smoking these days?"

● My view on this issue.
→ " This is a very negative social phenomena developing in our school communities, from which our high school students should free themselves.

● My three main points to discuss.
→ " This issue is to be discussed based on three perspectives: (1) the health related problems; (2) the image building; and, (3) the cost of purchasing tobacco products.

자, 지금까지 설명한 몇 가지 방법과 첫 문단(서론) 구성에 기초하여, 서론 문단을 써 보기로 하자.

첫 문단의 구성은 :

* 주제 : 십대들의 흡연
* 논의하게 될 구체적인 문제 : 고등학생들의 흡연 습관
* 이 문제에 대한 나의 입장 : 고등학생들은 흡연 습관에서 벗어나야 한다.
* 논의하게 될 세 가지 요지 : 흡연 습관에 대한 나의 세 가지 논점은 (1) 건강 관련 문제, (2) 이미지 만들기, (3) 담배 구매 비용

위의 포맷에 근거할 때, "십대들의 흡연"이라는 주제에 초점을 맞춰 다음과 같은 서론을 쓸 수 있다.

서론

이즈음 상당수의 고등학생들이 흡연 습관에 빠져드는 까닭은 무엇일까? 이것은 우리의 학교 공동체에서 전개되고 있는 매우 부정적인 사회 현상으로서, 우리 고등학생들은 응당 거기에서 벗어나야 한다. 이 문제는 (1) 건강 관련 문제, (2) 이미지 형성, (3) 담배 구매 비용이라는 세 가지 관점에서 논의되어야 한다.

● 앞으로 논의하게 될 구체적인 문제를 제시하며, 독자의 흥미를 유발시키고 글의 주제를 밝힘.
→ "이즈음 상당수의 고등학생들이 흡연 습관에 빠져드는 까닭은 무엇일까?"

● 이 문제에 대한 나의 입장
→ "이것은 우리의 학교 공동체에서 전개되고 있는 매우 부정적인 사회 현상으로서, 우리 고등학생들은 응당 거기에서 벗어나야 한다.

● 이 글에서 논의하게 될 세가지 요인
→ "이 문제는 (1) 건강 관련 문제, (2) 이미지 형성, (3) 담배 구매 비용이라는 세 가지 관점에서 논의되어야 한다.

4.1.2. Body Paragraphs (The second, third, and fourth).

Based on the format of the body previously presented, let's generate the second, third, and fourth paragraphs.

Body

Second Paragraph:
My first main point is _____.
Supporting evidence or examples for my first main point are _____.
Related sub-point
Details, description: Who, What, Where, When?
Add some information.
Include 1~4 transitional devices (conjunctions) if necessary.

Third Paragraph:
My second main point is _____.
Supporting evidence or examples for my second main point are _____.
Related sub-point
Details, description: Who, What, Where, When?
Add some information.
Include 1~4 transitional devices (conjunctions) if necessary.

Fourth Paragraph:
My third main point is _____.
Supporting evidence or examples for my third main point are _____.
Related sub-point.
Details, description: Who, What, Where, When?
Add some information.
Include 1~4 transitional devices (conjunctions) if necessary.

4.1.2. 본론(2, 3, 4단락)

앞에서 제시한 본론의 포맷에 근거하여 2, 3, 4 단락을 써 보자.

본론

두 번째 문단 :
나의 첫 번째 요지는 _____.
이 요지를 뒷받침하는 증거나 사례는 _____.
이와 관련된 부수적인 강조점.
세부 사항, 묘사 : 누가, 무엇을, 어디서, 언제?
몇 가지 정보를 첨가하라.
필요하다면 1 ~ 4개 정도의 이행 장치(접속사)를 포함시켜라.

세 번째 문단 :
나의 두 번째 요지는 _____.
이 요지를 뒷받침하는 증거나 사례는 _____.
이와 관련된 부수적인 강조점.
세부 사항, 묘사 : 누가, 무엇을, 어디서, 언제?
몇 가지 정보를 첨가하라.
필요하다면 1 ~ 4 정도의 이행 장치(접속사)를 포함시켜라.

네 번째 문단 :
나의 세 번째 요지는 _____.
이 요지를 뒷받침하는 증거나 사례는 _____.
이와 관련된 부수적인 강조점.
몇 가지 정보를 첨가하라.
세부 사항, 묘사 : 누가, 무엇을, 어디서, 언제?
필요하다면 1 ~ 4개 정도의 이행 장치(접속사)를 포함시켜라.

The second paragraph:

Line 1   My first main point is that smoking plays a key role in causing health problems. With each puff of a cigarette, scientists identify more than 3,000 different toxic, or poisonous chemicals. A cigarette that contains nicotine, carbon monoxide (a poisonous gas), carcinogens (substances that cause cancer), benzopyrene (one

L.5.   of the deadliest carcinogens), and a variety of harmful ingredients is actually a highly complex, and potentially lethal, chemical factory. This lethal factory producing carbon monoxide, benzopyrene, carcinogens and multifarious additives is responsible for the deaths of not only smokers, but of non-smokers as well. In the United States, more deaths and physical sufferings are closely

L.10.   related to smoking than any other single cause. According to a report presented by the Surgeon General, 1992, smoking contributed to the deaths of some 450,000 Americans every year. Most of the deaths are related to lung cancer, heart disease, and respiratory diseases for which smoking is largely responsible.

(1) The main idea (thesis) for the first main point: _____

(2) The supporting facts, statistics, and example(s) for the first main point are:
      (a) Facts: _____
      (b) Statistics_____
      (c) Example(s)_____

(3) Related sub-point(s):_____

(4) Details, description: Who, What, Where, When?:
    Who?:_____
    What?:_____
    Where?_____:
    When?: _____

(5) Add some information:_____

(6) Include 1~4 transitional devices (conjunctions) if necessary: _____

두 번째 문단

나의 첫 번째 요지는 흡연이 건강을 악화시키는 데 결정적인 역할을 한다는 점이다. 학자들은 담배 연기 한 모금 한 모금에 각각 3,000가지 이상의 유독하거나 유해한 화학 물질이 함유되어 있다는 사실을 입증하고 있다.

니코틴, 일산화탄소(유독 가스), 발암성 물질(암을 일으키는 물질), 벤조피렌(치명적인 발암 물질 가운데 하나) 외에도 온갖 해로운 성분을 함유하고 있는 담배 한 대는 실제로 아주 복잡한, 그리고 잠재적으로 치명적인 화학 공장이라 할 수 있다. 일산화탄소와 벤조피렌, 발암성 물질, 온갖 잡다한 첨가물 등을 생산하는 이 치명적인 공장은 흡연자뿐 아니라 비흡연자에게도 악영향을 끼친다.

미국의 경우, 사망 및 육체적 고통과 밀접한 관련을 가진 단일한 원인으로는 흡연이 단연 선두를 차지하고 있다. 공중 위생국장이 1992년 제출한 보고서에 따르면, 흡연은 매년 450,000명의 미국인을 죽음으로 내몰았다고 한다. 사망 원인은 대부분 흡연으로 야기되는 폐암, 심장 질환, 호흡기 질환 등과 관련이 있다.

Note

identify *v.* To recognize and acknowledge as being a certain person or thing
    --I identified my wallet by telling what was in it.
lethal *a.* Intended to cause or capable of causing death or extreme harm ; deadly.
multifarious *a.* Having a great variety of parts, forms, or kinds ; many and varied.
additive *n.* A substance added in small amounts to another to improve, preserve, or otherwise alter it.
    a. Involving, related to, or produced by addition.

(1) 첫 번째 요지(제목)는 :

My first main point is that smoking plays a key role in causing health problems.
(Line 1.)

(2) 첫 번째 요지를 뒷받침하는 사실, 통계, 사례:

(a) 사실 : ...scientists identify...3000 different toxic, ...chemicals. (Lines from 2 to 3)

(b) 통계 : According to...by the Surgeon General, 1992,...450,000 Americans... responsible. (Lines from 10 to 14.)

(c) 사례 : None(없음), but ...chemical factory. This lethal factory in Line 6, as metaphor, partially serves as function of examples.

(3) 주제와 관련된 부수적인 강조점 :

With each puff...different toxic, or poisonous chemicals. (Lines from 2 to 3)

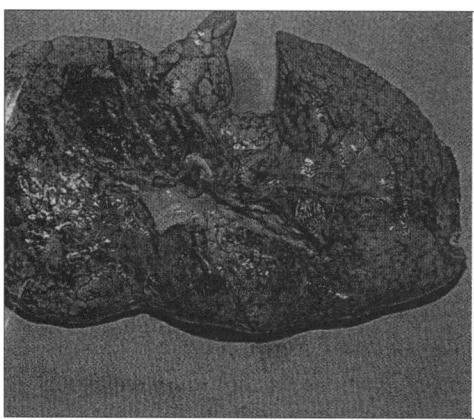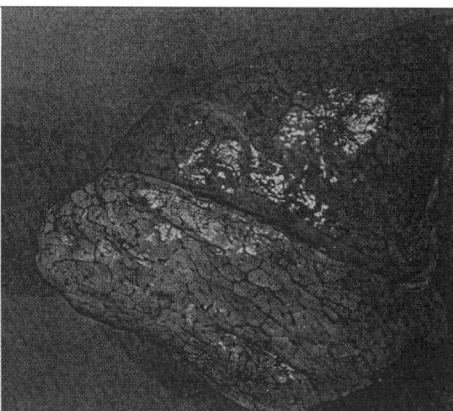

A cancerous lung(left)and a healthy lung(right). The white areas on the otherwise blackened lung show the development of lung cancer.

The third paragraph:

Line 1.   My second main point is that building a positive image is very important for high school students who would like to develop and maintain good relations with their parents, teachers, and adult community members. Those students who smoke hardly present

L.5.   positive images to their parents, teachers, adult relatives, and the community members, because they think that high school students are still too young to smoke. Half a century ago, smokers were portrayed in commercials and movies as heroes and heroines from all walks of life. The actors as "cool, tough guys," and

L.10.   actresses as "sophisticated dolls," puffed their way through film after film. With cigarette advertisements mushrooming in a variety of mass media, smokers had a time of portraying themselves as attractive, vigorous, and glamorous, which was often fostered by big tobacco companies. In conjunction with this trend, some high

L.15.   school students wanting to emulate their movie star idols took up smoking and passed themselves off as cool tough guys or sophisticated dolls. However, following a report issued by the Surgeon General entitled "Smoking and Health" in the mid 1960s, the smoker's glamorous image gradually began to fade into a much

C H A P T E R 4

(4) 세부사항, 묘사 : 누가, 무엇을, 어디서, 언제?

누가? : Americans

무엇을? : toxic, chemicals, nicotine, carbon monoxide, carcinogens, benzopyrene, ingredients, lung cancer, heart disease, respiratory diseases.

어디서? : In the U.S.

언제? : 1992

(5) 몇 가지 정보를 첨가하라 : Most of the deaths...is largely responsible. (Lines from 12 to 13.)

(6) 필요하다면 1 ~ 4개 정도의 이행 장치(접속사)를 포함시켜라 :

According to. (Line 10.)

세 번째 문단

나의 두 번째 요지는 부모, 선생님, 성인 공동체 구성원들과 좋은 관계를 발전시키고 유지하고픈 고등학생에게는 건설적인 이미지를 형성하는 것이 매우 중요하다는 점이다. 담배를 피지 않는 학생들은 부모, 선생님, 친척, 공동체 구성원들에게 건설적인 이미지를 보여준다. 그들은 담배를 피기에는 고등학생은 아직 어리다고 생각하기 때문이다. 반세기 전, 흡연자들은 광고와 영화에서 지위 고하를 막론하고 영웅과 여주인공으로 묘사되었다. '멋진 터프 가이' 역할을 맡은 남자 배우들과 '세련된 미녀' 역할을 맡은 여배우들은 영화가 바뀌어도 계속해서 담배 연기를 내뿜었다. 다양한 매스 미디어에서 담배 광고가 우후죽순처럼 생겨남에 따라, 흡연자들은 스스로를 매력적이고 정력적이며 매혹적으로 생각하게 되었고, 그것은 종종 거대한 담배 회사들에 의해 조장되었다. 이런 경향과 더불어, 우상으로 삼는 영화 배우를 흉내내려는 일부 고등학생들이 담배에 손을 댔고, 스스로 멋진 터프 가이나 세련된 미녀인 체했다.

그러나 1960년대 중반, 공중 위생국장이 '흡연과 건강'이라는 제목의 보고서를 발표한 이후, 흡연자의 매혹적인 이미지는 대부분 건강 관련 문제로 인해 차츰 덜 매혹적인 것으로 바뀌어가기 시작했다. 상당수의 공공 장소에 '금연' 표시가 나붙기 시작했고, 그런 장소에서의 흡연은 사회적으로 금지되었다. 이러한 변화하는 사회 환경에 발맞춰, 흡연 반대 조직들은 흡연에 반대하는 법령이나 규칙을 제정하는데 성공했다. 예를 들어, 1970년대 중반 이래로, 미국에서는 담배의 TV 광고가 금지되었고, 공공 장소에서의 금연 정책이 시행되었으며, 비흡연자들의 권리 장전(맑은 공기를 호흡할 수 있는 권리)이 도입되었다.

그 이후, 흡연자들은 '매력과는 거리가 먼' 사람으로 간주되는 경향이 있으며, 도시 범죄를 묘사한 일부 영화들은 흡연자들을 '나쁜 사람, 갱 단원, 마약 거래자, 범죄자, 이상 성격자 등'으로 묘사하였고, 그것은 결국 흡연자들에게 부정적인 이미지를 안겨주었다. 게다가 오늘날의 상업 광고들은 분별 있는 고등학생의 건설적인 이미지를, 흡연에 대해 '노'라고 말할 수 있는 사람으로 묘사하고 있다.

L.20.   less glamorous one, largely due to the health related issues.
"No Smoking" signs began to appear in many public places, and
smoking in those places became socially disapproved. In support of
this changing social phenomena, anti-smoking organizations have
been successful to make acts or regulations against smoking. For
L.25.   example, since mid-1970s, no T.V. commercial ads for tobacco
products have been allowed in the U.S.; smoking ban policy in
public places has been implemented; and, nonsmokers' Bill of
Rights (the rights to breathe clean air) are to be introduced.
Since then, smokers tend to be regarded as ·"much less glamorous,"
L.30.   and some films that depict urban crimes have portrayed smokers
as "bad guys, gangsters, drug dealers, criminals, deviants, and so on,"
which has eventually provided smokers with negative images.
Furthermore, today's commercials depict the positive image of
responsible high school students as those that say, "No" to smoking.

(1) The main idea (thesis) for the second main point:_____.

(2) The supporting facts, statistics, and examples for the first main point are:
    (a) Facts:_____.
    (b) Statistics:_____.
    (c) Example(s):_____.

(3) Related sub-point(s):_____.

(4) Details, description: Who, What, Where, When?:_____.
                    Who?:_____.
                    What?:_____.
                    Where?:_____.
                    When?: _____.

(5) Add some information: _____.

(6) Include 1~4 transitional devices (conjunctions) if necessary:_____.

C H A P T E R 4

Note

portray *v.* 1. To make a picture of. 2. To picture with use of words ; describe --The novel portray life in a small town.

sophisticated *a.* 1. Having or Showing signs of subtle or extensive knowledge or experience ; not naive or simple ; worldly-wise. 2. Very complicated or complex. 3. Appealing to knowledgeable, experienced, or refined persons. a sophisticated menu.

foster *v.* To aid the growth and development of --Concerts foster interest in music
   a. Receiving, Sharing, or giving care like that of a parent although not related by blood or adoption -- There are three foster children in our home.

glamorous *a.* Full of or characterized by fascination, allure, or excitement.

emulate *v.* To try to be the same as or better than (another person).

conjunction *n.* A word that joins other words or groups of words in a sentence. --And, or, but, and nor are conjunctions.

implement *n.* A specially made object used in doing a task or a kind of work ; tool --Plows, pitchforks, and rakes are farm implements.
   v. To carry out or put into effect. --I want to implement this plan.

depict *v.* 1. To represent in or as if in a painting 2. To represent in words.

(1) 두 번째 요지 : My second main point is...community members. (Lines from 1 to 4.)

(2) 두 번째 요지를 뒷받침하는 사실, 통계, 사례:

   (a) 사실 : Half a century ago...all walks of life. (Lines from 7 to 9.)

      ...following a report...1960s, (Lines from 17 to 18.)

      No Smoking...public places. (Line 21.)

      In support of...against smoking. (Lines from 22 to 24.)

   (b) 통계 : None(없음)

   (c) 사례: ....since mid-1970s,...to be introduced. (Lines from 25 to 28)

      ...some films... "No" to smoking. (Lines from 30 to 34.)

(3) 주제와 관련된 부수적인 강조점 :

   Those students who...to smoke. (Lines from 4 to 7.)

   Half a century ago...all walks of life. (Lines from 7 to 9.)

   However, following...health related issues. (Lines from 17 to 20.)

(4) 세부사항, 묘사 : 누가, 무엇을, 어디서, 언제?

   누가? : high school students, actors, actresses, Surgeon General, anti-smoking organizations, smokers, nonsmokers

   무엇을? : building a positive image, commercials & movies, tobacco companies, changing social phenomena, Bill of Rights, negative image, advertisements

   어디서? : In the U.S., public places

   언제? : Half a century ago, mid-1960s, since mid-1970s, today.

(5) 몇 가지 정보를 첨가하라 : No Smoking signs...to be introduced. (Lines from 21 to 28.)

(6) 필요하다면 1 ~ 4개 정도의 이행 장치(접속사)를 포함시켜라 : However. (Line 17)

The fourth paragraph:

L.1.   My third main point is that most high school students do not work. Although some of them work part-time jobs with minimum wage after school or during summer vacation, most of them are dependent on their parents' allowance for purchasing school supplies. With
L.5.   this limited allowance, it is impossible for them to purchase expensive tobacco products. In the past few years, the cost of cigarettes have nearly doubled. Three years ago in Pennsylvania, a pack of a premium brand of cigarettes could be obtained for under $1.85. Now, to purchase the same pack, it costs $3.50. If
L.10.   a student smokes two packs a day due to the addictive power of tobacco, then the average cost per day is $7, per week is $49, per month is $210, and, per year is $2,555, excluding all applicable sales tax. Are there any parents who are willing to pay this amount of money at the expense of their beloved children's health?

(1) The main idea (thesis) for the third main point:_____.

(2) The supporting facts, statistics, and examples for the first main point are:
    (a) Facts:_____.
    (b) Statistics:_____.
    (c) Example(s):_____.

(3) Related sub-point(s):_____.

(4) Details, description: Who, What, Where, When?:_____.
                 Who?:_____.
                 What?:_____.
                 Where?:_____.
                 When?: _____.

(5) Add some information:
    _____.

(6) Include 1~4 transitional devices (conjunctions) if necessary:
    _____.

In the early 1930s. smoking was considered a mark of sophistication. Today, slick advertising still lures many people to cigarettes.

네 번째 문단

　나의 세 번째 요지는 대부분의 고등학생들이 일을 하지 않는다는 점이다. 비록 일부 학생들이 방과 후 또는 여름 방학을 이용하여 최소한의 임금을 받는 시간제 노동을 하고 있긴 하지만, 대부분의 경우, 부모님이 주신 용돈으로 학용품을 구입하고 있다. 이 제한적인 용돈으로는 비싼 담배를 산다는 게 불가능하다. 지난 몇 년 동안, 담배 가격이 거의 두 배로 인상되었다. 펜실베이니아의 경우, 3년 전만 해도 1.85달러만 있으면 고급 담배를 한 갑 살 수 있었다. 지금은 똑같은 담배를 사는데 3.50달러가 필요하다. 담배의 중독성으로 인해 하루에 두 갑의 담배를 필 경우, 담배에 붙는 여타 영업세를 제외하더라도, 평균적으로 하루에 7달러, 일주일에 49달러, 한 달에 210달러, 1년에 2555달러가 든다. 이 정도의 돈을 지불해가면서 사랑스런 자녀의 건강을 희생시키려는 부모가 과연 있을까?

Cigarette manufacturers like to show active outdoor images in their advertisements to encourage people to associate cigarette smoking with successful living and good health.

(1) 세 번째 요지 :

　My third main point is that most high school students do not work. (Line 1.)

(2) 세 번째 요지를 뒷받침하는 사실, 통계, 사례:

　(a) 사실 : ...most of them...school supplies. (Lines from 3 to 4.)
　　　　　　　In the past few years...doubled. (Lines from 6 to 7.)
　(b) 통계 : Three years ago...sales tax. (Lines from 7 to 13.)
　(c) 사례 : Three years ago...sales tax. (In this case, we can consider the statistical facts as examples in rhetorical context.) (Lines from 7 to 13)

(3) 주제와 관련된 부수적인 강조점 : most of them...supplies. (Lines from 3 to 4.)
　a pack of premium brand...$1.85. (Lines from 8 to 9.)

(4) 세부사항, 묘사 : 누가, 무엇을, 어디서, 언제?
　누가? : high school students, parents
　무엇을? : tobacco products, minimum wage, the cost of cigarettes.
　어디서? : Pennsylvania, U.S. (implied in terms of context).
　언제? : In the past few years, three years ago.

(5) 몇 가지 정보를 첨가하라 :
　Although some of...tobacco products. (Lines from 2 to 6.)
　Are there...health? (Lines from 13 to 14.)

(6) 필요하다면 1 ~ 4개 정도의 이행 장치(접속사)를 포함시켜라 : Although. (Line 2)

So far, we have thoroughly seen a role model of the Introduction and the Body Paragraphs; however, this is just a model to help the writer create and structure his/her essay clearly and defensively. When writing an excellent paper, the writer should add some depth and complexity to the issue or topic. The following suggestions can be used to go below the surface and get to the core of the issue. You can use as many of the following suggestions as you like, since your essay can have a different emphasis or style that best fits your choice. However, some of the suggestions will be your favorites to be used more often.

Choose any of the following to develop each paragraph.

(1) Give an anecdote, example, maxim, or illustration related to the topic or issue.
(2) State some history or background focused on the main point of each paragraph.
(3) Use a documented quote or statistic.
(4) Use a contrasting example.
(5) Use a comparison such as metaphor, simile, or analogy.
(6) Clearly define your main point and its connection to the issue.
(7) Include a sequence list of events or things.
(8) Offer a short-term implication.
(9) Offer a long-term implication.
(10) Give the pros and cons.
(11) Ask yourself: "Who cares?" and write the response.
(12) Ask yourself: "So what?" and add in your response.
(13) Predict the future effect based on the main point.
(14) Use data from other areas such as anthropology, arts, economics, education, government, politics, law, chemistry, linguistics, literature, science, sociology, health, psychology, etc.,

지금까지 서론과 본론의 역할 모델을 자세히 살펴보았다. 그러나 이것은 그저 작가가 좀더 명확하고 조리 있게 글을 쓸 수 있게 하기 위한 하나의 모델에 불과하다. 훌륭한 글을 쓸 때, 작가는 논의할 문제나 주제에 대해 다소간의 깊이와 정교함을 덧붙여야 한다. 다음에 제시한 방법들은 좀더 깊이 들어가 문제의 핵심에 닿으려 할 때 쓰이곤 한다. 당신은 다음에 제시된 방법들을 원하는대로 다 쓸 수 있다. 글에 따라 각자의 선택과 가장 잘 어울리는 강조점이나 스타일이 다를 수 있기 때문이다. 그러나 게 중에는 당신이 선호하는 방법들이 생기게 될 것이다.

다음 중에서 각 문단을 전개시켜나갈 방법을 선택하라.

(1) 주제 또는 문제와 관련된 일화, 사례, 금언, 삽화 등을 삽입하라.

(2) 각 문단의 요지에 초점을 맞춘 일종의 역사 또는 배경을 서술하라.

(3) 문서화된 인용문이나 통계를 이용하라.

(4) 대조되는 사례를 이용하라.

(5) 은유, 직유, 유추 등과 같은 비유를 사용하라.

(6) 요지 및 요지와 문제와의 연관성을 분명히 밝혀라.

(7) 사건이나 상황의 전개 과정을 포함시켜라.

(8) 단기적인 암시를 이용하라.

(9) 장기적인 암시를 이용하라.

(10) 찬반양론을 제시하라.

(11) 자기 자신에게 '이게 무슨 상관이야?' 라고 묻고, 그 답을 적어라.

(12) 자기 자신에게 '그래서 어쨌다구?' 라고 묻고, 그에 대한 당신의 반응을 덧붙여라.

(13) 요지에 근거하여 미래의 효과를 예측하라.

(14) 인류학, 미술, 경제학, 교육, 정부, 정치학, 법, 화학, 언어학, 문학, 과학, 사회학, 건강, 심리학 등과 같은 여러 분야의 데이터를 이용하라.

4.1.3. Conclusion

Section 4.1. Structure, states that the conclusion as the final paragraph should restate the importance, significance, or purpose of the essay by tying all your major ideas together. The conclusion can be a few sentences, or it can be a whole paragraph. In either case, it should tell your readers that you have completed your essay, instead of leaving it behind. A good way to make a conclusion is by recalling the purpose of the essay and the information set forth to develop the topic/issue. Meanwhile, the conclusion should not merely repeat the introduction what the readers have already read in the essay. Rather, it should include a final statement that is an outgrowth of the points discussed in the body, so that the readers may get a final impression of your topic.

Read the following suggestions and choose a style/styles of your favorite.

Basic/defensive level for drawing a conclusion.

(1) Summarize all the major points stated in the essay.
(2) Restate the major points in different words.
(3) Restate the major points and give a thought or possibility for the readers to ponder.
(4) Offer a solution or make a recommendation.
(5) State where you are now after all the discussion.

Advanced/sophisticated level for drawing a conclusion

(6) Offer a new or unique solution or recommendation.
(7) Argue against, deny, or ridicule a belief, myth, or statement of fact.
(8) Make an educated or insightful prediction.
(9) Call for an action by a group or individual.
(10) Ask a deeper and probing question about the topic/issue.
(11) Use a relevant quotation to make the ending.
(12) Finish the essay with humor, satire, exaggeration, paradox, or irony, so as to make the conclusion creative or impressive.
(13) Quote the leading experts or organizations along with their current views on the topic/issue.

CHAPTER 4

4.1.3. 결론

4.1. 구조 부분에서 언급했듯이, 결론으로 기능하는 마지막 문단은 가능한 모든 아이디어를 종합해서 그 글의 중요성이나 의미, 또는 목적을 재차 밝혀야 한다. 결론은 몇 문장에 그칠 수도 있고, 문단 전체를 차지할 수도 있다. 어떤 경우든, 당신이 글을 그냥 뒤에 남겨놓고 가는 것이 아니라 완전히 끝마쳤다는 사실을 독자에게 밝혀야 한다. 결론을 내리는 좋은 방법 중 하나는 글의 목적과 주제/문제를 전개시키는데 사용한 정보를 상기시키는 것이다. 그런데 결론은 독자들이 이미 본문에서 읽은 도입부를 단순히 반복하는 것이어서는 안 된다. 도리어 독자들이 글의 주제에 대해 최종적인 인상을 받을 수 있도록, 본론에서 논의된 점들의 자연적 부산물로서 최종 진술을 담고 있어야 한다.

다음에 제시된 방법들을 읽고, 원하는 스타일을 선택하라.

결론을 이끌어내는 기본적/방어적 단계

(1) 글에서 밝힌 주요한 점들을 모두 요약하라.
(2) 주요한 점들을 표현만 바꿔서 재차 밝혀라.
(3) 주요한 점들을 재차 밝히고, 독자들이 생각해볼 의견이나 가능성을 덧붙여라.
(4) 해결책을 제시하거나 조언을 던져라.
(5) 모든 논의를 마친 후의 당신의 견해를 밝혀라.

결론을 이끌어내는 발전된/정교한 단계

(6) 새롭거나 독특한 해결책 또는 조언을 제시하라.
(7) 신념이나 신화 또는 진술된 사실에 대해 논쟁을 걸거나 부인하거나 비하하라.
(8) 근거 있는 예측 또는 통찰력 있는 예측을 제시하라.
(9) 그룹 또는 개인의 조치를 요구하라.
(10) 주제/문제에 대해 좀더 깊이 있고 예리한 질문을 던져라.
(11) 관련된 인용문을 사용하여 결론을 내려라.
(12) 결론이 좀더 창조적이거나 인상적으로 보일 수 있도록 유머, 풍자, 과장, 역설, 아이러니 등으로 글을 맺어라.
(13) 주제/문제에 대한 권위자 또는 조직의 최근 견해를 인용하라.

Based on the suggestions above, the conclusion related to the specific topic, "The smoking habit of high school students," is to be generated as follows:

Line 1   Smoking, as we have seen, does not offer any benefits at all
to the high school students who have chosen to risk their invaluable
lives, to tarnish their cool and positive appearances, and to throw their
parents' hard earned money out of the window. Smoking is a habit

L.5   that is definitely breakable. It is never unbreakable at all. It is just a
matter of choice. It is a choice between life or death, cool or ugly
appearance, and worthwhile or worthless spending of money.
Therefore, the answer is simple, and the choice is crystal clear.
Quit smoking right now.

1. "Smoking, as we have seen, ... out of the window." Lines from 1 to 4 satisfy the statements of (1) "Summarize all the major points stated," and, (2) "Restate the major points in different words."

2. "Smoking is a habit... It is never unbreakable... It is just a matter... It is a choice between... of money." Lines from 4 to 7 meet the statements of (3) "Restate the major points and give a thought for the readers to ponder," and, (4) "Offer a solution or make a recommendation."

3. Therefore, the answer is ... Quit smoking right now." Lines from 8 to 9 can satisfy the statement of (9) "Call for an action by a group or individual."

So far, we have seen an essay exemplified and illustrated based on a basic structure of the introduction, the body, and the conclusion. This type of essay called "The Five Paragraph Format," is provided below for review.

Why do so many high school students pick up the habit of smoking these days?
This is a very negative social phenomenon developing in our school communities, from which our high school students should free themselves. This issue is to be discussed based on three perspectives: (1) the health related problems; (2) the image building; and, (3) the cost of purchasing tobacco products.

My first main point is that smoking plays a key role in causing health problems.
With each puff of a cigarette, scientists identify more than 3,000 different toxic, or poisonous chemicals. A cigarette that contains nicotine, carbon monoxide (a poisonous gas), carcinogens (substances that cause cancer), benzopyrene (one of the deadliest carcinogens), and a variety of harmful ingredients is actually a highly complex, and potentially lethal, chemical factory. This lethal factory producing carbon monoxide, benzopyrene, carcinogens and multifarious additives is responsible for the deaths of not only smokers, but of non-smokers as well.

위의 방법에 근거해 볼 때, "고등학생의 흡연 습관"이라는 특정한 주제와 관련하여 다음과 같은 결론을 내릴 수 있다.

앞에서 살펴보았듯이, 흡연은 소중한 삶을 위험에 빠뜨리며, 멋지고 건설적인 모습을 흐트러뜨리고, 부모님이 열심히 일해서 번 돈을 어이없이 내던지게 하는 등, 고등학생들에게 아무런 혜택도 주지 않는다. 흡연은 분명히 깨뜨릴 수 있는 습관이다. 결코 깨뜨릴 수 없는 습관이 아닌 것이다. 단지 선택의 문제일 뿐이다. 그것은 삶과 죽음, 멋진 모습과 추한 모습, 가치 있는 소비와 아무 쓸모 없는 소비 사이의 선택이다. 따라서 대답은 간단하며, 선택은 명백하다. 지금 당장 담배를 끊어라.

1. "앞에서 살펴보았듯이... 주지 않는다."라는 문장은 〈(1) 글에서 밝힌 주요한 점들을 모두 요약하라〉와 〈(2) 주요한 점들을 표현만 바꿔서 재차 밝혀라.〉라는 방법을 만족시키고 있다.
2. "흡연은 분명히... 단지 선택의 문제일 뿐이다.. 선택이다."라는 부분은 〈(3) 주요한 점들을 재차 밝히고, 독자들이 생각해볼 의견이나 가능성을 덧붙여라.〉와 〈(4) 해결책을 제시하거나 조언을 던져라.〉를 만족시키고 있다.
3. "따라서, 대답은... 끊어라."라는 부분은 〈(9) 그룹 또는 개인의 조치를 요구하라.〉의 지시와 맞닿는 내용을 담고 있다.

지금까지 서론, 본론, 결론이라는 기본 구조에 근거하여 모범이 되는 에세이를 살펴보았다. '다섯 단락 구성'이라 불리는 이런 유형의 에세이를 다시 한 번 음미해보기로 하자.

이즈음 상당수의 고등학생들이 흡연 습관에 빠져드는 까닭은 무엇일까? 이것은 우리의 학교 공동체에서 전개되고 있는 매우 부정적인 사회 현상으로서, 우리 고등학생들은 응당 거기에서 벗어나야 한다. 이 문제는 (1) 건강 관련 문제, (2) 이미지 형성, (3) 담배 구매 비용이라는 세 가지 관점에서 논의되어야 한다.

나의 첫 번째 요지는 흡연이 건강을 악화시키는데 결정적인 역할을 한다는 점이다. 학자들은 담배 연기 한 모금 한 모금에 각각 3,000가지 이상의 유독하거나 유해한 화학 물질이 함유되어 있다는 사실을 입증하고 있다. 니코틴, 일산화탄소(유독 가스), 발암성 물질(암을 일으키는 물질), 벤조피렌(치명적인 발암 물질 가운데 하나) 외에도 온갖 해로운 성분을 함유하고 있는 담배 한 대는 실제로 아주 복잡한 그리고 잠재적으로 치명적인 화학 공장이라 할 수 있다. 일산화탄소와 벤조피렌, 발암성 물질, 온갖 잡다한 첨가물 등을 생산하는 이 치명적인 공장은 흡연자뿐 아니라 비흡연자에게도 악영향을 끼친다. 미국의 경우, 사망 및 육체적 고통과 밀접한 관련을 가진 단일한 원인으로는 흡연이 단연 선두를 차지하고 있다. 공중 위생국장이 1992년 제출한 보고서에 따르면, 흡연은 매년 450,000명의 미국인을 죽음으로 내몰았다고 한다. 사망 원인은 대부분 흡연으로 야기되는 폐암, 심장 질환, 호흡기 질환 등과 관련이 있다.

In the United States, more deaths and physical sufferings are closely related to smoking than any other single cause. According to a report presented by the Surgeon General, 1992, smoking contributed to the deaths of some 450,000 Americans every year. Most of the deaths are related to lung cancer, heart disease, and respiratory diseases for which smoking is largely responsible.

My second main point is that building a positive image is very important for high school students who would like to develop and maintain good relations with their parents, teachers, and adult community members. Those students who smoke hardly present positive images to their parents, teachers, adult relatives, and the community members, because they think that high school students are still too young to smoke. Half a century ago, smokers were portrayed in commercials and movies as heroes and heroines from all walks of life. The actors as "cool, tough guys," and actresses as "sophisticated dolls," puffed their way through film after film. With cigarette advertisements mushrooming in a variety of mass media, smokers had a time of portraying themselves as attractive, vigorous, and glamorous, which was often fostered by big tobacco companies. In conjunction with this trend, some high school students wanting to emulate their movie star idols took up smoking and passed themselves off as cool tough guys or sophisticated dolls. However, following a report issued by the Surgeon General entitled "Smoking and Health" in the mid 1960s, the smoker's glamorous image gradually began to fade into a much less glamorous one, largely due to the health related issues."No Smoking" signs began to appear in many public places, and smoking in those places became socially disapproved. In support of this changing social phenomena, anti-smoking organizations have been successful to make acts or regulations against smoking. For example, since mid-1970s, no T.V. commercial ads for tobacco products have been allowed in the U.S.; smoking ban policy in public places has been implemented; and, nonsmokers' Bill of Rights (the rights to breathe clean air) are to be introduced.

Since then, smokers tend to be regarded as "much less glamorous," and some films that depict urban crimes have portrayed smokers as "bad guys, gangsters, drug dealers, criminals, deviants, and so on," which has eventually provided smokers with negative images. Furthermore, today's commercials depict the positive image of responsible high school students as those that say, "No" to smoking.

My third main point is that most high school students do not work. Although some of them work part-time jobs with minimum wage after school or during summer vacation, most of them are dependent on their parents' allowance for purchasing school supplies. With this limited allowance, it is impossible for them to purchase expensive tobacco products. In the past few years, the cost of cigarettes have nearly doubled. Three years ago in Pennsylvania, a pack of a premium brand of cigarettes could be obtained for under $1.85. Now, to purchase the same pack, it costs $3.50. If a student smokes two packs a day due to the addictive power of tobacco, then the average cost per day is $7, per week is $49, per month is $210, and, per year is $2555, excluding all applicable sales tax. Are there any parents who are willing to pay this amount of money at the expense of their beloved children's health?

Smoking, as we have seen, does not offer any benefits at all to the high school students who have chosen to risk their invaluable lives, to tarnish their cool and positive appearances, and to throw their parents' hard earned money out of the window. Smoking is a habit that is definitely breakable. It is never unbreakable at all. It is just a matter of choice. It is a choice between life or death, cool or ugly appearance, and worthwhile or worthless spending of money. Therefore, the answer is simple, and the choice is crystal clear. Quit smoking right now.

　나의 두 번째 요지는 부모, 선생님, 성인 공동체 구성원들과 좋은 관계를 발전시키고 유지하고픈 고등학생에게는 건설적인 이미지를 형성하는 것이 매우 중요하다는 점이다. 담배를 피지 않는 학생들은 부모, 선생님, 친척, 공동체 구성원들에게 건설적인 이미지를 보여준다. 그들은 담배를 피기에는 고등학생은 아직 어리다고 생각하기 때문이다. 반세기 전, 흡연자들은 광고와 영화에서 지위 고하를 막론하고 영웅과 여주인공으로 묘사되었다. '멋진 터프 가이' 역할을 맡은 남자 배우들과 '세련된 미녀' 역할을 맡은 여배우들은 영화가 바뀌어도 계속해서 담배 연기를 내뿜었다. 다양한 매스 미디어에서 담배 광고가 우후죽순처럼 생겨남에 따라, 흡연자들은 스스로를 매력적이고 정력적이며 매혹적으로 생각하게 되었고, 그것은 종종 거대한 담배 회사들에 의해 조장되었다. 이런 경향과 더불어, 우상으로 삼는 영화 배우를 흉내내려는 일부 고등학생들이 담배에 손을 댔고, 스스로 멋진 터프 가이나 세련된 미녀인 체했다. 그러나 1960년대 중반, 공중 위생국장이 '흡연과 건강' 이라는 제목의 보고서를 발표한 이후, 흡연자의 매혹적인 이미지는 대부분 건강 관련 문제로 인해 차츰 덜 매혹적인 것으로 바뀌어가기 시작했다. 상당수의 공공 장소에 '금연' 표시가 나붙기 시작했고, 그런 장소에서의 흡연은 사회적으로 금지되었다. 이러한 변화하는 사회 환경에 발맞춰, 흡연 반대 조직들은 흡연에 반대하는 법령이나 규칙을 제정하는데 성공했다. 예를 들어, 1970년대 중반 이래로, 미국에서는 담배의 TV 광고가 금지되었고, 공공 장소에서의 금연 정책이 시행되었으며, 비흡연자들의 권리 장전(맑은 공기를 호흡할 수 있는 권리)이 도입되었다. 그 이후, 흡연자들은 '매력과는 거리가 먼' 사람으로 간주되는 경향이 있으며, 도시 범죄를 묘사한 일부 영화들은 흡연자들을 '나쁜 사람, 갱 단원, 마약 거래자, 범죄자, 이상 성격자 등'으로 묘사하였고, 그것은 결국 흡연자들에게 부정적인 이미지를 안겨주었다. 게다가 오늘날의 상업 광고들은 분별 있는 고등학생의 건설적인 이미지를, 흡연에 대해 '노' 라고 말할 수 있는 사람으로 묘사하고 있다.

　나의 세 번째 요지는 대부분의 고등학생이 일을 하지 않는다는 점이다. 비록 일부 학생들이 방과 후 또는 여름 방학을 이용하여 최소한의 임금을 받는 시간제 노동을 하고 있긴 하지만, 대부분의 경우, 부모님이 주신 용돈으로 학용품을 구입하고 있다. 이 제한적인 용돈으로는 비싼 담배를 산다는 게 불가능하다. 지난 몇 년 동안, 담배 가격이 거의 두 배로 인상되었다. 펜실베이니아의 경우, 3년 전만 해도 1.85달러만 있으면 고급 담배를 한 갑 살 수 있었다. 지금은 똑같은 담배를 사는데 3.50달러가 필요하다. 담배의 중독성으로 인해 하루에 두 갑의 담배를 필 경우, 담배에 붙는 여타 영업세를 제외하더라도, 평균적으로 하루에 7달러, 일주일에 49달러, 한 달에 210달러, 1년에 2555달러가 든다. 이 정도의 돈을 지불해가면서 사랑스런 자녀의 건강을 희생시키려는 부모가 과연 있을까?

　앞에서 살펴보았듯이, 흡연은 소중한 삶을 위험에 빠뜨리며, 멋지고 건설적인 모습을 흐트러뜨리고, 부모님이 열심히 일해서 번 돈을 어이없이 내던지게 하는 등, 고등학생들에게 아무런 혜택도 주지 않는다. 흡연은 분명히 깨뜨릴 수 있는 습관이다. 결코 깨뜨릴 수 없는 습관이 아닌 것이다. 단지 선택의 문제일 뿐이다. 그것은 삶과 죽음, 멋진 모습과 추한 모습, 가치 있는 소비와 아무 쓸모 없는 소비 사이의 선택이다. 따라서 대답은 간단하며, 선택은 명백하다. 지금 당장 담배를 끊어라.

We have studied a basic structure of an essay in the previous section, 4.1. Structure. In this section, 4.2. Types, we will see a

variety of essay types such as (1) Descriptive; (2) Expository; (3) Informative; (4) Narrative; (5) Personal; (6) Persuasive; and, (7) Research Paper in terms of their purposes and elements (what they are used for) First, read the following guidelines that define major purposes and elements of each essay type. Next, we will read a variety of models related to the types written by well-known writers or celebrities in the following section.

4.2 Types

Guidelines for Major Purposes and Elements of Each Essay Type

1. Descriptive:

(A) Purposes:
    (1) To describe a person, place, object, or situation.
    (2) To create a picture in writing so as to help readers see "details." (See (8) in Elements).
    (3) To describe specific characters of a person, or group(s).
    (4) To show readers how the topic looks, sounds, smells, tastes, & feels.

(B) Elements:
    (1) Use vivid & specific verbs & nouns.
    (2) Describe from vantage points.
    (3) Observing & taking notes.
    (4) Organize "details" in spatial order, or order of importance, whichever is more appropriate.
    (5) Write a topic sentence, & decide it'll be more effective positioned at the beginning or the end.
    (6) Gather & use as many good realistic details (color, size, appearance, sounds, tastes, smells) as you can.
    (7) Check the beginning & ending. The beginning should attract your readers to the description; the ending should bring the description to a natural stopping point.
    (8) To describe "details" for a target object, for example, (a) Define the type of object (tool, tree, wind) and its relationship to you; (b) Describe its physical parts (appearance, feature); (c) Compare it with others like it; (d) Determine how it is used or what its purpose is; (e) Analyze it (when it was discovered, built, first used, its strengths, and weaknesses); and, (f) Evaluate the importance of the object to you and others, or its place in the world.
    (9) Use specific words & figurative language effectively.
    (10) Make sure that the tone of the description is consistent.
    (11) Make sure that the description presents a clear emphasis or a main impression.
        Include 1~4 transitional devices (conjunctions) if necessary.

지금 까지 에세이의 기본 구조에 대해 공부했다. 이제부터는 (1) 묘사, (2) 설명, (3) 정보 제공, (4) 나레이션, (5) 사적인 이야기, (6) 설득, 그리고 (7) 연구 논문 등과 같은 에세이의 다양한 유형을 각각의 목적과 구성 요소라는 차원에서 살펴보기로 하겠다. 일단 에세이 각각의 유형별 주요 목적과 구성 요소를 정의한 아래의 지침을 읽어 보아라. 그리고 나서 다음 파트에서 각각의 유형과 관련된 유명 작가나 명사가 쓴 다양한 글을 살펴보기로 하겠다.

4.2. 에세이의 유형

각 에세이 유형별 주요한 목적 및 구성 요소

1. 묘사

(A) 목적 :

(1) 사람, 장소, 대상, 상황 등을 묘사한다.

(2) 독자들이 '세부사항' 을 볼 수 있도록 글로써 한 폭의 그림을 창조한다.

(3) 사람 또는 집단의 구체적인 캐릭터를 묘사한다.

(4) 독자들에게 시각적, 청각적, 후각적, 미각적, 촉각적으로 주제의 모습을 보여준다.

(B) 구성 요소 :

(1) 생생하고 구체적인 동사와 명사를 사용하라.

(2) 자신의 관점에서 묘사하라.

(3) 빈틈없고 흥미로운 묘사

(4) 공간적 순서든 중요도 순서든 보다 적절한 것을 선택하여 그 순서에 따라 '세부사항' 을 조직하라.

(5) 주제문을 쓰고, 그 주제문을 문두에 넣는 것이 나을지 문미에 넣는 것이 나을지 결정하라.

(6) 현실적인 세부사항들(색상, 크기, 모양, 소리, 맛, 냄새)을 가능한 한 많이 모아서 사용하라.

(7) 시작과 끝을 점검하라. 시작은 독자들로 하여금 묘사에 흥미를 느낄 수 있게 해야 하고, 끝은 그 묘사를 자연스런 귀착지로 끌어들여야 한다.

(8) 목표로 하는 대상의 '세부사항' 을 묘사하려면, 예를 들어, (a) 대상의 유형(연장, 나무, 바람) 및 대상과 당신과의 관계를 정의하고, (b) 대상의 물리적 부분(모양, 특징)을 묘사하며, (c) 그 대상을 그와 유사한 다른 것들과 비교하고, (d) 그것이 어떻게 사용되는지, 또는 그것의 목적이 무엇인지 결정하며, (e) 대상을 분석하고(그 대상이 발견되고 지어지고 처음 사용된 시기는 언제인지, 대상의 장점과 약점은 무엇인지 등), (f) 당신을 비롯한 여타 사람들에게 미치는 그 대상이 지니는 중요성이나 세계사적 위치 등을 평가한다.

(9) 구체적인 단어와 비유적인 표현을 효과적으로 사용하라.

(10) 묘사의 기조가 일관성을 잃지 않도록 하라.

(11) 묘사가 뚜렷한 강조점이나 지배적인 인상을 표현하도록 하라.(필요하다면 1~4개의 이행장치를 포함시켜라.)

2. Expository:

(A) Purposes:
  (1) To explain, interpret, or make a detailed statement.
  (2) To inform & explain the facts based on (a) process; (b) cause & effect; (c) comparison & contrast; (d) definition; (e) classification; and, (f) problem & solution.
  (3) To present information that should be accurate & understandable to readers.
  (4) To share facts, ideas, definitions, & directions with readers.
  (5) To share worthwhile information (i.e. giving directions, presenting facts, defining or identifying, comparing or giving reasons).

(B) Elements:
  (1) Use exact action verbs.
  (2) Avoid using sentence fragments.
  (3) Consider your target audience, their age, interest, & educational level.
  (4) When explaining a process, use such steps as (a) investigate, (b) observe, (c) arrange, (d) elaborate, (e) polish, & (f) review.
  (5) Use examples for comparison & contrast, cause & effect, definition or explanation to support the main idea.
  (6) Compare two persons, things, or ideas.
  (7) Explain why something happens.
  (8) Present your information in an accurate and clear way so that your readers can fully appreciate what you have said.
  (9) Make sure the topic is made clear with plenty of good details.
  (10) Make sure that the introduction captures reader's attention, and establishes the focus of the essay to be discussed.
  (11) Make sure that the essay is organized in a clear & easy-to-read way.
  (12) Make sure that the conclusion brings a satisfactory end.

3. Informative:

(A) Purposes:
  (1) To present factual information about one topic.
  (2) To explain "how to."
  (3) To give directions.
  (4) To answer questions, "who, what, when, how, where?"
  (5) To make something easier to understand.

(B) Elements:
  (1) Organize information into paragraphs that deal with one subject.
  (2) Introduce the main idea clearly with a topic sentence.
  (3) Include details & examples that support the topic sentence.
  (4) Use a concluding sentence that sums up the main idea.
  (5) Use smooth & logical transitions between paragraphs.

2. 설명

(A) 목적 :

(1) 설명, 해석 또는 세부적인 언급.

(2) (a) 과정, (b) 원인과 결과, (c) 비교와 대조, (d) 정의, (e) 분류, (f) 문제와 해답 등에 근거하여 사실을 알리고 설명한다.

(3) 독자들에게 정확하고 이해할 수 있을 만한 정보를 제시한다.

(4) 사실, 생각, 정의, 방향 등을 독자들과 공유한다.

(5) 가치 있는 정보를 공유한다.(예를 들어, 방향을 알려주고, 사실을 제시하며, 정의 또는 증명하고, 비교하거나 이유를 밝히는 것)

(B) 구성 요소 :

(1) 정확한 행위 동사를 사용하라.

(2) 불완전한 비문장을 사용하지 말라.

(3) 대상으로 삼을 독자를 설정하고, 그들의 나이, 관심사, 교육 수준 등을 고려하라.

(4) 과정을 설명할 때는 (a) 조사, (b) 관찰, (c) 정리, (d) 정교화, (e) 마무리, (f) 재검토 등의 단계를 사용하라.

(5) 주제를 뒷받침하기 위해 비교와 대조, 원인과 결과, 정의 또는 설명 등의 사례를 사용하라.

(6) 두 사람, 두 가지 상황, 두 가지 생각 등을 비교하라.

(7) 어떤 일이 일어난 이유를 설명하라.

(8) 글에서 말하고 있는 바를 독자들이 완전히 이해할 수 있도록 정확하고 분명하게 정보를 제시하라.

(9) 타당성 있는 세부자료를 많이 사용하여 주제를 명확히 하라.

(10) 서두는 독자의 관심을 끌 수 있어야 하며 이후에 논의될 글의 초점을 잡는 자리로 삼아라.

(11) 글은 분명하고 읽기 쉬운 방식으로 구성하라.

(12) 결론은 만족스런 결말을 끌어낼 수 있게 하라.

3. 정보 제공

(A) 목적 :

(1) 한 가지 주제에 대해 사실적인 정보를 제시한다.

(2) '방법적 측면' 을 설명한다.

(3) 방향을 제시한다.

(4) '누가, 무엇을, 언제, 어떻게, 어디서?' 라는 질문에 답한다.

(5) 이해하기 쉽게 한다.

(B) 구성 요소 :

(1) 한 가지 주제를 다루는 문단 안에 정보를 조직적으로 담아라.

(2) 주제문에 요지를 명확히 삽입하라.

(3) 주제문을 뒷받침하는 세부 사항 및 사례를 포함시켜라.

(4) 요지를 요약하는 마무리 문장을 사용하라.

(5) 문단 사이에는 매끄럽고 논리적인 이행 장치를 사용하라.

(6) Make sure that the introduction captures the reader's attention.

(7) Include all important information.

(8) Make sure that the essay brings a satisfactory end.

4. Narrative:

(A) Purposes:

(1) To tell what happened.

(2) To give a history of something.

(3) To narrate an account of an event.

(4) To describe something important based on the focused events & their significance.

(B) Elements:

(1) Use specific nouns, vivid verbs, precise adjectives to help readers share your excitement, sorrow, frustration, or anger.

(2) Use a chronological order or an order of importance, whichever is more appropriate.

(3) The narrative includes a plot, character, setting, & point of view.

(4) Give details in order using a beginning, middle, & end.

(5) Put yourself in the story.

(6) Don't use the same word over and over, especially, at the beginning of your sentences.

(7) Make sure the experience is described in a clear, yet colorful way.

(8) Consider basic elements such as (a) purpose of writing (to make readers smile, laugh, cry, ponder); (b) voice (Does the writing have the same enthusiasm & energy as if you are actually talking?); (c) audience (Have you written for specific readers?); (d) characters (Do your readers really get to know the people in your story?); (e) setting (Do your readers see & feel the setting of your story?); (f) dialogue (Have you used actual dialogue effectively?); (g) digression (Have you stretched your story in all possible directions to make your narrative more interesting & complete?); (h) personal thoughts & comments (Have you presented your comments or thoughts as they might have been at the time the narrative actually took place?); (i) figures of speech (Have you used any metaphors, similes, or personification to create effective images or word pictures for readers?); and, (j) purpose again (Does your narrative succeed in making your readers smile, laugh, or ponder?).

5. Personal:

(A) Purposes:

(1) To tell a real-life story that comes directly from your own experience.

(2) To express your feelings or thoughts about an experience that was/is significant to you.

(3) To reveal the feelings of the people who took part in the event.

(6) 서문은 독자의 흥미를 끌 수 있게 하라.

(7) 중요한 정보는 모두 포함시켜라.

(8) 글 전체를 만족스런 결말로 이끌어라.

4. 나레이션

(A) 목적 :

(1) 사건을 말한다.

(2) 어떤 것의 변천사를 말한다.

(3) 어떤 사건의 전말을 이야기한다.

(4) 초점이 된 사건 및 그 사건의 의미에 근거하여 중요한 점을 기술한다.

(B) 구성 요소 :

(1) 구체적인 명사, 생생한 동사, 정확한 형용사를 사용하여 독자들이 당신의 흥분, 슬픔, 좌절, 분노 등을 공유할 수 있게 하라.

(2) 연대기 순이든 중요도 순이든 적절한 순서를 사용하라.

(3) 이야기 속에 줄거리, 등장 인물, 무대 장치, 관점 등을 포함시켜라.

(4) 시작, 중간, 끝 등을 사용하여 순서에 따라 세부사항을 제시하라.

(5) 이야기 속에 당신 자신을 넣어라.

(6) 특히 문장을 시작할 때 똑같은 단어를 반복해서 사용하지 말라.

(7) 선명하면서도 다채롭게 경험을 묘사하라.

(8) 다음과 같은 기본적인 요소를 고려하라 : (a) 글쓰기의 목적(독자를 미소짓게 하고, 웃게 하고, 울게 하고, 생각하게 하는 것), (b) 음색(글에 당신이 직접 말할 때와 똑같은 열정과 에너지가 담겨 있는가?), (c) 청중(특정한 독자들을 위해 글을 썼는가?), (d) 등장 인물(독자들은 정말 당신의 이야기 속에 나오는 사람들을 알게 될까?), (e) 무대 장치(독자들은 당신의 이야기에 등장하는 주위 환경을 보고 느낄 수 있을까?), (f) 대화(실제 대화를 효과적으로 사용했는가?), (g) 지엽적인 이야기(이야기를 보다 흥미롭고 완전하게 하기 위해 가능한 모든 방향으로 이야기를 확장시켰는가?), (h) 개인적인 생각과 논평(당신의 생각이나 논평을 마치 이야기가 실제로 일어나는 순간에 그랬던 것처럼 표현했는가?), (i) 말의 형상(독자들에게 직접 다가설 수 있는 효과적인 이미지를 창조하거나 그림을 보는 듯한 서술을 위해 은유나 미소, 또는 의인화를 사용했는가?), (j) 목적의 재확인(당신의 이야기가 독자를 미소짓게 하거나 웃게 하거나 생각하게 하는데 성공했는가?)

5. 사적인 이야기

(A) 목적 :

(1) 당신 자신의 경험에서 나오는 실생활의 이야기를 말한다.

(2) 당신에게 중요했던/중요한 경험에 대해 당신의 느낌이나 생각을 표현한다.

(3) 그 사건에 참여한 사람들의 느낌을 밝힌다.

(4) 살면서 겪은 중요한 사건 및 그 사건의 의미에 근거하여 뭔가 중요한 점을 쓴다.

(4) To write something important based on the focused events of your life & their significance.

(B) Elements:
(1) Write in the first person pronoun: "I, me,my."
(2) Use vivid verbs & nouns to describe feelings & the events.
(3) Enliven your narrative with specific facts & details.
(4) Maintain 1st-person point of view.
(5) Use a beginning that captures the reader's attention.
(6) Draw a conclusion that explains what the experience meant to you.
(7) Describe the events in chronological order.
(8) Portray events, people, & places vividly.
(9) Make sure that the tone is friendly, honest, & informal.
(10) Show the experience rather than tell about it.

6. Persuasive:

(A) Purposes:
(1) To persuade your readers to agree with your point of view.
(2) To convince your readers of your value, belief, or attitude.
(3) To sell your ideas or products.
(4) To take a side on an issue.
(5) To persuade your readers to take some actions.
(6) To present your ideas clearly & convincingly based on logical or believable statements, instead of misleading, exaggerated, or only partial true idea.

(B) Elements:
(1) Introduce the issue while giving any background needed to help readers understand it fully.
(2) Take your position early in a clear, direct thesis statement.
(3) Support your position by giving convincing facts, strong reasons, & clear examples to respond to opposing points.
(4) Save your strongest fact, reason, or examples for last.
(5) Summarize your ideas & give a clear call to action as a conclusion.
(6) Make your concluding sentence strong or impressive so that your opinion can be memorable.
(7) Make sure that your opinions are clearly stated.
(8) Include appropriate emotional, logical, or ethical appeals, or reasons & evidence to convince your readers.
(9) Check if all of the reasons are strong, and the line of reasoning is clear & easy for readers to follow.
(10) Make sure that the first or two sentences capture the reader's attention.
(11) Make your conclusion be effective.

(B) 구성 요소 :

(1) 1인칭 대명사 '나'를 사용하라.

(2) 감정과 사건을 묘사하는데 생생한 동사와 명사를 사용하라.

(3) 구체적인 사실과 세부 사항으로 이야기에 생기를 주어라.

(4) 1인칭 시점을 유지하라.

(5) 시작 부분에서 독자의 주의를 끌어라.

(6) 그 경험이 당신에게 무엇을 의미하는지 설명하는 결론을 끌어내라.

(7) 연대기 순으로 사건을 서술하라.

(8) 사건, 사람, 장소 등을 생생하게 묘사하라.

(9) 어조는 정답고 솔직하며 구어체를 사용하라.

(10) 경험에 대해 이야기하기보다는 그 경험을 보여주어라.

6. 설득

(A) 목적 :

(1) 당신의 견해에 동의하도록 독자를 설득한다.

(2) 당신의 가치, 신념, 태도 등에 대해 독자들을 납득시킨다.

(3) 당신의 아이디어나 상품을 판다.

(4) 어떤 문제에 대해 한쪽 편을 든다.

(5) 독자들에게 모종의 조치를 취하라고 설득한다.

(6) 독자를 현혹시키거나 과장된 생각 또는 부분적으로만 옳은 생각이 아니라 논리적이거나 신뢰할 만한 제안에 근거하여 당신의 생각을 분명하고 설득력 있게 제시한다.

(B) 구성 요소 :

(1) 독자들이 충분히 이해할 수 있도록 이러저러한 배경 설명과 아울러 문제를 소개하라.

(2) 분명하고 직접적인 논제 서술을 통해 일찌감치 당신의 입장을 밝혀라.

(3) 반대되는 사실에 대응할 수 있는 설득력 있는 사실, 강력한 근거, 분명한 사례를 제시함으로써 당신의 입장을 뒷받침하라.

(4) 가장 강력한 사실이나 근거, 또는 사례를 마지막 순간을 위해 남겨두어라.

(5) 당신의 생각을 요약하고 결론에서 분명한 조치를 요구하라.

(6) 당신의 견해가 인상깊이 박히도록 결론이 담긴 문장은 강하게 표현하라.

(7) 당신의 견해를 분명하게 밝혀라.

(8) 독자들을 설득하기 위해서는 적절한 정서적, 논리적, 또는 윤리적 호소나 근거, 그리고 증거를 포함시켜라.

(9) 모든 근거가 설득력 있는지 점검하고, 논증 부분은 독자들이 잘 이해할 수 있도록 분명하고 쉽게 써라.

(10) 처음 한두 문장은 독자의 주의를 끌 수 있게 하라.

(11) 인상적으로 결론지어라.

7. Research Paper:

(A) Purposes:
 (1) To test student's ability to search out, recognize, accumulate, organize, & interpret a set of facts on a given or chosen topic.
 (2) To write a paper that shows the student's diligent studies into a particular subject.
 (3) To write a formal essay that reflects the student's reading, thinking, & writing ability about a particular subject.

(B) Elements:
 (1) Select a topic for your research, & find sources for the topic.
 (2) Locate & use both general & specific reference sources.
 (3) Make sure that the paper is developed with sufficient primary & secondary sources that satisfy the "4 Rs" test.
    (* "4 Rs"? = (a) Relevant (All the information is directly related to the topic.); (b) Reliable (The information is reliable since it is from respected scholars, professional journals, magazines, or organizations); (c) Recent (The information is not outdated); & (d) Representative (Show different points of view for discussing an issue based on well-balanced & representative interpretations).
 (4) Make sure that your topic is both interesting & informative.
 (5) Make sure that the thesis statement appears early in the paper.
 (6) Make sure that facts & ideas are stated mostly in your own words.
 (7) Do the following: (a) preliminary reading, (b) stating the purpose, (c) prepare bibliography cards, (d) take notes, (e) avoid plagiarism, (f) write the final outline & the draft, (g) revise the draft, (h) proofreading, and (i) cite all the sources used.

C H A P T E R 4

We have seen guidelines for major purposes and elements of each essay/writing type; however, remember that they are just general guidelines, not the rules. Most essays/writings include a variety of combined essay features, and we classify an essay type based on the major elements and purposes contained. There is no single essay that is totally "informative," "narrative," "persuasive," "personal," "expository," or "descriptive."

Now, we will see an analysis of each essay/writing evaluated based on the guidelines of major purposes and elements. Let's start from Model 1, "The November Afternoon" in the "descriptive" section. Read the following essay/writing and identify its major purposes and elements.

7. 연구 논문

(A) 목적 :

(1) 학생들이 주어진 또는 선택한 주제와 관련한 일련의 사실들을 조사, 인지, 축적, 편제, 해석하는 능력을 테스트한다.

(2) 학생들이 특정 주제에 대해 성실하게 연구했음을 보여주는 논문을 쓴다.

(3) 특정 주제에 대한 학생들의 읽기 능력과 사고 능력, 쓰기 능력 등을 반영하는 공식적인 에세이를 쓴다.

(B) 구성 요소

(1) 연구 주제를 선택하고 그 주제에 걸맞은 자료를 찾아라.

(2) 개괄적인 참고 자료와 특정한 참고자료를 모두 찾아서 사용하라.

(3) '4Rs' 테스트를 만족시키는 1차적인 자료와 보충자료를 충분히 활용하여 논문을 전개시켜라.

('4Rs' ? = (a) Relevant(관련성. 모든 정보는 주제와 직접적으로 관련이 있다.) (b) Reliable(신빙성. 모든 정보는 저명한 학자, 전문적인 신문, 잡지, 또는 조직에서 나온 것이므로, 신빙성이 있다.) (c) Recent (시의성. 주어진 정보가 시대에 뒤떨어져서는 안 된다.)

(d) Representative(대표성. 균형잡힌 전형적인 해석에 근거하고 있는 어떤 문제에 대해 논의할 때, 다양한 관점을 보여주어야 한다.)

(4) 주제는 재미있고 유익한 것이어야 한다.

(5) 논문 초반에 당신이 정립해야 할 논제를 밝혀라.

(6) 사실과 아이디어는 대부분 당신 자신의 언어로 표현하라.

(7) 다음 사항을 행하라. : (a) 예비 독서, (b) 목적 표명, (c) 참고 문헌 카드 준비, (d) 메모, (e) 표절 엄금, (f) 최종 개요 및 초고 작성, (g) 초고 교열, (h) 교정, (i) 참고 문헌 표기

지금까지 각 에세이 유형별 주요 목적 및 구성 요소에 대한 지침을 살펴보았다. 그러나 그것은 단지 일반적인 지침일 뿐, 규칙은 아니다. 대부분의 에세이는 여러 가지 특징을 포함하고 있으며, 우리는 거기 담긴 목적과 주요 구성요소에 근거하여 에세이의 유형을 분류한다. 전적으로 '정보 제공'을 목적으로 하는 에세이나 100% '나레이션,' '설득,' '사적인 이야기,' '설명,' 또는 '묘사'로만 이루어진 에세이는 없다.

지금부터 주요 목적 및 구성요소와 관련한 지침에 근거하여 평가한 유형별 에세이에 대해 분석해 보기로 하자. 먼저 '묘사' 영역의 에세이 '11월의 오후' 부터 읽어보기로 하겠다. 다음의 에세이를 읽고, 주요 목적과 구성 요소를 밝혀라.

4.2.1. Descriptive.

<u>Model 1</u>: "The November Afternoon" The New York Times

Line 1   It is not yet 4:30, and the sun is nearing the low ridge to the west. Soon the brightness of the late autumn afternoon will yield to twilight, to dusk, and to dark.

L.5.   The sun begins to set behind the ridge. The last, long light climbs from the valley's frosted pasture grass up the gray trunks of the naked maples and seems to pose on the hill tops to the east. Then it is gone. Twilight, the glow of November evening, possesses the day.

L.10.   At first there is a bright, shadowless light, a sunless daylight in which the growing moon, halfway up the eastern sky, is only a ghost. Then the glow comes, a rosy suffusion so subtle it could be a reflection of the maple leaves at the road side or the bronze-red grass in the neglected meadow. The air seems to thin and brighten, and the chill diminishes distances. The world comes close, the familiar world of this place called home.

L.15.   The glow fades. Dusk creeps in, on hurried but insistent, and the clarity of vision dims. In its place is a deceptive clarity of hearing. The farm dog barking just down the road sounds no closer than a truck shifting gears on a hill a mile away. The rustle of leathery leaves in an oak not ten feet away seems as far off as the hooting of the barred owl across the valley. And time somehow has lost its dimensions. It is evening and it is autumn, and the moon has begun to glow. The scuffle of leaves at the roadside just ahead could be a noontime cat or a midnight L.20.   fox or the evening breeze.

    Sunset, twilight, dusk, darkness, all by six o'clock on a mid-November evening, is late autumn's summary of serenity.

This writing, "The November Afternoon" includes a variety of "vivid details" for readers to see rather than to listen to them. The purposes of this writing are twofold: (1) to describe a natural phenomenon as an object, "The November Afternoon," and, (2) to create a picture in writing so as to help the readers see the target object through "vivid details (i.e. sights, sounds, smells, tastes, feelings)."

However, several summarized and easy-to-read guidelines related to the elements and purposes of a descriptive essay/writing should be established as criteria for the evaluation of each essay type. Some of the questions are as follows:

4.2.1. 묘사

'11월의 오후' (뉴욕 타임즈)

아직 4시 반도 지나지 않았건만, 태양은 서쪽의 낮은 산마루를 향해 다가가고 있다. 곧 늦가을 오후의 광휘도 차츰 어스름, 황혼, 그리고 어둠에게 굴복하리라.

태양이 산마루 너머로 지기 시작한다. 마지막 긴 빛이 골짜기의 서리 내린 목초지에서 잎사귀를 떨군 앙상한 단풍나무의 잿빛줄기로 올라가, 마치 언덕 꼭대기에서 동쪽을 향해 포즈를 취하고 있는 듯하다. 그러나 다음 순간, 그 빛은 사라진다. 어스름, 11월 저녁의 새빨간 빛이 낮을 지배한다.

처음엔 그림자 없는 투명한 빛, 태양이 사라진 상태의 빛이 있다. 그 빛 속에서 동쪽 하늘 위로 차츰 모습을 드러내는 달은 그저 허깨비에 불과하다. 뒤이어 새빨간 빛이 다가온다. 너무나 미세해서 길거리 한 켠의 단풍 잎이나 아무도 돌보지 않는 목초지의 청적색 풀이 투영된 듯 보이기도 하는 장미빛 충만함. 공기가 희박해지면서 빛을 내는 것처럼 보이고, 불쑥 다가서는 차가운 기운이 시계(視界)를 줄인다. 세상이 가까이 다가온다. 가정이라는 친숙한 세상이.

새빨간 빛이 희미해진다. 황급히, 그러나 뚜렷하게 황혼이 내려앉고, 투명하던 시야가 차츰 희미해진다. 그 속에서 청각의 혼란이 일어난다. 바로 저 밑에서 들려오는 개 짖는 소리가 여기서 1마일 떨어진 언덕 위에서 기어를 바꾸고 있는 트럭의 소리와 엇비슷하게 들리는 것이다. 10피트도 안 되는 곳에 자리한 가죽빛 오동나무 잎들의 살랑거리는 소리는 저 멀리 산골짜기를 날아다니는 올빼미 울음소리만큼 멀게 느껴진다. 그리고 시간은 그렇게 자신의 특질을 잃어버렸다. 지금은 저녁이고, 또한 가을이다. 달이 빛을 발하기 시작한다. 바로 앞 길가에 자리한 나뭇잎들의 수근거림이 한낮의 고양이나 한밤중의 여우, 또는 저녁의 미풍으로 느껴질 수도 있으리라.

일몰, 어스름, 황혼, 어둠, 11월 중순의 어느 날 저녁 6시, 이 모든 것들이 늦가을의 평온을 드러내고 있다.

Note

ridge *n.* 1. The line formed by two sloping surfaces that meet ; crest --A bird perched on the ridge of
the roof. 2. A long, narrow chain of mountains or hills. 3. A narrow raised strip, as in corduroy.
frost *n* 1. A covering of small ice particles formed from frozen water vapor --Our windows were
covered with frost. 2. Air temperatures below freezing.
v. 1. To cover with or as if with frost. 2. To cover with frosting.
pasture *n.* 1. Plants eaten by grazing animals. 2. Ground where animals graze.
v. To herd into a pasture to graze --We pastured the cattle in the south field.
scuffle *v.* To struggle in a disorderly way. *n.* A disorderly struggle.
twilight *n.* The light or time at dawn or sunset when the sun is below the horizon but there is a little
light in the sky.
chill *n.* 1. Unpleasant coldness --There was a chill in the dawn air. 2. A feeling of coldness, usually
with shivering --Chills and sneezing are signs of a cold

(1) Does the beginning of the description capture the reader's attention, and does the ending come to a natural stopping point?

(2) Has the description clearly identified what or who is being described?

(3) Does the description contain realistic sensory "details" (i.e. color, size, appearance, sounds, tastes, smells)?

(4) Are the description and "details" organized in spatial order, or order of importance?

(5) Has the writer described the object from his vantage (1st-person) points after carefully observing and taking notes related it?

(6) Has the writer used vivid words and figurative language effectively?

(7) Has the description presented a clear emphasis or a main impression?

Based on the established criteria for the evaluation of a descriptive essay/writing, let's answer for the questions, from (1) to (7)

(1) (A) Does the beginning of the description capture the reader's attention?
→ Yes, it does. Compare the following sentences.
(a) "It is not yet spring." vs. "It is not yet 4:30."
(b) "Call me in spring." vs. "Call me at 4:30."

The two words, "spring" and "4:30" are quite different in terms of capturing reader's attention. Compared to the specific and tense time factor, "4:30," the "spring" is less specific and tense because of its semantic meaning it represents. Therefore, "It is not yet 4:30,...to the west (L.1)," describes very specific time and situation to grab the reader's attention.

(B) Does the ending come to a natural stopping point?
→ Yes, it does. The ending of the description ("Sunset,...summary of serenity," Lines 21~22) leads to a natural stopping point, since it provides a precise, yet key summarization of the description it portrays.

(2) Has the description clearly identified what or who is being described?
→ Yes, it has clearly identified what is being described. The object described is a natural phenomenon, The November Afternoon; how it looks, how it sounds, and how the writer feels about it. To clearly identify this object, the description contains a variety of specific expressions as "realistic sensory details (sight, sound, and feeling)." Specific examples for " Sight, Sound, & Feeling" are:

이 글 '11월의 오후'는 독자들로 하여금 글을 읽는 것이 아니라 직접 그 광경을 보는 듯 느껴지게 하는 여러 가지 '생생한 세부 묘사'를 담고 있다. 이 글의 목적은 (1) 하나의 자연 현상으로서 '11월의 오후'를 묘사하는 것이면서, 동시에 (2) 독자들이 '생생한 세부 사항들(예를 들면, 시각, 청각, 후각, 미각, 촉각)'을 통해 목표로 삼은 대상을 볼 수 있도록, 글로써 하나의 그림을 창조하는 것이다.

그러나 각 에세이 유형의 평가 기준으로서 묘사적 에세이의 구성 요소 및 목적과 관련한 몇 가지 간단하고 읽기 쉬운 지침이 확립되어야 한다. 다음과 같은 몇 가지 질문을 던져보자.

(1) 시작 부분이 독자의 주의를 끄는가? 또한 끝 부분은 자연스런 귀착지로 이어지는가?

(2) 무엇 또는 누가 묘사되고 있는지 분명히 밝혀져 있는가?

(3) 묘사에 현실적인 감각적 '세부사항'(예를 들면, 색상, 크기, 모양, 소리, 맛, 냄새)이 담겨져 있는가?

(4) 묘사와 '세부 사항'이 공간이나 중요도 순서에 따라 배열되어 있는가?

(5) 작가는 대상을 주의깊게 관찰하고 메모를 한 뒤 자신에게 유리한 관점(1인칭 시점)에서 그것을 묘사했는가?

(6) 작가는 생생한 단어와 비유적인 표현을 효과적으로 사용했는가?

(7) 묘사에 분명한 강조점이나 지배적인 인상이 표현되었는가?

이러한 묘사적 에세이 평가 기준에 근거하여 (1)에서 (7)까지 각각의 질문에 답해 보자.

(1) (A) 시작 부분이 독자의 주의를 끄는가?

그렇다. 다음 문장들과 비교해 보자.

(a) '아직 봄은 아니다.'와 '아직 4시 반도 지나지 않았다.'

(b) '봄에 전화해.'와 '4시 반에 전화해.'

'봄'과 '4시 반'이라는 두 단어는 독자의 시선을 끈다는 차원에서 보면 상당히 다르다. '4시 반'이라는 구체적이고 팽팽한 시간 인자와 비교해 볼 때, '봄'이라는 단어는 그것이 표상하는 의미론으로 인해 그보다 덜 구체적이고 긴장감도 덜하다. 따라서, '아직 4시 반도... 다가가고 있다.'는 문장은 아주 구체적인 시간과 상황 묘사로 독자의 시선을 끌고 있다.

(B) 끝부분은 자연스런 귀착지로 이어지는가?

그렇다. 이 글의 끝 부분('일몰, 황혼... 드러내고 있다')은 자연스런 귀착지로 이어지고 있다. 이 글이 그려내고 있는 핵심적인 내용을 정확하게 요약해주고 있기 때문이다.

(2) 무엇 또는 누가 묘사되고 있는지 분명히 밝혀져 있는가?

그렇다. 이 글은 무엇을 묘사하고 있는지 분명히 밝히고 있다. 묘사한 대상은 11월 오후라는 자연 현상이다. 11월 오후의 풍경과 소리, 그리고 그에 대한 작가의 느낌을 묘사하고 있는 것이다. 이 대상을 분명히 인식시키기 위해, 이 글은 '현실적인 감각적 세부 사항(시각, 청각, 느낌)'으로서 여러 가지 구체적인 표현을 담고 있다. '시각, 청각, 느낌'의 구체적인 사례는 다음과 같다.

(A) Sight: (a) Lines 1 ~ 6. "It is not yet... the day- the sun... the west; the brightness... to dark; the sun... the ridge; the last... to the east; Then it is gone; Twilight... the day." (b) Lines 7 ~ 12. "At first...home; shadowless light...meadow." (c) Lines 13~21. "The glow fades...vision dims; Sunset,... darkness."

(B) Sound:(a) Lines 14~17. "In its place is ... across the valley."

(C) Feeling: (a) Lines 10~12. "The air seems to thin... called home." (b) Lines 17~22. "And time somehow... to glow; a mid-November evening ...of serenity."

(3) Does the description contain realistic sensory "details"?

→ Yes, it does. As we have seen previously at (2), the description includes vivid sensory details except the ones related to "taste and smell."

(4) Are the description and details organized in spatial order, or order of importance?

→ The description is organized in spatial order as exemplified below.

(a) Lines 1~5. "the sun... to the west; The sun... behind the ridge; The last, ... to the east." (b) Lines 8~12. "halfway up... sky; Then the glow... neglected meadow; The world comes... called home."(c) Lines 13~19. "Dusk creeps in ...insistent; down the road; a mile away; teṅ feet away as far off; across the valley; lost its dimensions; just ahead."

(5) Has the writer described the object from his vantage points of view after carefully observing and taking notes related to it?

→ Yes, the writer describes the object from his/her vantage points, which was keenly observed, well organized, and clearly written based on his/her own imaginative or realistic points of view.

(6) Has the writer used vivid and figurative language effectively?

→ (A) The writer has effectively used a variety of vivid words and phrases as we have seen at

(B) Figurative language:

(a) Lines 3~6. "The last, long light climbs... possesses the day." These lines are used as personification.

(b) Lines 8. "... is only a ghost," is used as a metaphor.

(c) Lines 18~20. "The scuffle of leaves ... the evening breeze," is a metaphor.

(7) Has the description presented a clear emphasis or a main impression?

→ The picturesque description as a simple yet precise unit presents a clear emphasis focused on a natural phenomenon, The November Afternoon; how it looks, how it sounds, and it is felt. This type of interpretation described based on the appeals from realistic sensory details provides us with a long lasting impression about the topic and the description.

(A) 시각　(a) "아직... 지배한다."

　　　　　(b) "처음엔 ... 장미빛 충만함."

　　　　　(c) "빨간색 빛이... 차츰 희미해진다; 일몰... 어둠."

(B) 청각　(a) "그 속에서... 멀게 느껴진다."

(C) 느낌　(a) "공기가...친숙한 세상이."

　　　　　(b) "시간은 그렇게... 느껴질 수도 있으리라; 11월 중순의... 드러내고 있다."

(3) 묘사에 현실적인 감각적 '세부사항'(예를 들면, 색상, 크기, 모양, 소리, 맛, 냄새)이 담겨져 있는가?

　(2)에서 이미 살펴보았듯이, 이 글은 '미각과 후각'을 제외한 나머지 생생한 감각적 세부사항들을 담고 있다.

(4) 묘사와 '세부 사항'이 공간이나 중요도 순서에 따라 배열되어 있는가?

　이 글은 다음과 같이 공간적 순서에 따라 짜여져 있다.

　(a) "태양은 서쪽의...; 태양이 산마루 너머로... ; 최후의 긴 빛이... 동쪽을 향해..."

　(b) "동쪽 하늘 위로...; 뒤이어... 장미빛 충만함; 세상이... 친숙한 세상이."

　(c) "황급히... 다가들고; 저 밑에서 ; 일 마일 떨어진 ; 10피트 가량 떨어진 곳; 산골짜기를 가로지르며 ; 특질을 잃어버렸다; 바로 앞"

(5) 작가는 대상을 주의깊게 관찰하고 메모를 한 뒤 자신에게 유리한 관점(1인칭 시점)에서 그것을 묘사했는가?

　작가는 대상을 자신의 관점에서 묘사하고 있는데, 자신의 상상 또는 현실적인 관점에 근거하여 대상을 예리하게 관찰하고 잘 배열한 뒤, 분명하게 글로 묘사했다.

(6) 작가는 생생한 단어와 비유적인 표현을 효과적으로 사용했는가?

　(A) (2)에서 이미 살펴보았듯이, 작가는 다양한 단어와 어구를 효과적으로 사용했다.

　(B) 비유적 표현

　　(a) "마지막 긴 빛이...낮을 지배한다." (의인법)

　　(b) "...그저 허깨비에 불과하다." (은유)

　　(c) "나뭇잎들의 수근거림이... 느껴질 수도 있으리라." (직유)

(7) 묘사에 분명한 강조점이나 지배적인 인상이 표현되었는가?

　단순하지만 정확한 구성 단위로서의 그림 같은 묘사는 11월 오후라는 자연 현상에 초점을 맞춰 그 대상이 어떻게 보이고, 어떻게 들리며, 또 어떤 느낌을 주는지 분명히 드러내고 있다. 현실적인 감각적 세부사항들에서 나오는 호소에 근거한 이런 유형의 해석은 주제 및 묘사에 대해 깊은 인상을 남겨준다.

<u>Model 2</u>: From a fiction, " The Street." by Ann Petry

Line 1   There was a cold November wind blowing through 116th Street. It rattled the top of garbage cans, sucked window shades out through the top of opened windows and set them flapping back against the windows; and it drove most of the people off the street in the block between Seventh and Eighth Avenues except for a few

L.5.   hurried pedestrians who bent double in an effort to offer the least possible exposed surface to its violent assault.

It found every scrap of paper along the street - theater throwaways, announcements of dances and lodge meetings, the heavy waxed paper that loaves of bread had been wrapped in, the thinner waxed paper that had enclosed

L.10.   sandwiches, old envelopes, newspaper. Fingering its way along the curb, the wind set the bits of paper to dancing high in the air, so that a barrage of paper swirled into the faces of the people on the street. It even took time to rush into doorways and areaways and find chicken bones and pork chop bones and pushed them along curb.

L.15.   It did everything it could to discourage the people walking along the street. It found all the dirt and dust and grime on the sidewalk and lifted it up so that the dirt got into their noses, making it difficult to breathe; the dust got into their eyes and blinded them; and the grit stung their skins. It wrapped newspaper around their feet entangling them until the people cursed deep in their throats, stamped their feet,

L.20.   kicked at the paper. The wind blew it back again and again until they were forced to stoop and dislodge the paper with their hands. And then the wind grabbed their hats, pried their scarves from around their necks, stuck its fingers inside their coat collars, blew their coats away from their bodies.

The wind lifted Lutie Johnson's hair away from the back of her neck so that she

L.25.   felt suddenly naked and bald, for her hair had been resting softly and warmly against her skin. She shivered as the cold fingers of the wind touched the back of her neck, explored the sides of her head. It even blew her eyelashes away from her eyes so that her eyeballs were bathed in a rush of coldness and she had to blink in order to read the words on the sign swaying back and forth over her head.

We have read the Model 2, "Street," and let's answer the questions from (1) to (7) as a way of evaluating the writing.

(1) (A) Does the beginning capture the reader's attention?

→ Yes, it does. How? Lines 1~6, The first sentence, " There was a cold November wind," starts from as a narrative introduction to the target object, "wind," and that object is described with specific action verb ("blowing") and noun phrase ("through

모델 2 앤 페트리의 소설 '거리' 중에서

차가운 11월의 바람이 116번가를 휩쓸고 있었다. 바람은 쓰레기통 뚜껑을 덜컹덜컹 움직이게 했고, 열려진 창문 밖으로 차양을 한껏 잡아당겼다가 다시금 창문을 향해 소리나게 내던졌다. 게다가 7번 가와 8번 가 사이에 위치한 이 거리에서 대부분의 사람들을 몰아내 버렸다. 예외가 있다면, 난폭한 바람의 공격에 가능한 한 적게 노출되려고 몸을 최대한 움츠린 성급한 보행자 몇 명 뿐.

바람은 이 거리를 따라 극장 광고 전단, 무도회와 모임 알림장, 빵을 포장하고 있던 기름기 묻은 두터운 종이, 샌드위치를 싸고 있던 그보다 얇은 종이, 낡은 봉투, 신문 등 온갖 종이 조각을 발견하였다. 바람은 고삐를 쥔 채 길을 더듬어 가면서, 종이 조각을 공중에 휘날려, 거리에 있는 사람의 얼굴 위로 소용돌이 치듯 날려보냈다. 심지어 문간방과 지하 출입구를 밀치고 들어가 닭과 돼지고기 뼈를 발견하고, 그것들을 흐트러 놓았다.

바람은 거리를 걷고 있던 사람들을 방해하기 위해 할 수 있는 일은 다 했다. 온갖 오물과 먼지는 다 찾아내서 인도를 더럽혔고, 그 오물을 사람들의 코로 들어갈 수 있도록 높이 날아 올려 숨쉬기조차 힘들게 만들었다. 먼지는 사람들의 눈에 들어가 앞을 볼 수 없게 했고, 잔모래는 살갗을 찔렀다. 바람은 사람들의 발에 신문지를 휘감았고, 사람들은 결국 목구멍까지 올라온 욕지거리를 내뱉으며 발을 굴러 종이를 차야 했다. 바람은 그 종이를 다시금 날려보냈고, 사람들은 결국 몸을 웅크린 채 손으로 종이를 떼어내야 했다. 그러고 나면, 바람은 그들의 모자를 잡아챘고, 목에서 스카프를 떼어냈으며, 코트 칼라 속으로 손가락을 밀어 넣어 코트마저 날려버렸다.

바람은 루티 존슨의 머리카락을 목덜미 위로 한껏 들어올렸고, 덕분에 그녀는 갑자기 대머리가 된 듯한 기분을 느꼈다. 그녀의 머리카락은 언제나 부드럽고 따스하게 그녀의 목덜미 위에 기대고 있었기 때문이다. 그녀는 바람의 손가락이 뒷목덜미를 건드리자, 부르르 몸을 떨면서 머리 양 옆을 살펴보았다. 바람은 심지어 그녀의 속눈썹까지 날려버렸고, 덕분에 그녀의 눈알은 밀려드는 냉기에 목욕을 해야 했으며, 그녀는 머리 위에서 앞뒤로 왔다갔다하는 표지판의 글자를 읽기 위해 눈을 깜빡여야 했다.

Note

rattle *v.* 1. To make or cause to make a quick series of short, sharp sounds --The wind rattled the windows. 2. To talk or say quickly and without pausing --I rattled off the list of manes. 3. To cause to be upset ; disturb --The size of my audience rattled me.

suck *v.* 1. To draw liquid into the mouth by inhaling or pulling in the cheeks. 2. To draw from in this way. 3. So much or so great --You read with suck speed!

shade *n.* 1. An area that is partly dark because light has been blocked off from it. 2. A device that blocks off part of the light --Pull down the window shade. 3. One of the degrees of lightness or darkness of a color --The garden has many shades of green. 4. A very small amount or degree.

lodge *n.* 1. A cottage or cabin, especially one used as a temporary place to stay. 2. A local branch or meeting place of and organization, such as a club.

v. 1. To provide with a place to sleep --We lodged our guest in a spare room. 2. To live in a place, especially a rented room --They lodged in a hotel for the night. 3. To become stuck or caught --A splinter lodged in my heel.

the 116th Street") Next, the object is described in a series of personifications, "It" (Line 1) and another "it" (L.3) followed with a variety of action verbs ("rattled, sucked, flapping, drove, bent."), which is strong enough to grab the reader's attention.

(B) Does the ending bring to a natural stopping point?

→ Not sure, since the description is excerpted from the fiction, The Street. However, the ending, "It even blew her eyelashes ... back and forth over her head," summarizes the description of a specific person, Lutie Johnson, in relation to the object, the wind, which comes to a natural stopping point.

(2) Has the description identified what is being described?

→ The introductory sentence (L.1), "There was a ... wind...," and numerous personifications, "It and it" (Lines 1,3,7,12,15,15,18,27) have all clearly identified that is being described.

(3) Does the description contain realistic sensory details?

→ Yes, it includes numerous details as follows:
(A) Sight: "except for a few ... assault (Lines 4~6)," "the dust got into... skins (Lines 17~18)."
(B) Sound: "It wrapped newspaper... at the paper (Lines 18~20)."
(C) Feeling: "It did everything... to breathe (Lines 15~17)," "The wind... of her head (Lines 24~27)."

(4) Are the description and details organized in spatial order, or order of importance?

→ They are organized in spatial order.

Examples: "through the 116th Street (L.1)," "the top of ... (L.2)," "between Seventh & Eighth Avenues (L.4)," "along the street (Lines 15)," "around their feet (Lines 18~19)," "around their necks (L.22)," "inside their coat collars (L. 22)," "back and forth over her head (L.29)."

(5) Has the writer described the object from her vantage points of view?

→ Yes, she describes the object, the wind, after carefully observing it, and generating a variety of specific words as well as figurative language (personification) based on her own creative imagination and insight.

(6) Has the writer used vivid and figurative language effectively?

→ Yes, she uses rich sensory details and phrases as we have seen at (3), and effectively uses numerous personifications as figurative language as shown at (2).

자, 이제 이 글의 유형을 평가하기 위해 (1)번부터 (7)번까지의 질문에 답해보기로 하자.

(1) (A) 시작 부분이 독자의 주의를 끄는가?

그렇다. 어떻게? "차가운 11월의 바람이 116번가를 휩쓸고 있었다."라는 첫 문장은 목표로 삼은 '바람'이라는 대상을 이야기체로 소개하고 있으며, 그 대상은 구체적인 행동 동사("불고 있다")와 명사구('116번가')로 묘사되고 있다. 뒤이어 그 대상은 일련의 의인법으로 묘사되고 있다. 바람을 지칭하는 대명사 'It' 뒤로 다양한 행동 동사가 뒤따르고 있는데("덜컹덜컹 움직이게 했다, 잡아당겼다, 내던졌다, 몰아냈다."), 이는 독자의 시선을 끌기에 모자람이 없다.

(B) 끝 부분은 자연스런 귀착지로 이어지는가?

반드시 그렇다고 볼 수는 없다. 이 글은 '거리'라는 소설에서 발췌한 것이기 때문이다. 그러나 "바람은 심지어... 깜빡여야 했다"라는 끝부분은 묘사 대상인 바람과 관련하여 루티 존슨이라는 구체적인 인물에 대해 묘사하고 있으며, 이는 자연스런 귀착지로 이어지고 있다.

(2) 무엇 또는 누가 묘사되고 있는지 분명히 밝혀져 있는가?

서두에 해당하는 첫 문장("차가운 11월의 바람이... 있었다.")과 수많은 의인법, 그리고 여러 번 등장하는 "It"이라는 표현은 묘사 대상을 명확히 밝히고 있다.

(3) 묘사에 현실적인 감각적 '세부사항'이 담겨져 있는가?

그렇다. 이 글에는 다음과 같은 다양한 보충 자료가 들어 있다.
(A) 시각 : "예외가 있다면... 보행자 몇 명뿐," "먼지는... 따끔거렸다."
(B) 청각 : "바람은 사람들의 발에... 차야 했다."
(C) 느낌 : "바람은 거리를 걷고 있던... 힘들게 만들었다." "바람은 루티 존슨의... 기대고 있었기 때문이다."

(4) 묘사와 '세부 사항'이 공간이나 중요도 순서에 따라 배열되어 있는가?

이 글은 다음과 같이 공간적 순서에 따라 짜여져 있다.

예] "116번가," "쓰레기통 뚜껑...," "7번가와 8번가 사이," "거리를 따라," "사람들의 발에," "사람들의 목에서," "코트 칼라 속으로," "머리 위에서 앞뒤로."

(5) 작가는 대상을 주의깊게 관찰하고 메모를 한 뒤 자신에게 유리한 관점에서 그것을 묘사했는가?

그렇다. 작가는 목표로 삼은 바람이라는 대상을 주의깊게 관찰한 뒤, 자신의 창조적 상상력과 통찰력에 근거하여 비유적 표현(의인화)뿐 아니라 구체적인 단어를 다양하게 사용하여 대상을 묘사하고 있다.

(6) 작가는 생생한 단어와 비유적인 표현을 효과적으로 사용했는가?

그렇다. (3)에서 살펴보았듯이, 그녀는 감각적 표현과 어구를 풍부하게 사용하고 있으며, (2)에서 본 것처럼, 비유적 표현으로서 효과적으로 의인법을 사용하고 있다.

(7) Has the description presented a clear emphasis or a main impression?

→ Although the description is excerpted from the fiction, The Street, the writer describes the target object in relation to specific people and various things in the streets. These descriptive elements displaying specific people and things in specific places make the description more impressive and memorable.

4.2.2. Expository

So far, we have read two models of descriptive writings the purpose of which is "to describe a specific person, object, place, or situation" so as to help readers see details; how they look, sound, smell, taste, or feel. Next, we will read two models of expository essays the purpose of which is "to explain, interpret, or make a detailed statement based on (a) process; (b) cause & effect; (c) comparison & contrast; (d) definition; and, (e) problem and solution." The word, "exposition" means "a systematic explanation of a subject."

Several guidelines formulated from Guidelines for Major Purposes and Elements of Each Essay Type are provided here for evaluating an expository essay.

(1) Does the introduction grab the reader's attention?
(2) Does the introduction establish the focus of the essay to be discussed with explanation or examples such as "comparison & contrast; cause & effect; definition or explanation" to support the main idea?
(3) Is the essay organized in a clear, and easy-to-read way?
(4) Is sufficient evidence given to show that the explanation is sound?
(5) Does the conclusion bring the essay to a satisfactory end?

CHAPTER 4

(7) 묘사에 분명한 강조점이나 지배적인 인상이 표현되었는가?

이 글이 〈거리〉라는 소설에서 발췌한 것임에도 불구하고, 작가는 거리의 구체적인 사람 및 다양한 사물들과의 연관성 속에서 목표로 삼은 대상을 묘사하고 있다. 특정한 장소의 구체적인 사람과 사물을 보여주는 이러한 묘사적 요소는 이 글을 보다 인상적으로 만든다.

4.2.2. 설명

지금까지 우리는 어떤 대상이 어떻게 보이고 들리는지, 냄새와 맛은 어떤지, 또 느낌은 어떤지를 독자들이 자세히 알 수 있도록 하기 위해 '구체적인 사람, 대상, 장소, 또는 상황 등의 묘사'를 목적으로 한 묘사적 글쓰기의 두 가지 사례를 살펴보았다. 그럼 이제 설명형 에세이의 모델 두 가지를 읽어보기로 하자. 이런 유형의 글은 '(a) 과정, (b) 원인과 결과, (c) 비교와 대조, (d) 정의, (e) 문제와 해결 등에 근거한 설명, 해석, 또는 상세한 진술'을 목적으로 한다. '설명'이라는 단어는 '어떤 주제에 대한 체계적 설명'을 의미한다.

다음은 각 에세이 유형별 주요 목적 및 구성 요소 지침에 근거하여 만들어진 설명형 에세이 평가 기준이다.

(1) 서론이 독자의 시선을 끄는가?
(2) 서론은 "비교와 대조, 원인과 결과, 정의 또는 설명"과 같은 주제를 뒷받침하는 설명 또는 예시와 더불어 앞으로 논의될 글의 초점을 밝히고 있는가?
(3) 에세이는 분명하고 쉽게 짜여져 있는가?
(4) 주어진 설명이 타당하게 여겨질 수 있도록 충분한 증거가 제시되었는가?
(5) 결론은 글 전체에 만족스런 결말을 안겨주는가?

Model 1: "How to read faster." by Bill Cosby

Bill Cosby

Line 1   When I was a kid in Philadelphia, I must have read every comic book ever published. I zipped through all of them in a couple of days, then reread the good ones until the next issues arrived. As I got older, my eyeballs must have slowed down or something! I mean, comic books started to pile up

L.5.   faster than my brother Russell and I could read them. It wasn't until much later, when I was getting my doctorate, that I realized it wasn't my eyeballs that were to blame. The problem is that there is too much to read these days, and too little time to read every word of it. That's when I started to look around for common-sense, practical ways to help me read faster. I found

L.10.   three that are especially good. And if I can learn them, so you can - and you can put them to use immediately.

    The first way is previewing. It is especially useful for getting a general idea of heavy reading like long magazine or newspaper articles and nonfiction books. To preview, read the entire first two paragraphs of whatever you've chosen.

L.15.   Next read only the first sentence of each successive paragraph. Then read the entire last two paragraphs. This will give a quick, overall view of long, unfamiliar material. It will keep you from spending time on things you don't really want - or need - to read.

    The second way to read faster is skimming. It is a good way to get a general

L.20.   idea of light reading like popular magazines or the sports and entertainment sections of the paper. It is also a good way to review material you've read before. To skim, think of your eyes as magnets. Force them to move fast. Sweep them across each and every line of type. Pick up only a few key words in each line. You will end up reading about half the words in less than the time it would

L.25.   take to read every word.

모델 1 '더 빨리 읽는 법' (빌 코스비)

　필라델피아에서 보낸 어린 시절, 나는 당시까지 출판된 만화책이란 만화책은 다 읽었음에 틀림이 없다. 나는 이틀만에 그 모든 것들을 휭하니 읽어치웠고, 그리고 나서 다음 호가 나올 때까지 좋은 것들만 다시 읽었다. 나이가 들어가면서, 내 눈알은 속도가 느려지거나 하여튼 그랬음에 틀림이 없다! 이유인즉, 만화책이 형 러셀과 내가 읽어나가는 속도보다 더 빨리 쌓여가기 시작했기 때문이다. 그게 내 눈알 탓이 아니라는 사실을 깨닫게 된 것은 그보다 훨씬 뒤, 내가 박사 학위를 딸 무렵이었다. 문제는 이즈음에는 읽어야 할 게 너무 많은 반면, 모든 단어를 다 읽기에는 시간이 턱없이 부족하다는 점이다. 그때부터 나는 글을 좀더 빨리 읽을 수 있는 상식적이고 실제적인 방법을 찾아보기 시작했다. 그리고 특히 좋은 방법을 세 가지 발견했다. 내가 배울 수 있다면, 당신도 그럴 수 있다. 그것도 지금 당장.

　첫 번째 방법은 사전 검토이다. 이 방법은 무거운 잡지나 신문 사설, 논픽션 등과 같은 무거운 읽을거리에서 대략적인 내용을 파악하려 할 때 특히 유용하다. 사전 검토를 하려면, 일단 당신이 선택한 책의 처음 두 문단을 꼼꼼이 읽어라. 그런 다음, 이어지는 각 문단의 첫 문장만 읽어라. 뒤이어 마지막 두 문단을 다시 꼼꼼이 읽어라. 이렇게 하면, 길고 낯선 소재를 신속하고 포괄적으로 볼 수 있게 될 것이다. 그리하여 당신이 읽고 싶지 않거나 읽을 필요가 없는 것들을 읽느라 시간을 낭비할 필요가 없어진다.

　글을 좀더 빨리 읽는 두 번째 방법은 대충 읽기이다. 이 방법은 대중 잡지 또는 신문의 스포츠면이나 연예면 같은 가벼운 읽을거리에서 대략적인 내용을 파악하려 할 때 좋다. 전에 읽었던 내용을 다시 검토할 때에도 이 방법이 유용하다. 대충 읽기를 하려면, 자신의 눈을 자석이라고 생각하라. 모든 줄 각각을 휙 둘러보면서, 각 줄에서 핵심적인 단어만 몇 가지씩 골라내라. 모든 단어를 다 읽는데 걸리는 시간의 반도 안 걸려서 대략 반 정도의 단어들을 읽게 될 것이다.

　읽기 속도를 증가시키는 세 번째 방법은 무리를 짓는 방법이다. 무리 짓기를 하게 되면, 한 번에 한 단어가 아니라 한번에 일련의 단어 집단을 보게 된다. 예를 들어, "나의 –형 – 러셀은– 괴물을–생각한다"라는 줄을 읽을 때면, "나의 형 러셀은 ––– 괴물을 생각한다."라는 식으로 읽게 되는 것이다. 대부분의 사람들에게 이러한 무리 짓기는 끊임없는 연습을 필요로 한다. 일반적으로 무언가를 읽어나가는 것과는 전적으로 다른 방법이기 때문이다. 무리짓기를 연습하려면, 일단 읽기 쉬운 책부터 시작하라. 그 책을 가능한 한 빨리 읽어라. 한번에 한 단어가 아니라 동시에 서너 단어를 보려고 노력하라. 그런 다음, 보통 속도로 읽으면서 당신이 놓친 것이 무엇인지 확인하라. 처음보다 많은 단어를 놓치지 않고 무리를 지어 단어를 읽을 수 있을 때까지, 매일 15분씩 연습하라.

The third way to increase your reading speed is clustering. Clustering trains you to look at the groups of words rather than one at a time. For example, instead of reading a line like this: "My - brother - Russell - thinks - monsters," you would read it like this: "My brother Russell ----- thinks monsters." For most
L.30. of us, clustering takes constant practice because it's a totally different way of seeing what we read. To practice clustering, begin with something easy to read. Read it as fast as you can. Concentrate on seeing three to four words at once rather than one word at a time. Then reread the piece at your normal speed to see what you missed the first time. Practice fifteen minutes every day until you can
L.35. read clusters without missing much the first time.

So now you have three ways to help you faster: previewing to cut down on unnecessary heavy reading; skimming to get a quick, general idea of light reading; and clustering to increase your speed and comprehension. With enough practice, you'll be able to handle more reading at school and at home in less
L.40. time. You should even have enough time to read your favorite comic books!

(1) Does the introduction grab the reader's attention?

→ Not strongly; however, the specific introductory information, "When I was a kid in Philadelphia...read every comic book ever published (Lines 1~2)," is sufficient enough to attract the reader's attention. Bill Cosby being a celebrity, his name can easily capture the reader's attention.

(2) Does the introduction establish the focus of the essay to be discussed with explanation or examples such as "comparison & contrast; cause & effect; definition or explanation" to support the main idea?

→ Yes, several introductory remarks establish the focus of the essay to be developed with examples and comparison & contrast to support the topic, "How to read faster." "I zipped...next issues arrived," (Lines 2~3) are an introduction related to the topic, reading fast. "As I got older,...that I realized it wasn't my eyeballs that were to blame." (Lines 3~7) are a cause & effect statement explaining the main idea. "The problem is...me read faster." (Lines 7~9) serves as an answer for the main topic; and, "I found three that are...to use immediately." (Lines 9~11) are the focus of the essay to be discussed based on forthcoming information and examples.

(3) Is the essay organized in a clear, and easy-to-read way?

→ Yes, it is. The introduction ("When I was a kid...to use immediately." (Lines 1~11)) captures the reader's attention, and the body is organized with three easy-to-read paragraphs.

이제 당신은 글을 좀더 빨리 읽을 수 있는 세 가지 방법을 알게 되었다. 두터운 책에서 불필요한 내용을 줄이기 위해 사전 검토 작업을 할 것. 가벼운 책의 전체적인 내용을 빨리 알아낼 때에는 대충 읽기를 이용할 것. 읽기 속도와 이해력을 높이기 위해서는 무리 짓기를 이용할 것. 충분한 연습이 뒷받침된다면, 당신은 학교에서나 집에서나 시간은 덜 들이고도 더 많은 책을 읽을 수 있게 될 것이다. 심지어 당신이 좋아하는 만화책을 읽을 시간도 충분히 가져야 한다.

Note

zip *v.* To fasten or close with a zipper.

pile *n* A mass of objects heaped together --A pile of old magazines lay in the attic.

　　v. 1. To place or heap in a pile the dishes in the sink. 2. To heap in great quantities --I piled my plate with food. 3. To move often in haste, in a group or mass.

doctorate *n.* The highest academic degree, esp. the Ph.D., awarded for completion of advanced work at the graduate level, or as an honorary degree, and conferring the title or status of doctor on the recipient; doctor's degree.

preview *v.* To show or see beforehand or in advance --The teacher previewed the film before showing it to the class.

skim *v.* 1. To remove from the surface of a liquid. 2. To move lightly and quickly over --The bird skimmed the water. 3. To read quickly, skipping over parts.

cluster *n.* A group of similar things growing or grouped close together. --We saw a cluster of stars in the night sky.

　　v. To grow or gather in a group --We all clustered around the warm fire.

(1) 서론이 독자의 주의를 끄는가?

강한 느낌은 아니다. 그러나 "필라델피아에서 보낸 어린 시절... 당시까지 출판된 만화책이란 만화책은 다 읽었다."라는 서두의 구체적인 정보는 독자의 시선을 끌기에 충분하다. 유명 인사인 빌 코스비는 그 이름만으로도 쉽사리 독자의 주의를 끌 수 있다.

(2) 서론은 '비교와 대조, 원인과 결과, 정의 또는 설명'과 같이 주제를 뒷받침하는 설명 또는 예시와 더불어 앞으로 논의될 글의 초점을 밝히고 있는가?

그렇다. 서두에 제시된 몇 가지 의견은 '더 빨리 읽는 법'이라는 주제를 뒷받침하는 예시 및 비유와 대조를 통해 에세이의 초점을 명확히 하고 있다. "나는 이틀만에... 다시 읽었다."라는 문장은 빨리 읽는다는 주제와 관련된 서두이다. "나이가 들어가면서... 박사학위를 딸 무렵이었다."는 '원인과 결과'를 이용하여 주제를 설명하고 있다. "문제는... 그것도 지금 당장."은 이후 정보와 예시에 근거하여 논의될 에세이의 초점이다.

Paragraph 1 : "The first way is previewing...to read." (Lines 12~18) serves as an explanation to support the main topic, previewing.

Paragraph 2 : "The second way...skimming...to read every word." (Lines 19~25) is an explanation to clarify and support the skimming.

Paragraph 3 : "The third way...clustering...without missing much the first time." (Lines 26~35) explains how to read faster by clustering while showing a specific example, "My brother Russell —— thinks monster," instead of reading word by word, "My - brother - Russell - thinks - monster."

Conclusion : The conclusion provides a summarized point of view for the description:(a) "So now...three ways to help you faster:" (Line 36) is a summarization of the main topic.(b) "Previewing to cut down...; skimming...; clustering..." (Lines 36~38) are the summarized review for the main idea.

  This essay is well organized considering the Five Paragraph Format previously introduced elsewhere.

(4) Is sufficient evidence given to show that the explanation is sound?

→ The evidence given in Paragraph 2, "To preview,...to read." (Lines 14~18); the one in Paragraph 3, "It is a good way...every word." (Lines 19~25); and, "Clustering trains you... the first time." (Lines 26~35) are sufficient enough to convince that the explanation is sound.

(5) Does the conclusion bring the essay to a satisfactory end?

→ Yes it does. The conclusion offers two satisfactory answers:
  (a) "With enough practice, you'll...in less time. (Lines 38~40), and
  (b) "You should even have enough time...comic books." (Line 40), which brings the essay to a satisfactory end.

Model 2: "Skiing - Then and Now." by Don Smith & Anne Marie Mueser

Line 1   We can't be sure just where skiing began. However, there is no doubt about how it began. In northern Europe and Asia, deep snow blanketed the land most of the year. Ancient peoples moving from place to place are known to have experimented with crude footwear for easier going in the snow. Those primitive

L.5.   efforts probably resulted in history's first snowshoe. This was a help, but not the answer.

(3) 에세이는 분명하고 쉽게 짜여져 있는가?

그렇다. 서론("필라델피아에서 보낸 어린 시절…. 지금 당장.")은 독자의 주의를 끌고 있고, 본론은 읽기 쉬운 세 문단으로 짜여져 있다.

문단 1: "첫번째 방법은… 없어진다."는 사전 검토라는 주제를 뒷받침하는 설명으로 기능하고 있다.

문단 2: "글을 좀더 빨리 읽는 두 번째 방법은… 읽게 될 것이다."는 대충 읽기라는 주제를 뒷받침하는 설명이다.

문단 3: "읽는 속도를 증가시키는… 15분씩 연습하라."는 구체적인 예를 통해 무리 짓기를 이용하여 글을 더 빨리 읽는 방법을 설명하고 있다.

결   론: 결론은 본론에서 제시한 견해를 요약하고 있다.

   (a) "이제 당신은…알게 되었다."는 주제의 요약이다.

   (b) "두터운 책에서… 이용할 것."은 주제를 다시금 요약하고 있다.

이 에세이는 앞에서 소개한 '다섯 문단 구성' 을 고려할 때, 아주 잘 짜여진 글이다.

(4) 주어진 설명이 타당하게 여겨질 수 있도록 충분한 증거가 제시되었는가?

문단 2에 제시된 증거, "사전 검토를 하려면… 필요가 없어진다."; 문단 3에 제시된 증거, "이 방법은… 읽게 될 것이다." ; 그리고 "무리 짓기를 하게 되면… 연습하라." 등은 설명이 타당하다는 것을 확신시켜주기에 부족함이 없다.

(5) 결론은 글 전체에 만족스런 결말을 안겨주는가?

그렇다. 결론은 (a) "충분한 연습이… 있게 될 것이다."와 (b) "심지어… 가져야 한다."라는 두 가지 만족스런 해답을 제공하고 있다.

모델 2   '스키 타기 — 옛날과 지금' (돈 스미스와 앤 마리 뮈세)

스키 타기가 어디서 시작됐는지는 명확히 알 수 없다. 그러나 어떻게 시작됐는지에 대해서는 의심의 여지가 없다. 북유럽과 아시아에서는 두텁게 쌓인 눈이 거의 일년 내내 땅을 뒤덮고 있었다. 여기저기 이동하던 고대 민족들은 눈 속을 더 쉽게 다닐 수 있게 하는 조잡한 신발류를 실험했던 것으로 알려져 있다. 아마도 그러한 선구적인 노력이 역사상 최초의 눈신을 낳았던 것 같다. 눈신이 도움이 되긴 했지만, 그렇다고 해답은 아니었다.

L.7.   We can guess that one day someone walking down a steep, icy hill started to slide. Amazingly, the trip to the bottom was accomplished in record time. And it was much easier than legging it one step at a time through the snow. History's

L.10.   first skier was probably quite pleased with the discovery and set about to improve his or her sliding shoes. Smooth wooden slats attached to the shoes were the result. We know this because the word ski comes from a northern European word meaning "a splinter cut from a log."

How old is skiing? Well, a pair of skis in a Swedish museum is thought to be

L.15.   at least five thousand years old. Stone carvings in a Norwegian cave, said to date back at least four thousand years, show skiing. And by the seventh century A.D. the Chinese were writing about it.

Skis helped people travel and hunt in the frigid Scandinavian countries for centuries before anyone thought about using them for sport. Then, in the

L.20.   eighteenth century, Norwegian soldiers on skis took part in a sporting contest in what is now the city of Oslo. Zigzagging between bushes and trees on their way down the slope, they accidentally hit on the idea of the slalom. The slalom today is one of skiing's most popular and demanding events.

L.25.   In the 1850s, the Norwegians began holding annual competitions in the valley of Telemark. They developed a means of holding the heel in place on the ski, thereby making the first ski jump possible, which took place on Norway's Huseby Hill, in 1879. In 1883, two main kinds of skiing - cross-country racing and jumping - were separated out for competition purposes.

L.30.   During the next few decades, the new and exciting sport from Norway spread to almost every country that had snow, including England. It was in England that standards and rules for the modern slalom were officially set down, even though slalom is a Scandinavian word (sla means "slope" and lom means "track left in the snow"). Skiing has grown extremely popular in the United

L.35.   States. The first U.S. ski club was organized in 1867 in, believe it or not, Laporte, California!

Today, wherever you can find a mountain and some snow, you are likely to see cars with ski racks on their roofs heading for the slopes and bumpers on the cars displaying stickers saying, "Think snow!"

추측컨대, 어느날 얼음으로 덮인 가파른 언덕을 걸어 내려가던 누군가가 활주를 시작했던 것 같다. 놀랍게도, 기록적인 시간만에 언덕 기슭까지 내려올 수 있었다. 게다가 눈 속을 한 번에 한 발자국씩 걷는 것보다 훨씬 더 쉬웠다. 역사상 최초의 스키어는 아마도 그러한 발견에 무척 기뻐하면서 자신의 눈신을 개량하는데 착수했을 것이다. 신에 부착된 부드러운 나무판이 그 결과물이었다. 그 점은 스키라는 단어가 '통나무에서 잘라낸 토막'을 의미하는 북유럽의 한 단어에서 유래한다는 사실로 충분히 알 수 있다.

스키 타기는 언제부터 시작됐을까? 스웨덴의 한 박물관에 소장된 스키 한 쌍은 최소한 5천 년 이상 된 것으로 여겨지고 있다. 적어도 4천 년 이전의 것으로 추정되는 노르웨이 동굴의 석기 시대 조각에는 스키 타는 모습이 묘사되어 있다. 중국인들 또한 서기 7세기 무렵, 스키 타기에 대해 쓰고 있었다.

냉혹한 추위에 시달려야 하는 스칸디나비아 반도의 여러 국민들은 누군가 스키를 스포츠용으로 사용하자는 생각을 하기 이전부터 수세기 동안 여행과 사냥에 스키를 이용했다. 그 뒤, 18세기에는 노르웨이 군인들이 스키를 타고 오늘날의 오슬로에서 열린 스포츠 경기에 참가했다. 그들은 덤불과 나무 사이의 길을 따라 지그재그로 움직이며 비탈을 내려오다가, 우연히 회전 경기에 대한 생각을 떠올렸다. 회전 경기는 오늘날 스키 경기 가운데 가장 대중적이고 힘든 종목 가운데 하나이다.

1850년대가 되자, 노르웨이인들은 일년에 한 번씩 텔레마크 계곡에서 경기를 개최하기 시작했다. 그들은 스키를 타고 발 뒤꿈치를 제자리에 붙이는 방법을 발전시켜 최초의 스키 점프를 가능하게 했고, 그 경기는 1879년, 노르웨이의 휴스비 힐에서 개최되었다. 1883년, 스키 타기의 주요한 두 경기 -- 크로스 컨트리 경주와 점핑 --이 경기를 목적으로 분리되었다.

이후 몇십 년 동안, 노르웨이에서 생겨난 새롭고 흥미진진한 스포츠는 영국을 포함, 눈이 내리는 거의 모든 나라에 전파되었다. 근대 회전경기의 표준과 규칙이 공식적으로 제정된 곳은 영국이었다. 그럼에도 불구하고, 회전 경기를 뜻하는 slalom이란 단어는 스칸디나비아 말이다(sla는 'slope,' 즉 비탈을 뜻하며, lom은 '눈에 남겨진 자국'을 의미한다). 스키 타기는 미국에서 매우 대중적인 스포츠로 성장해왔다. 미국 최초의 스키 클럽은, 믿거나 말거나, 1867년, 캘리포니아주의 라포트에서 조직되었다!

오늘날, 산과 약간의 눈이 있는 곳이라면, 지붕에 스키 랙을 설치하고, 범퍼에는 "눈을 생각하라!"라는 스티커를 붙인 차들이 슬로프를 향해 가고 있는 모습을 흔히 볼 수 있다.

(1) Does the introduction capture the reader's attention?

➡ The introduction, "We can't be sure just when skiing began." (Line 1), draws a question for curiosity regarding a history of the main topic, skiing, which captures the reader's attention.

(2) Does the introduction establish the focus of the essay to be discussed with explanation or examples such as "comparison & contrast; cause & effect; definition; or explanation" to support the main idea?

➡ Yes, the introduction establishes the focus of the essay to be developed with explanation. For example, "Ancient people... in the snow; Those primitive efforts...; This was a help, but not the answer." (Lines 3~6) introduces possible answers for the main topic, but the definite answer was not given. Instead, "but not the answer" (Lines 5~6) as a transitional device for introducing different points, serves as a phrase opening new information for different answers. In other words, "but not the answer" is a linguistic signal that draws quite different expository description as an answer for the focus of the essay to be discussed in a logical way.

(3) Is the essay organized in a clear, and easy-to-read way?

➡ Yes, the essay is organized with 7 expository paragraphs.
  (1) The first paragraph as the introduction (Lines 1~6).
  (2) The second paragraph (Lines 7~13) provides possible answers for the invention of the topic, skiing in relation to circumstance.
  (3) The third paragraph (Lines 14~17) gives details related to the topic in chronological order.
  (4) The fourth paragraph (Lines 18~24) illustrates details related to all the uses of skiing.
  (5) The fifth paragraph (Lines 25~29) narrates the details regarding the beginning of annual ski competitions.
  (6) The sixth paragraph (Lines 30~36) describes the details focused on the spread of skiing.
  (7) The last paragraph (Lines 37~39) as a brief review for associating the topic, "a mountain and some snow," (Line 37) provides details for the conclusion, "Think snow!" (Line 39).

(4) Is sufficient evidence given to show that the explanation is sound?

➡ Yes, the detailed evidence presented in each paragraph is sufficient to show that the explanation is solid.

(5) Does the conclusion bring the essay to a satisfactory end?

➡ Yes, the conclusion, "Today,..., Think snow!" as a brief review for the topic leads the essay to a satisfactory end by providing specific details: "mountain and snow" which are nicely associated with the closing remark, "Think snow!"

(1) 서론이 독자의 시선을 끄는가?

"스키 타기가 어디서 시작됐는지는 명확히 알 수 없다."라는 서두는 스키 타기라는 주제의 역사와 관련하여 호기심을 자극하며, 따라서 독자의 시선을 끌고 있다.

(2) 서론은 '비교와 대조, 원인과 결과, 정의 또는 설명'과 같은 주제를 뒷받침하는 설명 또는 예시와 더불어 앞으로 논의될 글의 초점을 밝히고 있는가?

그렇다. 서론은 설명과 더불어 앞으로 논의될 글의 초점을 밝히고 있다. 예를 들어, "고대 민족들은... 알려져 있다; 그러한 선구적인 노력이... ; 눈신이 도움이 되긴 했지만, 그렇다고 해답은 아니었다."라는 부분은 주제에 대한 여러 가지 해답을 제시하고 있지만, 명확한 대답은 제시하지 않았다. 대신, 다른 관점을 소개하는 이행 장치로서의 "그렇다고 해답은 아니었다"라는 부분은 다른 해답과 관련된 새로운 정보를 꺼내놓는 문구로 기능하고 있다. 다시 말해, "그렇다고 해답은 아니었다"라는 문장은 앞으로 논리적으로 전개될 글의 초점을 위한 해답으로서 기왕의 관점과 상당히 다른 설명을 이끌어내는 언어학적 신호이다.

(3) 에세이는 분명하고 쉽게 짜여져 있는가?

그렇다. 이 글은 7개의 설명형 문단으로 짜여져 있다.

(A) 첫 문단은 서론으로 기능하고 있다.

(B) 두 번째 문단은 스키 타기라는 주제의 발명에 대해 상황과 관련하여 가능한 해답을 제공하고 있다.

(C) 세 번째 문단은 주제와 관련된 세부 사항들을 연대기 순으로 제시하고 있다.

(D) 네 번째 문단은 스키 타기의 활용과 관련된 사항을 기술하고 있다.

(E) 다섯 번째 문단은 연례 스키 경기의 시초와 관련된 사항을 이야기하고 있다.

(F) 여섯 번째 문단은 스키의 확산에 초점을 맞춰 여러 가지 사항을 서술하고 있다.

(G) 주제를 연상시키는 "산과 약간의 눈"에 대한 간략한 재검토로서의 마지막 문단은 "눈을 생각하라!"라는 결론을 설명해주고 있다.

(4) 주어진 설명이 타당하게 여겨질 수 있도록 충분한 증거가 제시되었는가?

그렇다. 각 문단에 제시된 상세한 증거는 설명의 타당성을 보여주기에 충분하다.

(5) 결론은 글 전체에 만족스런 결말을 안겨주는가?

그렇다. 주제에 대한 간략한 재검토로서의 "오늘날...흔히 볼 수 있다"라는 결론은 '산과 눈'이라는 구체적인 사실과 "눈을 생각하라!"라는 마지막 말을 잘 결합시킴으로써 만족스런 결말을 이끌어내고 있다.

4.2.3. Informative.

As we have seen, the major purpose of the Informative essay/writing is "to give factual information about one topic." Previously we studied the Guidelines for Major Purposes and Elements of each Essay Type. Based on those guidelines, we can condense them as follows:

(1) Is the topic both interesting and informative so as to capture the reader's attention?
(2) Does the main idea clearly introduce a topic sentence?
(3) Is information organized into paragraphs that deal with one main subject?
(4) Does the information contain details and examples that support the topic sentence?
(5) Are there smooth and logical transitions between paragraphs?
(6) Does the conclusion bring a satisfactory end?

Keeping the condensed guidelines in mind, read and evaluate the following two essays: "Choosing a Part-Time Job," and, "How to Make Friends and Stop Being Lonely."

<u>Model 1</u>: "Choosing a Part-Time Job." by Kelli Mulholland

Line 1   Working a part-time job after school can be a fun and educating experience. By working after school, a young person can gain knowledge in the working field and make some extra money. There are many jobs out there for high school students. Two of the most popular jobs are telemarketing and working at fast-

L.5.   food restaurants. These two fields are world apart, but they also have a great deal in common.

Telemarketing, selling goods or services over the telephone, has been around for many years. Telemarketing offices are always looking for outgoing, enthusiastic people to fill the positions. It does not take much experience to be a

L.10.   telemarketer, just a good disposition. There are many advantages to telemarketing. You only have to work about four hours a day. Most telemarketing places pay their employees an hourly wage, although some places pay both an hourly wage and a commission. Another advantage is that some telemarketing places let employees work out of their homes. Imagine not even leaving the house and

L.15.   getting paid for it. Telemarketing is also good experience in sales. Unlike delivering papers or baby sitting, telemarketing is a very pleasant and easy

4.2.3. 정보 전달

정보 전달형 에세이/글쓰기의 주요 목적은 '한 가지 주제에 대해 사실적인 정보를 제공하는 것'이다. 앞에서 살펴본 각 에세이 유형별 주요 목적 및 구성 요소에 대한 지침에 근거해 볼 때, 정보 전달형 에세이의 평가 기준은 다음과 같이 요약될 수 있다.

(1) 주제는 독자의 시선을 끌 수 있을 만큼 재미있고 유익한가?

(2) 주제는 주제문을 명확히 전하고 있는가?

(3) 정보는 한 가지 주제를 다루는 문단들로 짜여져 있는가?

(4) 정보는 주제문을 뒷받침하는 세부사항과 예시문을 포함하고 있는가?

(5) 문단과 문단은 논리적이고 매끄럽게 연결되어 있는가?

(6) 결론은 만족스런 결말로 이어지는가?

이 응축된 지침을 명심하면서, "아르바이트 선택하기"와 "친구를 사귀어 외로움에서 벗어나는 방법"이라는 두 에세이를 읽고 평가해보자.

> **모델 2** **'아르바이트(시간제 일) 선택하기'** (켈리 멀홀랜드)

방과 후에 아르바이트를 한다는 것은 아주 재미있고 교육적인 일이 될 수 있다. 방과 후에 일함으로써, 젊은이들은 일터에 대한 지식을 획득할 수 있고, 약간의 용돈도 벌 수 있다. 학교 밖에는 고등학생을 위한 일거리가 많다. 가장 인기있는 일거리 가운데 두 가지가 텔레마케팅과 패스트푸트점 아르바이트이다. 이 두 분야는 서로 상당히 다르지만, 공통점도 아주 많다.

전화로 물건이나 서비스를 파는 텔레마케팅은 꽤 오랫동안 주위에 있었다. 텔레마케팅 사무소들은 자리를 채워줄 사교성 있고 열성적인 사람들을 항상 찾고 있다. 텔레마케터가 되는 데는 그다지 많은 경험이 필요치 않으며, 단지 적성만 맞으면 된다. 텔레마케팅에는 많은 이점이 있다. 근무 시간은 하루에 대략 네 시간 정도이다. 텔레마케팅 회사들은 대부분 시간급을 주는데, 시간급 외에 커미션까지 주는 곳도 있다. 또 다른 이점은 재택근무를 허용하는 회사도 있다는 점이다. 집에서 나가지도 않고 그에 대한 보수를 받는다고 상상해 보라. 텔레마케팅은 판매 업무에 좋은 경험이 되기도 한다. 전단을 뿌리거나 아이를 돌봐주는 일과 달리, 텔레마케팅은 다른 사람들과 이야기하기를 즐기는 사람들에게는 무척 유쾌하고 손쉬운 아르바이트이다.

아주 인기 있고 흥미로운 또 하나의 일이 바로 패스트푸드점에서 일하는 것이다. 패스트푸드점들은 항상 고등학생들을 고용하고 있다. 이런 종류의 일이 지닌 이점은 엄청나다. 일을 하면서 사람들을 만나고 돈을 번다는 것이 첫 번째 이점이다. 종업원은 요리법과 금전 등록기 사용법을 배우게 되며, 더 나아가 가게 매니저가 될 수도 있다. 또한 젊은이들이 고등학교 졸업 후 일자리를 찾으러 다닐 때, 고용주들은 장래의 고용인이 다른 사람들과 함께 일해왔는지, 또 약간의 압박감 속에서도 생산적으로 일할 수 있는지 알고 싶어한다. 패스트푸드 레스토랑에서 일하는 것은 바로 그 점을 보여주게 될 것이다.

part-time job for those who enjoy talking with other people.

Another very popular and exciting job is working at a fast-food place. Fast-food places are always hiring high school students. The benefits of this kind of job are great. Meeting people and making money while doing it is one advantage. An employee will learn how to cook and how to use a cash register and may even become manager of the whole store. Also, when young people apply for a job after high school, employers want to see that prospective workers have worked with other people and are able to productive under a little pressure. Working at a fast-food restaurant will show that.

Both jobs are very appealing in many ways. They will both look good on a resume after high school and show that you do have some work experience. Baby-sitting and delivery papers show responsibility, but they don't show punctuality and compatibility. Consider your options in choosing a part-time job. Find a job that fits your personality, and one that interests you most.

L.20.

L.25.

L.30.

(1) Is the topic both interesting and informative so as to capture the reader's attention?

→ The topic, "Choosing a Part-Time Job," is both interesting and informative to many readers, especially for those high school or college students including their parents and teachers. The first sentence, "Working a part-time job... can be a fun and educating experience (L.1)," is an interesting introduction so as to grab the reader's attention.

(2) Does the main idea introduce a topic sentence?

→ Yes, the main idea is stated in first three sentences, "Working a part-time... high school students (Lines 1~4)," which introduces the topic sentence, "Two of ... jobs are telemarketing and working at fast-food restaurant (Lines 4~5)." And then the topic sentence is supported by the details in second and third paragraphs as follows:
(a) "Telemarketing, selling... over the telephone,... with other people (Lines 7~17, 2nd paragraph)," which supports the topic, "telemarketing; and,
(b) "Another very popular... will show that (Lines 18~25, 3rd paragraph)," supports other topic, "working at fast-food restaurants."

(3) Is the information organized into paragraphs that deal with one main toipc/subject?

→ Yes. The man topic/subject, "telemarketing" is organized into second paragraph; and, the other one, "working at fast-food restaurant" is into third paragraph as we have seen at (2)

두 가지 일 모두 여러 가지 측면에서 무척 매력적이다. 졸업 후 이력서 쓰기에도 좋을 뿐 아니라 당신이 일을 해 본 경험이 있다는 것을 보여준다. 아이 돌보기와 전단 뿌리기는 신뢰성을 보여주긴 하지만, 정확성과 적합성을 보여주진 못한다. 아르바이트를 선택할 때에는 선택권을 고려하라. 당신의 성격과 잘 맞는 일, 그리고 당신이 가장 재미있게 할 수 있는 일을 찾아라.

Note

apart *ad.* 1. Away from each other in time or position --We saw two trees about ten feet apart.

2. In or into separate pieces ; to pieces --I took the camera apart.

3. One from another --It was almost impossible for us to tell the twins apart.

appeal *n.* 1. A request for something that is really needed --During the blizzard the governor made an appeal for everyone to stay home. 2. The power to attract or interest --That story has a strong appeal for me. 3. The bringing of a legal case from a lower court to a higher court to be heard again.

v. 1. To make a request for something really needed --I appealed to you to help me.

2. To be attractive or interesting --That game appeals to us.

3. To bring or ask to bring a legal case from a lower court to higher court to be heard again.

compatible *a.* able to exist or function harmoniously with another n. -compatibility.

(1) 주제는 독자의 시선을 끌 수 있을 만큼 재미있고 유익한가?

'아르바이트 선택하기'라는 주제는 특히 고등학생이나 대학생, 그리고 그들의 부모와 선생님 등 많은 독자들에게 흥미롭고 유익하다. "방과 후에 아르바이트를 한다는 것은 아주 재미있고 교육적인 일이 될 수 있다."는 첫 문장은 독자의 시선을 끄는 흥미로운 서두이다.

(2) 주제는 주제문을 명확히 전하고 있는가?

그렇다. 주제는 처음 세 문장, "방과후에... 일거리가 많다"에 진술되어 있으며, 그것은 "가장 인기 있는... 아르바이트이다."라는 주제문을 소개하고 있다. 그리고 나서 주제문은 다음과 같은 두 번째, 세 번째 문단에 나오는 자세한 사항들에 의해 뒷받침되고 있다.

(a) "전화로... 손쉬운 아르바이트이다."라는 두 번째 문단은 '텔레마케팅'이라는 주제를 뒷받침하고 있으며,

(b) "아주 인기 있고... 보여주게 될 것이다."라는 세 번째 문단은 또 하나의 주제인 '패스트푸드 레스토랑 아르바이트'를 뒷받침하고 있다.

(3) 정보는 한 가지 주제를 다루는 문단들로 짜여져 있는가?

그렇다. (2)에서 보았듯이, '텔레마케팅' 부분은 두 번째 문단에, '패스트푸드 레스토랑 아르바이트'는 세 번째 문단에 설명되어 있다.

(4) Does the information contain details and examples that support the topic sentence?

→ Yes, it does for the topic sentence, "Two of the most popular jobs are telemarketing and working at fast-food restaurants(Lines 4~5)."
  (a) Details for "telemarketing":
    "Telemarketing offices...to telemarketing (Lines 8~10)."
    "Most telemarketing places... their homes (Lines 11~14)."
    "Telemarketing... other people (Lines 15~17)."
  (b) Examples for telemarketing:
    "You only have... commission (Lines 11~13)."
    "Imagine not leaving ... other people (Line 14~17)."
  (c) Details for "working at a fast-food restaurants":
    "Fast-food places ... one advantage (Lines 18~21)."
  (d) Examples for "working at a fast-food restaurants":
    "An employee ... will show that (Lines 21~25)."

(5) Are there smooth and logical transitions between paragraphs?

→ Yes, there are two logical and smooth transitions that work as functional ones.
  (a) "Another very popular... (L.18)" is logical and smooth transition in the sense that the transition introduces a new topic while terminating the old one, "telemarketing."
  (b) "Both jobs are... (L.26)" summarizes all the details and examples provided earlier, paving a way for a conclusion.

(6) Does the conclusion bring a satisfactory end?

→ Yes, it does. "Find a job that fits your personality, and one that interests you most (L. 30)" serves as a good conclusion for a satisfactory end. It is because the writer does not ask the readers to choose the two part-time jobs described earlier, but he/she offers a wide variety of choices that really fits reader's personality and interest. Simply put, the conclusion neither imposes nor recommends any particular part-time jobs discussed, but gives free choices based on individual personality and interest.

(4) 정보는 주제문을 뒷받침하는 세부사항과 예시문을 포함하고 있는가?

그렇다. "가장 인기 있는 일거리 가운데 두 가지가 텔레마케팅과 패스트푸드점 아르바이트이다."라는 주제문을 세부 사항과 예시문으로 잘 뒷받침하고 있다.

(a) '텔레마케팅'에 대한 세부 설명

"텔레마케팅 사무소들은… 이점이 있다."

"텔레마케팅 회사들은 대부분… 회사도 있다는 점이다."

"텔레마케팅은… 손쉬운 아르바이트이다."

(b) 텔레마케팅과 관련한 예시

"근무시간은 하루에… 커미션까지 주는 곳도 있다."

"집에서 나가지도 않고… 손쉬운 아르바이트이다."

(c) "패스트푸드 레스토랑 아르바이트"에 대한 세부 설명

"패스트푸드점들은… 첫 번째 이점이다."

(d) "패스트푸드 레스토랑 아르바이트"에 대한 예시

"종업원은…보여주게 될 것이다."

(5) 문단과 문단은 논리적이고 매끄럽게 연결되어 있는가?

논리적이고 부드러운 연결 기능을 맡은 두 개의 이행 장치가 있다.

(a) "아주 인기 있고 흥미로운 또 하나의 일이…"는 이러한 이행 과정이 '텔레마케팅'이라는 이전의 주제를 종결하고 새로운 주제를 소개하고 있다는 면에서 매끄럽고 논리적이다.

(b) "두 가지 일 모두…"는 앞에서 제시한 모든 세부 사항과 예시문을 요약하면서 결론 짓기를 용이하게 하고 있다.

(6) 결론은 만족스런 결말로 이어지는가?

그렇다. "당신의 성격과 잘 맞는 일, 그리고 당신이 가장 재미있게 할 수 있는 일을 찾아라."라는 문장은 만족스런 결말로 이어지는 훌륭한 결론으로 기능하고 있다. 독자들에게 앞에서 서술한 두 가지 아르바이트를 선택하라고 말하는 것이 아니라 진정 독자의 성격과 관심에 맞는 다양한 선택의 자유를 부여하고 있기 때문이다. 간단히 말해서, 결론은 특정한 아르바이트를 강제하거나 추천하는 것이 아니라 개인의 성격과 관심에 근거한 자유로운 선택을 말하고 있다.

<u>Model 2</u> : "How to Make Friends and Stop Being Lonely."

Line 1   ... To be lonely means to feel alone. And at the heart of loneliness is low self-esteem, feelings of inadequacy, the nagging suspicion that "I am not loveable" and a reluctance to reach out for fear of being rejected. All of us have "attacks" of loneliness at some time or another. Even the most popular and well-adjusted among
L.5.   us.

   ... Suddenly a causal friend sees you from across the room, comes over and greets you warmly. While you barely know the person, you could kiss her for just walking over to say hello. Although it was a very small thing she did, you feel enormously grateful. You exchange pleasantries, discuss the weather, comment on her pretty
L.10.   blouse and she says she loves your haircut. Suddenly you aren't lonely anymore.

   By this time it should be clear that the way to overcome loneliness is to communicate with someone. And chances are good that when you go out of your way to do just that, you rescue another soul from the prison of his or her loneliness.

   Dr. Eugene Kennedy, a well-known author, said some profound and meaningful
L.15.   things about this subject in THE ANN LANDERS ENCYCLOPEDIA. He expressed it best in one paragraph:

   The concept of trying to help others as a practical approach to dealing with our own loneliness may sound corny, but it works. Volunteers work in hospitals, worthy causes, visiting the elderly, reading to crippled children, assisting the
L.20.   handicapped, being a good neighbor, investing one's self in constructive activities can break the shell that encases us in our loneliness. When a person asks that age-old question, "What can I do, I'm so terribly lonely?" The best answer is, "Do something for somebody else."

   No age group has a monopoly on loneliness. It hits almost everyone at some time
L.25.   or another. ... You want to get into the mainstream of life and be a part of what's happening. Here are several suggestions how to make friends and stop being lonely in terms of (1) being truly likeable; (2) developing friendship; and, (3) getting along with people.

   To be truly likeable, remember the following suggestions.
L.30.   (1) Don't criticize, condemn or complain.
   (2) Give honest, sincere appreciation.
   (3) Arouse in the other person an eager want.

C
H
A
P
T
E
R

4

모델 2 '친구를 사귀어 외로움에서 벗어나는 방법'

... 고독하다는 것은 외롭다는 것을 의미한다. 그리고 외로움의 심장부에는 자신감 결여, 무력감, "난 사랑스럽지 않다"는 끈질긴 의구심, 거절당할지도 모른다는 두려움 때문에 누구와도 접촉하기 싫어하는 마음이 자리하고 있다. 우리 모두가 가끔은 외로움의 "공격"을 받는다. 심지어 우리 중에 가장 인기 있고, 적응력이 뛰어난 사람조차도.

... 갑자기 뜻밖의 친구가 방 저편에서 당신을 보고, 이쪽으로 와서 따스하게 인사한다. 그 친구에 대해 잘 알지 못하면서도, 당신은 그녀를 향해 다가가 키스로 인사를 할 수도 있을 것이다. 비록 그녀가 한 일은 아주 사소한 것일지라도, 당신은 엄청난 고마움을 느낀다. 당신은 그녀와 농담을 주고받고, 날씨에 대해 이야기한다. 그리고 그녀의 블라우스가 예쁘다고 말하고, 그녀는 당신의 머리 모양이 참 예쁘다고 말한다. 갑자기 당신은 더 이상 외롭지 않다.

이쯤 되면 외로움을 극복하는 방법이 누군가와 의사를 소통하는 것이라는 사실이 분명해진다. 게다가 당신이 의도적으로 그렇게 할 때, 당신은 또 다른 사람을 외로움의 감옥에서 구출하게 될 것이다.

저명한 저술가 유진 케네디 박사는 이 문제에 대해 〈앤 랜더스 백과사전〉에서 다소 심오하고 의미 있는 점을 지적했다. 그는 그 점을 한 단락으로 멋지게 표현했다.

우리 자신의 외로움에 대처하는 실제적인 접근법으로서 다른 사람을 도우려 한다는 생각이 감상적으로 들릴지 모르지만, 사실이 그렇다. 병원에서 일하는 자원봉사자들이 숭고한 뜻을 품고 노인들을 방문하며, 장애가 있는 아이들에게 책을 읽어주고, 심신 장애자들을 도와주며, 좋은 이웃이 되고, 자신의 자아를 건설적인 활동에 바치는 것은 우리를 외로움 속에 가둬놓는 껍질을 깨뜨릴 수 있다. 누군가 "내가 뭘 할 수 있겠어요, 난 끔찍할 정도로 너무나 외로운데?"라는 오래된 질문을 던질 때, 그에 대한 최상의 대답은 "다른 누군가를 위해 뭔가를 하라."이다.

특정 연령대만이 외로움을 독점하고 있는 것은 아니다. 그것은 거의 모든 사람을 가끔씩 강타한다... 당신은 삶의 주류로 들어가 현실에서 벌어지는 일의 일부가 되고 싶어한다. 다음에 나오는 몇 가지 제안은 (1) 진정으로 호감 주기, (2) 우정 발전시키기, (3) 사람들과 의좋게 지내기 등 세 가지 차원에서 친구를 사귀어 외로움에서 벗어나는 방법이다.

진정으로 호감이 가게 하려면, 다음 제안을 항상 명심하라.
(1) 흠을 잡거나 힐난하거나 불평을 늘어놓지 말라.
(2) 솔직하고 성실하게 감사를 표하라.
(3) 상대방이 간절히 원하는 바를 일깨워라.
(4) 다른 사람에게 진정으로 관심을 가져라.
(5) 누군가의 이름이 그 사람에게는 어떤 언어로든 가장 감미로운 소리임을 기억하라.

(4) Become genuinely interested in other people.

(5) Remember that a person's name is to him or her the sweetest sound in any
language.

(6) Be a good listener. Encourage others to talk about themselves.

(7) Show interest in what he or she is saying. Ask questions.

(8) Make the other person feel important — and do it sincerely.

(9) The only way to get the best of an argument is to avoid it.

(10) Show respect for the other person's opinion. Never say, "You're wrong," even
if you think so.

(11) If you are wrong, admit it quickly and emphatically.

(12) Let the other person do a great deal of the talking.

(13) Never say, "I told you so." Be a gracious winner and don't crow about it.
You'll look twice as good in the eyes of the loser if you allow him to save face.

Developing friendship is a two-way street. The best way to have a friend is to
be one. True friendship cannot survive in an environment of broken dates, forgotten
promises, unpaid loans, unreturned phone calls, weak excuses and bald-faced lies.
If you are involved in such a relationship, end it. Freeloaders damage your self-
esteem and make you feel like a chump.

Finally, to get along well with other people, keep in mind the following rules.

(1) Keep skid chains on your tongue. Always say less than you think. Cultivate a
low, persuasive voice.How you say it often counts more than what you say.

(2) Make promises sparingly and keep them faithfully, no matter what the cost.

(3) Never let an opportunity pass to say a kind and encouraging word to or about
somebody. Praise good work, regardless of who did it.

(4) Be interested in others, their pursuits, their work, their homes and their
families. Make merry with those who rejoice; with those who weep, mourn.
Let everyone you meet, however humble, feel that you regard him as a
person of importance.

(5) Be cheerful. Don't burden or depress those around you by dwelling on your
aches and pains and smalldisappointments. Remember, everyone is carrying
some kind of burden.

(6) Keep an open mind. Discuss but don't argue. It is a mark of a superior mind
to be able to disagree without being disagreeable.

(7) Let your virtues speak themselves. Refuse to talk about the vices of others.
Discourage gossip. It is a waste of valuable time and can be destructive and
hurtful.

L.35.

L.40.

L.45.

L.50.

L.55.

L.60.

L.65.

(6) 상대방의 말을 경청하라. 다른 사람들이 자신에 대해 말할 수 있도록 용기를 북돋아라.

(7) 상대방이 하고 있는 말에 관심을 보이고, 질문을 던져라.

(8) 상대방이 중요한 사람이라고 느끼게 하라. 그것도 성실한 자세로.

(9) 논쟁에서 최상의 것을 얻기 위한 유일한 방법은 논쟁을 피하는 것이다.

(10) 상대방의 의견을 존중하라. 설령 당신과 의견이 다르더라도, 결코 "그게 아니야,"라고 말하지 말라.

(11) 당신이 잘못했을 경우, 그 즉시, 그리고 단호하게 그 사실을 인정하라.

(12) 상대방이 이야기를 많이 하게 하라.

(13) 절대 "내가 그렇게 말했잖아"라고 말하지 말라. 상냥한 승자가 되고, 승리에 대해 환성을 올리지 말라. 패자의 체면을 세워주면, 그 패자의 눈에는 당신이 두 배는 더 좋은 사람으로 보일 것이다.

우정을 발전시키는 데는 두 가지 방법이 있다. 친구를 사귀는 최선의 방법은 하나가 되는 것이다. 약속 시간을 어기고, 약속을 잊어버리며, 꾼 돈을 갚지 않고, 전화 한 번하지 않으며, 어줍잖은 변명이나 뻔뻔한 거짓말을 늘어놓는 상황에서는 진정한 우정이 자라날 수 없다. 그런 관계에 처해 있다면, 지금 당장 끝내라. 공짜로 얻어 먹는 사람들은 당신의 자존심을 손상시키며, 당신이 바보처럼 느껴지게 만들뿐이다.

마지막으로, 다른 사람들과 의좋게 지내려면 다음의 원칙들을 명심하라.

(1) 혀에 미끄럼 방지용 타이어 체인을 채워라. 당신이 생각하는 것보다 항상 적게 말하라. 낮고 설득력 있는 목소리를 가꿔라. 어떻게 말하느냐 하는 것이 종종 무엇을 말하느냐 하는 것보다 더 중요하다.

(2) 약속은 삼가고, 일단 한 약속은 어떤 대가를 치르더라도 충실히 이행하라.

(3) 누군가에게 또는 누군가에 대해 격려가 되는 친절한 말을 할 수 있는 기회는 절대 놓치지 말라. 누가 했든, 잘한 일에 대해서는 칭찬을 아끼지 말라.

(4) 다른 사람, 그 사람이 추구하는 것, 그 사람의 일, 그 사람의 가정과 가족 등에 대해 관심을 가져라. 기뻐하는 사람들과 흥겹게 떠들고, 또 우는 사람들과는 함께 슬퍼하라. 아무리 보잘 것 없는 사람이라도, 당신이 만나는 모든 사람들에게, 당신은 그 사람을 중요하게 생각한다고 느끼게 하라.

(5) 항상 쾌활하라. 당신의 아픔과 고통, 그리고 사소한 실망거리를 늘어놓음으로써 당신 주변의 사람들을 우울하거나 고민스럽게 만들지 말라.

(6) 열린 마음을 가져라. 토론을 하되 논쟁을 벌이지 말라. 비위를 거슬리지 않으면서 자신의 의견이 다르다고 말할 수 있는 것이 뛰어난 사람의 표시이다.

(7) 장점이 그냥 드러나게 하라. 다른 사람의 결점에 대해 말하지 말라. 뒷공론을 말려라. 그것은 귀중한 시간을 낭비하는 것이며, 파괴적이고 고통을 안겨주는 일이 될 수 있다.

(8) 다른 사람의 감정을 고려하라. 다른 사람을 희생양으로 삼는 위트와 유머는 결코 그 사람이 입을 고통에 값하지 못한다.

(9) 당신에 대한 심술궂은 말에 신경 쓰지 말라. 그냥 무시해버리고, 행동으로써 스스로를 변호하게 하라. 어느 누구도 험담꾼의 말을 믿지 않으리라고 확신하라.

(10) 당신이 응당 받아야할 인정에 대해 노심초사하지 말라. 최선을 다하고 느긋하게 기다려라. 당신 자신에 대해 잊어버리고 다른 사람들이 "기억하게" 하라. 그럴 때 성공은 훨씬 더 달콤하다.

L.70.
(8) Take into consideration the feelings of others. Wit and humor at the expense of another is never worth the pain that may be inflicted.

(9) Pay no attention to ill-natured remarks about you. Simply ignore the comments and let your actions speak for you. You can be sure no one will believe the backbiter.

L.75.
(10) Don't be anxious about the credit due you. Do your best and be patient. Forget about yourself and let others "remember." Success is much sweeter that way.

L.80.
And now a final word to all who sent for this booklet. The fact that you did is evidence that you want to improve the quality of your life by improving your relationships. You have taken the first step, which is the most important one. Now make this booklet your bible. Read it and reread it. Memorize the sentences that apply to you. Say them aloud, again and again. Tell yourself you are going to be the person you want to be and I promise, you'll feel the improvement in your bones. Good luck!

(Source: Adapted from Ann Landers' booklet).

(1) Is the topic both interesting and informative?

→ The topic is both interesting and informative, since it touches all of us in "practical" ("to make friends") and "psychological" ("stop being lonely") dimensions as described in this writing, "All of us have 'attacks' of loneliness at some time or another(L.3)... No age group has a monopoly on loneliness (L.24)."

(2) Does the main idea clearly introduce a topic sentence?

→ The main idea is "No age group... You want to get into the mainstream and be a part of what's happening (Lines 24~26)," and the topic sentence, "Here are ... suggestions... with people (Lines 26~28)." Therefore, the main idea, "...Be a part of what's happening" clearly introduces the topic sentence, "...several suggestions 'to make friends and stop being lonely'."

(3) Is the information organized into paragraphs that deal with one main subject/topic?

→ Yes, the information discussed the main ideas of the writing is organized into three paragraphs as follows:
(a) The main topic/subject of "Being truly likeable": "To be truly likeable, remember the following suggestions. (1) Don't... to save face (Lines 30~45)."
(b) The main subject of "Developing friendship": "Developing friendship is... like a chump (Lines 46~50)."
(c) The main topic of "Getting along with people.": Finally, to get along well ... is much sweeter that way (Lines 51~75)."

이제 이 책자를 읽는 모든 이들에게 마지막으로 한마디 덧붙이겠다. 이 책을 읽었다는 사실 자체가 당신이 관계를 개선시킴으로써 삶의 질을 개선시키고 싶어한다는 증거이다. 당신은 이미 그 첫 단계를 밟았으며, 그것이야말로 가장 중요하다. 이제 이 책자를 당신의 성전(聖典)으로 만들어라. 이 책자를 읽고 또 읽어라. 당신에게 해당되는 문장을 암기하라. 그 문장들을 반복해서 크게 말해보아라. 스스로에게 나는 내가 되고 싶어하는 사람이 될 거라고 말하라. 약속컨대, 당신은 그 사실을 확신하게 될 것이다. 행운이 있기를!

Note

inadequacy *n.* Insufficient or below standard.

nag *v.* To pester or annoy by complaining. scolding, or criticizing all the time.
    n. A horse, especially an old or worn-out horse.

pleasantry *n.* A casual remark intended to compliment or otherwise please another, esp. in a social situation of no great importance.

rescue *v.* To save from danger or harm --Lifeguards learn how to rescue swimmers.

corny *a.* 1. (informal) of humor, lacking subtlety ; obvious ; trite 2. of drama, foolishly sentimental or unoriginal.

cripple *n.* A person who is disabled, as because of injury to a leg.
    v. 1. To make into a cripple. 2. To disable ;damage --The sudden storm crippled the ship.

shell *n.* 1. The hard outer covering of such water animals as clams, crabs, oysters, and snails. 2. The hard outer covering of certain other animals or plants. Turtles, eggs, and nuts all have shells. 3. An outer covering or a frame. 4. A piece of ammunition for a gun, especially a case that holds a bullet and its explosive.

monopoly *n.* 1. Complete control over a product or service --The electric company has a monopoly on electricity. 2. A group or person having a monopoly.

condemn *v.* 1. To express strong feeling or opinion against --We condemn violence on television. 2. To declare someone guilty and say what the punishment is --The judge condemned the prisoner to 30 days in jail 3. To declare unsafe --The city has condemned that old building.

emphatically *ad.* 1.Expressed, performed, or uttered with emphasis 2.Forceful, determined, or insistent in speech or action. 3.Clearly delineated; bold in outline.

gracious *a.* Courteous and kind --Gracious hosts always try to make their guests comfortable.

(1) 주제는 독자의 시선을 끌 수 있을 만큼 재미있고 유익한가?

이 글의 주제는 재미있고 유익하다. "우리 모두가 가끔은 외로움의 '공격'을 받는다...특정 연령대만이 외로움을 독점하고 있는 것은 아니다."라는 표현에서 볼 수 있듯이, 이 글은 '실제적'('친구 사귀기')이고 심리학적('외로움에서 벗어나기')인 차원에서 우리 모두의 심금을 울리고 있기 때문이다.

(2) 주제는 주제문을 명확히 전하고 있는가?

주제는 "특정 연령대만이...당신은 삶의 주류로 들어가 현실에서 벌어지는 일의 일부가 되고 싶어한다."이며, 주제문은 "다음에 나오는 몇 가지 제안은... 벗어나는 방법이다."이다. 따라서 "...현실에서 벌어지고 있는 일의 일부가 되고 싶어한다"는 주제가 "다음에 나오는 몇 가지 제안은...친구를 사귀어 외로움에서 벗어나는 방법이다"라는 주제문에 명확히 소개되어 있다.

(4) Does the information contain details and examples that support the topic sentence?

→ (a) Details to support the topic sentence, " Here are ... with people (Lines 26~28)." "... To be lonely... among us (Lines 1~5)."

" (1) Don't criticize ... to save face (Lines 30~45)."

" Developing friendship is ... like a chump (Lines 46~50)."

" Keep skid chains ... that way (Lines 52~75)."

(b) Examples to support the topic sentence:

" ... Suddenly a casual friend ... anymore (Lines 6~10)."

" By this time ... or her loneliness (Lines 11~13)."

" Dr. Eugene Kennedy ... for somebody else (Lines 14~23)."

" And now a final word ... in your bones (Lines 76~82)."

(5) Are there smooth and logical transitions between paragraphs?

→ Yes, there are several smooth transitions that work as functional ones.

(a) "... Suddenly (L.6)."   (b) "By this time (L.11)."

(c) "Finally (L.51)."   (d) "And now (L.76)."

(6) Does the conclusion bring a satisfactory end?

→ Yes, it does effectively. The conclusion is very persuasive, since it asks some calls to action. The first sentence of the last paragraph, "And now a final word to all... for this booklet (L.76)" is a linguistic signal leading to the conclusion. The other sentences, "You have taken... Now,... Read... Memorize... Say them again and again (Lines 78~80)" include five Response-seekings techniques that call to action. And the sentence, "Tell yourself... and I promise, you'll feel ... in your bones (Lines 80~82)" is a statement for Confidence-building technique that assures your ability to succeed. In this sense, the conclusion as an end brings a feeling of satisfaction and success to readers.

(3) 정보는 한 가지 주제를 다루는 문단들로 짜여져 있는가?

그렇다. 이 글의 주제를 논의하는 정보는 다음과 같이 세 단락으로 짜여져 있다.

(a) '진정으로 호감 주기'

'진정으로 호감이 가게 하려면, 다음 제안을 항상 명심하라. (1)흠을 잡거나... (13)... 좋은 사람으로 보일 것이다."

(b) '우정 발전시키기'

"우정을 발전시키는 데는... 느껴지게 만들 뿐이다."

(c) '사람들과 의좋게 지내기'

"마지막으로... 더 달콤하다."

(4) 정보는 주제문을 뒷받침하는 세부사항과 예시문을 포함하고 있는가?

(a) "다음에 나오는 몇 가지 제안은... 벗어나는 방법이다."라는 주제문을 뒷받침하는 세부 사항

"...고독하다는 것은... 뛰어난 사람조차도."

"(1) 흠을 잡거나...(13)...좋은 사람으로 보일 것이다."

"우정을 발전시키는 데에는...느껴지게 만들뿐이다."

"혀에 미끄럼 방지용... 더 달콤하다."

(b) "주제문을 뒷받침하는 예시문

"...갑자기 뜻밖의 친구가... 더 이상 외롭지 않다."

"이쯤 되면... 구출하게 될 것이다."

"저명한 저술가 유진 케네디 박사는...다른 누군가를 위해 뭔가를 하라이다."

"이제 이 책자를 읽는 모든 이들에게...확신하게 될 것이다."

(5) 문단과 문단은 논리적이고 매끄럽게 연결되어 있는가?

그렇다. 연결을 매끄럽게 하는 몇 가지 이행 장치가 있다.

(a) '...갑자기'   (b) '이쯤되면'

(c) '마지막으로'   (d) '이제'

(6) 결론은 만족스런 결말로 이어지는가?

결론은 매우 설득력이 있다. 구체적인 행동을 요청하고 있기 때문이다. 마지막 문단의 첫 문장, "이제 이 책자를 읽는 모든 이들에게 마지막으로 한 마디 덧붙이겠다."는 결론에 이르는 언어학적 신호이다. "당신은 이미 그 첫 단계를...이제...읽어라...암기하라...반복해서 크게 말해 보아라." 등의 다른 문장들은 구체적으로 행동에 옮겨야할 다섯 가지 기법을 담고 있다. 그리고 "스스로에게... 확신하게 될 것이다."라는 말은 당신의 성공을 확실히 해 줄 자신감 증대 기법을 서술하고 있다. 이런 의미에서, 마지막으로서의 결론은 독자들에게 만족감과 성공에의 신념을 가져다 준다.

4.2.4. Narrative.

As we have seen earlier, one of the major purposes of an Narrative Essay is "to describe/tell an event based on a framework of topic related (a) plot, (b) characters, (c) setting, and, (d) point of view. Read the following essays, "The Gift," and "Pearl Harbor Day Stokes Memories" with the condensed guidelines in mind.

Condensed guidelines for a Narrative essay/writing.

(1) Does the narration include a plot, characters, setting, and point of view?
(2) Is the narration organized in chronological order, or order of importance?
(3) Does the narration contain specific and vivid nouns, verbs, and adjectives to share your excitement, sorrow, frustration, or a certain feeling with the readers?
(4) Has the writer put himself/herself in the story?
(5) Does the narration consider basic elements such as (a) purpose; (b) voice; (c) audience; (d) dialogue; (e) digression; (f) personal thoughts; (g) figures of speech; and, (j) purpose again?

<u>Model 1</u>: "The Gift." by Brenda Harms

Line 1   I met Gertrude as part of our Girl Scout project. We were to go to elderly people's homes in our town and do little odd jobs. To decide who went where, we drew names, and, well, I came up with Gertrude Hinkle. Gertrude is the oldest person in our town: she is ninety-four years old. She still lives in her own home and takes care

L.5.   of herself. At first, I was nervous. My mom's and dad's parents died when I was little. I never knew my grandparents, and I didn't know any other elderly people. But after my first visit with Gertrude, my nervousness vanished.

The first day I helped her do her dishes. She told me about her family. She had come from a large family with five boys and three girls. She was the youngest of

L.10.   the family and the only remaining member. The next Saturday I went back and helped herself clean her house. She told me more about her family and herself. When I was ready to leave, she asked me to come back on Monday. I did not ask why and cheerfully said I would.

On Monday I arrived at her house just after school was out. Scattered around the

L.15.   living room were square pieces of cloth. She told me that she was making a patchwork quilt for the granddaughter of one of her nieces. The pieces of cloth were all separated into colors and arranged in a pattern. I went to Gertrude's house

4.2.4. 나레이션

앞에서 살펴보았듯이, 나레이션형 에세이의 주요 목적 가운데 하나는 '(a) 플롯, (b) 등장 인물, (c) 무대 배경, (d) 관점과 관련된 주제의 틀에 입각하여 하나의 사건을 기술 또는 말하는 것'이다. 다음에 제시된 지침에 유의하면서 〈선물〉과 〈진주만 폭격일은 추억을 어루만지고〉라는 두 편의 에세이를 읽어보자.

나레이션 에세이 지침

(1) 나레이션에 플롯, 등장인물, 무대 배경, 관점 등이 포함되어 있는가?
(2) 나레이션은 연대기순 또는 중요도순으로 짜여져 있는가?
(3) 당신의 흥분, 슬픔, 좌절, 또는 특정한 감정을 독자들과 공유하기 위해 구체적이고 생생한 명사, 동사, 형용사를 사용하고 있는가?
(4) 작가는 이야기 속에 자신을 넣었는가?
(5) (a) 목적, (b) 음색, (c) 청중, (d) 대화, (e) 지엽적 이야기, (f) 개인적인 생각, (g) 말의 형상, (j) 목적의 재확인 등과 같은 기본적인 구성 요소가 고려되어 있는가?

모델 1 '선물' (브렌다 함스)

내가 게르트루드를 만난 것은 걸스카웃 프로젝트의 일환이었다. 우리 마을에 있는 노인 가정을 방문하여 잡일을 봐주기로 한 것이다. 누가 어디에 갈 것인지를 결정하기 위해, 우리는 이름이 적힌 제비를 뽑았고, 나는 게르트루드 힝클을 맡게 되었다. 게르트루드는 우리 마을에서 가장 연로한 사람으로, 아흔 네 살이다. 그녀는 아직도 자기 집에 살면서 스스로를 돌보고 있다. 처음에 나는 다소 신경이 예민해졌다. 친가, 외가를 막론하고, 나의 할아버지, 할머니는 모두 내가 어렸을 때 돌아가셨다. 나는 조부모님에 대해 전혀 알지 못했고, 동네의 여타 나이든 분들에 대해서도 마찬가지였다. 그러나 처음 게르트루드를 방문한 이후, 나의 두려움은 사라져 버렸다.

첫 날 나는 그녀가 설거지하는 것을 도와드렸다. 그녀는 자신의 가족에 대해 이야기했다. 그녀는 5남3녀의 대가족에서 자랐다. 그녀는 그 가족의 막내였고, 가족 구성원 가운데 유일하게 살아있는 사람이기도 했다. 그 다음 주 토요일, 나는 다시 그 집으로 가서 집 청소를 도왔다. 그녀는 가족과 자기 자신에 대해 더 많은 이야기를 들려주었다. 내가 떠날 준비를 끝내자, 그녀는 월요일 날 다시 와달라고 부탁했다. 나는 이유도 묻지 않고 흔쾌히 그러마고 대답했다.

every day after school for nearly a month. She taught me how to sew the pieces of cloth together evenly. Each piece had some sentimental meaning
L.20.   to her - each told a story - and she told me the stories.

When the quilt was finished, we both sat back and stared at it. So much had been put into it, not just work, but the lives of many people - people I had never known but felt I knew from her stories. Tears were in Gertrude's eyes as we took the quilt and packed it in a box. Both of us felt sad to send away the work that had given us
L.25.   many good times together. I would have loved to keep the quilt myself. However, I said nothing as we wrapped the box in brown paper so that it was ready to mail. Two days later a package arrived at my house. I knew what it was. Attached to the outside was a note that read:

Dear Sally,

L.30.   You worked hard on this. It's only fair that you should have it. I hope the quilt brings you as many memories as I have.

Love,
Gertrude

I went to thank Gertrude immediately, but she wasn't there. A neighbor said that
L.35.   she had gone to see relatives for a few days.

(1) Does the narrative include a plot, characters, setting, and point of view?

→ Yes, it does. The plot, characters, setting, and point of view are as follows:

   (a) The plot (sequences of a story):
       " I met Gertrude ... vanished (Lines 1~7)."
       " The first day... I would (Lines 8~13)."
       " On Monday ... the stories (Lines 14~20)."
       " When the quilt was finished... a note that read: (Lines 21~28)."
       " I went to thank ... a few days (Lines 34~35)."
   (b) Characters: I and Gertrude Hinkle
   (c) Setting: In our town.
   (d) Point of view:Each piece of clothes or items made at home has sentimental value or a memorable story, which is closely related to the lives of many people.

(2) Is the narrative organized in chronological order or order of importance?

→ The narrative is organized in chronological order as we have seen at (a) the plot in (1).

월요일이 되자, 나는 학교가 파한 뒤, 곧장 그녀의 집으로 갔다. 거실 여기저기에 네모난 천 조각들이 널려 있었다. 그녀는 조카의 손녀딸을 위해 퀼트를 만들고 있노라고 말했다. 천 조각들은 색깔에 따라 나뉘어 하나의 패턴으로 배열되었다. 나는 거의 한 달 동안 학교가 파한 뒤 매일 게르트루드의 집으로 갔다. 그녀는 내게 천 조각들을 고르게 바느질하는 방법을 가르쳐주었다. 각각의 조각이 그녀에게는 다소 감상적인 의미를 띠고 있었고 −− 각각 하나의 이야기를 담고 있었다 −− 그녀는 내게 그 이야기들을 들려주었다.

퀼트가 완성되자, 우리는 의자에 기대앉아 그것을 응시했다. 그 속에는 너무나 많은 것, 단순한 수고가 아니라 많은 사람들의 삶이 담겨 있었다. 내가 전혀 모르는, 그러면서도 그녀의 이야기 덕택에 마치 내가 알고 있는 듯 느껴지는 사람들의 삶 말이다. 그 퀼트를 잘 접어 상자에 포장하는 사이, 게르트루드의 눈에는 눈물이 가득 고였다. 우리는 우리 두 사람에게 함께 할 수 있는 좋은 시간을 많이 준 그 작품을 떠나보낸다는 사실이 무척 슬펐다. 그 퀼트를 내가 간직할 수 있다면. 그러나 갈색 종이로 상자를 포장하여 우편으로 보낼 준비를 하는 동안, 나는 아무런 내색도 하지 않았다. 이틀 뒤, 소포 꾸러미가 우리 집에 배달되었다. 나는 그것이 무엇인지 알고 있었다. 겉포장에는 다음과 같은 메모가 붙어 있었다.

샐리에게

넌 참 열심히 이 퀼트를 만들었어. 그러니 당연히 네가 가져야지.
이 퀼트가 네게도 내가 가진 것만큼 많은 추억을 가져오길 빌마.

게르트루드

나는 그 즉시 게르트루드에게 감사를 전하러 갔지만, 그녀는 집에 없었다. 이웃의 말로는 며칠간 친척을 만나러 갔다고 했다.

(1) 나레이션에 플롯, 등장인물, 무대 배경, 관점 등이 포함되어 있는가?

그렇다. 플롯, 등장인물, 무대 배경, 관점 등은 다음과 같다.

(a) 플롯

"내가 게르트루드를 만난 것은... 사라져 버렸다."

"첫날... 그러마고 대답했다."

"월요일이 되자... 들려주었다."

"퀼트가 완성되자... 메모가 붙어 있었다."

"나는 그 즉시...만나러 갔다고 했다."

(b) 등장인물 : 나와 게르트루드 힝클

(c) 무대 배경 : 우리 마을

(d) 관점 : 각각의 천 조각 또는 아이템들은 감상적인 가치 또는 잊혀지지 않는 이야기를 가지고 있으며, 그것은 많은 사람들의 삶과 긴밀하게 연관되어 있다.

(2) 나레이션은 연대기순 또는 중요도 순으로 짜여져 있는가?

(1)의 플롯에서 살펴보았듯이, 이 글은 연대기 순으로 짜여져 있다.

(3) Has the writer used specific and vivid words to help readers share his/her feeling of excitement or sorrow?

→ Yes, she did as follows:
  (a) Nouns: "Tears (L.23)" to show sorrow.
  (b) Adjectives: "the oldest (L. 3); ninety-four (L. 4); the only remaining (L. 10)" to share wonder.
  (c) Adverbs: "never (L. 6); only (L. 10); just (L. 14); immediately (L. 34)" to share a feeling of intensity.

(4) Has the writer put herself in the story?

→ Yes she did, since the writer acts and thinks as a protagonist in this story.

(5) Does the narrative include basic elements such as (a) purpose; (b) voice; (c) audience; (d) dialogue; (e) digression; (f) personal thoughts; (g) figure of speech; and, (h) purpose again?

→ (a) Purpose: To describe an important event with a focused topic. The writer describes "The Gift" as an important event based on the focused topic and its significance.
  (b) Voice: "Voice" means writing in a way that sounds like oneself, using language as natural and distinctive as possible without any phrases or sentences that are pretentious or knowledgeable. The whole passages in this essay include natural voice that reads and sounds like the writer's own tone.
  (c) Audience: This touching narrative can embrace various levels of readers, but the target audience is likely to be high school students. It is because the writer herself is a high school student who depicts this story based on her experience as a student.
  (d) Dialogue: The dialogue is not included.
  (e) Digression: "Digression" is a portion of a discourse deviating from the main theme. The digression in this essay is not found.
  (f) Personal Thoughts:
      "At first, I was nervous... my nervousness vanished (Ls. 5~7)."
      "- people I had never known... stories (Ls. 22~23)."
      "Both of us felt sad... quilt myself (Ls. 24~25)."
      "I knew... what it was (L. 27)" are all implicitly describing the writer's thoughts.
  (g) Figure of Speech: Figure of Speech involves some sort of imaginative comparison between seemingly unlike things. The most common are simile, metaphor, and personification, which are not found in this essay.
  (h) Purpose Again: "The Purpose Again" means that the narrative helps readers smile, laugh or ponder after reading the essay. Yes, this essay helps readersthink about the sentimental value of "The Gift" which is closely related to the lives of many people.

C H A P T E R 4

(3) 작가는 흥분이나 슬픔 등의 감정을 독자들과 공유하기 위해 구체적이고 생생한 단어를 사용하고 있는가?

  (a) 명사 : 슬픔을 보여주고 있는 명사 '눈물'

  (b) 형용사 : 경탄스러움을 느끼게 해 주는 '가장 연로한' ; '아흔 네 (살)' ; '유일하게 살아있는' 등의 형용사

  (c) 부사 : 강렬한 감정을 드러내는 '전혀' ; '유일하게' ; '곧장' ; '즉시' 등의 부사

(4) 작가는 이야기 속에 자신을 넣었는가?

  그렇다. 작가는 이 이야기의 주인공으로 행동하며 생각하고 있다.

(5) 이 나레이션 속에 (a) 목적, (b) 음색, (c) 청중, (d) 대화, (e) 지엽적 이야기, (f) 개인적인 생각, (g) 말의 형상, (j) 목적의 재확인 등과 같은 기본적인 구성 요소가 포함되어 있는가?

  (a) 목적 : 중요한 사건을 특정 주제에 맞춰 기술하는 것. 작가는 정해진 주제와 그 의미에 근거해서 '선물' 이라는 중요한 사건에 대해 기술하고 있다.

  (b) 음색 : ' 음색' 이란 뽐내거나 잘난 체 하는 구절이나 문장을 배제하고, 가능한 한 자연스럽고 특색 있는 언어를 사용하여 마치 자기 자신처럼 들리는 글쓰기를 의미한다. 이 에세이에 나오는 모든 구절들이 작가 자신의 어조처럼 읽히고 들리는 자연스런 음색을 담고 있다.

  (c) 청중 : 이 감동적인 나레이션은 다양한 수준의 독자를 포용할 수 있지만, 주요 타깃은 아무래도 고등학생들인 것 같다. 작가 자신이 학생으로서 자신의 경험에 근거하여 이 이야기를 묘사하는 고등학생이기 때문이다.

  (d) 대화 : 대화는 들어 있지 않다.

  (e) 지엽적 이야기 : ' 지엽적 이야기' 란 메인 테마에서 벗어나는 약간의 이야기이다. 이 에세이에서는 지엽적인 이야기가 발견되지 않는다.

  (f) 개인적인 생각 : "처음에 나는 다소... 사라져 버렸다." "내가 전혀 모르는... 삶 말이다." "우리는 우리 두 사람에게... 간직할 수 있다면." "나는 그것이 무엇인지 알고 있었다." 등의 문장이 모두 암묵적으로 작가의 생각을 드러내고 있다.

  (g) 말의 형상 : 말의 형상이란 겉보기에 서로 다른 두 가지를 가상으로 비유하는 것을 뜻한다. 가장 일반적인 것으로 직유, 은유, 의인화 등이 있으며, 이 에세이에서는 그런 비유가 발견되지 않는다.

  (h) 목적의 재확인 : ' 목적의 재확인' 이란 에세이를 읽고난 뒤, 독자들이 미소를 짓거나 웃거나 혹은 생각에 잠길 수 있도록 하는 것을 의미한다. 이 에세이는 독자들로 하여금 많은 사람들의 삶과 긴밀하게 연관되어 있는 '선물' 의 감상적 가치에 대해 생각하게 한다.

Note

odd *a.* Not ordinary or usual ; peculiar --The car is making an odd noise.
patchwork *n.* Pieces of cloth various colors, shapes, and sizes sewn together.
quilt *n.* A bed covering made by stitching together two layers of fabric with an inner layer of cotton, wool down, or feathers.
    v. 1. To work on or make a quilt. 2. To stitch together like a quilt, with an inner layer of padding.
stare *v.* To look with a steady, often wide-eyed gaze.

Model 2: "Pearl Harbor Day Stokes Memories."

Line 1   At about 8 a.m., Sunday, December 7,1941, the Japanese Imperial Navy launched a
surprise attack on Pearl Harbor, Hawaii, where about 100 U.S. Navy ships (battleships,
destroyers, cruisers and support ships) were docked, sinking five battleships.
Simultaneously, Hickham Field was bombed, destroying 18 Army Air Corps bombers
L.5.   and fighters on the ground. More than 4,500 Americans were killed or wounded.

The attack brought this country into World War II and was described by President
Roosevelt as "a day that will live in infamy." We were already supporting Great Britain
with lend-lease, but this act brought us directly into the war. Hitler almost immediately
joined in with a declaration of war against the United States. Winston Churchill later said, "I
L.10.   went to bed and slept the sleep of the saved and the thankful."

Today, judging from various Jay Leno TV man-on-the-street segments, most
Americans don't even seem to know where Pearl Harbor is much less what happened
there. At that time. however, Roosevelt said, "I ask that Congress declare, that since the
unprovoked and dastardly attack by Japan... a state of war has existed between the
L.15.   United States and the Japanese Empire."

Inevitably, as years passed, questions about Pearl Harbor developed. Was it really a
surprise? The Japanese code had been broken. Some say Roosevelt knew of the
impending attack, but did not act because of the certain knowledge that we had to enter
the war to stop Hitler and his Axis partners. It was not long after the attack that a song by
L.20.   Sammy Kaye and Don Reid became something of a rallying battle cry. The song was
"Remember Pearl Harbor."

One consequence of our entry in the war, described by Studs Terkel as "the last good
war," was a wonderful sense of, not merely unity, in this country, but for caring for one
another. I saw all this as a teen-ager when my father and brother were in the Army,
L.25.   mother working as a nurse and servicemen who were friends of my brother sleeping all
over the floor in our apartment so they would not have to pay for a hotel room that was
not that available in wartime New York in the first place. When I hitchhiked, drivers
would routinely stop to pick me up, thinking I might be a merchant seaman.
Servicemen everywhere were routinely offered free drinks at local bars. The USO was
L.30.   in full swing and some of the prettiest girls in this country would be there to dance with
lonely servicemen. More significant gestures were made by the nurse trapped on
Bataan in the Philippine sand recaptured in the recent book, "We Band of Angels."

This country was still plagued with segregation. Even in Philadelphia, certain movie
theaters restricted black audiences to the balcony. I heard of marvelous evasions of this
L.35.   injustice. A black man working in my building told me how his white friends would
surround the black kids going into a theater and escort them into the all-white sections.

CHAPTER 4

모델 2 '진주만 폭격일은 추억을 어루만지고'

1941년 12월 7일 일요일 오전 8시 무렵, 일본 해군이 백여 척의 미국 해군 함정(전함, 구축함, 순양함, 예비함정)이 주둔하고 있던 하와이의 진주만에 기습 공격을 감행하여 전함 다섯 척을 침몰시켰다. 그와 동시에, 히캄 필드에 폭탄이 투하되어 18대의 폭격기와 전투기가 현장에서 파괴되었다. 4,500명 이상의 미국인이 살해되거나 부상을 입었다.

일본의 기습 공격은 우리 나라를 제 2차 세계대전에 합류시켰고, 루스벨트 대통령에 따르면, "치욕의 날"로 묘사되었다. 우리는 이미 무기 대여를 통해 대영 제국을 지원하고 있었지만, 이 사건으로 말미암아 전쟁에 직접 참여하게 되었다. 히틀러는 거의 그와 동시에 미국에 대한 전쟁 선포에 동참했다. 윈스턴 처칠은 후에 "나는 잠자리에 들어 구원받은 느낌과 고마운 느낌 속에서 잠에 들었다."고 말했다.

제이 레노 TV 프로그램, '거리의 사람들'을 보며 판단컨대, 오늘날 대부분의 미국인은 진주만 사건의 내용은커녕 진주만이 어디인지조차 모르는 것 같다. 그러나 루스벨트 대통령은 그 당시 "일본이 정당한 사유도 없이 비열한 공격을 감행했으므로... 나는 의회가 미국과 일본 제국 사이에 전쟁 상태가 발발했다고 선언해 주기를 요청한다"고 말했다.

몇 년이 흐르는 사이, 부득이하게 진주만에 대한 의문이 터져나왔다. 그것은 진정 기습이었을까? 일본의 암호는 이미 파기되었다. 일부에서는 루스벨트가 공격이 임박했다는 사실을 알고 있었으나, 히틀러와 그의 핵심 동맹국들을 저지하려면 전쟁에 참여해야 한다는 인식 때문에 적절한 조치를 취하지 않았다고 말한다. 기습 이후 얼마 지나지 않아 새미 케이에와 돈 라이드의 노래가 전쟁의 함성을 규합하는 중요한 것으로 자리잡았다. 그 노래는 '진주만을 기억하라' 였다.

스터즈 터클이 '최후의 좋은 전쟁'이라 묘사한 그 전쟁에 우리가 참여한 뒤 나타난 하나의 결과는 단순한 일체감뿐만 아니라 서로에 대한 배려라는 훌륭한 의식이었다. 나는 십대로서 그 모습을 직접 지켜보았다. 나의 아버지와 형은 군인이었고, 어머니는 간호사로 일하고 있었으며, 형의 친구였던 많은 군인들이 전쟁 초기 뉴욕에서는 좀처럼 얻기 힘든 호텔 방에 투숙하는 대신 우리 아파트에서 지냈다. 내가 히치하이크를 하면, 운전자들은 나를 수병이라고 생각하면서 응당 태워주었다. 도처에 널린 군인들은 지방 술집에 가면 무료로 음료를 제공받았다. 미군 서비스 기관(United Service Organizations. 군대 위문 활동을 하는 민간 비영리 조직)은 총가동되고 있었고, 전국에서 가장 예쁘다는 소녀 일부는 직접 거기 가서 외로운 군인들과 춤을 추곤 했다. 보다 의미 있는 제스처들은 필리핀 바탄에서 함정에 빠진 간호사에 의해 이루어졌는데, 이 이야기는 "We Band of Angels"라는 최근의 책에 잘 나와 있다.

우리 나라는 여전히 인종 차별이라는 재앙에 시달리고 있었다. 필라델피아의 경우, 심지어 몇몇 영화관들이 흑인 관객의 2층 특별석 출입을 제한하고 있었다. 나는 이러한 부당 관행을 피해 가는 교묘한 방법에 대해 들었다. 내 건물에서 일하는 흑인 한 명의 말에 따르면, 그의 백인 친구들이 흑인 아이들을 에워싼 채 극장 안으로 들어가 그들을 백인 구역까지 데려다 준다는 것이었다.

This sense of caring prevailed even after the war. I recall returning from basic training in 1949 and being told by a conductor when I wondered if I would get the same meal as civilians, "Son, I would give you anything on this train without a moment's hesitation." That is, in fact, the way we were.

L.40.

(Source: True Van Deusen, Metro, December 7, 2000).

After bombing Pearl Harber, Japanese pilots radioed Tokyo with the message, "Tora, tora, tora." Tora, which means tiger, was a code word for: "We have succeeded." Despite the destruction shown here, the Japanese did not destory the entire American Pacific fleet. Three aircraft carriers were not in the harber during the attack. In the naval warfare of World War II , these aircraft carriers proved to be valuable weapons.

(1) Does the narrative include a plot, characters, setting, and point of view?

➡ Yes it does.

(a) Plot: The plot starts based on the following main ideas of each paragraph summarized as follows. The sequences of this writing include:

"the surprise attack on Pearl Harbor (Ls. 1~5),"

"U.S. entered the war (Ls. 6~10),"

"Today most Americans do not seem to know what happened at Pearl Harbor (Ls. 11~15),"

"There have been some developing questions about Pearl Harbor (Ls. 16~21),"

"There were unity and caring for one another during the wartime (Ls. 22~32),"

"This country had racial discrimination (Ls. 33~36),"

"This sense of caring was American social reality at that time (Ls. 37~40),"

(b) Characters: I, President Roosevelt, Winston Churchill, Jay Leno, Hitler, Sammy Kaye, Don Reid, Studs Terkel.

(c) Setting: Pearl Harbor, Hawaii; Hickham Field; New York; Bataan; This Country; Philadelphia; theater; all-white sections; basic training; train.

(d) Point of View: "This is, in fact, the way we were (L. 40)."

(2) Is the narrative organized in chronological order or order of importance?

➡ The narrative is organized in chronological order as evidenced at (a) Plot in (1).

이러한 배려 의식은 전쟁이 끝난 뒤에도 지속되었다. 1949년, 내가 신병 기초 훈련을 마치고 돌아오던 때의 일이다. 내가 일반인들과 똑같은 식사를 할 수 있겠느냐고 묻자, 차장은 이렇게 말했다. "이보게, 이 기차에서는 한 순간도 망설이지 않고 자네에게 아무거나 다 주겠네." 사실 그게 우리의 모습이었다.

(1) 나레이션에 플롯, 등장인물, 무대 배경, 관점 등이 포함되어 있는가?

그렇다.

(a) 플롯 : 플롯은 다음과 같이 요약된 각 문단의 주제에 근거하여 시작되고 있다.

"진주만 기습 공격"

"미국의 참전"

"오늘날 대부분의 미국인들은 진주만에서 무슨 일이 일어났는지 모르고 있는 것 같다."

"진주만에 대한 몇 가지 의문이 터져 나왔다."

"전시 기간 동안 일체감과 서로에 대한 배려가 있었다."

"우리 나라는 인종 차별이 있었다."

"이러한 배려 의식은 그 당시 미국 사회의 현실이었다."

(b) 등장인물 : 나, 루스벨트 대통령, 윈스턴 처질, 제이 레노, 히틀러, 새미 카이예, 돈 라이드, 스터즈 터클

(c) 무대 배경 : 하와이 진주만, 히캄 필드, 뉴욕, 바탄, 우리 나라. 필라델피아, 극장, 백인 구역, 신병 훈련, 기차

(d) 관점 : "사실 그게 우리의 모습이었다."

(2) 나레이션은 연대기 순 또는 중요도 순으로 짜여져 있는가?

나레이션은 (1) 플롯 부분에서 살펴보았듯이, 연대기 순으로 짜여져 있다.

(3) 작가는 흥분이나 슬픔 등의 감정을 독자들과 공유하기 위해 구체적이고 생생한 단어를 사용하고 있는가?

(a) 명사 : "공격" 대신 "기습 공격"

(b) 동사 : "가져오고" 대신 "어루만지고"(제목)

(c) 형용사 : "비겁한" 대신 "비열한"

(4) 작가는 이야기 속에 자신을 넣었는가?

그는 글 속에 자신을 삽입시켰다.

"나는 십대로서... 아파트에서 지냈다."

"이러한 배려 의식은... 우리의 모습이었다."

TRUE VAN DEUSEN
A Philadelphia freelance writer

(3) Has the writer used specific and vivid words to help readers share his excitement, sorrow, or frustration?

➡ (a) Nouns: "Surprise attack" instead of "attack" (L. 2)

   (b) Verbs: "Stokes" instead of "brings" (Title)

   (c) Adjective: "dastardly" instead of "cowardly" (L. 14)

(4) Has the writer put himself in the story?

➡ Yes he did in some parts of the essay.

   "I saw all this... in the first place (Ls. 24~27)."

   "This sense of caring... the way we were (Ls. 37~40)."

(5) Does the narrative include basic elements, (a) purpose, (b) voice, (c) audience, (d) dialogue, (e) digression, (f) personal thought, (g) figure of speech, and (h) purpose again?

➡ (a) Purpose: To share his wartime memories as Pearl Harbor Day approaches.

   (b) Voice: The voice in paragraph 1 (Ls. 1~5); 2 (Ls. 6~10); 3 (Ls. 11~15); and 4 (Ls. 16~21) sound to be more formal, since the writer describes much of the related public affairs at that time based on factual realities. The voice in paragraph 5 (Ls. 21~32); 6 (Ls. 33~36); and 7 (Ls. 37~40) sound to be more informal, since the writer describes the existing wartime social realities based on his own observation and experience in an informal tone.

   (c) Audience: This type of topic, "sharing memories" strongly appeals to the readers who can share the experiences or memories with the writer as contemporary fellows.

   (d) Dialogue: Not found in this essay.

   (e) Digression: Paragraph 6 (Ls. 33~36) shows a certain level of digression in meaning from the main theme, "The spirit of caring during the wartime." The paragraph depict the racial discrimination as existing social realities, but it destroys the unity of the essay.

   (f) Personal Thought: His personal thought are clearly expressed as "... but for caring for one another (Ls. 23~24); "This Sense of caring... after the war (L. 37); and, "That is, ... we were (L. 40)."

   (g) Figure of Speech: * Metaphor = "... slept the sleep of the saved and the thankful (L. 10)." The last good war (Ls. 22~23)."

    * Simile = "We Band of Angels (L. 32)."

   (h) Purpose Again: The narrative helps readers remember the caring spirit during the wartime and think about existing social realities today as Pearl HarborDay approaches.

(5) 이 나레이션 속에 (a) 목적, (b) 음색, (c) 청중, (d) 대화, (e) 지엽적 이야기, (f) 개인적인 생각, (g) 말의 형상, (j) 목적의 재확인 등과 같은 기본적인 구성 요소가 포함되어 있는가?

(a) 목적 : 진주만 공격이 다가오면서 자신의 전시 기억을 공유하는 것.

(b) 음색 : 문단 1, 2, 3, 4의 음색은 다소 딱딱하게 들린다. 작가가 사실에 근거하여 그 당시의 공적인 사건을 상당수 기술하고 있기 때문이다. 문단 5, 6, 6의 음색은 좀더 편안하게 들린다. 작가 자신의 관찰 및 경험에 근거하여 편안한 어조로 그 당시 사회 분위기를 기술하고 있기 때문이다.

(c) 청중 : "추억의 공유"라는 이런 유형의 주제는 작가와 동시대인으로서 함께 그 경험이나 추억을 공유할 수 있는 독자들에게 강한 호소력을 가진다.

(d) 대화 : 이 글에서는 대화가 발견되지 않는다.

(e) 지엽적인 이야기 : 문단 6은 "전쟁 중에 있었던 배려 의식"이라는 주제에서 의미상 약간의 이탈을 보여준다. 이 문단은 인종 차별을 실재하는 사회 현실로 묘사하고 있지만, 전체적으로 글의 통일성을 깨뜨리고 있다.

(f) 개인적인 생각 : 그의 개인적인 생각은 "...서로에 대한 배려라는 훌륭한 의식이었다."라든가 "이러한 배려 의식은... 지속되었다," "사실 그게 우리의 모습이었다." 등의 문장에 명확히 표현되어 있다.

(g) 말의 형상 :

* 은유 및 직유가 사용되었다.

(h) 목적의 재확인 : 이 글은 진주만 공격일이 다가옴에 따라 독자들로 하여금 전쟁 중의 배려의식을 상기하고 현재의 사회 현실에 대해 생각해 보게 한다.

Note

launch *v* 1. To throw --The coach taught us how to launch a javelin. 2. To send forcefully upward, as a rocket. 3 To set afloat --The new ship was launched today. 4. To begin or start --We launched a new project.

infamy *n.* 1. A deservedly evil fame or reputation, or the character or behavior that caused it. 2. A shameful or wicked act. 3. The loss of certain rights as a citizen consequent upon conviction for crimes such as treason.

segment *n.* A part into which something is or can be divided.

provoke *v.* 1. To bring on ; cause --The comedian provoked steady laughter. ≠ unprovoke

dastardly *ad.* Cowardly; mean; sneaky.

inevitable *a.* Unavoidable, regardless of the circumstances; certain to occur

merchant *n.* A person who buys and sells goods, especially a person who runs a store.

evasion *n.* 1.The act or an instance of escaping, avoiding, or failing to perform something. 2. The avoidance of giving a full or truthful response to a question, point of argument, or the like. 3. A means of avoiding, escaping, or otherwise evading; ruse.

recapture *v.* 1. To capture again. 2. To recall or find again --We tried to recapture the happy days of summer.

plague *n.* 1. A very contagious disease that often causes death.
2. Something that causes misery --A plague of locusts destroyed the farmer's crops.
v. 1. To torment with disease or misery

4.2.5. Personal.

One of the main purposes of a Personal Essay is "to describe a real-life story based on your own experience." Let's read the following Personal Essays, "Yes, Santa Exists and We Need Him" and "The Last Lesson," with the condensed guidelines in mind.

Condensed guidelines for a Personal essay/writing.

(1) Has the writer used the first person pronoun: "I, me, my," and maintained the first person's point of view?
(2) Has the writer enlivened his/her narratives with specific facts and details?
(3) Does the writer describe the events in chronological order?
(4) Is the tone friendly, honest, and informal?
(5) Has the writer drawn a conclusion that explains what the experience meant to him/her?

<u>Model 1</u>. "Yes, Santa Exists and We Need Him."

Line 1   Once upon a time when I wrote a column for a different newspaper, the city editor walked over to my desk with a letter in her hand and a look on her face. "Is this for real?" I asked the editor after I'd read the letter. There was a return address on the envelope and the phone number was listed, so I called. The little

L.5.   girl who wrote the letter answered the phone. She sounded much younger than her years. Hers was the tiny sweet voice of Christmas past, a tonic of innocence for ears sharpened to cynical points by the grindstone of insincere words.

   "Was this letter part of a school assignment," I asked. Had her parents helped her write it? No, the little girl said, she had written the letter by herself because she thought

L.10.   the newspaper would have the answer. Well, it was a very good letter, I told her. Thank you, she replied. I promised that I would try to find an answer. Thank you, she said again, good-bye. I looked at the letter for a long time, and I wished that she had asked about something easy, the theory of aerodynamics, perhaps, or why water in lakes doesn't sink into the ground. Instead, she wrote:

4.2.5. 사적인 이야기

사적 에세이의 주요 목적 가운데 하나는 "자신의 경험에 근거해서 실제 이야기를 기술하는 것"이다. 다음에 제시된 지침을 염두에 두면서 "그래, 산타클로스는 존재하고, 우린 그를 필요로 한단다."와 "마지막 수업"이라는 사적 에세이 두 편을 읽어보기로 하자.

사적 에세이 지침

(1) 작가는 1인칭 대명사 "나"를 사용하면서 1인칭 관점을 유지했는가?

(2) 작가는 구체적인 사실과 세부 설명으로 자신의 나레이션에 활기를 불어넣었는가?

(3) 작가는 사건을 연대기 순으로 서술하는가?

(4) 어조는 다정하고, 솔직하며, 편안한가?

(5) 작가는 그 경험이 자신에게 어떤 의미를 가지는지 알려주려는 결론을 이끌어냈는가?

> **모델 1** '그래, 산타클로스는 존재하고, 우린 그를 필요로 한단다.'

언젠가 내가 다른 신문에서 칼럼을 쓰던 시절, 사회 부장이 심각한 표정으로 손에 편지를 한 장 들고 내 책상으로 걸어왔다. "이게 사실이에요?" 편지를 읽고 나서 내가 그녀에게 물었다. 봉투에 회신할 주소와 전화번호가 적혀 있었으므로, 나는 전화를 걸었다. 편지를 쓴 어린 소녀가 전화를 받았다. 그녀의 목소리는 나이보다 훨씬 어리게 들렸다. 지난 크리스마스의 작고 감미로운 목소리, 성의 없는 말이라는 맷돌에 의해 냉소적 진의에 예리해진 귀에는 순결한 강장제 같은 그런 목소리였다.

"이 편지는 학교 숙제 때문에 쓴 거니?"라고 내가 물었다. 부모님이 도와주셨어? 아니오, 라고 어린 소녀가 대답했다. 신문이 대답해 줄 것 같아서 나 혼자서 쓴 거에요. 그래, 정말 멋진 편지구나, 라고 내가 그녀에게 말했다. 고맙습니다, 라고 그녀가 대답했다. 나는 답을 찾아보겠다고 약속했다. 고맙습니다, 안녕히 계세요. 나는 오랫동안 그 편지를 바라보았고, 그녀가 좀 쉬운 걸 물어봤더라면 좋았을걸, 하고 생각했다. 이를테면 항공 역학 이론이라든가 호수의 물은 왜 땅 속으로 스며들지 않는가 하는 문제 말이다. 대신 그녀는 이런 편지를 써보냈다.

> 편집자님께
> 전 아홉 살이고, 4학년이에요. 우리 반에서 가장 똑똑하죠. 하지만 제가 모르는 것도 너무나 많아요. 제가 이 편지를 쓰는 까닭은 여쭤보고 싶은 게 있기 때문이에요. 산타 클로스 같은 건 없다는 얘기를 들었어요. 옛날에는 있었지만, 지금은 없다는 얘기도 들었구요. 게다가 산타 클로스는 정말 있다는 얘기도 들었어요. 도대체 어떤 말이 진짜에요?
>
> 뉴저지주 우들린에서 마리 스타넥

L.15. Dear Editors,

I am nine and in fourth grade. I am the smartest person in the class. There are a lot of things I don't know. I am writing this letter to ask you a question. I have heard there is no such thing as Santa Claus. I have heard that there was a Santa Claus but there isn't now. I have also heard that there really is a Santa
L.20. Claus. Which of these is true?

Sincerely, Marie Stanek,
Woodlynne, N.J.

I am not the smartest person at the newspaper, Marie, but that's OK because you don't have to be smart to understand the truth about Santa Claus. Before I
L.25. answer your question, I must tell you about another little girl who wrote to a newspaper years before you, your parents and maybe even your grandparents were born. Her name was Virginia O'Hanlon, and she was just one year younger than you when she wrote to the editors of the New York Sun. Virginia was also confused by the things she had heard about Santa Claus,
L.30. and a wise editor named Francis P. Church answered her by writing, "Yes, Virginia, there is a Santa Claus. He exists as certainly as love and generosity and devotion exist, and you know that they abound and give your life its highest beauty and joy."

But terrible things have happened in the world since Virginia wrote her
L.35. letter, Marie, things beyond the imagination of the wisest or worst of men and women. Perhaps you have seen some of these terrible things on TV or in books. Perhaps you have seen the faces of children whose eyes have lost the hope of ever seeing Santa Claus, or of knowing love. How could Santa exist in a world where so many children live in pain and dies in despair? How
L.40. could he not? The world needs Santa Claus, Marie, now more than ever.

But what is Santa Claus? This, I think, is where your confusion sets in. You've been told that there is a Santa, that there was a Santa but there isn't one anymore, and that there isn't a Santa. My answer may confuse you even more, Marie, because all three are true. Santa is as
L.45. real as you or me. But Santa exists only if you believe. And Santa knows if you believe in him, the same way he knows if you've been naughty or nice. Santa knows these things because (and this is the important part) he lives in your heart. He lives in the
L.50. hearts of everyone who will let him. How? I don't know, he is Santa, he can do these things.

(Source: Clark Deleon, Metro, December 10, 2000)

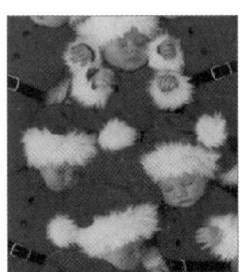

Santa Claus

난 신문사에서 가장 똑똑한 사람은 아니란다, 마리. 하지만 그건 괜찮아. 산타 클로스의 진실을 이해하는데 반드시 똑똑해야 할 필요는 없으니까. 네 질문에 답하기 전에, 너보다 몇 년 전에 한 신문사에 편지를 보낸 다른 소녀에 대해 이야기해야겠구나. 그 소녀의 이름은 버지니아 오핸론이고, 그 소녀는 너보다 한 살 어린 나이에 뉴욕 선지 편집자에게 편지를 보냈단다. 버지니아 역시 산타 클로스에 대한 갖가지 소문 때문에 혼란을 겪고 있었는데, 프랜시스 P. 처치라는 현명한 편집자는 이런 답신을 보냈어. "그래, 버지니아, 산타 클로스는 있단다. 사랑과 관용, 헌신이 존재하듯이, 산타 클로스도 분명히 존재하지. 아다시피, 그들은 많이 있고, 또 너의 삶에 최고의 아름다움과 즐거움을 선사한단다."

하지만 버지니아가 편지를 쓴 뒤, 세상에는 아주 끔찍한 일들이 일어났단다, 마리. 현명한 사람들의 상상을 뛰어넘는 일, 남녀 모두에게 최악의 일 말이야. 어쩜 너도 이런 끔찍한 일들을 TV나 책에서 봤을지도 모르겠구나. 행여라도 산타 클로스를 볼 수 있다거나 사랑을 알고 있다는 희망을 잃어버린 아이들의 얼굴을 본 적이 있을지도 모르지. 이렇게 많은 아이들이 고통 속에 살다가 절망 속에 죽어 가는 세상에 어떻게 산타 클로스가 존재할 수 있겠니? 또 어떻게 존재하지 않을 수 있겠니? 마리야, 세상은 지금 전보다 더욱 산타 클로스를 필요로 하고 있단다.

하지만 산타 클로스가 뭘까? 네가 혼란스러운 건 바로 이 문제라는 생각이 드는구나. 넌 산타가 있다는 이야기, 옛날에는 있었지만 지금은 없다는 이야기, 그리고 산타는 아예 없다는 이야기, 이렇게 세 가지 이야기를 다 들어봤을 거다. 내 대답은 너를 더욱 혼란스럽게 할 지도 모르겠구나, 마리. 세 가지 모두 사실이니까. 산타는 너와 나처럼 실재하고 있단다. 하지만 산타는 오직 네가 믿을 경우에만 존재하지. 게다가 산타는 네가 자신을 믿고 있는지 아닌지도 알고, 마찬가지로 네가 나쁜 앤지 착한 앤지도 안단다. 산타가 이런 걸 다 아는 건 바로 그가 네 마음 속에 살고 있기 때문이야(이게 가장 중요한 거지). 그는 자신을 받아 들이는 사람 모두의 마음 속에 살고 있단다. 그럼 어떻게 그럴까? 잘 모르겠지만, 산타니까 그럴 수 있는 거야.

Note

innocence *n.* The quality, condition, or fact of being innocent.

cynical *a.* 1. Showing little or no faith in human nature; distrustful or contemptuous of others motives.
2. Callously taking advantage of others or violating accepted morals.

grindstone *n.* A stone wheel that is rotated to sharpen implements or weapons, grind grain, or sand and shape items by abrasion.

aerodynamic *n.* (used with a sing. verb) A science that deals with the dynamics of air and other gases and with the forces acting on objects that move through them.

generosity *n.* 1. Willing readiness to give. 2. An act of ready giving. 3. Largeness of character.

devotion *n.* Loyalty and affection.

abound *v.* To be present in large numbers or amounts ; be full of --Fish abound in that river. The forest abounds in wildlife.

despair *n.* 1. Total lack of hope --They gave up in despair. 2. A cause of despair.
v. To be without or lose all hope.

(1) Has the writer used the first person pronoun: "I, me, my," and maintained the first person's point of view?

→ Yes, he did. Refer to the use of many "first person pronouns" in the paragraphs. And the writer maintains his points of view as follows:
(a) "I wished that she had asked... ground (Ls. 12~14)."
(b) "But terrible things... now more than ever (Ls. 34~40)."
(c) "But what is Santa Claus?... he can do these things (Ls. 41~51)."

(2) Has the writer enlivened his/her narratives with specific facts and details?

→ (a) Facts:* The phone call to the little girl, Marie and conversation between the writer and Marie.
　　　　* The contents of the letter from Marie (Ls. 15~22).
(b) Details & Examples:
　* "... I must tell you about... beauty and joy (Ls. 25~33)."
　* "But terrible things... now more than ever (Ls. 34~40)."
　* "But what is Santa Claus?... as you or me (Ls. 41~45)."
　* "But Santa exists... he can do these things (Ls. 45~51)."

(3) Has the writer described the events in chronological order?

→ Yes, he did as evidenced in the paragraphs arranged in chronological order.

(4) Is the tone friendly, honest, and informal?

→ Yes, the tone is very informal, friendly and honest, since the narrative describes the reliable and humanistic relationship between an innocent, nine-year-old girl and a newspaper columnist.

C H A P T E R 4

(5) Has the writer drawn a conclusion that explains what the experience meant to him/her?

→ The drawn propositions are (1) There is a Santa; (2) There was a Santa, but not anymore; and (3) There isn't a Santa. The writer has drawn a conclusion based on the first proposition, "But Santa exists only if you believe (Ls. 45~46)," and "He lives in the hearts... of everyone who will let him (L. 49~50)," which shows that the writer stresses a positive way of life."

(1) 작가는 1인칭 대명사 '나'를 사용하면서 1인칭 관점을 유지했는가?

그렇다. 이 글에 쓰인 수많은 '1인칭 대명사'를 참조하라. 게다가 작가는 다음과 같이 자신의 관점을 유지하고 있다.

(a) "나는 그녀가 좀 쉬운... 문제 말이다."

(b) "하지만 버지니아가... 필요로 하고 있단다."

(c) "하지만 산타 클로스가 뭘까?... 산타니까 그럴 수 있는 거야."

(2) 작가는 구체적인 사실과 세부 설명으로 자신의 나레이션에 활기를 불어넣었는가?

(a) 사실 : * 소녀 마리와의 전화 통화 및 작가와 마리 사이의 대화

　　　　　 * 마리가 보낸 편지 내용

(b) 세부 사항 및 예문 :

* "...네 질문에 답하기 전에... 아름다움과 즐거움을 선사한단다."

* "하지만 버지니아가... 필요로 하고 있단다."

* "하지만 산타 클로스가 뭘까?...실재하고 있단다."

* "하지만 산타는 오직... 그럴 수 있는 거야."

(3) 작가는 사건을 연대기 순으로 서술하는가?

그렇다. 연대기 순으로 배열된 문단이 이 사실을 증명하고 있다.

(4) 어조는 다정하고, 솔직하며, 편안한가?

어조는 매우 편안하고 다정하며 솔직하다. 나레이션 부분이 순진무구한 아홉 살 소녀와 신문사 칼럼니스트 사이의 믿음직하고 인도주의적인 관계를 기술하고 있기 때문이다.

(5) 작가는 그 경험이 자신에게 어떤 의미를 가지는지 알려주는 결론을 이끌어냈는가?

주어진 명제는 (1) 산타는 있다; (2) 옛날에는 있었지만, 지금은 없다; (3) 산타는 없다, 등이다. 작가는 첫 번째 명제에 근거하여 "산타는 오직 네가 믿을 경우에만 존재한다."와 "그는 자신을 받아들이는... 마음 속에 살고 있단다"라는 결론을 이끌어냈으며, 그것은 작가가 적극적인 생활 방식을 강조하고 있음을 보여준다.

Model 2: "The Last Lesson."

Line 1   I was very late to school that morning, and I was really worried. Mr. Hamel was going to test us, and I was unprepared. For a moment, I thought of running off and spending the day out of doors. It was a great day - warm and bright. The birds were chirping at the edge of the woods. In a large open field,
L.5.   I could see the foreign soldiers drilling. I was tempted to play hooky, but I hurried to school.

When I passed the town hall, I saw that a large crowd had gathered in front of the bulletin board. For the last two years, all our bad news had been posted there. The war had been going badly for France. We had lost so many battles.
L.10.   Without stopping, I thought to myself, "What can be the matter now?" Then I hurried by as fast as I could go. The blacksmith, Mr. Wachter, was reading a notice on the bulletin board. He called after me, "What's your rush? You'll get to school in plenty of time." I thought he was making fun of me, and I ran on. I reached the door of the little schoolhouse out of breath. Usually there was a
L.15.   great deal of noise inside. You could hear it in the street. There was the opening and closing of desks. There were students reciting their lessons. There was the rapping of the ruler on the table. But today, it was so still. I had counted on the noise and confusion to sneak to my desk without being seen. But today, everything was as quiet as a Sunday morning.

L.20.   Through the window, I saw my classmates. They were already in their places. I saw Mr. Hamel walking up and down with his iron ruler under his arm. I had to open the door and walk in front of everyone. You can imagine how scared and embarrassed I was! But nothing happened. When Mr. Hamel saw me, he said very kindly, "Go to your place quickly, Franz. We were
L.25.   beginning without you." I jumped over the bench and sat down at my desk. I saw that our teacher was wearing his best green jacket and his fancy white shirt. He wore them only on special days. Then I noticed that the whole school seemed strange and silent. What surprised me most were the benches in the back. They were always empty. But today, the village people were sitting
L.30.   there quietly. There was old Hauser, the former mayor. There was the postmaster and several others. Everybody looked sad. Hauser had brought an old book. It was open on his knees. His eye glasses were lying across the pages. I could not understand it.

Then Mr. Hamel got up from his chair. He spoke in the same soft and gentle
L.35.   tone in which he had spoken to me. He said, "My children, this is the last lesson I shall give you. The order has come from Berlin to teach only German in the schools here now. The new teacher will be here tomorrow. This is your last French lesson. I want you to listen very carefully."

모델 2 '마지막 수업'

그 날 아침, 나는 학교에 몹시 지각했고, 정말 불안했다. 하멜 선생님이 우리를 테스트할 예정이었는데, 나는 준비를 하지 못했던 것이다. 잠시나마, 나는 학교에서 도망쳐 밖에서 하루를 보내 버릴까도 생각했다. 따뜻하고 화창한, 정말 멋진 날이었다. 나뭇가지에서는 새들이 지저귀고 있었다. 탁 트인 커다란 운동장에서 외국 군인들이 훈련하는 모습이 보였다. 나는 학교를 빼먹고 싶은 마음이 솟아올랐지만, 서둘러 학교로 갔다.

읍사무소를 지나치는데, 수많은 사람들이 게시판 앞에 모여있는 모습이 보였다. 지난 2년 동안, 나쁜 소식이란 나쁜 소식은 죄다 거기에 붙여져 있었다. 전쟁은 프랑스에게 불리하게 돌아가고 있었다. 우리는 너무 많은 전투에서 패배했다. 나는 발걸음도 멈추지 않은 채 혼자 이렇게 중얼거렸다. "그게 지금 무슨 상관이람?" 그리고 나서 나는 가능한 한 발걸음을 재촉했다. 대장장이 와처 씨가 게시판의 벽보를 읽고 있었다. 그가 내 뒤에다 소리쳤다. "왜 그렇게 서두르냐? 학교엔 넉넉하게 도착할 수 있을 텐데." 나는 그가 나를 놀린다는 생각에 내쳐 뜀박질을 시작했다. 나는 숨을 헐떡이며 작은 교사 문 앞에 도착했다. 보통은 안에서 엄청난 소음이 들리게 마련이었다. 심지어 거리에서도 들을 수 있을 정도였다. 책상을 여닫는 소리. 학생들이 학과를 암송하는 소리. 탁자 위에 자를 세게 두드리는 소리... 그러나 웬일인지 오늘은 너무나 조용했다. 나는 그런 소음과 소란을 틈타 남의 눈에 띄지 않고 슬그머니 내 책상으로 들어가곤 했다. 그러나 오늘은 모든 것이 마치 일요일 아침처럼 너무나 조용했다.

나는 창문 너머로 반 친구들을 보았다. 그들은 이미 자리에 앉아 있었다. 하멜 선생님은 팔에 철자를 낀 채 걸어다니고 있었다. 나는 모든 사람이 보는 앞에서 문을 열고 들어가야 했다. 그러니 내가 얼마나 겁에 질리고 당황했겠는가! 그러나 아무 일도 일어나지 않았다. 하멜 선생님은 나를 보자 아주 친절한 목소리로 이렇게 말했다. "빨리 네 자리로 가라, 프란츠. 우리끼리 그냥 수업하고 있었다." 나는 의자를 뛰어넘어 내 책상에 앉았다. 선생님은 당신이 가지고 있는 옷 가운데 최고급 녹색 양복에 멋진 하얀색 셔츠를 입고 있었다. 특별한 날에만 입는 옷이었다. 그리고 보니 학교 전체가 왠지 이상하고 조용하게 느껴졌다. 무엇보다 나를 놀라게 한 것은 뒤쪽에 있는 긴 의자들이었다. 그 의자들은 보통 비어 있었다. 그러나 오늘만큼은 거기에 마을 사람들이 조용히 앉아 있었다. 옛 읍장 하우저 씨와 우체국장, 그리고 몇몇 다른 사람들까지. 모두들 슬픈 얼굴을 하고 있었다. 하우저 씨는 오래된 책을 가져왔다. 그 책은 그의 무릎 위에 펼쳐져 있었다. 그리고 그 책 위로 안경이 놓여져 있었다. 나는 도무지 그 상황을 이해할 수 없었다.

다음 순간, 하멜 선생님이 의자에서 일어났다. 그는 내게 말을 하던 때와 똑같이 부드럽고 온화한 목소리로 말을 시작했다. "여러분, 오늘 이 수업이 제가 여러분에게 해 줄 수 있는 마지막 수업입니다. 지금부터 이 고장 학교에서는 독일어만 가르치라는 지시가 베를린에서 내려왔습니다. 내일 새로운 선생님이 여기 오실 겁니다. 지금이 여러분이 받는 마지막 불어 수업입니다. 부디 주의 깊게 들어주기를 바랍니다."

What a blow those words were to me! So that was the notice they had put on the bulletin board! My last French lesson! Why I hardly knew how to write! And I would never learn any more! I would have to stop! How sorry I was that I had not learned my lessons better. I thought of all the days I had stayed away from school. I thought about Mr. Hamel, too. The idea that he was going away, that I would never see him again, made me forget about his ruler and how cranky he was.

Poor man. It was in honor of this lesson that he had put on his fine Sunday clothes. Now I understood why the old people of the village were sitting in the back of the room. It was because they, too, were sorry that they had not gone to school more. It was their way of thanking our teacher for his 40 years of faithful service. It was their way of showing respect for the country that was theirs no more.

While I was thinking of all of this, I heard my name called. It was my turn to recite. I got to my feet. I would have given anything to answer in a loud, clear voice, without any mistakes. But I got mixed up on the first words. I stood there, holding onto my desk, my heart beating, and not daring to look up. I heard Mr. Hamel say to me, "I won't scold you, little Franz. Everyday we say to ourselves, 'I have got plenty of time. I'll learn it tomorrow.' And now you see what happens. That's the great trouble. We always put off learning till tomorrow."

Mr. Hamel looked at me sadly. "Now," he continued, "those fellows out there will have the right to say to you: 'How is it you pretend to be Frenchmen, and yet you can neither speak nor write your own language?' But you are not the worst, poor little Franz. We all have a great deal to be sorry about." "Your parents were not anxious enough to have you learn. They preferred to put you to work on a farm or at the mills to have a little more money. And how about me? I've been to blame, too. Often I sent to you to water my flowers instead of learning your lessons. And when I wanted to go fishing, I gave you a holiday."

Then Mr. Hamel went on to talk about the French language. He said it was the most beautiful language in the world - the clearest, the most exact. He said that we must guard it among ourselves and never forget it. For when a people are enslaved, they must hold fast to their language. It is the key to their freedom. Then he opened a grammar book and read us our lesson. I was amazed at how well I understood it. All he said seemed so easy - so easy! I think, too, that I had never listened so well, and that he had never explained everything with so much care. It seemed almost as if the poor man wanted to give us all he knew before going away. It was as if he wanted to put it all into our heads at one stroke.

Line markers: L.40. L.45. L.50. L.55. L.60. L.65. L.70. L.75.

C H A P T E R 4

그 말은 나에게 얼마나 큰 충격이었던가! 게시판에 붙어 있던 통보는 바로 그것이었다! 나의 마지막 불어 수업! 나는 왜 쓰는 방법도 잘 몰랐단 말인가! 게다가 이제 더 이상 배울 수도 없다! 이제 수업은 끝나야 하는 것이다! 수업에 좀더 충실하지 못했다는 사실이 그렇게 안타까울 수 없었다. 나는 학교를 빼먹은 그 많은 날들에 대해 생각했다. 그리고 하멜 선생님에 대해서도. 그가 멀리 떠난다는 생각, 그리하여 다시는 그를 만날 수 없으리라는 생각에 나는 그의 자, 그리고 그가 얼마나 까다로운 사람인가 하는 문제는 다 잊어버리고 말았다.

불쌍한 선생님. 그가 그 멋진 옷을 입고 온 것은 바로 이 수업을 기리기 위해서였다. 그제서야 나는 나이든 동네 어른들이 교실 뒤켠에 앉아 있는 까닭을 알아차렸다. 그들 역시 더 이상 학교에 갈 수 없다는 사실이 유감스러웠던 것이다. 그것은 40년에 걸친 선생님의 충실한 봉사에 대한 그들 나름의 감사 표현이었다. 그것은 더 이상 그들의 것이 아닌 조국에 대한 그들 나름의 경의의 표현이었다.

이 모든 생각에 젖어있는 사이, 나는 내 이름이 불리는 것을 들었다. 내가 암송할 차례였다. 나는 자리에서 일어났다. 나는 사소한 실수도 없이 크고 명확한 목소리로 대답을 했어야 했다. 그러나 나는 첫 단어부터 갈피를 못잡고 말았다. 나는 책상에 의지한 채 거기 서서 차마 쳐다볼 엄두도 내지 못한 채 가슴만 쿵쾅거리고 있었다. 하멜 선생님의 말씀이 들려왔다. "널 꾸짖지 않으마, 프란츠. 우린 매일 우리 자신에게 이렇게 말하지. '난 시간이 많아. 내일 배우지 뭐.' 그러다 어떤 일이 일어나는지 이제 너희도 알 거다. 그건 정말 커다란 불행이야. 우린 항상 배움을 내일로 미룬다."

하멜 선생님이 슬픈 듯 나를 쳐다보았다. 그리고 말을 계속했다. "자, 저기 밖에 있는 저 사람들은 너희들에게 이렇게 말하게 될 거다. '너희들은 프랑스인인 체 하지만, 정작 네 나라 말을 말할 수도, 쓸 수도 없잖아?' 하지만 네가 제일 나쁜 건 아니다, 불쌍한 프란츠. 우리 모두가 유감스러운 게 참 많으니까." "너희 부모님들은 너희가 배움에 나서는데 대해 그다지 달가워하지 않았다. 도리어 농장이나 방앗간에서 일해서 조금이라도 돈을 벌어오는 걸 더 원했지. 그럼 난 어때? 나 역시 비난받아 마땅하다. 난 종종 수업 대신에 너희를 내 꽃에 물을 주러 보냈다. 게다가 낚시 가고 싶을 때면, 너희에게 휴가를 줬지."

그리고 나서 하멜 선생님은 계속해서 불어에 대해 이야기했다. 그는 불어가 세상에서 가장 아름답고, 가장 명료하며, 가장 정확한 언어라고 말했다. 그는 우리가 그것을 지켜야 하며, 결코 잊어서는 안 된다고 말했다. 한 민족이 노예가 되면, 언어를 꽉 붙들어야 한다는 것이었다. 그것이 곧 자유로 가는 열쇠이므로. 그리고 나서 그는 문법책을 펴서 우리에게 그 날 수업 부분을 읽어주었다. 나는 내가 그것을 너무나 잘 이해한다는 사실에 놀라고 말았다. 그가 하는 모든 말이 너무나 쉽게, 정말 너무나 쉽게 느껴졌다. 또한 내가 그렇게 제대로 들어본 적이 없었으며, 그가 모든 것을 그렇게 세심하게 설명해준 적도 없었다고 생각한다. 그 가련한 선생님은 떠나기 전에 당신이 알고 있는 모든 것을 우리에게 주고 싶어하는 것 같았다. 마치 그 모든 것을 단숨에 우리 머리 속에 넣어주고 싶어하는 것 같았다.

문법이 끝난 뒤, 우리는 쓰기 수업을 받았다. 모두들 얼마나 조용히 공부하고 있었는지 당신도 한번 봤어야 하는 건데. 오직 종이 위에 펜을 휘갈기는 소리뿐이었다. 지붕 위에서는 비둘기들이 아주 낮은 소리로 구구거리고 있었다. 나는 혼자 생각했다. "그들은 노래도 독일어로 부르게 할까, 비둘기들한테도?"

After grammar, we had a lesson in writing. You ought to have seen how quietly everyone was working. The only sound was the scratching of the pens over the paper. On the roof, the pigeons cooed very low. I thought to myself, "Will they make them sing in German, even the pigeons?"

L.80.   Whenever I looked up from my desk, I saw Mr. Hamel sitting motionless in his chair. He was staring first at one thing, then at another. It was as if he wanted to fix in his mind exactly how everything looked in the little classroom. Imagine! For forty years he had been there in the same place. His garden had been just outside the window. His class had been in front of him,

L.85.   just like that. Only the desks and benches had been worn smooth. The walnut trees in the garden were taller. And the vines he had planted himself grew up to the roof. How it must have broken his heart to leave it all! He could hear his sister moving about in the room above. She was packing their trunks. They had to leave the country the next day.

L.90.   After the writing, we had a lesson in spelling. At the back of the room, old Hauser had put on his glasses. He was holding his book in both hands. You could see that he was crying. His voice trembled, and it was so funny to hear him that we wanted to laugh and cry. Ah, how well I remember it, that last lesson.

L.95.   Suddenly the church clock struck twelve. At the same moment, we heard the trumpets of the soldiers returning from drill. Mr. Hamel stood up, very pale. I never saw him look so tall. "My friends," he said, "I - I -." But something choked him. He could not go on. Then he turned to the blackboard. He took a piece of chalk, and, pressing down with all his might,

L.100.   wrote as large as he could: Vive la France! Then he stopped. He leaned his head against the wall. The words stuck in his throat. He made a motion with his hand. "School is over," he said. "You may go."

(Source: "The Last Lesson," Alphonse Daudet (1840~1897)

Alphonse Daudet

책상에서 고개를 들 때마다 하멜 선생님이 자신의 의자에 정지한 듯 앉아있는 모습이 보였다. 그는 처음에는 이 물건을 응시하다가 다음에는 다른 것을 응시하고 있었다. 그는 마치 그 작은 교실에 있는 모든 것들의 모습을 마음 속에 정확히 새겨두려는 것 같았다. 상상해 보라! 그는 40년 동안 거기, 똑같은 자리에 있었다. 그의 정원은 바로 창문 밖에 있었다. 그의 반은 바로 그렇게 그의 앞에 있었다. 오직 책상과 의자만이 매끄럽게 닳아있었다. 정원의 호두나무는 키카 더 커졌다. 그리고 그가 심은 포도나무는 지붕까지 자랐다. 그 모든 것을 떠나야 한다니, 그의 마음이 오죽했으랴! 그는 자신의 여동생이 위층 방에서 이리저리 오가는 소리를 들을 수 있었다. 그녀는 짐을 싸고 있었다. 다음 날이면 그들 두 사람은 이 마을을 떠나야 했던 것이다.

글쓰기가 끝난 뒤, 우리는 철자법 수업을 받았다. 교실 뒤쪽에서 하우저 씨가 안경을 꼈다. 그는 양손에 책을 들고 있었다. 그는 울고 있었다. 그의 목소리는 떨렸고, 그이 목소리가 너무 웃겨서 우리는 웃고 싶기도 했고 또 울고 싶기도 했다. 아, 나는 그 마지막 수업이 얼마나 생생하게 기억나는지.

갑자기 교회 시계가 12시를 쳤다. 그와 동시에 우리는 훈련을 마치고 돌아오는 군인들의 트럼펫 소리를 들었다. 하멜 선생님이 아주 창백한 얼굴로 자리에서 일어섰다. 그가 그렇게 커 보였던 적이 없었다. "친구들." 그가 입을 열었다. "난–난–." 그러나 무언가 그의 목을 조이는 듯했다. 그는 말을 계속할 수 없었다. 그러자 그는 칠판을 향해 몸을 돌렸다. 그는 분필을 집어들고, 있는 힘을 다해 가능한 한 크게 글씨를 써나갔다. 프랑스 만세! 그리고 나서 그는 자리에 멈춰선 뒤, 머리를 벽에 기댔다. 그 말이 목에 걸려 말이 나오지 않았던 것이다. 그는 손으로 표현했다. "수업은 끝났다." 그가 말했다. "이제 가거라."

Note

chirp *n.* The short, high sound made by some small birds and insects.
  v. To make this sound.
hooky *n.* (informal) Illegal absence.
rap *v.* To strike a surface quickly and sharply ; knock --I rapped on the door.
count *v.* 1. To find the total of ; add up --Count your change. 2. To name the numbers in order up to and including a particular number --Count three and jump. 3. To name numbers in order --We counted from 1 to 10. 4. To include in counting or considering --There are seven in my family, counting me. 5. To have importance, force, or value --It is not how often you read but what you read that counts 6. To believe to be ; consider --Count yourself lucky to have a bicycle 7. To rely ; depend --You can count on my help.
sneak *v.* 1. To move or act in a sly or secret way.
scarce *a.* Not enough to meet a demand --Food is scarce in many countries.
postmaster *n.* The government official in charge of a post office
cranky *a.* 1. Cross-tempered; grouchy. -- The baby is cranky when he is hungry.
  2. Queer or peculiar; eccentric. 3. Difficult or unreliable of operation.
faithful *a.* 1. Fulfilling one's duty or obligations in life 2.Giving allegiance to a person, cause, or ideal 3. Reliable or trustworthy.
enslave *v.* 1. To cause to be a slave or to be in a condition of bondage.
choke *v.* 1. To stop from breathing, as by squeezing the windpipe blocked --If we eat slowly, we won't be so likely to choke on food. 3. To hold back ; control --I choked back my tears.
  4. To stop or slow down the growth or action of --Weeds choked the flowers.

(1) Has the writer used the first person pronoun: "I, me, my," and maintained the first person's point of view?

→ Yes, refer to the numerous use of the first person pronoun which starts from the beginning of the story until the end. The writer also describes the narratives while maintaining his point of view as depicted in most paragraphs of this story.

(2) Has the writer enlivened his/her narratives with specific facts and details?

→ (a) Facts: "I was... really worried (L.1)."
   "When I passed... board (Ls. 7~8)."
   "But today... Sunday morning (Ls. 17~19)."
   "Through the window... classmates (L. 20)."
   "Then Mr. Hamel... chair (L. 34)."
   "While I was... called (L. 52)."
   "Then Mr. Hamel... the French language (L. 67)."
   "Whenever I looked up... in his chair (Ls. 80~81)."
   "After the writing... spelling (L. 90)."
   "Suddenly... twelve (L. 95)."

   (b) Details: "Mr. Hamel was... bright (Ls. 1~4)."
   "For the last two years... as fast as I could go (Ls. 8~11)."
   "They were already... I could not understand it (Ls. 20~33)."
   "He spoke in the same soft... carefully (Ls. 34~38)."
   "It was my turn to recite... till tomorrow (Ls. 52~58)."
   "He said it was... one stroke (Ls. 67~75)."
   "He was staring first... the next day (Ls. 81~89)."
   "At the back... last lesson (Ls. 90~94)."
   "At the same moment... You may go (Ls. 95~102)."

(3) Has the writer described the events in chronological order?

→ Yes, he did as evidenced in the sequential order of the story.

(4) Is the tone friendly, honest, and informal?

→ Yes, from the protagonist, Franz's points, the narratives are described in honest sincere and informal tone.

(5) Has the writer drawn a conclusion that explains what the experience meant to him/her?

→ Yes, he did. The experience meant to Franz is that he deeply regrets his immature motivation for studying French, his mother tongue, which he realize after his mother tongue is forbidden to be taught at school by German authorities.

C H A P T E R 4

(1) 작가는 1인칭 대명사 "나"를 사용하면서 1인칭 관점을 유지했는가?

그렇다. 글 첫머리에서부터 끝까지 사용된 수많은 1인칭 대명사를 참조하라. 작가는 또한 이 글 대부분의 단락에 묘사된 자신의 관점을 유지하면서 이야기를 서술하고 있다.

(2) 작가는 구체적인 사실과 세부 설명으로 자신의 나레이션에 활기를 불어넣었는가?

    (a) 사　　실 : "그날 아침... 정말 불안했다."

                  "읍사무소를... 모습이 보였다."

                  "그러나 오늘은... 너무나 조용했다."

                  "나는 창문 너머로... 보았다."

                  "다음 순간... 일어났다."

                  "이 모든 생각에... 들었다."

                  "그리고 나서 하멜 선생님은... 불어에 대해 이야기했다."

                  "책상에서 고개를 들 때마다... 모습이 보였다."

                  "글쓰기가 끝난 뒤... 수업을 받았다."

                  "갑자기... 12시를 쳤다."

    (b) 세부 사항 : "하멜 선생님이 우리를... 생각했다."

                  "지난 2년 동안... 발걸음을 재촉했다."

                  "그들은 이미... 이해할 수 없었다."

                  "그는 내게... 들어주기를 바랍니다."

                  "내가 암송할... 내일로 미룬다."

                  "그는 불어가... 싫어하는 것 같았다."

                  "그는 처음에는... 떠나야 했던 것이다."

                  "교실 뒤쪽에서... 기억나는지."

                  "그와 동시에... 이제 가거라."

(3) 작가는 사건을 연대기 순으로 서술하는가?

이야기의 연속적인 순서에서 증명되고 있듯이, 그는 연대기 순으로 사건을 서술했다.

(4) 어조는 다정하고, 솔직하며, 편안한가?

이야기가 주인공 프란츠의 관점에서 솔직하고 진지하며 편안한 어조로 서술되고 있다.

(5) 작가는 그 경험이 자신에게 어떤 의미를 가지는지 알려주는 결론을 이끌어냈는가?

그렇다. 그 경험이 프란츠에게 의미하는 바는 그가 모국어인 불어에 대한 학습 의욕이 적었음을 깊이 후회한다는 것, 그리고 독일 당국에 의해 학교에서 모국어 수업이 금지 당한 뒤에 그 사실을 깨달았다는 점이다.

4.2.6. Persuasive.

One of the major purposes of a Persuasive Essay is "to make your readers to agree with your point of view and take some actions." Read the following two persuasive writings, "Come to St. Lucia for Your Vacation" and "To the Enemy Must Not be Left a Single Engine, Not a Single Pound of Grain or a Gallon of Fuel," with the condensed guidelines kept in mind.

Condensed guidelines for a Persuasive Essay/Writing.

(1) Do the first or two sentences capture the reader's attention?
(2) Has the writer introduced the key issue while giving background needed to help readers understand it fully?
(3) Has the writer taken his/her position early in a clear and direct statement?
(4) Has the writer supported his/her position by giving convincing facts, strong reasons, clear examples along with appropriate emotional or ethical appeals to persuade the target audience?
(5) Has the writer summarized his/her idea and given a clear and effective call to action?

<u>Model 1</u>. "Come to St. Lucia for Your Vacation."

Line 1   Escape to another world where wonders never cease. Where every moment becomes a romantic adventure. When you catch your first glimpse of the awesome sight from your champagne flight, you will grasp the true meaning of "The Greatest Week of Your Life."

L.5.   St.Lucia is an island of startling contrasts where nature's powerful forces left precious gifts behind. Get lost in more than 19,000 acres of rain forest teeming with sweet aromatic flowers, exotic sounds from colorful parrots and other rare species. Bananas, coconuts and papayas thrive as far as the eye can see. A ridge of richly adorned mountains stretches almost the length of the island rising 3,145 ft. then

L.10.   plunging 140 ft. below the seashore on the southern coast where bizarre sealife, coral pinnacles and spectacular sponges invites the curious to explore.

4.2.6. 설득

설득형 에세이의 주요 목적 가운데 하나는 "독자들이 당신의 관점에 동의하여 일련의 조치를 취하게 하는 것"이다. 다음의 지침을 염두에 두면서 "휴가는 세인트 루시아에서"과 "적에게 엔진 하나, 낟알 한 개, 연료 한 방울도 남겨서는 안됩니다"라는 두 편의 설득형 에세이를 읽어보자.

설득형 에세이 지침

(1) 처음 한두 문장이 독자의 시선을 끄는가?

(2) 작가는 핵심 문제를 소개하고, 독자들이 제대로 이해하는데 필요한 여타 배경 지식을 제공하였는가?

(3) 작가는 일찌감치 명확하고 직접적인 말로 자신의 입장을 밝혔는가?

(4) 작가는 목표로 삼은 청중을 설득하기 위해 적절한 정서적 또는 윤리적 호소와 더불어 설득력 있는 사실, 그럴 듯한 이유, 명확한 예시 등을 제시함으로써 자신의 입장을 뒷받침했는가?

(5) 작가는 자신의 아이디어를 요약하고 분명하고 효과적인 조치를 요구했는가?

모델 1 '휴가는 세인트 루시아에서'

경이가 그칠 날이 없는 또다른 세상으로 탈출하십시오. 모든 순간이 낭만적 모험으로 바뀌는 곳. 비행기 속에서 그 놀라운 풍경을 처음 보는 순간, 당신은 '인생 최고의 한 주'라는 말이 진정 무엇을 의미하는지 알게 될 것입니다.

세인트 루시아는 자연의 강력한 힘이 귀중한 선물을 남긴 놀라운 대비의 섬입니다. 달콤한 향기를 풍기는 꽃들, 화려한 앵무새들과 여타 진기한 종들의 이국적인 소리로 충만한 19,000에이커 이상의 열대 다우림에 몸을 맡기십시오. 시야가 닿는 곳이라면 어디서든 바나나와 코코넛, 파파야가 무성합니다. 풍성하게 치장한 산봉우리가 3,145피트 높이로 섬 거의 전역에 뻗어나가다가 기괴한 해양생물과 산호숲, 호화로운 해면 등이 호기심 강한 사람들을 유혹하는 남부 해안의 바다 속 140피트 아래로 잠깁니다.

다이아몬드 폭포에서 떨어지는 낙수로 활기찬 샤워를 즐기십시오. 세계 유일의 드라이브인 (차를 탄 채 이용할 수 있는) 화산에 있는 유황 목욕탕에서 젊음을 되찾고, 수프리에르라는 근처 낚시 마을에서 시간을 즐기십시오. 모든 각도에서 섬을 구경하십시오. 카스트리스와 수프리에르 사이의 멋진 해안을 따라 진행되는 30분간의 일주는 절대 빼놓을 수 없는 코스입니다. 헬리콥터에서 섬의 전경을 바라보십시오. 손을 뻗어 직접 만져보고 싶다면, 자전거를 이용하십시오. 말을 타고 섬을 구경하는 것도 좋겠습니다. 편안하게 즐기려면, 차로 운전하고 다니다가 피톤스를 내려다보며 잊을 수 없는 점심 식사를 즐기십시오. 그리고 반드시 잠수하십시오. 암초와 난파선, 벽과 화산 등성이를 잠수해보십시오. 해안 잠수, 보트 잠수, 그리고 밤중의 잠수까지. 꼬치고기와 고등어, 민어를 잡으십시오.

자, 망설이지 말고 원하는 시간만큼 "당신 인생의 가장 위대한 주"를 즐기십시오. 절대 떠나고 싶지 않겠지만, 떠날 때가 되면, 당신은 새로운 인생관을 가지고 집으로 돌아가게 될 것입니다.

Take an invigorating shower in cascading waterfalls at Diamond Falls. Rejuvenate your body in the sulfur baths at the world's only drive-in volcano and linger in the nearby fishing village of Soufriere. Take in the island from every perspective. The half-hour cruise along the inspiring coast between Castries and Soufriere is a must. Get a birds-eye-view from a helicopter. To reach out and touch it, hike it. Ride through it on horseback. For a leisure look, drive it, stopping for an unforgettable lunch overlooking the Pitons. And by all means, dive it. Dive reefs and wrecks, walls and volcanic ridges. Shore dives, boat dives and night dives. Catch barracuda, mackerel and kingfish.

L.15.

L.20.

So go ahead and stretch "The Greatest Week of Your Life" as long as you like. You'll never want to leave, but when you do, you'll return home with a whole new outlook on life.

(Source: Adapted from a travel brochure, "Your Vacation in St. Lucia." (1998) Air Jamaica).

(1) Do the first or two sentences capture the reader's attention?

→ Yes, they do. The first sentence, "Escape to another world where wonders never cease (L.1)," and the two romantic sentences that follow the first one, "Where every moment... 'the Greatest Week of Your Life'" are powerful enough to capture the readers' attention. To be specific, the first sentence serves as an "Attention getting," and the following two sentences as "Stimulating desire" in view of the "Motivated Sequences (* See the following reference)."

 * "Motivated Sequences": Alan Monroe (1982) defines motivated steps such as (1) Attention getting (Hey! Look at us. We have something special for you.); (2) Stimulating desire (Don't you like/want to have this?); (3) Establishing credibility for desire (We got what you want); (4) Benefits warranted (If you buy this, you can get more than you paid); and, (5) Urgency (Buy/Act now! If not you will regret it) These "Motivated Sequences" are used for commercial advertisements as a way of stimulating consumers to purchase commodities or services.

(2) Has the writer introduced the key issue while giving background needed to help readers understand it fully?

→ Yes, the writer did it very effectively. The issue here is "Come to St. Lucia for Your Vacation" as the topic indicates, and the background/reasons for coming to St. Lucia are fully supported as follows: "St. Lucia is an island... mackerel and kingfish (Ls. 5~20)," which serve as sound background/reasons why you as customers should enjoy your vacation at St. Lucia.

(1) 처음 한두 문장이 독자의 시선을 끄는가?

그렇다. "경이가 그칠 날이 없는 또 다른 세상으로 탈출하십시오."라는 첫 문장과 뒤이어 나타나는 낭만적인 두 문장, "모든 순간이... 알게 될 것입니다."는 독자의 시선을 끌 수 있을 만큼 충분히 강렬하다. "흥미 유발 과정"의 관점에서 좀더 구체적으로 보면, 첫 문장은 "시선 끌기"로 기능하고 있고, 이어지는 두 문장은 "욕망 자극"에 해당한다.

* **"흥미 유발 과정"** : 앨런 몬로(1982)는 흥미 유발 단계를 (1) 시선 끌기(헤이! 우릴 좀 보세요. 당신을 위해 아주 특별한 걸 준비했어요.); (2) 욕망 자극(이거 가지고 싶지 않으세요?); (3) 욕망의 신빙성 확립(우린 당신이 원하는 걸 가지고 있어요.); (4) 보증된 혜택(이걸 사면, 지불한 돈보다 더 많은 걸 얻을 수 있어요.); (5) 긴박성(지금 사세요/행동하세요! 그렇지 않으면, 후회하게 될 거에요.) 등으로 정의하고 있다. 이러한 "흥미 유발 과정"은 소비자가 상품이나 서비스를 구매하게 하는 한 방법으로 상업 광고에서 사용된다.

(2) 작가는 핵심 문제를 소개하고, 여타 배경지식을 제공함으로써 독자들이 제대로 이해할 수 있게 했는가?

작가는 매우 효과적으로 그렇게 했다. 이 글의 핵심은 "휴가는 세인트 루시아에서"이며, 세인트 루시아로 가야 하는 배경/이유는 "세인트 루시아는... 민어를 잡으십시오."에서 충분히 설명되어 있다. 이 부분은 고객이 세인트 루시아에서 휴가를 즐겨야 하는 타당한 배경/이유로 기능하고 있다.

(3) 작가는 일찌감치 명확하고 직접적인 말로 자신의 입장을 밝혔는가?

명확하고 직접적인 말로 입장을 밝히지는 않았다. 이 글은 상업적 목적을 위해 쓰여졌기 때문이다. 그러나 첫 문단의 자극적인 말들은 독자들에게 어떤 강요도 하지 않으면서 일찌감치 작가의 입장을 주장, 뒷받침하고 있다. 게다가 문단 2는 "욕망의 신빙성 확립(우린 당신을 원하는 걸 가지고 있어요)"으로 기능하고 있고, 이어지는 문단은 "보증된 혜택(세인트 루시아에 오신다면, 다른 곳에서는 쉽게 살 수 없는 모든 혜택을 얻을 수 있어요.)"으로 기능한다. 따라서 작가는 아주 암묵적이고 설득력 있는 방식으로 일찌감치 자신의 입장을 밝혔다.

Note

escape *n.* 1. To get free --The prisoners escaped by climbing the wall.
      2. To succeed in avoiding --I fell off the ladder but managed to escape injury.
glimpse *n.* A very quick look --We caught a glimpse of the house as we drove by.
      v. To get a quick look at.
champagne *n.* A sparkling white wine produced in the Champagne region of France.
grasp *v.* 1. To seize and hold firmly with or as if with the hand --I grasped the railing so I wouldn't fall. 2. To take into the mind ; understand --Do you grasp the problem?
teem *v.* To have in abundance -- The lake teems with fish.
thrive *v.* 1. To be or stay in a healthy condition --Some plants thrive in damp, sandy soil.
      2. To be successful ; flourish --The little town thrived.
bizarre *a.* Strikingly odd or unusual, esp. in appearance or behavior.

(3) Has the writer taken his/her position early in a clear and direct statement?

→ No, not in a clear and direct statement, since this writing is for commercial purposes. However, the stimulating statements in Ls. 1~4 claim and support the writer's position early without giving any forced pressure to the readers. Morever, the paragraph (Ls. 5~11) serves as "Establishing credibility for desire (We got what you want)"; and the following paragraph (Ls. 12~20) does as "Benefits warranted (If you come to St. Lucia, you can get all of its benefits which you cannot buy easily elsewhere)." Therefore, the writer has taken his position early in a very implicit and persuasive way.

(4) Has the writer supported his/her position by giving enticing facts, strong reasons, clear examples along with appropriate emotional or ethical appeals to persuade the target consumers?

→ Yes, he did.
   (a) Enticing facts: "St. Lucia is ... explore (Ls. 5~11)."
   (b) Examples: "Take an invigorating shower... mackerel and kingfish (Ls. 12~20)."
   (c) Emotional appeals: Escape to... of Your Life (Ls. 1~4)," serves as an enticing appeal for stimulating consumers. "Take an invigorating shower... kingfish (Ls. 12~20)," works as imaginary appeals leading to invited call to action. Refer to all of the sentences that start with "commanding statements," which strongly invites the call to action.

(5) Has the writer summarized his/her idea and given a clear and effective call to action?

→ Yes, the writer has summarized his idea and given an effective call to action.
   (a) Summarized idea: "So go ahead... as you like (Ls. 21~22)."
   (b) Effective call to action:
       "So go ahead and stretch... as you like (Ls. 21~22)," and
       "You will never want to leave... you'll return home with a new outlook on life (Ls. 22~23)," serve as an effective and skillful call to action, promising that "You will return home... on life" as persuasive skills related to Benefit warranted.

St. Lucia

(4) 작가는 목표로 삼은 청중을 설득하기 위해 적절한 정서적 또는 윤리적 호소와 더불어 설득력 있는 사실, 그럴 듯한 이유, 명확한 예시 등을 제시함으로써 자신의 입장을 뒷받침했는가?

그렇다.

(a) 매력적인 사실 : "세인트 루시아는... 140피트 아래로 잠깁니다."

(b) 예시문 : "다이아몬드 폭포에서... 민어를 잡으십시오."

(c) 정서적 호소 : "경이가 그칠 날이 없는... 알게 될 것입니다."는 고객들을 자극하는 매력 적인 호소로 기능하고 있다.

"다이아몬드 폭포에서... 민어를 잡으십시오."는 초대를 받아들이라는 상상의 호소로 기능하고 있다. "명령형"으로 시작하는 모든 문장을 참조하라. 이 문장들은 초대에 응하라고 강하게 호소하고 있다.

(5) 작가는 자신의 아이디어를 요약하고 분명하고 효과적인 조치를 요구했는가?

작가는 자신의 생각을 요약한 뒤, 직접 경험해보라며 효과적으로 설득하고 있다.

(a) 요약된 생각 : "자, 망설이지 말고... 즐기십시오."

(b) 효과적인 설득 : "자, 망설이지 말고... 즐기십시오."와 "절대 떠나고 싶지 않겠지만... 될 것입니다."는 효과적이고 교묘한 설득으로 기능하고 있으며, 보증된 혜택과 관련된 설득 기법으로서 "당신은 새로운...될 것입니다."라고 약속하고 있다.

<u>Model 2</u>: "To the enemy must not be left a single engine, a single railway car, not a single pound of grain or a gallon of fuel."

Line 1   Comrades! Citizens! Brothers and Sisters! Men of our Army and Navy! I am addressing you, my friends! The perfidious military attack on our fatherland, begun on June 22 by Hitler's Germany, is continuing.

L.5.   In spite of heroic resistance of the Red Army, and although the enemy's finest divisions and finest air-force units have already been smashed and have met their doom on the field of battle, the enemy continues to push forward, hurling fresh forces into the attack. Hitler's troops have succeeded in capturing Lithuania, a considerable part of Latvia, the western part of White Russia, and a part of the western Ukraine. The fascist air force is extending the range of
L.10.   operations of its bombers and is bombing Murmansk, Orsha, Mogilev, Smolensk, Kiev, Odessa, and Sevastopol.

    A grave danger hangs over our country. How could it have happened that our glorious Red Army surrendered a number of our cities and districts to the Fascist armies? Is it really true that German Fascist troops are invincible, as is
L.15.   ceaselessly trumpeted by boastful Fascist propagandists? Of course not!

    History shows that there are no invincible armies, and never have been. Napoleon's army was considered invincible, but it was beaten successfully by Russian, English, and German armies. Kaiser Wilhelm's German army in the period of the first imperialist war was also considered invincible, but it was
L.20.   beaten several times by Russian and Anglo-French forces, and was finally smashed by Anglo-French forces.

    The same must be said of Hitler's German Fascist army today. This army has not yet met with serious resistance on the Continent of Europe. Only on our territory has it met serious resistance, and if as a result of this resistance the
L.25.   finest divisions of Hitler's German Fascist army have been defeated by our Red Army, it means that this army, too, can be smashed and will be smashed as were the armies of Napoleon and Wilhelm.

    As to part of our territory having nevertheless been seized by German Fascist troops, this is chiefly due to the fact that the war of Fascist Germany on the
L.30.   U.S.S.R. began under conditions favorable for German forces and unfavorable for Soviet forces. The fact of the matter is that troops of Germany, as a country at war, were already fully mobilized, and 170 divisions hurled by Germany against the U.S.S.R. and brought up to the Soviet frontiers were in a state of complete readiness, only awaiting the signal to move into action, whereas Soviet
L.35.   troops had little time to effect mobilization and move up to the frontiers.

모델 2 "적에게 단 하나의 엔진, 단 한 대의 철도 차량, 단 한 알의 낟알,
단 한 방울의 연료도 남겨서는 안됩니다."

동지여! 시민이여! 형제자매여! 육해군 군인들이여! 제가 지금 여러분을 부르고 있습니다, 친구들이여! 히틀러의 독일이 6월 22일부터 시작한 우리 조국에 대한 비열한 군사 공격이 지금도 계속되고 있습니다.

우리 적군의 영웅적인 저항에도 불구하고, 그리고 적의 최정예 사단과 최정예 공군 부대가 이미 대패하여 전쟁터에서 죽었음에도 불구하고, 적은 진격을 계속하여 신예 부대를 공격에 합류시키고 있습니다. 히틀러 군은 리투아니아와 라트비아의 상당 부분, 백러시아 서부 지구, 우크라이나 서부 지구 등을 점령하는데 성공했습니다. 파시스트 공군은 폭격기 운행 범위를 확대시키면서 무르만스크, 오르샤, 모질레프, 스몰렌스크, 키에프, 세바스토폴 등에 폭격을 가하고 있습니다.

우리 나라에 심각한 위험이 닥치고 있습니다. 영예로운 우리 적군이 우리의 도시와 지방을 파시스트 군에게 넘겨주다니 어떻게 그런 일이 생길 수 있습니까? 파시스트 선동가들이 끊임없이 날조하고 있듯이, 파시스트 독일군은 천하무적이라는 말이 진정 사실입니까? 물론, 그렇지 않습니다!

역사는 정복할 수 없는 군대는 존재하지도 않았고, 또 존재하지도 않는다는 사실을 보여주고 있습니다. 나폴레옹군은 무적으로 여겨졌지만, 러시아, 영국, 독일군에게 패배하고 말았습니다. 제1차 제국주의 전쟁 동안에는 빌헬름 황제의 독일군 역시 무적으로 간주되었지만, 러시아와 영불 군대에게 몇 차례 패배하였고, 마침내 영불군에 의해 격퇴되었습니다.

오늘날 히틀러의 파시스트 독일군에 대해서도 동일한 사례가 적용되어야 합니다. 이 군대는 아직까지 유럽 대륙에서 심각한 저항에 부딪치지 않았습니다. 오직 우리 영토에서 심각한 저항에 부딪쳤고, 이러한 저항의 결과로서 히틀러의 파시스트 군 최정예 사단이 우리 적군에게 패배한다면, 그것은 곧 이 군대 역시 나폴레옹 군대나 빌헬름 군대처럼 격퇴될 수 있으며, 또한 격퇴되리라는 것을 의미합니다.

그럼에도 불구하고 우리 영토 일부가 파시스트 독일군에게 점령된 점에 관한 한, 그것은 주로 파시스트 독일군의 소련에 대한 전쟁이 독일군에게는 우호적인 반면 소비에트군에게는 불리한 조건하에서 시작되었다는 사실에서 기인합니다. 중요한 것은 전쟁 중인 나라로서의 독일군은 이미 전시체제가 갖춰졌고, 독일이 소련에 파견하여 소비에트 국경에 출정시킨 170개 사단은 완벽한 준비를 갖춘 채 오직 작전 명령만 기다리고 있었던 반면, 소비에트군은 효과적으로 동원되어 전선으로 이동할 시간이 거의 없었다는 점입니다.

이런 점에서 파시스트 독일이 전세계인들에게 침략국으로 간주되리라는 사실을 간과한 채 1939년 소련과 맺은 불가침 조약을 갑자기 그리고 비열하게 깨뜨렸다는 사실은 그리 중요하지 않습니다. 평화를 사랑하는 우리 나라는 당연히 솔선해서 조약을 파기하고 싶지 않았기 때문에 배반에 의존할 수 없었습니다.

Of little importance in this respect is the fact that Fascist Germany suddenly and treacherously violated the nonaggression pact she concluded in 1939 with the U.S.S.R., disregarding the fact that she would be regarded as an aggressor by the whole world. Naturally, our peace-loving country, not wishing to take L.40. the initiative of breaking the pact, could not resort to perfidy. It may be asked: how could the Soviet government have consented to conclude a nonaggression pact with such treacherous fiends as Hitler and Ribbentrop? Was not this an error on the part of the Soviet government? Of course not! Nonaggression pacts are pacts of peace between two states. It was such a pact that Germany L.45. proposed to us in 1939. Could the Soviet government have declined such a proposal? I think that not a single peace-loving state could decline a peace treaty with a neighboring state, even though the latter was headed by such fiends and cannibals as Hitler and Ribbentrop.

But that, of course, only on one indispensable condition - namely, that this L.50. peace treaty does not infringe either directly or indirectly on the territorial integrity, independence, and honor of a peace-loving state. As is well known, the nonaggression pact between Germany and the U.S.S.R. is precisely such a pact.

What did we gain by concluding a nonaggression pact with Germany? We secured for our country peace for a year and a half and the opportunity of L.55. preparing its forces to repulse Fascist Germany should she risk an attack on our country despite the pact. This was a definite advantage for us and a disadvantage for Fascist Germany. What has Fascist Germany gained and what has she lost by treacherously tearing up the pact and attacking the U.S.S.R.? She gained a certain advantageous position for her troops for a short L.60. period, but she has lost politically by exposing herself in the eyes of the entire world as a bloodthirsty aggressor. There can be no doubt that this short-lived military gain for Germany is only an episode, while the tremendous political gain of the U.S.S.R is a serious and lasting factor that is bound to form the basis for development of decisive military successes of the Red Army L.65. in the war with Fascist Germany...

In case of a forced retreat of Red Army units, all rolling stock must be evacuated; to the enemy must not be left a single engine, a single railway car, not a single pound of grain or a gallon of fuel. Collective farmers must drive off all their cattle and turn over their grain to the safekeeping of state L.70. authorities for transportation to the rear. All valuable property including nonferrous metals, grain, and fuel which cannot be withdrawn must be without fail destroyed. In areas occupied by the enemy, guerrilla units, mounted and foot, must be formed, diversionist groups must be organized to combat enemy troops, to foment guerrilla warfare everywhere, to blow up bridges, roads,

이런 의문이 생길 수도 있습니다. 소비에트 정부가 어째서 히틀러와 리벤트롭 같은 믿을 수 없는 친구들과 불가침 조약을 체결하는데 동의할 수 있었던 것일까요? 소비에트 정부 입장에서 보면, 그것은 실수가 아니었을까요? 물론, 아닙니다! 불가침 조약은 두 국가 사이의 평화 조약입니다. 독일이 1939년에 우리에게 제안한 것은 바로 그런 조약이었습니다. 소비에트 정부가 그런 제안을 거부할 수 있었을까요? 평화를 사랑하는 국가라면 이웃 나라와의 평화 협정을 거부할 수 없었으리라고 생각합니다. 설령 후자가 히틀러나 리벤트롭 같은 친구 겸 식인종을 수반으로 하고 있다고 해도 마찬가지입니다.

그럼에도 불구하고, 한 가지 필수 불가결한 조건이 있습니다. 다시 말해, 이러한 평화 조약이 평화를 사랑하는 국가의 영토 보전, 독립, 그리고 명예를 직접적으로든 간접적으로든 침해하지 않는다는 조건 말입니다. 잘 알려져 있는 바와 같이, 독일과 소련 사이의 불가침 조약은 정확히 그런 조약입니다.

그렇다면, 독일과의 불가침 조약 체결로 우리가 얻은 것은 무엇입니까? 우리는 1년 반동안 우리 나라의 평화를 확보했고, 파시스트 독일이 그 조약에도 불구하고 우리 나라를 공격할 경우, 그들을 격퇴할 힘을 키울 수 있는 기회를 가졌습니다. 그것은 우리 입장에서는 명확한 이득이었지만, 파시스트 독일의 입장에서는 손실이었습니다. 파시스트 독일이 그 조약을 비열하게 깨뜨리고 소련을 공격함으로써 얻은 것과 잃은 것은 무엇일까요? 독일은 군 전력상 짧은 기간 동안 어느 정도 유리한 위치를 확보했지만, 전세계인들에게 피에 굶주린 침략자의 이미지를 노출시킴으로써 정치적으로는 손해를 입었습니다. 독일의 이 일시적인 군사적 이득이 단지 하나의 삽화에 불과하다면, 소련이 얻은 엄청난 정치적 이득은 파시스트 독일과의 전쟁에서 적군의 결정적인 승리를 발전시키는 토대로서 작용하게 될 중대하고도 지속적인 요인이라는 데에는 의심의 여지가 있을 수 없습니다...

적군 부대가 불시에 퇴각할 경우, 주변에 있는 모든 비축물은 전부 소개되어야 합니다. 적에게 단 하나의 엔진, 단 한 대의 철도 차량, 단 한 알의 낟알, 단 한 방울의 연료도 남겨서는 안됩니다. 농부들은 모든 가축들을 쫓아버리고, 곡물은 국가 당국에 인계하여 배후로 운송, 보관할 수 있게 해야 합니다. 회수할 수 없는 비철 금속, 곡물, 연료 등을 포함한 모든 귀중품은 반드시 없애버려야 합니다. 적의 점령 하에 있는 지역에서는 기병과 보병 중심의 게릴라 부대를 형성하고, 파괴 활동가 그룹을 조직하여 적군과 싸우고, 도처에서 게릴라전을 벌여야 하며, 교량과 도로를 파괴하고, 전화와 전화선을 끊어버려야 하며, 숲, 가게, 수송선 등에 불을 질러야 합니다. 점령 지역에서는 적군을 비롯한 모든 공범자들이 도저히 참을 수 없는 조건을 만들어야 합니다. 그들은 도처에서 괴롭힘을 당하고 근절되어야 하며, 그들이 취하는 모든 대책은 실패해야 합니다.

파시스트 독일과의 이 전쟁은 평범한 전쟁으로 볼 수 없습니다. 그것은 두 군대간의 전쟁일 뿐 아니라 전체 소비에트 인민과 독일 파시스트 무리와의 전쟁이기도 합니다. 파시스트 압제자들에 대항하여 우리 나라를 수호하려는 이 국가적 전쟁의 목표는 우리 나라에 닥친 위험을 제거하는 것일 뿐 아니라 독일 파시즘의 멍에 아래 신음하고 있는 전체 유럽 인민들을 돕는 것이기도 합니다.

L.75.　damage telephone and telegraph lines, and to set fire to forests, stores, and transports. In occupied regions conditions must be made unbearable for the enemy and all his accomplices. They must be hounded and annihilated at every step and all their measures frustrated.

L.80.　　This war with Fascist Germany cannot be considered as an ordinary war. It is not only a war between two armies, it is also a great war of the entire Soviet people against the German Fascist forces. The aim of this national war in defense of our country against the Fascist oppressors is not only elimination of the danger hanging over our country, but also aid to all European peoples groaning under the yoke of German Fascism. In this war of liberation we shall not be

L.85.　alone. In this great war we shall have loyal allies in the peoples of Europe and America, including German people who are enslaved by Hitlerite despots. Our war for the freedom of our country will merge with the struggle of the peoples of Europe and America for their independence, for democratic liberties. It will be a united front of peoples standing for freedom and against enslavement and threats

L.90.　of enslavement by Hitler's Fascist armies. In this connection the historic utterance of British Prime Minister Churchill regarding aid to the Soviet Union and the declaration of the U.S.A.government signifying readiness to render aid to our country, which can only evoke a feeling of gratitude in the hearts of the peoples of the Soviet Union, are fully comprehensible and symptomatic.

L.95.　　Comrades, our forces are numberless. The overweening enemy will soon learn this to his cost. Side by side with the Red Army and Navy thousands of workers, collective farmers, and intellectuals are rising to fight the enemy aggressor. The masses of our people will rise up in their millions. The working people of Moscow and Leningrad already have commenced to form vast popular levies in

L.100.　support of the Red Army. Such popular levies must be raised in every city that is in danger of an enemy invasion; all working people must be roused to defend our freedom, our honor, our country - in our patriotic war against German Fascism.

　　In order to insure a rapid mobilization of all forces of the peoples of the U.S.S.R., and to repulse the enemy who treacherously attacked our country, a

L.105.　State Committee of Defense has been formed in whose hands the entire power of the state has been vested. The State Committee of Defense has entered into its functions and calls upon all our people to rally around the party of Lenin-Stalin and around the Soviet government so as self-denyingly to support the Red Army and Navy, demolish the enemy, and secure victory.

L.110.　　All our forces for the support of our heroic Red Army and our glorious Red Navy! All the forces of the people - for the demolition of the enemy! Forward, to our victory!

(Joseph Stalin's Radio Broadcast on July 3, 1941).

자유를 향한 이 전쟁에서 우리는 결코 외롭지 않을 것입니다. 이 위대한 전쟁에서 우리는 유럽과 미국의 인민들을 비롯하여 히틀러의 독재에 시달리고 있는 독일 인민에 이르기까지 충실한 동맹자를 얻게 될 것입니다. 우리 나라의 자유를 향한 우리의 전쟁은 유럽과 미국 인민들의 독립 및 민주주의적 자유를 향한 투쟁과 결합될 것입니다. 그것은 자유를 상징하는, 그리고 히틀러의 파시스트 군대에 의한 노예화 및 노예화의 위협에 대항하는 민족들의 공동 전선이 될 것입니다. 이런 연관 속에서 볼 때, 소비에트 원조와 관련한 영국 처칠 수상의 역사적인 발언과 우리 나라를 원조할 준비가 되어 있다는 미국 정부의 천명은, 소비에트 인민의 가슴에는 오직 감사의 마음만을 불러일으킬 수 있으나, 사실은 충분히 이해가능한 일입니다.

동지여, 우리의 부대는 무수히 많습니다. 오만한 적군은 곧 뼈아픈 경험을 통해 이 사실을 알게 될 것입니다. 우리 육해군과 아울러 수천의 노동자, 농민, 지식인들이 침략자들과 싸우려 일어나고 있습니다. 우리 인민 대중은 무리를 지어 일어설 것입니다. 모스코바와 레닌그라드의 노동자 계급은 이미 적군을 지지하는 거대한 지원군을 형성하기 시작했습니다. 적의 침략 위험에 처해있는 모든 도시에서 바로 그러한 대중적 지원군이 발기해야 합니다. 모든 노동 계급은 독일 파시즘과 대항하는 우리의 이 애국적인 전쟁에서 우리의 자유, 우리의 명예, 우리의 나라를 수호하기 위해 일어서야 합니다.

소련내 모든 인민군을 신속하게 동원하고 비열하게 우리나라를 공격한 적을 격퇴하기 위해서는 국가 방위 위원회를 조직하여 국가에 귀속된 모든 권력을 거기에 위임시켜야 합니다. 국가 방위 위원회는 자체 기능에 들어갔고, 모든 인민이 레닌-스탈린 당과 소비에트 정부 주위로 재집결하여 자기를 잊은 채 우리 육해군을 뒷받침하고 적을 섬멸하며 승리를 지켜내자고 요청하고 있습니다.

영웅적인 육군과 영예로운 해군을 뒷받침하는 모든 인민군이여! 적을 섬멸하는 그 날까지, 승리를 향해 돌진합시다!

Note

perfidious *a.* Purposely disloyal or treacherous ; faithless.

smash *v.* 1. To break or be broken into pieces. 2. To throw, move, or strike violently. 3. To destroy or defeat completely.
　　　　n. The act or sound of smashing.

hurl *v.* To throw with a great force ; fling.

invincible *a.* 1. Too strong to be defeated, overcome, or surmounted.

treacherously *a.* 1. Betraying or likely to betray trust ; traitorous ; faithless. 2. Not to be trusted or depended upon; risky, dangerous, or unreliable.

consent *v.* To give permission --My parents consented to my plans.
　　　　n. Permission --I have my teacher's consent to go to the library.

fiend *n.* 1. An evil spirit or demon; devil. 2. A cruelly malicious or wicked person 3. (informal) One who is addicted to or has a consuming enthusiasm for something..

infringe *v.* 1. To cross established limits ; encroach ; trespass (usu. fol. by on or upon). --Censorship infringes on the right of free speech.

foment *v.* 1. To encourage the development of; instigate or foster. --The troublemakers fomented discontent. 2. To treat (the surface of the body) with warm water, medicated liquids, or the like.

repulse *v.* 1. To force backward or repel (an attack or the like) 2. To reject coldly or rudely.

(1) Do the first or two sentences grab the reader's attention?

→   Yes, they do.

   (a) The forms of address used in the first paragraph are very powerful so as to grab the reader's attention. Specifically, first Stalin appeals to his party members ("comrades"), next, to Soviet people (all "citizens"), ethnic and kinship group members ("brothers & sisters"), active service men ("Men of our Army and Navy"), and fellows who share the common grounds with Stalin ("my friends").

   (b) The two sentences, "I am addressing... The perfidious military attack... begun on June 22 by Hitler's Germany, is still continuing (Lines 1~3)" include specific and vivid expressions such as "The perfidious military attack," "begun on June 22," "by Hitler's Germany," "...is still continuing (Ls. 2~3)" are powerful enough to capture the reader's or listener's attention, since the expressions provide very specific details based on (a) nature ("perfidious attack"); (b) time ("on June 22"); (c) agent ("Hitler's Germany"); and, (d) action ("is still continuing")

(2) Has the speaker/writer introduced the key issue while giving background needed to help audience understand it fully?

→   Yes, he did very effectively.

   (A) The key issues are based on (a) Fact as a major premise; (b) Question as a minor premise; and, (c) Answer as a conclusion. Stalin proposes an interesting format as a syllogism based on the above factors.

      (a) Fact as a major premise: "... the enemy continues to push forward... Sevastopol (Ls. 6~11)."

      (b) Question as a minor premise: "Is it really true... Fascist propagandist (Ls. 14~15)?"

      (c) Answer as a conclusion: "Of course not! (L. 15)."

   (B) Background: Stalin provides comprehensive background based on clear facts, details,and examples.

      (aa) Fact: "History shows that... never have been (L. 16)."

      (ab) Examples to support the fact: "Napoleon's army... by Anglo-French forces (Ls. 16~21)."

      (ba) Fact: "The same must be... army today (L. 22)."

      (bb) Details to support the fact: "This army has... Wilhelm (Ls. 22~27)."

      (ca) Fact: "As to part of... Soviet forces (Ls. 28~31)."

      (cb) Details: "The fact... to the frontiers (Ls. 31~35)."

      (da) Fact: "Of little importance... whole world (Ls. 36~39)."

      (db) Details: "Naturally... and Ribbentrop (Ls. 39~47)."

      (ea) Question for the fact: "What did we gain... with Germany? (L. 53)"

      (eb) Answer for the fact: "We secured... for Fascist Germany (Ls. 53~57)."

      (fa) Question for the fact: "What has... U.S.S.R.? (Ls. 57~59)"

      (fb) Answer for the fact: "She gained... with Fascist Germany (Ls. 59~65)."

(1) 처음 한두 문장이 독자의 시선을 끄는가?

그렇다.

(a) 첫 문단에 쓰인 인사말의 형태는 독자의 시선을 끌 수 있을 정도로 무척 강력하다. 구체적으로 보면, 스탈린은 먼저 자신의 당원들("동지")에게, 그 다음으로 소비에트 인민들(모든 "시민"), 민족 집단 및 혈족 구성원들("형제자매"), 현역 군인들("육해군 군인들"), 그리고 스탈린과 공통의 기반을 갖고 있는 사람들("친구들")에게 호소하고 있다.

(b) "제가 지금 여러분을 부르고 있습니다… 히틀러의 독일이 6월 22일부터 시작한 우리 조국에 대한 비열한 군사 공격이 지금도 계속되고 있습니다"라는 두 문장은 "비열한 군사 공격," "6월 22일부터 시작한," "히틀러의 독일이," "…계속되고 있습니다" 등 구체적이고 생생한 표현을 담고 있어서 독자나 청취자의 주목을 끌 수 있을 정도로 무척 힘있다. 이 표현들이 (a) 본질("비열한 공격"), (b) 시간("6월 22일"), (c) 행위자("히틀러의 독일"), (d) 행위("지금도 계속되고 있습니다") 등에 근거한 아주 구체적인 세부 사항을 제공하고 있기 때문이다.

(2) 작가는 핵심 문제를 소개하고, 독자들이 제대로 이해하는데 필요한 여타 배경 지식을 제공하였는가?

(A) 핵심 문제는 (a) 대전제로서의 사실, (b) 소전제로서의 의문, (c) 결론으로서의 해답에 근거하고 있다. 스탈린은 위의 요인들에 근거한 연역법으로서 재미있는 포맷을 제안하고 있다.

(a) 대전제로서의 사실 : "…적은 진격을 계속하여… 폭격을 가하고 있습니다."

(b) 소전제로서의 의문 : "파시스트 선동가들이… 진정 사실입니까?"

(c) 결론으로서의 해답 : "물론 그렇지 않습니다!"

(B) 배경 : 스탈린은 명확한 사실과 세부 사항, 사례 등에 근거하여 납득할만한 배경을 제공하고 있다.

(aa) 사실 : "역사는… 보여주고 있습니다."

(ab) 사실을 뒷받침하는 사례 : "나폴레옹군은… 격퇴되었습니다."

(ba) 사실 : "오늘날… 적용되어야 합니다."

(bb) 사실을 뒷받침하는 세부 사항 : "이 군대는… 의미합니다."

(ca) 사실 : "그럼에도 불구하고 우리 영토 일부가… 기인합니다."

(cb) 세부 사항 : "중요한 것은… 없었다는 점입니다."

(da) 사실 : "이런 점에서… 중요하지 않습니다."

(db) 세부 사항 : "평화를 사랑하는… 마찬가지입니다."

(ea) 사실에 대한 질문 : "그렇다면… 무엇입니까?"

(eb) 사실에 대한 대답 : "우리는 1년 반 동안… 손실이었습니다."

(fa) 사실에 대한 질문 : "파시스트 독일이… 무엇일까요?"

(fb) 사실에 대한 대답 : "독일은… 있을 수 없습니다."

(3) Has the speaker/writer taken his position early in a clear and direct statement?

→ Following the paragraph for "Attention getting (Ls. 1~3)," and second paragraph for the "Background information (Ls. 4~11)," Stalin clearly takes his position claiming that the Russians can surely defeat the German Fascist troops, since they are not invincible (Refer to Ls. 12~15, 3rd paragraph, especially "Of course not!").

(4) Has the writer supported his position by convincing facts, strong reasons, clear examples along with appropriate emotional or ethical appeals to persuade his audience?

→ Yes, Stalin supports his position effectively by giving numerous facts, reasons, examples, and emotional and ethical appeals for his persuasions.
  (a) Facts: "Hitler's troops... Sevastopol (Ls. 7~11)."
         "Of little importance... the whole world (Ls. 36~39)."
  (b) Reasons: "As to part of... to the frontiers (Ls. 28~35)."
         "Of little importance... such a pact (Ls. 36~52)."
         "In order to... secure victory (Ls. 103~109)."
  (c) Examples: "Napoleon's army... by Anglo-French forces (Ls. 17~21)."
         "As is well known... such a pact (Ls. 51~52)."
         "In cases of a forced retreat... frustrated (Ls. 66~78)."
  (d) Ethical appeals: "Of little importance... Ribbentrop (Ls. 36~48)."
         "This was a definite... Fascist Germany (Ls. 56~65)."
         "This war... symptomatic (Ls. 79~94)."
  (e) Emotional appeals: "Comrade... against German Fascism (Ls. 95~102)," in an appealing and encouraging tone.
         "All our forces... our victory (Ls. 110~112)," in a very heightened voice.

(5) Has the speaker/writer summarized his idea and given a clear and effective call to action?

→ Yes, Stalin summarized his idea to encourage and solidify his people.
  "This war... against the German Fascist forces (Ls. 79~81)" is a summarized idea.
  "The aim of this national war... In this war of liberation we shall not be alone... symptomatic (Ls. 81~94)" are stated as a way of encouraging his people.
  "Comrades, our forces are numberless... against German Fascism (Ls. 95~102)" helps Stalin solidify his people against the enemy.
  The last paragraph "All our forces... Forward, to our victory! (Ls. 110~112)" serves as a clear and an effective call to action. The ultimate goal of calling to action is "for the demolition of the enemy (L. 111)."

(3) 작가는 일찌감치 명확하고 직접적인 말로 자신의 입장을 밝혔는가?

"시선 끌기" 문단과 "배경 정보"로서의 두 번째 문단에 이어 스탈린은 자신의 입장을 분명히 밝히고, 파시스트 독일 군대가 천하무적이 아니므로 러시아인들은 반드시 그들을 이길 수 있다고 주장하고 있다 (세 번째 문단, 특히 "물론 그렇지 않습니다!"를 참조하라).

(4) 작가는 목표로 삼은 청중을 설득하기 위해 적절한 정서적 또는 윤리적 호소와 더불어 설득력 있는 사실, 그럴 듯한 이유, 명확한 예시 등을 제시함으로써 자신의 입장을 뒷받침했는가?

그렇다. 스탈린은 다양한 사실, 근거, 사례, 그리고 자신의 신념에 대한 정서적이고 윤리적인 호소를 제공함으로써 자신의 입장을 효과적으로 뒷받침하고 있다.

(a) 사실 : "히틀러군은… 폭격을 가하고 있습니다."

　　　　 "이런 점에서… 중요하지 않습니다."

(b) 이유 : "그럼에도 불구하고 우리 영토 일부가… 없었다는 점입니다."

　　　　 "이런 점에서…정확히 그런 조약입니다."

　　　　 "소련 내 모든 인민군을… 요청하고 있습니다."

(c) 사례 : "나폴레옹군은… 격퇴되었습니다."

　　　　 "잘 알려져 있는 바와 같이… 그런 조약입니다."

　　　　 "적군 부대가 불시에… 실패해야 합니다."

(d) 윤리적 호소 : "이런 점에서… 마찬가지입니다."

　　　　　　　 "그것은 우리 입장에서는… 있을 수 없습니다."

　　　　　　　 "파시스트 독일과의 이 전쟁은… 이해가능한 일입니다."

(e) 정서적 호소 : "동지여… 일어서야 합니다."(호소 및 격려의 어조)

　　　　　　　 "영웅적인 육군과… 돌진합시다!"(아주 높아진 목소리로)

(5) 작가는 자신의 아이디어를 요약하고 분명하고 효과적인 조치를 요구했는가?

그렇다. 스탈린은 자신의 생각을 요약하여 국민을 고무하고 결속시켰다.

"파시스트 독일과의 이 전쟁은… 전쟁이기도 합니다." 부분이 요약된 생각.

"파시스트 압제자들에 대항하여… 이해가능한 일입니다." 부분은 국민을 고무하기 위한 진술.

"동지여, 우리의 부대는… 일어서야 합니다." 부분은 적에 대항하여 국민을 결속시키는 역할을 담당하고 있다.

"영웅적인 육군과… 돌진합시다!"라는 마지막 문단은 행동에 나서라며 효과적이고 분명하게 촉구하고 있다. 행동에 나서는 최종 목표는 "적을 섬멸시키는 것"이다.

Joseph Stalin

4.2.7. Research Paper

Research paper is a composition based on research drawn from books, periodicals, and interviews with other people. There are thousands of topics to choose for your paper, but choosing a suitable topic is crucially important. The chosen topic should be not only interesting and informative to you and your readers, but also it should be suitable/manageable to cover adequately in a short period of time. Below are provided several topics that are either manageable for a short period of time or not. Circle X on the manageable topic.

(1) Korean Culture and Customs.................................(   ).
(2) Animals: Habitats, Types, Reproduction.................(   ).
(3) The Structure of Cells...(   ).
(4) Japanese Traditional Music Through the Ages.......(   ).
(5) How Crystals are Formed.......................................(   ).

As you may know, the topics (3) and (5) are manageable, and there is likely to be sufficient information in the library for the manageable topics. Let's read the following Research Papers, "The Divided World of Pearl Buck" and "Saving the Elephant" with the condensed guidelines kept in mind.

Condensed guidelines for a Research Paper.

(1) Is the topic interesting, informative, and manageable?
(2) Does the thesis statement appear early in the paper?
(3) Is the paper developed with sufficient primary and secondary sources that are (a) relevant; (b) reliable; (c) recent; and, (d) representative?
(4) Are the facts and ideas stated mostly by the student/writer?
(5) Are the citations and the research paper format structured based on your instructor's recommendation?

4.2.7. 연구 논문

연구 논문은 책, 정기 간행물, 그리고 다른 사람들과의 인터뷰에서 끌어낸 연구에 근거한 작문이다. 선택할 수 있는 주제는 다양하지만, 적절한 주제를 선택하는 것이야말로 가장 중요하다. 선택된 주제는 당신과 독자들에게 흥미롭고 유익해야 할 뿐 아니라 짧은 기간 안에 충분히 다룰 수있을 만큼 적당해야 한다. 다음은 짧은 기간에 다룰 수 있는 주제와 그렇지 않은 주제들이다. 다루기 쉬운 주제에 표시하라.

(1) 한국의 문화와 관습 ....(   )
(2) 동물 : 서식지, 유형, 생식 ....(   )
(3) 세포의 구조 ....(   )
(4) 시대에 따른 일본의 전통 음악...................................(   )
(5) 수정은 어떻게 형성되는가.......................................(   )

아다시피, 주제 (3)과 (5)는 다루기 쉬우며, 다루기 쉬운 주제들에 대해서는 도서관에 충분한 정보가 있을 듯하다. 다음에 제시된 지침을 명심하면서 "펄벅의 분열된 세계"와 "코끼리 구하기"라는 두 편의 연구 논문을 읽어보자.

연구 논문 지침

(1) 주제는 흥미롭고 유익하며 다루기 쉬운가?
(2) 논문 초반에 논제를 제시하고 있는가?
(3) 논문은 (a) 관련성, (b) 신빙성, (c) 시의성, (d) 대표성을 지닌 1, 2차 자료를 충분히 활용하고 있는가?
(4) 사실과 아이디어는 대부분 학생/작가에 의해 진술되고 있는가?
(5) 인용문과 연구 논문 구성은 교사의 권고에 근거하여 짜여져 있는가?

Mummensnchanz's 　Next,　presented by Dance Celebration, will perform at the Zellerbach Theatre at the Annenberg Center through Sunday.

Model 1: "The Divided World of Pearl Buck." by Tim Loughman

OUTLINE

Thesis : Conflict between East and West affected Pearl Buck's life, but she was
able to resolve the conflict in her life and in her work.

Introduction: Pearl Buck and the conflict that divided her life.

I. Buck's life
  A. First half
    1. Childhood in China
        a. Parents' background
        b. Boxer Rebellion
    2. Escape of 1927
    3. Decision to leave China
  B. Second half
    1. Humanitarian projects
    2. Denial of permission to return to China

II. Buck's works
    A. Early works
      1. <u>The Good Earth</u>
      2. Chinese or Americans in China as subjects.
    B. Later works
      1. <u>Letter from Peking</u>
      2. "The Golden Bowl"
      3. <u>All Under Heaven</u>
      4. Americans forced out of Asia as subjects

III. Buck's response to conflict
    A. Personal friendships
    B. Adoption agency for orphans
    C. Desire to return to China

Conclusion : Buck's ability — through life and work — to bridge the conflict

모델 1 '펄벅의 분열된 세계' (팀 러프만)

개요

논제 : 동서양의 갈등은 펄벅의 삶에 영향을 끼쳤으나, 그녀는 자신의 삶과 작품 속에서 그 갈등을 해소할 수 있었다.

서문 : 펄벅과 그녀의 삶을 분열시킨 갈등

Pearl S. Buck
A Chinese portrait of Pearl S. Buck, at the time. 'The Good Earth' was published, in 1931. Buck was still in China when her book became a bestseller in America.

   I. **벅의 생애**
     A. 전반기
       1. 중국에서의 유년기
         a. 부모의 배경
         b. 의화단 사건
       2. 1927년의 도피
       3. 중국을 떠나다

     B. 후반기
       1. 인도주의적 프로젝트
       2. 중국으로의 귀환을 거부당하다

   II. **벅의 작품**
     A. 초기 작품
       1. 대지
       2. 주제로 쓰인 중국의 중국인 또는 미국인
     B. 후기 작품
       1. 북경에서 온 편지
       2. "The Golden Bowl"
       3. All Under Heaven
       4. 주제로 쓰인 아시아에서 쫓겨난 미국인

   III. **갈등에 대한 벅의 반응**
     A. 개인적 우정
     B. 고아들을 위한 결연 기구
     C. 중국으로 돌아가려는 욕망

결론 : 삶과 작품을 통해 갈등을 돌파하는 벅의 능력

Line 1   Pearl Buck, an American who grew up in Asia, was a living contradiction of Rudyard Kipling's famous line, "Oh, East is East and West is West, and never the twain shall meet." [1] Buck was one of the most popular and widely-translated writers of all time, the first American woman to win the Noble Prize for
L.5.   Literature, and a tireless crusader for peace and international goodwill. In the world in which she lived, however, the division between East and West was real enough. This division had a profound impact on Buck's life and on her writing.

Born in Hillsboro, West Virginia, in 1892, Pearl Buck was just three months old when her parents first took her to China, where her father worked as a
L.10.   missionary. Buck spent most of the next forty-three years there amid the turmoil of rebellion and civil war. She was eight years old when the Boxer Rebellion broke out. The Boxer Rebellion represented an attempt by the Chinese to expel the foreign powers—mostly Westerners—that had seized various Chinese port cities for use as trading bases. [2]

L.15.   The Boxer Rebellion impressed upon the little girl for the first time, the deep anger many Chinese felt toward the foreigners in their midst. During the rebellion, old friends became afraid to talk to her family, for talking with foreigners might have cost them their lives. [3] The rebellion was crushed, but with it was crushed the secure world of Buck's early childhood. "Afterward," she
L.20.   wrote later, "...it was never the same again, never secure, never safe." [4]

At least outwardly, however, life returned to normal. Buck continued to absorb both the culture of her parents and that of China itself. She returned to the United States to attend college in Virginia, but she returned to China just as World War I was breaking out in Europe. In the dozen years that
L.25.   followed, she taught school, married, worked as a nurse, began raising children, and started writing the stories that were to make her world-famous.

Then, on March 27, 1927, the calm of her life was shattered once again when an anti-foreign mob swept through Nanking, where she was living with her family at the time. While the mob ransacked their home, Buck's
L.30.   family hid in the home of a servant, then fled to Japan. Within a year, when the danger had subsided, they returned, but it became increasingly clear to Buck that her days in China were numbered. China was becoming more and more dangerous for foreigners and Chinese alike; for, as Buck foresaw, the civil war that was developing between Nationalists and Communists was
L.35.   only going to become worse. [5]

C H A P T E R 4

아시아에서 자란 미국인 펄벅은 "오, 동양은 동양이며 서양은 서양이니, 그 둘은 결코 만나지 못하리." [1] 라는 루디야드 키플링의 유명한 구절을 정면으로 반박하는 살아있는 표본이다. 벅은 시대를 통틀어 전세계적으로 널리 번역되어 읽히는 가장 인기 있는 작가 중의 한 명이자 노벨 문학상을 수상한 최초의 미국 여성이며, 평화와 국제적 친선을 위해 노력하는 지칠 줄 모르는 개혁 운동가이다. 그러나 그녀가 살았던 세상에서는 동양과 서양 사이의 분열이 현실이었다. 이러한 분열은 벅의 삶과 작품에 심오한 영향을 미쳤다.

1892년, 웨스트 버지니아주 힐스보로에서 태어난 펄벅은 생후 3개월만에 부모님을 따라 처음 중국에 갔다. 아버지는 거기서 선교사로 일했다. 벅은 폭동과 내란의 소용돌이 속에서 이후 43년 간 거기서 보냈다. 의화단 사건이 일어났을 때, 그녀는 여덟 살이었다. 의화단 사건은 중국인들이 중국의 다양한 항구 도시를 무역 거점으로 사용하고 있던 외국 세력 대부분 서양인들 을 몰아내려는 시도의 일환이었다. [2]

의화단 사건은 어린 소녀에게 처음으로 중국인들이 중국에 사는 외국인들에게 느끼는 깊은 분노를 알 수 있게 해주었다. 폭동 기간 동안, 오랜 친구들은 그녀의 가족에게 말 걸기를 두려워하게 되었다. 외국인과 이야기하다가 잘못하면 목숨을 잃을 수도 있었기 때문이다. [3] 폭동은 진압되었지만, 폭동과 더불어 어린 시절 벅의 안전한 세계도 사라지고 말았다. 나중에 그녀가 쓴 글에 따르면, "그 후, 세상은 결코 전과 같아지지 않았다. 결코 안전하지도 않았고, 안정적이지도 못했다." [4]

그러나 적어도 표면상으로는 평범한 생활로 돌아갔다. 벅은 계속해서 부모님들의 문화와 중국 자체의 문화를 동시에 흡수해나갔다. 그녀는 대학 입학을 위해 미국 버지니아주로 돌아왔지만, 유럽에서 제1차 세계대전이 발발하자마자 다시 중국으로 돌아왔다. 이후 12년간, 그녀는 학교에서 가르쳤고, 결혼했으며, 간호사로 일했고, 아이들을 기르기 시작했고, 그녀를 전세계적으로 유명하게 해 줄 이야기들을 글로 쓰기 시작했다.

그러다 1927년 3월 27일, 그녀의 평온한 삶이 또 한번 산산조각나고 말았다. 그 당시 그녀가 가족과 함께 살고 있던 난징 전역에 반외세 기운이 몰아쳤던 것이다. 폭도가 그들의 집을 수색하는 동안, 벅의 가족은 하인의 집에 숨어있다가 급기야 일본으로 도망쳤다. 1년이 채 지나지 않아, 위험이 가라앉자, 그들은 중국으로 돌아왔지만, 벅은 차츰 중국에서 보낼 날도 이제 다했다는 생각을 지울 수 없었다. 중국은 외국인에게나 중국인에게나 점점 더 위험한 곳으로 변해가고 있었다. 벅이 예견했듯이, 국민당과 공산당 사이에 진행되던 내전이 갈수록 악화되고 있었기 때문이다. [5]

나중에 그녀는 이렇게 썼다:

...내가 막을 수도 없고 또 도울 수도 없는 그런 소동 속에서 평생을 보내고 싶지 않다면, 내 조국을 바꾸고 그와 더불어 내 세계를 바꿔야 한다는 생각이 더욱 분명해졌다. 나는 그러한 변화가 두려웠다. 중국을 너무나 사랑했고, 내게는 중국인들이 바로 내 동포 같았기 때문이다. [6]

1935년, 그녀는 미국으로 영구 귀국했다.

Later, she wrote:

...it became clear to me that unless I wanted to spend my life in a turmoil I could neither prevent nor help, I would have to change my country, and with it my world. I dreaded the change, for I deeply loved China, and her people to me were as my own.[6]

In 1935, she returned to the United States for good.

1935 marked a critical turning point in Buck's writing as well as in her life. Until that point, she had concentrated in her writing largely on Chinese subjects or on Americans in China. In <u>The Good Earth</u>, for example, Buck's most famous work, for which she won the Pulitzer Prize in 1932, she presented a moving story of a Chinese peasant family. After leaving China, however, she tended to fill her stories with Americans who, like herself, had been forced out of Asia after living there for many years. In <u>Letter from Peking</u>, Elizabeth MacLeod flees the civil war in China with her son, while her husband, a university president, feels duty-bound to his students to stay behind.[7] In "The Golden Bowl," the impending outbreak of World War II drives missionary James Briony from Japan, where he had been toiling for twenty-five years.[8] In <u>All Under Heaven</u>, the fall of Peking to the Communists spells the end of another twenty-five year career abroad, that of diplomat Malcolm MacNeil in China.[9]

All of these American characters are victims of circumstances. They each love the Asian country in which they have been living, but they are each compelled to leave it because they are foreigners. Moreover, back in the United States, each finds the same sort of prejudice in reverse: they find themselves the objects of suspicion from their fellow Americans because they have just returned from foreign countries. Unhappily, each of these characters must endure the mutual distrust between East and West.

Pearl Buck, however, was no pessimist, and it would be wrong to interpret her stories in a pessimistic light. In her stories she acknowledged the suspicion and distrust between East and West — the gulf that divided her own life in two and that runs through the lives of so many of her characters — but she never admitted that the gulf could not be crossed. True, her stories are full of characters who, like Buck herself, build individual bridges of personal friendship over that gulf, only to be barred from crossing them by war, prejudice, or official decree.

(margin line markers: L.40, L.45, L.50, L.55, L.60, L.65)

(vertical margin text: CHAPTER 4)

1935년은 벅의 생애뿐 아니라 그녀의 글쓰기에서도 결정적인 전환점이 되었다. 그 때까지 그녀는 대부분 중국 문제나 중국의 미국인들에 대한 글쓰기에 집중해왔다. 예를 들어, 벅의 가장 유명한 작품이자 1932년, 그녀에게 퓰리처 상을 안겨준 [대지]에서 그녀는 중국 농부 가족의 감동적인 이야기를 묘사했다. 그러나 중국을 떠난 뒤, 그녀는 자신과 마찬가지로 아시아에서 오랫동안 살다가 쫓겨난 미국인들의 이야기로 작품을 채워나가는 경향이 있었다. [북경에서 온 편지]에서, 엘리자베스 맥레오드는 내전을 피해 아들과 함께 중국을 떠나지만, 대학교수인 그녀의 남편은 제자들에 대한 의무감 때문에 뒤에 남는다.[7] "The Golden Bowl"에서는 제2차 세계 대전이 임박하면서 선교사 제임스 브리오니는 자신이 25년 간 일해오던 일본에서 쫓겨난다.[8] [All Under Heaven]의 경우, 북경이 공산주의자들에게 함락당하자, 중국에서 일하던 말콤 맥닐은 25년 간의 해외 외교관 생활에 종지부를 찍어야 했다.[9]

이들 미국인들은 모두 상황의 희생자들이다. 그들은 각각 자신이 살고 있던 아시아 국가를 사랑하지만, 외국인이라는 이유 때문에 그곳을 떠나야 한다. 게다가 미국으로 돌아오자, 그들은 각각 똑같은 종류의 편견을 역으로 경험하게 된다. 그들이 단지 외국에서 살다 왔다는 이유로 동료 미국인들로부터 의심의 대상이 되는 것이다. 불행하게도, 이들 각각의 등장인물들은 동양과 서양 사이의 상호 불신을 감내해야 한다.

그러나 펄벅은 결코 염세주의자가 아니었고, 그녀의 작품을 염세주의적 관점으로 해석하는 것은 분명 잘못된 것이다. 그녀는 작품 속에서 동양과 서양 사이의 의심과 불신 -- 그녀 자신의 삶을 둘로 나눴고, 그녀가 창조한 상당수 인물들의 삶을 관통하고 있는 격차 --을 인정했지만, 그 격차가 해소될 수 없다고 인정한 적은 단 한 번도 없었다. 사실 그녀의 이야기에는 벅 자신처럼 그 격차를 넘어 사적인 우정이라는 개인적 다리를 건설했으나 결과적으로 전쟁이나 편견, 또는 정부 법령에 의해 그 다리를 건너지 못하게 되는 사람들로 가득하다. 그러나 벅은 결코 그런 다리를 건설하는 것이 쓸모 없다고 말하지 않았을 것이다. 그녀는 개인적이고 사적인 우정을 신뢰했고, 국제적 알력에도 불구하고 사적인 우정의 힘과 중요성을 믿어 의심치 않았다.[10] "The Golden Bowl"에서 미국인 선교사 제임스 브리오니는 일본에서 강제로 출국당하기 전날, 일본인 친구들로부터 그에 대한 애정을 상징하는 도자기 사발을 선물 받는다. 미국으로 돌아온 뒤, 브리오니는 진주만 공격 이후 일본에 대한 반감이 커져가는 가운데 자신의 지적인 여자 친구마저 그 사발을 깨뜨리고 싶어한다는 사실을 알게 된다. 그 사발이 상징하는 우정과 마찬가지로, 그 사발 역시 전쟁통에도 무사히 살아남아 브리오니의 남은 평생 내내 손상되지 않은 채 온전히 보존된다.[11]

펄벅 자신의 삶은 키플링의 그 유명한 구절을 반박하고 있다. 그녀는 자신의 삶 그 자체와 글쓰기의 상당 부분을 동양과 서양이 개인적 차원에서든 국가적 차원에서든 우정으로 만날 수 있다는 점을 보여주는 데 할애했다. 그녀는 제2차 세계대전 기간 동안 중국 구호 사업에 적극적으로 참여했고, 나중에는 한국과 일본에서 버려지거나 고아가 된 아시아계 미국인 아이들을 위해 미국에 가정을 찾아주는 양자 결연 단체의 창립을 도왔다.[12]

1972년, 미국인들에게 오랫동안 문을 닫아왔던 중국이 다시금 문호를 개방했다. 그러나 중국 정부는 펄벅이 "새로운 중국 사람들과 그 지도자들"에 대해 비판적이었다는 이유로 그녀의 입국을 거부했다.[13] 1973년, 펄벅은 중국에 돌아가 보지 못한 채 사망하고 말았다.

L.70.   Buck, however, would have been the last to suggest the uselessness of building such bridges. She believed in the individual and in personal friendship, and in the strength and importance of personal friendship in the face of international discord.[10] In "The Golden Bowl," on the eve of his forced departure from Japan, the American missionary James Briony is presented by his Japanese friends with

L.75. a porcelain bowl symbolic of their affection for him. Back in the United States, Briony finds that, amid the strong feelings against Japan in the wake of Pearl Harbor, even his intelligent girl friend wants to smash the fragile bowl to bits. The bowl, however, endures. Like the friendship it symbolizes, it survives the war and remains intact throughout the rest of Briony's life.[11]

L.80. Pearl Buck's own life contradicts Kipling's famous lines. She devoted much of her life and her writing to showing that East and West could meet in friendship, whether on a personal or a national level. She was active in relief work for China during World War II, and she later helped set up an adoption agency to find homes in the United States for unwanted or orphaned Asian-American children

L.85. from Korea and Japan.[12]

In 1972, China which had for so long been closed to Americans, reopened its doors. The Chinese government, however, denied Pearl Buck permission to return to the land of her youth on the grounds that she had been critical of "the people of the new China and their leaders."[13] In 1973, Pearl Buck died, never

L.90. having returned to China.

The bridge to the East that Buck built, however, endures. It endures in the lives of those for whom she found homes, in the ongoing work of her adoption agency, and in her stories — stories that testify to the love and respect Buck felt throughout her life for the people among whom she grew up. Conflict between

L.95. East and West tore Pearl Buck from Asia, but nothing could ever take her love for Asia or its people from her.

---

[1] Rudyard Kipling, "The Ballad of East and West," <u>Rudyard Kipling's Verse</u> (New York: Doubleday and Company, Inc., 1940), p. 233.

[2] Unlike England, Russia, Germany, France, and Japan, the United States never actually took over any Chinese cities. It simply demanded and got the same sort of special trading privileges these other countries enjoyed.

[3] Theodore F. Harris, <u>Pearl S. Buck</u>: A Biography (New York: The John Day Company, 1969), p. 79.

[4] Pearl S. Buck, as quoted in Harris, p. 80.

[5] Pearl S. Buck, <u>My Several Worlds: A Personal Record</u> (New York: The John Day Company, 1954), pp.263-265.

CHAPTER 4

그러나 벽이 건설한 동양으로 가는 다리는 지속되고 있다. 그녀가 집을 찾아준 사람들의 삶 속에, 그녀가 제창한 양자 결연 조직의 지속적인 활동 속에, 그리고 그녀의 이야기들 ㅡㅡ 벽이 유년 시절을 함께 한 사람들에 대해 평생 사랑과 존경을 느꼈음을 입증하는 이야기들 ㅡㅡ 속에 계속 살아 있는 것이다. 동양과 서양의 갈등은 펄벅을 아시아에서 떼놓았지만, 그 어떤 것도 그녀에게서 아시아나 아시아 사람들에 대한 사랑을 빼앗을 수는 없었다.

'The Good Earth' brought the author wealth. fame, and social prominence. In 1934, Pearl Buck also became an editor at John Day, the company which published her novels.(The Pearl S. Buck family trust)

One of Buck's greatest concerns was the walfare of children, especially Amerasian children in countries like China and Japan. In 1949, she founded Welcome House, the first international, interracial adoption agency in the world.(The Pearl S. Buck family trust)

Note

twain *n.* two of anything ; pair ; couple

turmoil *n.* Great confusion ; uproar.

crush 1. To press, squeeze, or beat down on with enough force to break or injure --The tree fell on the car and crushed it. 2. To grind or pound into very find particles --This machine crushes rocks into powder. 3. To crumple ; winkle --Don't crush your suit. 4. To put down ; subdue.

shatter *v.* 1. To break suddenly into many pieces ; smash. 2. To destroy ; ruin.

ransack *v.* To search through thoroughly, esp. for items to steal ; plunder.

mob *n.* 1. A large, disorderly crowd. 2. A large group of people ; crowd around and jostle or annoy -- Fans mobbed the movie star.

subside *v.* 1. To sink to a lower or more normal level --The flood waters finally subsided. 2. To become less intense or active --The cheers for the winner finally subsided.

dread *n.* Great fear. v. To fear greatly. a. Causing great fear ; dreadful --Smallpox is a dread disease.

toil *v.* 1. To work hard and for a long time. 2. To move or go with a lot of effort.

distrust *n.* Lack of trust ; suspicion. v. To have no trust in.

gulf *n.* 1. A large area of a sea or ocean that is partly enclosed by land. 2. A deep break in the earth, as one caused by an earthquake. 3. A big difference, as of opinions.

intact *a.* Not harmed or damaged.

[6] Buck, <u>Worlds</u>, p. 265.

[7] Anthony Arlsberg, "The Life and Meaning of Pearl Buck," Norwood Literacy Review, Apr., 1973, pp. 59-62.

[8] Arlsberg, p. 60.

[9] Arlsberg, p. 61.

[10] Harris, p. 242.

[11] Arlsberg, p. 61.

[12] Harris, p. 252.

[13] H. L. Yuan, Second Secretary of the Embassy of the People's Republic of China in Canada, letter reproduced in Pearl S. Buck, <u>China Past and Present</u> (New York: The John Day Company, 1972), p. 171.

<u>Bibliography</u>

Arlsberg, Anthony. "The Life and Meaning of Pearl Buck." Norwood Literary Review, April, 1973, pp. 59-62.

Buck, Pearl S. <u>China Past and Present</u>. New York: The John Day Company, 1972.
_____. <u>The Good Earth</u>. New York: The John Day Company, 1931.
_____. <u>My Several Worlds: A Personal Record</u>. New York: The John Day Company, 1954.

"Buck, Pearl S." <u>Collier's Encyclopedia</u> (1980), IV, 650
Deas, Malcolm, et al. <u>Civilization: Journey to the Modern World</u>. Volume II. Del Mar, California: CRM Books, 1973.

Harris, Theodore F. <u>Pearl S. Buck: A Biography</u>. New York: The John Day Company, 1969.

Kipling, Rudyard. "The Ballad of East and West." <u>Rudyard Kipling's Verse</u>. New York: Doubleday and Company, Inc., 1940.

(1) Is the topic interesting, informative, and manageable?

→ The topic, "The Divided World of Pearl Buck" is both interesting and informative for those good world citizens who respect human dignity based on "humanistic love and view" instead of a type of Kipling's "egocentrism and racism (Ls. 2~3)." The topic is also manageable, since it deals with Pearl Buck's egalitarian human respect and love toward all the people regardless of the East or the West.

(2) Does the thesis statement appear early in the paper?

→ Yes, it does. The first two sentences, "Pearl Buck,... was a living contradiction of Rudyard Kipling's famous line, 'Oh, East is East and West is West, and never the twain (two) shall meet,'" are thesis statements, and they clearly show that Pearl Buck's idea, unlike Kipling's claim, can pave a way for universal peace and prosperity based on humanistic love and multicultural understanding.

(3) Is the paper developed with sufficient primary and secondary sources that are (a) relevant; (b) reliable; (c) recent; and, (d) representative?

→ Yes, it is. Refer to the Bibliography section as a way of answering these questions.

(1) 주제는 흥미롭고 유익하며 다루기 쉬운가?

"펄벅의 분열된 세계"라는 주제는 키플링의 "자기 중심성과 인종적 차별" 유형 대신 "인도주의적 사랑과 관점"에 근거하여 인간의 존엄성을 존중하는 선한 세계 시민들에게 매우 흥미롭고 유익한 주제이다. 게다가 다루기도 쉽다. 펄벅의 평등주의적 인간 존중과 동서양을 막론한 모든 사람들에 대한 사랑을 다루고 있기 때문이다.

(2) 논문 초반에 논제를 제시하고 있는가?

그렇다. "아시아에서 자란 ... 살아있는 표본이다"라는 처음 두 문장은 논제 진술이며, 키플링의 주장과 달리, 펄벅의 생각은 인도주의적 사랑과 다문화적 이해에 근거한 보편적 평화와 번영을 용이하게 한다는 점을 분명히 보여주고 있다.

(3) 논문은 (a) 관련성, (b) 신빙성, (c) 시의성, (d) 대표성을 지닌 1, 2차 자료를 충분히 활용하고 있는가?

그렇다. 이 질문에 답하는 한 방법으로서 참고 자료 부분을 참조하라.

(a) 관련성 : 인용된 모든 자료가 주제와 관련이 있다. [문명: 근대 세계로의 여행 2권]은 2차적인 자료로 기능하고 있는 반면, 다른 모든 자료들은 1차 자료이다.

(b) 신빙성 : 각주 13을 제외하면, 인용된 모든 자료들이 객관적 시각, 학문적 내용, 호의적 평가 등의 차원에서 신빙성이 있다.

(c) 시의성 : 인용된 자료 대부분은 최신 자료가 아니며, 이 점은 자연 과학 분야와 관련된 연구에서는 권장되지 않는다. 그러나 이 주제는 문학 및 "인간을 인간적 견지에서 인간화한다"는 문학의 목적과 관련되어 있다. 이런 의미에서, 이 주제를 전개시키는데 비교적 이전 자료를 사용한 것이 그다지 큰 흠은 아니다.

(d) 대표성 : 인용된 자료 대부분은 펄벅의 문학적 견지를 반영하고 있으며(예를 들면, [중국의 과거와 현재] ; [대지] ; [나의 몇몇 세계 :개인적 기록]), 벅을 위대한 작가로 묘사하고 있다("펄벅의 생애와 그 의미" ; 펄벅 전기). 그러나 키플링의 "동양과 서양의 발라드"나 H.L. 유안의 공적 편지와 같은 자료들은 이 연구 논문이 다양화된 다각적 관점을 "대표"하는데 도움을 주고 있다.

(a) Relevant: All the sources cited are relevant to the topic. Civilization: Journey to the Modern World, Vol. II serves as a secondary source, while all others are primary.

(b) Reliable: Except the footnote 13, all cited sources are reliable in terms of objective points of view, academic contents, and recognized acceptance.

(c) Recent: Most of the cited sources are not up-to-date, which is not recommended for research related to the natural science field. The area for this topic, however, is related to literature and its goal: "To humanize human beings humanly." In this sense, it does not hurt too much using the sources that are not up-to-date for this topic.

(d) Representative: Most of the sources cited reflect Pearl Buck's literary perspectives (eg. China Past and Present; <u>The Good Earth</u>; <u>My Several Worlds: A Personal Record</u>), and describes Buck as a great writer ("The Life and Meaning of Pearl Buck"; and <u>Pearl S. Buck: A Biography</u>) However, sources such as Kipling's "The Ballad of East and West," and H. L. Yuan's official letter help this research paper be "representative" for diversified points of view.

(4) Are the facts and ideas stated mostly by the student/writer?

→ Yes, they are as evidenced as follows:

(a) Footnotes 2, 3, 5, 12, and 13: The writer clearly summarizes with his own words drawn from the sources cited.

(b) The first paragraph (Ls 1~7): As the introduction and thesis statements, the paragraph is clearly stated with the writer's own ideas.

(c) The last paragraph (Ls 91~96): As the conclusion, the paragraph clearly summarizes all the details that support the topic (Refer to Ls. 95~96, "but nothing could ever take her love from Asia or its people from her.")

(5) Are the citations and the research paper format structured based on your instructor's recommendation?

→ The citations and the format employed for this research paper is a well established traditional format, which has been widely used for many years in the academic communities. However, since the early 1980s, a new format called "APA" (American Psychological Association) has been widely used, which we will see a sample in the next paper, "Saving the Elephants."

Carie and Absalom Sydenstricker brought their daughter Pearl to China when she was only three months old.(The Pearl S.Buck family trust)

(4) 사실과 아이디어는 대부분 학생/작가에 의해 진술되고 있는가?

그렇다.

(a) 각주 2, 3, 5, 12, 13 : 작가는 인용된 자료에서 도출한 내용을 자기 자신의 언어로 명확히 요약하고 있다.

(b) 첫 문단 : 서론 및 논제 제시 성격을 띠는 이 문단은 작가 자신의 아이디어로 명확히 진술되어 있다.

(c) 마지막 문단 : 결론으로 기능하고 있는 이 문단은 주제를 뒷받침하는 모든 세부 사항들을 명확히 요약하고 있다 (마지막 줄에 나오는 "그 어떤 것도 그녀에게서 아시아나 아시아 사람들에 대한 사랑을 빼앗을 수는 없었다."라는 문장을 참조하라.)

(5) 인용문과 연구 논문 포맷은 교사의 권고에 근거하여 짜여져 있는가?

이 논문에 쓰인 인용문과 포맷은 잘 짜여진 전통적 포맷으로서, 학계에서 오랫동안 광범위하게 사용되어왔다. 그러나 1980년대 초반 이후, "APA"(미국 심리학 협회)라 불리는 새로운 포맷이 광범위하게 사용되어왔는데, "코끼리 구하기"라는 다음 논문에서 그 실례를 보게 될 것이다.

The Metro - Goldwyn - Mayer movie version of 'The Good Earth' was released in 1937. Actor Paul Muni played the farmer Wang Lung. Here shown toiling in the toiling in the fields. Today, the use of white actors to portray Asian characters is controversial.

Model 2: "Saving the Elephants." by Jullian Polaski

Line 1   In the nineteenth century, Africa contained an estimated 5 million elephants, a number that had slowly decreased to an estimated 3 million by 1970 (Chadwick 3). But then something started to happen. The numbers began to decrease at an alarming rate. By 1979, the number had decreased to an estimated

L.5   1.3 million, and by 1990, to an estimated 609,000 (Morell 10) The cause of this sudden decrease is not hard to determine. It was "M-O-N-E-Y" (Chadwick 39).

    The money came from the sale of ivory, or "white gold," as it is called in most of the sources read. The demand for ivory was unending. It was used to produce everything from rings, necklaces, and earrings to musical instruments and

L.10   elaborately carved sculptures of all sizes, and it was in demand everywhere - from Germany, Italy, France, and the United States to India, Southeast Asia, China, and Japan, the "world's largest consumer of ivory" (Underwood). This demand "sent the price of ivory skyrocketing into the rarefied realm where the likes of gold, rhinoceros horn, diamonds, and hard drugs mingle with potent

L.15   human fantasies and cravings" (Chadwick 41). Between 1983 and 1988 alone, the price increased approximately $55 a pound, from $27 a pound in 1983 to $82 a pound in 1988 (Morell 11). And ivory was bought by the ton.

    It's no wonder poachers went on a rampage. During the 1980s, the elephant opulation in Kenya alone decreased from around 130,000 to around

L.20   16,000 (Contreras 87; Morell 6). As the slaughter continued, the poachers' methods became more and more sophisticated and destructive. As Chadwick has pointed out,

> [the] poachers resembled the field forces of drug operations in
> the Golden Triangle and Columbia: They traveled in large,
>
> L.25 well-armed, paramilitary groups supported by vehicles,
> radios, an occasional spotting plane, and a network of
> informants that sometimes reached to the highest level of
> government. Their weapon of choice was the semiautomatic
> rifle or machine gun. Few ever stopped to take so much as one
>
> L.30 steak from the tons of meat left lying to rot after the tusks
> were hacked out of the animals with an ax or chain saw. (43)

    In 1989, in an effort to combat the poaching and to end the slaughter, the Convention on International Trade in Endangered Species (CITES) issued a "moratorium on international trade in ivory," a temporary ban that went into

L.35   effect in 1990 ("Poachers' pause"). Although there was some opposition to the original moratorium, CITES voted to retain it at a meeting in March 1992 ("When Is Culling").

모델 2 '코끼리 구하기' (줄리안 폴라스키)

19세기 아프리카에는 대략 5백만 마리의 코끼리가 서식하고 있었는데, 그 수치는 천천히 줄어들어 1970년에는 대략 3백만 마리가 남게 되었다(채드윅 3). 그러나 그때부터 중요한 변화가 생기기 시작했다. 그 수치가 놀라운 비율로 감소하기 시작한 것이다. 1979년, 코끼리 수치는 대략 1백 3십만 마리로 줄어들었고, 1990년이 되자, 대략 6십만 9천마리로 감소되었다(모렐 10). 이 갑작스런 감소 원인을 알아내기란 어렵지 않다. 바로 '돈' 이었다(채드윅 39).

돈은 상아, 또는 대부분의 자료에서 쓰여지는 명칭대로라면, '화이트 골드'의 판매에서 생겨났다. 상아 수요는 끝이 없었다. 그것은 반지, 목걸이, 귀고리에서부터 다양한 크기로 정성스레 조각된 조각품과 악기에 이르기까지, 모든 물건을 제작하는데 사용되었고, 독일, 이탈리아, 프랑스, 미국 등은 물론 인도, 동남아시아, 중국을 비롯하여 '세계에서 가장 거대한 상아 소비국' 일본에 이르기까지 세계 도처에 수요가 있었다(언더우드). 이러한 수요는 상아 가격을 "금, 무소뿔, 다이아몬드, 마약 같은 물건이 인간의 막강한 공상 및 갈망과 뒤섞이는 희귀한 영역으로까지 급등시켰다"(채드윅 41). 1983년에서 1988년까지만 보더라도, 상아 가격은 파운드 당 대략 55달러나 치솟았는데, 1983년에 파운드 당 27달러이던 것이 1988년에는 파운드 당 82달러로 올라버렸다(모렐 11). 게다가 상아는 톤 단위로 판매되었다.

밀렵꾼들이 날뛰는 것도 이상한 일은 아니다. 1980년대 케냐 한 나라의 코끼리 수만 해도 대략 130,000 마리에서 대략 16,000마리로 줄어들었다(컨트레라스 87; 모렐 6). 살육이 계속됨에 따라, 밀렵꾼들의 방식도 점점 더 복잡하고 파괴적으로 변해갔다. 채드윅이 지적했듯이,

> 밀렵꾼들은 황금의 삼각지대 및 콜롬비아의 마약 공급 세력과 유사했다. 그들은 무장이 잘 된 거대한 준군사조직 단위로 차량, 라디오, 임시 동향 탐지 비행기, 그리고 때로 정부 고위층까지 뻗어있는 정보망의 뒷받침을 받으며 여행했다. 그들이 엄선한 무기는 반자동 소총이나 기관총이었다. 도끼나 사슬톱으로 엄니(상아)를 빼낸 뒤에는 썩을 때까지 방치된 수 톤의 고기 중에서 스테이크 한 접시 분량조차도 가져가려는 사람이 없다. (43)

1989년, 멸종 위기에 처한 야생 동식물의 국제 거래에 관한 협약(CITES)에서는 밀렵을 없애고 도살을 막으려는 노력의 일환으로, 1990년에 효력을 발하는 일시적 금지령으로서 '상아의 국제 거래 유예'를 선포했다('밀렵꾼들의 휴지기'). 본래의 유예에 대한 다소간의 반대가 있긴 했지만, CITES는 1992년 3월의 회합에서 그것을 존속시키기로 가결했다("동물을 죽이는 것이 아니라 도태시키는 것은 언제인가?").

전체적으로 보면, 이 유예 선포가 효과를 거둔 것 같다. 실제로 국제 야생 생물 보호 협회 회장 데이빗 웨스턴은 "상아 금지령은 아프리카 전역의 코끼들에게 엄청난 도움이 되었다"고 말했다(컨트레라스 87에서 인용). 1989년 7월, 케냐의 다니엘 아랍 모이 대통령은 금지령을 찬성하는 뜻에서 "산더미처럼 쌓인 엄청난 양의 몰수된 엄니들 -- 거의 3백만 달러에 달하는 상아 12톤 --에 불을 질렀다.

Overall, the moratorium seems to have worked. Indeed, David Western, the director of Wildlife Conservation International, has stated that "the ivory

L.40.   ban has done an enormous amount of good for the elephants all over Africa" (qtd. in Contreras 87) In support of the ban, in July 1989, the president of Kenya, Daniel arap Moi, set fire to "a confiscated mountain of tusks - 12 tons of ivory, worth nearly $3 million - while camera crews filmed the costly conflagration. The message: 'Ban the Ivory Trade'" (Morell 7) In Kenya, at

L.45.   least, the poachers seem to have received the message, for just 55 elephants were killed in 1990, compared to the thousands that were being killed each year during the preceding two decades (Contreras 87) To enforce the ban, both Kenya and Tanzania passed laws that provide for mandatory terms of five years in prison for poachers (Morell 10).

L.50.   Even modern technology, in the form of DNA testing, has entered the picture to help protect the elephants and to capture poachers. With DNA testing, experts can establish a "fingerprinting database of elephant tusks...[to] help pinpoint the types of elephants from which confiscated tusks are obtained as well as the exact location in Africa of those elephant types" ("Elephants' Telltale Tusks").

L.55.   And believe it or not, there is even a natural substitute for ivory, a substitute called tagua, which grows on trees.

Tagua, or vegetable ivory, is made from the dried and polished nuts of several South American palms. "It is remarkably similar to animal ivory in both looks and feel," says Marlene Kanas... Tagua is durable

L.60.   and easily carved and it even mimics the porosity of animal ivory. Evidently, those similarities were not lost on early botanists, who named the palm genus Phytelephas - "elephant plant." (Underwood)

While tagua is small in comparison with the ivory taken from elephants (it can be used only for such items as buttons and small pieces of jewelry), it is

L.65.   <u>renewable</u>. As Underwood further points out, a single female tagua tree can produce almost twenty pounds of nuts a year, the same amount a female elephant can produce only once.

Unfortunately, the decrease in the quest for ivory has created a major problem: the elephant population has started to expand in areas where the

L.70.   human population has increased drastically. In mid-1992, the population of Botswana, Kenya, Malawi, Namibia, South Africa, Tanzania, Zambia, and Zimbabwe was estimated to be 131,600,000 with an estimated average yearly increase of 3.3% (<u>1993 Information</u> 145-296). As Chadwick has pointed out, the population increase is "causing more and more wildlife

L.75.   habitat to be converted to cropland and livestock pastures" (40).

In order to combat the problem of the increasing elephant population, a number of countries have resorted to "culling" the elephant herds. In other words, they have started to kill the elephants to reduce the herds to more manageable numbers and to sell the ivory through an "ivory trading

L.80.   association... to pay for conservation" ("Poachers' pause"). As an example, Botswana, in mid-1992, culled 300-600 elephants and plans to increase the number to about 3,000 a year to stabilize the numbers (Contreras 88).

그 사이 카메라 기자들은 그 호사스러운 화재를 필름에 담았다. '상아 거래 금지' 메시지를 알린 것이다"(모렐 7). 적어도 케냐에서는 밀렵꾼들이 그 메시지를 받은 것 같다. 이전 2십년간 매년 수천 마리가 도살되었던 점에 비춰볼 때, 1990년에 도살된 코끼리 수는 55마리에 그쳤기 때문이다(컨테라스 87). 금지령을 시행하기 위해 케냐와 탄자니아 두 나라는 밀렵꾼들을 5년간 투옥할 수 있게 하는 법을 통과시켰다(모렐 10).

근대 과학기술 조차도 DNA 테스트의 형태로 코끼리를 보호하고 밀렵꾼들을 잡는 상황에 이르렀다. DNA 테스트를 통해, 전문가들은 "코끼리 엄니의 지문 데이터베이스를 확립하여...몰수된 엄니들이 어떤 유형의 코끼리로부터 얻어진 것인지 파악하고 그런 유형의 코끼리가 정확히 아프리카 어느 지역에 있는지 알 수 있다"("자동적으로 드러나는 코끼리의 엄니").

게다가 믿거나 말거나 상아의 자연 대체품, 다시 말해 나무에서 자라는 타구아라는 대체품까지 있다.

> 야채 상아 타구아는 윤기 나게 잘 말린 남아메리카 일부 종려나무 열매로 만들어진다. "그것은 모양과 감촉 면에서 동물 상아와 놀라울 정도로 유사하다,"고 말렌 카나스는 말한다... 타구아는 튼튼하고 조각하기도 쉬우며, 동물 상아의 다공성(多孔性)까지 닮아 있다. 초기 식물학자들 역시 그러한 유사성을 놓치지 않았던 것 같다. 종려나무 속명을 Phytelephas, 즉 "코끼리 식물"이라고 명명했기 때문이다. (언더우드)

타구아는 코끼리로부터 포획한 상아에 비하면 크기가 작지만(타구아는 단추나 작은 보석류 같은 아이템에만 사용될 수 있다), 계속 부활한다는 장점이 있다. 언더우드가 계속해서 지적하고 있듯이, 암컷 타구아 나무 한 그루가 1년에 거의 20파운드의 열매를 생산할 수 있는데, 그것은 암컷 코끼리가 단 한 번 생산할 수 있는 양과 똑같다.

불행히도, 상아 밀렵의 감소는 거대한 문제를 낳았다. 인구가 맹렬히 증가하는 지역에서 코끼리 수가 팽창하기 시작한 것이다. 1992년 중반, 보츠와나, 케냐, 말라위, 나미비아, 남아프리카, 탄자니아, 잠비아, 짐바브웨 등의 인구는 연평균 3.3.%의 증가율과 더불어 대략 131,600,000명으로 추정되었다 (1993 연감 145-296). 채드윅이 지적했듯이, 인구 증가는 "야생 생물 서식지를 농경지와 가축 목초지로 변경시키는 상황을 야기하고 있다."(40)

코끼리 수의 증가 문제를 해결하기 위해, 많은 나라들이 코끼리 떼를 "도태시키는" 방법에 의지해왔다. 다시 말해, 그들은 코끼리를 죽여 좀더 다루기 쉬운 정도만 남기고, "보존에 따른 대가를 치르면서...상아 거래 협회"를 통해 상아를 팔기 시작했다("밀렵꾼들의 휴지기"). 예를 들어, 보츠와나는 1992년 중반에 300-600마리의 코끼리를 도태시켰고, 일년에 대략 3000마리까지 그 수를 증가시켜 전체 코끼리 수를 안정화시킬 계획이다.

However, the culling itself presents a major problem. As described in several sources, the elephants have strong social ties (DiSilvestro 83-107; L.85. Moss 121-143). Thus, the elephants cannot be culled individually. The poaching of the 1970s and 1980s has eliminated that possibility. As Morell has pointed out, the older elephants, the ones with the largest tusks, were killed first. These were followed by the matriarchs, the leaders who were at least 30 years of age or older. Currently there are not many over the age of 25. What is left is possibly "a whole lot of scared, neurotic, and sad L.90. teenagers" (11). Moss describes just such a culling operation:

> A family is herded by helicopter or light aircraft toward waiting
> marksmen and all members, except calves about one to three
> years old, are shot and killed in a matter of a couple minutes.
> The calves are captured for sale to zoos and safari parks. It
> L.95. would be a clean, quiet operation except for the babies, who
> scream and mill about and climb over their dead relatives in an
> effort to find and stay with their mothers. (315-316)

And those that are left are impossible to relocate, for as Contreras states: "Elephants are territorial creatures that would resist being driven from their L.100. regions. Despite their circus image, they're not as docile as longhorn steers" (88).

What remains, then, is a dilemma, a dilemma which is based on what Morais calls a "struggle between man and beast" (338). As much as some individuals may not like it, there must be "efficient and effective game-management policies" (Tattersall). And those policies must include culling L.105. entire herds, despite the cries of "those animal rights advocates who, unlike conservationists, focus, misty-eyed, on the realistic goal of saving every individual animal rather than on preserving a species" (Tattersall). Considering what is going on in Africa today - the expanding population, the droughts, and the wars - this complete culling may be the only way of L.110. ensuring the existence of "one of the Earth's most magnificent beasts" (Underwood) well into the twenty-first century.

Work Cited

Chadwick, Douglas H. The Fate of the Elephant. San Francisco: Sierra Club, 1992.

Contreras, Joseph. "The Killing Fields." Newsweek. November 18, 1991: 86-88.

DiSilvestro, Roger L. The African Elephant: Twilight in Eden. New York: Wiley, 1991.

"The Elephant's Telltale Tusks." Futurist. March/April 1990: 51.

Morais, Richard C. "Save the Elephants!" Forbes. September 14, 1992: 338-345.

Moss, Cynthia. Elephant Memories: Thirteen Years in the Life of an Elephant Family. New York: Morrow, 1988.

The 1993 Information Please Almanac. 46th ed. New York: Simon and Schuster, 1993. "Poachers' Pause." Economist. March 2, 1991: 42.

Tattersall, Ian. "The Elephant Wars." Rev. of At the Hand of Man: Peril and Hope for Africa's Wildlife, by Raymond Bonner. New York Times Book Review. May 2, 1993: 13.

Underwood, Anne. "The Good Fake." International Wildlife. 21 (July/August 1991): 29.

"When Is Culling the Animal Not Killing the Animal?" Africa Report. May/June 1992: 10.

그러나 도태 그 자체는 거대한 문제를 낳고 있다. 몇몇 자료에 기술되어 있듯이, 코끼리들은 강한 사회적 유대를 가지고 있다(디실베스트로 83-107 ; 모스 121-143). 따라서 코끼리들은 개별적으로 도태시킬 수 없다. 1970년대와 1980년대의 밀렵이 그러한 가능성을 제거시켜버렸다. 모렐이 지적했듯이, 나이 든 코끼리들, 다시 말해 커다란 엄니를 가진 코끼리들이 먼저 살해되었다. 뒤이어 족장, 그러니까 최소한 30살 이상의 지도자들이 살해되었다. 지금 25살 이상의 코끼리들은 그리 많지 않다. 남아 있는 것은 아마도 "상당수가 겁에 질리고, 신경이 예민하며, 슬픈 십대들"인 것 같다(11). 모스는 그러한 도태 과정을 다음과 같이 묘사한다.

> 한 살에서 세 살까지의 새끼들을 제외하고, 헬리콥터나 경비행기에 의해 대기하고 있던 저격병들과 모든 구성원들한테 이끌어진 한 가족은 단 2분만에 사살 당한다. 새끼들은 포획되어 동물원과 사파리 공원으로 팔려간다. 어머니를 찾아 그 곁에 있으려고 비명과 함께 이리저리 돌아다니며 죽은 친척들 위로 올라가는 어린 새끼들만 아니라면, 그것은 깨끗하고 조용한 작전일지도 모른다.

게다가 남아있는 코끼리들은 다른 장소로 이동시키기가 불가능하다. 컨테라스가 지적하고 있듯이, "코끼리들은 자기 구역에서 쫓겨나는데 저항하는 지역적 동물이다. 그들이 보여주는 서커스 이미지에도 불구하고, 그들은 롱혼 수송아지만큼 온순하지 않다."(88)

그렇다면 남아있는 코끼리들은, 모리스의 표현대로라면, "인간과 야수의 투쟁"이라는 딜레마를 안겨준다(338). 어떤 사람들은 싫어할지 모르지만, "능률적이고 효과적인 게임 매니지먼트 정책"이 있어야 한다(태터솔). 그리고 그 정책들은, "자원보호론자들과 달리, 종의 보전보다는 모든 동물 개인을 구하자는 비현실적 목표에 초점을 맞추는 감상적인 동물 권리 옹호론자들"(태터솔)의 요구에도 불구하고, 무리 전체를 도태시키는 것까지 포함하고 있어야 한다. 오늘날 아프리카에서 진행되고 있는 일 -- 인구 팽창, 가뭄, 전쟁 --을 고려할 때, 이 완전한 도태야말로 "지구상에서 가장 웅장한 동물"(언더우드)을 21세기까지 보존시키기 위한 유일한 방법일지도 모른다.

Note

skyrocket *v.* To rise or cause to rise with the speed, suddenness, and height of a rocket.

rarefy *v.* To make purer; refine.

potent *a.* 1. Having strength; powerful. 2. Producing strong effects, as a drug. 3. persuasive or influential 4. of a male, able to have an erection of the penis.

poacher *n.* One who illegally hunts on another's property.

hack *v.* To chop or cut up or off with repeated heavy blows

moratorium *n.* 1. A legal right or authorization to delay the performance of some obligation, or the period of such a delay. 2. A temporary ban on, or suspension of, some activity considered to be bad or unhealthful.

confiscate *v.* To take something away from someone, in some cases because one has the legal right to do so. --The police confiscated the stolen television sets.

porosity *n.* 1. The state, quality, or condition of being porous. 2. The ratio of the volume of a substance's pores or interstices to the total volume of its mass, expressed as a percentage.

calves *n.* Plural of calf.

(1) Is the topic interesting, informative, and manageable?

➡ Yes, the topic, "saving the elephants" is both interesting and informative. It's interesting since the topic does not deal with the elephants in the zoo, but the wild ones inhabiting exotic and faraway places. The topic is also manageable in the sense that it deals with the conservation of the elephants instead of "destruction, training, lifestyle, and character of the elephants" for multiple purposes.

(2) Does the thesis statement appear early in the paper?

➡ The thesis statements are, "The (elephant) numbers began to decrease at an alarming rate (Ls. 3~4) The cause of the sudden decrease is not hard to determine. It was "M-O-N-E-Y." (L. 6)." In other words, because of human greed for money, elephant populations are decreasing significantly.

(3) Is the paper developed with sufficient primary and secondary sources that are
   (a) relevant; (b) reliable; (c) recent; and, (d) representative?

➡ (a) Relevant: The citations, The Fate of the Elephant; The African Elephant: Twilight in Eden; serves as primary sources. "The Killing Fields"; "The Elephant's Telltale Tusks"; "Save the Elephant!"; Thirteen Years in the Life of an Elephant Family; The 1993 Information Please Almanac; "Poacher's Pause"; "The Elephant War"; "The Good Fake" and "When Is Culling the Animal Not Killing the Animal?" are used as secondary sources. All these sources are relevant to the topic.

   (b) Reliable: The primary sources cited are highly reliable. The secondary sources support the primary ones, which helps the paper be "more reliable."

   (c) Recent: Most of the cited sources are within a decade, which gives a credit for "recent"

   (d) Representative: Not really, except the claim from Tattersall who favors culling of the elephants.

(4) Are the facts and ideas stated mostly by the student/writer?

➡ Yes, most of the parts of this paper. However, there are three major direct quotations (Ls. 23~31; 57~62; 91~97), which may weaken his own ideas. Direct quotes, if more then three lines, can be simplified without changing the original meaning while citing the author's last name and the year.

(5) Are the citations and the research paper format structured based on your instructor's recommendation?

➡ This is a good sample for "APA" (American Psychological Association), which is strongly recommended for use in the international academic communities..

(1) 주제는 흥미롭고 유익하며 다루기 쉬운가?

그렇다. '코끼리 구하기' 라는 주제는 흥미롭고 유익하다. 이 주제가 재미있는 까닭은 동물원의 코끼리가 아니라 낯선 이국에서 살고있는 야생 코끼리를 다루고 있기 때문이다. 이 주제는 '코끼리의 파괴, 훈련, 라이프 스타일, 특징' 이 아니라 코끼리 보존 문제를 다각적으로 논의한다는 점에서 다루기도 쉽다.

(2) 논문 초반에 논제를 제시하고 있는가?

이 글의 논제는 "(코끼리) 수치가 놀라운 비율로 감소하기 시작했다. 이 갑작스런 감소 원인을 알아내기란 어렵지 않다. 바로 '돈' 이었다."이다. 다시 말해, 인간의 돈 욕심 때문에 코끼리 수가 두드러지게 감소하고 있다.

(3) 논문은 (a) 관련성, (b) 신빙성, (c) 시의성, (d) 대표성을 지닌 1, 2차 자료를 충분히 활용하고 있는가?

(a) 관련성 : 〈코끼리의 운명〉; 〈아프리카 코끼리 : 에덴의 여명〉 등의 인용문이 1차 자료로 기능하고 있다. '킬링 필즈' ; '자동적으로 드러나는 코끼리의 엄니' ; '코끼리를 구하라!' ; 〈한 코끼리 가족의 13년간 삶〉; 〈1993년 연감〉; '밀렵꾼들의 휴지기' ; '코끼리 전쟁' ; '선의의 사기' ; "동물을 죽이는 것이 아니라 도태시키는 것은 언제인가?" 등이 2차 자료로 사용되고 있다. 이 자료들은 모두 주제와 관련이 있다.

(b) 신빙성 : 인용된 1차 자료들은 신빙성이 매우 높다. 2차 자료들은 1차 자료를 뒷받침하고 있으며, 그것은 논문을 보다 신빙성 있게 만들어주고 있다.

(c) 시의성 : 인용된 자료 대부분이 십 년 이내의 것들이며, 그것은 시기상의 문제에 신뢰를 안겨준다.

(d) 대표성 : 코끼리 도태에 찬성하는 태터솔의 주장을 제외하면, 반드시 그렇다고 볼 순 없다.

(4) 사실과 아이디어는 대부분 학생/작가에 의해 진술되고 있는가?

이 논문 대부분이 그렇다. 그러나 이 글에 등장하는 세 번의 직접 인용문의 경우, 작가 자신의 아이디어를 약화시키는 면이 있다. 직접 인용은, 세 줄 이상일 경우, 본래의 의미를 바꾸지 않는 선에서 단순화시키고 작가의 성과 연도를 인용할 수도 있다.

(5) 인용문과 연구 논문 포맷은 교사의 권고에 근거하여 짜여져 있는가?

이 글은 'APA' 형 글쓰기를 보여주는 좋은 샘플로서, 이런 포맷은 국제 학계에서 강력하게 추천하는 방법이다.

4.3. Chapter Summary & Exercises

So far, we have studied a general outline of an essay. First, we have examined how the essay is structured. It contains an introduction, a body paragraph, and a conclusion. The introduction tells the readers what the main points or responses will be about, while the main idea of the essay is expressed in the topic or the topic sentence. The body is usually structured with several paragraphs providing all the related details to support the main topic. The conclusion as the last paragraph of the essay summarizes all of the main points previously given or illustrated to support the main topic or issue.

Second, we have seen a variety of essay types including their major purposes and elements. The type of the essay is classified into (1) descriptive; (2) expository; (3) informative; (4) narrative; (5) personal; (6) persuasive; and, (7) research paper. The major purpose of the descriptive essay is "to describe specific features of a person, place, object, or situation." The major purpose of the expository essay is "to explain the facts," that of the informative one, "to present factual information about one topic," and, that of the narrative one, "to describe an account of an event." Likewise, the major purpose of the personal essay is "to tell a real-life story based on your own experience," that of the persuasive one, "to make your readers agree with your points of view and take some actions by changing their points of view, value, or attitude," and, finally that of the research paper, "to test student's ability related to his/her researching, organizing, and interpreting a set of facts given or chosen."

EXERCISE SECTION:

I. Read the following statements and decide which statement serves as
   (1) the Introduction;
   (2) Part of the Body Paragraph; or
   (3) the Conclusion, in terms of its meaning, purposes, and elements. Select the best answer among the choices provided in the parenthesis.

1. (1) Like children, cats do not always want to take medicine.
   (a) Introduction ( )   (b) Part of the Body Paragraph ( )   (c) Conclusion ( )
   (2) Cats are neat, so they will lick it right off.
   (a) Introduction ( )   (b) Part of the Body Paragraph ( )   (c) Conclusion ( )
   (3) Pour the medicine on its fur.
   (a) Introduction ( )   (b) Part of the Body Paragraph ( )   (c) Conclusion ( )

4.3. 요약과 연습

지금 까지 우리는 에세이의 개요에 대해 공부했다. 먼저 우리는 에세이가 어떻게 구성되는지 살펴보았다. 에세이는 서론, 본론, 결론으로 이루어진다. 서론은 독자들에게 요점이나 반응이 어떤 것일지 말해주며, 글의 요지는 주제 또는 주제문으로 표현된다. 본론은 보통 전체 주체를 뒷받침하는 관련 세부 사항이 담긴 몇 개의 문단으로 짜여진다. 글의 마지막 문단으로서의 결론은 앞에서 제시하거나 설명한 모든 요지들을 요약함으로써 주제나 핵심 문제를 뒷받침한다.

둘째로, 우리는 주요 목적과 구성 요소를 중심으로 다양한 에세이 유형들을 살펴보았다. 에세이 유형은 (1) 묘사, (2) 설명, (3) 정보전달, (4) 나레이션, (5) 사적인 이야기, (6) 설득, (7) 연구 논문 등으로 분류된다. 묘사형 에세이의 주요 목적은 '사람, 장소, 대상, 또는 상황의 구체적인 특징을 묘사하는 것'이다. 설명형 에세이의 주요 목적은 '사실을 설명하는 것'이며, 정보 전달형 에세이는 '한가지 주제에 대한 사실적 정보를 제시하는 것,' 나레이션은 '한 사건에 대해 이야기하는 것'을 주요 목적으로 하고 있다. 마찬가지로, 사적인 에세이의 주요 목적은 '작가 자신의 경험에 근거하여 실제 이야기를 말하는 것'이며, 설득형 에세이는 '독자들로 하여금 작가의 관점에 동의하게 하고, 각자의 관점이나 가치관, 또는 태도 등을 바꿔 일련의 조치를 취하게 하는 것'을 목적으로 한다. 마지막으로 연구 논문의 주요 목적은 '학생들이 주어진 또는 선택한 일련의 사실들을 연구하고, 조직하며, 해석하는 능력이 어느 정도인지 테스트하는 것'이다.

연습 문제

I. 다음 제시문을 읽고, 의미, 목적, 구성 요소 등의 측면에서 볼 때, 그 문장이 (1) 서론, (2) 본론의 일부, (3) 결론 중 어디에 해당하는지 판정하고, 괄호 안에 제시된 것들 가운데 답을 골라라.

1. (1) 아이들과 마찬가지로, 고양이들이 항상 약을 먹고 싶어하는 것은 아니다.
   (2) 고양이들은 깔끔해서 그 즉시 그것을 핥아먹을 것이다.
   (3) 고양이털에 약을 부어라.
   정답 (1). (a); (2). (c); (3) (b).

2. (1) 그것은 빨간색과 하얀색 줄무늬 13개가 있고, 파란 바탕에 하얀색 별 50개가 그려져 있는 미국 국기이다.
   (2) 장미처럼 빨갛고, 하늘처럼 파랗고, 또 눈처럼 하얀 것은 무엇일까?
   (3) '성조기'라는 표현은 빨갛고, 하얗고, 파란 이 깃발을 지칭하는 가장 유명한 명칭이다.
   정답 (1). (b); (2) (a); (3) (c).

2. (1) It is the American flag, with its thirteen red and white stripes and its 50 white stars on a field of blue.

     (a) Introduction ( )   (b) Part of the Body Paragraph ( )   (c) Conclusion ( )

   (2) What is red as a rose, blue as the sky, and white as the snow?

     (a) Introduction ( )   (b) Part of the Body Paragraph ( )   (c) Conclusion ( )

   (3) "The Stars and Stripes" is the best known-name for this banner of red, white, and blue.

     (a) Introduction ( )   (b) Part of the Body Paragraph ( )   (c) Conclusion ( )

3. (1) Today medicine is used to help repair or restore body parts.

     (a) Introduction ( )   (b) Part of the Body Paragraph ( )   (c) Conclusion ( )

   (2) As more facts about the body became known, schools began to teach doctors about medicine.

     (a) Introduction ( )   (b) Part of the Body Paragraph ( )   (c) Conclusion ( )

   (3) Medicine has been used to help sick or wounded people since long before history was written.

4. (1) It was 1902. Two convicts had been found in the same prison with the same names and appearances.

     (a) Introduction ( )   (b) Part of the Body Paragraph ( )   (c) Conclusion ( )

   (2) To provide foolproof identification, Bertillon pioneered fingerprint photography.

     (a) Introduction ( )   (b) Part of the Body Paragraph ( )   (c) Conclusion ( )

   (3) Thanks to a pair of look-alike convicts, the science of fingerprinting was founded.

     (a) Introduction ( )   (b) Part of the Body Paragraph ( ) (c) Conclusion ( )

5. (1) A way had been paved for the invention of the stethoscope: an invention that was to save thousands of lives.

     (a) Introduction ( )   (b) Part of the Body Paragraph ( ) (c) Conclusion ( )

   (2) Was there any way to magnify chest sounds?

     (a) Introduction ( )   (b) Part of the Body Paragraph ( ) (c) Conclusion ( )

   (3) Inspired, Dr. Rene Laennec rolled up a cylinder of paper and placed it against the patient's chest.

     (a) Introduction ( )   (b) Part of the Body Paragraph ( ) (c) Conclusion ( )

6. (1) Long ago, people went to feasts for their entertainment. These feasts lasted for days or weeks.

     (a) Introduction ( )   (b) Part of the Body Paragraph ( ) (c) Conclusion ( )

   (2) Feasts were entertaining, but they were often dangerous.

     (a) Introduction ( )   (b) Part of the Body Paragraph ( ) (c) Conclusion ( )

   (3) At a single feast, thousands of people might be present. Herds of cattle were killed for food. But food often spoiled and many people became sick after a feast.

     (a) Introduction ( )   (b) Part of the Body Paragraph ( ) (c) Conclusion ( )

3. (1) 오늘날 약은 몸을 고치거나 회복시키는 데 사용된다.

   (2) 몸에 대한 사실들이 더 많이 알려지게 되자, 학교에서는 의사들에게 약에 대해 가르치기 시작했다.

   (3) 약은 역사가 기록되기 훨씬 이전부터 병들거나 다친 사람들을 돕는데 사용되었다.

   정답 (1). (c); (2) (b); (3) (a).

4. (1) 때는 1902년. 같은 감방에서 이름과 생김새마저 똑같은 두 명의 죄수가 발견되었다.

   (2) 아주 간단한 신원 확인을 위해, 버틸론은 지문 사진술을 개척했다.

   (3) 아주 닮은 두 명의 죄수 덕택에, 지문 채취술이 창시되었다.

   정답 (1). (a); (2). (b); (3) (c).

5. (1) 청진기라는 수천 명의 목숨을 구할 발명품을 위한 길이 닦여졌다.

   (2) 가슴 속 소리를 증대시킬 방법이 있었을까?

   (3) 영감을 얻은 레니 래넥 박사는 종이를 원통형으로 말아 환자의 가슴 위에 얹었다.

   정답 (1). (c); (2). (a); (3) (b).

6. (1) 오랜 옛날, 사람들은 여흥을 즐기러 축제에 갔다. 이러한 축제는 며칠 또는 몇 주 동안 계속되었다.

   (2) 축제는 유쾌했지만, 종종 위험하기도 했다.

   (3) 단 하나의 축제에 수천 명의 사람들이 참석하곤 했다. 소 떼들이 도살되어 식량으로 사용되었다. 그
   러나 그 식량은 종종 부패해버렸고, 축제가 끝나면 많은 사람들이 아프곤 했다.

   정답 (1). (a); (2). (c); (3) (b).

7. (1) 오늘날에는 4년마다 열리는 올림픽 외에도 많은 마라톤 경기가 있다.

   (2) "마라톤 경주"는 페이디피데스와 그의 그 유명한 공적을 기려, 1896년 제 1회 근대 올림픽 대회에
   서 치러진 경기 가운데 하나였다.

   (3) 그리스의 마라톤 평원에서 치러진 전투는 역사상 가장 중요한 전투 가운데 하나였다. 그리스군 사
   령관은 페이디피데스에게 아테네까지 달려가서 "기뻐하라, 우리가 승리했도다!"라는 메시지를 전
   달하라고 명령했다. 그는 그 메시지를 전한 뒤, 달리기 때문에 지쳐 쓰러져 죽고 말았다.

   정답 (1). (c); (2). (b); (3) (a).

8. (1) 세상에서 가장 긴 길은 미국에서 남부 칠레까지 뻗어 있다.

   (2) 판 어메리칸 하이웨이의 목적은 라틴 아메리카 국가들과 미국을 좀더 긴밀하게 연결하는 것이다.

   (3) 요컨대, 그 길은 17개국의 수도를 연결하고 있으며, 애초의 목적을 달성했다.

   정답 (1). (a); (2). (b); (3) (c).

7. (1) Today there are many marathon races besides the one every 4 years at the Olympics.

    (a) Introduction ( ) (b) Part of the Body Paragraph ( ) (c) Conclusion ( )

   (2) In honor of Pheidippides and his famous feat, the "Marathon Race" was one of the contests at the first modern Olympic Games in 1896.

    (a) Introduction ( ) (b) Part of the Body Paragraph ( ) (c) Conclusion ( )

   (3) The battle on the plains of Marathon in Greece was one of the most important ones in history. The commander of the Greek force summoned Pheidippides to run to Athens to deliver the message, "Rejoice, we conquered!" After speaking the message, he fell down and died because of the exhausting run.

    (a) Introduction ( ) (b) Part of the Body Paragraph ( ) (c) Conclusion ( )

8. (1) The longest road in the world stretches from the United States to Southern Chile.

    (a) Introduction ( ) (b) Part of the Body Paragraph ( ) (c) Conclusion ( )

   (2) The purpose of the Pan American Highway is to bring the Latin American countries and the United States closer together.

    (a) Introduction ( ) (b) Part of the Body Paragraph ( ) (c) Conclusion ( )

   (3) In short, the road connects the capitals of 17 countries and has achieved its goal.

    (a) Introduction ( ) (b) Part of the Body Paragraph ( ) (c) Conclusion ( )

9. (1) Tahiti's scenery is what impresses most travelers. Waterfalls drop from tall mountains to lush lowlands. Beaches of both white and black sands circle its shore. There are green forests and tropical jungles.

    (a) Introduction ( ) (b) Part of the Body Paragraph ( ) (c) Conclusion ( )

   (2) To many world travelers, the island of Tahiti is the most beautiful place on earth.

    (a) Introduction ( ) (b) Part of the Body Paragraph ( ) (c) Conclusion ( )

   (3) The economy of Tahiti is very sound. Agriculture flourishes in the climate and fertile soil producing a variety of tropical fruits, which contributes to the island's economy. In addition, tourism is increasing each year.

    (a) Introduction ( ) (b) Part of the Body Paragraph ( ) (c) Conclusion ( )

10.(1) Airports, large or small, have always held a fascination not only for those who fly, but also for those who wish to fly.

    (a) Introduction ( ) (b) Part of the Body Paragraph ( ) (c) Conclusion ( )

   (2) As we have seen, airports for air carrier, aviation, and air bases are utilized as a means of fast transportation.

    (a) Introduction ( ) (b) Part of the Body Paragraph ( ) (c) Conclusion ( )

   (3) Airports are of three major types. The large ones used by airlines for scheduled flights to other cities are called air carrier airports... The final major type of airport is air bases used by military planes.

    (a) Introduction ( ) (b) Part of the Body Paragraph ( ) (c) Conclusion ( )

CHAPTER 4

9. (1) 타히티의 풍경은 대부분의 여행가들에게 깊은 인상을 남긴다. 높은 산에서 풀이 무성한 저지대로 폭포가 떨어진다. 흰 모래와 검은 모래가 공존하는 해변이 해안을 에워싸고 있다. 푸른 숲과 열대의 정글도 있다.

(2) 전세계의 수많은 여행가들에게 타히티 섬은 지상에서 가장 아름다운 장소이다.

(3) 타히티의 경제는 매우 견실하다. 다양한 열대성 과일을 생산하는 기후와 비옥한 토양 속에서 농업이 번창하는데, 그 점이 섬 경제에 이바지하고 있다. 게다가 관광객도 매년 증가하고 있다.

정답 (1). (b); (2). (a); (3) (c).

10. (1) 크든 작든, 공항은 날고 있는 사람뿐 아니라 날고 싶어하는 사람에게도 매력을 끌어왔다.

(2) 앞에서 살펴보았듯이, 수송기, 항공기, 공군 기지를 위한 공항은 빠른 수송 수단으로서 이용된다.

(3) 공항에는 주요한 세 가지 유형이 있다. 다른 도시로의 비행이 예정된 비행기들이 사용하는 커다란 공항은 수송기 공항이라 불린다... 공항의 마지막 유형은 군용 비행기가 사용하는 공군 기지이다.

정답 (1). (a); (2). (c); (3) (b).

11. (1) "Who discovered America?" is no longer a simple
    question to answer. Once, the answer to the
    question was simple it is Christopher Columbus,
    the well-known Italian navigator. In recent years,
    however, many theories have evolved suggesting
    that a variety of other explorers might have
    arrived at the American continents before
    Columbus.
    (a) Introduction (   )(b) Part of the Body Paragraph (   )
    (c) Conclusion (   )

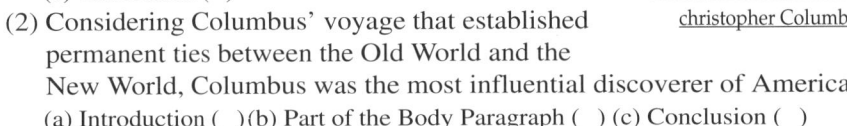

christopher Columbus

   (2) Considering Columbus' voyage that established
    permanent ties between the Old World and the
    New World, Columbus was the most influential discoverer of America.
    (a) Introduction (   )(b) Part of the Body Paragraph (   ) (c) Conclusion (   )

   (3) Some theories are supported by more concrete evidence...
    (a) Introduction (   )(b) Part of the Body Paragraph (   ) (c) Conclusion (   )

12. (1) The first side of the Leopoldskron Castle was used as the von Trapp family
    house.The children were boating on the lake and fell into the water. The
    Venetian room was copied from this castle and used as the ballroom.
    (a) Introduction (   )(b) Part of the Body Paragraph (   ) (c) Conclusion (   )

   (2) Welcome aboard our comfortable Panorama buses. Sit back and reminisce
    the scenes from this world famous movie, The Sounds of Music.
    (a) Introduction (   )(b) Part of the Body Paragraph (   ) (c) Conclusion (   )

   (3) We hope you have enjoyed your wonderful ride with breathtaking views of
    the landscape where the opening scenes were filmed. Relax and listen to the
    original Sounds of Music soundtrack.
    (a) Introduction (   )(b) Part of the Body Paragraph (   ) (c) Conclusion (   )

C H A P T E R 4

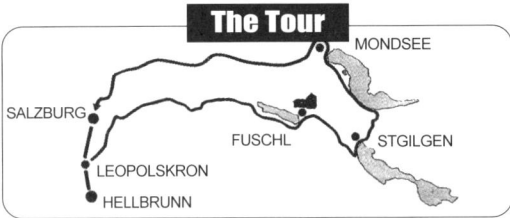

The Tour

MONDSEE
SALZBURG
FUSCHL
STGILGEN
LEOPOLSKRON
HELLBRUNN

Original Comment
regarding our Sound of
Music Tour by;

11. (1) "누가 미국을 발견했나?"라는 질문은 더 이상 간단히 대답할 수 있는 질문이 아니다. 한 때는 그 질문에 대한 대답이 단순했다. 이탈리아의 해양 탐험가 크리스토퍼 콜럼버스라고 대답하면 되니까. 그러나 최근에는 다른 다양한 탐험가들이 콜럼버스 이전에 미 대륙에 도착했다고 제기하는 많은 이론들이 발전되었다.

(2) 구대륙과 신대륙 사이의 영원한 유대를 확립한 콜럼버스의 여행을 고려할 때, 콜럼버스는 가장 영향력 있는 미대륙 발견자였다.

(3) 몇몇 이론들은 좀더 구체적인 증거에 의해 뒷받침되고 있다...

정답 (1). (a); (2) (c); (3). (b).

12. (1) 레오폴드스크론성의 앞면은 폰 트랩 가족의 집으로 사용되었습니다. 아이들은 호수에서 뱃놀이를 하다가 물에 빠졌죠. 베니스풍 방은 이 성을 모방했는데, 무도장으로 사용되었습니다.

(2) 편안한 파노라마 버스에 타신 것을 환영합니다. 편안히 앉으셔서 전세계적으로 유명한 영화 〈사운드 오브 뮤직〉에 나오는 경치를 떠올려보십시오.

(3) 영화 첫 장면에 나오는 굉장한 풍경과 함께 멋진 여행이 되셨기를 바랍니다. 편안한 마음으로 〈사운드 오브 뮤직〉 오리지널 사운드 트랙을 감상하십시오.

정답 (1). (b); (2). (a); (3) (c).

The sound of subtitles
Maria(Julie Andrews) and the Von Trapp children get ready for another song in the film "The sound of Music." All of the songs in the original film have been subtitled for "Sing-a-Long Sound of Music," which is on stage at the Prince Music Theater through Sunday. Attendees can also come dressed up in costume for a contest.

II. Read the following topic carefully. If you are asked to write an essay/paragraph focused on that topic, then what type of essay/paragraph would you choose in terms of meaning, purposes, and elements? Select the best answer among the choices provided in the parenthesis. For convenience, the abbreviation for the Descriptive essay type is DS; Expository, EX; Informative, IN; Narrative, NA; Personal, PE; and Persuasive, PR.

1. "Spring Festival on the River," Zhang Zeduan.
   (a) DS ( ) (b) EX ( ) (c) IN ( ) (d) NA ( ) (e) PE ( ) (f) PR ( )

2. How to change a flat tire.
   (a) DS ( ) (b) EX ( ) (c) IN ( ) (d) NA ( ) (e) PE ( ) (f) PR ( )

3. We should go to the front to fight for our country.
   (a) DS ( ) (b) EX ( ) (c) IN ( ) (d) NA ( ) (e) PE ( ) (f) PR ( )

4. When I lost my beloved sweetheart.
   (a) DS ( ) (b) EX ( ) (c) IN ( ) (d) NA ( ) (e) PE ( ) (f) PR ( )

5. The day I left Saigon in 1975.
   (a) DS ( ) (b) EX ( ) (c) IN ( ) (d) NA ( ) (e) PE ( ) (f) PR ( )

6. Events leading to Mr.Kim's alcoholic addiction.
   (a) DS ( ) (b) EX ( ) (c) IN ( ) (d) NA ( ) (e) PE ( ) (f) PR ( )

7. The causes and effects of World War I.
   (a) DS ( ) (b) EX ( ) (c) IN ( ) (d) NA ( ) (e) PE ( ) (f) PR ( )

8. Directions for catching carp.
   (a) DS ( ) (b) EX ( ) (c) IN ( ) (d) NA ( ) (e) PE ( ) (f) PR ( )

9. Mosque of Selim, Edirne, Turkey.
   (a) DS ( ) (b) EX ( ) (c) IN ( ) (d) NA ( ) (e) PE ( )   (f) PR ( ).

10. Comparisons and contrasts between sperm whales and killer whales.
    (a) DS ( ) (b) EX ( ) (c) IN ( ) (d) NA ( ) (e) PE ( ) (f) PR ( )

11. My first school day in Los Angeles, California.
    (a) DS ( ) (b) EX ( ) (c) IN ( ) (d) NA ( ) (e) PE ( ) (f) PR ( )

12. Why we should quit smoking.
    (a) DS ( ) (b) EX ( ) (c) IN ( ) (d) NA ( ) (e) PE ( ) (f) PR ( )

13. "Christ and John the Baptist as Children," Francois Boucher.
    (a) DS ( ) (b) EX ( ) (c) IN ( ) (d) NA ( ) (e) PE ( ) (f) PR ( )

14. Paraguay: Its Land, People, and Language.
    (a) DS ( ) (b) EX ( ) (c) IN ( ) (d) NA ( ) (e) PE ( ) (f) PR ( )

15. Similarities and differences between Seoul and Pyongyang.
    (a) DS ( ) (b) EX ( ) (c) IN ( ) (d) NA ( ) (e) PE ( ) (f) PR ( )

II. 다음 주제를 주의 깊게 읽어라. 그 주제에 초점을 맞춘 에세이/문단을 써야 한다면, 의미, 목적, 구성 요소 등의 측면에서 당신은 어떤 유형의 에세이/문단을 선택하겠는가? 괄호 안에 제시된 것들 가운데 가장 알맞은 답을 골라라. 편의상 묘사형 에세이는 약어로 DS, 설명형은 EX, 정보 전달 IN, 나레이션 NA, 사적 이야기 PE, 설득형은 PR로 표현하겠다.

1. "강가의 봄 축제" 정답 (a)

Zhang Zeduan. Detail of Spring Festival on the River. Northern Song dynasty, early 12th century. Handscroll, ink and colors on silk,(24.8cm × 2.28m). The Palace Museum, Beijing

2. 바람 빠진 타이어 갈아 끼우는 방법 정답 (c)
3. 조국을 위해 우리는 전선으로 싸우러 나가야 한다. 정답 (f)
4. 사랑하는 연인을 잃었을 때 정답 (e)
5. 1975년, 내가 사이공을 떠나던 날 정답 (e)
6. 김씨를 알콜 중독으로 이끈 사건들 정답 (d)
7. 제1차 세계대전의 원인과 결과 정답 (b)
8. 잉어 잡는 요령 정답 (c)
9. 터키의 셀림사원 정답 (a)

Sinan. Selimiye Cami(Mosque of Selim), Edirne, Turkey. 1570-74

The minarets that pierce the sky around the prayer hall of this mosque, their sleek, fluted walls and needle - nosed spires soaring to more than 295 feet, are only 12 1/2 feet in diameter at the base, an impressive feat of engineering. Only royal mosques were permitted multiple minarets, and more than two was highly unusual.

16. How to fill out the U.S. Federal Income Tax Form, 1040.

    (a) DS (　) (b) EX (　) (c) IN (　) (d) NA (　) (e) PE (　) (f) PR (　)

17. Seated Buddha, Yungang, Datong, Shanxi Province.

    (a) DS (　) (b) EX (　) (c) IN (　) (d) NA (　) (e) PE (　) (f) PR (　)

18. An unforgetful event for Miss Korea at the Miss Universe Beauty Contest.

    (a) DS (　) (b) EX (　) (c) IN (　) (d) NA (　) (e) PE (　) (f) PR (　)

19. What happened to Rev. Jessie Jackson at the 76th Democratic Convention.

    (a) DS (　) (b) EX (　) (c) IN (　) (d) NA (　) (e) PE (　) (f) PR (　)

20. How to write a resume.

    (a) DS (　) (b) EX (　) (c) IN (　) (d) NA (　) (e) PE (　) (f) PR (　)

21. When I was at Pearl Harbor on December 7, 1941.

    (a) DS (　) (b) EX (　) (c) IN (　) (d) NA (　) (e) PE (　) (f) PR (　)

22. Okhee's heart pounded, and her knees felt like jelly when she walked on stage.

    (a) DS (　) (b) EX (　) (c) IN (　) (d) NA (　) (e) PE (　) (f) PR (　)

23. Our school needs a larger parking lot.

    (a) DS (　) (b) EX (　) (c) IN (　) (d) NA (　) (e) PE (　) (f) PR (　)

24. As we peered out the window, the sound became deafening.

    (a) DS (　) (b) EX (　) (c) IN (　) (d) NA (　) (e) PE (　) (f) PR (　)

25. The four cute mini monks.

    (a) DS (　) (b) EX (　) (c) IN (　) (d) NA (　) (e) PE (　) (f) PR (　)

26. My last teaching day at St. John's University in Bangkok.

    (a) DS (　) (b) EX (　) (c) IN (　) (d) NA (　) (e) PE (　) (f) PR (　)

27. Let's vote Mr. Shin for our next President.

    (a) DS (　) (b) EX (　) (c) IN (　) (d) NA (　) (e) PE (　) (f) PR (　)

28. The imposition of the Japanese language on the Korean students during the colonial period.

    (a) DS (　) (b) EX (　) (c) IN (　) (d) NA (　) (e) PE (　) (f) PR (　)

29. The fogged Golden Gate Bridge.

    (a) DS (　) (b) EX (　) (c) IN (　) (d) NA (　) (e) PE (　) (f) PR (　)

30. The Mummy Returns is a great movie. You had better see it.

    (a) DS (　) (b) EX (　) (c) IN (　) (d) NA (　) (e) PE (　) (f) PR (　)

10. 향유 고래와 범고래의 유사점과 차이 정답 (b)
11. 캘리포니아주 로스앤젤레스에서 맞은 나의 등교 첫 날 정답 (e)
12. 금연해야 하는 이유 정답 (f)
13. "예수와 세례 요한의 어린 시절" 정답 (a)
14. 파라과이 : 영토, 국민, 언어 정답 (b)
15. 서울과 평양의 유사점과 차이점 정답 (b)
16. 미 연방 소득세 신고서 1040 메우는 법 정답 (c)
17. 산시성 윤강 다퉁의 좌불 정답 (a)
18. 미스 유니버스 선발대회에서 생긴 미스 코리아의 잊을 수 없는 사건 정답 (d)
19. 76회 민주당 전당대회에서 제시 잭슨 목사에게 무슨 일이 일어났나 정답 (d)
20. 이력서 쓰는 법 정답 (c)
21. 1941년 12월 7일, 내가 진주만에 있었을 때 정답 (e)
22. 무대에 올랐을 때, 옥희의 마음은 두근거렸고, 무릎이 마치 젤리처럼 느껴졌다. 정답 (d)
23. 우리 학교에는 더 큰 주차장이 필요하다. 정답 (f)
24. 창밖을 응시하자, 소리가 귀를 멍멍하게 했다. 정답 (d)
25. 귀여운 네 명의 동자승 정답 (a)
26. 방콕의 세인트 존 대학에서 내가 마지막으로 수업하던 날 정답 (e)
27. 신씨를 차기 대통령으로 뽑읍시다. 정답 (f)
28. 식민지 시대 조선 학생들에 대한 일본어 과제 정답 (b)
29. 안개에 젖은 금문교 정답 (a)
30. 〈미이라 속편〉은 멋진 영화야. 너도 보는 게 나을 거야. 정답 (f)

Mini monks--South Korean little monks enjoy ice cream during a picnic at a park in Seoul.

Mummy Returns

III. Read the following paragraph/essay, and decide the type of writing in terms of its meaning, purposes, and elements. Select the best answer among the choices provided in the parenthesis. For convenience, the abbreviation for the Descriptive essay type is DS; Expository, EX; Informative, IN; Narrative, NA; Personal, PE; and Persuasive, PR.

1. I lived in a large white house on a tree-shaded street. After classes, my friends would often play at my house. My mom would have cookies and lemonade for us, or hot chocolate during the cold months. The school was only 5 blocks away. A stream ran right by it. When the weather was warm, we would take off our shoes and socks. At recess, we would wade in the stream. In winter, we could ice skate on the frozen stream. On weekends, my family would go on picnics in the nearby hills. In spring, those rolling hills were covered with wild flowers. My town had two movie theaters, a small department store, five grocery stores, and a few other shops. Everyone living in town was proud of our small and clean town.

   (a) DS ( ) (b) EX ( ) (c) IN ( ) (d) NA ( ) (e) PE ( ) (f) PR ( )

2. The Wilderness Road was a trail which Daniel Boone blazed the Cumberland Gap from Virginia to Kentucky. Later, Boone led settlers along the trail that he had first marked out in 1771. At first the Wilderness Road was named "Boone's Trace" from the slashings of trees which Boone had cut as a guide for others who were to follow.

   (a) DS ( ) (b) EX ( ) (c) IN ( ) (d) NA ( ) (e) PE ( ) (f) PR ( )

3. Haiku writing contests are very popular in Japan. A haiku is a very short poem with only 17 syllables. The words are usually written in three line of five, seven, and five syllables. In these few words, the haiku writers sketches a picture of a thing or a happening. The writer does not tell what he or she feels or thinks. The reader must create a response to this described picture. Thus the writer and the reader are to collaborate in a unique experience.

   (a) DS ( ) (b) EX ( ) (c) IN ( ) (d) NA ( ) (e) PE ( ) (f) PR ( )

4. I rise at first light and I start by rereading and editing I have written to the point I left off. That way I go through a book I'm writing several hundred times. Most writers slough off the toughest but most important part of their trade — editing their stuff, honing it and honing it until it gets an edge like a bullfighter's killing sword. One time my son Patrick brought me a story and asked me to edit it for him. I went over it carefully and changed one word. "but, Papa," he said, "you've only changed one word." I said: "If it's the right word, that's a lot."
   (Source: "Writers on Writing," Ernest Hemingway).

   (a) DS ( ) (b) EX ( ) (c) IN ( ) (d) NA ( ) (e) PE ( ) (f) PR ( )

III. 다음 문단/에세이를 읽고, 의미, 목적, 구성 요소 등의 측면에서 각 글의 유형을 정하라. 괄호 안에 제시된 것들 가운데 가장 알맞은 답을 골라라. 편의상 묘사형 에세이는 약어로 DS, 설명형은 EX, 정보 전달 IN, 나레이션 NA, 사적 이야기 PE, 설득형은 PR로 표현하겠다.

1. 나는 나무가 그늘을 드리운 거리 옆, 크고 하얀 집에 살았다. 방과후면, 친구들은 종종 우리 집에서 놀곤 했다. 엄마는 우리를 위해 과자와 레모네이드, 또는 추운 날이면 핫 초콜릿을 만들어주셨다. 학교는 기껏 다섯 블록 떨어진 곳에 있었다. 바로 그 옆으로 개울이 흐르고 있었다. 날씨가 따뜻해지면, 우리는 구두와 양말을 벗어 던지곤 했다. 쉬는 시간이면, 우리는 개울을 건너곤 했다. 겨울에는 얼음이 언 개울 위에서 스케이트를 탈 수 있었다. 주말이면, 우리 가족은 근처 언덕으로 소풍을 가곤 했다. 봄에는 그 완만한 언덕들이 야생화로 뒤덮였다. 우리 마을에는 영화관 두 개, 작은 백화점, 야채 가게 다섯 개, 그리고 다른 가게 몇몇 등이 있었다. 마을 사람들은 누구나 작고 깨끗한 우리 마을을 자랑스러워했다. 정답 (a)

2. 윌더니스 로드는 다니엘 분이 컴버랜드 고개에 낸, 버지니아주에서 켄터키주에 이르는 길이었다. 나중에 분은 1771년, 자신이 처음 표시해둔 길을 따라 이주자들을 데려왔다. 애초에 윌더니스 로드는 다음에 따라올 사람들을 위한 이정표로서 분이 나무들을 베어냈다는 의미에서 "분의 자취"라고 명명되었다. 정답 (c)

3. 하이쿠 경연은 일본에서 매우 인기가 높다. 하이쿠는 기껏해야 17음절로 이루어지는 아주 짧은 시이다. 단어들은 보통 다섯 음절, 일곱 음절, 다섯 음절로 된 삼행으로 이루어진다. 이 몇 안 되는 단어들을 가지고 하이쿠 작가들은 어떤 물건이나 사건의 모습을 스케치한다. 작가는 자신의 느낌이나 생각을 말하지 않는다. 독자는 이 문자화된 그림에 대해 나름의 반응을 보여줘야 한다. 따라서 작가와 독자는 독특한 경험으로 협력하게 된다. 정답 (b)

4. 나는 새벽녘에 일어나 내가 쓰다 만 부분까지 다시 읽으면서 수정을 시작한다. 그런 식으로 나는 내가 쓰고 있는 책을 수백 번 다시 본다. 대부분의 작가들은 직업상 가장 힘들면서도 가장 중요한 부분을 버린다. 글을 수정하고, 투우사의 날카로운 칼 같은 날을 얻을 때까지 갈고 또 갈고 또 가는 일 말이다. 언젠가 내 아들 패트릭이 글을 한 편 가져오더니, 수정 좀 해달라고 부탁했다. 나는 그 글을 주의 깊게 읽은 뒤, 단어 하나를 바꿨다. 아들이 이렇게 말했다. "하지만, 아빠, 기껏 단어 하나만 고치셨잖아요." 그러자 내가 대답했다. "그게 적절한 단어라면, 그것만으로도 엄청난 일이란다." 정답 (e)

Ernest Hemingway

5. Tax dollars spent on city parks give pleasure to many people. The dollars pay for land and trees as well as recreational facilities. Parks offer relief from the summer heat and the noise of city streets. Moreover, they are located near the places where the people live. In addition, if parks are large enough, hiking trails can be laid out for joggers to use for exercise. Furthermore, nature trails can be constructed to help citizens learn identity trees and plants. For these reasons, city government should budget more money for park development.
   (a) DS ( ) (b) EX ( ) (c) IN ( ) (d) NA ( ) (e) PE ( ) (f) PR ( )

6. Maryla Jonas, a brilliant pianist, was born in Warsaw, Poland, in 1911. She toured Europe in the 1930s, won many prizes, and was acclaimed as one of the best women pianists. When the Nazis attacked Poland, Maryla's husband, parents, and brother were killed. Maryla escaped from a concentration camp and fled 300 miles to safety. Her musical career was almost destroyed by the horror of that experience, but she managed to begin anew. She decided to devote herself entirely to her music and made her North American debut at Carnegie Hall in 1946.
   (a) DS ( ) (b) EX ( ) (c) IN ( ) (d) NA ( ) (e) PE ( ) (f) PR ( )

7. I can still remember so many details of that day, so far away and still so recent, when my feet finally came to rest on the soil of the kingdom of liberality—the United States of America. I can still feel the cold thrill in my chest that I experienced when I saw the Statue of Liberty. I could hardly believe that it was not just another dream of freedom. I was still not completely certain that I wasn't going to wake up and find myself in my old home, in my old bed, in my old country. But it was real; my dream HAD come true! What I fantasized about for seven years was finally no longer a wish. The great turning point in my life had arrived.

   Sadly, one of the first words I learned in the United States was Chink. On my second day of school, in January, 1981, I found five big letters on the outside of my locker. The fat black letters spelled C-H-I-N-K. Not comprehending its derisive nature, I wanted to know what the word meant. My previous experiences with my peers, however, made me afraid to ask.

   After two months, I finally summoned enough courage to ask the boy sitting next to me. He didn't answer. Instead, he said mischievously to the crowd, "Hey, the Chink wants to know Chink means! Ha-Ha-Ha!" Everyone around me laughed so hard that it was easy to get the feeling that those five black letters on my locker were the letters of a word that insulted Chinese.
   Suddenly, after Christmas of 1981, my school year became a happy time. Purely by chance I met a girl named Susanna Russell, who was as bitter as I, but for different reasons.

5. 시민 공원에 들어갈 때 내는 세금은 많은 사람들에게 즐거움을 준다. 그 돈은 오락 시설뿐 아니라 땅과 나무에게 지불된다. 공원은 여름의 열기와 도시 거리의 소음으로부터 잠시나마 휴식을 제공한다. 그리고 사람들이 사는 곳 근처에 자리하고 있다. 게다가 넓은 공원에는 산책로가 조성되어 조깅하는 사람들이 운동용으로 이용할 수 있다. 더 나아가 자연적인 오솔길이 생겨나 시민들이 나무와 식물에 대해 배울 수도 있다. 이런 이유들로 해서, 시 당국은 공원 발전을 위해 더 많은 돈을 예산에 넣어야 한다. 정답 (f)

6. 훌륭한 피아니스트 마릴라 조나스는 1911년, 폴란드의 바르샤바에서 태어났다. 그녀는 1930년대에 유럽을 순회했고, 많은 상을 탔으며, 최고의 여성 피아니스트 가운데 한 명으로 대접받았다. 나치가 폴란드를 공격했을 때, 마릴라의 남편과 부모, 형제들이 살해당했다. 마릴라는 포로 수용소에서 탈출하여 300마일을 달린 끝에 안전 지대에 도착했다. 그녀의 음악적 재능은 그때의 공포로 거의 파괴되고 말았지만, 그녀는 가까스로 새 삶을 시작했다. 그녀는 남은 생애를 온전히 음악에 바치기로 결심했고, 1946년, 카네기 홀에서 미국 무대에 데뷔했다. 정답 (d)

7. 나는 아직도 그 날의 일들을 생생히 기억할 수 있다. 너무 까마득한 옛날인데도 여전히 엊그제처럼 느껴지는 그날, 내가 마침내 자유의 땅 미국에 발을 내딛던 그 날 말이다. 나는 자유의 여신상을 보았을 때 경험했던 내 가슴의 짜릿한 전율을 아직도 느낄 수 있다. 나는 그것이 자유를 염원한 나머지 꾸게 된 또 하나의 꿈이 아니라는 사실을 믿을 수 없었다. 나는 아직도 잠에서 깼을 때 내가 나의 옛 조국에 있는 그 낡은 집에 있지 않으리라는 사실을 100퍼센트 확신하지 못했다. 그러나 그것은 현실이었다. 나의 꿈이 실현된 것이다! 내가 7년 가량 그려왔던 것이 마침내 이제 더 이상은 꿈이 아니었다. 내 삶의 거대한 전환점이 다가왔다.

슬프게도, 내가 미국에서 처음 배운 단어들 가운데 하나가 '칭크(Chink : 중국 사람을 경멸적으로 부르는 단어)' 였다. 1981년 1월, 학교에 다닌 지 이틀째 되던 날, 나는 로커 바깥에 써 있는 다섯 개의 커다란 문자를 발견했다. 굵고 까만 그 글자들은 C-H-I-N-K라고 쓰여져 있었다. 조롱 섞인 그 말의 의미를 몰랐으므로, 나는 그 단어가 무슨 뜻인지 알고 싶었다. 그러나 동료들과 겪었던 이전의 경험으로 인해 물어보기가 두려웠다.

두달 뒤, 나는 마침내 용기를 내어 내 옆에 앉아있던 남학생에게 물었다. 그는 대답 대신 장난스럽게 반친구들에게 이렇게 말했다. "이봐, 칭크가 칭크의 뜻을 알고 싶대! 하—하—하!" 내 주변에 있던 모든 사람들이 너무나 열심히 웃어댔기 때문에 내 로커에 쓰여져 있던 다섯 개의 까만 문자가 중국인을 모욕하는 단어라는 사실을 알아차리기란 너무나 쉬웠다.

시간이 흐를수록, 더 많은 사람들이 내 생김새에 대해 놀려댔다. "쟤 좀 봐! 저 코 말야, 풍뚱한 얼굴에 배가 붙어 있는 것 같지 않냐!" "아유, 저 눈 좀 봐! 어찌나 작은지 바늘 같다야. 쟨 어쩜 저렇게 못생길 수 있니?"

As time passed, more people made fun of my appearance: "Look at that creature! Look at that nose—just like a pear stuck on her big fat face!" "What ugly eyes! So small they look like needles! How can she be so ugly?"

...Consequently, I changed entirely. The girl who tended to talk too much, who had a large number of friends, who was an optimist and proud of her new country had become a quiet, eccentric, ascetic, pessimistic person. I could never speak loudly at school again. I was afraid to talk to the other students. I became so paranoid that when I heard people laughing, I naturally assumed that I was the source of their levity. I withdrew into myself and despised myself for doing so. It was a vicious circle. For the first time in my life, I experienced the feeling of being a lose and a loner. Instead of feeling buoyant, joyous, and elated—as I used to dream—I was alone, friendless, disappointed, and unhappy. Because I was the only foreigner in the school, everyone could easily ignore me—the "problem" student who knew no English. This first half-year of school passed with me sitting at my desk, moving to each successive class like a sleepwalker. I would wait for the dismissal bell signaling the time when I could go home to lock my door and cry.

Luckily for my sanity, one history teacher whose father was from Japan undertook the task of helping me. She used every method imaginable to try to teach me the alphabet, some simple words, basic conversation, and pronunciation. She bought many simple stories for me to read. She wanted me to teach her Chinese, so I would have company learning a new language, and wouldn't feel so stupid when I couldn't pronounce or understand a word.
The experience of relearning communication skills was alien to me. In Taiwan, I had been at the top of my class, loud, giggly, and very popular. Writing came so easily that I even had some poetry published. But, in this school, I suddenly felt like a small and helpless child.
My teacher's devotion and kindness helped restore a measure of my self-confidence and gave me at least a few hours to look forward to each day without dread.

...On my first day [of high school], a tall boy said to his crowd of friends, "Hey, our school has the ugliest creature in the world now! Look at her. Even the Elephant Man' is too cute for her." He was joined with cries of "Yoo hoo, Chink! We don't sell egg rolls here. Go home to Chinkland, will you? You can phone home like E.T., but no one would cry for you, you ugly ———."

I tried not to cry, as I knew this would only make them laugh more. But they had hurt me deeply. I wondered how Americans could be so tender towards animals, but so prejudiced against me. I questioned why my family had thought that by coming to this country they would be enjoying freedom and welcoming arms.

... 그 결과, 나는 완전히 변했다. 말 많고 친구 많고 낙천적인데다 새로운 조국에 대해 자부심을 느끼던 소녀가 조용하고 괴벽스러우며 금욕적이고 염세적인 사람이 되어버린 것이다. 나는 다시는 학교에서 결코 큰 소리로 말할 수 없었다. 나는 다른 학생들에게 말을 걸기가 두려웠다. 어찌나 과대망상에 사로잡혀 있었던지, 사람들이 웃는 소리라도 들리면, 나는 자연스럽게 그 경솔한 웃음의 원료가 나라고 단정하곤 했다. 나는 나 자신 속으로 움츠러들었고, 그런 나 자신을 경멸했다. 악순환이었다. 나는 난생 처음으로 패자이자 고독한 사람이 되었다는 느낌에 사로잡혔다. 내가 꿈꿨던 것처럼 낙천적이고 쾌활하고 의기양양한 대신, 나는 외롭고, 친구도 없었고, 절망감을 느꼈고, 불행했다. 내가 학교에서 유일한 외국인이었으므로, 모두들 나를 영어도 모르는 "문제" 학생이라며 쉽게 무시할 수 있었다. 처음 반 년 동안 나는 책상에 앉아 있다가 몽유병자처럼 다음 수업 장소로 이동하며 보냈다. 빨리 수업이 끝났음을 알리는 종이 울려서, 집에 가서 방문을 잠그고 울 수 있기만 기다리고 있었던 것이다.

운좋게도, 아버지가 일본계인 역사 선생님이 나를 돕는 임무를 맡았다. 그녀는 내게 알파벳과 몇 가지 간단한 단어들, 기본적인 대화, 발음 등을 가르치기 위해 상상할 수 있는 모든 방법을 다 동원했다. 그녀는 나한테서 중국어를 배우고 싶어했고, 덕분에 나는 새로운 언어를 배우는 동료를 얻게 되어, 내가 어떤 단어를 발음하지 못하거나 이해할 수 없을 때에도 그다지 절망감을 느끼지 않게 되었다. 의사 소통 기법을 다시 배운다는 경험이 내게는 낯설게만 느껴졌다. 대만에서 나는 공부도 잘했고, 목소리도 컸으며, 낄낄 잘 웃고, 인기도 아주 좋았다. 작문이 너무 쉬워서 심지어 시집을 출판하기도 했다. 그러나 이 학교에서 나는 갑자기 작고 무기력한 아이처럼 느껴졌다. 선생님의 헌신과 친절은 자신감을 회복하는데 도움이 되었고, 하루에 최소한 몇 시간은 두려움 없이 고대할 수 있는 시간을 주었다.

...[고등학교에] 들어간 첫 날, 키 큰 남학생이 모여있던 자기 친구들에게 이렇게 말했다. "이봐, 이제 우리 학교에 세상에서 가장 못생긴 애가 다니게 됐어! 저 애 좀 봐. 저 애에 비하면 '엘리펀트 맨' 조차 너무 귀엽게 느껴지는 걸." 그러자 다른 친구들의 함성이 이어졌다. "야, 칭크! 여기선 달걀말이(야채, 고기의 달걀말이. 중화요리 가운데 하나) 안 팔아. 칭크들 나라로 돌아가, 응? E.T.처럼 집에 전화할 수도 있겠지만, 아무도 널 위해 울어주지 않을 거야, 이 못생긴――――――."

나는 울지 않으려고 애썼다. 눈물을 보였다가는 더 큰 웃음거리가 될 것이었기 때문이다. 나는 미국인들이 동물한테는 그렇게 다정하면서 나한테는 왜 그렇게 편견을 가지는지 의아스러웠다. 나는 우리 가족이 왜 이 나라에 오면 자유와 환대를 누릴 거라고 생각했는지 의심스러웠다.

1981년 크리스마스 이후, 나의 학교 생활은 갑자기 행복해졌다. 순전히 수잔나 러셀이라는 소녀를 만났기 때문이었다. 그녀는 나만큼이나 고통에 차 있었지만, 이유는 달랐다. 그 당시에는 그 이유를 몰랐지만, 그녀는 내가 그녀를 필요로 하는 만큼이나 나를 필요로 하고 있었다. 그녀는 개인적으로 나를 가르치는 프로젝트에 착수했다. 그녀는 매일 나의 숙제를 도와주었고, 정신적 문제도 함께 풀어주었다. 그녀는 다른 아이들이 내게 그렇게 심술궂게 구는 것은 나의 인격 때문이 아니라고 가르쳐주었다. 단지 새로운 상황과 다른 사람들에 대해 적응할 수 없기 때문이라는 것이었다. 문제는 내가 상상한 나의 결점들이 아니라 그들의 불확실성이었다. 그녀는 내게 자신의 친구들을 소개시켜 주었고, 그들 또한 그녀만큼이나 다정하고 이해심이 많았다. 일년간의 고통 끝에, 나는 마침내 친구들을 사귀었다.

Suddenly, after christmas of 1981, my school year became a happy time Purely by chance I met a girl named Susanna Russell,who was as bitter as I, but for different reasons.

I didn't know it at the time, but she needed me as much as I needed her. She was easy going, unprejudiced, compassionate, understanding, and sweet. She launched into the project of tutoring me. Every day, she helped me with both my homework and my mental problems. She taught me that the other kids were not so nasty to me because of who I was. They were merely unable to adapt to new situations and different people. The problem was their insecurity, not my imagined shortcomings. She introduced me to her friends, who were as sweet and understanding as she. Finally, after a year of suffering, I had some friends. Susanna was talkative, so I had a chance to practice my English. She took me to movies, called me, listened to my dissatisfactions with patience, and even stood up to the teachers and counselors who felt that I was incapable of handling an advanced curriculum.

Thanks to her stubbornness, I was once again the top student I had been before coming to the U.S. She was my tutor, my best friend, and even my psychologist. Although some of the school kids still pestered me, I began to see the bright side of life. I regained my self-esteem. From my experience at school, I found out the dark side of a foreigner's life. I saw the cruelty of which some Americans were capable. But I also saw the kindness. And I gained insight into myself. I had seen my life when it was dark and moody, and when it was carefree and wild. I had seen it when it was quiet, serene, and hopeful. In all its stages, I saw myself—more clearly than I would have if I had not endured that nightmare of darkness.

"Nightmare," Judy Cheng

Judy Cheng, 16, is an 11th grader at Friendswood High School in Friendswood, Texas. She wrote the first five drafts of this essay in Chinese before translating it into English. Her friend Susanna Russell advised her on grammar. Judy excels in art and math and plays both piano and soccer.

(a) DS ( ) (b) EX ( ) (c) IN ( ) (d) NA ( ) (e) PE ( ) (f) PR ( )

8. George Gershwin (1898~1937), A Great American Musician.

George Gershwin grew up with music and performance. His mother, Rose Gershwin, frequently entertained family and friends from Europe who were Yiddish theater performers. And his father, Morris Gershwin, moved the family to New York City's Lower East Side, where George became interested in the music of Tin Pan Alley. When George was twelve years old, his parents bought a used piano for his brother, Ira. When George promptly sat down and played a tune on the piano, his parents immediately consented to him getting piano lessons along with his brother. From these early experiences, his love and involvement with music intensified.

Gershwin said that he had more tunes in his head than he could write down in a lifetime.

C H A P T E R 4

수잔나는 말이 많았고, 덕분에 나는 영어를 실습할 수 있는 기회를 갖게 되었다. 그녀는 나를 극장에 데려갔고, 전화도 걸어주었으며, 인내심을 가지고 나의 불평을 들어주었다. 심지어 내가 앞선 커리큘럼을 소화할 수 없다고 생각하는 선생님이나 카운셀러들에게 대들기까지 했다.

그녀의 완고함 덕택에, 나는 미국에 오기 전에 그랬던 것처럼 또다시 우등생이 되었다. 그녀는 나의 개인 교사이자 가장 친한 친구였으며, 심지어 나의 심리 상담가이기도 했다. 비록 학생들 중에 아직도 나를 못살게 구는 아이들이 있긴 하지만, 나는 생의 밝은 면을 보기 시작했다. 나는 나의 자존심을 회복했다. 학교에서의 경험을 통해, 나는 외국인들의 삶의 어두운 면을 알게 되었다. 나는 일부 미국인들이 저지를 수 있는 잔인함을 보았다. 그러나 친절함 또한 보았다. 그리고 나는 나 자신에 대한 통찰력을 갖게 되었다. 나는 내 인생의 어둡고 우울한 시기도 겪었지만, 즐겁고 흥분된 시기도 겪었다. 조용하고, 평화로우며, 희망에 찬 시절도 보았다. 그 모든 단계에서 나는 나 자신을 보다 뚜렷하게 보았다. 만약 내가 그 어둠의 악몽을 견뎌내지 못했더라면, 아마도 그러지 못했으리라. 정답 (e)

Note

derisive *a.* Ridiculing, mocking, or scoffing.
summon *v.* 1 To ask to come or appear ; call or send for. 2. To find in oneself and use --Summon your courage and go onto the stage.
mischievous *a.* 1 Full of mischief ; naughty --Newborn kittens can be mischievous. 2. Playful or teasing --There's a mischievous look on your face. 3. Causing harm or damage.

8. 미국의 위대한 음악가, 조지 거쉰(1898 - 1937)

조지 거쉰은 음악과 연주와 함께 자랐다. 어머니 로즈 거쉰은 이디시 극장 연주자로 일하는 유럽에서 온 가족과 친구들을 자주 접대했다. 그리고 그의 아버지 모리스 거쉰은 뉴욕 시의 로어 이스트 사이드로 데려갔고, 거기서 조지는 틴 판 앨리(뉴욕시의 포퓰러 음악 관계자들이 모이는 지역) 음악에 관심을 가지게 되었다. 조지가 열두 살이 되었을 때, 부모님은 그의 형 아이라에게 중고 피아노를 사주었다. 조지가 곧바로 피아노 앞에 앉아 한 곡을 연주하자, 부모님은 그 즉시 그가 형과 함께 피아노 레슨을 받게 했다. 어린 시절의 이런 경험에서부터 음악에 대한 그의 사랑과 관심은 강렬해졌다.

18세 때, 그는 자신의 첫 노래, "웬 유 원트 뎀, 유 캔트 겟 뎀"을 발표하여 5달러를 벌었다. 형 아이라와의 첫 번째 합작품은 "진정한 미국의 포크 송은 래그(래그 타임 리듬으로 작곡된 곡)"였다. 1919년, 그는 첫 번째 뮤지컬 코미디 스코어 〈라 라 루실〉을 작곡했고, 그의 첫 번째 히트작 "스와니"는 앨 졸슨의 테마 음악이 되었다. 1920년대가 되자, 그는 "섬바디 러브스 미," "오, 레이디 비 굿," "패시네이팅 리듬," "'S 원더풀," "더 맨 아이 러브" 등 그의 이름을 들으면 떠오르는 많은 노래들을 작곡했다.

거쉰의 노래에 나타나는 특징은 잃어버린 사랑, 우연히 찾은 사랑, 사랑에의 갈망, 심지어 사랑하고픈 마음에 이르기까지 사랑을 찬미한다는 것이다. 오직 〈포기와 베스〉에서만 거쉰의 노래 한곡이 죽음이라는 문제를 다루고 있다. 거쉰의 음악은 청중들이 죽음이라는 최후의 결말을 생각할 수 없을 정도로 지나치게 삶으로 충만하다.

At the age of 18, he published his first song, "When You Want 'Em, You Can't Get 'Em," for which he earned five dollars. The first collaboration with his brother Ira was "TheReal American Folk Song is a Rag." In 1919, he wrote his first musical comedy score, La La Lucille, and his first hit, "Swanee," became Al Jonson's signature song. In the 1920s, he wrote many of the songs which have come to be identified with him: "Somebody Loves Me," "Oh, Lady Be Good," "Fascinating Rhythm," "'S Wonderful," and "The Man I Love."

A distinctive characteristic of the Gershwin songs is that they celebrate love — lost, found, longed for and even disposed. Only in Porgy and Bess does a Gershwin song touch the subject of death. The Gershwin music is too full of life for its listeners to contemplate the finality of death.

He slowly began experimenting with orchestral music. His first major effort was "Rhapsody in Blue," introduced by bandleader Paul Whiteman in February 1924. Whitemand, like Gershwin, was a pioneer in the movement which sought to make jazz respectable and part of the musical mainstream. The success of "Rhapsody" was followed by "Concerto in F," which premiered at Carnegie Hall in New York in 1925. These two works brought Gershwin international fame.

The European premiere of the "Concerto" took place in 1928 at the Paris Opera; it was a resounding success. The year 1928 also saw the premiere of his great symphonic poem, "An American in Paris." In this piece, he sought to portray the impressions of an American visitor as he strolls through the city. He described the music as more suited to ballet than symphony, and admitted that it was his modern music he had ever attempted. It is animated, lively, and restless, with elements if jazz, blues and the famous French dance known as the can-can.

Gershwin's 1931 political satire musical, Of Thee I Sing, was one of only four Depression - era musicals to pass the 400 performance mark on Broadway. It won the Pulitzer Prize as best play of the year, and is still regarded as the first significant musical comedy produced in the United States. The show's hit song included "Love is Sweeping the Country."

Gershwin's biggest success was his opera Porgy and Bess, which opened in 1935, first in Boston and then in New York. He moved to Hollywood in 1937 where he was offered contracts to write the scores of several movies. He was not happy on the west coast. In New York City, he was a famous composer, but in Hollywood he was seen as just another composer. He and Ira went to work writing the music to the film A Damsel in Dustress. It had some of the finest songs they ever wrote. It included: "Nice Work If You Can Get It," "Lady Be Good," and "A Foggy Day."

그는 천천히 오케스트라 음악을 실험하기 시작했다. 그 첫 번째 성과물이 1924년 2월, 밴드리더 폴 화이트만이 소개한 "랩소디 인 블루"였다. 화이트맨은 거쉰과 마찬가지로 재즈를 품격있는 음악적 주류의 위치로 끌어올리려는 운동의 선구자였다. "랩소디"에 이어 "콘체르토 인 에프"도 성공을 거두었는데, 이 작품은 1925년, 뉴욕의 카네기 홀에서 초연되었다. 이 두 작품은 거쉰에게 국제적인 명성을 안겨주었다.

"콘체르토"의 유럽 초연은 1928년, 파리 오페라에서 이루어졌는데, 대성공이었다. 1928년에는 그의 위대한 교향시 "파리의 미국인"이 초연되기도 했다. 이 작품에서 그는 미국 관광객이 도시를 한가히 거닐면서 받은 인상을 묘사하려 했다. 그는 그 음악을 심포니보다는 발레에 더 적합하게 만들었고, 그 작품은 그가 항상 시도해온 근대 음악이라고 시인했다. 그것은 재즈와 블루스, 그리고 캉캉으로 알려진 유명한 프랑스 춤곡의 요소를 지닌 생기있고 경쾌하며 들뜬 곡이다.

거쉰이 1931년 작곡한 정치 풍자 뮤지컬 〈나 그대를 찬미해〉는 대공황기에 브로드웨이에서 400회 이상 공연된 네 개의 뮤지컬 가운데 하나였다. 그 작품은 퓰리처상 최우수 희곡상을 받았고, 지금도 미국에서 만들어진 최초의 뜻깊은 뮤지컬 코미디로 평가받고 있다. "러브 이즈 스위핑 더 컨트리"도 바로 그 뮤지컬에 나오는 히트곡이다.

거쉰에게 가장 큰 성공을 안겨준 것은 오페라 〈포기와 베스〉였는데, 이 작품은 1935년, 처음에는 보스턴에서, 다음으로 뉴욕에서 공연되었다. 1937년, 그는 몇몇 영화 음악을 작곡해달라는 의뢰를 받아 헐리우드로 갔다. 서부에서 그는 행복하지 않았다. 뉴욕시에서 그는 유명한 작곡가였지만, 헐리우드에서는 그저 그런 또 한 명의 작곡가로 비쳐졌다. 그와 아이라는 〈더스트리스의 처녀〉라는 영화 음악 작곡에 들어갔다. 이 작품에는 "나이스 워크 이프 유 캔 겟 잇," "레이디 비 굿," "어 포기 데이" 등 그들이 그때껏 썼던 가장 멋진 곡들이 들어 있었다.

1937년 7월 11일 일요일, 조지 거쉰은 심한 뇌종양으로 사망했다. 그러나 그가 남긴 음악의 단순성과 우아함은 지금까지도 살아 있고, 그의 천재성에 필적하는 사람도 없었거니와 그를 능가하는 사람도 거의 없었다. 그와 그의 형 아이라는 그들이 남긴 음악 및 서정시와 뗄래야 뗄 수 없는 모습으로 미국인의 마음 속에 남아 있다. 정답 (c)

Note

collaborate *v.* 1.To cooperate or work with someone else, esp. on an artistic or intellectual project.
　　　　　　2. To cooperate or work with an enemy force, esp. one occupying one's own country.
contemplate *v.* To look at or think about carefully.
mainstream *n.* 1. the principal or dominant direction or trend of a human activity or movement.
surpass *v.* 1. To be better, greater, or stronger than ; exceed. 2. To go beyond the limit or powers of --
　　　　　　The beauty of the valley surpasses description
intertwine *v.* To twist together, one about the other; interlace or interlock.

On Sunday, July 11, 1937, George Gershwin died of a severe brain tumor. But the simplicity and grace of his music have lived on, and his genius seldom matched and hardly surpassed. He and his brother Ira have become inseparable with their music and lyrics intertwined in American mind.

   (a) DS ( ) (b) EX ( ) (c) IN ( ) (d) NA ( ) (e) PE ( ) (f) PR ( )

9. "... He was a great fat fellow, neither old nor young, and he had been lying naked in his bed, doubtless with a pretty woman, for his naked body gaped through a purple satin robe he held about him. The great yellow rolls of his flesh doubled over his breasts and over his belly and in the mountains of his cheeks his eyes were small and sunken as a pig's eyes. When he saw Wang Lung he shook all over and yelled out as though his flesh had been stuck with a knife, so that Wang Lung, weaponless as he was, wondered and could have laughed at the sight. But the fat fellow fell upon his knees and knocked his head on the tiles of the floor and he cried forth, "Save a life — save a life — do not kill me. I have money for you — much money—.""

   (Source: From The Good Earth (1934) Pearl S. Buck).
   (a) DS ( ) (b) EX ( ) (c) IN ( ) (d) NA ( ) (e) PE ( ) (f) PR ( )

10. Former President Jimmy Carter grew up on a small rural farm outside of Plains,Georgia, in an era when blacks and whites lived side by side but were worlds apart. He recalls having to take the train to see a movie at the Rylander Theater in Americus with his best friend. He also remembers having to split up and sit in separate seats marked "white" and "colored."

   No one would want to return to the old days of unchallenged racial segregation, when `blacks knew their place'." Carter writes in his current best seller, An Hour Before Daylight: Memories of a Rural Boyhood. "But in the dramatic changes we have witnessed, something has been lost as well as gained. My own life was shaped by a degree of personal intimacy between blacks and white people that is now almost completely unknown and largely forgotten." The book, released earlier this month, is Carter's first collection of memoirs focusing primarily on his childhood in South Georgia.

   Carter, 76, describes what it was like to walk in his shoes, sharecropping, segregation, the Depression and the New Deal to bouts with boils, hookworms and medicinal castor oil. He looks back to those days in Archery, Georgia, with mixed emotions and a sense of pride.
   He often found himself in a precarious position, watching his father, James Earl Carter Sr., reject the racist organizations of the times, yet refuse to let blacks enter their home. His mother, Lillian, was a registered nurse and often broke the rules of a segregated society, caring for blacks in the community.

9. "...그는 아주 뚱뚱했고, 늙지도 젊지도 않았다. 그리고 그는 분명 예쁜 여자와 함께 벌거벗은 채 침대에 누워있었던 모양이었다. 몸에 두른 자주색 공단 겉옷 너머로 벌거벗은 그의 몸이 모습을 내밀고 있었기 때문이다. 가슴과 배에는 누런 살덩이가 겹으로 접혀 있었고, 팽팽한 양 볼에 묻힌 두 눈은 작을 뿐 아니라 돼지 눈처럼 움푹 들어가 있었다. 왕룽을 보자, 그는 칼에 찔리기라도 한 것처럼 몸을 부르르 떨며 비명을 내질렀다. 비록 흉기를 가지고 있진 않았지만, 왕룽은 그 광경에 의아해하며 웃음을 터뜨리지 않을 수 없었다. 그러나 그 뚱뚱한 녀석은 무릎을 꿇고 방바닥에 연신 머리를 조아리며 이렇게 외쳤다. "목숨만 살려주십쇼 — 목숨만은 살려주십쇼 — 제발 날 죽이지 마십쇼. 돈은 드리겠습니다 — 얼마든지 —." 정답 (a)

10. 지미 카터 전 대통령은 흑인과 백인이 바로 옆에 있으면서도 마치 딴 세상 사람들처럼 살던 시대에 조지아주 대초원 외곽의 작은 시골 농가에서 자랐다. 그는 아메리쿠스의 릴랜더 극장에서 영화를 보기 위해 가장 친한 친구와 함께 기차를 탔던 시절을 상기한다. 또한 그 친구와 떨어져 각각 '백인'과 '유색인'으로 나뉜 격리된 좌석에 앉았던 것도 기억한다.

"어느 누구도 인종 차별을 당연시하던 그 옛날로 돌아가고 싶지 않을 것이다. '흑인들이 자기 분수를 알던' 그런 시절 말이다." 카터는 [동트기 한 시간 전 : 시골 소년 시절의 추억]이라는 이즈음의 베스트셀러에 그렇게 쓰고 있다. "그러나 우리가 목격한 극적인 변화들 속에서 우리는 중요한 것을 얻었을 뿐 아니라 잃기도 했다. 나의 인생은 지금은 거의 완벽한 미지의 것이거나 대부분 잊혀져버린, 흑인과 백인 사이의 일정 정도의 개인적 친밀감에 의해 형성되었다." 이 달 초 출판된 그 책은 카터가 사우스 조지아에서 보낸 어린 시절에 초점을 맞춰 펴낸 첫 번째 회고록이다.

76세의 카터는 구두를 신고 걷는 기분, 토지 경작, 인종차별, 한바탕 세상을 들끓게 한 대공황과 뉴딜 정책, 십이지장충, 약효 있는 비버 기름 등에 대해 나름의 생각을 기술하고 있다. 그는 감동과 자부심 속에서 그 당시의 조지아주 아처리를 돌아다본다. 그는 종종 아버지 제임스 얼 카터가 당시의 인종차별주의자 조직을 거부하면서 동시에 흑인들로 하여금 집에 들어오지 못하게 하는 모습을 지켜보면서 자기 자신이 불안정한 처지에 있다는 사실을 발견했다. 그의 어머니 릴리안은 정식 간호사였으며, 종종 인종 차별 사회의 원칙을 깨고 마을의 흑인들을 돌봐주었다.

"때로 임의적인 이 추억들이 내게는 가장 생생한 것들이다,"라고 카터는 사이먼 앤 슈스터에서 발간된 그 책에서 설명하고 있다. "일부는 고통스럽고, 특히나 지금은 이 세상을 떠난, 내가 사랑하는 사람들에 대한 추억은 더욱 그렇다. 또한 모두 흑인이었던 우리 이웃들...그 당시 우리가 단 한 번의 의구심도 품지 않았던 사회적 관습 속에 살던 사람들에 대한 처리 부분을 포함하여 나머지 추억들은 곤혹스럽다."

책을 15권이나 저술한 카터는 미국 39대 대통령으로 활약한 뒤, 1981년, 고향인 조지아주로 돌아갔다. 다음 해, 그와 그의 아내 로잘린은 애틀랜타에 초당파적 비영리 조직인 카터 센터를 창립했다.

These sometimes random recollections are my most vivid ones," Carter explains in the Simon & Schuster book. "Some of them are painful, especially those about people I love who are no longer with us. Other memories are embarrassing, including the treatment of our immediate neighbors, all of them black, under societal customs that ... we never questioned at the time."

The author of 15 books, Carter returned to his native Georgia in 1981 after serving as the 39th president of the United States. The next year, he and his wife, Rosalynn, founded the nonpartisan, nonprofit organization the Carter Center, in Atlanta.

Carter weaves humor and honesty throughout the book. He talks about plowing the fields, picking cotton, and on days off, hunting, fishing, or wading in muddy creeks.

Last year, the National Park Service dedicated Carter's boyhood farm as part of the Jimmy Carter National Historic Site. The historic site shows how rural families lived during the Great Depression, and is the place where Carter says he learned the values of hard work, family and a sense of community.

(Source: Adapted from Tania Fuentez's article, Phildelphia Sunday SUN, Feb.4, 2001)
(a) DS (　) (b) EX (　) (c) IN (　) (d) NA (　) (e) PE (　) (f) PR (　)

11. Cooperative education is a type of higher education that combines work and study. One student may study biology while working part-time in a laboratory; another student may learn secretarial and other office skills while working part-time in an office. Usually some credit toward graduation is given for part-time work related to a student's field of study. In some school systems, students work certain hours

Jimmy Carter's postpresidential career included building houses for the homeless. In 1992 he and Rosalynn lent a hand in Washington, D.C.

each week and attend classes at other times during the week. In other systems, students may spend one whole semester working and another semester going to school full-time. Whatever the work-study arrangement, a student has an opportunity to learn both in the classroom as well as on the job.
(a) DS (　) (b) EX (　) (c) IN (　) (d) NA (　) (e) PE (　) (f) PR (　)

카터는 책 전체에 유머와 정직을 짜넣었다. 그는 밭갈기, 목화 따기, 그리고 쉬는 날에 즐기던 사냥, 낚시, 또는 진흙 투성이 시냇물 건너기등에 대해 이야기한다.

지난해, 국립 공원 공단은 카터의 소년시절 농장을 지미 카터 국립 사적지의 일부로 헌정했다. 그 사적지는 대공황기에 시골의 가족들이 어떻게 살았는지 보여주고 있으며, 카터의 말에 따르면, 그가 고된 노동의 가치와 가족, 그리고 공동체 의식을 배운 곳이다. 정답 (d)

Jimmy Carter

Note

segregate *v.* To separate and set apart from others or from a main body or group.
intimacy *n.* The condition of being close in friendship or otherwise intimate.
sharecrop *v.* To work (farmland) as a sharecropper, giving a portion of the crop to the landowner.
precarious *a.* 1. So unstable or insecure as to be dangerous ; risky 2. dependent on chance or uncertain conditions 3. based on unproved or questionable premises.
dedicate *v.* To set apart for a special purpose ; devote --The scientists dedicated themselves to research.

11. 공동 교육은 일과 공부를 결합시킨 일종의 고등 교육이다. 한 학생이 생물학을 공부하면서 연구소에서 파트 타임으로 일한다. 또 한 학생은 비서학과 여타 사무 기술을 배우면서 동시에 사무실에서 파트 타임으로 일한다. 보통 학생들의 전공 분야와 관련된 파트 타임 일에 대해서는 보통 졸업 때까지 일정 정도의 학점이 주어진다. 일부 학교에서는 학생들이 매주 일정 시간 일하고 나머지 시간에는 수업에 참여한다. 또 다른 일부 학교에서는 학생들이 한 학기 내내 일하고 다음 학기에는 내내 수업만 받기도 한다. 일과 공부가 어떻게 배열되어 있든, 학생은 직장뿐 아니라 교실에서도 배울 기회를 얻게 된다. 정답 (b)

12. 우리 군대와 많은 사람들이 탈출에 성공했습니다. 그 분들을 아끼는 많은 사람들은 지옥 같은 한 주를 보냈을 겁니다. 그런데 그에 대한 고마운 마음 때문에 프랑스와 벨기에에서 일어난 일이 바로 어마어마한 군사적 실패라는 사실에서 눈을 돌려서는 안됩니다. 프랑스군은 약체화되었고, 벨기에 군은 패배하였으며, 너무나 많은 신뢰를 받고 있던 요새화된 전선 상당 부분이 사라졌습니다. 귀중한 광산 지구와 공장 상당수가 적의 휘하에 넘어갔고, 영국 해협 항구 전체가 적의 손에 있으며, 그 이후 뒤따른 온갖 비극적 결과에도 불구하고, 우리는 조만간 우리나 프랑스를 향해 또 다른 일격이 가해지리라고 예상해야 합니다. 우리는 히틀러가 영국 제도를 침공할 계획을 가지고 있다는 말을 듣고 있습니다. 이 점은 전에도 종종 고려되어 왔습니다. 나폴레옹은 바닥이 평평한 배와 당당한 군대를 이끌고 1년 동안 불로뉴를 공격했을 때, 누군가로부터 "영국에는 끈질긴 민초들이 있습니다" 라는 말을 들었습니다. 영국 원정군이 돌아온 이래, 확실히 그런 사람들이 더 많아지고 있습니다.

12. Our thankfulness at the escape of our Army and so many men, whose loved ones have passed through an agonizing week, must not blind us to the fact that what has happened in France and Belgium is a colossal military disaster. The French Army has been weakened, the Belgium Army has been lost, a large part of those fortified lines upon which so much faith had been reposed is gone, many valuable mining districts and factories have passed into the enemy's possession, the whole of the Channel ports are in his hands, with all the tragic consequences that follow from that, and we must expect another blow to be struck almost immediately at us or at France. We are told that Herr Hitler has a plan for invading the British Isles. This has often been thought of before. When Napoleon lay at Boulogne for a year with his flat-bottomed boats and his Grand Army, he was told by someone, "There are bitter weeds in England." There are certainly a great many more of them since the British Expeditionary Force returned.

I have, myself, full confidence that if all do their duty, if nothing is neglected, and if the best arrangements are made, as they are being made, we shall prove ourselves once again able to defend our Island home, to ride out the storm of war, and to outlive the menace of tyranny, if necessary for years, if necessary alone. At any rate, that is what we are going to try to do. That is the resolve of His Majesty's Government — every man of them. That is the will of Parliament and the nation. The British Empire and the French Republic, linked together in their cause and in their need, will defend to the death their native soil, aiding each other like good comrades to the utmost of their strength.

Even though large tracts of Europe and many old and famous States have fallen or fall into the grip of the Gestapo and all the odious apparatus of Nazi rule, we shall fight on the seas and oceans, we shall fight with growing confidence and growing strength in the air, we shall defend our Island, whatever the cost may be, we shall fight on the beaches, we shall fight on the landing grounds, we shall fight in the fields and in the streets, we shall fight in the hills; we shall never surrender, and even if, which I do not for a moment believe, this Island or a large part of it were subjugated and starving, then our Empire beyond the seas, armed and guarded by the British Fleet, would carry on the struggle, until in God's good time, the New World, with all its power and might, steps forth to the rescue and the liberation of the Old.

(The Address, called "The Miracle of Dunkirk," Winston Churchill, Radio broadcast on June 4,1940)

(a) DS ( ) (b) EX ( ) (c) IN ( ) (d) NA ( ) (e) PE ( ) (f) PR ( )

저 자신으로 말하자면, 모두가 각자의 의무를 다하고, 어떤 것도 소홀히 하지 않으며, 지금처럼 최상의 준비만 갖춘다면, 우린 다시 한 번 우리 조국을 수호하고, 전쟁이라는 난관을 극복할 수 있으며, 필요하다면 몇 년이라도, 필요하다면 혼자서라도, 독재자의 횡포를 견뎌낼 수 있으리라고 백 퍼센트 확신하고 있습니다. 그게 바로 우리가 해야 할 일입니다. 그게 바로 황제의 정부의 결의이자 모든 사람의 결의입니다. 그것은 의회와 국가의 의지입니다. 대의와 필요 차원에서 서로 연관된 대영 제국과 프랑스 공화국은 목숨 바쳐 자국 영토를 수호할 것이며, 좋은 친구처럼 있는 힘을 다하여 서로를 도울 것입니다.

비록 유럽과 유서 깊고 유명한 국가들 상당수가 게쉬타포 및 나치 통치라는 가증스런 체제에 함락되었거나 함락하고 있지만, 우리는 바다에서도 싸울 것이고, 커져가는 자신감과 커져가는 힘을 가지고 하늘에서도 싸울 것이며, 어떤 희생을 치르더라도 우리 나라를 수호할 것입니다. 우리는 해변에서도 싸우고, 경비행장에서도 싸울 것이며, 들판에서도, 거리에서도, 언덕에서도 싸울 것입니다. 우리는 결코 굴복하지 않을 것이며, 이런 일이 일어나지야 않겠지만, 설령 이 나라 또는 이 나라 상당 부분이 함락되거나 굶주린다면, 영국 함대가 무장하고 호위하는 바다 건너 우리 제국은 투쟁을 계속할 것이며, 마침내 신세계가 구세계의 해방과 자유를 위해 앞으로 나아갈 것입니다. 정답 (f)

Winston S. Churchill (left)

Note

colossal *a.* Extremely large in size, magnitude, or effect; enormous; gigantic; huge.

fortify *v.* 1. To make strong, as against attack --They fortified the castle by digging deep trenches around it.

　　2. To improve the quality of, as by adding ; enrich --The flour was fortified with vitamins.

menace *n.* A threat or danger.

　　v. To put into danger --An oil spill menaced the lives of birds, fish, and plants.

odious *a.* Provoking or deserving of hatred; loathsome or repellent.

subjugate *v.* 1. To win mastery over, as by military conquest ; subdue ; vanquish 2. To force into submission or subservience; enslave

weed *n.* A plant that grows where it is not wanted and is considered to be useless or harmful.

CHAPTER 5

효과적인 글 쓰기

Effective Writing

Since writing is a highly creative process, it is difficult to write. Furthermore, "writing well" or "writing effectively" is more difficult whether you are native or non-native speakers of Chinese, French, Thai, Spanish, German, Korean, Japanese, English, or any language. As we may know, writing well in English is not easy at all. English has not only an enormous vocabulary (about half a million), but also monstrously difficult grammatical rules. In addition, English encompasses an amalgam of numerous Indo-European and world languages, which causes us difficulty to write English well. In support of this, William Somerset Maugham, well-known British novelist and playwright, claims that "English is not an easy one to write... None of us can expect never to make mistakes. The best we can hope is that we shall not make many."

Nevertheless, we do not have to be discouraged by the notion that "English writing is difficult." We do not write it for money or for power. We write it for pleasure even though we may make mistakes. Making mistake is a necessary step for learning, especially in studying a foreign/second language. For example, Joseph Conrad (1857~1924), Poland-born novelist, is recognized as a master of English prose in a series of brilliant tales. We conclude that he had made countless mistakes in writing before he became a master of English prose. He just practiced writing, since "practice makes perfect." Likewise, we should not be ashamed of making mistakes; instead we should be ashamed of not practicing at all. Learning to write without making mistakes does not serve as an art of creation; it is merely an art of imitation. The consistent practice with mistakes can indeed create an art. For this writing as a creative art, William Faulkner mentions, "There is nothing that can match the pleasure of creation — creating some form of art... 'I was here for a while; I left this mark'." Faulkner enjoyed writing, so will we.

In PART 5, the final part of this text, we will study a variety of strategies for clear and effective writing. <u>Clear and effective writing refers to being (a) succinct ('Brief & to the point'); (b) easy to understand; and, (c) concrete and vivid</u>. In essence, good sentences should not include unnecessary words or phrases that might create confusion or misunderstanding to the readers. Instead, they should be precise, to the point, and vivid so as to create a strong and clear picture to the target readers.

How can we prepare ourselves for effective writing? There are hundreds of strategies for clear and effective writing; however, several key strategies such as (1) Choosing Word; (2) Reducing Wordiness; (3) Concise Writing; (4) Condensing; (5) Sentence Completeness; (6) Replacing Faulty Conjunctions; and, (7) Avoiding Fallacies, are introduced in the following sections of this text so as to help us write effectively.

글 쓰기는 고도로 창조적인 과정이므로, 글을 쓴다는 것은 어려운 일이다. 하물며 중국어, 불어, 타이어, 스페인어, 독일어, 한국어, 일본어, 영어 등 모든 언어를 막론하고 당신이 원어민이든 그렇지 않든, '글을 잘 쓴다'거나 '효과적으로 쓴다'는 것은 더욱 어렵다. 알다시피, 영어로 글을 잘 쓴다는 것은 결코 쉽지 않다. 영어는 어휘가 방대할 뿐 아니라(대략 오십만 단어) 문법 또한 터무니없이 어렵다. 게다가 영어는 인도유럽어를 비롯한 전세계 언어의 혼합물이며, 그로 인해 영어로 글을 잘 쓴다는 것은 더욱 어렵다. 이 점을 들어, 영국의 저명한 소설가 겸 극작가인 윌리엄 서머셋 모옴은 다음과 같이 주장하고 있다. "영어는 쓰기 쉬운 언어가 아니다. 어느 누구도 단 한 번의 실수도 하지 않으리라고 기대할 수 없다. 우리가 바랄 수 있는 최상은 그저 그 실수가 많지 않게 해달라는 것뿐이다."

그럼에도 불구하고, "영어 작문은 어렵다"는 생각에 지레 주눅이 들 필요는 없다. 우리는 돈이나 권력을 위해 글을 쓰는 것이 아니라, 설령 실수는 할지언정, 즐거움을 위해 글을 쓴다. 실수란 배움의 필수적인 단계이며, 외국어/제 2외국어를 공부할 때는 특히 더 그렇다. 예를 들어, 폴란드 태생의 소설가 조지프 콘래드(1857-1924)는 일련의 멋진 이야기들 속에서 영산문의 거장으로 인정받고 있다. 우리는 그가 영산문의 거장이 되기 전에 글을 쓰면서 셀 수 없이 많은 실수를 했었다고 추정하지 않을 수 없다. 그는 끊임없이 글 쓰기를 연습했다. "익혀 안 될 일 없기 때문"이다. 마찬가지로, 우리는 실수를 부끄러워해서는 안된다. 대신 연습을 하지 않는 것을 부끄러워해야 한다. 실수도 없이 글 쓰기를 배우는 것은 창조의 예술로 기능하지 않는다. 그것은 단지 모방의 기술일 뿐이다. 실수와 함께 하는 끊임없는 연습은 실제로 예술을 창조할 수 있다. 윌리엄 포크너는 이러한 창조의 예술로서의 글 쓰기에 대해 다음과 같이 말하고 있다. "창조의 기쁨에 필적할 수 있는 것은 아무 것도 없다. --- 일정한 형태의 예술을 창조하는 것... '나 잠시 여기 있었나니, 여기 이 표시를 남겼네.'" 포크너는 글 쓰기를 즐겼고, 우리도 그럴 것이다.

이 책의 마지막 장인 5장에서 우리는 명확하고 효과적인 글쓰기를 위한 다양한 전략을 공부하게 될 것이다. 명확하고 효과적인 글쓰기란 (a) 간명하고 (간결하고 적절해야 하고), (b) 이해하기 쉬우며, (c) 구체적이고 생생한 글을 가리킨다. 본질적으로, 좋은 문장에는 독자들에게 혼란이나 오해를 불러일으킬 수 있는 불필요한 단어나 구가 들어있지 않다. 대신 목표로 삼은 독자들에게 강하고 명확한 상을 창조할 수 있도록 정확하고, 적절하며, 생생해야 한다.

그렇다면 효과적인 글 쓰기를 위해 우리는 어떤 준비를 갖춰야 할까? 명확하고 효과적인 글 쓰기 전략은 수백 가지나 있다. 그러나 여기에서는 (1) 단어 선택, (2) 장황함 줄이기, (3) 간결한 글 쓰기, (4) 압축하기, (5) 문장의 완결성, (6) 잘못된 접속사 바꾸기, (7) 오류 피하기 등 효과적인 글 쓰기를 위한 핵심 전략을 몇 가지 살펴보기로 하겠다.

5.1. Choosing Word

The words you choose and the way you place them in a sentence play a key role for effective writing. It is because each word makes a difference in meaning and style. A well-chosen word helps the meaning of a sentence be more "accurate" and "effective." "Accurate words" refer to the specific words as contrasted to abstract or general ones; and, "effective words" are the expressive ones that catch vividly what you attempt to say.

5.1.1. Accurate Words

Choosing an accurate word is essential for effective writing. Below are provided some troublesome or confusing words, and several words that need correct usage in grammatical rules. Read the following sentences carefully, and select the most accurate word among the choices provided in the parenthesis.

(1) Colds are ((a) ordinary; (b) customary; (c) general; (d) common) in winter.

(2) Why don't you ((a) minimize; (b) reduce; (c) belittle; (d) restrain) your workload?

(3) David's academic progress deserves his parent's ((a) compliment; (b) complement; (c) completion; (d) compliance).

(4) The mousetrap made by John is a/an ((a) ingenious; (b) ingenuous; (c) imaginative; (d) illuminating) device.

(5) It is up to the principal's ((a) discredit; (b) discretion; (c) discreteness; (d) discrepancy) to punish Jim's poor attendance.

(6) The police should be ((a) disinterested; (b) uninterested; (c) disintegrated; (d) disjointed) in investigating this homicide case.

(7) A ((a) practicable; (b) practicing; (c) practical; (d) practiced) person does not spend money foolishly.

5.1. 단어 선택

당신이 선택한 단어와 당신이 문장 속에 그 단어를 배치하는 방식은 효과적인 글 쓰기에서 핵심적인 역할을 담당하고 있다. 각각의 단어는 의미와 스타일 면에서 차이가 있기 때문이다. 잘 선택된 단어는 문장의 의미를 보다 '정확하고' '효과적으로' 만든다. '정확한 단어'는 추상적이거나 일반적인 단어와 달리 구체적인 단어를 지칭하며, '효과적인 단어'는 당신이 말하고자 하는 바를 생생하게 포착하는 표현이 풍부한 단어이다.

5.1.1. 정확한 단어

정확한 단어 선택은 효과적인 글 쓰기의 본질적인 요소이다. 다음에 제시된 단어들은 애매하거나 혼란스런 단어와 문법상 올바른 사용법이 필요한 단어들이다. 다음 문장을 주의 깊게 읽고, 괄호 안에 제시된 단어들 가운데 가장 정확한 단어를 골라라.

(1) 겨울에는 감기가 흔하다. 정답 (d)

Note

ordinary *n.* 1. Commonly met with ; usual -- After the flood the river returned to its ordinary course.
2. Not distinguished in any way ; average -- This bread you baked is much tastier than ordinary bread.
common *n.* 1. Belonging to or shared equally by everybody--The swamp was drained for common use.
2. Found or occurring often ; widespread --Cats and dogs are common pets. 3. Often seen ; ordinary.

(2) 일을 좀 줄이는 게 어때? 정답 (b)

(3) 데이빗의 학문적 진보는 그의 부모님의 칭찬을 받을 만하다. 정답 (a)

(4) 존이 만든 쥐덫은 독창적인 장치이다. 정답 (a)

(5) 짐의 출석률 저조를 처벌하는 것은 교장의 재량에 달려 있다. 정답 (b)

(6) 경찰은 이 살인 사건을 조사하는 데 이해관계를 초월해야 한다. 정답 (a)

(7) 실용적인 사람은 돈을 어리석게 쓰지 않는다. 정답 (c)

Note

practicable *a.* Capable of being done or put into practice.
practicing *a.* Actively pursuing an occupation or profession.
practical *a.* 1. Having or serving a useful purpose. 2. Coming from experience, practice, or use rather than theory or study.
practiced *a.* 1. Having experience or proficiency 2. Acquired by means of practice.

(8) The houses made of wood, mud, and straw are ((a) likely; (b) liable; (c) answerable; (d) responsible) to collapse in a heavy storm.

(9) A thick fog ((a) laid; (b) lain; (c) had laid; (d) lay) over the London Bridge yesterday.

(10) The little cat ((a) lies; (b) lays; (c) has lain; (d) has laid) on the porch, sunning itself.

(11) The President, together with the Secretary of Defense and the Chief of Staff ((a) were; (b) was; (c) are; (d) had been) at the Inchon International Airport.

(12) A number of books about "The Korean Reunification" ((a) has; (b) have; (c) had; (d) was) been translated into Chinese, Japanese, Russian, and English.

(13) The academic advisor for foreign students recommended that Okhee ((a) study; (b) studied; (c) had studied; (d) should have studied) more English before enrolling at the University.

(14) I have been looking forward ((a) meet; (b) to meet; (c) to meeting; (d) to have met) you and your wife.

(15) Like humans, zoo animals must have a dentist ((a) to fill; (b) fill; (c) to be filled; (d) filled) their teeth.

(16) The cost of living ((a) has raised; (b) has risen; (c) raised; (d) had raised) over thirty percent in the past five years.

(17) Jacqueline Kennedy used to collect many beautiful antiques and ((a) sat; (b) set; (c) sit; (d) sets) them among the original pieces in the White House.

(18) Helen Keller, (1880-1968) blind, deaf, and mute by illness at the age of 19 months, became a well-known American author and lecturer. She received her education from Ann Sullivan by overcoming her handicap. Thus, to many handicaps, she proved herself as a/an ((a) incredulously (b) incredible; (c) incremental; (d) incriminatory) role-model.

(8) 나무, 진흙, 밀짚으로 지어진 집은 심한 폭풍우에 무너지기 쉽다. 정답 (b)

Note

likely *a.* Having or showing a strong chance of happening.
liable *a.* Inclined or disposed; tending.

(9) 어제 런던 다리 위로 두꺼운 안개가 덮여 있었다. 정답 (d)/자동사에 과거형(yesterday), lie–lay–lain

(10) 어린 고양이가 현관에 누워 햇볕을 쬐고 있다. 정답 (a) / 현재형에 자동사이므로 lies

(11) 국방 장관 및 비서실장과 함께 인천 국제 공항에 있었다. 정답 (b) / 3인칭 단수형이므로

(12) "남북 통일"에 대한 수많은 책들이 중국어, 일본어, 러시아어, 영어로 번역되었다.

정답 (b) / a number of가 주어일 경우 동사는 복수형

(13) 외국 학생들을 위한 진학 상담사는 옥희에게 대학에 입학하기 전에 영어를 좀더 공부하라고

권고했다. 정답 (a) / Recommend와 같은 요구, 명령 동사는 that절에서 조동사와 동사원형을 쓴다.

조동사는 생략가능.– I recommend that we (should) repeal the law.

(14) 당신과 당신 부인을 만날 날을 고대해왔습니다. 정답 (c) / looking forward to ~ing.

(15) 인간과 마찬가지로, 동물원의 동물들도 치과의사한테 이를 치료받아야 한다. 정답 (b) /
사역동사 + 목적어 + 동사원형

(16) 지난 5년 동안, 생활비가 30퍼센트 이상 올랐다. 정답 (b) / 자동사에 완료형

(17) 재클린 케네디는 아름다운 골동품을 수집하여 백악관에 원래 있던 작품들 사이에 놓아두곤

했다. 정답 (b)

Note

sit - sat - sat ; To rest on the lower part of the body where hips and legs join.
set - set - set ; To put ; place.

(18) 헬렌 켈러(1880 - 1968)는 생후 19개월에 병으로 인해 장님에 귀머거리, 벙어리가 되었지

만, 미국의 저명한 저술가 겸 강연자가 되었다. 그녀는 앤 설리반으로부터 교육을 받아 자신

의 장애를 극복했다. 따라서 많은 장애자들에게 그녀는 엄청난 역할 모델로서 자신을 입증해

보였다. 정답 (b)

Note

incredulously *ad.* In a state of skepticism, wonder.
incredible *a.* 1. Difficult or impossible to believe. 2, Extraordinary; astonishing. --Your silly excuse is
incredible.
incremental *a.* A rise or addition in number or value, often small.
incriminatory *ad.* To indicate the involvement of (someone) in a criminal or immoral act ; implicate.

Attack on Pearl Harbor

(19) The Japanese surprise attack on Pearl Harbor on December 7, 1941 brought the U.S. into World War II and was declared by President Roosevelt as "a day that will live in((a) scandal; (b) immorality; (c) discredit; (d) infamy)."

(20) Believe it or not, they ((a) censure; (b) censor; (c) celebrate; (d) census) your mails in North Korea according to the instructions of the government.

(21) If you want to ((a) flout; (b) flaunt; (c) defy; (d) cajole) your valuable possessions, display them in a public place for public admiration.

(22) None of the candidates who ((a) is; (b) are; (c) was; (d) had) campaigning in New York is willing to talk about abortion.

(23) If dinosaurs ((a) would; (b) had; (c) have; (d) would have) continued roaming the earth, man would have evolved quite differently.

(24) Dr. Albert Schweitzer (1875-1965), a good-natured French theologian, philanthropist, music scholar, and ((a) hostile; (b) bellicose; (c) malignant; (d) hospitable) physician founded Lambarene Hospital in French Equatorial Africa in 1913. He received a Noble prize for peace in 1952.

Dr. Albert Schweitzer

Al Capone

(25) Al Capone (1899-1947), one of the ((a) famous; (b) celebrated; (c) notorious; (d) renowned) American gangsters, was actively engaged in many illegal activities such as winning control of bootlegging and vice in Chicago, and controlling political campaigns and police. Morever, he ordered the St. Valentine's Day Massacre of Bugs Moran gang in 1929.

(19) 1941년 12월 7일, 일본의 진주만 기습 공격은 미국을 제2차 세계대전에 참전시켰고, 루스벨트 대통령에 의해 "치욕으로 남을 날"로 선포되었다. 정답 (d)

> **Note**
>
> scandal *n.* 1. A wrong or immoral act that shocks people. 2. Harmful gossip.
> immortality *n.* 1. The condition of being immortal. 2. Fame that will last forever.
> infamy *n.* 1. A deservedly evil fame or reputation, or the character or behavior that caused it.
> 2. A shameful or wicked act. 3.The loss of certain rights as a citizen consequent upon conviction for crimes such as treason.

(20) 믿거나 말거나, 북한에서는 정부 지침에 따라 우편물을 검열한다. 정답 (b)

(21) 당신의 소중한 재산을 과시하고 싶으면, 공공 장소에 전시해 대중의 찬탄을 받으십시오. 정답 (b)

> **Note**
>
> flout *v.* To show scorn or contempt for, esp. by openly or deliberately disobeying.
> defy *v.* 1. To challenge to do something thought of as impassible ; dare --I defy you to jump that high hurdle 2. To resist boldly 3. To be beyond the power of
> cajole *v.* To coax or persuade insistently, as by flattery or false promises.

(22) 뉴욕에서 선거운동을 벌이고 있는 후보들은 누구도 자발적으로 낙태에 대해 말하려 하지 않는다. 정답 (b) / candidates가 복수이므로 복수동사 필요.

(23) 공룡이 계속해서 지구상을 배회하고 있었다면, 인간은 사뭇 다르게 진화했을 것이다. 정답 (b) / 가정법 과거완료형

(24) 마음씨 좋은 프랑스의 신학자이자 박애주의자이며, 음악학자 겸 공손한 의사인 알버트 슈바이처 박사는 1913년, 프랑스령 적도 아프리카에 람바렌 병원을 개원했다. 그는 1952년, 노벨 평화상을 받았다. 정답 (d)

(25) 미국의 갱으로 악명높은 알 카포네(1899 - 1947)는 술 밀매와 시카고에서의 악행, 선거 운동과 경찰 통제 관리 등 온갖 불법 행위에 적극적으로 개입했다. 게다가 그는 1929년, 벅스 모간의 성 발렌타인 데이 대학살을 지시했다. 정답 (c)

> **Note**
>
> famous *a.* Very well known.
> celebrated *a.*1. Having a party or other such activity to honor a special occasion.
> 2. Performing with the proper ceremony or rite.
> notorious *a.* Well known for something bad or unpleasant.
> renowned *a.* Widely known and acclaimed; famous

5.1.2. Effective Words

Choosing an effective/specific word is essential for your effective writing. The more specific your words are, the more effective your writing will be. Different words convey different ideas. Compare the underlined words provided below: one is "general," while the other is "specific."

(a) It rained last night, so the grass is wet. ("General")
(b) It poured last night, so the grass is soaked. ("Effective")

Do the following exercises as a way of studying "effective words."

Exercise 1: Read the following sentences, and based on the context select the most effective word among the choices provided in the parenthesis.

(1) It was a ((a) nice; (b) wonderful; (c) good; (d) sparkling) day to golf.
(2) The sun ((a) blazed; (b) illuminated; (c) reflected; (d) blinked) brightly in the cloudless sky.
(3) Audrey Hepburn turned and presented her ((a) outline; (b) look; (c) profile; (d) silhouette) to the cameras.
(4) The roofs got ((a) flooded; (b) saturated; (c) engulfed; (d) submerged) with the silent rain of autumn moonlight.
(5) Suddenly, the lightning ((a) opened; (b) unzipped; (c) disclosed; (d) spread) the dark sky, and let the water out.

Audrey Hepburn

(6) Everything seemed familiar and kind — the white faces of buildings ((a) melting; (b) cooking; (c) broiling; (d) sizzling) in the soft September afternoon sun.
(7) The red-tailed hawk ((a) flew; (b) flitted; (c) fluttered; (d) glided) silently over the mountain.
(8) The soccer match between the Brazilian team and that of Italy was ((a) wonderful; (b) great; (c) interesting; (d) suspenseful).
(9) Larry offered to ((a) transport; (b) snatch; (c) carry; (d) drag) Jane's books for her.
(10) The old woman ((a) trudged; (b) walked; (c) moved along on foot; (d) traveled) home.

5.1.2. 효과적인 단어

효과적인/구체적인 단어 선택은 효과적인 글 쓰기의 본질적 요소이다. 단어가 구체적이면 구체적일수록, 당신의 글 또한 더욱 효과적이다. 서로 다른 단어는 서로 다른 사상을 전달한다. 다음에 제시된 밑줄 친 단어들을 비교하라. 하나는 '보편적' 인 반면, 다른 하나는 '구체적' 이다.

(a) 어제밤 비가 와서, 잔디가 축축하다. (보편적)
(b) 어제밤 비가 퍼부어서 잔디가 흠뻑 젖어 있다. (효과적)

> 다음 연습 문제를 풀면서 '효과적인 단어'를 공부해 보자.

1. 다음 문장을 읽고, 괄호 안에 주어진 단어들 가운데 문맥에 근거하여 가장 효과적인 단어를 골라라.

(1) 골프치기에 안성맞춤인 날이었다. 정답 (d)

sparkling *a.* Throwing off or reflect little flashes or gleams of light.

(2) 구름 한 점 없는 하늘에 태양이 찬란히 타오르고 있었다. 정답 (a)

blazed *a.* Burning or shining with or as though with fire

(3) 오드리 햅번은 카메라 쪽으로 고개를 돌려 자신의 옆모습을 보여주었다. 정답 (c)

profile *n.* A side view or drawing of something, especially the human head. outline *n.* 1. A line that forms the outer edge, limit, or boundary of something and shows its shape. 2. A picture or drawing that consists only of the outline of something 3. A short description or account ; summery

(4) 지붕들은 조용히 쏟아져 내리는 가을 달빛에 흠뻑 젖어들었다. 정답 (b)

(5) 갑자기 번개가 어두운 하늘을 열어제치더니 물을 쏟아냈다. 정답 (b)

(6) 모든 것이 익숙하고 친절해 보였다. 하얀 빌딩 겉면이 부드러운 9월 오후의 태양에 녹아들고 있었던 것이다. 정답 (a) / broiling *a.* Being subjected to high heat.

(7) 붉은 꼬리 매는 조용히 산 너머로 날아갔다. 정답 (d)

(8) 브라질과 이탈리아의 축구 경기는 서스펜스가 넘쳤다. 정답 (d)

(9) 래리는 제인의 책을 들어다 주겠다고 제안했다. 정답 (c) / snatch *v.* To grasp quickly

(10) 나이 든 할머니가 터벅터벅 집으로 걸어갔다. 정답 (a)

(11) Sally was so angry that she ((a) shut; (b) slammed; (c) closed; (d) sealed) the door when she left the room.

(12) Freedom ((a) danced; (b) produced; (c) spread; (d) whispered) in the streets of Seoul when Hirohito, the Emperor of Japan, announced the unconditional surrender to the Allies.

Hirohito

(13) In Minnesota 1943, a severe ((a) storm; (b) wind; (c) tornado; (d) air currents) destroyed everything in its path, exploding buildings with a whirling funnel of air that spun at a velocity of more than 200 mph.

(14) Marcelo looked at us and began to cry for his brother's death. His anguish ((a) stirred; (b) disturbed; (c) motivated; (d) vitalized) an aching fear in me.

(15) After the marathon, the first runner ((a) settled; (b) collapsed; (c) exhausted; (d) languished) on the ground.

Exercise 2: Select the least effective word among the choices provided in the parenthesis.

(1) There are several ((a) cottages; (b) houses; (c) huts; (d) cabins) near the lake.

(2) We enjoyed dancing to ((a) music; (b) jazz; (c) waltz; (d) polka) last night.

(3) The angry lady ((a) shrieked; (b) blustered; (c) grunted; (d) said), "No! Get lost, you, skunk!."

(4) Two ((a) pick-up trucks; (b) passenger cars; (c) station wagons; (d) vehicles)collided into each other.

(5) The robber ((a) went; (b) strode; (c) paced; (d) stalked) over to the window and looked outside.

(6) The severely wounded soldier ((a) howled; (b) cried loudly; (c) bawled;(d) outcried) for help.

(7) The old woman ((a) strolled; (b) sauntered; (c) rambled; (d) walked slowly & carelessly) in her large backyard.

(8) The teenager ((a) rushed; (b) dashed; (c) flitted; (d) moved) toward the towering redwood tree.

(9) Pearl Harbor is a ((a) thrilling; (b) breathtaking; (c) dramatic; (d) great) movie produced recently.

(10) The suspect ((a) answered sharply & briefly; (b) retorted; (c) rebutted; (d) refuted) to the police who were investigating the homicide case.

(11) 샐리는 너무나 화가 난 나머지 방을 나가면서 문을 쾅 닫았다. 정답 (b)

  slam *v.* 1. To shut forcefully and noisily. 2. To put forcefully. 3. To strike forcefully ; crash.

(12) 일황 히로히토가 연합국에 대해 무조건적인 항복을 발표하자, 서울 거리에는 자유가 넘실거렸다. 정답 (a)

(13) 1943년, 미네소타에서는 심한 대선풍이 길에 있던 모든 것을 파괴했고, 시속 200마일의 속도로 움직이는 깔때기 모양의 공기 회전 통로와 함께 건물을 파열시켰다. 정답 (c)

  tornado *n.* A violent, whirling wind;a tornado is accompanied by a funnel-shaped cloud that comes down from a thundercloud.

(14) 마르첼로는 우리를 쳐다보더니, 죽은 형을 생각하며 울기 시작했다. 그의 고통은 내게서 쑤시는 듯한 두려움을 불러일으켰다. 정답 (a)

  stir *v.* 1. To mix by using repeated circular motions 2. To move or cause to move slightly.

(15) 마라톤이 끝난 뒤, 첫 번째 주자는 땅 위에 무너져 내렸다. 정답 (b)

  collapse *v.* 1. To fall down suddenly ; cave in 2. To break down in strength or health. 3. To fold together.

2. 괄호 안에 주어진 단어들 가운데 가장 비효과적인 단어를 골라라.

(1) 호수 근처에 (작은 별장, 오두막)이 몇 채 있다. 정답 (b)

(2) 우리는 어젯밤 (재즈, 왈츠, 폴카)에 맞춰 춤추며 놀았다. 정답 (a)

(3) 성난 여자는 이렇게 (소리질렀다, 고함쳤다, 불평을 터트렸다). "안돼! 길을 잃다니, 이런 바보 같은 녀석!" 정답 (d)

(4) (픽업 트럭, 승합차, 스테이션 왜건) 두 대가 서로 충돌했다. 정답 (d)

(5) 강도는 창문으로 (성큼 다가가더니, 천천히 걸어가더니, 젠체하며 걸어가더니) 밖을 내다보았다. 정답 (a)

(6) 심한 부상을 입은 병사가 (악쓰듯, 울부짖으며, 큰 소리로 외치며) 도움을 청했다. 정답 (b)

(7) 나이 든 여자가 커다란 뒤뜰에서 (산책했다, 이리저리 어슬렁거렸다, 거닐었다). 정답 (d)

(8) 틴에이저가 높이 치솟은 아메리카 삼나무를 향해 (돌진했다, 달려들었다, 빠르게 달려갔다). 정답 (d)

(9) 『진주만』은 최근에 제작된 (스릴 만점의, 아슬아슬한, 극적인) 영화이다. 정답 (d)

(10) 용의자는 살인 사건을 수사중인 경찰에게 (반박했다, 항변했다, 논파했다). 정답 (a)

Note

retort *v.* To make a sharp answer.
rebut *v.* To prove false by means of contradictory evidence or argument; refute.
refute *v.* To demonstrate the falseness or error of ; disprove.
bluster *n.* A loud, hard blowing, as of the wind
grunt *n.* 1. A short, deep, harsh sound made by a pig. 2. A similar sound made deep in the throat.
howl *n.* 1 A long wailing cry, such as the one made by a dog, wolf, or coyote. 2. A loud cry or scream.

Exercise 3: Read the following sentences from(1) to(20). Based on the context of the base sentence, select the most effective sentence among the choices given.

(1) The tired, old man walked home slowly.

    (a) The tired, old man went home slowly. ( )
    (b) The tired, old man moved home slowly. ( )
    (c) The tired, old man trudged home. ( )

(2) The mud was very thick and sticky.

    (a) The mud was so thick and sticky that we could not walk. ( )
    (b) The mud was too thick and sticky to walk. ( )
    (c) The mud sucked our shoes off. ( )

(3) The woman's girdle was very tight.

    (a) The girdle split when she bent over. ( )
    (b) The girdle made her very uncomfortable. ( )
    (c) The girdle squeezed her waist. ( )

(4) Things are extremely expensive these days.

    (a) The price is soaring up. ( )
    (b) The price is skyrocketing. ( )
    (c) I paid $50 for a watermelon. ( )

(5). That chemistry test was extremely difficult.

    (a) The chemistry test was so difficult that no one passed it. ( )
    (b) The chemistry test was monstrously difficult. ( )
    (c) 99 % out of 100 students failed in the chemistry test. ( )

(6) Sally's room is very untidy.

    (a) Sally's room is filled with all dirty stuffs. ( )
    (b) Sally's room is full of all dirty things. ( )
    (c) Sally's room is littered with old newspapers, dirty clothes, broken dolls, milk cartons, and several boxes of leftover Chinese food. ( )

3. 다음 문장을 읽고, 기본 문장의 문맥에 근거하여 주어진 보기들 가운데
   가장 효과적인 문장을 골라라.

(1) 지친 노인은 천천히 집으로 걸어갔다. 정답 (c)

   (a) 지친 노인은 천천히 집에 갔다.

   (b) 지친 노인은 천천히 집으로 움직였다.

   (c) 지친 노인은 터벅터벅 집으로 걸어갔다.

(2) 진흙은 아주 두텁고 질척질척했다. 정답 (c)

   (a) 진흙이 너무 두텁고 질척거려서 우리는 걸을 수 없었다.

   (b) 걸어가기에는 진흙이 너무 두텁고 질척거렸다.

   (c) 진흙이 우리 구두를 벗겨갔다.

(3) 그 여자의 거들은 몸에 꼭 낀다. 정답 (a)

   (a) 그녀가 몸을 구부리자, 거들이 찢어졌다.

   (b) 거들 때문에 그녀는 매우 불편했다.

   (c) 거들은 그녀의 허리를 압박했다.

(4) 이즈음 물건값이 지나치게 비싸다. 정답 (c)

   (a) 가격이 폭등하고 있다.

   (b) 가격이 급등하고 있다.

   (c) 나는 수박 한 통에 50달러나 냈다.

(5) 그 화학 시험은 너무 어려웠다. 정답 (c)

   (a) 화학 시험이 너무 어려워서 아무도 통과하지 못했다.

   (b) 화학 시험은 엄청나게 어려웠다.

   (c) 100명 가운데 99명의 학생이 화학 시험에 낙제했다.

(6) 샐리의 방은 매우 난잡하다. 정답 (c)

   (a) 샐리의 방은 지저분한 물건으로 가득 차 있다.

   (b) 샐리의 방은 더러운 물건들로 가득하다.

   (c) 샐리의 방은 오래된 신문, 더러운 그릇, 부서진 인형, 우유팩, 먹다 남은 중국 요리 상자 등이 어지럽게
       널려 있다.

(7) Snow fell in my city all day.

    (a) It snowed all day in my city. (   )
    (b) Snow made my city all white. (   )
    (c) Snow blanketed my city. (   )

(8) A skinny brown dog sat in a doorway.

    (a) A skinny brown dog was in a doorway. (   )
    (b) A skinny brown dog huddled in a doorway. (   )
    (c) A skinny brown dog flocked in a doorway. (   )

(9) People who had been pleasant became sad.

    (a) Pleasant people became sad. (   )
    (b) Happy people became sad. (   )
    (c) Pleasant people stopped smiling. (   )

(10) The woman ate the food and liked it.

    (a) The woman ate all the good food offered. (   )
    (b) The woman hastily filled her empty stomach with food. (   )
    (c) The woman devoured the spicy chicken, scrambled eggs, and enjoyed each
       mouthful. (   )

(11) I felt extremely lonely.

    (a) I felt as lonely as the last leaf on a tree. (   )
    (b) I felt as lonely as a single bird on a tree. (   )
    (c) I felt as lonely as a single wild goose flying over the late fall sky. (   )

(12) Moses (14th~13th century B.C.), a Hebrew prophet and lawgiver who led the
    Israelites out of Egypt through the wilderness to Canaan, and his followers
    drank the water heartily by a well in a desert.

    (a) Moses, ..., & his followers swallowed the water heartily... desert. (   )
    (b) Moses, ..., & his followers gulped the water like thirsty camels... desert. (   )
    (c) Moses, ..., & his followers took in the water wholeheartedly... desert. (   )

(13) I ate too much. I can't eat any more.

    (a) I am so full that I can't eat any more. (   )
    (b) I ate like a vulture. (   )
    (c) I am as full as a satisfied mosquito. (   )

CHAPTER 5

(7) 도시에 하루 종일 눈이 내렸다. 정답 (c)

    (a) 도시에 하루 종일 눈이 왔다.

    (b) 눈은 도시를 온통 하얗게 만들었다.

    (c) 눈이 도시를 뒤덮었다.

(8) 삐쩍 마른 갈색 개 한 마리가 현관에 앉았다. 정답 (b)

    (a) 삐쩍 마른 갈색 개 한 마리가 현관에 있었다.

    (b) 삐쩍 마른 갈색 개 한 마리가 현관에 기어들었다.

    (c) 삐쩍 마른 갈색 개 한 마리가 현관에 몰려들었다.

(9) 쾌활했던 사람들이 슬퍼졌다. 정답 (c)

    (a) 쾌활한 사람들이 슬퍼졌다.

    (b) 행복한 사람들이 슬퍼졌다.

    (c) 쾌활한 사람들이 웃음을 그쳤다.

(10) 그 여자는 음식을 먹었고, 그것을 좋아했다. 정답 (c)

    (a) 그 여자는 제공된 좋은 음식을 모두 먹었다.

    (b) 그 여자는 음식으로 성급히 빈 배를 채웠다.

    (c) 여자는 맛있는 치킨과 스크램블드 에그를 게걸스레 먹었고, 입 안의 음식을 즐겼다.

(11) 나는 극심한 외로움을 느꼈다. 정답 (a)

    (a) 나는 나무에 달린 마지막 잎새처럼 외로움을 느꼈다.

    (b) 나는 나무 위의 한 마리 새처럼 외로움을 느꼈다.

    (c) 나는 늦가을 하늘을 나는 한 마리 기러기처럼 외로움을 느꼈다.

(12) 유대의 선지자이자 이스라엘 민족을 이집트에서 탈출시켜 가나안 광야로 데려간 모세(기원전 14세기–13세기)와 그의 추종자들은 사막의 한 우물 옆에서 실컷 물을 마셨다. 정답 (b)

    (a)...모세와 그의 추종자들은 ... 물을 실컷 들이켰다.

    (b)...모세와 그의 추종자들은 ... 목마른 낙타처럼 꿀꺽꿀꺽 물을 마셨다.

    (c)...모세와 그의 추종자들은...전심전력을 다해 물을 마셨다.

(13) 난 너무 많이 먹었어. 더 이상 먹을 수가 없어. 정답 (c)

    (a) 난 배가 너무 불러서 더 이상 먹을 수 없다.

    (b) 난 욕심장이처럼 먹었다.

    (c) 나는 흡족한 모기처럼 배가 부르다.

(14) A group of us set off for the mountains early in the morning.

    (a) A group of us set off for the mountains at dawn. (　)
    (b) A group of us set off for the mountains at the first hint of daylight. (　)
    (c) A group of us set off for the mountains at the first light in the east. (　)

(15) The climb was worth it, because the scene below was great.

    (a) The climb was worth it, because the scene below was spectacular. (　)
    (b) The climb was worth it, because the scene below was breathtaking. (　)
    (c) The climb was worth it, because the scene below was as pretty as a picture. (　)

(16) My uncle, Larry, lived in poverty.

    (a) My uncle, Larry, lived poor like a church mouse. (　)
    (b) My uncle, Larry, was very poor. (　)
    (c) My uncle, Larry, lived very poorly. (　)

(17) The pretty actress smiled at me happily.

    (a) The pretty actress beamed at me. (　)
    (b) The pretty actress giggled at me. (　)
    (c) The pretty actress hooted at me. (　)

(18) After two hours of heavy climbing, we sat down on the grass.

    (a) After two hours of heavy climbing, we rested on the grass. (　)
    (b) After two hours of heavy climbing, we took seats on the grass. (　)
    (c) After two hours of heavy climbing, we plopped down on the grass. (　)

(19) Some distant lamp or lighted window shone below.

    (a) Some distant lamp or lighted window glittered below. (　)
    (b) Some distant lamp or lighted window gleamed below. (　)
    (c) Some distant lamp or lighted window emitted light. (　)

(20) Napoleon Bonaparte (1769~1821) walked proudly toward the cheering crowd.

    (a) Napoleon ... strolled toward the cheering crowd. (　)
    (b) Napoleon ... proudly went to the cheering crowd. (　)
    (c) Napoleon ... strutted toward the cheering crowd. (　)

(14) 우리 팀은 아침 일찍 산으로 출발했다. 정답 (b)

    (a) 우리 팀은 새벽녘에 산으로 출발했다.

    (b) 우리 팀은 동틀 기미가 보이자 산으로 출발했다.

    (c) 우리 팀은 동쪽에 동이 트자마자 산으로 출발했다.

(15) 등산은 그만한 가치가 있었다. 눈 아래 펼쳐진 풍경이 굉장했기 때문이다. 정답 (c)

    (a) 등산은 그만한 가치가 있었다. 눈 아래 펼쳐진 풍경이 장관이었기 때문이다.

    (b) 등산은 그만한 가치가 있었다. 눈 아래 펼쳐진 풍경이 감동적이었기 때문이다.

    (c) 등산은 그만한 가치가 있었다. 눈 아래 펼쳐진 풍경이 그림처럼 아름다웠기 때문이다.

(16) 나의 삼촌 래리는 가난하게 살았다. 정답 (a)

    (a) 나의 삼촌 래리는 교회 쥐처럼 가난하게 살았다.

    (b) 나의 삼촌 래리는 매우 가난했다.

    (c) 나의 삼촌 래리는 매우 가난하게 살았다.

(17) 그 예쁜 여배우가 나를 보며 행복하게 미소지었다. 정답 (a)

    (a) 그 예쁜 여배우가 나를 보고 싱글싱글 웃었다.

    (b) 그 예쁜 여배우가 나를 보며 낄낄 웃었다.

    (c) 그 예쁜 여배우가 나를 야유했다.

(18) 두 시간의 힘든 산행 뒤, 우리는 풀밭에 앉았다. 정답 (c)

    (a) 두 시간의 힘든 산행 뒤, 우리는 풀밭에서 쉬었다.

    (b) 두 시간의 힘든 산행 뒤, 우리는 풀밭에 자리를 잡았다.

    (c) 두 시간의 힘든 산행 뒤, 우리는 풀밭에 털썩 주저앉았다.

(19) 저 멀리 아래쪽에서 등불 또는 불켜진 창문이 비쳤다. 정답 (b)

    (a) 저 멀리 아래쪽에서 등불 또는 불켜진 창문이 반짝반짝 빛났다.

    (b) 저 멀리 아래쪽에서 등불 또는 불켜진 창문이 어슴푸레 빛났다.

    (c) 저 멀리 아래쪽에서 등불 또는 불켜진 창문이 빛을 발했다.

(20) 나폴레옹 보나파르트(1769~1821)는 환호하는 군중을 향해 거만하게 걸어갔다. 정답 (c)

    (a) 나폴레옹...환호하는 군중을 향해 한가로이 걸어갔다.

    (b) 나폴레옹...환호하는 군중을 향해 거만하게 다가갔다.

    (c) 나폴레옹...환호하는 군중을 향해 점잔빼며 걸어갔다.

5.2. Reducing Wordiness

Writing style is partly a matter of personal taste. You can write either in a "long/wordy" or "short/brief" way as long as you make a point. A good sentence makes a point clearly while expressing an idea in a direct and interesting way. As we have seen in the beginning of PART 5, effective writing should be <u>(a) brief; (b) easy to understand; and, (c) concrete and vivid.</u>

Wordiness comes from using more words than you need to get your message across, and it often makes your writing dull and unclear. Therefore, this section, Reducing Wordiness, is designed for you to write effectively: "brief and easy to understand," by reducing unnecessary words.

5.2.1. Eliminating Repeated or Unnecessary Synonyms

Read the following examples and see how repeated words and unnecessary synonyms are eliminated. Pay your attention to the underlined words.

1. Repeated Words:

(1) My grandfather's <u>watch</u> is the oldest <u>watch</u> of the six <u>watches</u>.
= My grandfather's watch is the oldest of the six.

(2) My history teacher scheduled a <u>test</u>. The test is on The Industrial Revolution.
= My history teacher scheduled a test on The Industrial Revolution.

(3) This <u>time</u> can be a very difficult <u>time</u> in your life.
= This time can be a very difficult one in your life.
= This time can be very difficult in your life.

(4) <u>Most women</u> love to have <u>jewelry</u>. <u>Jewelry</u> is <u>most women</u>'s favorite possession.
= Most women love to have jewelry; it is their favorite possession.

5.2. 장황함 피하기

글 쓰는 스타일은 어느 정도는 개인적 취향의 문제이다. 당신은 논지를 입증하는 한 '길게/장황하게' 글을 쓸 수도 있고, 반대로 '짧게/간결하게' 글을 쓸 수도 있다. 좋은 문장은 논지를 명확히 입증하면서 직접적이고 흥미롭게 어떤 생각을 표현한다. 5장 서두에서 보았듯이, 효과적인 글 쓰기란 **(a) 간명하고, (b) 이해하기 쉬우며, (c) 구체적이고 생생해야** 한다.

장황함은 필요 이상으로 많은 단어를 사용할 때 나타나는 현상이며, 그것은 종종 글을 지루하고 모호하게 만든다. 따라서 이 부분에서는 불필요한 단어를 줄임으로써 '간명하고 이해하기 쉽게' 글 쓰는 방법을 배워보기로 하겠다.

5.2.1. 반복되는 단어나 불필요한 동의어 없애기

다음 예를 읽고, 반복되는 단어와 불필요한 동의어가 어떻게 삭제되는지 살펴보아라. 밑줄친 단어에 주목하라.

1. 반복되는 단어들

(1) 할아버지의 시계는 여섯 개의 시계들 가운데 가장 오래된 시계이다.
→ 할아버지의 시계는 여섯 개 중에서 가장 오래된 것이다.

(2) 역사 선생님이 시험 일정을 잡았다. 그 시험은 산업 혁명에 관한 것이다.
→ 역사 선생님은 산업 혁명에 관한 시험 일정을 잡았다.

(3) 지금 시기는 네 인생에서 매우 힘든 시기일 수 있다.
→ 지금 시기는 네 인생에서 매우 힘든 것일 수 있다.
→ 지금 시기는 네 인생에서 매우 힘들 수 있다.

(4) 대부분의 여성들은 보석을 가지고 싶어한다. 보석은 대부분의 여성들이 가장 좋아하는 재산이다.
→ 대부분의 여성들은 보석을 가지고 싶어한다. 그것은 그들이 가장 좋아하는 재산이다.

(5) Michael Jordan was the best basketball <u>player</u> of the five Chicago Bull's <u>players</u>.
= Michael Jordan was the best of the five Chicago Bull's basketball players.

(6) I <u>dreamt</u> a horrifying <u>dream</u> last night.
= I had a horrifying dream last night.

(7) My father <u>lived</u> a miserable <u>life</u>.
= My father had a miserable life.
= My father's life was miserable.

Michael Jordan

(8) <u>The height of a mountain can depend on how you measure the</u> height of the mountain.
= The height of a mountain can depend on how you measure it.

(9) As <u>Russian explorers and traders</u> traveled through Alaska and the Northern Coast from 1741 to 1867, <u>the Russian explorers and traders</u> collected samples of the Eskimo's local arts and crafts.
= As Russian explorers and traders traveled through Alaska and the Northern Coast from 1741 to 1867, they collected samples of the Eskimo's local arts and crafts.

(10) <u>Some Indians</u> picked <u>pokeberries or jack-in-the-pulpits</u>. Then <u>the Indians</u> mashed up <u>pokeberries or jack-in-the-pulpits</u> and dropped them into little ponds or slow-moving streams. The poisonous plants killed <u>the fish</u>. <u>The dead fish</u> floated to the top, only to be gathered and eaten by <u>the Indians</u>. The poison in the fish did not seem to bother <u>the Indians</u>.
= Some Indians picked pokeberries or jack-in-the-pulpits. Then they mashed up these plants and dropped them into little ponds or slow-moving streams. The poisonous plants killed the fish. The dead ones floated to the top, only to be gathered and eaten by them. The poison in the fish did not seem to bother them.

2. Unnecessary Synonyms:

(1) Paul threw away the <u>broken</u> electric oven that <u>does not work</u>.
= Paul threw away the broken electric oven.

(2) Elizabeth <u>carefully</u> opened the door <u>cautiously</u>.
= Elizabeth carefully opened the door.

(5) 마이클 조단은 시카고 불스의 다섯 선수들 가운데 가장 뛰어난 농구 선수였다.

→ 마이클 조단은 시카고 불스의 농구 선수 다섯 명 가운데 가장 뛰어났다.

(6) 나는 어젯밤 무서운 꿈을 꾸었다.

(7) 아버지는 불행한 삶을 살았다.

→ 아버지의 삶은 불행했다.

(8) 산의 높이는 당신이 산의 높이를 어떻게 평가하느냐에 달린 문제일 수 있다.

→ 산의 높이는 당신이 그것을 어떻게 평가하느냐에 달린 문제일 수 있다.

(9) 러시아 탐험가들과 상인들은 1741년부터 1867년까지 알래스카와 북부 연안을 두루 여행하면서, 러시아 탐험가들과 상인들은 에스키모인들의 공예품 견본을 수집했다.

→ 러시아 탐험가들과 상인들은 1741년부터 1867년까지 알래스카와 북부 연안을 두루 여행하면서, 에스키모인들의 공예품 견본을 수집했다.

(10) 일부 인디언들은 미국자리공이나 천남성류를 채집했다. 그리고 나서 인디언들은 미국자리공이나 천남성류를 으깬 뒤, 작은 연못이나 흐름이 느린 개울에 떨어뜨렸다. 그 유독한 식물은 물고기를 죽였다. 죽은 물고기가 떠오르면, 인디언들은 모아서 먹었다. 물고기의 독은 인디언들을 괴롭히지 않았던 것 같다.

→ 일부 인디언들은 미국자리공이나 천남성류를 채집했다. 그리고 나서 이 식물을 으깨어 작은 연못이나 흐름이 느린 개울에 떨어뜨렸다. 그 유독한 식물은 물고기를 죽였다. 죽은 물고기가 떠오르면, 모아서 먹었다. 물고기의 독은 그들을 괴롭히지 않았던 것 같다.

2. 불필요한 동의어

(1) 폴은 작동되지 않는 고장난 전기 오븐을 던져버렸다.

→ 폴은 고장난 전기 오븐을 던져버렸다.

(2) 엘리자베스는 조심스럽게 그 문을 주의하여 열었다.

→ 엘리자베스는 조심스럽게 그 문을 열었다.

(3) The truck was traveling at an <u>unsafe</u> speed <u>that was extremely dangerous</u>.
  = The truck was traveling at an extremely dangerous speed.

(4) It is surprising how many notable <u>events</u> and <u>happenings</u> in Korean history occurred between <u>the dates</u> of <u>June 25, 1950</u> and <u>July 27, 1953</u>.
  = It is surprising how many notable events in Korean history occurred between June 25,1950 and July 27, 1953.

(5) The task of writing a dictionary <u>begins</u> and <u>commences</u> with the reading of vast amount of the <u>written</u> literature of the period or subject that is <u>intended</u> and <u>planned</u> to cover.
  = The task of writing a dictionary begins with the reading of vast amount of the literature of the period or subject that is intended to cover.

(6) The auto-mechanic gave me an <u>approximate</u> estimate of $2,000 for the trouble-making transmission in my car.
  = The auto-mechanic gave an estimate of $2,000 for the trouble-making transmission in my car.

(7) <u>Each</u> and <u>every</u> moment in Tahiti was <u>exciting</u> and <u>stimulating</u> for us.
  = Each moment in Tahiti was exciting for us.

(8) There was lots of <u>excitement</u> and <u>enthusiasm</u> as our family prepared for its first trip to Switzerland.
  = There was lots of excitement as our family prepared for its first trip to Switzerland.

(9) Jane emptied all her <u>superfluous</u> and <u>unnecessary</u> <u>stuffs</u> and <u>details</u> from her drawers.
  = Jane emptied all her unnecessary stuffs from her drawers.

(10) The chemistry teacher <u>combined</u> the liquids <u>together</u>.
  = The chemistry teacher combined the liquids.

(11) My mother told the <u>honest</u> <u>truth</u>.
  = My mother told the truth.

(12) Oh my God! I have never seen a <u>dead</u> <u>corpse</u>.
  = Oh my God! I have never seen a corpse.

(3) 그 트럭은 극히 위험한 안전하지 않은 속도로 움직이고 있었다.

→ 그 트럭은 극히 위험한 속도로 움직이고 있었다.

(4) 한국사에서 1950년 6월 25일에서 1953년 7월 27일 사이에 주목할만한 일과 사건이 너무나 많이 일어났다는 점은 놀랍다.

→ 한국사에서 1950년 6월 25일에서 1953년 7월 27일 사이에 주목할만한 사건이 너무나 많이 일어났다는 점은 놀랍다.

(5) 사전 편찬 작업은 포함시키기로 예정하고 계획한 시대의 문자화된 방대한 양의 문헌이나 주제를 읽는 것에서 시작하고 개시된다.

→ 사전 편찬 작업은 포함시키기로 한 시대의 문자화된 방대한 양의 문헌이나 주제를 읽는 것에서 시작된다.

(6) 자동차 정비사는 말썽 많은 내 차 변속기 값으로 대략 추정액 2,000달러를 제시했다.

→ 자동차 정비사는 말썽 많은 내 차 변속기 값으로 대략 2,000달러를 제시했다.

(7) 우리한테는 타히티의 각각의 모든 순간이 흥미롭고 자극적이었다.

→ 우리한테는 타히티의 각각의 순간이 흥미로웠다.

(8) 우리 가족은 엄청난 흥분과 열정 속에서 스위스로의 첫 여행을 준비했다.

→ 우리 가족은 엄청난 흥분 속에서 스위스로의 첫 여행을 준비했다.

(9) 제인은 장롱에서 남아도는 불필요한 물건과 잡동사니를 모두 치워버렸다.

→ 제인은 장롱에서 불필요한 물건들을 모두 치워버렸다.

(10) 화학 선생님은 액체들을 함께 섞었다.

→ 화학 선생님은 액체들을 섞었다.

(11) 어머니는 솔직한 진실을 말했다.

→어머니는 진실을 말했다.

(12) 이런! 난 죽은 시체는 한 번도 본 적이 없었다.

→ 이런! 난 시체는 한 번도 본 적이 없었다.

(13) We got up just before <u>sunrise</u> <u>in the morning</u>.

= We got up just before sunrise.

(14) Jane <u>repeatedly</u> cursed her husband <u>again and again</u>.

= Jane repeatedly cursed her husband.

(15) The Old Manse in Concord, Massachusetts, was home to <u>poet and essayist</u> Ralph Waldo Emerson, <u>writer</u> Henry David Thoreau, and <u>novelists</u> Nathaniel Hawthorne and Louisa May Alcott.

= The Old Manse in Concord, Massachusetts, was home to writers such as Ralph Waldo Emerson, Henry David Thoreau, Nathaniel Hawthorne, and Louisa May Alcott.

| <u>Ralph Waldo Emerson</u> (1803-1882) | <u>Henry David Thoreau</u> (1817-1862) | <u>Nathaniel Hawthorne</u> (1804-1864) | <u>Alcott, Louisa May</u> (1832-1888) |

(16) The <u>nomadic</u> Tuarey people <u>who wander from place to place</u> live in <u>the Sahara desert, the largest dry barren area incapable of supporting a population without water supply</u>.

= The nomadic Tuarey people live in the Sahara desert.

(17) <u>At one time</u>, other American Indians once called the Inuit people as Eskimos, which means "eaters of raw meat." The home of the Inuit is the North American <u>tundra, a treeless plain of northern arctic regions</u>. In this frozen and barren land the Inuit have struggled to find food and shelter.

= Once other American Indians called the Inuit people as Eskimos, which means "eaters of raw meat." The home of the Inuit is the North American tundra. In this frozen and barren land the Inuit have struggled to find food and shelter.

(13) 우리는 아침 해돋이 바로 전에 일어났다.
→ 우리는 해돋이 바로 전에 일어났다.

(14) 제인은 몇 번이고 반복해서 남편을 저주했다.
→ 제인은 반복해서 남편을 저주했다.

(15) 매사추세츠주 콘코드의 올드 맨스는 시인 겸 수필가 팔프 왈도 에머슨, 작가 헨리 데이빗 소로우, 그리고 소설가 나타니엘 호돈과 루이자 메이 올콧에게는 마음의 고향이었다.
→ 매사추세츠주 올드 맨스는 랄프 왈도 에머슨, 헨리 데이빗 소로우, 나타니엘 호돈, 루이자 메이 올콧 등과 같은 작가에는 마음의 고향이었다.

(16) 이곳 저곳 유랑하는 유목민 투아리족은 물 공급이 없으면 단 한 명도 살 수 없는 세상에서 가장 건조한 불모지, 사하라 사막에 살고 있다.
→ 유목민 투아리족은 사하라 사막에 살고 있다.

(17) 일찍이, 다른 미국 인디언들은 한때 이뉴잇족을 에스키모라 불렀는데, 그 말은 '날고기를 먹는 사람들' 을 의미했다. 이뉴잇의 고향은 수목이 없는 북극 지방의 벌판인 북아메리카의 툰드라이다. 이 꽁꽁 언 불모의 땅에서 이뉴잇은 음식과 피난처를 찾기 위해 분투해왔다.
→ 한때 다른 미국 인디언들은 이뉴잇족을 에스키모라 불렀는데, 그 말은 '날고기를 먹는 사람들' 을 의미했다. 이뉴잇의 고향은 북아메리카의 툰드라이다. 이 꽁꽁 언 불모의 땅에서 이뉴잇은 음식과 피난처를 찾기 위해 분투해왔다.

Inuit people means "eaters of raw meat";
They were called by other American
Indians as 'Eakimos.'

(18) Thank you very much for your kind and generous invitation to the <u>sumptuous</u> and <u>extravagant</u> dinner, which shall live with us <u>long</u> <u>for many years to come</u>.

= Thank you very much for your kind invitation to the sumptuous dinner, which shall live with us long.

(19) How can I forget our <u>memorable</u> and <u>unforgettable</u> events we <u>shared</u> <u>together</u> in Salzburg, Austria? I felt the Austrian magnetism in <u>that city</u>, <u>Salzburg</u>: birthplace of Mozart and spiritual home of <u>the movie</u>, "<u>The Sound of Music</u>."

= How can I forget our memorable events we shared in Salzburg, Austria? I felt the Austrian magnetism in that city: birthplace of Mozart and spiritual home of "The Sound of Music."

(20) Katharine Drexel (1858~1955) was declared a <u>holy</u> <u>saint</u> on March 12, <u>2000</u>, and her canonization date was set on October 1, <u>2000</u> in Rome.

= Katharine Drexel was declared a saint on March 12, 2000, and her canonization date was set on October 1, in the same year.

Katharine Drexel

3. Redundancies:

(1) <u>In my opinion</u>, I believe that two of the prisoners have already died.

= I believe that two of the prisoners have already died.

(2) The school psychologists evaluated that Jim is a <u>brilliant</u> <u>genius</u>.

= The school psychologists evaluated that Jim is a genius.

(3) These scarves are free <u>gifts</u> <u>from</u> the Korean ambassador.

= These scarves are gifts from the Korean ambassador.

(4) He will be cast as the <u>evil</u> <u>villain</u> in the forthcoming production.

= He will be cast as the villain in the forthcoming production.

(5) It is <u>absolutely</u> <u>essential</u> to set your goal realistically.

= It is essential to set your goal realistically.

(18) 화려하고 호사스런 저녁 식사에 초대해주신 당신의 친절과 관대에 매우 감사드립니다. 앞
으로 오랫동안 기억에 남을 겁니다.

→ 화려한 저녁 식사에 초대해주신 당신의 친절에 매우 감사드립니다. 오랫동안 기억에 남을
겁니다.

(19) 우리가 오스트리아의 슬라츠부르그에서 함께 공유한 그 기억할만한 잊을 수 없는 사건을
내가 어떻게 잊을 수 있겠습니까? 나는 모차르트의 탄생지이자 영화 〈사운드 오브 뮤직〉의
영적인 고향인 그 도시, 슬라츠부르그에서 오스트리아의 매력을 느꼈습니다.

→ 우리가 오스트리아의 슬라츠부르그에서 공유한 잊을 수 없는 사건을 내가 어떻게 잊을 수
있겠습니까? 나는 모차르트의 탄생지이자 영화 〈사운드 오브 뮤직〉의 영적인 고향인 그 도
시에서 오스트리아의 매력을 느꼈습니다.

(20) 캐더린 드렉셀(1858-1955)은 2000년 3월 12일 신성한 성인으로 선포되었고, 그녀의 시성
식은 2000년 10월 1일, 로마에서 거행되기로 정해졌다.

→ 캐더린 드렉셀은 2000년 3월 12일, 성인으로 선포되었고, 그녀의 시성식은 같은 해 10월
1일로 잡혔다.

3. 쓸데없는 말

(1) 내 생각으로는, 나는 죄수 가운데 두 명이 이미 죽었다고 믿고 있다.
→ 나는 죄수 가운데 두 명이 이미 죽었다고 믿고 있다.

(2) 대학 심리학자들은 짐이 뛰어난 천재라고 평가했다.
→ 대학 심리학자들은 짐이 천재라고 평가했다.

(3) 이 스카프는 한국 대사관에서 주는 무료 선물입니다.
→ 이 스카프는 한국 대사관에서 주는 선물입니다.

(4) 그는 다음 작품에서는 사악한 악한으로 연기하게 될 것이다.
→ 그는 다음 작품에서는 악한으로 연기하게 될 것이다.

(5) 목표를 현실적으로 잡는 것이 절대적으로 가장 중요하다.
→ 목표를 현실적으로 잡는 것이 가장 중요하다.

(6) Political differences <u>still</u> <u>persist</u> between the North and the South Koreas.

= Political differences persist between the North and the South Koreas.

(7) Land is <u>totally</u> <u>useless</u> without labor.

= Land is useless without labor.

(8) With all his experience abroad he is a major <u>valuable</u> <u>asset</u> to the company.

= With all his experience abroad he is a major asset to his company.

(9) These tiny creatures are hardly <u>visible</u> <u>to the naked eyes</u>.

= These tiny creatures are hardly visible.

(10) Such treatment never gets down to root causes, to <u>basic</u> <u>fundamentals</u>.

= Such treatment never gets down to root causes, to fundamentals.

(11) Della had to save <u>each</u> and <u>every</u> penny to buy a Christmas present for Jim.

= Della had to save every penny to buy a Christmas present for Jim.

(12) By good fortune the leak has done no damage <u>as of</u> <u>yet</u>.

= By good fortune the leak has done no damage yet.

(13) We have greatly <u>advanced</u> <u>forward</u> in our understanding of our human body.

= We have greatly advanced in our understanding of our human body.

(14) <u>Both</u> Jane and Sally are invited <u>together</u> to a dinner at the White House.

= Both Jane and Sally are invited to a dinner at the White House.

(15) President Bush <u>rose</u> <u>up</u> to greet Dalai Lama, and they had a talk for preserving Tibet's heritage.

= President Bush rose to greet Dalai Lama, and they had a talk for preserving Tibet's heritage.

<u>Bush and Dalai Lama</u>

(6) 남한과 북한 사이에는 아직도 정치적 차이가 지속되고 있다.

➡ 남한과 북한 사이에는 정치적 차이가 지속되고 있다.

(7) 땅은 노동이 없으면 전적으로 무용지물이다.

➡ 땅은 노동이 없으면 무용지물이다.

(8) 해외 경험과 더불어, 그는 그 회사에 중요한 귀중한 자산이다.

➡ 해외 경험과 더불어, 그는 그 회사의 주요한 자산이다.

(9) 이 작은 생명체들은 육안으로는 눈에 거의 보이지 않는다.

➡ 이 작은 생명체들은 거의 눈에 보이지 않는다.

(10) 그런 방법은 결코 근본 원인, 기본적인 원리까지 파고들지 못한다.

➡ 그런 방법은 결코 근본 원인, 기본까지 파고들지 못한다.

(11) 델라는 짐에게 줄 크리스마스 선물을 사기 위해 각각의 모든 돈을 저축해야 했다.

➡ 델라는 짐에게 줄 크리스마스 선물을 사기 위해 모든 돈을 저축해야 했다.

(12) 운이 좋아서 누전은 현재 아직 아무런 손해도 입히지 않았다.

➡ 운이 좋아서 누전은 아직 아무런 손해도 입히지 않았다.

(13) 인간의 몸에 대한 이해는 엄청나게 앞으로 진보했다.

➡ 인간의 몸에 대한 이해는 엄청나게 진보했다.

(14) 제인과 샐리 둘다 백악관의 저녁 식사에 함께 초대받았다.

➡ 제인과 샐리 둘다 백악관의 저녁 식사에 초대받았다.

(15) 부시 대통령은 달라이 라마를 환영하기 위해 자리에서 위로 일어났고, 그들은 티벳의 유산 보호에 대해 환담을 나눴다.

➡ 부시 대통령은 달라이 라마를 환영하기 위해 자리에서 일어났고, 그들은 티벳의 유산 보호에 대해 환담을 나눴다.

5.2.2. Replacing a Long Phrase with One Word.

A group of words can be replaced with a single word for a clear and effective sentence. Read the following sentences while paying a close attention to the underlined parts.

(1) Henry is serving a life sentence <u>at the present time</u>.
  = Henry is serving a life sentence <u>now</u>.

(2) Dr. Neill will <u>conduct a test</u> on my blood type.
  = Dr. Neill will <u>test</u> my blood type.

(3) They kept on fighting although they <u>arrived at an agreement to</u> a cease-fire.
  = They kept on fighting although they <u>agreed to</u> a cease-fire.

(4) <u>Considering the fact that</u> he easily passed the preliminary examinations leading to his Ph.D. degree, he is predicted to complete his dissertation.
  = <u>Because</u> he easily passed the preliminary examinations leading to his Ph.D. degree, he is predicted to complete his dissertation.

(5) The police <u>conducted a search</u> for the missing child.
  = The police <u>searched</u> for the missing child.

(6) He and his older brother <u>had a ferocious argument</u> about their jointly owned car.
  = He and his older brother ferociously <u>argued</u> about their jointly owned car.

(7) My son will learn to take responsibility for others <u>during the course of</u> military training.
  = My son will learn to take responsibility for others <u>during</u> military training.

(8) My mother did not <u>give approval of</u> my marriage to Chulsoo Kim.
  = My mother did not <u>approve</u> my marriage to Chulsoo Kim.

5.2.2. 긴 어구를 한 단어로 바꾸기

서로 모여 구를 이루고 있는 단어들은 명확하고 효과적인 문장을 위해 한 단어로 대체될 수 있다. 밑줄 친 부분에 주의하면서 다음 문장을 읽어보아라.

(1) 헨리는 현재 시각 종신형을 살고 있다.
→ 헨리는 지금 종신형을 살고 있다.

(2) 닐 박사가 혈액형에 대한 테스트를 수행할 것이다.
→ 닐 박사가 내 혈액형에 대해 테스트할 것이다.

(3) 그들은 정전 합의에 도달했음에도 불구하고 계속 싸우고 있었다.
→ 그들은 정전에 합의했음에도 불구하고 계속 싸우고 있었다.

(4) 그가 박사 학위 논문 자격 시험을 쉽게 통과한 사실을 고려할 때, 그는 논문을 완성할 것으로 보인다.
→ 박사 학위 논문 자격 시험을 쉽게 통과했기 때문에 그는 논문을 완성할 것으로 보인다.

(5) 경찰은 행방불명된 아이에 대한 수색을 지휘했다.
→ 경찰은 행방불명된 아이를 수색하였다.

(6) 그와 그의 형은 공동 소유의 차 때문에 맹렬한 논쟁을 벌였다.
→ 그와 그의 형은 공동 소유의 차 때문에 맹렬하게 논쟁했다.

(7) 내 아들은 군사 훈련 과정 동안 다른 사람들을 책임지는 것을 배우게 될 것이다.
→ 내 아들은 군사 훈련 동안 다른 사람들을 책임지는 것을 배우게 될 것이다.

(8) 어머니는 김철수씨와 나의 결혼에 찬성 의사를 표하지 않았다.
→ 어머니는 김철수씨와 나의 결혼에 찬성하지 않았다.

(9) We are <u>in need of</u> more money.

  = We <u>need</u> more money.

(10) President Lyndon Johnson with his staff <u>made an analysis of</u> the existing sociopolitical realities in Vietnam.

  = President Lyndon Johnson with his staff <u>analyzed</u> the existing sociopolitical realities in Vietnam.

(11) The soldiers <u>made an inspection of</u> this area.

  = The soldiers <u>inspected</u> this area.

President Lyndon Johnson

(12) John and I <u>had a discussion</u> about the coming election.

  = John and I <u>discussed</u> about the coming election.

(13) People in Kwangjoo <u>held strong protests</u> against the military coup de'tat in 1981.

  = People in Kwangjoo strongly <u>protested</u> against the military coup de'tat in 1981.

(14) We are <u>a long distance away</u> from Seoul.

  = We are <u>faraway</u> from Seoul.

(15) "Do you really want to study *philosophy*?" the professor asked, <u>placing emphasis on</u> each word.

  = "Do you really want to study *philosophy*?" the professor asked, <u>emphasizing</u> each word.

CHAPTER 5

(9) 우리는 더 많이 돈이 필요한 상태에 있다.
➡ 우리는 더 많은 돈이 필요하다.

(10) 린든 존슨 대통령은 참모들과 함께 베트남의 현존 사회정치적 현실에 대한 분석을 단행했다.
➡ 린든 존슨 대통령은 참모들과 함께 베트남의 현존 사회정치적 현실을 분석했다.

(11) 군인들이 이 지역에 대한 시찰을 단행했다.
➡ 군인들이 이 지역을 시찰했다.

(12) 존과 나는 다가오는 선거에 대해 토론을 벌였다.
➡ 존과 나는 다가오는 선거에 대해 토론했다.

(13) 광주 사람들은 1981년 군사 쿠데타에 대항하여 완강한 저항을 벌였다.
➡ 광주 사람들은 1981년 군사 쿠데타에 대항하여 완강하게 저항했다.

(14) 우리는 서울에 멀리 떨어져 있다.
➡ 우리는 서울에서 멀리 있다.

(15) "자네 정말 철학을 공부하고 싶은가?" 교수님이 단어 하나하나에 강조점을 두며 물었다.
➡ "자네 정말 철학을 공부하고 싶은가?" 교수님이 각각의 단어를 강조하며 물었다.

5.3. Concise Writing

"Concise writing" is another way for effective writing, and it refers to keeping your sentences concise by removing unnecessary words, phrases, or empty expressions. Read the following sentences while paying a close attention to the underlined parts. Write a concise sentence after removing all unnecessary parts as exemplified below.

> <u>Example</u>: The theater at 15th Avenue shows movies continuously all the time.
> = The theater at 15th Avenue shows movies continuously.

(1) <u>As a rule</u>, I <u>generally</u> jog in the morning.

= _____.

(2) We can not hold our breath long <u>due to the fact that</u> carbon dioxide builds up in our cells.

= _____.

(3) KeoJae-Do, <u>which is an island off the southeastern coast of Korea</u>, is visited by many tourists.

= _____.

(4) Not many flowers are <u>white or black</u> <u>in color</u>.

= _____.

(5) From the cabin in the Kilimanjaro in the northeast Tanzania, I saw two mountains <u>whose</u> <u>summits were covered with snow</u>.

= _____.

(6) Cars and televisions are manufactured from parts <u>that are mass-produced</u>.

= _____.

5.3. 간결한 글 쓰기

'간결한 글 쓰기'란 효과적인 글 쓰기를 위한 또 하나의 방법이다. 그것은 불필요한 단어, 어구, 또는 무의미한 표현을 삭제함으로써 문장을 간결하게 하는 것과 관련이 있다. 밑줄 친 부분에 주의하면서 다음 문장을 읽어보아라. 다음 예와 같이 불필요한 부분을 모두 없앤 뒤 간결한 문장을 써 보아라.

예] 15번 가의 극장은 항상 끊임없이 영화를 보여준다.
➡ 15번 가의 극장은 끊임없이 영화를 보여준다.

(1) 일반적으로, 나는 대개 아침에 조깅한다.
모범정답 : I generally jog in the morning.

(2) 이산화탄소가 세포 안에 쌓인다는 사실로 인해 우리는 숨을 오래 참을 수 없다.
모범정답 : We can not hold our breath long because carbon dioxide builds up in our cells.

(3) 한국 남동 해안에 저편에 위치한 섬 거제도는 관광객들이 많이 찾는다.
모범정답 : KeoJae-Do, an island off the southeastern coast of Korea, is visited by many visitors

(4) 색상이 하얗거나 까만 꽃들은 많지 않다.
모범정답 : No many flowers are white or black.

(5) 탄자니아 남동쪽 킬리만자로의 오두막집에서, 나는 꼭대기가 눈으로 뒤덮인 두 개의 산을 보았다.
모범정답 : From the cabin in the Kilimanjaro in the northeast Tanzania, I saw two snow-capped mountains

(6) 자동차와 텔레비전은 대량생산되는 부문에서 제조된다.
모범정답 : Cars and televisions are manufactured from mass-produced parts.

(7) A paddle <u>that is made for a canoe</u> is usually carved from spruce or white cedar.

= _____.

(8) President Carter wrote an <u>autobiography</u> <u>of his life</u>.

= _____.

(9) <u>What I am trying to say is that</u> we can't survive without water and air.

= _____.

(10) Tires <u>that are made for race cars</u> are steel-belted.

= _____.

(11) Computers use chips <u>that are made of</u> silicon.

= _____.

(12) The magazines <u>that my sister subscribe to</u> all deal with computer science.

= _____.

(13) Pears and apricots <u>that have been dried</u> can be used in cooking.

= _____.

(14) In the operetta, Marian Anderson sang three <u>solos</u>, "La Favorita; Un Ballo in Maschera; O Mio Fernando," <u>by herself</u>.

= _____.

(15) <u>It is true</u> that many people are colorblind.

= _____.

(16) Animals <u>that live in the desert</u> usually sleep in the shade during the day.

= _____.

(7) 카누용으로 만들어지는 패들(짧고 폭넓은 노)은 보통 전나무나 흰색 삼나무로 조각된다.

모범정답 : A canoe paddle is usually carved from spruce or white cedar

(8) 카터 대통령은 인생의 자서전을 썼다.

모범정답 : President Carter wrote an autobiography

(9) 내가 말하고자 하는 것은 우리는 물과 공기 없이는 생존할 수 없다는 점이다.

모범정답 : We can not survive without water and air.

(10) 경주 자동차용으로 만들어진 타이어는 강철을 대고 있다.

모범정답 : Race car tires are steel-belted

(11) 컴퓨터는 실리콘으로 만들어진 칩을 사용한다.

모범정답 : Computers use silicon chips.

(12) 여동생이 구독하는 잡지들은 모두 컴퓨터 사이언스를 다루고 있다.

모범정답 : My sisters magazines all deal with computer science.

(13) 잘 말린 배와 살구는 요리에 사용될 수 있다.

모범정답 : Dried pears and apricots can be used in cooking.

(14) 그 오페레타에서, 마리안 앤더슨은 '라 라보리타; 운 발로 인 마셰라; 오 미오 페르난도' 등 세 곡의 솔로곡을 혼자 불렀다.

모범정답 : In the operetta, Marian Anderson sang three solos, La Favorita; Un Ballo in Maschera; O Mio Fernando.

Marian Anderson

(15) 많은 사람들이 색맹인 것은 사실이다.

모범정답 : Many people are colorblind.

(16) 사막에 사는 동물들은 보통 낮 동안 그늘에서 잔다.

모범정답 : Desert animals usually sleep in the shade during the day.

(17) The <u>round,</u> <u>full moon</u> rose over the mountains.

= _____ .

(18) The Canary Islands, <u>which are islands off the coast of Africa</u>, belong to Spain.

= _____ .

(19) Tourists in Mexico visit many ancient pyramids <u>that are made of stone</u>.

= _____ .

(20) Brazil, <u>which is the fifth largest country in the world</u>, covers half of South America.

= _____ .

(21) <u>It is known by most people</u> that too much fat in the diet is unhealthy.

= _____ .

(22) Fried foods, <u>due to the fact that</u> they are covered with fat, are digested more slowly than <u>boiled or broiled foods</u> are.

= _____ .

(23) Sally works <u>at a job</u> <u>in the supermarket</u>.

= _____ .

(24) Some traditional Thai boats have sails <u>that are square in shape</u>.

= _____ .

(25) In the ruins of ancient cities <u>that were built by the Mayans</u> are the remains of ball courts.

= _____

_____ .

(17) 둥근 보름달이 산 위로 떠올랐다.

모범정답 : The full moon rose over the mountains

(18) 아프리카 해안 저 편에 위치한 섬들, 카나리아 제도는 스페인령이다.

모범정답 : The Canary Islands, off the coast of Africa, belong to Spain

(19) 멕시코 관광객들은 돌로 만들어진 많은 고대의 피라미드들을 방문한다.

모범정답 : Tourists in Mexico visit many ancient stone pyramids.

(20) 세계에서 15번째로 큰 나라 브라질은 남아메리카의 반을 차지하고 있다.

모범정답 : Brazil, the worlds fifth largest country, covers half of South America.

(21) 음식물에 지방이 너무 많으면 건강에 해롭다는 사실은 대부분의 사람들에게 알려져 있다.

모범정답 : Most people know that too much fat in the diet is unhealthy.

(22) 기름에 튀긴 음식은 지방으로 덮여있다는 점으로 인해 삶거나 구운 음식들보다 더 천천히 소화된다.

모범정답 : Because fried foods are covered with fat, they are digested more slowly then those boiled or broiled.

(23) 샐리는 슈퍼마켓의 일자리에서 일한다.

모범정답 : Sally works at the supermarket.

(24) 타이의 전통적인 배 일부는 모양이 정사각형인 돛을 달고 있다.

모범정답 : Some traditional Thai boats have square sails

(25) 마야인에 의해 지어진 고대 도시 잔해에는 공놀이 경기장 유적이 있다.

모범정답 : In the ruins of ancient Mayan cities are the remains of ball courts.

5.4. Condensing

We have seen "Concise Writing" as a way of writing effectively. "Condensing" compared to "Concise Writing" expresses the main ideas and the most important supporting details more briefly with fewer words without altering the original meaning. Read each sentence provided below, counting the number of words used. Write the number in the blank from (1) to (15). Then rewrite the sentence by eliminating all unnecessary parts, while condensing the main ideas and the important supporting details. Make your sentence as short as possible as exemplified below:

Examples:
(a) Everything that glitters is not necessarily made of gold. (9 words)
 = All that glitters is not gold. (Condensed in 6 words)
(b) Whatever you do, everything that comes to an end without a failure is said to be good. (17 words)
 = All is good that ends well. (6 words)

(1) Owing to the fact that he was sick, he did not go to school at that day. (17)

= _____.

(2) Collecting stamps is one of my absolute favorite hobbies, one that appeals to me as much as anything in the whole world. (22)

= _____.

(3) When you live in Korea, but at the same time you don't speak the language of the Korean people, it is just exactly the same as you are locked up in prison. (32)

= _____.

(4) After the milk bottle has been knocked over to be shattered into small pieces, all the milk has spilled out. Then there is no point in crying out about the spilled milk. (32)

= _____.

5.4. 압축하기

효과적으로 글을 쓰는 한 방법으로서 '간결한 글 쓰기'에 대해 공부했다. '간결한 글 쓰기'와 비교할 때, '압축하기'는 주제와 가장 중요한 세부 사항들을 원 뜻을 바꾸지 않고 더 작은 단어로 더 간략하게 표현하는 것이다. 다음에 지시된 각 문장을 읽으면서 사용된 단어의 수를 확인하라. 괄호 안에 그 숫자를 써넣어라. 그리고 나서 불필요한 부분은 모두 삭제하고 문장을 다시 쓰면서 주제와 중요 보충 자료들을 압축시켜 보아라. 아래의 예처럼 문장은 가능한 한 짧게 할 것.

예] (a) 반짝이는 것들이 반드시 금으로 만들어진 것은 아니다.

➡ 반짝이는 것이 다 금은 아니다.

(b) 당신이 무엇을 하든, 실패 없이 끝나는 것은 모두 좋은 것이라고 말해진다.

➡ 끝이 좋으면 다 좋다.

(1) 그가 아팠다는 사실 때문에, 그는 그 날 학교에 가지 않았다.

모범정답 : Because he was sick, he didn't go to school.(9 words)

(2) 우표 수집은 내가 가장 좋아하는 취미 가운데 하나인데, 내게는 이 세상 그 어떤 것 보다도 흥미로운 것이다.

모범정답 : I love collecting stamps. (4 words)

(3) 한국에 사는데 한국 사람들의 언어를 말할 수 없을 때, 그것은 바로 감옥에 갇혀있는 것과 똑같다.

모범정답 : Living in Korea without speaking Korean is like being in prison. (11)

(4) 우유병이 깨어져 산산조각이 난 뒤, 모든 우유가 엎질러졌다. 그때는 엎질러진 우유를 놓고 울어봐야 아무 소용도 없다.

모범정답 : There is no use crying over spilled milk. (8)

(5) Gas prices are soaring drastically these days, but they do not show any signs that they will fall down. (19)

= _____.

(6) Despite the fact that Mary was extremely heavy by being 8 months pregnant, she could walk up to the hill as fast as the other women did. (27)

= _____.

(7) If you keep telling lies, it is certain that you will lose your credibility and friends.(16)

= _____.

(8) Do not believe in anything unless you actually see it by yourself. (12)

= _____.

(9) It is just about impossible to drag a stubborn mule to the stream to drink water. (16)

= _____.

(10) You should treat other people the same way that you would like them to treat you. (15)

= _____.

(11) When you try to do something in a hurry, it turns out to take even longer very often than when you do it slowly and steadily. (26)

= _____.

(12) A thousand years ago, Iceland had many forests and little ice. Many Norse emigrated to Iceland where they proceeded to cut down most of the trees. Their only fuel was wood. They brought sheep with them, and the sheep also destroyed trees by eating the bark. Even today Icelanders depend on sheep for most of their income. Now they protect their few forests with fences, and they are planting trees by the thousands. They hope to recreate an Iceland of many forests and little ice. (85)

= _____

_____.

(5) 이즈음 가스 값이 엄청나게 급등하고 있지만, 그것이 떨어지리라는 신호는 전혀 보이지 않는다.

모범정답 : Skyrocketing gas prices show no signs of landing. (8)

(6) 임신 8개월에 이르러 메리가 엄청나게 무거워졌다는 사실에도 불구하고, 그녀는 다른 여자들
    만큼 빠르게 언덕에 오를 수 있었다.

모범정답 : Although Mary was 8 months pregnant, she quickly walked up the hill like the
           other women. (16)

(7) 계속 거짓말을 한다면, 당신은 신용과 친구를 잃게 될 것이 분명합니다.

모범정답 : Lying makes you lose your credibility and friends. (8)
           Honesty is the best policy. (5)

(8) 눈으로 직접 보기 전에는 어떤 것도 믿지 말라.

모범정답 : Seeing is believing. (3)

(9) 고집 센 노새를 개울가로 끌고 가 물을 먹인다는 것은 정말 불가능하다.

모범정답 : You can lead a horse to water but can't make him drink. (12)
           You can't get anything by force. (6)

(10) 다른 사람들이 당신을 어떻게 대했으면 좋을 지에 맞춰 그와 똑같은 방식으로 다른 사람들을
     대해야 한다.

모범정답 : Do to others as you would have them do to you. (11)

(11) 뭔가를 성급히 하려고 할 때면, 천천히 그리고 꾸준히 할 때보다 훨씬 더 오래 걸리는 경우가
     많다.

모범정답 : Haste makes waste. (3) / Slow and steady wins the race. (6)

(12) 천년 전, 아이슬란드에는 숲이 많았고 얼음은 거의 없었다. 많은 노르웨이인들이 아이슬란드
     로 이주하여 계속해서 대부분의 나무를 베어냈다. 그들의 유일한 연료는 나무였다. 그들은
     자신들과 함께 양을 데려왔고, 그 양 또한 나무껍질을 먹음으로써 나무를 파괴했다. 오늘날
     에도 아이슬란드 사람들은 대부분의 수입을 양에 의존한다. 이제 그들은 울타리를 쳐서 몇 안
     되는 숲을 보호하며, 나무를 아주 많이 심고 있다. 그들은 다시금 숲이 많고 얼음은 적은 아이
     슬란드를 만들고 싶어한다.

(13) If you are extremely hungry, you can eat any foods that are available. (13)

= _____.

(14) It is a common social phenomenon to find out that the Korean people get married among the Koreans, the Japanese, the Germans, the Vietnamese, the Afro-Americans amongthemselves. (28)

= _____.

(15) It is of no use for a blind man to be angry with the ditch into which he has fallen, because the fall is due to his own lack of sight. (31)

= _____.

(16) People in different countries eat somewhat different foods. Europeans and Americans eat bread made of wheat flour and raised by yeast. Mexicans prefer tortillas, a flat bread made of ground corn. Tibetans drink yak milk; Iranians drink goat milk. Koreans eat kimchee.

   Many Americans would not enjoy being served snails, grasshoppers, or turtles' eggs, but these are considered delicacies in some countries. We are all likely to prefer the foods popular in our own country.

= _____

_____.

(17) If I speak in the tongues of men and of angels, but have not love, I am only a resounding gong or a clanging cymbal. If I have the gift of prophecy and can fathom all mysteries and all knowledge, and if I have a faith that can move mountains, but have not love, I am nothing. If I give all I posses to the poor and surrender my body to the flames, but have not love, I gain nothing.
(Source: 1 Corinthians 13)

= _____

_____.

모범정답 : Although Iceland once had many forests, they were cut down for fuel or destroyed by sheep. Today, Icelanders are protecting and planting trees. (23)

(13) 몹시 허기진 상태라면, 얻을 수 있는 음식은 아무거나 먹을 수 있다.

모범정답 : Hunger is the best sauce. (5)

(14) 한국인은 한국인끼리, 일본인은 일본인끼리, 독일인은 독일인끼리, 베트남인은 베트남인끼리, 미국 흑인은 미국 흑인끼리 결혼하는 것은 흔히 볼 수 있는 사회 현상이다.

모범정답 : Marriage among the same ethnic group members is common. (9)

　　　　　 Birds of a feather flock together. (6)

(15) 맹인이 자기가 빠진 도랑에 대고 화를 내는 것은 아무 소용이 없다. 도랑에 빠진 것 자체가 자신의 시력 결핍에서 기인하기 때문이다.

모범정답 : The blind man blames the ditch. (6)

　　　　　 It's easy to blame others. (5)

(16) 국적이 다른 사람들은 다소 다른 음식을 먹는다. 유럽인과 미국인은 밀가루로 만들어 이스트로 부풀린 빵을 먹는다. 멕시코인은 옥수수를 주원료로 만들어진 둥글넙적한 빵, 토르티야를 선호한다. 티벳인은 야크(티벳산 들소) 우유를 마시며, 이란인들은 염소 우유를 마신다. 한국인은 김치를 먹는다.

　　많은 미국인들은 달팽이 요리나 메뚜기 요리, 또는 거북이 알을 즐기지 않지만, 다른 나라에서는 이 음식들이 맛있는 것으로 간주되고 있다. 우린 모두 각자의 고향에서 인기있는 음식을 선호하는 것 같다.

모범정답 : People in different countries eat different foods such as tortillas, yak milk, and kimchee. Most people like to eat the foods they are accustomed to.

(17) 내가 사람의 방언과 천사의 말을 할지라도, 사랑이 없으면 소리나는 징이나 울리는 심벌즈 같다. 내가 예언의 재능이 있어서 모든 비밀과 모든 지식을 간파할 수 있고, 또한 산을 옮길 수 있는 믿음이 있더라도, 사랑이 없으면 소용이 없다. 내가 가진 모든 것을 가난한 자에게 주고 내 몸을 불사를지라도, 사랑이 없으면 아무 소득도 없다.

모범정답 : Love is above all. / Love conquers all.

(18) Death of an Innocent

I went to a party, Mom,
I remembered what you said.
You told me not to drink, Mom,
so I drank soda instead.

I really felt proud inside, Mom,
the way you said I would.
I didn't drink and drive, Mom,
even though the others said I should.

I know I did the right thing, Mom,
I know you are always right.
Now the party is finally ending, Mom,
as everyone is driving out of sight.

As I got into my car, Mom,
I knew I'd get home in one piece.
Because of the way you raised me,
so responsible and sweet.

I started to drive away, Mom,
but as I pulled out into the road,
the other car didn't see me, Mom,
and hit me like a load.

As I lay there on the pavement, Mom,
I hear the policeman say,
the other guy is drunk, Mom,
and now I'm the one who will pay.

I'm lying here dying, Mom.
I wish you'd get here soon.
How could this happen to me, Mom?
My life just burst like a balloon.

(18) 무고한 자의 죽음

파티에 갔어요, 엄마,
엄마 말씀을 기억했죠.
술 마시지 말라고 그러셨잖아요, 엄마,
그래서 난 대신 소다수를 마셨어요.

난 마음 속으로 뿌듯함을 느꼈어요, 엄마,
엄마 말씀대로 했으니까요.
난 술 마시고 운전하지 않았어요, 엄마,
비록 다른 사람들은 내가 그랬다고 말하지만.

난 내가 옳은 일을 했다는 걸 알아요, 엄마,
난 엄마가 항상 옳다는 걸 알아요.
이제 파티가 마침내 끝나가고 있어요, 엄마,
모두들 차를 타고 사라지고 있네요.

차에 탔을 때, 엄마,
난 내가 곧장 집에 도착하리란 걸 알았어요.
엄마가 날 그렇게 키우셨잖아요,
책임감 있고, 상냥하게.

난 차를 몰기 시작했어요, 엄마,
하지만 내가 길가로 움직이기 시작했을 때,
다른 차가 날 보지 못했어요, 엄마,
그리고 마치 짐짝처럼 날 치고 말았죠.

거기, 차도에 누워서, 엄마,
난 경찰의 말을 들어요,
상대방 남자애는 술에 취했어요, 엄마,
그리고 지금 그 대가를 치러야 하는 건 바로 나에요.

난 여기 누워서 죽어가고 있어요, 엄마.
엄마가 빨리 여기 오면 좋겠는데.
어떻게 나한테 이런 일이 일어날 수 있어요, 엄마?
내 인생은 이제 막 풍선처럼 부풀어올랐는데.

There is blood all around me, Mom,
and most of it is mine.
I hear the medic say, Mom,
I'll die in a short time.

I just wanted to tell you, Mom,
I swear I didn't drink.
It was the others, Mom.
The others didn't think.

He was probably at the same party as I.
The only difference is,
he drank and I will die.

Why do people drink, Mom?
It can ruin your whole life.
I'm feeling sharp pains now.
Pains just like a knife.

The guy who hit me is walking, Mom,
and I don't think it's fair.
I'm lying here dying
and all he can do is stare.

Tell my brother not to cry, Mom.
Tell Daddy to be brave.

(Source: Anonymous)

= _____

_____

_____

_____.

내 옆으로 온통 피가 흘러요, 엄마,
그 피는 대부분 내 피죠.
난 의사의 말을 들어요, 엄마,
내가 곧 죽게 되리라는.

난 그냥 말하고 싶어요, 엄마,
맹세코 난 술마시지 않았어요.
그건 걔들이었어요, 엄마.
걔들은 그렇게 생각하지 않았지만.

그 앤 아마도 나와 같은 파티에 있었을 거에요.
유일한 차이가 있다면,
그 앤 술을 마셨고, 난 죽을 거라는 거죠.

사람들은 왜 술을 마실까요, 엄마?
그건 인생 자체를 파괴할 수 있는데.
지금 예리한 통증이 느껴져요, 엄마.
칼날 같은 통증.

나를 친 애가 걸어가고 있어요, 엄마,
난 이게 공정하지 않다고 생각해요.
난 여기 누워서 죽어가고 있고
그가 할 수 있는 일이라곤 빤히 쳐다보는 것 뿐.

오빠한테 울지 말라고 전해주세요, 엄마.
아빠한테 용감하라고 전해주세요.

모범정답 : The innocent are sometimes victimized.

(19) Thought for today...

A basketball in my hands is worth about $19.
A basketball in Michael Jordan's hands is worth about $33 million.
It depends whose hands it's in.

A baseball in Mark McGwire's hands is worth $19 million.
It depends whose hands it's in.

A tennis racket is useless in my hands.
A tennis racket in Pete Sampras' hands is a Wimbeldon Championship.
It depends whose hands it's in.

A rod in my hands will keep away a wild animal.
A rod in Moses' hands will part the mighty sea.
It depends whose hands it's in.

A sling shot in my hands is a kid's toy.
A sling shot in David's hands is a mighty weapon.
It depends whose hands it's in.

Two fish and five loaves of bread in my hands is a couple of fish sandwiches.
Two fish and five loaves of bread in God's hands will feed thousands.
It depends whose hands it's in.

Nails in my hands might produce a birdhouse.
Nails in Jesus Christ's hands will produce salvation for the entire world.
It depends whose hands it's in.

 As you see now it depends whose hands it's in. So put your concerns, your worries, your fears, your hopes, your dreams, your families and your relationship in God's hands because it depends whose hands it's in.

(Source: Anonymous)

= _____

_____.

(19) 오늘의 단상...

내 손에 있는 농구공의 가치는 대략 19달러.
마이클 조단의 손에 있는 농구공의 가치는 대략 3,300만 달러.
그것은 오직 누구의 손에 있느냐에 달려 있네.

마크 맥과이어의 손에 있는 야구공의 가치는 대략 1,900만 달러.
그것은 오직 누구의 손에 있느냐에 달려 있네.

내 손에 있는 테니스 라켓은 쓸모가 없지만,
피트 샘프라스의 손에 있는 테니스 라켓은 윔블던 참피언.
그것은 오직 누구의 손에 있느냐에 달려 있네.

내 손의 지팡이는 야생 동물을 멀리 쫓겠지만,
모세의 손에 있는 지팡이는 강력한 바다를 가를 것이니,
그것은 오직 누구의 손에 있느냐에 달려 있네.

내 손의 고무총은 아이들 장난감.
다윗의 손에 있는 고무총은 강력한 무기.
그것은 오직 누구의 손에 있느냐에 달려 있네.

내 손의 물고기 두 마리와 빵 다섯 덩어리는 피시 샌드위치 두 개이겠지만,
신의 손에 있는 물고기 두 마리와 빵 다섯 덩어리는 수천 명을 먹일 것이니,
그것은 오직 누구의 손에 있느냐에 달려 있네.

내 손의 손톱은 새장을 만들어내겠지만,
예수 그리스도의 손에 있는 손톱은 전 세계의 구원을 낳으리니,
그것은 오직 누구의 손에 있느냐에 달려 있네.

방금 보았듯이, 그것은 오직 누구의 손에 있느냐에 달려 있네. 그러니 당신의 걱정, 당신의 근심, 당신의 두려움, 당신의 희망, 당신의 꿈, 당신의 가족과 당신이 맺고 있는 관계, 그 모든 것을 신의 손에 놓아라. 그것은 오직 누구의 손에 있느냐에 달려 있으므로.

모범정답 : Believe in Gods hands. Work hard with trust in Gods hands.

(20) One of the most attractive tourist spots in Bangkok, Thailand, is The Grand Palace. The Palace was built by King Rama I (1782 ~ 1809) who is the founder of the Chakri Dynasty.

  The king had the palace built in 1782 at the same time Bangkok was made the capital city of Siam. The Grand Palace is divided into three sections: (a) the Outer Palace; (b) the Middle Palace; and, (c) the Inner Palace. The Outer Palace has the Royal Temples and administrative offices. The Middle Palace includes several principal palace buildings, and the Inner Palace had the Royal Residences and dwellings for principal and minor queens.

  The Grand Palace is exceptionally beautiful that many tourists from all over the world visit this palace all year round.

= _____

_____

_____.

The Grand Place of Thailand

(20) 타이의 방콕에서 가장 매력적인 관광 명소 가운데 하나가 바로 그랜드 팰리스이다. 이 궁전은 차크리 왕조의 설립자인 라마 왕(1782-1809)에 의해 건조되었다.

왕은 1782년, 방콕을 샴의 수도로 만들면서 그와 동시에 궁전을 짓게 했다. 그랜드 팰리스는 (a) 외부 궁전, (b) 중간 궁전, (c) 내부 궁전 등 세 부분으로 나뉘어져 있다. 외부 궁전에는 왕실 신전과 행정 관청들이 있다. 중간 궁전에는 주요 궁전 건물 몇 채, 그리고 내부 궁전에는 왕의 침소와 왕비 및 후궁들의 처소가 있었다.

그랜드 팰리스는 무척 아름다워서 전세계의 많은 관광객들이 일년 내내 이 궁전을 찾고 있다.

모범정답 : The Grand Palace, a well-known tourist spot in Bangkok was built in 1782 by King Rama I, the founder of the Chakri Dynasty. The Palace includes three sections: the Outer Palace, the Middle Palace, the Inner Palace. The Palace always attracts countless tourists for its beauty.

5.5. Sentence Completeness

Two types of sentence errors are common: sentence fragments and run-on sentences. The first type of error, the sentence fragment, occurs when a part of sentence is written as if it were a complete sentence often with a capital letter and a period. The second type, the run-on sentence, occurs when two or more sentences are run together with only a comma, or no punctuation between them. Neither the fragment nor the run-on sentences are complete sentences.

5.5.1. Sentence Fragments

"Fragments" refer to carelessly split sentences that were used as if they were complete. These split pieces are just "fragments," not complete sentences. Read the following sentence fragments, and rewrite them into complete sentences.

Examples: (a) The plane ran out of gas. <u>And landed on an island</u>. (Fragmented)
= The plane ran out of gas and landed on an island.
(b) We were lined up at the door. <u>Waiting for the store to open</u>.
(Fragmented)
= _____.

(1) The game was won by Michael. The oldest player on our team.

= _____.

(2) We noticed a dark cloud. As we were rowing toward the remote island.

= _____.

(3) I was brought up by my aunt. Who gave me lots of love and care.

= _____.

(4) John received an urgent letter from his father. But neglected to answer it.

= _____.

(5) The children often went swimming, living near a lake.

= _____.

5.5. 문장의 완결성

문장에서 나타나는 실수 가운데 가장 일반적인 것으로 문장의 파편과 다음 행으로 이어지는 문장 등 두 가지 유형이 있다. 실수의 첫 번째 유형인 문장의 파편은 문장 일부가 종종 대문자 및 마침표와 함께 완결된 문장인 것처럼 쓰여질 때 나타난다. 두 번째 유형인 다음 행으로 이어지는 문장은 둘 이상의 문장이 단지 쉼표나, 심지어 구두점도 없이 서로 뒤섞일 때 나타난다. 두 경우 모두 완전한 문장은 아니다.

5.5.1. 문장의 파편

'문장의 파편' 이란 마치 완결된 것처럼 사용된 부주의하게 잘린 문장을 가리킨다. 이 잘린 조각들은 완전한 문장이 아니라 그저 '파편' 에 불과하다. 다음에 나오는 문장의 파편들을 읽고, 완전한 문장으로 바꿔라.

예] (a) 비행기는 가스가 바닥났다. 그리고 섬에 착륙했다.
  ➡ 비행기는 가스가 바닥나서 섬에 착륙했다.
  (b) 우리는 문 앞에 줄지어 서 있었다. 가게가 문 열기를 기다리면서.
  ➡ 우리는 가게가 열리기를 기다리면서 문 앞에 줄지어 서 있었다.

(1) 게임은 마이클 덕분에 승리했다. 우리 팀에서 가장 나이든 선수.
모범정답 : The game was won by Michael, the oldest player on our team.

(2) 우리는 어두운 구름을 주목했다. 우리가 외딴 섬을 향해 노를 젓고 있었을 때.
모범정답 : We noticed a dark cloud as we were rowing toward the remote island.

(3) 난 숙모에 의해 길러졌다. 내게 많은 사랑과 보살핌을 주신.
모범정답 : I was brought up by my aunt who gave me lots of love and care.

(4) 존은 아버지로부터 긴급한 편지를 받았다. 그러나 거기에 답장하는 것을 잊어버렸다.
모범정답 : John received an urgent letter from his father, but neglected to answer it.

(5) 아이들은 종종 수영하러 갔다. 호수 근처에 살고 있어서.
모범정답 : The children often went swimming since they lived near a lake.

(6) We spent three days at Cheju-Do. One of the well-known resorts in Korea.

= _____.

(7) The crocodile is a good swimmer. It is sometimes seen hundreds of miles from land.

= _____.

(8) After the flood the barn roof lying in the yard.

= _____.

(9) The earthquake occurs because of a fault. Which is a break in the crust of the earth.

= _____.

(10) Henrik Ibsen, a Norwegian playwright whose works include Peer Gynnt (1867) and A Doll's House (1879), was born in 1828. And died in 1906.

= _____.

5.5.2. Run-on Sentences

When a comma, (instead of a period, a semicolon, or a conjunction), is used between two complete sentences, the result is a run-on sentence. A comma does not have power to connect two sentences. There are four ways of correcting the error in the run-on sentences.

Examples: The lights dimmed, the audience quieted down. (Run-on sentence)

(1) The lights dimmed. The audience quieted down.
(2) Since the lights dimmed, the audience quieted down.
(3) The audience quieted down, for the lights dimmed.
(4) The audience quieted down; the lights dimmed.

(6) 우리는 제주도에서 사흘을 보냈다. 한국의 유명한 휴양지 가운데 하나.

모범정답 : We spent three days at Cheju-Do, one of the well-known resorts in Korea

(7) 악어는 훌륭한 수영선수이다. 그것은 때로 육지에서 수백 마일이나 떨어진 곳에서도 보인다.

모범정답 : The crocodile is a good swimmer since it is sometimes seen hundreds of miles from land

(8) 홍수가 지나간 뒤, 휑뎅그렁한 지붕이 마당에 누워있는.

모범정답 : After the flood, the barn roof lay in the yard.

(9) 지진은 결함 때문에 일어난다. 지구 표면에 나타나는 균열.

모범정답 : The earthquake occurs because of a fault, which is a break in the crust of the earth.

(10) <Peer Gynnt(1867)>와 〈인형의 집(1879)〉 등의 작품을 쓴 노르웨이의 극작가 헨릭 입센은 1828년에 태어났다. 그리고 1906년에 죽었다.

모범정답 : Henrik Ibsen, a Norwegian playwright whose works include Peer Gynnt and A Doll's House, was born in 1828, and died in 1906.

Henrik Ibsen

5.5.2. 다음 행으로 이어지는 문장

두 개의 완전한 문장 사이에 (마침표나 세미 콜론, 또는 접속사 대신) 쉼표가 사용될 때, 그 결과는 다음 행으로 이어지는 문장이 된다. 쉼표는 두 문장을 연결한 능력을 가지고 있지 않다. 다음 행으로 이어지는 문장의 실수를 교정하는 방법은 네 가지가 있다.

예] 불빛이 어두워졌다, 관객은 조용해졌다.

    (1) 불빛이 어두워졌다. 관객은 조용해졌다.
    (2) 불빛이 어두워지자, 관객은 조용해졌다.
    (3) 관객이 조용해졌다. 불빛이 어두워졌기 때문이다.
    (4) 관객이 조용해졌고, 불빛이 어두워졌다.

Read the following run-on sentences and correct them by inserting a period or using appropriate conjunction such as "therefore, and, but, or any other conjunctive adverbs (then, as a result, however, nevertheless, indeed, thus, etc.) as shown in the examples below.

Examples: (a) <u>The signature was illegible, none of us could read it.</u> (Run-on sentence) = The signature was illegible. None of us could read it.
(b) <u>I lit a match the wind blew it out at once.</u> (Run-on)
= I lit a match, but the wind blew it out at once.

(1) I began to speak, my nervousness disappeared.

= _____.

(2) The meeting was long, it lasted until midnight.

= _____.

(3) The line broke, therefore, the fish got away.

= _____.

(4) There were no other people around the park I spent my days hiking alone.

= _____.

(5) I did not know she had a baby, I had not spoken with her in years.

= _____.

(6) The English system of measurement is used in the United States, it is not widely used elsewhere.

= _____.

(7) Scientists need a uniform system of measurement, this system enables them to communicate easily with one another.

= _____.

다음 행으로 이어지는 다음 문장들을 읽고, 아래 예문과 같이, 마침표를 삽입하거나 "따라서, 그리고, 그러나, 또는 여타 접속 부사(그리고 나서 그 결과, 그런데, 그럼에도 불구하고, 실제로, 그리하여, 등)" 등의 적절한 접속사를 사용하여 교정하라.

예] (a) 서명은 판독하기 어려웠다, 우리 가운데 어느 누구도 그것을 읽을 수 없었다.

　→ 서명은 판독하기 어려웠다. 우리 가운데 어느 누구도 그것을 읽을 수 없었다.

　(b) 나는 성냥불을 켰다 바람이 그 즉시 그것을 꺼버렸다.

　→ 나는 성냥불을 켰지만, 바람이 그 즉시 꺼버렸다.

(1) 나는 말하기 시작했다, 나의 과도한 걱정은 사라졌다.

모범정답 : After I began to speak, my nervousness disappeared

(2) 모임은 길어졌다, 그것은 한밤중까지 계속되었다.

모범정답 : The meeting was long. It lasted until midnight

(3) 줄이 끊어졌다, 따라서, 물고기는 도망쳐버렸다.

모범정답 : The line broke. Therefore, the fish got away.

(4) 공원 주위에 아무도 없었다 나는 하루 종일 혼자 하이킹하면서 보냈다.

모범정답 : There were no other people around the park. I spent my days hiking alone.

(5) 나는 그녀에게 아기가 있다는 것을 몰랐다, 나는 몇 년 동안 그녀와 이야기해보지 않았다.

모범정답 : I didn't know she had a baby. I had not spoken with her in years.

(6) 영국식 도량법이 미국에서 사용되고 있다, 다른 곳에서는 그것이 널리 사용되지 않는다.

모범정답 : The English system of measurement is used in the United States, but it is not widely used elsewhere.

(7) 과학자들은 단일한 도량법을 필요로 한다, 이 체제는 그들이 서로 쉽게 의사소통 할 수 있게 해 준다.

모범정답 : Scientists need a uniform system of measurement. This system enables them to communicate easily with one another.

(8) The restaurant was crowded as we had no time to wait.

= _____ .

(9) If your car swerves when stopping, your brakes need adjusting.

= _____ .

(10) Fires do not just happen, they are usually caused by carelessness.

= _____ .

(11) If you try your best, no one can blame you.

= _____ .

(12) Food is scarce for wild animals in the winter you can help by feeding them.

= _____ .

(13) Peanuts were more than just food for George Washington Carver (1864 ~ 1943), in his laboratory he used them to make such things as ink and shampoo.

= _____ .

(14) Victoria Falls in southern Africa is named for Queen Victoria one of the world's most well-known queens.

= _____

_____ .

Victoria

(15) The heart of Amish country is Pennsylvania there you can see a variety of beautiful samples of their arts works.

= _____

_____ .

CHAPTER 5

(8) 그 레스토랑은 만원이었다 우리가 기다릴 시간이 없었을 때.

모범정답 : The restaurant was crowded, and we had no time to wait.

(9) 정지할 때 차가 빗나간다면, 브레이크는 조정할 필요가 있다.

모범정답 : If your car swerves when stopping, then your brakes need adjusting.

(10) 화재는 그냥 일어나는 것이 아니다, 보통 부주의에 의해 발생된다.

모범정답 : Fires do not just happen, instead they are usually caused by carelessness

(11) 최선을 다하려 한다면, 아무도 당신을 비난할 수 없다.

모범정답 : If you try your best, then no one can blame you.

(12) 야생동물들은 겨울에 음식이 부족하다. 당신은 먹이를 줌으로써 그들을 도울 수 있다.

모범정답 : Food is scarce for wild animals in the winter, but you can help by feeding them.

(13) 조지 워싱턴 카버(1864 -1943)에게는 땅콩이 단순한 음식 이상의 것이었다. 연구실에서 그는 그것으로 잉크와 샴푸 같은 것들을 만들었다.

모범정답 : Peanuts were more than just food for George Washington Carver (1864 ~ 1943). In his laboratory he used them to make such things as ink and shampoo.

George Washington Carver

(14) 남부 아프리카의 빅토리아 폭포는 세상에서 가장 유명한 여왕 가운데 한 명인 빅토리아 여왕의 이름을 따서 명명되었다.

모범정답 : Victoria Falls in southern Africa is named for Queen Victoria, one of the worlds most well-known queens.

Amish

(15) 암만파 신도들의 중심지는 펜실베이니아이다. 거기서 당신은 그들이 만든 다양한 예술 작품의 아름다운 견본을 볼 수 있다.

모범정답 : The heart of Amish country is Pennsylvania. There you can see a variety of beautiful samples of their arts works.

5.5.3. Parallel Structure

Parallelism is a rhetorical technique in which a writer emphasizes an equal weight/value of two or more ideas by expressing them in the same syntactical forms. This arrangement in parallel structure contributes clarity and effectiveness to writing. There are two elements which commonly require parallel arrangements: Coordinated Ideas and Correlative Constructions.

5.5.3.1. Coordinated Ideas

"Coordinated Ideas" refers to the same syntactical arrangement in which words, phrases, or clauses are paralleled with equal weight/value. This arrangement is joined by coordinate conjunctions such as "and, but, or, nor." Read the following parallel structures while paying a close attention to the underlined parts.

(1) Give me liberty, or give me death. (Coordinated ideas in two clauses) (Patrick Henry, 1736~1799)

(2) To err is human, to forgive divine. (Coordinated ideas in two noun phrases) (Alexander Pope, 1688~1744)

(3) ...government of the people, by the people, for the people shall not perish from the earth. (In three adjective/prepositional phrases). (Abraham Lincoln, 1821~1882)

(4) The love of liberty is the love of others. The love of power is the love of ourselves. (In four noun phrases) (William Hazlitt, 1778~1830)

(5) Let every nation know, whether it wishes us well or ill, that we shall pay any price, bear any burden, meet any hardship, support any friend, or oppose any foe to assure the survival and the success of liberty. (In five noun clauses) (John F. Kennedy, 1917~1963)

Read the following faulty parallel structures, and rewrite the sentence based on parallelism.

(1) I like receiving letters much better than to write them.

= _____ .

(2) Most of my classmates went swimming, sunbathing, and had a picnic.

= _____.

5.5.3. 병렬 구조

대구법이란 작가가 둘 또는 그 이상의 아이디어를 똑같은 구문으로 표현함으로써 거기에 동등한 무게/가치를 두는 수사학 기법이다. 이러한 병렬 구조 배열은 글의 명확성과 효과를 높이는데 기여한다. 병렬식 배열에 흔히 요구되는 두 가지 요소로서, 대등한 아이디어와 상관 구성이 있다.

5.5.3.1. 대등한 아이디어

'대등한 아이디어' 란 단어, 구, 또는 절이 동등한 무게/가치로 비교되는 똑같은 구문상의 배열을 가리킨다. 이러한 배열은 '그리고, 그러나, 또는, --도 아니다' 등과 같은 대등 접속사에 의해 연결된다. 밑줄 친 부분에 유의하면서 다음 병렬 구조를 읽어보아라.

(1) 내게 자유를 달라, 그게 아니면 내게 죽음을 달라.

(2) 잘못은 인간 상사요, 용서는 신의 일이다.

(3) …국민의, 국민에 의한, 국민을 위한 정부는 지구상에서 멸망하지 않을 것입니다.

(4) 자유에 대한 사랑은 타인에 대한 사랑이요.
권력에 대한 사랑은 우리 자신에 대한 사랑이요.

(5) 우리가 잘 되기를 바라는 나라든 안되기를 바라는 나라든, 그 모든 나라에게 알려줍시다. 우리는 자유의 생존과 성공을 보장하기 위해 어떤 대가라도 치를 것이며, 어떤 짐이라도 질 것이고, 어떤 친구라도 도울 것이며, 또한 어떤 적이라도 대항할 것입니다.

다음에 나오는 불완전한 병렬 구조를 읽고, 대구법에 근거하여 문장을 수정하라.

(1) 나는 편지 쓰는 것보다 편지 받는 것을 훨씬 더 좋아한다.
모범정답 : I like receiving letters much better than writing them.

(2) 우리 반 친구 대부분은 수영과 일광욕, 그리고 들놀이에 갔다.
모범정답 : Most of my classmates went swimming, sunbathing, and picnicking

(3) Counseling will help you understand the problem better and to solve it more quickly.

= _____ .

(4) I decided that I would rather be a diplomat than being a pharmacist.

= _____ .

(5) That you learn responsibility is as important as doing your schoolwork.

= _____ .

(6) Candidates for a scholarship may qualify either by writing an English essay or by pass a mathematics test.

=

_____ .

(7) Sleeping sickness is a terrible disease which runs a slow course and ending in coma and death.

= _____ .

(8) A good friend should be loyal, sensitive, and showing consideration.

= _____ .

(9) The mountain villages in Japan stay open throughout the year offering beautiful views.

= _____ .

(10) And I made a rural pen,
　　　And I stain'ed the water clear,
　　　And I wrote my songs happily
　　　Every child may joy to hear. (William Blake, 1757~1827)

= _____

_____ .

(3) 카운슬링은 당신이 문제를 더 잘 이해하고 보다 빨리 풀 수 있게 하는데 도움이 될 것이다.

모범정답 : Counseling will help you understand the problem better and solve it more quickly.

(4) 나는 약사보다는 외교관이 되는 게 낫겠다고 결심했다.

모범정답 : I decided that I would rather be a diplomat than be a pharmacist

(5) 책임감을 배우는 것은 숙제를 하는 것만큼이나 중요하다.

모범정답 : That you learn responsibility is as important as that you do your schoolwork.

(6) 장학금을 받으려는 학생은 영어 에세이를 쓰거나 수학 시험에 통과하거나 하는 자격을 갖춰야 할 것이다.

모범정답 : Candidates for a scholarship may qualify either by writing an English essay or by passing a mathematics test.

(7) 수면병은 천천히 진행되다가 혼수 상태와 죽음으로 끝나는 끔찍한 질병이다.

모범정답 : Sleeping sickness is a terrible disease which runs a slow course and ends in coma and death.

(8) 좋은 친구란 충실하고, 민감하며, 생각이 깊어야 한다.

모범정답 : A good friend should be loyal, sensitive, and considerate

(9) 일본의 산골 마을들은 일년 내내 개방되어 있으며, 아름다운 경치를 자랑한다.

모범정답 : The mountain villages in Japan stay open throughout the year and offer beautiful views

(10) 그리고 나는 촌스런 펜을 만들었고, 그리고 나는 물을 온전히 물들였으며, 그리고 나는 행복하게 나의 노래를 썼나니, 모든 아이들이 듣고 기뻐하리라.

William Blake

모범정답 : And I made a rural pen,

And I stained the water clear,

And I wrote my happy songs

Every child may joy to hear.

(William Blake, 1757~1827)

5.5.3.2. Correlative Constructions

"Correlative constructions" refer to parallel structures when describing two things that always exist or happen together for an effect on one another. These structures are usually formed with correlative conjunctions such as "both ~ and; either ~ or; neither ~ nor; not only ~ but (also)."

Read the following faulty and the revised correlative constructions with a close attention to the underlined parts.

(1) At the gate they tried both <u>persuasion</u> and <u>to force</u> their way in. (Faulty)
= At the gate they tried <u>both persuasion and force</u>. (Revised)

(2) The new secretary proved herself to be <u>not only capable but also a lady who could be trusted</u>. (Faulty)
= The new secretary proved herself to be <u>not only capable but trustworthy</u>. (Revised).

(3) In Switzerland people speak <u>not only French, Italian,</u> <u>but also German is spoken</u>.(Faulty)
= In Switzerland people speak <u>not only French, Italian, but German</u>. (Revised)

Revise the following faulty correlative parallel structures.

(1) The poem has neither clear image nor it rhymes in a natural way.

= _____.

(2) John must have spoken either quickly or in a nervous manner throughout his speech.

= _____.

(3) To escape detection from the police, the secret agent both changed his name and his address.

= _____.

(4) My mother was not only friendly to my friends but she also helped them.

= _____.

5.5.3.2. 상관 구성

'상관 구성'이란 서로에 대한 영향 때문에 항상 함께 존재하거나 일어나는 두 가지 것들을 묘사할 때의 병렬 구조를 가리킨다. 이러한 구조는 보통 "A와 B 둘다; A 또는 B; A도 B도 아니다; A뿐 아니라 B도" 등의 상관 접속사와 함께 만들어진다.

밑줄 친 부분에 유의하면서 다음 불완전한 상관 구성과 개정된 상관 구성을 읽어 보아라.

(1) 문 앞에서 그들은 설득과 강압을 둘 다 시도했다.

(2) 새로운 비서는 자신이 유능할 뿐 아니라 신뢰할 수 있는 사람임을 입증했다.

(3) 스위스 사람들은 불어와 이탈리아어뿐 아니라 독일어로도 말한다.

다음의 불완전한 상관 병렬 구조를 알맞게 고쳐라.

(1) 그 시는 뚜렷한 이미지도, 자연스런 운율도 없다.

모범정답 : The poem has neither clear image nor natural rhyme.

(2) 존은 연설 내내 빠르게 또는 신경질적으로 말했음에 틀림없다.

모범정답 : John must have spoken either quickly or nervously throughout his speech.

(3) 경찰의 추적을 피하기 위해, 비밀 요원은 이름과 주소 모두 바꿨다.

모범정답 : To escape detection from the police, the secret agent changed both his name and his address.

(4) 어머니는 내 친구들에게 다정할 뿐 아니라 도움이 되기까지 한다.

모범정답 : My mother was not only friendly to my friends but also helpful.

(5) She not only brought home wild guys but also some girls who talked too much.

= _____.

(6) We neither accepted his hospitality nor his bribe.

= _____.

(7) The two leaders could neither agree on the time nor the place for their next meeting.

= _____.

(8) The team both felt the satisfaction of victory and the disappointing defeat.

= _____.

(9) President Kennedy not only supported the creation of the Peace Corps but also the space program to restore America's pride.

= _____.

(10) American artist, Georgia O'Keefe (1887 ~ 1986) is best known not only for her vivid close-ups of individual flowers but also for her desert landscapes.

= _____.

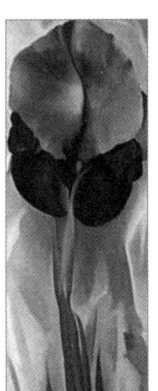

O'keefe's masterpieces (Left; Iris(1929). Right; White Trumpet Flower(1932))

(5) 그녀는 난폭한 남자들뿐 아니라 수다스런 여자들까지 집으로 데려왔다.

모범정답 : She brought home not only wild guys but also talkative girls.

(6) 우리는 그의 환대도 뇌물도 받지 않았다.

모범정답 : We accepted neither his hospitality nor his bribe.

(7) 두 정상은 다음 번 모임의 시간도 장소도 합의할 수 없었다.

모범정답 : The two leaders could agree on neither the time nor the place for their next meeting.

(8) 그 팀은 승리의 만족과 패배의 절망을 둘 다 느꼈다.

모범정답 : The team felt both the satisfaction of victory and the disappointment of defeat.

(9) 케네디 대통령은 평화 봉사단의 창설뿐 아니라 미국의 자부심을 회복시킬 우주 계획도 지지했다.

모범정답 : President Kennedy supported not only the creation of the Peace Corps but also the restoration of Americas pride in the space program.

(10) 미국의 예술가 조지아 오키프는 개별 꽃들의 생생한 클로즈업뿐 아니라 사막 풍경화로도 잘 알려져 있다.

모범정답 : American artist, Georgia O'Keefe (1887~1986) is best known for not only her vivid individual flower close-ups but also her desert landscapes.

Georgia O'keefe

5.6. Replacing Faulty Conjunctions

"Faulty conjunctions" refers to the conjunctions that are used inappropriately without clearly expressing the relationship between two ideas. These faulty conjunctions make your writing inconsistent and ineffective. Common coordinate conjunctions that deal with two ideas equally as independent clauses are as follows:

and; or; but; instead; however; so; for; therefore; yet; nor.

Common correlative conjunctions that connect words or groups of words with equal weight/value are:

both ~ and; not only ~ but (also); whether ~ or; either ~ or; neither ~ nor.

Common subordinate conjunctions that do not deal with two ideas equally, but one clause as a dependent clause are:

after; although; as; as well as; as if; as though; before; because; if; in order that; provided; how; since; so that; than; unless; until; when whenever; whereas; where; wherever; while; why.

Read the following base sentence that includes a faulty conjunction. Based on the context of the sentence, select the best conjunction among the choices provided in the parenthesis.

(1) Give me liberty, ((a) and; (b) therefore; (c) or; (d) but; (e) if) give me death.

(2) I think; ((a) because; (b) therefore; (c) or; (d) but; (e) if), I am. (Rene Descartes, 1596 ~ 1650)

(3) The plane took off, ((a) although; (b) therefore; (c) or; (d) but; (e) if) the control tower had not given permission.

(4) The sea turtle, heavy with eggs, lumbered slowly through the shallows, ((a) although; (b) therefore; (c) or; (d) but; (e) as) the scientists looked on.

5.6. 잘못된 접속사 바꾸기

'잘못된 접속사'란 두 아이디어 사이의 관계를 명확히 표현하지 못한 채 부적절하게 사용된 접속사를 가리킨다. 이러한 그릇된 접속사는 글을 모순되고 비효율적으로 만든다. 두 아이디어를 동등하게 독립된 절로 다루는 일반적인 대등 접속사는 다음과 같다.

그리고 ; 또는 ; 그러나 ; 대신 ; 그런데 ; 그래서 ; 왜냐하면 ; 그러므로 ; 그럼에도 불구하고 ; ～도 않다

동등한 무게/가치를 가진 단어나 단어 집단을 연결하는 일반적인 상관 접속사는 다음과 같다.

A와 B 둘 다 ; A뿐만 아니라 B도 ; A든 B든 ; A 또는 B; A도 B도 아니다

두 아이디어를 동등하게 다루는 것이 아니라 한 절을 독립절로서 다루는 일반적인 종속 접속사는 다음과 같다.

～후에 ; 비록 ～일지라도 ; ～처럼 ; B뿐만 아니라 A도 ; 마치 ～인 것처럼 ; ～전에 ; 만일 ～라면 ; ～하기 위해서 ; 만일 ～이라면 ; 이렇게 해서 ; ～이래로 ; ～하기 위해서 ; ～보다 ; 만일 ～하지 않으면 ; ～할 때까지 ; ～할 때, ～할 때마다 ; 반면 ; ～하는 곳에 ; ～하는 곳은 어디든지 ; ～하는 동안 ; ～한 이유

다음의 기본 문장에는 잘못된 접속사가 들어 있다. 문장의 문맥에 근거하여 괄호 안에 주어진 보기들 가운데 가장 적합한 접속사를 골라라.

(1) 내게 자유를 달라, 그게 아니면 죽음을 달라. 정답 (c)

(2) 나는 생각한다; 그러므로 나는 존재한다. 정답 (b)

(3) 관제탑에서 허가를 하지 않았음에도 불구하고, 비행기가 이륙했다. 정답 (a)

(4) 바다거북은 과학자들이 관찰하는 가운데 알을 실은 채 육중한 몸을 이끌고 얕은 물가를 천천히 기어갔다. 정답 (e)

(5) The rain stopped, ((a) although; (b) because; (c) or; (d) but; (e) so) we played soccer.

(6) The oil works kept drilling, ((a) since; (b) therefore; (c) or; (d) but; (e) if) they never did strike oil.

(7) At camp we get up ((a) until; (b) if; (c) when; (d) unless; (e) during) the sun rises.

(8) We arrived at the theater very late; ((a) however; (b) but; (c) while; (d) instead; (e) therefore) we couldn't find seats.

(9) There is no rule ((a) but; (b) that; (c) because; (d) which; (e) yet) has no exceptions.

(10) ((a) But; (b) Although; (c) And; (d) Since; (e) After) Dr. Kwak was the least renowned member of the executive team, he contributed the most sales ideas.

(11) The work is good, ((a) despite; (b) that; (c) because; (d) which; (e) yet) it could be better.

(12) We shall go to protest, ((a) unless; (b) that; (c) because; (d) which; (e) yet) it rains.

(13) The squirrel bit open the acorn easily, ((a) unless; (b) that; (c) because; (d) which; (e) yet) its teeth are very sharp.

(14) Dr. Rhee was the only candidate for the Presidential Election; ((a) however; (b) but; (c) while; (d) instead; (e) therefore) he was elected.

(15) Oh my sweetheart! Come to me at once; ((a) unless; (b) that; (c) because; (d) otherwise;(e) yet) you will be too late.

(16) That bastard, Mr. Lee, will do anything, ((a) unless; (b) provided; (c) that; (d) otherwise; (e) yet) he is well paid.

(5) 비가 그쳤다. 그래서 우리는 축구를 했다. 정답 (e)

(6) 유전 탐사기가 계속해서 구멍을 뚫었지만, 석유를 뽑아내지는 못했다. 정답 (d)

(7) 캠프에서 우리는 해가 뜰 때 일어난다. 정답 (c)

(8) 우리는 극장에 매우 늦게 도착했다. 그래서 자리를 찾을 수 없었다. 정답 (e)

(9) 예외 없는 규칙은 없다. 정답 (a)

(10) 곽 박사는 임원들 가운데 지명도는 가장 떨어졌지만, 세일즈 아이디어는 대부분 그가 낸 것이었다. 정답 (b)

(11) 일은 훌륭하다. 하지만 더 나아질 수도 있을 텐데. 정답 (e)

(12) 비가 오지 않으면, 우리는 항의하러 갈 것이다. 정답 (a)

(13) 다람쥐는 도토리를 쉽사리 깨문다. 이가 매우 날카롭다. 정답 (b)

(14) 이 박사는 유일한 대선 후보였다. 따라서 그가 선출되었다. 정답 (e)

(15) 오, 내 사랑! 당장 내게 오라. 그렇지 않으면 너무 늦으리. 정답 (d)

(16) 이씨, 그 녀석은 돈만 많이 주면 무슨 일이든 할 것이다. 정답 (b)

(17) Sherlock Holmes listened quietly ((a) and; (b) but; (c) since; (d) while; (e) provided) Dr. Watson explained his story.

(18) Seeds were removed from cotton balls by hand ((a) and; (b) but; (c) since; (d) while;(e) until) Eli Whitney (1765 ~ 1825) invented the cotton gin.

Eli Whitney

(19) Jim behaved ((a) and; (b) but; (c) since; (d) while; (e) as if) he were extremely angry.

(20) Air goes downward ((a) wherever; (b) however; (c) whereas; (d) so that; (e) until) the temperature is cold.

(21) I used to think that money was incredibly important, ((a) whereas; (b) because; (c) as if; (d) while; (e) until) I look at it now in quite a different way.

(22) Everything around the President was blown to pieces, ((a) so; (b) yet; (c) as if; (d) how; (e) whenever) he escaped without a scratch.

(23) ((a) While; (b) When; (c) During; (d) As; (e) Although) Alfred Hitchcock, the well-known director, died in 1980, people mourned the loss of this master of suspense.

(24) Emily Dickinson (1830~1886) wrote more than a thousand verses, ((a) and; (b) but; (c) because; (d) since; (e) or) only six of them were published in her lifetime.

(25) Emily Dickinson was not a person who wanted to see the world, ((a) but; (b) instead;(c) and; (d) while; (e) because) she lived her whole life in her hometown, Amherst, Massachusetts.

(17) 셜록 홈즈는 왓슨 박사가 자기 이야기를 늘어놓는 동안 조용히 듣고만 있었다. 정답 (d)

(18) 엘리 휘트니(1765-1825)가 조면기를 발명할 때까지, 목화에서 손으로 씨를 빼야 했다. 정답 (e)

(19) 짐은 자신이 마치 극도로 화난 것처럼 행동했다. 정답 (e)

(20) 공기는 기온이 차가운 곳에서는 어디서나 아래로 내려간다. 정답 (a)

(21) 나는 돈이 매우 중요하다고 생각했으나, 지금은 전혀 다르게 생각한다. 정답 (a)

(22) 대통령 주위의 모든 것들이 박살났지만, 그는 생채기 하나 없이 탈출했다. 정답 (b)

(23) 1980년, 유명한 감독 알프레드 히치콕이 사망했을 때, 사람들은 이 서스펜스 거장의 죽음을 애도했다. 정답 (b)

Alfred Hitchcock

(24) 에밀리 디킨슨(1830-1886)은 수천 편의 시를 썼지만, 살아 생전에는 오직 여섯 편만이 출판되었다. 정답 (b)

(25) 에밀리 디킨슨은 세상을 보고 싶어하지 않았고, 대신 고향인 매사추세츠주 암허스트에서 평생 살았다. 정답 (b)

Emily Dickinson

5.7. Avoiding Fallacies

"Fallacies" refers to a statement drawn from an erroneous or invalid inference. Errors in reasoning or deliberately misleading arguments can make you irresponsible writers. Responsible writers avoid using these fallacies, whereas irresponsible writers often use them for immediate political or commercial gains. They attempt to support their claims or conclusions based on these fallacies, which seriously damages not only the fundamental value of democracy, but also the rights and reputation of individuals.

Some fallacies violate the formal rules of logic; others function by clouding the issues; still others rely on faulty definitions. These fallacies often sound plausible if you do not know how to detect them. Learning to recognize some common fallacies enables you to construct better and effective writing. You as responsible writers should avoid using these false or invalid claims while creating an art of writing for effective and logical purposes. Common fallacies such as (1) Appeal to Ignorance; (2) Attacking the Person; (3) Bandwagon; (4) Circular Reasoning; (5) False Analogy; (6) False Dichotomy; (7) Overgeneralization; (8) Post hoc Fallacy; (9) Prestige Suggestion; and, (10) Stereotyping, are introduced here so as to help you be more responsible and effective writers.

5.7.1. Appeal to Ignorance

This fallacy assumes and concludes that something cannot be or must not be because we have neither evidence of it nor other explanation of it.

> Examples: (a) There cannot be life in other galaxies because astronomers have found no evidence of it.
>
> (b) We must have been born with an innate inclination to process language. No other explanation accounts for the rapid acquisition of language.

5.7. 오류 피하기

'오류'란 잘못되거나 가치 없는 추론에서 도출된 진술을 가리킨다. 추리의 실수나 의도적으로 그릇된 인상을 주는 주장은 당신을 무책임한 작가로 만들 수 있다. 책임 있는 작가는 이러한 오류의 사용을 피하는 반면, 무책임한 작가는 즉각적인 정치적 또는 상업적 이익을 위해 종종 그것을 사용한다. 그들은 이러한 오류에 근거하여 자신들의 주장이나 결론을 뒷받침하고자 하지만, 그것은 민주주의의 기본 가치뿐 아니라 개인의 권리와 명성에도 심각한 손상을 끼친다.

일부 오류는 형식 논리상의 원칙에 위배되고, 다른 일부는 논점을 애매하게 하는 기능을 한다. 또 다른 일부는 잘못된 정의에서 나오기도 한다. 이러한 오류들은 그 오류를 간파하지 못할 때면 그럴 듯하게 들리기도 한다. 일반적인 오류 식별법을 배우게 되면, 더 멋있고 효과적인 글을 쓸 수 있을 것이다. 책임 있는 작가는 이러한 잘못된 또는 무가치한 주장을 피하고 효과적이고 논리적인 글쓰기 기법을 창조해야 한다. 당신이 좀더 책임 있고 효과적인 작가로 성장하는데 반드시 피해야 할 몇 가지 오류로는 **(1) 무지에의 호소, (2) 인신 공격, (3) 시류에 편승하기, (4) 순환 논법, (5) 잘못된 유추, (6) 잘못된 이분법, (7) 지나친 일반화, (8) 포스트 학 팰러시(전후관계와 인과관계를 혼동하는 오류), (9) 세력 암시, (10) 정형화** 등이 있다.

5.7.1. 무지에의 호소

이 오류는 증거도 없고 여타의 설명도 찾을 수 없으므로 어떤 것이 존재할 수도, 존재해서도 안된다고 추정하고 결론짓는 것이다.

예 (a) 다른 은하계에는 생명체가 있을 리 없다. 천문학자들이 그에 대한 증거를 전혀 발견하지 못했기 때문이다.

(b) 우리는 언어를 진행시키는 타고난 기호를 가지고 태어났음에 틀림이 없다. 급속한 언어 습득의 원인을 밝혀주는 설명이 전혀 없기 때문이다.

5.7.2. Attacking the Person

Instead of discussing opponent's points of view, or providing the reasons and evidence given to support the opposing views, you attack the opponent's character or situation. This type of illogical argument can be often detected during political campaigns when candidates attack their opponents instead of facing the issues.

(a) People who oppose Dr. Rhee and his strong leadership are communists.
(b) Those who do not work hard for our party and fatherland without using "comrade" as a proper form of address are counter-revolutionists.

5.7.3. Bandwagon

"Bandwagon" attempts to persuade you with appeals that you should take some action because everyone is doing it.

(a) Don't be the last person to buy this book for writing skills.
   More than 99% of your school students have bought this book.
(b) All the juniors of this college go to Hawaii for the spring vacation.
   Why don't you go with them?

5.7.4. Circular Reasoning

This fallacy is to attempt to prove or support your opinion without distinct reasons.

(a) I hate Ms Kim's English class because I am never happy in there.
(b) Mr. Yoo is the best English teacher at my school. In character, experience, and intellectual ability, he is superior to any other English teachers.

5.7.2. 인신 공격

상대방의 관점 또는 그것을 뒷받침하는데 사용된 이유와 증거에 대해 논의하는 대신, 상대방의 성격이나 상황을 공격하는 것을 말한다. 이런 유형의 비논리적 주장은 후보자들이 논쟁점을 직시하는 대신 상대방을 공격하는 선거 유세 기간 동안 종종 감지될 수 있다.

(a) 이 박사 및 그의 강력한 지도력에 반대하는 사람은 공산주의자다.

(b) '동지'라는 호칭도 쓰지 않고 우리 당과 조국을 위해 열심히 일하지 않는 사람들은 반혁명 분자이다.

5.7.3. 시류에 편승하기

'시류에 편승하기'란 모두가 그렇게 하고 있으니 당신도 일련의 조치를 취하라는 말로 당신을 설득하려는 것을 말한다.

(a) 이 작문 책을 마지막으로 사는 사람이 되지 않기를.

여러분이 다니는 학교 학생들 중에 99% 이상이 이 책을 샀으므로.

(b) 이 대학 3학년 학생들은 봄방학 때 모두 하와이로 갑니다.

당신도 함께 가는 게 어때요?

5.7.4. 순환논법

이 오류는 명확한 이유 없이 자신의 견해를 증명하거나 뒷받침하려는 것을 말한다.

(a) 나는 김 선생님의 영어 수업을 증오한다. 그 시간에는 전혀 행복하지 않기 때문이다.

(b) 유 선생님은 우리 학교에서 가장 뛰어난 영어 선생님이다. 성격과 경험, 지적 수준 면에서 그는 다른 어떤 영어 선생님보다 더 우수하다.

5.7.5. False Analogy

This fallacy occurs when an essential likeness is asserted in the face of significant dissimilarities.

(a) America has no right to complain about the human rights in Tibet
in view of its own suppressions of American Indians.
(b) Like the manager of a wild animal circus, the principal of an American high
school is engaged in the business of training students.

5.7.6. False Dichotomy

This fallacy assumes that there are just two possibilities while ignoring all other possibilities.

(a) If I don't get accepted at Seoul National University, I will never be able to attend college.
(b) To reunify Korea, we must either negotiate with Mr. Jeongil Kim or invade North Korea.

5.7.7. Overgeneralization

This fallacy bases a conclusion draw from insufficient evidence. A generalization should be based on a great deal of evidence or on many observations, not just one or two experiences.

(a) Mr. Neill went to Seoul on business. The hotel he stayed in was very expensive.
When he returned, he said, "All hotels in Seoul are unbelievably expensive."
(b) One of the American tourists got pickpocketed in a crowded bus in Bangkok.
"All buses in Bangkok are very crowded so as to provide a haven for pickpockets."

Note : To avoid making overgeneralization, it is advised to use "qualifying words" instead of "absolute words."

Absolute Words	Qualifying Words
All	Most
Everyone	Many
Nobody	Few
Never	Rarely

5.7.5. 그릇된 유추

이 오류는 중요한 차이점을 마주하고 있으면서도 본질적인 유사점이 주장될 때 나타난다.

(a) 미국은 미국 인디언들에 대한 억압을 고려할 때, 티벳의 인권에 대해 말할 자격이 없다.
(b) 야생 동물 서커스단의 매니저처럼, 미국 고등학교의 교장은 학생들을 훈련시키는 일을 담당하고 있다.

5.7.6. 잘못된 이분법

이 오류는 다른 모든 가능성을 무시하고 오직 두 가지 가능성만 있다고 가정하는 것을 말한다.

(a) 서울 대학에 입학하지 못한다면, 나는 결코 대학에 입학 할 수 없을 것이다.
(b) 한국을 통일하기 위해서는 김정일과 협상을 벌이든 북한을 침략하든 둘 중의 하나를 선택해야 한다.

5.7.7. 지나친 일반화

이 오류는 충분치 않은 증거에서 도출된 결론에 근거를 두고 있다. 일반화란 한두 가지 경험이 아니라 상당량의 증거 또는 수많은 관찰에 근거해야 한다.

(a) 닐 씨는 사업차 서울에 갔다. 그가 머물렀던 호텔은 매우 비쌌다. 고향으로 돌아온 뒤, 그는 "서울의 호텔은 하나같이 엄청나게 비싸다"고 말했다.
(b) 미국인 관광객 한 명이 방콕의 만원 버스에서 소매치기를 당했다. "방콕의 버스들은 소매치기들에게 피난처를 제공하기 위해 하나같이 사람들로 붐빈다."

참고 : 지나친 일반화를 피하기 위해서는 '절대적인 단어' 대신 '제한적 단어'를 사용하는 것이 좋다.
절대적 단어 : 모든, 모두, 아무도 ~않다, 결코 ~않다.
제한적 단어 : 대부분, 많은, 거의 없는, 좀처럼 ~않는.

5.7.8. Post hoc Fallacy

This fallacy assumes that merely because one event precedes another, it must be its cause.

(a) I had a severe cold. One day I had a bowl of very hot and spicy bean sprout soup with sojoo. Several hours later, the cold was gone. A bowl of hot and spicy bean sprout soup with a shot of sojoo is the best treatment for colds.

(b) The production of nuclear plants in this country has slowed considerably since the protests at Seabrook, New Hampshire. Those protesters were really effective.

5.7.9. Prestige Suggestion

This fallacy attempts to seek the validity of a claim or conclusion solely on the basis of statement or testimony from a prestige source.

(a) We cannot open the North Korean society by economic aid alone.
The President said that in his speech.

(b) We can cure all sorts of terminal diseases such as cancer and HIV within five years.
Dr. Jeong, Chief Executive Officer at the Korean Cancer Center, affirmed that.

5.7.10. Stereotyping

Stereotyping is an assumption or belief that all members of a particular group show certain characteristics or qualities just because they are members of the group. This type of fallacy often leads to prejudice.

(a) All graduates of Harvard University are pedantic.

(b) I love to rent Bruce Lee movies. All Chinese men must be kung fu experts.

5.7.8. 포스트 학 팰러시

이 오류는 A라는 사건이 B라는 사건에 선행한다는 이유만으로 A는 B의 원인이라고 추정하는 것을 말한다.

(a) 나는 심한 감기에 걸렸다. 어느 날 나는 소주와 함께 아주 맵고 짜릿한 콩나물국을 한 사발 먹었다. 몇 시간 뒤, 감기는 사라졌다. 감기 치료에는 소주 한 잔에 맵고 짜릿한 콩나물국 한 사발이 제일 좋다.

(b) 이 나라 원자력 발전소의 생산량이 뉴햄프셔주 씨브룩에서의 항의 이후 눈에 띄게 떨어졌다. 항의자들은 정말 인상적이었다.

5.7.9. 세력 암시

이 오류는 권위 있는 기관의 진술이나 증언 하나에 근거하여 어떤 주장이나 결론의 유효성을 얻고자 하는 것을 말한다.

(a) 경제 원조만으로는 북한 사회의 문을 열 수 없다. 대통령은 연설에서 그렇게 말했다.

(b) 우리는 5년 이내에 암이나 AIDS와 같은 치명적 질병들을 모두 치료할 수 있다. 한국 암센터 병원장인 정박사가 그렇게 단언했다.

5.7.10. 정형화

정형화란 특정 그룹의 모든 구성원들이 단지 자신들이 그 그룹 구성원이라는 이유만으로 일정한 특성이나 성격을 보여준다는 가정 또는 믿음이다. 이런 유형의 오류는 종종 편견으로 이어진다.

(a) 하버드대 졸업생들은 모두 현학적이다.

(b) 나는 브루스 리의 영화들을 자주 빌려다 본다. 중국인들은 모두 쿵푸 전문가들임에 틀림이 없다.

Now, identify the fallacies imbedded in the following sentences/passages by selecting its name from the choices provided in the parenthesis.

(1) All politicians are dishonest and manipulative.

    (a) False Dichotomy   (b) Overgeneralization   (c) Post hoc Fallacy
    (d) Prestige Suggestion   (e) Stereotyping

(2) One of my teenage sons does not study hard. Instead he likes to party and hang out with his undisciplined friends. Teenagers are irresponsible revelers.

    (a) False Dichotomy   (b) Overgeneralization   (c) Post hoc Fallacy
    (d) Prestige Suggestion   (e) Stereotyping

(3) Since everyone is going to see the movie, <u>Pearl Harbor</u>, it must be very exciting.

    (a) Appeal to Ignorance   (b) Attacking the Person (c) Bandwagon
    (d) Circular Reasoning   (e) False Analogy

(4) Gentlemen! We don't know what will happen to us on our tomorrow night's bombing mission. Tonight, let's drink like fish and be drunk like skunks.

    (a) Appeal to Ignorance   (b) Attacking the Person (c) Bandwagon
    (d) Circular Reasoning   (e) False Analogy

(5) Tipping is like giving a handout to a beggar.

    (a) Appeal to Ignorance   (b) Attacking the Person (c) Bandwagon
    (d) Circular Reasoning   (e) False Analogy

(6) If we don't reelect Dr. Rhee, our country will be invaded again by the communists.

    (a) False Dichotomy   (b) Overgeneralization   (c) Post hoc Fallacy
    (d) Prestige Suggestion   (e) Stereotyping

(7) The North Koreans have no sense of humor because they live in a closed society.

    (a) False Dichotomy   (b) Overgeneralization   (c) Post hoc Fallacy
    (d) Prestige Suggestion   (e) Stereotyping

자, 이제 다음 문장/구절에 들어 있는 오류를 밝히고, 괄호 안의 보기들 가운데 그 유형을 골라라.

(1) 모든 정치가들은 부정직하고 속임수에 능숙하다. 정답 (e)

(2) 십대인 내 아들 가운데 한 명은 열심히 공부하지 않는다. 대신 그는 파티에 가거나 규율이 없는 친구들과 놀러나가는 걸 좋아한다. 십대들은 무책임한 난봉꾼이다. 정답 (b)

(3) 모두가 〈진주만〉이란 영화를 보러 가는 것으로 보아, 그 영화는 무척 흥미진진한 게 분명하다. 정답 (c)

The movie, Pearl Harbor

(4) 여러분! 내일 밤의 폭격 임무 중 우리에게 무슨 일이 일어날지 아무도 모릅니다. 오늘밤, 진탕 마시고 맘껏 취해봅시다. 정답 (a)

(5) 팁이란 거지에게 동냥을 주는 것과 같다. 정답 (e)

(6) 이 박사를 재당선시키지 않는다면, 우리나라는 또다시 공산주의자들의 침공을 받게 될 것입니다. 정답 (a)

(7) 북한 사람들은 폐쇄 사회에 살기 때문에 유머 감각이 없다. 정답 (e)

(8) If the budget for the défense program isn't increased, Korea will be seriously risking her national security.

    (a) False Dichotomy   (b) Overgeneralization   (c) Post hoc Fallacy
    (d) Prestige Suggestion   (e) Stereotyping

(9) Sir, he got a doctoral degree from Harvard. He should be one of the cabinet members.

    (a) False Dichotomy   (b) Overgeneralization   (c) Post hoc Fallacy
    (d) Prestige Suggestion   (e) Stereotyping

(10) Television programs focus on violence, crime, and abnormality.

    (a) False Dichotomy   (b) Overgeneralization   (c) Post hoc Fallacy
    (d) Prestige Suggestion   (e) Stereotyping

(11) Everyone on the team wears high-tops. It's the only way to go.

    (a) Appeal to Ignorance   (b) Attacking the Person (c) Bandwagon
    (d) Circular Reasoning   (e) False Analogy

(12) Life is like a play. People are not serious for their commitments; they just pretend to be.

    (a) Appeal to Ignorance   (b) Attacking the Person (c) Bandwagon
    (d) Circular Reasoning   (e) False Analogy

(13) Those who would like to live abroad do not have patriotism; they have just egocentrism.

    (a) Appeal to Ignorance   (b) Attacking the Person (c) Bandwagon
    (d) Circular Reasoning   (e) False Analogy

(14) Show me one study that proves our average life span will be 300 after a century later.

    (a) Appeal to Ignorance   (b) Attacking the Person (c) Bandwagon
    (d) Circular Reasoning   (e) False Analogy

(8) 방위비 예산이 증액되지 않는다면, 한국은 국가 안보를 심각하게 위협받을 것이다. 정답 (a)

(9) 각하, 그는 하버드에서 박사학위를 받았습니다. 그는 내각에 입각해야 합니다. 정답 (d)

(10) 텔레비전 프로그램들은 폭력, 범죄, 기형적인 것에 초점을 맞춘다. 정답 (b)

(11) 팀원 모두가 하이 탑을 신고 있다. 그래야 갈 수 있다. 정답 (c)
    * high-tops : Sneakers or athletic shoes that lace up the ankle.

(12) 인생은 마치 연극과 같다. 사람들은 자신의 말에 대해 진지하지 않다. 그저 그런 척 할 뿐이다.
    정답 (e)

(13) 외국에 살고 싶어하는 사람들은 애국심이 없다. 오직 자기 중심성만 가지고 있다. 정답 (b)

(14) 우리의 평균 수명이 1세기 뒤에는 300살이 되리라고 증명한 연구 논문 하나만 보여다오.
    정답 (a)

high - tops

(15) Mr. Park has proposed a series of plausible reforms to clean up the corruption existing in our government. But, it is an irony to hear about corruption from Mr. Park. Everyone knows that he is corrupt. He has accumulated millions of dollars through those scandalous briberies as all of us know.

(a) Appeal to Ignorance   (b) Attacking the Person (c) Bandwagon
(d) Circular Reasoning   (e) False Analogy

(16) Mr. Lee, the candidate I strongly support, is the best qualified of all. In education, experience, and ability, he is superior to any other candidates. Therefore, he deserves your vote.

(a) Appeal to Ignorance   (b) Attacking the Person (c) Bandwagon
(d) Circular Reasoning   (e) False Analogy

(17) The North Korean leaders made an all-out war against the South in 1950. If our military power is not strong, they will wage another one.

(a) False Dichotomy   (b) Overgeneralization (c) Post hoc Fallacy
(d) Prestige Suggestion (e) Stereotyping

(18) She is proud of driving her new Rolls Royce after she hit a multi-million dollar lottery.

(a) False Dichotomy   (b) Overgeneralization (c) Post hoc Fallacy
(d) Prestige Suggestion (e) Stereotyping

(19) When John traveled by plane last winter, the airport was closed because of a blizzard. Now, John is going to travel by train to avoid being stuck at the airport.

(a) False Dichotomy   (b) Overgeneralization (c) Post hoc Fallacy
(d) Prestige Suggestion (e) Stereotyping

(20) Leo Tolstoy (1828-1910) is a fine writer because his works such as <u>War and Peace</u>, <u>What is Art?</u>, and <u>Anna Karenina</u> are so well written.

(a) Appeal to Ignorance   (b) Attacking the Person (c) Bandwagon
(d) Circular Reasoning   (e) False Analogy

(15) 박 선생은 우리 정부에 만연한 부패를 척결하는 그럴듯한 일련의 개혁을 제안했다. 그러나 박 선생의 부패에 대한 소식을 듣게 된 것은 일종의 아이러니이다. 모두들 그가 부패하다는 사실을 잘 알고 있다. 그는 우리 모두가 알고 있는 것처럼 창피하기 짝이 없는 뇌물 수수를 통해 수백만 달러를 축적했다. 정답 (b)

(16) 내가 강력하게 지지하는 후보 이 박사는 모든 후보 중에서 가장 적임자다. 교육으로나 경험, 능력 등으로 볼 때, 그는 다른 어떤 후보보다 월등하다. 따라서 그는 당신의 한 표를 받을 가치가 있다. 정답 (d)

(17) 북한의 지도자들은 1950년, 남한에 대한 전면전을 감행했다. 우리의 군사력이 강하지 않다면, 그들은 또 한 번의 전쟁을 벌일 것이다. 정답 (c)

(18) 그녀는 수백만 달러 짜리 복권에 당첨된 뒤 새로운 롤스로이스를 몰게 된 것을 자랑스럽게 생각한다. 정답 (d)

(19) 지난 겨울, 존이 비행기로 여행할 때, 공항이 폭설로 인해 폐쇄되었다. 지금 존은 공항에 갇히는 일이 없도록 기차로 여행할 생각이다. 정답 (c)

(20) 레오 톨스토이(1828-1910)는 〈전쟁과 평화〉, 〈예술이란 무엇인가?〉, 〈안나 카레리나〉와 같은 훌륭한 작품을 썼기 때문에 뛰어난 작가이다. 정답 (d)

Leo Tolstoy

5.8. Chapter Summary & Exercises

In this part, Effective Writing, we have seen several key strategies for effective writing. There are hundreds of strategies for effective writing such as (1) Analyzing parts of speech; (2) Identifying and restructuring the phrases, the clauses, and the sentences; (3) Agreement of Subject/Pronouns - Verb; and, (4) Using pronouns and verbs correctly. These strategies are primarily geared for syntactical studies. Effective writing, as we have studied, should be (a) Brief and to the point; (b) Easy to understand; and, (c) Concrete and vivid. Such syntactical studies as those seldom help us write effectively, although they provide us with a clear concept and analysis of a sentence structure. We should study syntactical and other grammatical rules as a way of improving our reading and writing skills for practical purposes, not for grammar's sake.

The seven strategies carefully selected in this part for practical purposes serve as powerful tools for effective writing. A well-chosen word makes a difference in meaning and style as shown in 5.1. Choosing Word, and using a right word while eliminating unnecessary words as studied in 5.2. Reducing Wordiness, makes a point clearly and effectively. Both "Concise Writing" and "Condensing" are also powerful devices for effective writing, since they briefly and clearly express the main idea and the important supporting details. When we make a sentence, the sentence should be complete both syntactically and semantically. These deformed sentence structures (i.e. Sentence Fragments; Run-on Sentences; Parallel Structures) are to be corrected as demonstrated in 5.5. Sentence Completeness. The proper use of a conjunction is also important for a smooth flow of communication, since it clearly expresses the relationship between two ideas as we have seen in 5.6. Replacing Faulty Conjunctions.

Finally, we have seen several fallacies: (a) Appeal to Ignorance; (b) Attacking the Person; (c) Bandwagon; (d) Circular Reasoning; (e) False Analogy; (f) False Dichotomy; (g) Overgeneralization; (h) Post hoc Fallacy; (i) Prestige Suggestion; and, (j) Stereotyping.

Since all these fallacies do not help us be responsible and effective writers, we should avoid making these errors in reasoning as much as possible. We should be proud of ourselves for being responsible writers in a democratic society where we write for the creation of an art based on truth instead of seeking immediate political or commercial gains.

5.8. 요약과 연습

이 장, 효과적인 글 쓰기를 통해, 우리는 효과적인 글 쓰기를 위한 몇 가지 핵심 전략을 살펴보았다. 효과적인 글 쓰기를 위한 전략으로는 (1) 품사 분석, (2) 구, 절, 문장의 구축 및 재구성, (3) 주어/대명사–동사의 일치, (4) 대명사와 동사 제대로 사용하기 등 수백 가지가 있다. 이러한 전략들은 일차적으로 구문 공부와 관련이 있다. 효과적인 글 쓰기는, 앞에서 공부했듯이, (a) 간결하며 적절해야 하고, (b) 이해하기 쉬우며, (c) 구체적이고 생생한 글을 가리킨다. 그러한 구문론적 공부는 문장 구조에 대한 명확한 개념과 분석을 제공하지만, 그럼에도 불구하고 효과적으로 글을 쓰는 데는 거의 도움이 되지 않는다. 우리는 문법을 위해서가 아니라 실제적 목적을 위해 우리의 읽기와 쓰기 기법을 개선시키는 한 방법으로서 구문 및 문법적 원칙을 공부해야 한다.

이 장에서 실제적 목적을 위해 신중하게 선택된 일곱 가지 전략은 효과적인 글 쓰기의 강력한 도구로 기능한다. 5.1 단어 선택에서 보았듯이, 잘 선택된 단어 하나가 의미와 스타일에 차이를 가져오며, 5.2. 장황함 피하기에서 공부했듯이, 불필요한 단어를 삭제하고 적절한 단어 하나를 사용하는 것은 요점을 명확하고 효과적으로 드러낸다. '간결한 글 쓰기'와 '압축하기' 또한 효과적인 글 쓰기를 위한 강력한 장치들이다. 주제를 비롯한 여타 중요한 보충 자료들을 간결하고 명확하게 표현해주기 때문이다. 문장을 만들 때, 그 문장은 구문상으로나 의미론적으로 완결적이어야 한다. 이러한 변형된 문장 구조(예를 들면, 문장의 파편; 다음 행으로 이어지는 문장 ; 병렬 구조)는 5.5. 문장의 완결성에서 보았듯이, 바르게 고쳐져야 한다. 접속사의 올바른 사용 또한 이야기의 부드러운 흐름이라는 측면에서 매우 중요하다. 5.6. 잘못된 접속사 바꾸기에서 보았듯이, 접속사는 두 아이디어 사이의 관계를 명확히 표현해주기 때문이다. 마지막으로, 우리는 (a) 무지에의 호소, (b) 인신 공격, (c) 시류에 편승하기, (d) 순환 논법, (e) 잘못된 유추, (f) 잘못된 이분법, (g) 지나친 일반화, (h) 포스트 학 팰러시, (i) 세력 암시, (j) 정형화 등 몇 가지 오류들을 살펴보았다. 이러한 오류들은 책임 있고 효과적인 글 쓰기에 전혀 도움이 되지 않으므로, 우리는 추론 과정에서 이러한 실수들을 가능한 한 피해야 한다. 민주주의 사회에서 책임있는 작가로서 즉각적인 정치적 또는 상업적 이익을 추구하는 것이 아니라 진실에 바탕한 하나의 예술을 창조하기 위해 글을 쓴다는 것은 무척 흐뭇한 일이다.

EXERCISES:

1. Read the following poems, and based on the context of the poem select the most appropriate and effective word among the choices provided in the parenthesis.

(1) In the golden age of Asia
Korea was one of its lamp bearers
And that lamp is waiting
To be lighted again
For the ((a) brilliance; (b) illumination; (c) insight; (d) inspiration)in the East.

- Rabindranath Tagore (1861~1941)

(2) Come, let's go
Snow - viewing
Till we're ((a) buried; (b) covered; (c) drowned; (d) entombed).

- Matsuo Basho (1644~1694)

(3) "Friendship"

Friend, whatever hardship threaten
If thou call me,
I'll ((a) befriend; (b) benefit; (c) encourage; (d) sustain) thee;
All-enduring, fearlessly,
I'll befriend thee.

- A Sioux Verse (American Indian tribe)

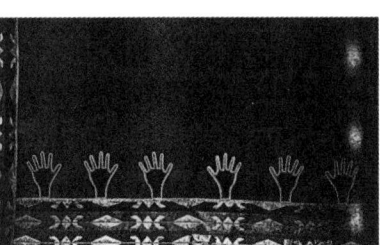
Osage Friendship Blanket,1990.

(4) "Tears"

Tears of loneliness rinse my memory;
Tears of memory cleanse my heart;
Tears of sadness ((a) bathe; (b) moisten; (c) rinse; (d) wet) my eyes;
Tears of hate build up to drown me.

- Alonzo Lopez

연습 문제

1. 다음 시를 읽고, 시의 문맥에 근거하여 괄호 안에 주어진 보기들 가운데 가장 적절하고 효과적인 단어를 골라라.

(1) 아시아의 황금 시대에
한국은 그 등불을 간직하고 있던 나라 중 하나였나니,
그 등불
다시 타올라
동방을 밝히리라.
– 타고르(1861–1941)
정답 (b)

Rabindranath Tagore

(2) 오라, 가자,
눈 구경하러.
눈에 파묻힐 때까지.
– 마츠오 바쇼(1644–1694)
정답 (a)

Matsuo Basho

(3) '우정'
친구여, 어떤 고난이 닥칠지라도
그대 날 부르면,
나 그대의 편이 되리라.
영원히, 두려움 없이,
나 그대의 편이 되리라.
– 북미 인디안 수 부족의 시
정답 (a)

(4) '눈물'
외로움의 눈물은 내 추억을 씻어내고,
추억의 눈물은 내 마음을 정화하네.
슬픔의 눈물은 내 눈을 적시고,
증오의 눈물은 나를 익사시키네.
– 알론조 로페즈
정답 (a)

Alonzo Lopez

(5) "Youth to Age"

Aged one and wise,
Were you twenty-two again
Would you risk all your fame?
Conform?
Or go your way alone?

But how can you reply, being seventy-two?
Your path is ((a) clouded; (b) confused; (c) fogged; (d) obscured) with memories
As mine with fears.

- Paul Murky

(6) "The Azalea"

When you take your leave,
Tired of seeing me,
Gently and silently I'll bid you go.

From Mountain Yak of Yongbyon
An armful of azaleas I shall pick,
And strew them in your path

Go now, I pray, with short steps!
Let each footstep gently tread
The flowers I have spread for you.

When you take your leave,
Tired of seeing me.
Though I should die., I shall not ((a) cry; (b) sob; (c) wail; (d) weep)

- Sowol Kim (1902~1934)

Azalea

(5) '젊음이 노년에게'

> 현명한 늙은이여,
> 다시 스물 두 살이 된다면,
> 모든 명예를 걸고 감행하시겠습니까?
> 그러시겠습니까?
> 아니면 홀로 당신의 길을 가시겠습니까?
>
> 하지만 일흔 둘이라면, 어떻게 대답하시겠습니까?
> 당신의 길은 추억의 안개로 뒤덮여 있으나,
> 나의 길은 두려움으로 뒤덮여 있나니.
> – 폴 머키

정답 (c)

(6) '진달래꽃'

> 나 보기가 역겨워
> 가실 때에는
> 말 없이 고이 보내 드리우리다.
>
> 영변에 약산
> 진달래꽃
> 아름 따다 가실 길에 뿌리우리다.
>
> 가시는 걸음걸음
> 놓인 그 꽃을
> 사뿐히 즈려 밟고 가시옵소서.
>
> 나 보기가 역겨워
> 가실 때에는
> 죽어도 아니 눈물 흘리우리다.
> – 김소월(1902–1934)

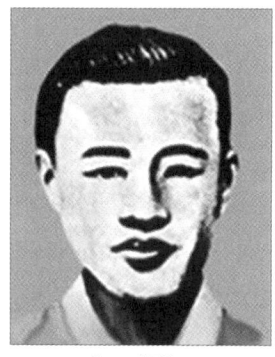

Sowol Kim

정답 (d)

(7) "Waking from Drunkenness on a Spring Day"

"Life in the world is but a big dream;
I will not spoil it by any labor or care."
So saying, I was drunk all the day,
Lying helpless at the porch in front of my door.
When I woke up, I ((a) blinked; (b) fluttered; (c) glittered ; (d) looked)
at the garden-lawn;
A lonely bird was singing amid the flowers.
I asked myself, had the day been wet or fine?
The Spring wind was telling the mango-bird.
Moved by its song I began to sigh,
And as wine was there I filled my own cup.
Wildly singing I waited for the moon to rise;
When my song was over, all my senses had gone.

- Li Po (701~762, Tang Dynasty)

(8) Oh, Champa! When I sense your fragrance,
A thousand memories ((a) affect; (b) agitate; (c) motivate; (d) stir) in my heart.
Your sweet scent reminds me of the garden of my father.
And I recall all my dreams, all my melancholy, and all my childhood joys.

Champa, you are for me the flower of my childhood.
Your perfume awakens in me delightful memories.
When I inhale your fragrance I seem to recall in my heart
My beloved whom I have lost.

Champa, the most beautiful flower of Laos,
You are for me
The flower of my love.

- Champa, Flower of Laos.

(7) '봄날 술에서 깨어'

"이승의 삶은 그저 꿈에 지나지 않으니,
나는 그 어떤 노동이나 걱정으로 그것을 망치지 않으리."
그렇게 말하며, 나 하루 종일 술을 마셨네.
내 문 앞마루에 무력하게 누워서.
깨어나 뜰을 바라본즉,
꽃들 사이에서 외로운 새 한 마리 노래하고 있었지.
나 홀로 중얼거렸나니, 날씨가 화창했던가 아니면
비가 오고 있었던가?
봄바람이 망고 새에게 말하고 있었네.
그 노래에 감동 받아 나, 한숨쉬기 시작했나니,
술이 있기에 술잔을 가득 채웠네.
미친 듯 노래하며, 나, 달이 뜨기를 기다렸지.
내 노래가 끝났을 때, 의식도 사라졌다네.

– 이백(701-762, 중국 당나라)

정답 (a)

(8) 오, 챰파! 너의 향기를 맡으면,
내 가슴의 수많은 기억들이 되살아나네.
너의 달콤한 향기는 아버지의 정원을 상기시키지.
그리고 나는 생각하네. 내 모든 꿈, 내 모든 우울, 그리고 어린 시절의 내 모든 기쁨들까지.

챰파, 내게 너는 내 유년의 꽃.
너의 향내는 내 안의 즐거운 추억들을 일깨운다네.
너의 향기를 마시면, 나는 마치 내 마음 속
지금은 잃어버린 나의 연인을 떠올리는 것 같아라.

챰파, 라오스의 가장 아름다운 꽃이여,
내게 너는
내 사랑의 꽃.

– 챰파, 라오스의 꽃

정답 (d)

(9) "A Psalm of Life"

Tell me not, in mournful numbers,
Life is but an empty dream!
For the soul is dead that slumbers,
And things are not what they seem.

Life is real! Life is earnest!
And the grave is not its goal;
Dust thou art, to dust returnest,
Was not spoken of the soul.

Not enjoyment, and not sorrow,
Is our destined end or way;
But to act, that each to-morrow
Find us farther than to-day.

Henry Wadsworth Longfellow

Art is long, and Time is ((a) agile; (b) fleeting; (c) hasty; (d) rapid)
And our hearts, though stout and brave,
Still, like muffled drums, are beating
Funeral marches to the grave.

In the world's broad field of battle,
In the bivouac of Life,
Be not like dumb, driven cattle!
Be a hero in the strife!

- Henry Wadsworth Longfellow (1807~1882)

(9) '인생 찬가'

슬픈 곡조로, 나에게
인생은 한낱 공허한 꿈이라고 말하지 말라!
잠자는 영혼은 죽은 영혼,
만물은 겉보기와는 다른 것.

삶은 실재하는 것! 삶은 진지한 것!
무덤은 결코 그의 목표가 아니니,
본디 흙으로 된 존재이니, 그대 다시 흙으로 돌아가야 한다는 그 말이
영혼을 두고 한 말은 아니었다.

기쁨도 슬픔도
숙명적으로 정해진 우리의 목적이나 길은 아니다.
그러나 행동하라, 각각의 내일이
오늘보다 더 멀리 있는 우리를 발견하도록.

예술은 길고, 세월은 덧없이 흐르는 것.
오늘 우리의 가슴은 튼튼하고 용감하지만,
지금 이 순간에도 무덤을 향해
소리 없이 행진하고 있다.

세상이라는 광대한 싸움터에서,
인생의 야영장에서,
말없이 쫓기는 가축의 무리는 되지 말아라!
투쟁의 영웅이 되어라!

– 헨리 워즈워드 롱펠로우

정답 (b)

(10) "Last Poem"

> They have put my bed beside the unpainted screen;
> They have shifted my stove in front of the blue curtain.
> I listen to my grandchildren, reading me a book;
> I watch the servants, heating up my soup.
> With rapid pencil I answer the poems of friends;
> I feel in my pockets and pull out medicine-money.
> When this superintendence of trifling affairs is done,
> I ((a) lay; (b) lie; (c) move; (d) set) back on my pillows
> With my face to the South.

- Po Chu-i (772~846, Tang Dynasty)

2. The following is a letter from Thomas Jefferson to his daughter, Patsy. Read it and answer the questions.

Annapolis, Nov.28, 1783
To Martha Jefferson

My dear Patsy,

After four days journey I arrived here without any accident and in as good health as when I left Philadelphia. The conviction that you would be more improved in the situation I have placed you than if still with me has solaced me on my parting with you, which my love for you has rendered
L.5   a difficult thing. The skills which I hope you will acquire under the tutors I have provided for you will render you more worthy of my love, and if they cannot increase it they will prevent its diminution...

With respect to the distribution of your time the following is what I should approve:
L.10   from 8 to 10 o'clock practice music.
from 10 to 1 dance one day and draw another.
from 1 to 2 draw on the day you dance, and write a letter the next day.
from 3 to 4 read French.
from 4 to 5 exercise yourself in music.
L.15   from 5 till bedtime read and write English.

Communicate this plan to Mrs. Hopkinson and if she approves of it pursue it... I expect you will write to me by every post. Inform me what

(10) '마지막 시'

그들은 그림 없는 병풍 곁에 내 침대를 놓았고,

파란 커튼 앞에 내 난로를 옮겼네.

나는 내게 책을 읽어주는 손주들의 말에 귀 기울이고,

하인들이 내 국물을 데우는 모습을 지켜보네.

나는 빠른 속도로 친구들의 시에 답하노니,

호주머니를 뒤져 약 값을 꺼내지.

이 사소한 일들이 끝나면,

나는 머리를 남쪽으로 한 채

반듯이 베개에 몸을 누이네.

– 백거이(白居易)(772–846, 중국 당나라)

정답 (b)

2. 다음은 토마스 제퍼슨이 딸 팻시에게 보낸 편지이다. 잘 읽고 질문에 답하라.

1783년 11월 28일, 아나폴리스에서

마사 제퍼슨에게

사랑스런 팻시,

   나흘 간의 여행 끝에 이 애비는 아무 사고 없이, 게다가 필라델피아를 떠날 때처럼 건강한 모습으로 여기 도착했단다. 나와 함께 있을 때보다 네가 더욱 좋아졌으리라는 확신이 너와 헤어져 있다는 사실에도 불구하고 그나마 위안이 되는구나. 너에 대한 내 사랑은 너와 헤어져 있다는 사실을 힘든 것으로 만들었으니까. 내가 소개해준 가정 교사들 밑에서 내가 바라는 기술들을 잘 배우면, 넌 더욱 내 사랑에 값하는 사람이 될 것이며, 만일 그들이 그것을 증진시킬 수 없다면, 그들은 그것의 감소를 예방할 것이다...

시간 배분에 관해서는 이렇게 하도록 해라.

8시부터 10시까지는 음악을 연습해라.

10시부터 1시까지는 하루는 춤을, 또 하루는 그림을 그려라.

1시부터 2시까지는 춤을 춘 날에는 그림을 그리고, 그 다음 날에는 편지를 써라.

3시부터 4시까지는 불어를 공부해라.

4시부터 5시까지는 음악을 연습해라.

5시부터 잠잘 때까지는 영어를 읽고 써라.

books you read, what tunes you learn, and enclose me your best copy of every lesson in drawing. Write also one letter every week either to your
L.20 Aunt Eppes, your Aunt Skip with, your Aunt Carr, or the little lady from whom I now enclose a letter, and always put the letter you so write under cover to me. Take care that you never spell a word wrong. Always (L.22) you write a word consider how it is spelled, and if you do not remember it, turn to a dictionary. It produces great praise to a lady to spell well.

L.25   I have placed my happiness on seeing you good and accomplished, and no distress which this world can bring on me could equal that of disappointing my hopes. If you love me, (L. 27) , strive to be good under every situation and to all living creatures, and to acquire those accomplishments which I have put in your power, and which will go
L.30 far towards ensuring you the warmest love of your affectionate father,

Thomas Jefferson

P.S. Keep my letters and read them, so that you may always have present in your mind those things which will endear you to me.

(1) Based on the context of the letter, choose the most appropriate conjunction among the choices provided in the parenthesis.
(a) : (a) after   (b) before   (c) but   (d) since) in Line 22.
(b) : (a) and   (b) then   (c) therefore   (d) thus) in Line 27.

(2) In the letter, Jefferson took an attitude toward his daughter, which is a tone.
His tone taken toward his daughter sounds as ((a) casual; (b) coaxing; (c) sarcastic; (d) stern).

(3) What subjects does he suggest his daughter to study?

= _____.

(4) Line 16, "Communicate ... Mrs. Hopkinson," gives a clue regarding her role. What do you think she is? Based on your inference related to the early American social realities in 1780s, and the wealth of Jefferson's family, write a sentence regarding her role.

= _____.

(5) Condense the main idea of his letter as short as possible.

= _____.

CHAPTER 5

이 계획표에 대해 홉킨슨 부인과 상의하고, 부인이 승인하면 그대로 따라라... 난 네가 우편으로 내게 글을 써보내기를 고대하고 있단다. 무슨 책을 읽는지, 어떤 곡을 배우는지 내게 알려다오. 그리고 네가 그림을 그릴 때마다 가장 좋은 것들을 내게 동봉해라. 또한 매주 한 번은 엡스 숙모나 스킵위드 숙모, 카 숙모, 또는 지금 내가 편지에 동봉하는 어린 숙녀께도 편지를 써라. 그리고 그렇게 쓴 편지는 내게 보내는 편지에 동봉해서 보내도록 해라. (a) 철자 틀리지 않도록 주의해라. 단어를 하나 쓸 때마다 철자가 어떻게 되는지 항상 주의하고, 만약 기억이 나지 않으면, 사전을 찾아봐라. 그것은 철자를 제대로 쓰는 숙녀에게는 엄청난 칭찬을 낳는단다.

나의 행복은 착하고 교양 있는 네 모습을 보는 데 있단다. 이 세상이 내게 어떤 고난을 안겨주더라도, 그것은 내 희망이 좌절되는 고통보다는 적다. 날 사랑한다면, (b) 어떤 상황에서든 살아있는 모든 생물에 대해 선량하고자 노력하고, 내가 네게 부과한 교양을 획득하기 위해 노력하거라.
그렇게 해야 이 애비의 따스한 사랑으로 좀더 다가올 수 있을 게다.

토마스 제퍼슨

추신 : 내 편지들을 보관해 뒀다가 잘 읽어라. 그래야 네가 나의 사랑을 받을 수 있게 하는 그런 일들을 마음 속에 항상 떠올릴 수 있을 테니까.

(1) 편지의 문맥에 근거하여 괄호 안의 보기들 가운데 가장 적절한 접속사를 골라라.
 정답 (a) - b, (b) -b

(2) 편지에서 제퍼슨은 딸에 대해 일정한 태도를 취했으며, 그것이 곧 어조이다. 딸에 대해 취한 그의 어조는 --하게 들린다. 정답 (a)

(3) 그는 딸에게 어떤 과목을 공부하라고 제안하는가?
정답 The subjects are music, dance, drawing, French, and reading & writing English.

(4) "이 계획표에 대해 홉킨슨 부인과 상의하고"라는 부분은 그녀의 역할에 대한 단서를 제공한다. 그녀가 담당한 역할은 무엇이라고 생각되는가? 1780년대 미국의 사회 현실과 관련된 추론 및 제퍼슨 가의 부에 근거하여 그녀의 역할을 한 문장으로 써 보아라.
정답 : She is a private tutor.

(5) 편지의 주제를 가능한 한 짧게 압축하라.
정답 : Study hard as much as I love you.

Thomas Jefferson

3. Read the adapted "Farewell Address" by George Washington (1732~1799), the first President of the United States (1789~1797), and select the best answer among the choices provided in the parenthesis.

Friends and Fellow Citizens: My second term as President of the United States will soon expire. The term for another presidential election is drawing near. Your thoughts should be turning in that direction. It is in the public interest; therefore, that I disclose a decision I have reached.
L.5.   I will not be a candidate for reelection. I will not seek a third term as president.

For some time now, I have wished to retire from public life, but the affairs of state were unsettled. A sense of duty compelled me to stay on. I am happy to say my services are no longer needed. The Foreign and
L.10.   Domestic affairs of our country are now in order. I can pursue my inclination with a clear conscience. Here, perhaps, I should stop. But my concern for your welfare will not end with my term in office. My affection for you will only end with my death. Therefore, I will offer for your consideration some advice. These sentiments are the result of many years of experience and much
L.15.   observation of human nature. They are the thoughts of a parting friend, uncolored by personal or political motive.

Love of liberty is woven through every fiber of your hearts. You need no counsel from me to strengthen that attachment. Remember, though, that the one nation you forged from thirteen colonies is the pillar on which that
L.20.   liberty stands. It is that unity of government which is the source of your real independence. The union makes possible your tranquillity at home and peace abroad. You are all Americans. It is to America that you owe your first allegiance, not the region of your birth. That name, America, embraces all the common bonds you share: your manners, customs, and political beliefs.
L.25.   You have fought and triumphed together in a common cause. The independence and liberty you now possess result from those joint efforts and shared suffering.

Regional loyalties are a threat to your liberty. More dangerous yet is party allegiance. Party spirit is rooted in human nature. Political parties exist to some extent under all forms of government. But it is in a democracy that they are seen
L.30.   in their most dangerous form. Parties win some elections and lose others. A party newly come to power may be tempted to take revenge for earlier defeats.

3. 미국의 초대 대통령 조지 워싱턴의 "고별 연설"을 읽고, 괄호 안에 주어진 보기들 가운데 가장 알맞은 답을 골라라.

친구들과 동료 시민 여러분 : 미국 대통령으로서 제 두 번째 임기가 곧 끝나게 됩니다. 또 다른 대통령 선거 기간이 다가오고 있습니다. 여러분의 생각은 그 방향으로 돌려져야 합니다. 그것은 공적인 관심사이므로, 따라서 저는 제 입장을 밝히고자 합니다. 저는 재선 후보로 출마하지 않겠습니다. 대통령으로서 세 번째 임기를 추구하지 않겠습니다.

한동안 저는 공직에서 은퇴하고 싶었지만, 국가 상황이 불안정했습니다. 일종의 의무감이 저를 계속 이 자리에 있게 했습니다. 이제 더 이상 제 봉사가 필요하지 않다고 말할 수 있게 되어 무척 기쁩니다. 우리나라의 대외 문제와 대내 문제는 이제 자리가 잡혔습니다. 저는 양심에 거리낌 없이 제 취향을 추구할 수 있습니다. 아마도 이쯤에서 저는 그만두어야 할 것 같습니다. 그러나 여러분의 복지에 대한 제 관심은 임기와 더불어 끝나지 않을 것입니다. 여러분에 대한 제 사랑은 오직 죽음과 더불어 끝날 것입니다. 따라서 저는 여러분께 몇 가지 조언을 드리고자 합니다. 지금 말씀드리는 소견은 인간 본성에 대한 오랜 경험과 충분한 관찰 끝에 얻어진 것입니다. 그것은 떠나가는 친구의, 개인적 또는 정치적 동기에 물들지 않은 있는 그대로의 소견입니다.

자유에 대한 사랑은 여러분의 가슴 구석구석에 스며 있습니다. 여러분은 그러한 애착을 강화시키기 위해 제게서 그 어떤 조언도 들을 필요가 없습니다. 그럼에도 불구하고, 기억하십시오. 여러분이 동부 13주의 영국 식민지로부터 만들어낸 한 국가야말로 자유를 지탱시키는 기둥이라는 것을. 여러분의 진정한 독립의 근원은 바로 통합된 정부입니다. 연방이야말로 집에서의 평온과 외국에서의 평화를 가능하게 합니다. 여러분 모두 미국인들입니다. 여러분이 맨 먼저 충성을 바쳐야 할 곳은 여러분이 태어난 지역이 아니라 바로 미국입니다. 미국이라는 이름은 여러분이 공유하고 있는 모든 계약, 다시 말해 풍습, 관례, 정치적 신념을 포괄하고 있습니다. 여러분은 공통의 대의 속에서 함께 싸워 승리를 일궈냈습니다. 여러분이 지금 향유하고 있는 독립과 자유는 바로 그러한 공동의 노력과 아픔의 공유로부터 나왔습니다.

지방에 대한 충성은 여러분의 자유에 위협이 됩니다. 게다가 더욱 위험한 것은 바로 파벌적 충성입니다. 파벌 정신은 인간 본성에 근거하고 있습니다. 정치적 파벌은 어느 정도는 온갖 형태의 정부 하에서 존재합니다. 그러나 민주주의에서는 그 파벌이 가장 위험한 형태로 비춰집니다. 정당들은 어떤 선거에서는 이기기도 하지만, 또 어떤 선거에서는 지기도 합니다. 새로 권력을 잡은 정당은 이전의 패배를 설욕해야겠다는 유혹에 빠질지도 모릅니다. 프랑스의 파벌 경쟁이 대중의 지지를 잃은 지도자들의 처형으로 이어진 것은 여러분도 알고 계실 겁니다. 그러한 사악함은 혼돈으로 이어집니다.

You have seen how party rivalry in France has led to the execution of leaders who lost public favor. Such wickedness leads to chaos.

L.35. The public, alarmed at the threat of lawlessness, becomes inclined to place absolute power in the hands of one strong leader who can restore order. Sooner or later, this leader raises himself above the law and becomes a tyrant. Liberty is left in ruins. Such a calamity need not happen. A wise people can prevent it by discouraging and restraining party loyalty. The framers of the Constitution wisely gave no one branch of government absolute power.

L.40. The president, the congress, and the courts have separate spheres of influence. No one of the three branches can be permitted to encroach upon the powers of the others. Consolidation of power in any one branch leads to tyranny. The need for Constitutional change may arise. Consolidation of power may seem a convenient means of effecting change. But it is the customary weapon

L.45. by which free governments are destroyed. The permanent evil it sets loose outweighs the temporary benefit that results. If change is needed, let it come through a Constitutional amendment ratified by the people. Public morality and an educated citizenry are indispensable to the preservation of liberty. Life, reputation, and property are only safe in a land which values virtue.

L.50. Only an informed public can make wise choices. Encourage, therefore, public education and the growth of educational institutions.

Be honest and generous in dealing with other nations. Strive to be at peace with all peoples but maintain a strong defense. A strong defense is the surest guarantee of peace. Do not be drawn into European affairs. Expand trade

L.55. relations but avoid permanent political alliances. The nations of Europe have warred upon each other for centuries and will continue to do so. Honor these temporary treaties signed in a time of emergency but do not extend them. European quarrels are not our quarrels. We are separated by an ocean. Our destiny lies in the future. Do not be drawn into Europe's past. And in both

L.60. public and private affairs, remember the maxim, "Honesty is the best policy."

I offer these thoughts as an old and true friend. I realize my words alone are no safeguard against an uncertain future. It is enough if now and then the nation remembers a friend's counsel: Discourage and restrain party allegiance. Guard against those who would use patriotism to conceal selfish interests.

L.65. Avoid entanglement in European intrigues. As president, I committed no intentional errors, but I am aware of my own human frailties. Whatever mistakes I have made, I ask God to correct in the course of time. I hope my countrymen will forgive my failings, realize my good intentions, and remember my zeal to serve this land to the best of my ability.

C H A P T E R 5

무법(無法)의 위협에 놀란 국민 대중은 질서를 회복시킬 수 있는 강한 지도자의 손에 절대 권력을 쥐어주는 경향이 있습니다. 조만간, 이 지도자는 자신을 초법적 지위에 올려놓고, 전제군주가 됩니다. 자유는 황폐해집니다. 그런 불행은 일어날 필요가 없습니다. 현명한 국민은 파벌적 충성을 말리고 제지함으로써 그것을 예방할 수 있습니다. 헌법 기초자들은 현명하게도 정부의 어느 한 부분에도 절대 권력을 주지 않았습니다. 대통령, 의회, 법원 모두 각자 독립된 세력 범위를 가지고 있습니다. 세 부분 가운데 어느 하나도 상대방의 권력을 침해할 수 없습니다. 어느 한 부분으로의 권력 통합은 전제정치로 이어집니다. 헌법 개정 요구가 대두될 수도 있습니다. 권력 통합은 변화를 일궈내는 편리한 수단처럼 보일지도 모릅니다. 그러나 바로 그런 관습적인 무기야말로 자유로운 정부를 파멸시킵니다. 한번 느슨해진 영원한 악은 그 결과 얻게 되는 일시적인 혜택을 능가하고 맙니다. 개정이 필요하다면, 헌법 수정안을 만들어 국민의 비준을 받게 하십시오. 공적 윤리와 교양 있는 국민은 자유 수호에 없어서는 안될 존재입니다. 목숨과 덕망, 재산은 오직 미덕을 존중하는 나라에서만 안전합니다. 학식 있는 국민만이 현명한 선택을 할 수 있습니다. 따라서 공교육과 교육 기관의 발전을 장려하십시오.

다른 국가들을 상대할 때에는 정직하고 관대하십시오. 모든 민족과 평화를 유지하려 노력하면서 동시에 강한 방위력을 유지하십시오. 강력한 방위력은 평화를 지켜주는 가장 확실한 담보물입니다. 유럽의 문제에 말려들지 마십시오. 무역 관계를 확대하되, 영원한 정치 동맹은 피하십시오. 유럽 국가들은 수세기 동안 서로 싸워왔고, 앞으로도 그렇게 할 것입니다. 비상시에 맺은 일시적인 조약을 존중하되, 그것을 연장하지 마십시오. 유럽인들의 싸움이 우리의 싸움이 아닙니다. 우리는 바다 너머에 떨어져 있습니다. 우리의 운명은 미래에 놓여 있습니다. 유럽의 과거에 끌려 들어가지 마십시오. 그리고 공적인 일에서든 사적인 일에서든, "정직이 최선의 방책"이라는 금언을 기억하십시오.

저는 지금 오랜, 그리고 진정한 친구로서 이런 소견을 제안하고 있습니다. 그러나 제 말만으로는 불확실한 미래에 대한 안전 장치가 될 수 없다는 점을 잘 알고 있습니다. 가끔씩 이 친구의 조언을 기억해주시는 것으로 충분합니다. 파벌적 충성을 말리고 못하게 하십시오. 이기적 이해관계를 숨기기 위해 애국심을 사용하는 무리들을 경계하십시오. 유럽의 음모에 휘말리지 마십시오. 대통령으로서 저는 국제적인 실수는 결코 저지르지 않았지만, 그럼에도 불구하고 제 자신의 인간적 약점들을 잘 알고 있습니다. 제가 어떤 실수를 했더라도, 시간이 지나면 저는 신께 바

George Washington

로잡아 달라고 청합니다. 국민 여러분께서 제 부족함을 용서해주시고, 다만 제 의도가 선했다는 점을 알아주시기 바랍니다. 그리고 능력이 닿는 한, 이 나라에 봉사하려는 제 열정을 기억해 주십시오.

(1) In which paragraph do you identify the introduction of the address?
(a) 1   (b) 2   (c) 3   (d) 7

(2) The body of the address can be found in paragraph(s) of
(a) 1~3   (b) 2~5   (c) 2~6   (d) 2~7

(3) The conclusion of the address is found in paragraph(s) of
(a) 1~3   (b) 2~5   (c) 6   (d) 7

(4) The statements, "My second term...in that direction (Lines 1~3)," is the _____ of his address.
(a) background   (b) issue   (c) personal reason   (d) thesis

(5) "I will not be...as president (Lines 5~6)," is a personal _____ for his address.
(a) justification   (b) opinion   (c) proposition   (d) reason

(6) "Therefore, I will offer for your consideration...political motive (Lines 13~16)," are statements leading to his _____.
(a) background   (b) conclusion   (c) reason   (d) thesis

(7) The main idea of "Love of liberty is...joint efforts and shared suffering (Lines 17~26)," is
_____.
(a) Prosperity & liberty should be considered first.
(b) The benefit for the region of your birth is important.
(c) The need for unity for the nation's liberty is to be preserved.
(d) Tranquillity at home & peace abroad should be maintained.

(8) "Regional loyalties are...leads to chaos (Lines 27~33)," is a warning against .
(a) all forms of government (b) party politics (c) party spirit (d) regional loyalties

(9) The public, alarmed...educational institutions (Lines 34~51)," is a warning against _____.
(a) absolute power/tyranny (b)Constitute amendment (c) party loyalty (d) public morality

(10) "Be honest and generous...policy (Lines 52~60)," is a warning against _____.
(a) European affairs   (b) foreign entanglement   (c) permanent political allies   (d) trade relations

(11) "I offer these thoughts...European intrigues (Lines 61~65)," is a conclusion _____ and _____ his main points.
(a) concluding & emphasizing   (b) concluding & proposing
(c) summarizing & stating   (d) summarizing & restating

(12) Identify his three main points in paragraph 7, and condense those points.

(1) 어느 문단이 연설문의 서두로 기능하고 있는가? 정답 (a)

(2) 연설문의 본론은 (   )문단에서 찾아볼 수 있다. 정답 (c)

(3) 연설문의 결론은 (   )문단에서 찾아볼 수 있다. 정답 (d)

(4) "미국 대통령으로서 제 두 번째 임기가... 돌려져야 합니다."라는 말은 연설의 (   )이다.
   정답 (a)

(5) "저는 재선 후보로... 않겠습니다"라는 말은 연설을 하게 된 개인적 (   )이다. 정답 (d)

(6) "따라서 저는 여러분께... 소견입니다."는 그가 말하려는 (   )로 이어지는 진술이다. 정답 (d)

(7) "자유에 대한 사랑은... 공유로부터 나왔습니다."라는 문단의 요지는 (   )이다. 정답 (c)

(8) "지방에 대한 충성은... 혼돈으로 이어집니다."라는 문단은 (   )에 대한 경고이다. 정답 (b)

(9) "무법의 위협에... 장려하십시오."라는 문단은 (   )에 대한 경고이다. 정답(a)

(10) "다른 국가들을... 기억하십시오."라는 문단은 (   )에 대한 경고이다. 정답 (b)

(11) "저는 지금 오랜... 휘말리지 마십시오."라는 부분은 그의 요지를 (   )하고 (   )한 결론이다.
   정답 (d)

(12) 마지막 문단에서 그가 말하고자 한 요지 세 가지를 고르고, 그 세 가지 요점을 압축시켜 표현하라.
   정답 : (a) Discourage party allegiance.
        (b) Beware of crooked patriots.
        (c) Avoid European affairs